C₁ 3~

# PRINCIPLES OF MACRO-
# CONOMICS
## AND THE CANADIAN ECONOMY

D1501276

# PRINCIPLES OF MACRO-ECONOMICS
## AND THE CANADIAN ECONOMY

### SECOND EDITION

## JOSEPH E. STIGLITZ
STANFORD UNIVERSITY

## ROBIN W. BOADWAY
QUEEN'S UNIVERSITY

W • W • NORTON & COMPANY • NEW YORK • LONDON

Copyright © 1997, 1994, 1993 by W. W. Norton & Company, Inc.

All rights reserved.
Printed in the United States of America.

The text of this book is composed in Zapf Book
with the display set in Kabel
Composition by TSI Graphics
Manufacturing by Rand McNally
Book design by Antonina Krass
Cover painting: Laszlo Moholy-Nagy, *LIS*, 1922
Oil on canvas, 131 × 100 centimeters
Courtesy of the Kunsthaus, Zurich
Special thanks to Hattula Moholy-Nagy

Library of Congress Cataloging-in-Publication Data

Stiglitz, Joseph E.
    Principles of macroeconomics and the Canadian economy / Joseph E. Stiglitz,
Robin W. Boadway.—2nd ed.
        p.   cm.
    Includes bibliographical references and index.
    **ISBN 0-393-97054-X (pbk.)**
    1. Macroeconomics.   I. Boadway, Robin W., 1943–   .   II. Title.
HB172.S753   1997
339—dc20                                                                        96-9681

W. W. Norton & Company, Inc., 500 Fifth Avenue, New York, N.Y. 10110
  http://www.wwnorton.com

W. W. Norton & Company Ltd., 10 Coptic Street, London WCIA 1PU

1 2 3 4 5 6 7 8 9 0

To Andrew

# CONTENTS IN BRIEF

# CONTENTS

# PART TWO

# FULL-EMPLOYMENT MACROECONOMICS

CHAPTER **6** MACROECONOMIC GOALS AND MEASURES • 105

CHAPTER **7** MICROFOUNDATIONS • 128

CHAPTER **8** **THE FULL-EMPLOYMENT MODEL** • 156

CHAPTER **9** **USING THE FULL-EMPLOYMENT MODEL** • 180

## PART THREE

# UNEMPLOYMENT MACROECONOMICS

CHAPTER **10** **OVERVIEW OF UNEMPLOYMENT MACROECONOMICS** • 201

CHAPTER **11** **AGGREGATE DEMAND** • 221

CHAPTER **15** FISCAL AND MONETARY POLICY • 311

**PART FOUR**

## DYNAMICS OF ADJUSTMENT

CHAPTER **16** INFLATION: WAGE AND PRICE DYNAMICS • 327

CHAPTER **17**

# UNEMPLOYMENT: UNDERSTANDING WAGE RIGIDITIES • 354

CHAPTER **18**

# INFLATION VERSUS UNEMPLOYMENT: APPROACHES TO POLICY • 372

## PART FIVE

## TOPICS IN MACROECONOMIC POLICY

### CHAPTER 19 GROWTH AND PRODUCTIVITY • 397

### CHAPTER 20 INTERGENERATIONAL TRANSFERS: DEFICITS AND PUBLIC PENSIONS • 424

# P REFACE

**B**eginning students should know the vitality of modern economics, and this book is intended to show them. When we wrote the First Edition, we felt that none of the available texts provided an adequate understanding of the principles of *modern* economics—both those that are necessary to understand how modern economists think about the world around them and those that are required to understand current economic issues. Apparently, our feelings were shared by many others, as reflected by the success the First Edition has enjoyed, by the feedback we have received from the market, and especially by the responses our own students have had to the book. With the benefit of this feedback, we have made a painstaking effort to improve the book from cover to cover, focusing both on clarity and on conciseness. We believe both students and their instructors will be pleased with the result.

As with the First Edition, this edition closely parallels the Second Edition prepared for the American market by Joseph Stiglitz alone. Both versions have benefited from his role in U.S. policy making as chairman of President Clinton's Council of Economic Advisers and as a member of the Cabinet. His experience has confirmed the view that the traditional principles course is far removed from economic policy concerns and the modern economic advances that can illuminate them.

The need to confront modern economic policy problems with modern economic analysis is no less true in Canada. Indeed, many of the problems are essentially the same. Through our collaboration we have been able to combine Stiglitz's policy experience with Boadway's intimate knowledge of the Canadian economy and the policy problems it faces.

Economics is the science of choice, and writing a textbook involves many choices. As we began working on the Second Edition, we were convinced that the choices made in the First Edition—for instance, the attention to new topics, such as technological change and finance, and the increased emphasis on information—moved the book in the right direction. But we were even more convinced that an understanding of these new topics had to be based on a solid foundation in established fundamentals, such as the law of supply and demand, the theory of household and firm decision making, and traditional perspectives on unemployment, inflation, and economic growth. Thus, the revision faced several seemingly conflicting challenges, not the least of which was the need to reinforce the exposition of the fundamentals while at the same time strengthening the discussion of new topics.

Several of the dramatic changes that loomed large in the early 1990s while the First Edition was being prepared still occupy centre stage, and new issues and perspectives have also emerged. The economic systems of formerly communist countries are still in collapse, with Eastern Europe and the former Soviet Union making slow and painful transitions to market economies. International investors, losing confidence in Mexico in 1995, precipitated a financial crisis that threatened to spread quickly and was only arrested through international cooperation. The countries of Africa have seen their desperate economic conditions worsen. The countries of East Asia, a bright spot in a world facing disappointment, have experienced unprecedented growth, in some cases at rates in excess of 10 percent year after year. Japan remains an economic powerhouse, while South Korea, Taiwan, and the other Asian "tigers" went from being poor backward countries to being major players by taking advantage of opportunities in international markets.

Beginning around 1973, growth in the industrialized countries, including Canada, slowed markedly. Here and in Europe, unemployment rates that in the 1960s had remained extremely low, often soared into double digits and stubbornly remained there. Economic inequality increased, with those at the bottom actually seeing their living standards deteriorate. The mid-1990s brought Canada signs of the reversal of some of these trends. Inflation fell to levels that had not been seen for a quarter of a century, and productivity began to pick up. The poverty rate began to decline, and incomes of all groups, especially those at the bottom, began to rise. But among many workers, anxiety remained high; while their real wages and incomes had begun to rise, they still had not recovered to their earlier peaks, and no one was sure these increases would continue. And unemployment remained stubbornly high, especially for new entrants into the labour force. Moreover, the enormous government debt that had built up over the past 15 years dramatically reduced the government's options: with a high proportion of the budget needed simply to pay interest on the debt, governments were hard pressed to maintain public services and to provide assistance to those in need. Moreover, another time bomb was on the horizon: aging baby boomers would soon put an unprecedented strain on the public pension and health care systems.

As the world has changed, expectations have changed as well. While there has been enormous improvement in the quality of air in our major cities and while Lake Erie has been rescued from becoming polluted to the point where life could not survive, our expectations about the environment have grown even faster; we have become increasingly aware of environmental costs. Longevity has increased, but our knowledge of how to prolong life has outstripped it, and rising health care costs have become a major political issue. The economic role of women has changed: not only have they taken a more active part in the labour force, but there has also been a revolution in expectations concerning the kinds of jobs women can hold.

And in virtually every one of the major issues facing the economy, there is a debate about the role of government. Government at all levels in Canada has grown enormously, largely due to the rapid growth of social programmes and of cash transfers to various groups in the economy. Before World War II, government took about one out of every six dollars of wages in taxes; today it takes more than one out of every three. There are differing views of government responsibility. For instance, people expect, even demand, that government do something about unemployment and provide free health care and education to all. But at the same time, there is a wider understanding of the limitations of government in an increasingly globalized economy. The increasing government deficits over the past decade, the largest in Canada's peacetime history, have meant that one of the wealthiest countries in the world seems short of money to maintain basic public programmes. Issues concerning the responsibilities, capabilities, and strategies of government in the economy have come to the centre of political debates.

These are exciting issues and events, and they fill the front pages of our newspapers and the evening television news shows. Yet in the recent past, teachers of the introductory course in economics have felt frustrated: none of the textbooks really conveyed this sense of excitement. Try as they might, none seemed to prepare the student adequately for interpreting and understanding these important economic events.

On reflection, one of the reasons for this becomes clear: the principles expounded in Alfred Marshall's classic textbook of a hundred years ago, or Paul Samuelson's now almost fifty years old, are not the principles for today. The way we economists understand our discipline has changed to reflect the changing world, but textbooks have not kept pace. Our professional discourse is built on a *modern* economics, but these new developments are simply not adequately reflected in any of the vast array of textbooks available to us as teachers.

Indeed, changes in economics over the past half century have been as significant as the changes in world events. The basic competitive model of the economy was perfected in the 1950s. Since then, economists have gone beyond that model in several directions as they have come to understand its limitations better. Earlier researchers paid lip service to the importance of incentives and to problems posed by limited information. However, it was only in the last two decades that real progress was made in understanding these issues. The 1996 Nobel Prize in economics was awarded to two economists who pioneered our understanding of the role of information and incentives in the economy. Their work, and the work of others in this field, have found immediate applications. The collapse of the Soviet bloc economies, the debt crisis facing many less developed countries, the rash of major bankruptcies in the financial sector, and the escalating costs of health and unemployment insurance programmes can all be viewed as consequences of the failure to provide appropriate incentives. Thus, a central question in the debate over growth and productivity should be: How can an economy provide stronger incentives for innovation? The debate over pollution and the environment centres around the relative merits of regulation and providing incentives not to pollute and to conserve resources.

The past fifty years have also seen a reexamination of the boundary between economics and business. Subjects like finance and management used to be relegated to business schools, where they were taught without reference to economic principles. Today we know that to understand how market economies actually work, we have to understand how firms finance and manage themselves. Tremendous insights can be gleaned through the application of basic economic principles, particularly those grounded in an understanding of incentives. Stories of corporate takeovers have been replaced on the front page by stories of bankruptcies as acquiring corporations have found themselves overextended. The 1990 Nobel Prize was awarded to three economists who made the greatest contribution to the integration of finance and economics. Yet introductory textbooks had not yet built in the basic economics of finance and management.

We have also come to appreciate better the virtues of competition. We now understand, for instance, how the benefits of competition extend beyond price to competition for technological innovation. At the same time, we have come to see better why, in so many circumstances, competition appears limited. Again, none of the available textbooks seemed to provide students with a sense of this new understanding.

Samuelson's path-breaking textbook is credited with being the first to integrate successfully the (then) new insights of Keynesian economics with traditional microeconomics. Samuelson employed the concept of the neoclassical synthesis—the view that once the economy was restored to full employment, the old classical principles applied. In effect, there were two distinct regimes to the economy. In one, when the economy's resources were underemployed, macroeconomic principles applied; in the other, when the economy's resources were fully employed, microeconomic principles were relevant. The belief that these were distinct regimes was reflected in how texts were written and courses were taught; it made no difference whether micro was taught before macro, or vice versa. In the last decades, economists came to question the split that had developed between microeconomics and macroeconomics. The profession as a whole came to believe that macroeconomic behaviour had to be related to underlying microeconomic principles; there was one set of economic principles, not two. But this view simply was not reflected in any of the available texts.

This book differs from most other texts in several ways. Let us highlight some of the most prominent distinctions.

- Reflecting the role of economics in policy making, we have introduced examples throughout the text to relate economic theory to recent policy discussions. In each chapter, a Policy Perspective box provides a vignette on a particular issue both to enliven the course and to enrich the student's command over the basic material.

- Economists are a contentious lot, yet on most issues differences among economists pale in comparison to differences among noneconomists. Indeed, there is a high degree of consensus among economists, and we have drawn attention to this throughout the book with fourteen points of consensus in economics.

- The organization of the macroeconomic presentation has been changed to reflect more closely the microeconomic foundations of macroeconomics. It begins in Part Two with an analysis based on perfect markets—a full-employment model with perfectly flexible wages and prices. This model has the virtue of being pedagogically simple and yet remarkably powerful. From there we move to the other extreme—and the focus of traditional macroeconomics—an unemployment model with rigid wages and prices (Part Three). This leads to a discussion of the dynamics of adjustment, where we present the analysis of an economy in which wages and prices are neither perfectly flexible nor perfectly rigid and in which a principal concern is the rate of inflation (Part Four).

- One of the virtues of the new organization is that we can turn, in Chapter 9, to the important topics of economic growth and fiscal deficits as applications of the full-employment model. Later, in Chapters 19 and 20, we return to consider economic growth and the deficit in greater detail. Students are eager to learn about these fundamental macroeconomic subjects, which are the focus of considerable attention in current policy debates.

- Throughout the book, we integrate modern advances in economics—such as those provided by endogenous growth theory, rational expectations, and theories of credit rationing and credit availability—with traditional topics. This approach lends insight into both the modern advances and the traditional perspectives.

- We have integrated international considerations into macroeconomic analysis. For instance, after setting forth the full-employment model in Chapter 8, we use it in Chapter 9 to explain international capital flows and the determination of exchange rates. Then, in presenting the model of unemployment (Part Three) and the dynamics of adjustment (Part Four), international dimensions are carefully addressed, especially in relation to monetary theory and policy.

- In addition to the extensive integration of international concerns throughout the book, we have added a new chapter on international trade policy (Chapter 21), focusing on trade practices including commercial policy, 'fair trade' laws, and the role of trade agreements and organizations such as the North American Free Trade Agreement (NAFTA) and the World Trade Organization (WTO).

# ACKNOWLEDGMENTS

It has been an honour and a delight to have the privilege of working with Joe Stiglitz in the preparation of this book. As most economists know, he is a remarkable person. Over the years, his writings in many fields have taught my cohort of teachers much. By the clarity and breadth of his work, Joe has served not only to define individual fields of economics (including risk and uncertainty, asymmetric information, tax and public expenditure theory, technological innovation, product diversity and market structure, capital theory, the operation of labour markets in both industrialized and developing countries, and decision making within institutions and bureaucracies, to name a few) but in many cases also to point out the common features of these various fields and the important role that incentives and information play in determining economic outcomes in each of them.

In particular, his application of economic analysis has always been motivated by a wish to explain important real-world phenomena. Writing technical articles for other teachers obviously did not go far enough. So he worked to create the *Journal of Economic Perspectives*, which has succeeded in making available the most abstract of advances in our discipline to a very wide audience of economists. His recent experience with President Clinton's Council of Economic Advisers allowed him to hone his skills at policy analysis further to the benefit of the country as well as economics. That he found time to work on a major revision of this text is testimony to his dedication to economics education.

My role in this venture has been to adapt the textbook to the special features of the Canadian economy and to the particular policy problems it faces. I am fortunate to have been given a free hand to do so and have tried to take advantage of the opportunity. This was not a difficult task. The principles of analysis are universal and apply to any market economy. It was simply a matter of showing their relevance to various issues of Canadian interest. These include our special industrial structure, which results from the combination of a relatively small population for our size, a rich endowment of natural resources, and a historic reliance on inflows of capital from abroad for our development; the importance of trade and financial flows with the rest of the world; the special relationship we have with our giant neighbour to the south, a relationship that has resulted in a sequence of negotiated trading arrangements; the role our government has assumed in providing an array of social programmes and programmes for regional development; and the importance of our relatively decentralized federal system of government. Not surprisingly, many of the current policy problems facing Canada are similar to those facing the United States as well as other developed economies, including lagging productivity growth, difficulties in balancing our trade in the face of increased international competition, and concerns about the way our governments go about their business, both in terms of the services they provide and the difficulty of covering their costs. These issues are all reflected in the Canadian Edition of this book.

Previous users of the book will recognize a considerable shortening of the text and a corresponding reduction in the number of chapters. This is in direct response to the advice of the several reviewers of the First Edition who recognized better than I that students have more to do than devote all their attention to economics during their first year of study. The ideas have not changed, only the economy and efficiency with which they have been presented.

In addition to my deep debt to Joe Stiglitz for giving me the opportunity to participate in this venture, I have also received some exceptional help in preparing the Second Canadian Edition. I am particularly indebted to my colleague Ian Cromb, whose assistance and advice was invaluable in preparing the various Close-up, Policy Perspective, and Using Economics boxes in the text and in helping compile the data for the many tables and graphs. He brought to the collaboration not only his good judgment and good humour but also his wide experience as a principles instructor at Queen's and elsewhere in Canada. Alan Harrison of McMaster University also provided very helpful advice on how to approach various topics in student-friendly ways. My wife, Bernie, helped on this edition, as on the first one, with many of the editorial matters. I also benefited greatly from the reactions of my students in the introductory course at Queen's.

This edition and the previous one have benefited from numerous reviewers. The book has been improved immeasurably by their advice—some of which, quite naturally, was conflicting. In particular, I would like to thank: Douglas W. Allen, Simon Fraser University; James Feehan, Memorial University of Newfoundland; Hugh Grant, University of Winnipeg; Geoffrey B. Hainsworth, University of British Columbia; Michael J. Hare, University of Toronto; Ian J. Irvine, Concordia University; David Johnson, Wilfrid Laurier University; Rashid Khan, University of New Brunswick; Robert R. Kerton, University of Waterloo; Robert F. Lucas, University of Saskatchewan; Henry Rempel, University of Manitoba; Ian Rongve, University of Regina; Peter Sinclair, Wilfrid Laurier University; and Leon P. Sydor, University of Windsor.

This book bears more than the logo of W. W. Norton, a company that reflects many of the aspects of organizational design that we discuss in the text. The book would not be nearly the one it is without the care, attention, and most important, the deep thought devoted to it by so many there. We cannot sufficiently acknowledge our indebtedness to Drake McFeely, who served as our editor on the First Edition (and succeeded Don Lamm as president of Norton), and Ed Parsons, who served as our editor on the Second Edition. Both have been concerned about the ideas *and* their presentation and both have been tough, but constructive, critics. Kate Scott, the manuscript editor, and Kelly Nusser, the project editor, contributed to the book with uncompromising care and precision. And Rosanne Fox showed that the practice of proofreading is indeed an art and that she is a wonderfully accomplished artist. All five made our work harder, so that readers of this book would have an easier time. Three others at Norton also deserve mention: Claire Acher, for outstanding editorial assistance, and Roy Tedoff and Jane Carter for coordinating the production of the book.

Three other people have worked closely with Joe Stiglitz on the two American Editions, and many of their contributions carry over to the Canadian Edition: Timothy Taylor on the First Edition and Felicity Skidmore and John Williams on the Second. All gave their energy and creativity to the enterprise, applying their deep understanding of economics with a commitment to the notion that it is important for modern economic ideas to be communicated widely. The book is immeasurably better as a result.

Necessary and valuable adjuncts to the book are the *Study Guide* for students and the *Instructor's Manual* and test bank for teachers. The *Study Guide* was very capably revised for the Second Canadian Edition by Alan Harrison of McMaster University. It was based on the U.S. Edition prepared by Lawrence Martin of Michigan State University. I took on the *Instructor's Manual* with the careful and helpful assistance of Travis Armour. Alan Harrison also prepared the test bank, and Stephen R. King and Rick M. McConnell are responsible for the unusual and effective computer tutorials.

Finally, though I tried to complete this task with minimal disruption to my family, I am sure that is not the way it seemed to them. At least they know that if it were not this, it would have been something else. In any case, they showed characteristic patience with my preoccupations. My only defence is to suggest that a good understanding of the principles of economics by whomever should study it at colleges and universities in Canada can only help to serve the interests of my sons' generation.

I especially dedicate this book to Andrew, who has struggled with a disease that few can understand. The plight of those like him should remind us that the study of economics serves a broader social purpose than just the self-interest of market participants.

## OUTLINE FOR A SHORT COURSE IN MACROECONOMICS

This book is suitable for short courses offered under a semester system or other abbreviated schedules. Below we offer a provisional outline for such a short course, omitting several chapters. Naturally, to a large extent *which* topics get omitted is a matter of taste. The following is our selection for a short course using fifteen chapters.

| Chapter Number | Chapter Title |
|---|---|
| 2 | Thinking Like an Economist |
| 3 | Trade |
| 4 | Demand, Supply, and Price |
| 6 | Macroeconomic Goals and Measures |
| 7 | Microfoundations |
| 8 | The Full-Employment Model |
| 10 | Overview of Unemployment Macroeconomics |
| 11 | Aggregate Demand |
| 13 | Money, Banking, and Credit |
| 14 | Monetary Theory |
| 15 | Fiscal and Monetary Policy |
| 16 | Inflation: Wage and Price Dynamics |
| 18 | Inflation versus Unemployment: Approaches to Policy |
| 20 | Intergenerational Transfers: Deficits and Public Pensions |
| 21 | Trade Policy |

## OUTLINE FOR A ONE-SEMESTER FULL COURSE

This book may be used with its companion volume, *Principles of Micro-economics and the Canadian Economy* (Second Edition), in either a one- or two-semester course covering both microeconomics and macroeconomics. Below is our suggested outline for a one-semester course, including chapters from both books. Chapters from the microeconomics volume are indicated with asterisks. The outline includes most of the fundamentals, but of necessity it must leave out some of the exciting new topics. Naturally, *which* topics get omitted is a matter of taste. The following is our selection for a short course using twenty chapters.

| Chapter Number | Chapter Title |
| --- | --- |
| 2* | Thinking Like an Economist |
| 3* | Trade |
| 4* | Demand, Supply, and Price |
| 5* | Using Demand and Supply |
| 6* | The Consumption Decision |
| 8* | Saving and Investing |
| 9* | The Firm's Costs |
| 10* | Production in a Competitive Industry |
| 12* | Monopolies and Imperfect Competition |
| 16* | Imperfect Information |
| 18* | Government and Public Decision Making |
| 6 | Macroeconomic Goals and Measures |
| 8 | The Full-Employment Model |
| 10 | Overview of Unemployment Macroeconomics |
| 11 | Aggregate Demand |
| 13 | Money, Banking, and Credit |
| 14 | Monetary Theory |
| 16 | Inflation: Wage and Price Dynamics |
| 20 | Intergenerational Transfers: Deficits and Public Pensions |
| 21 | Trade Policy |

# PART ONE

# INTRODUCTION

These days economics is big news. If we pick up a newspaper or turn on the television for the prime-time news report, we are likely to be bombarded with statistics on unemployment rates, inflation rates, exports, and imports. How well are we doing in competition with other countries, such as Japan? Everyone seems to want to know. Political fortunes as well as the fortunes of countries, firms, and individuals depend on how well the economy does.

What is economics all about? That is the subject of Part One. Chapter 1 uses the story of the automobile industry to illustrate many of the fundamental issues with which economics is concerned. The chapter describes the four basic questions at the heart of economics and how economists attempt to answer these questions.

Chapter 2 introduces the economists' basic model and explains why notions of property rights, profits, prices, and cost play such a central role in economists' thinking.

A fact of life in the modern world is that individuals and countries are interdependent. Even a wealthy country like Canada is dependent on foreign countries for vital imports. Chapter 3 discusses the gains that result from trade—why trade, for instance, allows greater specialization and why greater specialization results in increased productivity. It also explains the patterns of trade—why each country imports and exports the particular goods it does.

Prices play a central role in enabling economies to function. Chapters 4 and 5 take up the question of what determines prices. What causes prices to change over time? Why is water, without which we cannot live, normally so inexpensive, while diamonds, which we surely can do without, are very expensive? What happens to the prices of beer and cigarettes if the government imposes a tax on these goods? What happens if the government restricts the quantities that can be produced and sold, as in the case of some agricultural products? Sometimes the government passes laws requiring firms to pay wages of at least so much or forbidding landlords to charge rents that exceed a certain level; what are the consequences of these government interventions?

# CHAPTER 1

# THE AUTOMOBILE AND ECONOMICS

Imagine the world a hundred years ago: no cars, airplanes, computers (and computer games!), movies—to say nothing of atomic energy, lasers, and transistors. The list of inventions since then seems almost endless.

Of all the inventions that have shaped the world during the past century, perhaps none has had so profound an effect as the automobile. It has changed how and where people work, live, and play. But like any major innovation, it has been a mixed blessing: traffic jams on the one hand, access to wilderness on the other. And the new opportunities it created for some were accompanied by havoc for others. Some occupations—such as blacksmiths—virtually disappeared. Others—such as carriage makers—had to transform themselves (into car body manufacturers) or go out of business. But the gains of the many who benefited from the new industry far outweighed the losses of those who were hurt.

The story of the automobile is familiar. But looking at it from the perspective of economics can teach us a great deal about the economic way of thinking.

## KEY QUESTIONS

**1** What *is* economics? What are the basic questions it addresses?

**2** In economies such as that of Canada, what are the respective roles of government and the private, or "market," sector?

**3** What are markets, and what are the principal markets that make up the economy?

**4** Why is economics called a social science?

**5** Why, if economics is a science, do economists so often seem to disagree?

## THE AUTOMOBILE: A BRIEF HISTORY

The idea of a motorized carriage occurred to many in North America and Europe at roughly the same time. An automobile was actually built in Canada as early as 1867, well before cars were first imported from the United States. But ideas alone are not enough. Translating ideas into marketable products requires solving technical problems and persuading investors to finance the venture.

If you visit a museum of early cars, you will see that the technical problems were resolved in a variety of ways, by many people working independently. At the turn of the century, the area around Detroit was full of innovators developing cars—Ransom E. Olds, the Dodge brothers, and Henry Ford. The spirit must have been much like that of "Silicon Valley" (the area in California between San Francisco and San Jose) in the past quarter century, which has been at the center of computer technology development: a spirit of excitement, breakthroughs made, and new milestones reached. The various automobile innovators could draw upon a stock of ideas "in the air." They also had the help of specialized firms that had developed a variety of new technologies and skills: new alloys that enabled lighter motors to be constructed and new techniques for machining that allowed for greater power, precision, and durability.

Henry Ford is generally given credit for having recognized the potential value of a vehicle that could be made and sold at a reasonable price. Before Ford, automobiles were luxuries, affordable only by the very rich. He saw the potential benefit of providing inexpensive transportation. After he introduced the Model T in 1909 at a "bargain" price of U.S.\$900, he continued to cut the price—to U.S.\$440 in 1914 and U.S.\$360 in 1916. Sales skyrocketed from 58,000 in 1909 to 730,000 in 1916. Ford's prediction of a mass market for inexpensive cars had proved correct.

But success was not sudden or easy. To translate his idea into action Ford had to put together a company to produce cars, figure out how to produce them cheaply, and raise the capital required to make all this possible.

Raising capital was particularly difficult, since the venture was extremely risky. Would Ford be successful in developing his automobile? Would someone else beat him to it? Would the price of a car be low enough for many people to buy it? If he was successful, would imitators copy his invention, robbing him of the mass market he needed to make money?

Ford formed a partnership to develop his first car. He was to supply the ideas and the work, while his partners supplied the funds. It took three partnerships before Ford produced a single car. The first two went bankrupt, with the financial partners in each case accusing Ford of spending all of his time developing ideas instead of acting on them.

But were the first two sets of partners treated unfairly? After all, they knew the risks. Ford could have entered each partnership in good faith and simply been unable to deliver. Even in the third case his partners were unhappy, claiming that he managed to get the lion's share of the profits for himself.

Whatever the truth in Ford's case, the general problem of who contributes more in a partnership and who should get what share of any profits occurs often. Ford may have argued that his ideas were far more important than the mere dollars that the financiers provided to carry them out.

Ford's success was due as much to his ability to come up with innovative ways of providing incentives and organizing production as to his skill in solving technical problems. He demonstrated this ability with his original labour policies. He offered more than double the going wage and paid his workers the then princely sum of U.S.$5 a day. In exchange, Ford worked his employees hard; the moving assembly line he invented enabled him to set his workers a fast pace and push them to keep up. The amount produced per worker increased enormously. Still, it was clear that the high wages were ample compensation for the extra effort. Riots almost broke out as workers clamoured for the jobs he offered. Ford had rediscovered an old truth: in some cases, higher wages for employees can repay the employer in higher productivity, through greater loyalty, harder work, and less absenteeism.

Ford's success in increasing productivity meant that he could sell his cars far more cheaply than his rivals could. The lower prices and the high level of sales that accompanied them made it possible for him to take full advantage of the mass production techniques he had developed. At one point, however, Ford's plans were almost thwarted when a lawyer-inventor named George Baldwin Selden claimed that Ford had infringed on his patent.

Governments grant patents to enable inventors to reap the rewards of their innovative activity. These are generally for specific inventions, like a new type of braking system or transmission mechanism, not for general ideas. Ford's idea of an assembly line, for example, was not an invention that could be patented, and it was imitated by other car manufacturers. A patent gives the inventor the exclusive right to produce his invention for a limited time, thus helping to assure that inventors will be able to make some money from their successful inventions. Patents may lead to higher prices for these new products, since there is no competition from others making the same product. But the presumption is that the gains to society from the innovative activity more than compensate for the losses to consumers from the temporarily higher prices.

Selden had applied for, and been granted, a patent for a horseless, self-propelled carriage. He demanded that other car manufacturers pay him a royalty, which is a payment for the right to use a patented innovation. Ford challenged Selden's patent in court on the grounds that the concept of a "horseless, self-propelled carriage" was too vague to be patentable. Ford won. Providing cars to the masses at low prices made Ford millions of dollars and many millions of North Americans better off, by enabling them to go where they wanted to go more easily, cheaply, and speedily.

Automobile production quickly spread to Canada, largely through foreign investment in and around the Windsor, Ontario, area. The founding of Ford Motor Company of Canada in 1904 marked the beginning of the Canadian automobile industry. It became the heart of the manufacturing industry in central Canada, providing thousands of high-paying jobs both directly and indirectly to Canadian workers.

## CRISIS IN THE NORTH AMERICAN AUTOMOBILE INDUSTRY

Today people think of computers and gene-splicing, not automobiles, as the new technologies. The story of the automobile is no longer emblematic of the latest technological breakthroughs. The changing fortunes of the automobile industry during the past two decades reflect a redefinition of North American industry.

There were more than a hundred automobile manufacturers in the fall of 1903, twenty-seven of which accounted for more than 70 percent of the total sales of the industry. By the early 1960s, however, only three companies were responsible for 88 percent of North American auto sales. Of the car manufacturers that existed at the beginning of the century, many had gone bankrupt or had given up on the automobile business, and the remainder had been consolidated into or taken over by the dominant firms.

The most serious problems faced by the auto industry in the 1960s involved air pollution and automobile safety. To reduce pollution, the Canadian and U.S. governments regulated the kind of exhaust fumes a car could produce, and design changes

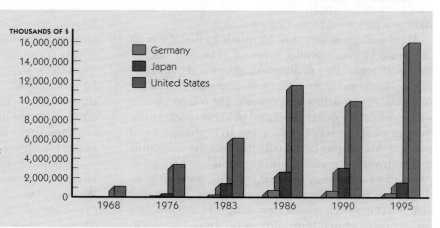

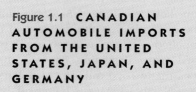

**Figure 1.1 CANADIAN AUTOMOBILE IMPORTS FROM THE UNITED STATES, JAPAN, AND GERMANY**

Imports from Germany and, especially, Japan rose from the 1960s until 1990. Imports from the United States fell in the late 1980s but have surged in the 1990s. *Source:* Statistics Canada (65-006, 65007), CANSIM Database, 1996.

followed. On the safety front, automobile companies quickly responded to demands for increased safety by providing seat belts.

This relatively rosy picture changed dramatically in 1973. That year, the Organization of Petroleum Exporting Countries (OPEC)—mainly countries in the Middle East—combined forces to hold down the supply of oil, create a scarcity, and thus push up its price. OPEC actually cut off all oil exports for a few tense weeks late in 1973. Its power was a surprise to many, including the automobile industry. North American cars then tended to be bigger and heavier than those in Japan and Europe. This was easily explained: incomes in the United States and Canada were higher; consumers could afford larger cars and the gasoline they guzzled. Also, Japan and Europe imposed much heavier taxes on gasoline, encouraging consumers in those countries to buy smaller, more fuel-efficient cars.

The North American auto industry thus was ill-prepared for the higher gas prices caused by OPEC's move. But other countries, especially Japan, stood ready to gain, with smaller, cheaper, and more fuel-efficient cars. Figure 1.1 shows the rapid growth of imports of new passenger cars into Canada between 1968 and 1994 from the United States, Japan, and Germany. The figures tell a story: car imports, which account for over a quarter of sales in Canada, rose rapidly over the period. However, those from outside

North America initially garnered a larger and larger share, rising from about 7 percent in 1968 to over 22 percent by the end of the 1980s before falling off to 13 percent by 1994.

It was clear that the Japanese firms were supplying what Canadian consumers wanted, but the effect on the domestic automobile industry was devastating. Profits fell and many workers, those whose high wages could not be justified by the level of productivity, were laid off.

## PROTECTION FROM FOREIGN COMPETITION

In the early 1980s, the Big Three—Canadian subsidiaries of Chrysler, General Motors, and Ford—began to make a recovery from the hard times of the 1970s, for several reasons. Unions dramatically reduced their wage demands. Smaller and more fuel-efficient cars were developed. And the government stepped in to help protect the industry from foreign competition. Rather than imposing a tariff (tax) on car imports, the Canadian and U.S. governments negotiated with the Japanese government to restrain Japan's automobile exports. Although the export limits were called voluntary, they were actually negotiated under pressure. If the Japanese had not taken the "voluntary" step of limiting exports, Parliament

The intent of the North American Free Trade Agreement (NAFTA) is to eliminate all tariffs on goods and services produced in one member country and exported to another. However, that does not mean that all cars made in Canada can cross the border into the United States tariff-free; cars made in Canada may be assembled from parts manufactured elsewhere, including outside North America. To be eligible, goods must satisfy the "rules of origin" provisions of NAFTA, which spell out various formulae for determining whether the goods "originated" in North America.

When NAFTA is fully phased in, cars, light trucks, and their engines and transmissions will only be eligible for duty-free status if it can be demonstrated that they contain at least 62.5 percent North American content. For the automobile industry, the content percentage is calculated using the net-cost method: North American

content is defined as total eligible costs less the value of non–North American materials, divided by total eligible costs, where eligible costs are total costs less ineligible costs such as royalties, shipping and packing, sales promotion, and marketing.

These rather arcane rules are of more than mere academic interest. In recent years Japanese automakers have invested in several plants in Canada, partly to avoid having to pay the tariff. The cars built in these plants have been challenged as to whether they satisfy the North American rule of origin, a challenge that has threatened their tariff-free status. Any adverse ruling would clearly affect the profitability of these plants and the desire of overseas automakers to invest in Canada.

*Source:* External Affairs and International Trade Canada, *NAFTA—What's it all about?* (1993), Chapter 4, "Rules of Origin."

and Congress probably would have passed laws forcing them to do so.

The reduced supply of Japanese cars led not only to increased sales of North American cars, but also to higher prices, for both Japanese and domestic cars. The domestic industry was subsidized not by the taxpayers in general but by those who bought cars, through these higher prices. The Japanese car manufacturers had little to complain about, since they too benefited from the higher prices. Had Japanese manufacturers gotten together and agreed to reduce their sales and raise prices, the action would have been viewed as a violation of Canadian anti-combines laws, which were designed to enforce competition. But here the government itself was encouraging less competition!

The Japanese responded in still another way to these restrictions. They decided to circumvent the limitations imposed on their exports by manufacturing cars here in Canada and the United States. Figure 1.2 shows the fraction of total Canadian production accounted for by General Motors, Ford, Chrysler, Honda, and "other" firms in 1971, 1991, and 1994. This picture reflects three phenomena. First, production in Canada is highly concentrated in a few firms. Thus, GM, with about 44 percent of total production, is shown as having close to one half of the pie. Second, whereas in 1971 Honda was not producing cars in Canada, by 1991 its production rose to over 11 percent of total Canadian production and was larger than that of the smallest American-owned producer, Chrysler. Third, by 1994 Chrysler had

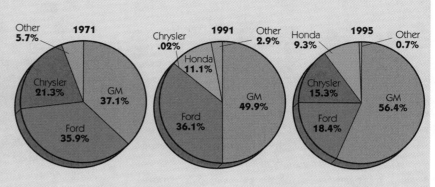

**Figure 1.2 SHARES OF AUTOMOBILE PRODUCTION IN CANADA**

These pie charts show some of the changes in Canadian automobile production in recent decades. They show that production has remained concentrated, but that the shares of various companies have changed. Honda's production in Canada grew from zero to over 10 percent in the 1990s. Although Chrysler's production initially fell dramatically, it has since recovered its market share. *Source:* Statistics Canada, CANSIM Database 1995.

rebounded dramatically, overtaking not only Honda but also Ford. Honda roughly held its own.

What would have happened had the automobile industry not been given the breather that the Japanese export restraints provided? We cannot tell. Perhaps it would have been forced to transform itself more quickly. Perhaps one or more firms would have gone out of business. What we do know is that during the 1980s, the industry worked hard to compete effectively with its Japanese rivals.

## CANADA'S PLACE IN THE AUTOMOBILE INDUSTRY

More than any other industry, the automobile industry typifies the "openness" of the Canadian economy— its reliance on foreign investment and technology and its interrelationship with its American counterpart. The same companies that came to dominate the American industry also dominated the Canadian one, largely through branch plants or subsidiaries. Automobiles and parts produced in each country served the entire North American market. The fortunes of the Canadian automobile industry were interwoven with those of the U.S. automobile industry; these were formalized with the signing of the so-called Auto Pact in 1965 (technically called the Canada-U.S. Automotive Products Trade Agreement).

By the early 1990s, Canadian vehicle production

was over two million units, employing more than 45,000 workers. Under the Auto Pact, as discussed below, the allocation of production was rationalized between Canada and the United States, with each country specializing in certain vehicle lines. In Canada, most activity is in light vehicle production (automobiles, minivans, and light trucks) and is dominated by the Big Three. But as a result of the relative ease of entry, efficient and competitive foreign automobile producers have been able to set up production facilities and gain a substantial share of the North American market. Asian-owned production from companies such as Toyota, Hyundai, and Suzuki has been growing rapidly and now accounts for over 30 percent of industry output. Part of the reason for setting up plants in Canada is to avoid the tariff levied on imported vehicles coming into Canada and the United States. In Canada, the tariff ranges from 6.0 to 9.2 percent of the value of vehicles, while the U.S. tariff rates are slightly lower.

Foreign producers have put considerable pressure on the Canadian industry, and are likely to continue to do so. For example, Japanese corporations are moving towards the production of more specialized and expensive midrange automobiles from the traditional smaller ones. As well, Japanese parts manufacturers are poised to begin making parts in Canada. The Big Three are responding partly by adopting Japanese methods, such as building stronger ties to component manufacturers, and partly by closing down existing plants and investing in modernization.

The development of the Canadian automobile industry has been heavily influenced by the Canada-U.S. Auto Pact, whose provisions remained the same under both the 1988 Canada-U.S. Free Trade Agreement and the subsequent North American Free Trade Agreement (NAFTA). The Auto Pact essentially stipulates that there be limited duty-free movement of automobile products across the Canada-U.S. border. This is **sectoral free trade,** or free trade in the products of a particular industry. Its two main goals are to integrate the North American auto industry to bring about more efficient patterns of investment, production, and trade, and to strengthen trade relations between the two countries. The main provision of the Auto Pact concerns the circumstances under which products can be imported duty-free. A manufacturer may import vehicles and original parts into Canada free of duty, provided the manufacturer maintains a ratio of production to sales in Canada at least as great as its 1964 production-to-sales ratio and at least 3 to 4.

The Auto Pact has apparently served Canada well, as attested by the relative success of the automotive industry. The Canadian automobile industry attracted over $12 billion of investment during the 1980s. The industry now faces the challenges of the 1990s, including continued competition from Asian automobile producers as well as the prospects for increased competition from Mexico as a result of the North American Free Trade Agreement.

Although the Canadian industry has been dominated by foreign-owned companies, there have been attempts in the past to produce a made-in-Canada car. Back in the 1950s, the Studebaker was produced in Walkerville, Ontario, largely to serve the British market. The company produced up to 15,000 cars per year but was unable to compete against the larger U.S.-based companies. A more spectacular case was that of the Bricklin car, a dream car intended to capture some of the upper end of the luxury market. It was to be produced in New Brunswick, though with franchises in the United States. The New Brunswick government agreed to provide financial support for the enterprise in the hope of creating permanent jobs in the province. As it turned out, the corporation declared bankruptcy in 1975 after two years in operation and after producing 2,800 cars. The New Brunswick government lost a total of $23 million in the venture.

More recently, some independence was achieved on the labour side of the industry. In 1985 the Canadian Autoworkers Union (CAW) split from the International Union of United Automobile Workers of America (UAW), and now represents most automobile workers in Canada. At the time of the split, the CAW had about 140,000 workers, making it the sixth largest union in Canada.

## WHAT IS ECONOMICS?

This narrative illustrates many facets of economics, but now a definition of our subject is in order. **Economics** is the study of how individuals, firms, governments, and other organizations within our society make **choices,** and how those choices determine the way the resources of society are used. **Scarcity** figures prominently in economics: choices matter because resources are scarce. Imagine an enormously wealthy individual who can have everything he wants. We might think that scarcity is not in his vocabulary—until we consider that time is a resource, and he must decide what expensive toy to devote his time to each day. When one takes time into account, scarcity is a fact in everyone's life.

To produce a single product, like an automobile, thousands of decisions and choices have to be made. Since any economy is made up not only of automobiles but of millions of products, it is a marvel that the economy functions at all, let alone as well as it does most of the time. This marvel is particularly clear if you consider instances when things do not work so well: the worldwide Great Depression in the 1930s, when almost 20 percent of the Canadian work force could not find a job; the countries of the former Soviet Union today, where ordinary consumer goods like carrots or toilet paper are often simply unavailable; the less developed economies of many countries in Africa, Asia, and Latin America, where standards of living have remained stubbornly low, and in some places have even been declining.

The fact that choices must be made applies to the economy as a whole as much as it does to each individual. Somehow, decisions are taken—by individuals, households, firms, and government—that together determine how the economy's limited resources, including its land, labour, machines, oil, and other natural resources, are used. Why is it that land used at one time for growing crops may, at another time, be used for an automobile plant? How was it that over the space of a couple of decades, resources were transferred from making horse carriages to making automobile bodies? that blacksmiths were replaced by auto mechanics? How do the decisions of millions of consumers, workers, investors, managers, and government officials all interact to determine the use of the scarce resources available to society? Economists reduce such matters to four basic questions concerning how economies function:

**1. *What is produced, and in what quantities?***
There have been important changes in consumption over the past fifty years. Spending for medical care, for example, was only 2 percent of total personal consumption in 1950. By 1990, more than one out of every ten dollars was spent on medical care, most of it by the government. What can account for changes like these? The economy seems to spew out new products like videocassette recorders and new services like automated bank tellers. What causes this process of innovation? The overall level of production has also shifted from year to year, often accompanied by large changes in the levels of employment and unemployment. How can economists explain these changes?

In Canada, the question of what is produced, and in what quantities, is answered largely by the private interaction of firms and consumers, but government also plays a role. Prices are critical in determining what goods and services are produced. When the price of some good rises, firms are induced to produce more of that good, to increase their profits. Thus, a central question for economists is, why are some goods or services more expensive than others? And why has the price of some goods increased or decreased?

**2. *How are these goods and services produced?***
There are often many ways of making something.

Textiles can be made with hand looms. Modern machines enable fewer workers to produce more cloth. Very modern machines may be highly computerized, allowing one worker to monitor many more machines than was possible earlier. The better machines generally cost more, but they require less labour. Which technique will be used, the advanced technology or the labour-intensive one? Henry Ford introduced the assembly line. More recently, car manufacturers have begun using robots, and automated machines have replaced tellers in providing banking services. What determines how rapidly technology changes?

In the Canadian economy, firms answer the question of how goods and services are produced, again with help from the government, which sets regulations and enacts laws that affect everything from the overall organization of firms to the ways they interact with their employees and customers.

**3. *For whom are these goods and services produced?*** Individuals who have higher incomes can consume more goods and services. But that answer only pushes the question back one step: What determines the differences in income and wages? What is the role of luck? of education? of inheritance? of savings? of experience and hard work? These questions are difficult to answer. For now, suffice it to say that while incomes are primarily determined by the private interaction of firms and households, government also plays a strong role, with taxes that redistribute income as well as programs like education and health care that enhance the ability of persons to earn incomes.

Figure 1.3 shows the relative pay in a variety of different occupations. To judge by income, each computer specialist receives almost twice as much of the economy's output as the average worker, and over four times as much as a bank teller.

**4. *Who takes economic decisions, and by what processes?*** In a **centrally planned economy,** as the Soviet Union used to be, the government takes responsibility for virtually every aspect of economic activity. The government provides the answers to the first three questions. A central economic planning agency works through a bureaucracy to say what will be produced and by what method, and who

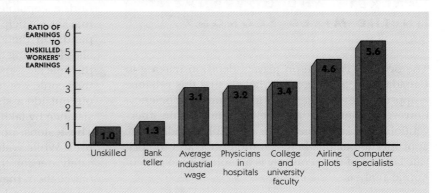

**Figure 1.3 WHO TAKES HOME CANADA'S OUTPUT?**

This chart, using data for 1990, compares the earnings of workers in various occupations to the earnings of the unskilled worker. The average worker makes 3.0 times as much as the unskilled worker, and computer specialists make 5.6 times as much. *Source:* Statistics Canada, *Employment Earnings and Hours* (1993).

shall consume it. At the other end of the spectrum are economies that rely primarily on the free interchange of producers and their customers to determine what, how, and for whom. Canada, which lies towards this latter end, has a **mixed economy;** that is, there is a mix between public (governmental) and private decision making. Within limits, producers make what they want to make; they use whatever method of production seems appropriate to them; and the output is distributed to consumers according to their income.

When economists examine an economy, they want to know to what extent economic decisions are taken by the government, and to what extent they are taken by private individuals. In Canada, while individuals for the most part take their own decisions about what kind of car to purchase, the government has inserted itself in a number of ways: it has taken actions that affect the imports of Japanese cars, that restrict the amount of pollutants a car can produce, and that promote fuel efficiency and automobile safety.

A related question is whether economic decisions are taken by individuals for their own interests or for the interest of an employer such as a business firm or government agency. This is an important distinction. We can expect people acting on their own behalf to take decisions that benefit themselves. When they act on behalf of organizations, however, a conflict of interest may arise. Observers often refer to corporations and governments as if they were a single individual. Economists point out that organizations consist, by definition, of a multitude of individuals and that the interests of these individuals do not necessarily coincide with one another or, for that matter, with the interests of the organization itself. Organizations bring a number of distinctive problems to the analysis of choice.

As you can see by their concern with decision making, economists are concerned not only with *how* the economy answers the four basic questions, but also *how well.* They ask, is the economy efficient? Could it produce more of some goods without producing fewer of others? Could it make some individuals better off without making some other individuals worse off?

## BASIC QUESTIONS OF ECONOMICS

**1** What is produced, and in what quantities?

**2** How are these goods and services produced?

**3** For whom are these goods and services produced?

**4** Who takes economic decisions, and by what processes?

## MARKETS AND GOVERNMENT IN THE MIXED ECONOMY

The primary reliance on private decision making in Canada reflects economists' beliefs that this reliance is appropriate and necessary for economic efficiency; however, economists also believe that certain interventions by government are desirable. Finding the appropriate balance between the public and the private sectors of the economy is a central issue of economic analysis.

### MARKETS

The economic concept of markets is used to include any situation where exchange takes place, though this exchange may not necessarily resemble what takes place in traditional village markets. In department stores and shopping malls, customers rarely haggle over the price. When manufacturers purchase the materials they need for production, they exchange money for them, not other goods. Most goods, from cameras to clothes, are not sold directly from producers to consumers. They are sold from producers to distributors, from distributors to retailers, from retailers to consumers. All of these transactions are embraced by the concepts of **market** and **market economy.**

In market economies with competition, individuals make choices that reflect their own desires, and firms make choices that maximize their profits; to do so, they must produce the goods and services that consumers want, and they must produce them at lower cost than other firms. As firms compete in the quest for profits, consumers are benefited, both in the kinds of goods and services produced and the prices at which they are supplied. The market economy thus provides answers to the four basic economic questions—what is produced, how it is produced, for whom it is produced, and how these decisions are taken. And on the whole, the answers the market gives ensure the efficiency of the economy.

The market provides answers to the question of whom goods are produced for that not everyone finds acceptable. As with bidders at an auction, what market participants are willing and able to pay depends on their income. Some groups of individuals—including those without skills that are valued by the market—may receive such a low income that they could not feed and educate their children without outside assistance. Government provides the assistance by taking steps to increase income equality. These steps, however, often blunt economic incentives. While welfare payments provide an important safety net for the poor, the taxation required to finance them may discourage work and savings. If the government takes one out of three or even two dollars that an individual earns, that individual may not be inclined to work so much, whatever her income level. And if the government takes one out of two or three dollars a person earns from interest on savings, the person may decide to spend more and save less. Like the appropriate balance between the public and private sectors, the appropriate balance between concerns about equality (often referred to as **equity concerns**) and efficiency is a central issue of modern economics.

### THE ROLE OF GOVERNMENT

The market provides answers to the basic economic questions *that on the whole* ensure efficiency. But in certain areas the solutions appear inadequate to many. There may be too much pollution, too much inequality, and too little concern about education, health, and safety. When the market is not perceived to be working well, people often turn to government.

Government plays a major role in modern economies. We need to understand both what that role is and why governments undertake the activities they do. Historically, governments in Canada have always taken an active role in economic affairs. The construction of the trans-Canadian railroad in the 1880s, which was instrumental in unifying the country, was only accomplished with the active financial support of the government. The system of tariff protection for manufacturing under the National Policy implemented by the 1889 Conservative government of Sir

While the mixed economy now is the dominant form of economic organization, it is not the only possible way of answering the basic economic questions. Beginning in 1917, an experiment in almost complete government control was begun in what became the Soviet Union.

What was produced in such an economy, and in what quantities? Government planners set the targets, which workers and firms then struggled to meet.

How were these goods produced? Again, since government planners decided what supplies would be delivered to each factory, they effectively chose how production occurred.

For whom were these goods produced? The government took decisions about what each job was paid, which affected how much people could consume. In principle, individuals could choose what to buy at government-operated stores, at prices set by the government. But in practice, many goods were unavailable at these stores.

Who took economic decisions, and by what process? The government planners decided, basing the decisions on their view of national economic goals.

At one time, all this planning sounded very sensible, but as former Soviet premier Nikita Khrushchev once said, "Economics is a subject that does not greatly respect one's wishes." Many examples of Soviet economic woes could be cited, but two will suffice. In the shoe market, the Soviet Union was the largest national producer in the world. However, the average shoe was of such low quality that it fell apart in a few weeks, and inventories of unwanted shoes rotted in warehouses. In agriculture, the Soviet government had traditionally allowed small private plots. Although the government limited the time farmers could spend on these plots, publicly run farming was so unproductive that the 3 percent of Soviet land that was privately run produced about 25 percent of the total farm output.

Today the standard of living in the former Soviet Union is not only below that in industrialized nations like those of North America, Japan, and Western Europe, but it is barely ahead of developing nations like Brazil and Mexico. Workers in the Soviet Union shared a grim one-liner: "We pretend to work and they pretend to pay us."

The collapse of the former Soviet Union was to a large extent the result of the failure of its economic system. Much of this text is concerned with explaining why mixed economies work as well as they do.

John A. Macdonald formed the basis of industrial policy for most of the twentieth century. The encouragement of high levels of immigration in the early 1900s was undertaken to develop the agricultural economy of the Prairie provinces. Government-owned corporations have been important in such industries as transportation, communications, and energy. Government has virtually taken over the provision of services in the areas of health, education, and welfare, services that were originally offered either by the private sector or by charitable organizations such as the churches. By tax and subsidy policies, governments have changed the fortunes of entire industries or segments of the nation. The National Energy Policy of the 1970s had an enormous impact on the oil and gas industry. Federal transportation policies have helped to economize on the costs of getting grain to foreign markets. And an active program of regional development subsidies has attempted to encourage industry to locate in high-unemployment regions of the Atlantic provinces and parts of Quebec. Many observers have noted the seemingly greater tendency to resort to government intervention in the Canadian economy than in the American.

The government sets the legal structure under which private firms and individuals operate. It regulates businesses to ensure that they do not discriminate by race or gender, do not mislead customers, are careful about the safety of their employees, and do not pollute the air and water. In some cases, such as telecommunications, even the prices that firms can charge are regulated. In many industries, government firms, called **Crown corporations,** operate as private businesses, sometimes in competition with private firms: examples have included PETRO Canada in the oil industry, Air Canada and Canadian National in transportation, the Canadian Broadcasting Corporation in entertainment, Canada Post, several provincial electrical utilities, as well as telephone companies and even automobile insurance plans in some provinces. Most schools as well as virtually all universities and hospitals are government-owned. In other cases, the government supplies goods and services that the private sector does not, such as providing for the national defence, building roads, and printing money. Government programmes provide for the elderly through Old Age Security, which pays income to retired individuals, and health care, which is fully funded by the government. The government helps those who have suffered economic dislocation, through unemployment insurance for those temporarily unemployed and disability insurance for those who are no longer able to work. The government also provides a "safety net" of support for the poor through various welfare programs.

One can easily imagine a government controlling the economy more directly. In countries where decision-making authority is centralized and concentrated in the government, government bureaucrats might decide what and how much a factory should produce and set the level of wages that should be paid. At least until recently, governments in countries like the former Soviet Union and China attempted to control practically all major decisions regarding resource allocation.

## THE THREE MAJOR MARKETS

The market economy revolves around exchange between individuals (or households), who buy goods and services (products) from firms, and firms, which take **inputs,** the various materials of production, and produce **outputs,** the goods and services that they sell. In thinking about a market economy, economists focus their attention on three broad categories of markets in which individuals and firms interact. The markets in which firms sell their outputs to households are referred to collectively as the **product market.** Many firms also sell goods and services to other firms; the outputs of the first firm become the inputs of the second. These transactions too are said to occur in the product market.

On the input side, firms need (besides the materials that they buy in the product market) some combination of labour and machinery with which their goods can be produced. They purchase the services of workers in the **labour market.** They raise funds with which to buy inputs in the **capital market.** Traditionally, economists have also highlighted the importance of a third input, land, but in modern industrial economies, land is of secondary importance. For most purposes, it suffices to focus attention on the three major markets listed here, and this text will follow this pattern.

As Figure 1.4 shows, individuals participate in all three markets. When individuals buy goods or services, they act as **consumers** in the product market. When people act as **workers,** economists say they "sell their labour services" in the labour market. When individuals buy shares of stock in a firm or lend money to a business, economists note that they are participating in the capital market, and refer to them as **investors.**

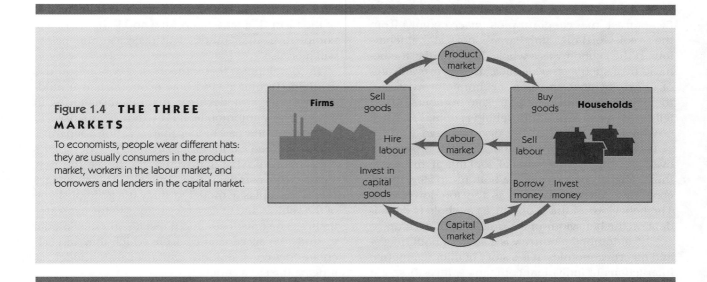

**Figure 1.4 THE THREE MARKETS**

To economists, people wear different hats: they are usually consumers in the product market, workers in the labour market, and borrowers and lenders in the capital market.

## TWO CAVEATS

Terms in economics often are similar to terms in ordinary usage, but they can take on special meanings. The terms "market" and "capital" illustrate the problem.

Though the term "market" is used to conjure an image of a busy **marketplace,** there is no formal marketplace for most goods and services. There are buyers and sellers, and economists analyze the outcome *as if* there were a single marketplace in which all the transactions occurred.

Moreover, economists often talk about the "market for labour" as if all workers were identical. But workers obviously differ in countless ways. In some cases, these differences are important. We might then talk about the "market for skilled workers," or "the market for plumbers." But in other cases—such as when we are talking about the overall state of the economy and are focusing on the unemployment rate (the fraction of workers who would like jobs but cannot get them)—these differences can be ignored.

When newspapers refer to the **capital market,** they mean the bond traders and stockbrokers and the companies they work for on Bay Street in Toronto and other financial districts. When economists use the term "capital market" they have in mind a broader

concept. It includes all the institutions concerned with raising funds (and, as we will see later, sharing and insuring risks), including banks and insurance companies.

The term "capital" is used in still another way—to refer to the machines and buildings used in production. To distinguish this particular usage, in this book we refer to machines and buildings as **capital goods.** "Capital markets" thus refers to the markets in which funds are raised, borrowed, and lent. **Capital goods markets** refers to the markets in which capital goods are bought and sold.

## MICROECONOMICS AND MACROECONOMICS: THE TWO BRANCHES OF ECONOMICS

The detailed study of product, labour, and capital markets is called **microeconomics.** Microeconomics (*micro* is derived from the Greek word meaning "small") focuses on the behaviour of the units—the firms, households, and individuals—that make up the economy. It is concerned with how the individual units take decisions and what affects those decisions. By contrast, **macroeconomics** (*macro* comes from the Greek word meaning "large") looks at the behaviour of the economy as a whole, in particular the behaviour of such aggregate measures as overall rates of unemployment, inflation, economic growth, and the balance of trade. The aggregate numbers do not tell us what any firm or household is doing. They tell us what is happening in total, or on average.

It is important to remember that these perspectives are simply two ways of looking at the same thing. Microeconomics is the bottom-up view of the economy; macroeconomics is the top-down view. The behaviour of the economy as a whole is dependent on the behaviour of the units that make it up.

The automobile industry is a story of both micro- and macroeconomics. It is a story of microeconomic interactions of individual companies, investors, and labour unions. It is also a story of global macroeconomic forces like oil shortages and economic fluctuations. When auto companies laid off workers in the late 1970s, their problems boosted the overall unemployment rate. The recession of the early 1990s brought heavy reductions in car sales.

## THE SCIENCE OF ECONOMICS

Economics is a **social science.** It studies the social problem of choice from a scientific viewpoint, which means that it is built on a systematic exploration of the problem of choice. This systematic exploration involves both the formulation of theories and the examination of data.

A **theory** consists of a set of assumptions (or hypotheses) and conclusions derived from those assumptions. Theories are exercises in logic: *if* the assumptions are correct, *then* the results follow. If all university graduates have a better chance of getting jobs and Ellen is a university graduate, then Ellen has a better chance of getting a job than a nongraduate. Economists make predictions with their theories. They might use a theory to predict what will happen if a tax is increased or if imports of foreign cars are limited. The predictions of a theory are of the form "If a tax is increased and if the market is competitive, then output will decrease and prices will increase."

In developing their theories, economists use **models.** To understand how economists use models, consider a modern car manufacturer trying to design a new automobile. It is extremely expensive to construct a new car. Rather than creating a separate, fully developed car for every engineer's or designer's conception of what she would like to see the new car be, the company uses models. The designers might use a plastic model to study the general shape of the vehicle and to assess reactions to the car's aesthetics. The engineers might use a computer model to study the air resistance, from which they can calculate fuel consumption, and a separate model for judging the car's comfort.

Just as the engineers construct different models to study a particular feature of a car, so too economists construct models of the economy—in words or equations—to depict particular features of the economy. An economic model might describe a general relationship ("When incomes rise, the number of cars purchased increases") or a quantitative relationship ("When incomes rise by 10 percent, the number of cars purchased rises, on average, by 12 percent") or make a general prediction ("An increase in the tax on gasoline will decrease the demand for cars").

### DISCOVERING AND INTERPRETING RELATIONSHIPS

A **variable** is any item that can be measured and that changes. Prices, wages, interest rates, quantities bought and sold, are all variables. What interests economists is the connection among variables. When economists see what appears to be a systematic relationship among variables, they ask, could it have arisen by chance, or is there indeed a relationship? This is the question of **correlation.**

Economists use statistical tests to measure and test correlations. Consider the problem of deciding whether a coin is biased. If you flip a coin 10 times and get 6 heads and 4 tails, is the coin a fair one? Or is it weighted to heads? Statistical tests will say that the result of 6 heads and 4 tails could easily happen by chance, so the evidence does not prove that the coin is weighted. This does not prove that it is *not* slightly weighted. The evidence is just not strong enough for either conclusion. But if you flip a coin 100 times and get 80 heads, statistical tests will tell you that the possibility of this happening by blind chance with a fair coin is extremely small. The evidence supports the assertion that the coin is weighted.

A similar logic can be used on correlations in economic data. People with more education tend to earn higher wages. Is the connection merely chance? Statistical tests show whether the evidence is too weak for a conclusion, or whether it supports a particular answer.

## CAUSATION VERSUS CORRELATION

Economists would like to accomplish more than just assert that different variables are indeed correlated. They would like to conclude that changes in one variable *cause* the changes in the other variable. The distinction between correlation and **causation** is important. If one variable "causes" the other, then changing one variable necessarily will change the other. If the relationship is just a correlation, this may not be true.

For instance, Figure 1.5 shows the relationship between level of schooling completed and annual income. There is no doubt that those with more years of schooling receive a higher income. But there are at least two possible explanations. One is that firms are willing to pay more for workers who are more productive and that education increases individuals' productivity. In this explanation, there is causation. More education "causes" greater productivity, which "causes" higher wages. The other explanation is that firms are willing to pay higher wages to those who are smarter even though they may not yet have many productive skills (and what skills they possess may have little to do with what they have learned in school), and those who are smarter survive longer in school. In this view, more able individuals stay in school longer and receive higher wages, but the schools do not "cause" increased productivity. There is a correlation, but no causation.

Sometimes there are systematic relationships between variables in which it is difficult to tell which variable is the cause, which the effect. For example, there is a systematic relationship between the number of children a woman has and the wages she earns. But the explanation for this relationship is not clear. Low wages mean that the income the woman must give up when she takes off work to have a child is less since less money is lost as a result of not working. Do low wages, then, induce women to have more children? Or does having more children

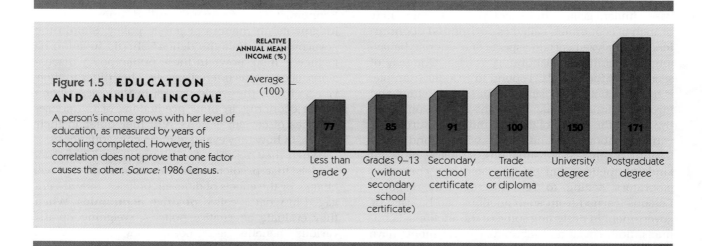

Figure 1.5 **EDUCATION AND ANNUAL INCOME**

A person's income grows with her level of education, as measured by years of schooling completed. However, this correlation does not prove that one factor causes the other. *Source:* 1986 Census.

RELATIVE ANNUAL MEAN INCOME (%)

Average (100)

| Less than grade 9 | Grades 9–13 (without secondary school certificate) | Secondary school certificate | Trade certificate or diploma | University degree | Postgraduate degree |
|---|---|---|---|---|---|
| 77 | 85 | 91 | 100 | 150 | 171 |

distract a woman from pursuing her career as avidly, and thus lead to low wages? Or is there a third factor, accounting for both the level of wages and the number of children?

## EXPERIMENTS IN ECONOMICS

Many sciences use laboratory experiments to test alternative explanations, since experiments allow the scientist to change one factor at a time and see what happens. But the economy is not a chemistry lab. Instead, economics is like astronomy, in that both sciences must use the experiments that the natural world provides. Economists look for situations in which only one factor changes, and study the consequences of changing that factor. A change in the income tax system is an example of a natural experiment. But nature is usually not kind to economists; the world does not hold still. As the tax system changes, so do other features of the economy, and economists often have a difficult time deciding whether changes are the result of the new tax system or of some other economic change. Sometimes they can use what is called **econometrics,** the branch of statistics developed to analyze the particular measurement problems that arise in economics.

In a few cases, economists have engaged in social experiments. For example, they have given a selected group of individuals a different income tax schedule or welfare program from that given to another, otherwise similar, group. In recent years, a major new branch of economics, called **experimental economics,** has analyzed certain aspects of economic behaviour in a controlled laboratory setting. One way of seeing how individuals respond to risk, for example, is to construct a risky situation in such a setting and force individuals to take decisions and act on them. By varying the nature of the risk and the rewards, one can learn about how individuals will respond to different risks in real-life situations. Similarly, different kinds of auctions can be simulated in a controlled laboratory setting to see how bidders respond. Lessons learned from such auctions can be used by government in designing some of the auctions it conducts. Both social and laboratory experiments have

provided economists with valuable insights concerning economic behaviour.

But even with all available tools, the problem of finding a variety of correlations between several different types of data and having to discern which connections are real and which are only apparent is a difficult one. Economists' interest in these questions is motivated by more than just curiosity. Often, important policy questions depend on what one believes is really going on. Whether a country thinks it worthwhile to pour more resources into higher education may depend on whether it believes that the differences in wages observed between those with and without a postsecondary education are largely due to the skills and knowledge acquired during college or university, or whether they are mainly related to differences in ability between those who make it through college or university and those who do not.

The important lessons to remember here are (1) the fact of a correlation does not prove a causation; (2) the way to test different explanations of causation is to hold all of the factors constant except for one, and then allow that one to vary; (3) data do not always speak clearly, and sometimes do not allow any conclusions to be drawn.

## WHY ECONOMISTS DISAGREE

Economists are frequently called upon to make judgments on matters of public policy. Should the government reduce the deficit? Should inflation be reduced? If so, how? In these public-policy discussions, economists often disagree. They differ in their views of how the world works, in their *description* of the economy, in their predictions of the consequences of certain actions. And they differ in their values, in how they evaluate these consequences.

When they describe the economy, and construct models that predict either how the economy will change or the effects of different policies, they are engaged in what is called **positive economics.** When they evaluate alternative policies, weighing up the various benefits and costs, they are engaged

## CLOSE-UP: ECONOMISTS AGREE!

Try the following six statements out on your classmates or your family to see whether they, like the economists surveyed, disagree, agree with provisos, or agree:

| | Percentage of economists who | | |
| | Disagree | Agree with provisos | Agree |
| --- | --- | --- | --- |
| 1. Tariffs and import quotas usually reduce general economic welfare. | 6.5 | 21.3 | 71.3 |
| 2. A minimum wage increases unemployment among young and unskilled workers. | 20.5 | 22.4 | 56.5 |
| 3. A ceiling on rents reduces the quantity and quality of housing available. | 6.5 | 16.6 | 76.3 |
| 4. The cause of the rise in gasoline prices that occurred in the wake of the Iraqi invasion of Kuwait is the monopoly power of large oil companies. | 67.5 | 20.3 | 11.4 |
| 5. The trade deficit is primarily a consequence of the inability of domestic firms to compete. | 51.5 | 29.7 | 18.1 |
| 6. Cash payments increase the welfare of recipients to a greater degree than do transfers-in-kind of equal cash value. | 15.1 | 25.9 | 58.0 |

Among the general population, these are controversial questions. You will find many people who believe that restricting foreign imports is a good thing; that government regulation of wages and rents has few ill effects; that the trade deficit is mainly caused by the inability of domestic companies to compete; that government should avoid giving cash to poor people (because they are likely to waste it); and that oil companies are the cause of higher oil prices.

But when professional economists are surveyed, there is a broad agreement that many of those popular answers are misguided. The percentages listed above are from a survey carried out in the United States in 1990. Notice that healthy percentages of economists apparently believe that most import quotas are economically harmful; that government control of wages and rents does lead to adverse consequences; that oil companies are not to blame for higher oil prices; that the trade deficit is not caused by the competitive problems of individual companies; that cash payments benefit the poor more than direct (in-kind) transfers of food, shelter, and medical care.

*Sources:* Richard M. Alston, J. R. Kearl, and Michael B. Vaughan, "Is There a Consensus Among Economists in the 1990s?" *American Economic Review* (May 1992); J. R. Kearl, Clayne L. Pope, Gordon C. Whiting, and Larry T. Wimmer, "A Confusion of Economists?" *American Economic Review* (May 1979), pp. 28–37.

in what is called **normative economics.** Positive economics is concerned with what "is," with describing how the economy functions. Normative economics deals with what "should be," with making judgments about the desirability of various courses of action. Normative economics makes use of positive economics. We cannot make judgments about whether a policy is desirable unless we have a clear picture of its consequences. Good normative economics also tries to be explicit about precisely what values or objectives it is incorporating. It tries to couch its statements in the form "If these are your objectives . . . , then this is the best possible policy."

Consider the normative and positive aspects of the proposal to restrict imports of Japanese cars. Positive economics would describe the consequences: the increased prices consumers have to pay; the increased sales of domestic cars; the increased employment and increased profits; the increased pollution and oil imports, because domestic cars on average are less fuel-efficient than Japanese cars. In the end, the question is, *should there be restraints on imports of Japanese cars?* This is a normative question: normative economics would weigh these various effects— the losses of the consumers, the gains to workers, the increased profits, the increased pollution, the increased oil imports—to reach an overall judgment. Normative economics develops systematic frameworks within which these complicated judgments can be conducted in a systematic way.

## DISAGREEMENTS WITHIN POSITIVE ECONOMICS

Even when they describe how the economy works, economists may differ for two main reasons. First, economists differ over what is the appropriate model of the economy. They may disagree about how well people and firms are able to perceive and calculate their self-interest, and whether their interactions take place in a competitive or a noncompetitive market. Different models will produce different results. Often the data do not allow us to say which of two competing models provides a better description of some market.

Second, even when they agree about the appropriate theoretical model, economists may disagree about quantitative magnitudes, which will cause their predictions to differ. They may agree, for instance, that reducing the tax on interest income will encourage individuals to save more, but they may produce different estimates about the amount of the savings increase. Again, many of these disagreements arise because of inadequate data. We may have considerable data concerning savings in Canada over the past century. But institutions and economic conditions today are markedly different from those of fifty or even ten years ago.

## DISAGREEMENTS WITHIN NORMATIVE ECONOMICS

There are generally many consequences of any policy, some beneficial, some harmful. In comparing two policies, one may benefit some people more, another may benefit others. One policy is not unambiguously better than another. It depends on what you care more about. A cut in the tax on the profits from the sale of shares might encourage savings, but at the same time, most of the benefits accrue to the very wealthy; hence, it increases inequality. A reduction in taxes to stimulate the economy may reduce unemployment, but it may also increase inflation. Even though two economists agree about the model, they may make different recommendations. In assessing the effect of a tax cut on unemployment and inflation, for instance, an economist who is worried more about unemployment may recommend in favour of the tax cut, while the other, concerned about inflation, may recommend against it. In this case, the source of the disagreement is a difference in values.

But while economists may often seem to differ greatly among themselves, in fact they agree more than they disagree: their disagreements get more attention than their agreements. (See box, page 17.) Most important, when they do disagree, they seek to be clear about the source of their disagreement: 1) to what extent does it arise out of differences in models, 2) to what extent does it arise out of differences in estimates of quantitative relations, and 3) to what extent does it arise out of differences in values? Clarifying the sources of and reasons for disagreement can be a very productive way of learning more.

## CONSENSUS ON THE IMPORTANCE OF SCARCITY

Most of what we have discussed in this chapter fits within the areas on which there is broad consensus among economists. This includes the observation that the Canadian economy is a mixed economy and that there are certain basic questions that all economic systems must address. We highlight the most important points of consensus throughout the book, beginning here, with our first. The most important point of consensus in this chapter concerns scarcity:

**1 Scarcity**

*There is no free lunch. Having more of one thing requires giving up something else. Scarcity is a basic fact of life.*

## REVIEW AND PRACTICE

### SUMMARY

**1** Economics is the study of how individuals, firms, and governments within our society make choices. Choices are unavoidable because desired goods, services, and resources are inevitably scarce.

**2** There are four basic questions that economists ask about any economy. (1) What is produced, and in what quantities? (2) How are these goods and services produced? (3) For whom are these goods and services produced? (4) Who takes economic decisions, and by what processes?

**3** Canada has a mixed economy; there is a mix between public and private decision making. The economy relies primarily on the private interaction of individuals and firms to answer the four basic questions, but government plays a large role as well. A central question for any mixed economy is the balance between the public and private sectors.

**4** The term "market" is used to describe any situation where exchange takes place. In Canada's market economy, individuals, firms, and government interact in product markets, labour markets, and capital markets.

**5** Economists use models to study how the economy works and to make predictions about what will happen if something is changed. A model can be expressed in words or equations, and is designed to mirror the essential characteristics of the particular phenomena under study.

**6** A correlation exists when a change in one variable is associated with a predictable change in another variable. However, the simple existence of a correlation does not prove that one factor causes the other to change. Additional outside factors may be influencing both.

**7** Positive economics is the study of how the economy works. Disagreements within positive economics centre on the appropriate model of the economy or market and on the value of different empirical estimates of the consequences of change. Normative economics deals with the desirability of various actions. Disagreements within normative economics centre on differences in the values placed on the various costs and benefits resulting from change.

## KEY TERMS

| | | | |
|---|---|---|---|
| sectoral free trade | Crown corporations | capital goods | model |
| scarcity | inputs | microeconomics | correlation |
| centrally planned economy | outputs | macroeconomics | causation |
| mixed economy | product market | social science | positive economics |
| market economy | labour market | theory | normative economics |
| | capital market | | |

## REVIEW QUESTIONS

**1** Why are choices unavoidable?

**2** How are the four basic economic questions answered in the Canadian economy?

**3** What is a mixed economy? Describe some of the roles government might play, or not play, in a mixed economy.

**4** Name the three main economic markets, and describe how an individual might participate in each one as a buyer and seller.

**5** Give two examples of economic issues that are primarily microeconomic, and two that are primarily macroeconomic. What is the general difference between microeconomics and macroeconomics?

**6** What is a model? Why do economists use models?

**7** When causation exists, would you also expect a correlation to exist? When a correlation exists, would you also expect causation to exist? Explain.

**8** "All disagreements between economists are purely subjective." Comment.

## PROBLEMS

**1** Characterize the following events as microeconomic, macroeconomic, or both.
   (a) Unemployment increases this month.
   (b) A drug company invents and begins to market a new medicine.
   (c) A bank lends money to a large company but turns down a small business.
   (d) Interest rates decline for all borrowers.
   (e) A union negotiates for higher pay.
   (f) The price of oil increases.

**2** Characterize the following events as part of the labour market, the capital market, or the product market.
   (a) An investor tries to decide which company to invest in.
   (b) With practice, the workers on an assembly line become more efficient.
   (c) The opening up of the economies in East-ern Europe offers new markets for Canadian products.
   (d) A big company that is losing money decides to offer its workers a special set of incentives to retire early, hoping to reduce its costs.
   (e) A consumer roams around a shopping mall, looking for birthday gifts.
   (f) The federal government needs to borrow more money to finance its level of spending.

**3** Discuss the incentive issues that might arise in each of the following situations. (Hint: Remember the history of the automobile industry at the start of this chapter.)
   (a) You have some money to invest, and your financial adviser introduces you to a couple of software executives who want to start their own company. What should you worry about as you decide whether to invest?

(b) You are running a small company, and your workers promise that if you increase their pay, they will work harder.

(c) A large industry is going bankrupt and appeals for government assistance.

**4** Name ways in which government intervention has helped the automobile industry in the last two decades, and ways in which it has injured the industry.

**5** On the back of a bag of cat litter it is claimed, "Cats that use cat litter live three years longer than cats that don't." Do you think that cat litter actually causes an increased life expectancy of cats, or can you think of some other factors to explain this correlation? What evidence might you try to collect to test your explanation?

**6** Life expectancy in Sweden is 78 years; life expectancy in India is 57 years. Does this prove that if an Indian moved to Sweden he would live longer? That is, does this prove that living in Sweden causes an increase in life expectancy, or can you think of some other factors to explain these facts? What evidence might you try to collect to test your explanation?

# CHAPTER 2

# THINKING LIKE
# AN ECONOMIST

E veryone thinks about economics, at least some of the time. We think
about money (we wish we had more of it) and about work (we wish
we had less of it). But there is a distinctive way that economists approach economic issues, and one of the purposes of this course is
to introduce you to that way of thinking. This chapter begins with a
basic model of the economy. We follow this with a closer look at how the
basic units that the economy comprises—individuals, firms, and governments—take choices in situations where they are faced with scarcity. In
Chapters 3 through 5, we study ways in which these units interact with one
another, and how those interactions "add up" to determine how society's
resources are allocated.

## KEY QUESTIONS

**1** What is the basic competitive model of the economy?

**2** What are incentives, property rights, prices, and the profit motive, and what roles do these essential ingredients of a market economy play?

**3** What alternatives to the market system are there for allocating resources, and why do economists tend not to favour these alternatives?

**4** What are some of the basic techniques economists use in their study of how people make choices? What are the various concepts of costs that economists use?

## THE BASIC COMPETITIVE MODEL

Though different economists employ different models of the economy, they all use a basic set of assumptions as a point of departure. The economist's basic model has three components: assumptions about how consumers behave, assumptions about how firms behave, and assumptions about the markets in which these consumers and firms interact. The model ignores government, not because government is not important, but because before we can understand the role of government we need to see how an economy without a government might function.

### RATIONAL CONSUMERS AND PROFIT-MAXIMIZING FIRMS

The fact of scarcity, which we encountered in Chapter 1, implies that individuals and firms must make choices. Underlying much of economic analysis is the basic assumption of **rational choice,** that people weigh the costs and benefits of each possibility. This assumption is based on the expectation that individuals and firms will act in a consistent manner, with a reasonably well-defined notion of what they like and what their objectives are, and with a reasonable understanding of how to attain those objectives.

In the case of an individual, the rationality assumption is taken to mean that he makes choices and decisions in pursuit of his own self-interest. Different people will, of course, have different goals and desires. Sally may want to drive a Porsche, own a yacht, and have a large house; to attain those objectives, she knows she needs to work long hours and sacrifice time with her family. Andrew is willing to accept a lower income to get longer vacations and more leisure throughout the year.

Economists make no judgments about whether Sally's preferences are "better" or "worse" than Andrew's. They do not even spend much time asking why different individuals have different views on these matters, or why tastes change over time. These are important questions, but they belong more to the province of psychology and sociology. What economists are concerned about are the consequences of these different preferences. What decisions can they expect Sally and Andrew, rationally pursuing their respective interests, to take?

In the case of firms, they are in the business of making profits for their owners. The rationality assumption is taken to mean that they choose their inputs and outputs to maximize profits.

### COMPETITIVE MARKETS

To complete the model, economists make assumptions about the places where self-interested consumers and profit-maximizing firms meet: markets. Economists begin by focusing on the case where there are many buyers and sellers, all buying and selling the same thing. You might picture a crowded farmers' market to get a sense of the number of buyers and sellers—except that you have to picture everyone buying and selling just one good. Let's say we are in Ontario in the autumn, and the booths are all full of peaches.

Each of the farmers would like to raise his prices.

---

INGREDIENTS IN THE BASIC COMPETITIVE MODEL

**1** Rational, self-interested consumers

**2** Rational, profit-maximizing firms

**3** Competitive markets with price-taking behaviour

---

That way, if he can still sell his peaches, his profits go up. Yet with a large number of sellers, each is forced to charge close to the same price, since if any farmer charged much more, he would lose business to the farmer next door. Profit-maximizing firms are in the same position. In an extreme case, if a firm charged any more than the going price, it would lose *all* its sales. Economists label this case **perfect competition.** In perfect competition, each firm is a **price taker,** which simply means that because it cannot influence the market price, it must accept that price. The firm takes the market price as given because it cannot raise its price without losing all sales, and at the market price it can sell as much as it wishes. Even if it sold ten times as much, this would have a negligible effect on the total quantity marketed or the price prevailing in the market. Perhaps the best example of real markets that in the absence of government intervention would probably be perfectly competitive is the markets for agricultural goods. There are so many wheat farmers, for instance, that each farmer believes he can grow and sell as much wheat as he wishes and have no effect on the price of wheat. (Later in the book, we will encounter markets with limited or no competition, like monopolies, where firms can raise prices without losing all their sales.)

On the other side of our farmers' market are rational individuals, each of whom would like to pay as little as possible for her peaches. Why can't she pay less than the going price? Because the seller sees another buyer in the crowd who will pay the going price. Thus, the consumers also take the market price as given, and focus their attention on other factors—their taste for peaches, primarily—in deciding how many to buy.

This model of consumers, firms, and markets—rational, self-interested consumers interacting with rational, profit-maximizing firms, in competitive markets where firms and consumers are both price takers—is the **basic competitive model.** The model has one very strong implication: if actual markets are well described by the competitive market, then the economy will be efficient: resources are not wasted, it is not possible to produce more of one good without producing less of another, and it is not even possible to make anyone better off without making someone else worse off. These results are obtained without government.

Virtually all economists recognize that actual economies are not *perfectly* described by the competitive model, but most still use it as a convenient benchmark—as we will throughout this book. We will also point out important differences between the predictions of the competitive model and observed outcomes, which will guide us to other models which may provide a better description of particular markets and situations. Economists recognize too that while the competitive market may not provide a *perfect* description of some markets, it may provide a good description—with its predictions matching actual outcomes well, though not perfectly. As we shall see, economists differ in their views about how many such markets there are, how good the "match" is, and how well alternative models do in rectifying the deficiency of the competitive model in any particular case.

## PRICES, PROPERTY RIGHTS, AND PROFITS: INCENTIVES AND INFORMATION

For market economies to work efficiently, firms and individuals must be informed and have incentives to act on available information. Indeed, incentives can be viewed as at the heart of economics. Without incentives, why would individuals go to work in the morning? Who would undertake the risks of bringing out new products? Who would put aside savings for a rainy day? There is an old expression about the importance of having someone "mind the store." But without incentives, why would anyone bother?

Market economies provide information and incentives through *prices, profits, and property rights.* Prices provide information about the relative scarcity of different goods and services. The **price system** ensures that goods and services go to those individuals who are most willing and able to pay for them, and are supplied by the firms that can provide them at least cost. Prices convey information to firms about how individuals value different goods.

The desire for profits motivates firms to respond to the information provided by prices. By producing what consumers want in the most efficient way, in ways that use the least scarce resources, they increase their profits. Similarly, rational individuals' pursuit of self-interest induces them to respond to prices: they buy goods and services that are more expensive—in a sense relatively more scarce—only if the goods and services provide commensurately greater benefits.

For the profit motive to be effective, firms need to be able to keep at least some of their profits. Households, in turn, need to be able to keep at least some of what they earn or receive as a return on their investments. (The return on their investments is simply what they receive back in excess of what they invested. If they receive back less than they invested, the return is negative.) There must, in short, be **private property,** with its attendant **rights.** Property rights include both the right of the owner to use the property as she sees fit and the right to sell it.

These two attributes of property rights give individuals the incentive to use property under their control efficiently. The owner of a piece of land tries to figure out the most profitable use of the land, for example, whether to build a store or a restaurant. If he makes a mistake and opens a restaurant when he should have opened a store, he bears the consequences: the loss in income. The profits he earns if he takes the right decisions—and the losses he bears if he takes the wrong ones—give him an incentive to think carefully about the decision and do the requisite research. The owner of a store tries to make sure that her customers get the kind of merchandise and the quality of service they want. She has an incentive to establish a good reputation, because if she does so, she will do more business and earn more profits.

The store owner will also want to maintain her property—which is not just the land anymore, but includes the store as well—because she will get more for it when the time comes to sell her business to someone else. Similarly, the owner of a house has an incentive to maintain *his* property, so that he can sell it for more when he wishes to move. Again, the profit motive combines with private property to provide incentives.

## INCENTIVES VERSUS EQUALITY

While incentives are at the heart of market economies, they come with a cost: inequality. Any system of incentives must tie compensation with performance. Whether through differences in luck or ability, performance of different individuals will differ. In many cases it will not be possible to identify why performance is high. The salesperson may claim that the reason his sales are high is superior skill and effort, while his colleague may argue that it is dumb luck.

If pay is tied to performance, there will inevitably be

## HOW THE PROFIT MOTIVE DRIVES THE MARKET SYSTEM

In market economies, incentives are supplied to individuals and firms by the chance to own property and to retain some of the profits of working and producing.

some inequality. And the more closely tied compensation is to performance the greater the inequality. The fact that the greater the incentives, the greater the resulting inequality is called the **incentive-equality trade-off.** If society provides greater incentives, total output is likely to be higher, but there will also probably be greater inequality.

One of the basic questions facing society in the choice of tax rates and welfare systems concerns how much incentives would be diminished by an increase in tax rates to finance a better welfare system and thus reduce inequality? What would be the results of those reduced incentives?

## WHEN PROPERTY RIGHTS FAIL

Prices, profits, and property rights are the three essential ingredients of market economies. We can learn a lot about why they are so important by examining a few cases where property rights and prices are interfered with. Each example highlights a general point. Whenever society fails to define the owner of its resources and does not allow the highest bidder to use them, inefficiencies result. Resources will be wasted or not used in the most productive way.

***Ill-Defined Property Rights*** Fish are a valuable resource. Not long ago, the area southeast of Newfoundland, called the Grand Banks, was teeming with fish, especially cod. Not surprisingly, it was also teeming with fishermen, who saw an easy livelihood scooping out the fish from the sea. Since there were no property rights, everyone tried to catch as many fish as he could. A self-interested fisherman would rationally reason that if he did not catch the fish, someone else would. The result was a tragedy: the Grand Banks was overfished, to the point where not only was it not teeming with fish, but commercial fishing became unprofitable. Beginning in 1977, foreign fishing was reduced by the extension of Canada's offshore jurisdiction to include most of the Grand Banks. Canada and the United States agreed to a treaty limiting the amount of fish that each country's fishermen could take. More recently, fishing for some species, such as the northern cod, has

been stopped altogether. Only by limiting the quantity taken can the fish stocks be restored.

Similar problems arise in the use of freshwater bodies of water. For many years, industrial firms flushed waste containing harmful chemicals into the lakes, rivers, and streams of the country, essentially treating water as a free resource. The result was a deterioration of the quality of water to an extent that was harmful to other users. Again, the problem arose because of a lack of definition of property rights. Governments have gradually intervened with a variety of regulatory measures to attempt to redress the costs that had been imposed by pollution.

The problem of ill-defined property rights is more general than the situation of fishermen and freshwater users. *Any* time society fails to define the owners of its resources and does not allow the highest bidder to use them, we can expect inefficiencies to result. Resources will be wasted or will not be used in the most productive way.

***Restricted Property Rights*** In some instances, those who have property rights are not allowed the full freedom to use the property as they wish for as long as they wish, or to buy and sell it. In Canada, much of the timberland is provincial Crown land that is leased to firms wishing to cut trees for profit. The sale of licences combined with taxes imposed on the basis of the number of trees cut (stumpage fees) was a valuable and seemingly inexhaustible source of revenue to provincial governments. However, leases were only temporary, thus conferring only partial property rights to the leaseholders. The value of timber as a resource depends upon the extent to which reforestation is undertaken. However, the benefit of reforestation accrues sometime in the future, perhaps many years later. Since leasehold only confers temporary property rights on the logging industry, the incentive does not exist to engage in reforestation practices that will generate the largest long-term benefit from the forests, and the forests may be inefficiently used. When forest resources seemed endless, insufficient reforestation may not have been perceived as a great problem. However, recent concern has led governments to attempt to regulate reforestation practices on Crown lands held in leasehold by timber firms.

***Entitlements as Property Rights*** Property rights do not always mean that you have full ownership or control. A **legal entitlement,** such as the right to occupy an apartment for life at a rent that is controlled, common in some large cities, is viewed by economists as a property right. Individuals do not own the apartment and thus cannot sell it, but they cannot be thrown out, either. Because the individual in a rent-controlled apartment cannot (legally) sell the right to live in her apartment, as she gets older she may have limited incentives to maintain its condition, let alone improve it.

A similar situation exists with the use of frequencies on the airwaves. They are allocated by a federal regulatory agency, the Canadian Radio-television and Telecommunications Commission (C.R.T.C.). The result is that those who value the slots most are not necessarily those to whom they are allocated. Thus, for example, a large commercial station would be willing to pay a great deal of money for the frequency held by a nonprofit organization, such as a university. But the nonprofit organization is not allowed to sell its entitlement to the frequency. The result is that frequencies are allocated differently from how a market would allocate them.

## CONSENSUS ON INCENTIVES

Incentives, prices, profits, and property rights are central features of any economy. Our second consensus point concerns incentives:

**2  Incentives**

> *Providing appropriate incentives is a fundamental economic problem. In modern market economies, profits provide incentives for firms to produce the goods individuals want, and wages provide incentives for individuals to work. Property rights also provide people with important incentives, not only to invest and to save, but to put their assets to the best possible use.*

## RATIONING

The price system is only one way of allocating resources, and a comparison with other systems will help to clarify the advantages of markets. When individuals get less of a good than they would like at the terms being offered, the good is said to be **rationed.** Different rationing schemes are different ways of deciding who gets society's scarce resources.

***Rationing by Queues*** Rather than supplying goods to those willing and able to pay the most for them, a society could give them instead to those most willing to wait in line. This system is called **rationing by queues.** Tickets are often allocated by queues, whether they are for movies, sporting events, or rock concerts. A price is set, and it will not change no matter how many people line up to buy at that price. (The high price that scalpers can get for "hot" tickets is a good indication of how much more than the ticket price people would be willing to pay.)

Rationing by queues is thought by many to be a more desirable way of supplying medical services than the price system. Why, it is argued, should the rich—who are most able to pay for medical services—be the ones to get better or more medical care? Using this reasoning, Canada provides free medical care to everyone. To see a doctor, all you have to do is wait in line. Rationing medicine by queues turns the allocation problem around: since the value of time for low-wage workers is lower, they are more willing to wait, and therefore they get a disproportionate share of (government-supplied) medical services.

In general, rationing by queues is an inefficient way of distributing resources because the time spent in line is a wasted resource. There are usually ways of achieving the same goal within a price system that can make everyone better off. Returning to the medical example, if some individuals were allowed to pay for doctors' services instead of waiting in line, more doctors could be hired with the proceeds, and the lines for those unable or unwilling to pay could actually be reduced.

***Rationing by Lotteries*** **Lotteries** allocate goods by a random process, like picking a name from a hat. University dormitory rooms are usually assigned by lottery. So are seats in popular courses; when more students want to enroll in a section of a principles of economics course than the size of the section allows, there may be a lottery to determine who gets to enroll. In another example of distribution by lottery, the Ontario Ministry of Natural Resources conducted public meetings to determine how to rehabilitate the moose population by controlling the annual moose harvest. The results of the meetings showed that the public preferred the lottery draw to the first-come, first-served technique on the grounds that it would provide an equal chance for all residents. However, lotteries are also inefficient because the scarce resources do not go to the individual or firm that values them the most and is willing and able to pay the most.

***Rationing by Coupons*** Most governments in wartime use **coupon rationing.** People are allowed so many litres of gasoline, so many kilograms of sugar, and so much flour each month. To get the good, you have to pay the market price *and* produce a coupon. The reason for coupon rationing is that without coupons prices might soar, inflicting a hardship on poorer members of society.

Coupon systems take two forms, depending on whether coupons are tradable or not. Coupons that are not tradable give rise to the same inefficiency that occurs with most of the other nonprice systems—goods do not in general go to the individuals who are willing and able to pay the most. There is generally room for a trade that will make all parties better off. For instance, I might be willing to trade some of my flour ration for some of your sugar ration. But in a nontradable coupon system, the law prohibits such transactions. When coupons cannot be legally traded, there are strong incentives for the establishment of a **black market,** an illegal market in which the goods or the coupons for goods are traded.

***Rationing by Government Regulation*** Sometimes direct **government regulation** is used to ration the amounts that can be bought or sold. There are numerous examples of this. Many countries have operated capital controls that restrict the amount of foreign currency that can be purchased. The amount of game that can be taken by recreational hunters is often subject to regulation. Some communities limit the number of bags of garbage that can be left out by households for collection. Quantity controls are often used to restrict the amounts of pollutants emitted by firms. In each of these cases, the quantity restriction typically bears no direct relation to the value put on the item by the various users of it. As a result, the item is likely to be inefficiently allocated among users.

In some cases this inefficiency is overcome by allowing persons to trade their quotas. This is typically the case with agricultural and fishing quotas, and has been suggested by economists for pollution controls. Being able to buy and sell quotas will ensure that those who value the restricted item most will have the opportunity to use it.

## OPPORTUNITY SETS

We have covered a lot of ground so far in this chapter. We have seen the economist's basic model, which relies on competitive markets. We have seen how the profit motive and private property supply the incentives that drive a market economy. And we have gotten our first glimpse at why economists believe that market systems, which supply goods to those who are willing and able to pay the most, provide the most efficient means of allocating what the economy produces. They are far better than the nonprice rationing schemes that have been employed. It is time now to return to the question of choice. Market systems leave to individuals and firms the question of what to consume. How are these decisions taken?

For a rational individual or firm, the first step in the economic analysis of any choice is to identify what is possible—what economists call the **opportunity set,** which is simply the group of available options. If you want a sandwich and you have only roast beef and tuna fish in the refrigerator, then your op-

POLICY PERSPECTIVE:
ASSIGNING FREQUENCIES—AUCTION OR BUREAUCRATIC
DISCRETION?

The spectrum of radio frequencies is a scarce resource and therefore has economic value. As with other scarce resources, society is best served if it is used in the most efficient way. In Canada, as in most countries, government is the steward of the use of these frequencies. The Canadian government has exercised this prerogative by assigning frequencies on the basis of applications by potential users. Thus, radio stations must be granted a licence to use a particular frequency by the Canadian Radio-television and Telecommunications Commission on the basis of a written submission. There is no reason to believe that such licences will go to those who are able to use them most efficiently, or to those who will best satisfy consumer preferences.

Now, a new use for part of the radio frequency spectrum has been developed, and that is to transmit signals over long distances for the next generation of cellular telephones. This will free cellular telephone companies from the need to use the transmission systems of standard telephone companies, and would immediately increase the convenience and flexibility of cellular phone use. The government must decide how to allocate the scarce frequency spectrum among alternative cellular telephone companies. Two alternatives are possible. One is to adopt the procedure of allocating them on the basis of bureaucratic discretion as to which companies

will best serve Canada's interest, as outlined above. As with any rationing system, there is no guarantee that the allocations will go to the firms that can use them most efficiently and produce the best service for potential consumers.

The alternative is to use the price system. One way to do this is for the government to sell the rights to use the frequencies by auction. As Professor Daniel Vincent of the University of Western Ontario has argued, auctioning the rights to the highest bidders will have two advantages. First, it will ensure that some of the value of the property rights to the frequencies accrues to the public rather than ending up as profits in the hands of the companies. And second, it will ensure that the companies that can use the frequencies most efficiently and at least cost are the ones that obtain the licences. They are the ones that will earn the most profits, and so can make the highest bids for the licences.

There is a lot at stake. On the basis of experience in the United States, where such licences have been allocated by auction, Professor Vincent estimates that up to $3 billion would be bid for the rights to use these frequencies in Canada.

*Source:* Daniel R. Vincent, "Industry Canada Is Taking Itself to the Cleaner's," *The Globe and Mail,* December 7, 1995.

portunity set consists of a roast beef sandwich, a tuna fish sandwich, a strange sandwich combining roast beef and tuna fish, or no sandwich. A ham sandwich is out of the question. Defining the limitations facing an individual or firm is a critical step in economic analysis. One can spend time yearning after the ham sandwich, or anything else outside the opportunity set, but when it comes to making choices and facing decisions, only what is within the opportunity set is relevant.

## BUDGET AND TIME CONSTRAINTS

**Constraints** limit choices and define the opportunity set. In most economic situations, the constraints that limit a person's choices—that is, those constraints that actually are relevant—are not sandwich fixings, but time and money. Opportunity sets whose constraints are imposed by money are referred to as **budget constraints;** opportunity sets whose constraints are prescribed by time are called **time constraints.** A billionaire may feel that his choices are limited not by money but by time; while for an unemployed worker, time hangs heavy—lack of money rather than time limits his choices.

The budget constraint defines a typical opportunity set. Consider the budget constraint of Alfred, who has decided to spend $100 on either cassette recordings or compact discs. A CD costs $10, a cassette $5. So Alfred can buy 10 CDs or 20 cassettes; or 9 CDs and 2 cassettes; or 8 CDs and 4 cassettes. The various possibilities are set forth in Table 2.1. And they are depicted graphically in Figure 2.1:[1] Along the vertical axis we measure the number of cassettes purchased, and along the horizontal axis we measure the number of CDs. The line marked $B_1B_2$ is Alfred's budget constraint. The extreme cases,

[1] See the Chapter Appendix for help in reading graphs.

### Table 2.1 ALFRED'S OPPORTUNITY SET

| Cassettes | CDs |
|-----------|-----|
| 0 | 10 |
| 2 | 9 |
| 4 | 8 |
| 6 | 7 |
| 8 | 6 |
| 10 | 5 |
| 12 | 4 |
| 14 | 3 |
| 16 | 2 |
| 18 | 1 |
| 20 | 0 |

where Alfred buys only CDs or cassettes, are represented by the points $B_1$ and $B_2$ in the figure. The dots between these two points, along the budget constraint, represent the other possible combinations. The cost of each combination of CDs and cassettes must add up to $100. The point actually chosen by

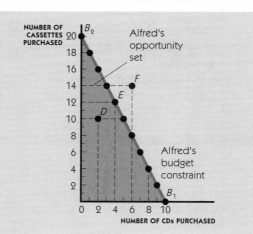

### Figure 2.1 ALFRED'S BUDGET CONSTRAINT

The budget constraint identifies the limits of an individual's opportunity set between CDs and cassettes. Points $B_1$ and $B_2$ are the extreme options, where he chooses all of one and none of the other. His actual choice is point $E$. Choices from the shaded area are possible, but less attractive than choices actually on the budget constraint.

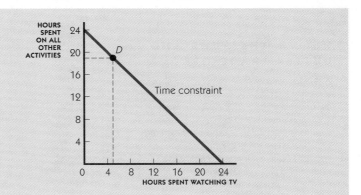

**Figure 2.2 AN OPPORTUNITY SET FOR WATCHING TV AND OTHER ACTIVITIES**

This opportunity set is limited by a time constraint, which shows the trade-off a person faces between spending time watching television and spending it on other activities. At 5 hours of TV time per day, point *D* represents a typical choice for a Canadian.

Alfred is labeled *E*, where he purchases 4 CDs (for $40) and 12 cassettes (for $60).

Alfred's budget constraint is the line that defines the outer limits of his opportunity set. But the whole opportunity set is larger. It also includes all points below the budget constraint. This is the shaded area in the figure. The budget constraint shows the maximum number of cassettes Alfred can buy for each number of CDs purchased, and vice versa. Alfred is always happiest when he chooses a point on his budget constraint rather than below it. To see why, compare the points *E* and *D*. At point *E*, he has more of both goods than at point *D*. He would be even happier at point *F*, where he has still more cassettes and CDs, but that point, by definition, is unattainable.

Figure 2.2 depicts a time constraint. The most common time constraint simply is that the sum of what an individual spends her time on each day—including sleeping—must add up to 24 hours. The figure plots the hours spent watching television on the horizontal axis and the hours spent on all other activities on the vertical axis. People—no matter how rich or how poor—have only 24 hours a day to spend on different activities. The time constraint is quite like the budget constraint. A person cannot spend more than 24 hours or fewer than zero hours a day watching TV. The more time she spends watching television the less time she has available for all other activities. Point *D* (for "dazed") has been added to the diagram at 5 hours a day—this is the amount of time the typical Canadian chooses to spend watching TV.

## THE PRODUCTION POSSIBILITIES CURVE

Business firms and whole societies face constraints. They too must make choices limited to opportunity sets. The amounts of goods a firm or society could produce, given a fixed amount of land, labour, and other inputs, are referred to as its **production possibilities.**

As one commonly discussed example, consider a simple description of a society in which all economic production is divided into two categories, military spending and civilian spending. Of course, each of these two kinds of spending has many different elements, but for the moment, let's discuss the choice between the two broad categories. For simplicity, Figure 2.3 refers to military spending as "guns" and civilian spending as "butter." The production of guns is given along the vertical axis, the production of butter along the horizontal. The possible combinations of military and civilian spending—of guns and butter—is the opportunity set. Table 2.2 sets out some of the possible combinations: 90 million guns and 40 million tonnes of butter, or 40 million guns and 90 million tonnes of butter. These possibilities are depicted in the figure. In the case of a choice involving production decisions, the boundary of the opportunity set—giving the maximum amount of guns that can be produced for each amount of butter and vice versa—is called the **production possibilities curve.**

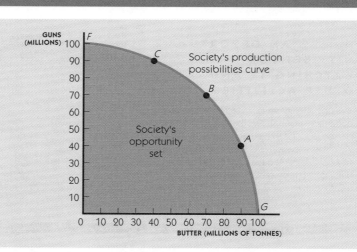

### Figure 2.3 THE GUNS AND BUTTER TRADE-OFF

A production possibilities curve can show society's opportunity set. This one describes the trade-off between military spending ("guns") and civilian spending ("butter"). Points *F* and *G* show the extreme choices, where the economy produces all guns or all butter. Notice that unlike the budget and time constraints, the production possibilities line curves, reflecting diminishing returns.

### Table 2.2 PRODUCTION POSSIBILITIES FOR THE ECONOMY

| Guns (millions) | Butter (millions of tonnes) |
|---|---|
| 100 | 0 |
| 90 | 40 |
| 70 | 70 |
| 40 | 90 |
| 0 | 100 |

When we compare the individual's opportunity set and that of society, reflected in its production possibilities curve, we notice one major difference. The individual's budget constraint is a straight line, while the production possibilities curve bows outwards. There is a good reason for this. An individual typically faces fixed **trade-offs:** if Alfred spends $10 more on CDs (that is, he buys one more CD), he has $10 less to spend on cassettes (he can buy two fewer cassettes).

On the other hand, the trade-offs faced by society are not fixed. If a society produces only a few guns, it will use those resources—the men and machines—that are best equipped for gun making. But as society tries to produce more and more guns, doing so becomes more difficult; it will increasingly have to rely on those who are less and less good at producing guns. It will be drawing these resources out of the production of other goods—in this case, butter. Thus, when the economy increases its production of guns from 40 million a year (point *A*) to 70 million (*B*), butter production falls by 20 million tonnes, from 90 million to 70 million tonnes. But if production of guns is increased further, to 90 million (*C*), an increase of only 20 million, butter production has to decrease by 30 million tonnes, to only 40 million tonnes. For each increase in the number of guns, the reduction in the number of tonnes of butter produced gets larger. That is why the production possibilities curve is curved.

The importance of the guns-butter trade-off was seen dramatically during World War II, when car production plummeted almost to zero as the automobile factories' production was diverted to tanks and other military vehicles.

In another example, assume that a firm owns land that can be used for growing wheat but not corn, and land that can grow corn but not wheat. In this case,

## Table 2.3 DIMINISHING RETURNS

| Labour in cornfield (no. of workers) | Corn output (bushels) | Labour in wheat field (no. of workers) | Wheat output (bushels) |
|---|---|---|---|
| 1,000 | 60,000 | 5,000 | 200,000 |
| 2,000 | 110,000 | 4,000 | 180,000 |
| 3,000 | 150,000 | 3,000 | 150,000 |
| 4,000 | 180,000 | 2,000 | 110,000 |
| 5,000 | 200,000 | 1,000 | 60,000 |

the only way to increase wheat production is to move workers from the cornfields to the wheat fields. As more and more workers are put into the wheat fields, production of wheat goes up, but each successive worker increases production less. The first workers might pick the largest and most destructive weeds. Additional workers lead to better weeding, and better weeding leads to higher output. But the additional weeds rooted up are smaller and less destructive, so output is increased by a correspondingly smaller amount. This is an example of the general principle of **diminishing returns.** Adding successive units of any input such as fertilizer, labour, or ma-

chines to a fixed amount of other inputs—seeds or land—increases the output, or amount produced, but by less and less.

Table 2.3 shows the output of the corn and wheat fields as labour is increased in each field. Assume the firm has 6,000 workers to divide between wheat production and corn production. Thus, the second and fourth columns together give the firm's production possibilities, which are depicted in Figure 2.4.

### INEFFICIENCIES: BEING OFF THE PRODUCTION POSSIBILITIES CURVE

There is no reason to assume that a firm or an economy will always be on its production possibilities curve. Any inefficiency in the economy will result in a point such as *A* in Figure 2.4, below the production possibilities curve. One of the major quests of economists is to look for instances in which the economy is inefficient in this way.

Whenever the economy is operating below the production possibilities curve, it is possible for us to have more of every good—more wheat and more corn, more guns and more butter. No matter what goods we like, we can have more of them. That is why we can unambiguously say that points below the production possibilities curve are undesirable. But this does not mean that every point on the production possibilities curve is better than any point below it. Compare points *A* and *C* in Figure 2.4. Corn

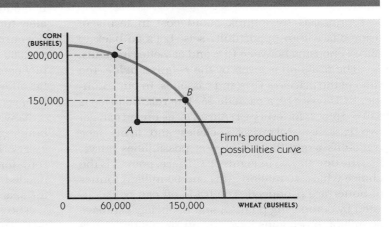

### Figure 2.4 THE WHEAT AND CORN TRADE-OFF

This production possibilities curve shows that as wheat production increases, it becomes necessary to give up larger and larger amounts of corn. Or to put the same point a different way, as corn production falls, the resulting increase in wheat production gets smaller and smaller. Point *A* illustrates an inefficient outcome in this opportunity set.

production is higher at *C*, but wheat production is lower. If people do not like corn very much, the increased corn production may not adequately compensate them for the decreased wheat production.

There are many reasons why the economy may be below the production possibilities curve. If land better suited for the production of corn is mistakenly devoted to the production of wheat, the economy will operate below its production possibilities curve. If some of society's resources—its land, labour, and capital goods—are simply left idle, as happens when there is a depression, the economy operates below the production possibilities curve. The kinds of inefficiencies discussed earlier in the chapter with inadequately or improperly defined property rights also result in operating below the production possibilities curve.

## COST

The beauty of an opportunity set like the budget constraint, the time constraint, or the production possibilities curve is that it specifies the cost of one option in terms of another. If the individual, the firm, or the society is operating on the constraint or curve, then it is possible to get more of one thing only by sacrificing some of another. The "cost" of one more unit of one good is how much you have to give up of the other.

Economists thus think about cost in terms of trade-offs within opportunity sets. Let's go back to Alfred choosing between CDs and cassettes in Figure 2.1. The trade-off is given by the **relative price,** the ratio of the prices of CDs and cassettes. In our example, a CD cost $10, a cassette $5. The relative price is $10 ÷ $5 = 2; for every CD Alfred gives up, he can get two cassettes. Likewise, societies and firms face trade-offs along the production possibilities curve, like the one shown in Figure 2.3. There, point A is the choice where 40 million guns and 90 million tonnes of butter are produced. The trade-off can be calculated by comparing points *A* and *B*. Society can have 30 million more guns by giving up 20 million tonnes of butter.

Trade-offs are necessary because resources are scarce. If you want something, you have to pay for it; you have to give up something. If you want to go to the library tomorrow night, you have to give up going to the movies. If a sawmill wants to make more two-by-four beams from its stock of wood, it will not be able to make as many one-by-four boards.

## OPPORTUNITY COSTS

If someone were to ask you right now what it costs to go to a movie, you would probably answer, "Eight dollars," or whatever you paid the last time you went to the movies. But with the concept of trade-offs, you can see that a *full* answer is not that simple. To begin with, the cost is not the $8 but what that $8 could otherwise buy. Furthermore, your time is a scarce resource that must be figured into the calculation. Both the money and the time represent opportunities forgone in favour of going to the movie, or what economists refer to as the **opportunity cost** of the movie. To apply a resource to one use means that it cannot be put to any other use. Thus, we should consider the next-best, alternative use of any resource when we think about putting it to any particular use. This next-best use is the formal measurement of opportunity cost.

Some examples will help to clarify the idea of opportunity cost. Consider a student, Sarah, who enrolls in university. She thinks that the cheque for tuition and room and board represents the costs of her education. But the economist's mind immediately turns to the job she might have had if she had not enrolled at university. If Sarah could have earned $15,000 from September to June, this is the opportunity cost of her time, and this forgone income must be added to the university bills in calculating the total economic cost of the school year.

Now consider a business firm that has bought a building for its headquarters that is bigger than necessary. If the firm could receive $20 per month in rent for each square metre of space that is not needed, then this is the opportunity cost of leaving the space idle.

The analysis can be applied to the government as well. The British Columbia government owns a vast amount of wilderness. In deciding whether it is

# CLOSE-UP: OPPORTUNITY COSTS AND SMOKING

Since the 1970s when evidence began to accumulate that smoking is potentially harmful to one's health, governments have used regulations and tax policy both to discourage smoking and to raise revenues to cover the costs imposed on society by smokers. Not surprisingly, this has given rise to a battle of rights between smokers and nonsmokers. Nonsmokers claim that smokers impose large external costs on the rest of society which are not reflected in the price paid for cigarettes. On the other hand, smokers argue that the price and taxes they pay are more than enough compensation for any costs they impose on society, and that these policies unnecessarily interfere with their freedom to choose the amount of perfectly legal products they should consume.

The concept of opportunity cost can help us evaluate the net costs imposed on society by smokers. The question is whether the price paid by smokers covers all the costs to society of the activity. In the case of cigarettes, in addition to the production costs and the costs voluntarily assumed by smokers in deciding to smoke, there are certain external costs imposed on society at large. These include especially the health services provided to smokers and nonsmokers alike for smoking-related diseases. In addition, some economists count as part of social costs the opportunity cost of potential output lost due to the premature death of some smokers. On the other hand, smokers compensate society over and above the costs of producing cigarettes. This compensation takes two forms. One is the substantial government revenues from taxes on tobacco products. The other is the reduction in transfer payments that results from the fact that early death results in a reduction in public pension benefits that would otherwise accrue to elderly persons. In addition, premature death also economizes on certain types of public services used by the elderly, especially health services and residential care facilities.

A recent study by economists André Raynauld and Jean-Pierre Vidal of the University of Montreal attempted to place dollar values on these various amounts. They estimated that, using 1986 data, the social costs attributable to smoking were $669 million for all of Canada. These include both the total hospitalization and medical services costs and the cost to properties of accidental fires blamed on smokers' negligence. Against this, however, reductions in future hospital, medical, and residential care costs amounted to $462 million, leaving a net cost of $207 million. Note that the authors assume that smokers know that smoking is bad for their health and that they internalize the risk of premature death in their decision to smoke. Therefore, loss of years of a smokers' life is not an extra cost. The authors also state that there is no evidence that smoking is a cause of death for nonsmokers.

These costs are more than made up for by the taxes paid by smokers, estimated to be $3.17 billion and the savings in pension plan payments of $1.42 billion. When set against the net external costs imposed on nonsmokers, this leads Raynauld and Vidal to conclude that it is a myth that smokers impose a cost on society. Of course, many persons will dispute the choice of items to include in the costs of smoking and the way in which they are measured. Because of the difficulty of computing some costs, other economists may differ in their conclusions about the net costs of smoking.

*Source:* André Raynauld and Jean-Pierre Vidal, "Smokers' Burden on Society: Myth and Reality In Canada," *Canadian Public Policy* 18 (September 1992): 300–317.

worthwhile to convert some of that land into a provincial park, the government needs to take into account the opportunity cost of the land. The land might be used for growing timber or for grazing sheep. Whatever the value of the land in its next-best use, this is the economic cost of the provincial park. The fact that the government does not have to buy the land does not mean that the land should be treated as a free good.

Thus, in the economist's view, when rational firms and individuals take decisions—whether to undertake one investment project rather than another, whether to buy one product rather than another—they take into account *all* of the costs, the full opportunity costs, not just the direct expenditures.

## SUNK COSTS

Economic cost includes costs, as we have just seen, that noneconomists often exclude, but it also ignores costs that noneconomists include. If an expenditure has already been made and cannot be recovered no matter what choice is made, a rational person would ignore it. Such expenditures are called **sunk costs.**

To understand sunk costs, let's go back to the movies, assuming now that you have spent $8 to buy a movie ticket. You were skeptical about whether the movie was worth $8. Half an hour into the movie, your worst suspicions are realized: the movie is a disaster. Should you leave the movie theatre? In making that decision, the $8 should be ignored. It is a sunk cost; your money is gone whether you stay or leave. The only relevant choice now is how to spend the next 90 minutes of your time: watch a terrible movie or go do something else.

Or assume you have just purchased a fancy laptop computer for $2,000. But the next week, the manufacturer announces a new computer with twice the power for $1,000; you can trade in your old computer for the new one by paying an additional $400. You are angry. You feel you have just paid $2,000 for a computer that is now almost worthless, and you have gotten hardly any use out of it. You decide not to buy the new computer for another year, until you have gotten at least some return for your investment. Again, an economist would say that you are not ap-

proaching the question rationally. The past decision is a sunk cost. The only question you should ask yourself is whether the extra power of the fancier computer is worth the additional $400. If it is, buy it. If not, don't.

## MARGINAL COSTS

The third aspect of cost that economists emphasize is the extra costs of doing a little more of something, what economists call the **marginal costs.** These are weighed against the (additional) **marginal benefits** of doing it. The most difficult decisions we take are not whether to do something or not. They are whether to do a little more or a little less of something. Few of us waste much time deciding whether or not to work. We have to work; the decision is whether to work a few more or a few less hours. A country does not consider whether or not to have an army; it decides whether to have a larger or smaller army.

Jim has just obtained a job for which he needs a car. He must decide how much to spend on the car. By spending more, he can get a bigger and more luxurious car. But he has to decide whether it is worth a few hundred (or thousand) marginal dollars for a larger car or for extra items like cute hubcaps, power windows, and so on.

Polly is thinking about flying to Banff for a ski weekend. She has three days off from work. The air fare is $200, the hotel room costs $100 a night, and the ski ticket costs $35 a day. Food costs the same as at home. She is trying to decide whether to go for two or three days. The *marginal* cost of the third day is $135, the hotel cost plus the cost of the ski ticket. There are no additional transportation costs involved in staying the third day. She needs to compare the marginal cost with the additional enjoyment she will have from the third day.

People, consciously or not, think about the trade-offs at the margin in most of their decisions. Economists, however, bring them into the foreground. Like opportunity costs and sunk costs, marginal analysis is one of the critical concepts that enable economists to think systematically about the costs of alternative choices.

## BASIC STEPS OF RATIONAL CHOICE

Identify the opportunity sets.

Define the trade-offs.

Calculate the costs correctly, taking into account opportunity costs, sunk costs, and marginal costs.

# REVIEW AND PRACTICE

## SUMMARY

**1** The economists' basic model consists of rational, self-interested individuals and profit-maximizing firms, interacting in competitive markets.

**2** The profit motive and private property provide incentives for rational individuals and firms to work hard and efficiently. Ill-defined or restricted property rights can lead to inefficient or counterproductive behaviour.

**3** Society often faces choices between equality, which means allowing people more or less equal amounts of consumption, and efficiency, which requires incentives that enable people or firms to receive different benefits depending on their performance.

**4** The price system in a market economy is one way of allocating goods and services. Other methods include rationing by queues, by lottery, by coupon, and by government regulation.

**5** An opportunity set illustrates what choices are possible. Budget constraints and time constraints define individuals' opportunity sets. Both show the trade-offs of how much of one thing a person must give up to get more of another.

**6** A production possibilities curve defines a firm's or society's opportunity set, representing the possible combinations of goods that the firm or society can produce. If a firm or society is producing below its production possibilities curve, it is said to be inefficient, since it could produce more of either good (or both goods) without producing less of the other.

**7** The opportunity cost is the cost of using any resource. It is measured by looking at the next-best, alternative use to which that resource could be put.

**8** A sunk cost is a past expenditure that cannot be recovered, no matter what choice is made in the present. Thus, rational decision makers ignore them.

**9** Most economic decisions concentrate on choices at the margin, where the marginal (or extra) cost of a course of action is compared with its extra benefits.

## KEY TERMS

perfect competition

price taker

basic competitive model

property rights

incentive-equality trade-off

rationing systems

opportunity sets

budget constraints

time constraints

production possibilities curve

diminishing returns

opportunity cost

sunk costs

marginal costs and benefits

## REVIEW QUESTIONS

**1** What are the essential elements of economists' basic competitive model?

**2** Consider a lake in a provincial park where everyone is allowed to fish as much as he wants. What outcome do you predict? Might this problem be averted if the lake were privately owned, or fishing licences were sold?

**3** Why might government policy to make the distribution of income more equitable lead to less efficiency?

**4** List advantages and disadvantages of rationing by queues, by lottery, by coupon, and by government regulation. If the government permitted a black market to develop, might some of the disadvantages of these systems be reduced?

**5** What are some of the opportunity costs of going to university? What are some of the opportunity costs a province should consider when deciding whether to widen a highway?

**6** Give two examples of a sunk cost, and explain why they should be irrelevant to current decisions.

**7** How is marginal analysis relevant in the decision about which car or which house to purchase? After you have decided which car to purchase, how is marginal analysis relevant?

## PROBLEMS

**1** Imagine that many businesses are located beside a river into which they discharge industrial waste. There is a city downstream that uses the river as a water supply and for recreation. If property rights to the river are ill defined, what problems may occur?

**2** Suppose an underground reservoir of oil resides under properties owned by several different individuals. As each well is drilled, it reduces the amount of oil that others can take out. Compare how quickly the oil is likely to be extracted in this situation with how quickly it would be extracted if one person owned the property rights to drill for the entire pool of oil.

**3** In some provinces, hunting licences are allocated by lottery; if you want a licence, you send in your name to enter the lottery. If the purpose of the system is to ensure that those who want to hunt the most get a chance to do so, what are the flaws of this system? How would the situation improve if people who won licences were allowed to sell them to others?

**4** Imagine that during time of war, the government imposes coupon rationing. What are the advantages of allowing people to buy and sell their coupons? What are the disadvantages?

**5** Kathy, a university student, has $20 a week to spend; she spends it either on junk food at $2.50 a snack, or on gasoline at $.50 per litre. Draw Kathy's opportunity set. What is the trade-off between junk food and gasoline? Now draw each new budget constraint she would face if
  (a) a kind relative started sending her an additional $10 per week
  (b) the price of a junk food snack fell to $2
  (c) the price of gasoline rose to $.60 per litre.
In each case, how does the trade-off between junk food and gasoline change?

**6** Why is the opportunity cost of going to medical school likely to be greater than the opportunity cost of going to university? Why is the opportunity cost of a woman with a university education having a child greater than the opportunity cost of a woman with just a secondary education having a child?

**7** Bob likes to divide his recreational time between going to movies and listening to compact discs. He has twenty hours a week available for recreation; a movie takes two hours, and a CD takes one hour to listen to. Draw his "time budget constraint." Bob also has a limited amount of income to spend on recreation. He has $60 a week to spend on recreational activities; a movie costs $5, and a CD costs $12. (He never likes to listen to the same CD twice.) Draw his budget constraint. What is his opportunity set?

## APPENDIX: READING GRAPHS

Whether the old saying that a picture is worth a thousand words under- or overestimates the value of a picture, economists find graphs extremely useful.

For instance, look at Figure 2.5; it is a redrawn version of Figure 2.1, showing the budget constraint—the various combinations of CDs and cassettes an individual, Alfred, can purchase. More generally, a graph shows the relationship between two variables—here, the number of CDs and the number of cassettes that can be purchased. The budget constraint gives the maximum number of cassettes that can be purchased, given the number of CDs that have been bought.

In a graph, one variable (here, CDs) is put on the horizontal axis and the other variable on the vertical axis. We read a point such as E by looking down to the horizontal axis and seeing that it corresponds to 4 CDs, and by looking across to the vertical axis and seeing that it corresponds to 12 cassettes. Similarly, we read point A by looking down to the horizontal axis and seeing that it corresponds to 5 CDs, and by looking across to the vertical axis and seeing that it corresponds to 10 cassettes.

In the figure, each of the points from the table has been plotted, and then a curve has been drawn through those points. The "curve" turns out to be a straight line in this case, but we still use the more general term. The advantage of the curve over the individual points is that with it, we can read off from the graph points on the budget constraint that are not in the table.

Sometimes, of course, not every point on the graph is economically meaningful. You cannot buy half a cassette or half a CD. For the most part, we ignore these considerations when drawing our graphs; we simply pretend that any point on the budget constraint is actually possible.

## SLOPE

In any diagram, the amount by which the value along the vertical axis increases from a change in a unit along the horizontal axis is called the **slope,** just like the slope of a mountain. Slope is sometimes described as "rise over run," meaning that the slope of a line can be calculated by dividing the change on the vertical axis (the "rise") by the change on the horizontal axis (the "run").

Look at Figure 2.5. As we move from E to A, increasing the number of CDs by 1, the number of cassettes purchased falls from 12 to 10. For each

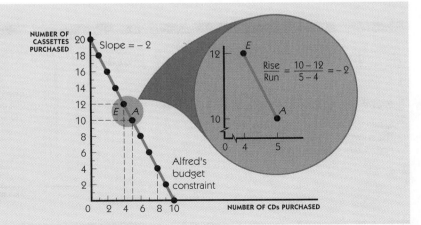

**Figure 2.5 READING A GRAPH: THE BUDGET CONSTRAINT**

Graphs can be used to show the relationship between two variables. This one shows the relationship between the variable on the vertical axis (the number of cassettes Alfred can buy) and the variable on the horizontal axis (the number of CDs).

The slope of a curve like the budget constraint gives the change in the number of cassettes that can be purchased as Alfred buys one more CD. The slope of the budget constraint is negative.

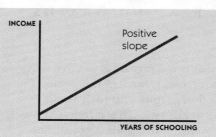

**Figure 2.6 POSITIVELY SLOPED CURVE**

Income increases with the number of years of schooling.

additional CD bought, the feasible number of cassettes that can be purchased falls by 2. So the slope of the line is

$$\frac{\text{rise}}{\text{run}} = \frac{10 - 12}{5 - 4} = \frac{-2}{1} = -2.$$

When, as in Figure 2.5, the variable on the vertical axis falls when the variable on the horizontal axis increases, the curve, or line, is said to be **negatively sloped.** A budget constraint is always negatively sloped. But when we describe the slope of a budget constraint, we frequently omit the term "negative." We say the slope is 2, knowing that since we are de-

scribing the slope of a budget constraint, we should more formally say that the slope is negative 2. Alternatively, we sometimes say that the slope has an absolute value of 2.

Figure 2.6 shows the case of a curve that is **positively sloped.** The variable along the vertical axis, income, increases as schooling increases, giving the line its upward tilt from left to right.

In later discussions, we will encounter two special cases. A line that is very steep has a very large slope; that is, the increase in the vertical axis for every unit increase in the horizontal axis is very large. The extreme case is a perfectly vertical line, and we say then that the slope is infinite (Figure 2.7, panel A). At the

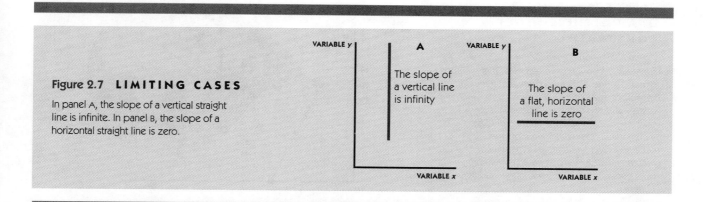

**Figure 2.7 LIMITING CASES**

In panel A, the slope of a vertical straight line is infinite. In panel B, the slope of a horizontal straight line is zero.

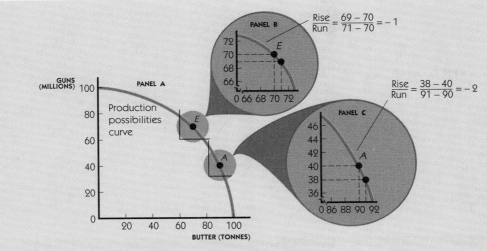

**Figure 2.8  THE GUNS AND BUTTER TRADE-OFF**

Panel A shows a trade-off between military spending ("guns") and civilian spending ("butter"), where society chooses point E. Panel B is an enlargement of the area around E, which focuses on the slope there, which also measures the marginal trade-offs society faces near that point. Similarly, panel C is an enlargement of the area around A and shows the marginal trade-offs society faces near that point.

other extreme is a flat, horizontal line; since there is no increase in the vertical axis no matter how large the change along the horizontal, we say that the slope of such a curve is zero (panel B).

Figures 2.5 and 2.6 both show straight lines. Everywhere along the straight line, the slope is the same. This is not true in Figure 2.8, which repeats the production possibilities curve shown originally in Figure 2.3. Look first at point E. Panel B of the figure blows up the area around E, so that we can see what happens to the output of guns when we increase the output of butter by 1. From the figure, you can see that the output of guns decreases by 1. Thus, the slope is

$$\frac{\text{rise}}{\text{run}} = \frac{69 - 70}{71 - 70} = -1.$$

Now look at point A, where the economy is producing more butter. The area around A has been blown up in panel C. Here, we see that when we increase butter by 1 more unit, the reduction in guns is greater than before. The slope at A is

$$\frac{\text{rise}}{\text{run}} = \frac{38 - 40}{91 - 90} = -2.$$

With curves such as the production possibilities curve, the slope differs as we move along the curve.

## INTERPRETING CURVES

Look at Figure 2.9. Which of the two curves has a larger slope? The one on the left appears to have a slope that has a larger absolute value. But look carefully at the axes. Notice that in panel A, the vertical axis is stretched relative to panel B. The same distance that represents 20 cassettes in panel B represents only 10 cassettes in panel A. In fact, both panels

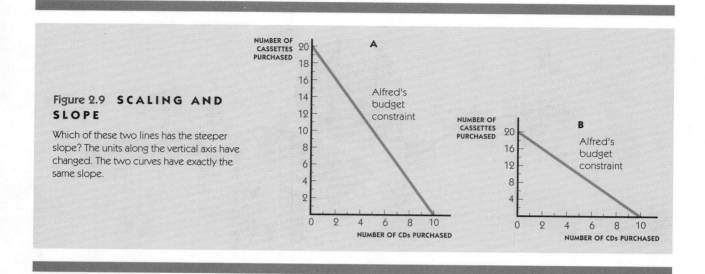

**Figure 2.9 SCALING AND SLOPE**

Which of these two lines has the steeper slope? The units along the vertical axis have changed. The two curves have exactly the same slope.

represent the same budget constraint. They have exactly the same slope.

This kind of cautionary tale is as important in looking at the graphs of data that were common in Chapter 1 as it is in looking at the relationships presented in this chapter that produce smooth curves. Compare, for instance, panels A and B of Figure 2.10.

Which of the two curves exhibits more variability? Which looks more stable? Panel B appears to show that car production does not change much over time. But again, a closer look reveals that the axes have been stretched in panel A. The two curves are based on exactly the same data, and there is really no difference between them.

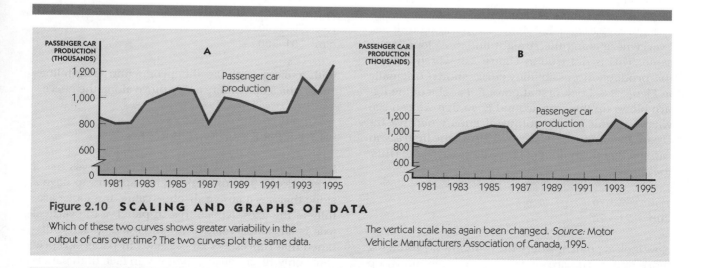

**Figure 2.10 SCALING AND GRAPHS OF DATA**

Which of these two curves shows greater variability in the output of cars over time? The two curves plot the same data.

The vertical scale has again been changed. *Source:* Motor Vehicle Manufacturers Association of Canada, 1995.

# CHAPTER 3

# TRADE

A creature on another planet looking down at a developed modern economy on earth might compare human activity to an enormous ant colony. Each ant seemingly has an assigned task. Some stand guard. Some feed the young. Some harvest food and others distribute it. Some shuffle paper, scribble notes in books, and keyboard at computer consoles. Others work in factories, tightening screws, running machines, and so on. How is all of this activity coordinated? No dictator or superintelligent computer is giving instructions. Yet somehow an immense amount is accomplished in a reasonably coordinated way. Understanding how a complex economy operates—how it is that certain individuals do one task, others do another, how information is communicated and decisions taken—is a central objective of economics.

This chapter discusses the problem of economic interdependence at two levels: individuals and firms within a country, and countries within the world economic community. Many of the same principles apply at both levels.

## KEY QUESTIONS

**1** Why is trade (exchange) mutually beneficial?

**2** What are the similarities and differences between trade (exchange) between individuals within a country and trade between countries?

**3** What determines what any particular country produces and sells on the international market? What is meant by

comparative advantage, and why does it play such an important role?

**4** What are the gains from specialization?

**5** How valid is the argument, so often heard in political circles, that trade should be restricted?

## THE BENEFITS OF ECONOMIC INTERDEPENDENCE

We begin by considering the benefits of trade, specifically the exchange of goods that are already available in the economy.

### THE GAINS FROM TRADE

When individuals own different goods or have different desires, or both, there is an opportunity for trades that benefit all parties to the trade. Kids trading hockey cards learn the basic principles of exchange. One has two Mario Lemieux cards, the other has two Eric Lindros cards. A trade will benefit both of them. The same principle applies to countries. Canada has more natural gas than it can use, but it does not produce enough fruit to feed its populace. The United States has more fruit than Americans can consume, but needs natural gas. Trade can benefit both countries.

Voluntary trade involves only winners. If a trade would make a loser of any party, that party would choose not to trade. Thus, a fundamental consequence of voluntary exchange is that it benefits everyone involved.

### FEELING "JILTED" IN TRADE

In spite of the seemingly persuasive argument that individuals engage in trade voluntarily only if they think they will be better off as a result, people often walk away from a deal believing they have been hurt.

It is important to understand that when economists say that a voluntary trade makes the two traders better off, they do not mean that it makes them both happy.

Imagine, for example, that Frank brings an antique rocking chair to a flea market to sell. He is willing to sell it for $100 but hopes to sell it for $200. Helen comes to the flea market planning to buy such a chair, hoping to spend only $100, but willing to pay as much as $200. They argue and negotiate, eventually settle on a price of $125, and make the deal. But when they go home, they both complain. Frank complains the price was too low, and Helen that it was too high.

From an economist's point of view, such complaints are self-contradictory. If Frank *really* thought $125 was too low, he would not have sold at that price. If Helen *really* thought $125 was too high, she would not have paid the price. Economists argue that people reveal their preferences not by what they say, but by what they do. If one voluntarily agrees to make a deal, one also agrees that the deal is, if not perfect, at least better than the alternative of not making it.

Two common objections are made to this line of reasoning. Both involve Frank's or Helen's "taking advantage" of the other. The implication is that if a buyer or a seller can take advantage, then the other party may be a loser rather than a winner.

The first objection is that either Frank or Helen may not really know what is being agreed to. Perhaps Frank doesn't realize that the chair is an antique; Helen does, and by neglecting to tell Frank, manages to buy it for only $125. Perhaps Frank knows the rockers fall off but sells the chair without telling this to Helen, thus keeping the price high. In either case, lack of relevant information makes someone a loser after the trade.

The second objection concerns equitable division of the **gains from trade.** Since Helen would have been willing to pay as much as $200, anything she pays less than that is **surplus,** the term economists use for a gain from trade. Similarly, since Frank would have been willing to sell the chair for as little as $100, anything he receives more than that is also surplus. The total dollar value of the gain from trade is $100—the difference between the maximum price Helen was willing to pay and the minimum price at which Frank was willing to sell. At a price of $125, $25 of the gain went to Frank, $75 to Helen. The second objection is that such a split is not fair.

Economists do not have much patience with these objections. Like most people, they favour making as much information public as possible, and they think vendors and customers should be made to stand behind their promises. But economists also point out that second thoughts and "If only I had known" are not relevant. If Frank sells his antique at a flea market instead of having it evaluated by reputable antique dealers, he has made a voluntary decision to save his time and energy. If Helen buys an antique at a flea market instead of going to a reputable dealer, she knows she is taking a risk.

The logic of free exchange, however, does not say that everyone must express happiness with the result. It simply says that when people choose to make a deal, they prefer making it to not making it. And if they prefer the deal, they are by definition better off *in their own minds* at the time the transaction takes place.

The objections to trade nonetheless carry an important message: most exchanges that happen in the real world are considerably more complicated than the Frank-Helen chair trade. They involve problems of information, estimating risks, and expectations about the future. These complications will be discussed throughout the book. So without going into too much detail at the moment, let's just say that if you are worried that you do not have the proper information to make a trade, shop around, get a guarantee or expert opinion, or buy insurance. If you choose to plunge ahead without these precautions, don't pretend you didn't have other choices. Like those who buy a ticket in a lottery, you know you are taking chances.

## ECONOMIC RELATIONS AS EXCHANGES

Individuals in our economy are involved in masses of voluntary trades. They "trade" their labour services (time and skills) to their employer for dollars. They then trade dollars with a multitude of merchants for goods (like gasoline and groceries) and services (like plumbing and hair styling). The employer trades the goods it produces for dollars, and trades those dollars for labour services. Even your savings account can be viewed as a trade: you give the bank $100 today in exchange for the bank's promise to give you $105 at the end of the year, your original deposit plus 5 percent interest.

Unlike Frank's sale of the rocking chair to Helen, most trades take place anonymously at prices that are posted beforehand rather than decided by one-on-one bargaining. But even though neither party has any influence over the market price, there are still gains from trade associated with market transactions. When the price of a loaf of bread is $1.50, consumers will purchase it if the value they place on a loaf is at least $1.50. That goes not only for the first loaf they purchase but for the second, third, and so on. The excess of the value they place on all loaves of bread they purchase above what they actually pay for them is referred to as their **consumer surplus**— simply, their individual gain from trade. Similarly, producers will supply the bread as long as the cost of supplying the bread is no more than $1.50. The excess of the price of bread over the cost of producing it is called **producer surplus.** The total gain from trade in the bread market is the sum of consumer and producer surpluses of all buyers and sellers. The notions of consumer and producer surplus are important in understanding the benefits of the market system of allocating resources and will be returned to in later chapters.

## TRADE BETWEEN COUNTRIES

Why is it that people engage in this complex set of economic relations with others? The answer is that people are better off as a result of trading. Just as individuals *within* a country find it advantageous to trade with one another, so too do countries find trade advantageous. Just as it is impossible for any individual to be self-sufficient, it is impossible for a country to be self-reliant without sacrificing its standard of living. Canada has long been part of an international economic community, and this participation has grown in recent decades. How has this affected the three main markets in the Canadian economy?

***Interdependence in the Product Market***   In 1994, close to a third of the good and services sold in Canada were **imports,** goods produced abroad but sold domestically. Roughly two thirds of motor vehicles sold in Canada were imported, along with a third of the oil, virtually all of the CDs and VCRs, and some basic foodstuffs like bananas, coffee, and tea. Not surprisingly, two thirds of the imports into Canada came from the United States, and that proportion may even rise as the Canada-U.S. Free Trade Agreement negotiated by the two countries in 1987 continues to work its way through. At the same time, Canadian producers sell a third of everything they produce as **exports,** goods produced domestically but sold abroad; almost three quarters of Canada's exports go to the United States. Fully 70 percent of motor vehicles produced in Canada are exported, as are 30 percent of oil and gas produced, and even higher proportions of wheat and forest products.

The Canadian economy has always been heavily dependent on trade, though the extent of dependency has changed over time. The share of both exports and imports plummeted dramatically during the Great Depression and rose rapidly in World War II. Figure 3.1 shows how exports and imports have varied as a proportion of national income, known as gross domestic product (GDP), over the postwar period. The proportions initially declined from the immediate postwar levels of just over one quarter of GDP to less than one fifth in the mid-1950s. They have been increasing for much of the postwar period, reaching almost one third, with temporary declines during major recessions. Canadian trade as a share of GDP is comparable to that of Britain and France, and over twice as high as that of the United States. This reflects the fact that smaller countries tend to be more dependent than larger ones on international trade.

Earnings from exports constitute a major source of income for some of our largest corporations, accounting for 85 percent of sales for Chrysler Canada, 84 percent for Pratt & Whitney Canada, and 60 percent for IBM Canada. Table 3.1 gives some other examples of large companies that rely heavily on exports. It is interesting to note that over half of these companies are foreign-owned, which is another feature of a highly open economy like Canada's.

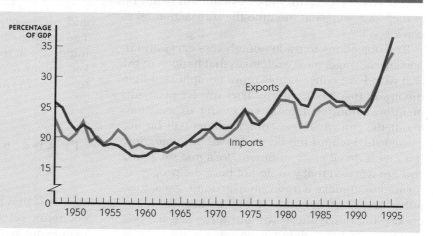

**Figure 3.1  INTERNATIONAL TRADE**

Here, Canadian imports and exports are both expressed as a percentage of the gross domestic product (GDP). Notice that trade has increased in the last thirty years and that imports have grown relative to exports in recent years. *Source:* Statistics Canada, CANSIM Database 1996.

## Table 3.1 EXPORT-DEPENDENT BIG COMPANIES

| Company and product | Rank by export sales | Exports as percentage of sales |
|---|---|---|
| Chrysler Canada (automobiles) | 2 | 85 |
| Pratt & Whitney Canada (aerospace) | 14 | 84 |
| Canfor (forest products) | 18 | 81 |
| Stone Consolidated (forest products) | 23 | 73 |
| Canadian Reynolds (metals) | 26 | 73 |
| General Motors Canada (automobiles) | 1 | 67 |
| Falconbridge (mining) | 17 | 67 |
| IBM Canada (computers) | 4 | 60 |
| Abitibi-Price (forest products) | 16 | 55 |
| Fletcher Challenge Canada (forest products) | 19 | 53 |
| Ford Canada (automobiles) | 3 | 52 |
| Bombardier (engineering) | 7 | 47 |
| Inco (nickel) | 13 | 41 |
| MacMillan Bloedel (forest products) | 11 | 36 |
| Amoco Canada (energy) | 9 | 35 |
| Noranda (resources) | 8 | 34 |

Source: The Globe and Mail Report on Business Magazine, July 1995, p. 89.

***Interdependence in the Labour Market*** International interdependence extends beyond the mere shipping of goods between countries. More than 98 percent of Canadian citizens either immigrated here from abroad or are descended from people who did so. The flow of immigrants has varied considerably over time. The numbers increased rapidly from the 1850s until World War I. In the period 1910–14, about three million settlers arrived from Europe and Britain, mainly to the Prairie provinces. Immigration fell dramatically during the war and did not pick up again until the mid-1920s, again largely from the British Isles and Europe. It fell off considerably after the Crash of 1929 and was virtually nonexistent until after World War II. In the late 1940s and early 1950s, the numbers of immigrants started to increase rapidly; again they were mainly Europeans, many of them having been displaced by the war. By the end of the 1950s, the immigrant profile started to change considerably: from rural to urban workers, and from European to other nationalities. The annual number of immigrants tripled between 1961 and 1967, when it reached 220,000. It then fell off and averaged about 140,000 per year until the early 1980s. With the recession of 1981–82, immigration began to fall to less than 100,000, but since then it has gradually recovered to 200,000. By 1989, almost one half of all immigrants came from Asia, about one quarter from Europe, one eighth from North and Central America, and the remainder mostly from Africa and South America. These proportions have held steady in the 1990s.

The nations of Europe have increasingly recognized the benefits that result from this international movement of workers. One of the important provisions of the treaty establishing the European Union (EU), an agreement among most countries within Western Europe, allows for the free flow of workers between member nations of the EU.

***Interdependence in the Capital Market*** Canada has always borrowed heavily from abroad, but the country also invests heavily overseas. In 1994, Canadians invested approximately $13 billion in foreign countries (factories, businesses, buildings, loans, etc.), while foreign investors invested over $30 billion in Canada. Canadian companies have sought out profitable opportunities abroad, where they can use their special skills and knowledge to earn high returns. They have established branches and built factories in the United States, Europe, Latin America, and elsewhere in the world.

Just as the nations of Western Europe have recognized the advantages that follow from the free flow of goods and labour among their countries, so too have they recognized the gains from the free flow of capital. Funds can be invested where they yield the highest returns. Knowledge and skills from one country can be combined with capital from another to produce goods that will be enjoyed by citizens of all countries. Though the process of liberalizing the flow of goods, labour, and capital among countries of the European Union has been going on for more than twenty years, 1992 marks the crucial date at which all remaining barriers were officially removed.

## MULTILATERAL TRADE

Many of the examples to this point have emphasized two-way trade. Trade between two individuals or countries is called **bilateral trade.** But exchanges between two parties is often less advantageous than trade between several parties, called **multilateral trade.** Such trades are observed between sports teams. The Toronto Blue Jays send a catcher to the St. Louis Cardinals, the Cardinals send a pitcher to the Montreal Expos, and the Expos send an outfielder to the Blue Jays (see Figure 3.2A). No two of the teams was willing to make a two-way trade, but all can benefit from the three-way swap.

Countries function in a similar way. Japan has no domestic oil; it imports oil from Arabian countries. The Arabian countries want to sell their oil, but they want wheat and food, not the cars and television sets that Japan can provide. Canada can provide the missing link by buying cars and televisions from Japan and selling food to the Arab nations. Again, this three-way trade, shown in Figure 3.2B, offers gains that two-way trade cannot. The scores of na-

tions active in the world economy create patterns far more complex than these simplified examples.

Figure 3.3 illustrates the construction of a Ford Escort in Europe, and dramatizes the importance of multilateral and interconnected trade relations. The parts that go into an Escort come from all over the world. Similar diagrams could be constructed for many of the components in the diagram; the aluminum alloys may contain bauxite from Jamaica, the chrome plate may use chromium from South Africa, the copper for wiring may come from Chile.

Multilateral trade means that trade between any two participants may not balance. In Figure 3.2B, the Arab countries send oil to Japan but get no goods (only yen) in return. No one would say that the Arab countries have an unfair trade policy with Japan. Yet some politicians, newspaper columnists, and business executives complain that since Canada imports more from a particular country (often Japan) than it exports to that country, the trade balance is "unfair." There is a popular saying, "Trade is a two-way street." But trade in the world market involves hundreds of possible streets between nations. While there are legitimate reasons to be concerned with the overall

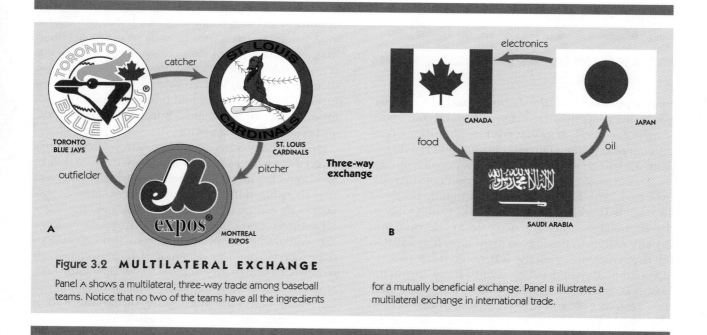

**Figure 3.2 MULTILATERAL EXCHANGE**

Panel A shows a multilateral, three-way trade among baseball teams. Notice that no two of the teams have all the ingredients for a mutually beneficial exchange. Panel B illustrates a multilateral exchange in international trade.

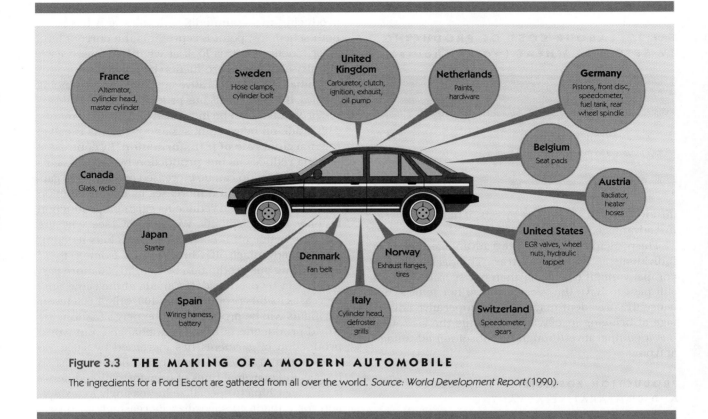

**Figure 3.3 THE MAKING OF A MODERN AUTOMOBILE**

The ingredients for a Ford Escort are gathered from all over the world. *Source: World Development Report* (1990).

Canadian trade deficit, there is no reason why Canadian exports and imports with any particular country should be balanced.

## COMPARATIVE ADVANTAGE

We have so far focused on exchanges of existing goods. But clearly, most of what is exchanged must first be produced. Trade allows individuals and countries to concentrate on what they produce best.

Some countries are more efficient at producing almost all types of goods and services than other countries. The possession of superior production skills is called having an **absolute advantage,** and these advanced countries are said to have an absolute advantage over the others. How can the countries with disadvantages successfully engage in trade? The answer lies in the principle of **comparative advantage,** which states that individuals and countries specialize in producing those goods in which they are *relatively,* not absolutely, more efficient.

To see what comparative advantage means, let's say that both Canada and Japan produce two goods, TV sets and wheat. The amount of labour needed to produce these goods is shown in Table 3.2. (These numbers are all hypothetical.) Canada is more efficient (spends fewer worker hours) at making both products. Canada can rightfully claim to have the more efficient TV industry, and yet it imports TV sets from Japan. Why? The opportunity cost, or *relative* cost, of making a TV set (in terms of labour used) in Japan relative to the cost of producing a tonne of wheat is low compared with Canada. That is, in Japan, it takes 15 times as many hours (120/8) to produce a TV set as a tonne of wheat; in Canada, it takes 20 times as many hours (100/5) to produce a TV set as a tonne of wheat. While Japan has an absolute

## Table 3.2 LABOUR COST OF PRODUCING TV SETS AND WHEAT (worker hours)

|  | Canada | Japan |
|---|---|---|
| Labour required to make a TV set | 100 | 120 |
| Labour required to make a tonne of wheat | 5 | 8 |

*dis*advantage in producing TV sets, it has a *comparative* advantage.

The principle of comparative advantage applies to individuals as well as countries. The president of a company might type faster than her secretary, but it still pays to have the secretary type her letters, because the president may have a comparative advantage at bringing in new clients, while the secretary has a comparative (though not absolute) advantage at typing.

### PRODUCTION POSSIBILITIES SCHEDULES AND COMPARATIVE ADVANTAGE

The easiest way to understand the comparative advantage of different countries is to use the production possibilities schedule first introduced in Chapter 2. Figure 3.4 depicts hypothetical production possibili-

ties schedules for two countries, China and Canada, producing two commodities, textiles and buses. In both schedules, point E represents the current level of production. Let us look at what happens if each country changes its production by 100 buses.

China has a comparative advantage in producing textiles. If it reduces its bus production by 100, its textile production can be increased by 10,000 garments. This trade-off between buses and garments is called the **marginal rate of transformation.** By contrast, if Canada reduces its bus production by 100 buses, its textile production can be increased by only 1,000 garments. Conversely, if it increases its bus production by 100, it will have to reduce its garment production by only 1,000 garments. We can now see why the world is better off if each country exploits its comparative advantage. If China moves from E to E' (decreasing bus production by 100), 10,000 more garments can be produced. If Canada at the same time increases its bus production by 100, only 1,000 fewer garments will be produced. In the new situation, the world production of buses is unchanged, but world production of garments has increased by 9,000. So long as the production trade-offs differ—that is, so long as the marginal rates of transformation differ— it pays for China to specialize increasingly in textiles, and for Canada to specialize increasingly in buses. Notice that the analysis only requires knowledge about the production trade-offs. We do not need to know how much labour or capital is required in either country to produce either buses or garments.

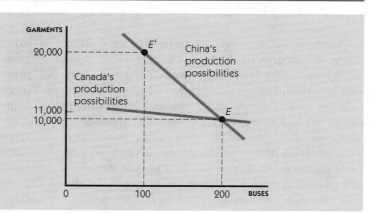

### Figure 3.4 EXPLOITING COMPARATIVE ADVANTAGE

The production possibilities schedules for China and Canada, each manufacturing two commodities, garments and buses, illustrate the trade-offs at different levels of production. Point E shows the current level of production for each country; E' illustrates a production decision that better exploits each country's comparative advantage.

## USING ECONOMICS: COMPARATIVE ADVANTAGE AND THE GAINS FROM TRADE

**Problem:** Using the earlier example of Japan and Canada, producing wheat and TV sets, calculate the trade-offs and show the gains from specialization.

Assume that both countries have 240,000 worker hours, initially divided equally between producing wheat and TV sets.

**Solution:** First, draw the production possibilities curves, as in the figure below. Since the costs (in worker hours) of producing each unit of each commodity are fixed, the production possibilities schedule is a straight line. If Canada used all its labour to produce TV sets, it would produce 2,400 TV sets; if it used all its labour to produce wheat, it would produce 48,000 tonnes of wheat. If Japan used all its labour to produce TV

sets, it would produce 2,000 TV sets; if it used all its labour to produce wheat, it would produce 30,000 tonnes of wheat.

In both curves, use point A to mark the current point of production, at which labour is equally divided between TV sets and wheat.

Next, calculate the slope of the production possibilities curve, giving the trade-offs: in Canada, increasing wheat output by 1,000 tonnes leads to a reduction of TV sets by 50, while reducing wheat output by 1,000 tonnes in Japan leads to an increase in TV sets of 66⅔. Thus, each shift of wheat production by 1,000 tonnes from Japan to Canada increases world TV set production by 16⅔.

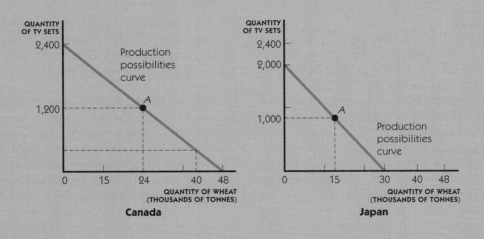

Though it pays countries to increase production and export of goods in which they have a comparative advantage and to import goods in which they have a comparative disadvantage, this may not lead to complete specialization. Thus, Canada continues to be a producer of textiles in spite of heavy imports from the Far East. This does not violate the principle

of comparative advantage: not all textiles require the same skill and expertise in manufacturing. Thus, while China may have a comparative advantage in inexpensive textiles, Canada may have a comparative advantage in higher-quality textiles. At the same time, the comparative advantage of other countries is so extreme in producing some goods that it does not pay for Canada to produce them at all: TVs, VCRs, and a host of other electronic gadgets, for example.

## COMPARATIVE ADVANTAGE AND SPECIALIZATION

To see the benefits of specialization, consider the pencil. A tree containing the right kind of wood must be felled; it must be transported to a sawmill and cut into pieces that can be further processed into pencil casings. Then the graphite that runs through the pencil's center, the eraser at its tip, and the metal that holds the two together must each be produced by specially trained people. The pencil is a simple tool. But to produce it by oneself would cost a fortune in money and an eternity in time.

***Why Specialization Increases Productivity*** Specialization increases productivity, thus enhancing the benefits of trade, for three reasons. First, specializing avoids the time it takes a worker to switch from one production task to another. Second, by repeating the same task, the worker becomes more skilled at it. And third, specialization creates a fertile environment for invention.

Workers may possess roughly equal skills before they begin specializing. But after workers have begun specializing, switching them back and forth between jobs will make production less efficient.

Dividing jobs so that each worker can practice a particular skill, called the **division of labour,** may increase productivity hundreds or thousands of times. Almost anyone who practices simple activities—like sewing on a button, shooting a basketball, or adding a column of numbers—will be quite a lot better at them than someone who has not practiced. Similarly, a country that specializes in producing sports cars may develop a comparative advantage. With its relatively large scale of production, it can divide tasks into separate assignments for different people; as they become better at their own tasks, productivity is increased.

At the same time, the division of labour often leads to invention. As someone learns a particular job extremely well, she might figure out ways of doing it better—including inventing a machine to do it. Specialization and invention reinforce each other. A slight initial advantage in some good leads to greater production of that good, thence to more in-

vention, and thence to even greater production and further specialization.

***Limits of Specialization*** The extent of division of labour, or specialization, is limited by the size of the market. There is greater scope for specialization in mass-produced manufactured goods like picture frames than in custom-made items like the artwork that gets framed. That is one reason why the costs of production of mass-produced goods have declined so much. Similarly, there is greater scope for specialization in a big city than a small town. That is why small stores specializing in a particular food or type of clothing thrive in cities but are rarer in smaller places.

The very nature of specialization limits gains. Repetitive jobs can lead to bored and unproductive workers. And single-track specialization inhibits the new insights and ideas that can come from engaging in a variety of work activities.

## WHAT DETERMINES COMPARATIVE ADVANTAGE?

Earlier we learned that comparative advantage determines the pattern of trade. But what determines comparative advantage? In the modern world, this turns out to be a complex matter.

***Natural Endowments*** In first laying down the principle of comparative advantage in the early 1800s, the great British economist David Ricardo used the example of Portugal's trade with Britain. In Ricardo's example, Portugal had an absolute advantage in producing both wool and wine. But it had a comparative advantage in producing wine, because compared with Britain it could produce wine better than it could produce wool. Thus, Britain had a comparative advantage in producing wool. In this and other early examples, economists tended to assume that a nation's comparative advantage was determined largely by its **natural endowments.** Countries with soil and climate that are *relatively* better for grapes than for pasture will produce wine; countries with soil and climate that are relatively better for pasture than for grapes will produce sheep and hence wool. Canada's abundance of arable land gives us a comparative advantage in agriculture.

Natural endowments still count in the modern

Three lists of goods define Canada's comparative advantage today. The first are those of which Canada exports a great deal and imports little—presumably the goods in which we have a strong comparative advantage. The second consists of goods of which Canada imports a great deal and exports little in which we have a strong comparative disadvantage. The third are goods of which Canada is both a high importer and high exporter in which we have neither a comparative advantage nor disadvantage and in which trade is presumably based on the gains from specialization.

*Category 1: High Exports, Low Imports*   Pulp and paper, lumber, wheat and other grains, fish and fish products, ores and concentrates, precious metals, aluminum, copper, nickel and other metals, nonmetallic minerals, fertilizers, coal, electricity. Notice that most of these goods are based on natural resources, as might be expected.

*Category 2: High Imports, Low Exports* Communications and electronics equipment, fruit and vegetables, cotton, wool and textiles, chemicals, consumer goods. In contrast with category 1, these goods tend either to be manufactured goods or agricultural goods for which the Canadian climate is unsuited.

*Category 3: High Imports and Exports*   Vehicles and parts, aircraft and parts, other transport equipment, oil and natural gas, industrial machinery, agricultural machinery, iron and steel, plastics, food products. Some of these goods are exported from one area of the country and imported into another, so transport costs play an important role. Others are manufactured goods that represent global industries in which products are shipped around the world.

---

economy: countries that have an abundance of low-skilled labour relative to other resources, such as South Korea and Hong Kong, have a comparative advantage in producing goods like textiles, which require a lot of handwork. But in today's technological age nations can also act to *acquire* a comparative advantage.

***Acquired Endowments***   The Japanese have little in the way of natural resources, yet they are a major player in international trade, in part because they have **acquired endowments.** Their case underscores the principle that by saving and accumulating capital and building large factories, a nation can acquire a comparative advantage in goods that, like steel, require large amounts of capital in their production. And by devoting resources to education, a nation can develop a comparative advantage in goods whose production requires a skilled labour force. Thus, the resources—human and physical—that a country has managed to acquire for itself can also give rise to comparative advantage.

***Superior Knowledge***   In the modern economy, comparative advantage may come simply from expertise in using resources productively. Switzerland has a comparative advantage in watches because over the years the country has accumulated superior knowledge and expertise in watchmaking. Belgium has a comparative advantage in fine lace; its workers have developed the requisite skills. A quirk of fate might have led Belgium to acquire a comparative advantage in watches and Switzerland one in lace.

Although sometimes patterns of specialization occur as an accident of history, in modern economies they are more likely to be a consequence of deliberate decisions. The U.S. semiconductor industry is a case in point. This industry manufactures the tiny silicon chips that control computers. Semiconductors were invented by an American, Robert Noyce,

## THE FOUR BASES OF COMPARATIVE ADVANTAGE

**1** Natural endowments, which consist of geographical determinants such as land, natural resources, and climate

**2** Acquired endowments, which are the physical capital and human skills a nation has developed

**3** Superior knowledge, including technological advantages, which may be acquired either as an accident of history or through deliberate policies

**4** Specialization, which may create comparative advantages between countries that are similar in all other respects

and in the 1970s the United States had a powerful comparative advantage in manufacturing semiconductors; Japan managed to become a close competitor in the 1980s, but in the 1990s the United States has regained its leadership. The rise of the U.S. semiconductor industry was built in part on decisions by the federal government to fund the necessary research—primarily so the semiconductors could be used in guided missiles and other weapons. The rise of the Japanese industry was similarly based on decisions by that government to support its semiconductor industry.

Stories like that of the semiconductor industry have led some economists to argue that a government that wants to gain a technological advantage in a certain industry should encourage that industry by, for instance, supporting research relevant to that industry. In Canada, government support for the nuclear energy and aerospace industries have resulted in the country's occupying a niche in world markets for nuclear reactors and commuter airplanes.

*Specialization*   Earlier we saw how comparative advantage leads to specialization. Specialization may also lead to comparative advantage. The Swiss make fine watches and have a comparative advantage in that market based on years of unique experience. Such superior knowledge, however, does not explain why Britain, Germany, and the United States, which are at roughly the same level of technological expertise in building cars, all trade cars with one another. How can each country have a comparative advantage in making cars? The answer lies in specialization.

Both Britain and Germany may be better off if Britain specializes in producing sports cars and Germany in producing luxury cars, because specialization increases productivity. Countries enhance, or simply develop, a comparative advantage by specializing, just as individuals do. As a result, similar countries enjoy the advantages of specialization even when they specialize in different variations of basically similar products.

## THE PERCEIVED COSTS OF INTERNATIONAL INTERDEPENDENCE

If the argument that voluntary trade must be mutually beneficial is so compelling, why has there been from time to time such strong antitrade sentiment in Canada and many other countries? This antitrade feeling is often labelled **protectionism,** because it calls for protecting the economy from the effects of trade. Those who favour protectionism raise a number of concerns. Some of the objections to international trade parallel the objections to trade among individuals noted earlier. Did they get a fair deal? Was the seller in a stronger bargaining position? For individuals and countries, such concerns revolve around how the *surplus* associated with the gains from trade is divided. Weak countries may feel that they are being taken advantage of by stronger countries. Their weaker bargaining position may mean that the stronger countries get *more* of the gains from trade. But this does not contradict the basic premise: both parties gain from voluntary exchange. All countries—weak as well as strong—are better off as a result of voluntary exchange.

But an important difference exists between trade among individuals and trade among countries. Some individuals within a country benefit from trade and

Despite the fact that the Canadian Constitution gives the federal government jurisdiction over international and interprovincial trade, the provinces have effectively been able to undertake policies that protect their own producers of some products within provincial borders. Beer is a case in point. Until recently, Ontario residents were unable to purchase Moosehead beer in Ontario, despite the fact that this Maritime brand is the most popular Canadian beer sold in the United States. The Ontario government did this by restricting distribution of beer to government-regulated outlets operated by the Ontario breweries, and these outlets only sold beer brewed in Ontario plants. Other provinces with breweries accomplished the same thing by other means, such as by selling the beer in provincially owned retail stores. The effect of this was not only to restrict the number of brands available but also to increase the cost of beer to the consumer and to induce inefficient methods of production. Thus, the major breweries were forced to operate small-scale plants in many provinces rather than concentrating their efforts in larger plants that could produce at lower costs.

The signing of the Canada–U.S. Free Trade Agreement in 1988 signalled the beginning of the end of this form of protection of the Canadian breweries. The practice has also been found to be in contravention of the General Agreement on Tariffs and Trade (GATT), which establishes rules of conduct for international trade with most other countries in the world. Provinces such as Ontario were forced to admit imported beer for sale in order to comply with these rules. They have begun to do so only gradually, recognizing that large-scale producers in the United States could underprice inefficient Canadian producers by a considerable margin, at least until the latter have a chance to rationalize their operations.

In fact, the provinces have found other ways to provide implicit protection to domestic breweries. In Ontario, a significant "handling" charge was imposed on imported beers. As well, a large "environmental tax" was imposed on beer cans and not on beer bottles or soft-drink cans. Since beer imported from the United States tends to be canned rather than bottled, this effectively imposed a differential cost on imported beer. (It also incidentally hurt Ontario can producers.) More recently, the Ontario government has imposed a "minimum price" on beer, allegedly for social reasons. This also tends to eliminate the cost advantage of imported beer.

As is often the case, entrepreneurs will find ways to skirt regulations that artificially keep prices high. In Ontario, firms have sprung up in most cities that specialize in assisting consumers to brew their own beer. Not only can this be done at relatively low cost, it can also avoid the punitive taxes imposed on alcoholic beverages by the federal and provincial governments.

some lose. Since the trade as a whole is beneficial to the country, the gains to the winners exceed the losses to the losers. Thus, in principle, those who benefit within the country could more than compensate those who lose. In practice, however, those who lose remain losers and obviously oppose opening up trade, using the argument that trade results in lost jobs and reduced wages. These concerns have become particularly acute as unskilled workers see themselves competing against the low-wage unskilled workers in Asia and Latin America: How can they compete without lowering their wages?

These concerns played a prominent role first in the debate in the late 1980s over the signing of the Canada-U.S. Free Trade Agreement, which allows American goods and services into Canada with no duties at all, and then in the early 1990s with the prospect of the North American Free Trade Agreement (NAFTA), which extends the privilege to Mexico. Advocates of freer trade pointed out that (1) more jobs would be created by the new export opportunities than would be lost through competition from American and Mexican firms, and (2) the jobs created pay higher wages, reflecting the benefits from specialization in comparative advantage.

Textile workers in Quebec who lose their jobs as a result of imports of inexpensive clothing from China cannot instantly convert themselves into forest workers in New Brunswick or engineers working for Bombardier. But the fact is that jobs are being destroyed and created all the time, irrespective of trade. Over the long run, the economic incentive of the new jobs at Bombardier may induce some in Manitoba to leave their semiskilled jobs and get the training that makes them eligible for the skilled jobs at Bombardier. The vacancy that that creates may be filled by someone who moves in from Ontario, leaving a vacancy there for the laid-off textile worker in Quebec.

Because of the practical complications and the very real costs of retraining and relocation, there is increasing recognition that government may need to play a role in facilitating job movements. To the extent that such assistance increases the number of winners from trade, it should reduce opposition to trade.

## CONSENSUS ON BENEFITS OF TRADE

While the perceived costs of economic interdependence cannot be ignored—especially when they become the subject of heated political debate—the fact that the country as a whole benefits from freer trade is one of the central tenets on which there is a consensus among the vast majority of economists. Trade is our third consensus point:

**3 Trade**

*There are gains from voluntary exchanges. Whether between individuals or across national borders, all can gain from voluntary exchange. Trade allows parties to specialize in those activities in which they have a comparative advantage.*

## REVIEW AND PRACTICE

### SUMMARY

**1** The benefits and costs of economic interdependence apply to individuals and firms within a country as well as to countries within the world. No individual and no country is self-sufficient.

**2** Both individuals and countries gain from voluntary trade. There may be cases when there are only limited possibilities for bilateral trade (exchange between two parties), but the gains from multilateral trade (exchange among several parties) may be great.

**3** The principle of comparative advantage asserts that countries should export the goods in which their production costs are *relatively* low.

**4** Specialization tends to increase productivity for three reasons: specializing avoids the time it takes a worker to switch from one production task to another; workers who repeat a task become more skilled at it; specialization creates a fertile environment for invention.

**5** A country's comparative advantage can arise from natural endowments or can result from acquired endowments, superior knowledge, or specialization.

**6** There is a basic difference between trade among individuals and trade among countries: with trade among countries, some individuals within the country may actually be worse off. Though in principle, those who gain could more than compensate those who lose, such compensation is seldom provided. Though free trade enhances national income, fears about job loss and wage reductions among low-skilled workers have led to demands for protection. Government assistance to facilitate the required adjustments may be desirable.

## KEY TERMS

| | | | |
|---|---|---|---|
| gains from trade | imports | absolute advantage | specialization |
| surplus consumer | exports | comparative advantage | natural endowments |
| producer surplus | bilateral trade | division of labour | acquired endowments |
| | multilateral trade | marginal rate of transformation | protectionism |

## REVIEW QUESTIONS

**1** Why are all voluntary trades mutually beneficial?

**2** Describe a situation (hypothetical, if need be) where bilateral trade does not work, but multilateral trade is possible.

**3** What are some of the similarities of trade between individuals and trade between countries? What is a key way in which they differ?

**4** Does a country with an absolute advantage in a product necessarily have a comparative advantage in that product? Does a country with an absolute disadvantage in a product necessarily not have a comparative advantage in that product? Explain.

**5** Why does specialization tend to increase productivity?

**6** "A country's comparative advantage is dictated by its natural endowments." Discuss.

**7** "If trade with a foreign country injures anyone in this country, the government should react by passing protectionist laws to limit or stop that particular trade." Comment.

## PROBLEMS

**1** Four players on a bantam hockey team discover that they have each been collecting hockey cards, and they agree to get together and trade. Is it possible for everyone to benefit from this agreement? Does the fact that one player starts off with many more cards than any of the others affect your answer?

**2** Leaders in many less developed countries of Latin America and Africa have often argued that because they are so much poorer than the wealthy nations of the world, trade with the more developed economies of North America and Europe will injure them. They maintain that they must first become self-sufficient before than can benefit from trade. How might an economist respond to these claims?

**3** If Canada changes its immigration quotas to allow many more unskilled workers into the country, who is likely to gain? Who is likely to lose? Consider the impact on consumers, on businesses that hire low-skilled labour, and on low-skilled labour in both Canada and the workers' countries of origin.

**4** David Ricardo illustrated the principle of comparative advantage in terms of the trade between England and Portugal in port wine and wool. Suppose that in

England it takes 120 labourers to produce a certain quantity of wine, while in Portugal it takes only 80 labourers to produce that same quantity. Similarly, in England it takes 100 labourers to produce a certain quantity of wool, while in Portugal it takes only 90. Draw the opportunity set for each country, assuming that each has 72,000 labourers. Assume that each country commits half its labour to each product in the absence of trade, and designate that point on your graph. Now describe a new production plan, with trade, that can benefit both countries.

**5** In 1981, the Canadian government prodded Japanese automakers to limit the number of cars they would export to Canada. Who benefited from this protectionism in Canada and in Japan? Who was injured in Canada and in Japan? Consider companies that produce cars, their workers, and consumers who buy cars.

**6** For many years an international agreement called the Multifiber Agreement has limited the amount of textiles that the developed economies of North America and Europe can buy from poor countries in Latin America and Asia. Textiles can be produced by relatively unskilled labour with a reasonably small amount of capital. Who benefits from the protectionism of the Multifiber Agreement, and who suffers?

# CHAPTER 4

# DEMAND, SUPPLY, AND PRICE

hoice in the face of scarcity, as we have seen, is the fundamental concern of economics. **Price,** to an economist, is what is given in exchange for a good or service and is a signal of choice. When the forces of supply and demand operate freely, price measures scarcity. As such, prices convey critical economic information. When the price of a resource used by a firm is high, the company has a greater incentive to economize on its use. When the price of a good that the firm produces is high, the company has a greater incentive to produce more of that good, and its customers have an incentive to economize on its use. In these ways and others, prices provide our economy with incentives to use scarce resources efficiently.

## KEY QUESTIONS

**1** What is meant by demand? Why do demand curves normally slope downwards? On what variables, other than price, does the quantity demanded depend?

**2** What is meant by supply? Why do supply curves normally slope upwards? On what variables other than price does the quantity supplied depend?

**3** Why do economists say that the equilibrium price occurs at the intersection of the demand and supply curves?

**4** How do shifts in the demand and supply curves affect the equilibrium price?

## THE ROLE OF PRICES

Prices are the way participants in the economy communicate with one another. Assume a drought hits the country, reducing drastically the supply of corn. Households will need to reduce their consumption of corn or there will not be enough to go around. But how will they know this? Suppose newspapers across the country ran an article informing people they would have to eat less corn because of a drought. What incentive would they have to pay attention to it? How would each family know how much it ought to reduce its consumption? As an alternative to the newspaper as a means of communication, consider the effect of an increase in the price of corn. The higher price conveys all the relevant information. It tells families corn is scarce at the same time as it provides incentives for them to consume less of it. Consumers do not need to know anything about why corn is scarce.

Price changes and differences present interesting problems and puzzles. In the late 1980s, while the price of an average house in Toronto went up by 20 percent, the price of a house in Regina increased by only 2 percent. Why? During the same period, the price of computers fell dramatically, while the price of bread rose, but at a much slower rate than the price of housing in Toronto. Why? The "price" of labour is just the wage or salary that is paid. Why does a physician earn twice as much as a university professor, though the university professor may have performed better in the university courses they took together? Why did average wage rates rise in Canada in the postwar period? Why is the price of water, without which we cannot live, very low in most cases, but the price of diamonds, which we can surely live without, very high? The simple answer to all these questions is that in market economies like that of Canada, price is determined by supply and demand. Changes in prices are determined by changes in supply and demand.

Understanding the causes of changes in prices and being able to predict their occurrence is not merely of academic interest. One of the events that precipitated the French Revolution was the rise in the price of bread, for which the people blamed the government. Large price changes have also given rise to recent political turmoil in several countries, including Morocco, the Dominican Republic, Russia, and Poland.

The public sees much more in prices than the impersonal forces of supply and demand: the landlord raised the rent on the apartment; the oil company or the gas station owner raised the price of gasoline. These people and companies *chose* to raise their prices, says the average citizen, in moral indignation. True, replies the economist, but there must be some factor that made these people and companies believe that a higher price was not a good idea yesterday, but is today. And economists point out that at a different time, these same impersonal forces can force the same landlords and oil companies to cut their prices. Economists see prices, then, as symptoms of underlying causes, and focus on the forces of demand and supply behind price changes.

# DEMAND

Economists use the concept of **demand** to describe the quantity of a good or service that a household or firm chooses to buy at a given price. It is important to understand that economists are concerned not just with what people desire, but with what they choose to buy given the spending limits of their budget constraint and the prices of various goods and services. In analyzing demand, the first question they ask is how the quantity of a good or service purchased by an individual changes as the price changes, keeping all other determinants of demand constant.

## THE INDIVIDUAL DEMAND CURVE

Think about what happens as the price of chocolate bars changes. At a price of $5.00 you might never buy one. At $3.00 you might buy one as a special treat. At $1.25 you might buy a few, and if the price declined to $.50, you might buy a lot. The table in Figure 4.1 summarizes the weekly demand of one individual, Roger, for chocolate bars at these different prices. We can see that the lower the price, the larger the quantity demanded. We can also draw a graph that shows the quantity Roger demands at each price. The quantity demanded per week is measured along the horizontal axis, and the price is measured along the vertical axis. Figure 4.1 plots the points.

A smooth curve can be drawn to connect the points. This curve is called the **demand curve.** The demand curve gives the quantity demanded at each price. Thus, if we want to know how many chocolate bars a week Roger will demand at a price of $1.00, we simply look along the vertical axis at the price $1.00, find the corresponding point *A* along the demand curve, and then read down to the horizontal axis. At a price of $1.00, Roger buys 6 chocolate bars each week. Alternatively, if we want to know at what price he will buy just 3 chocolate bars, we look along the horizontal axis at the quantity 3, find the corresponding point *B* along the demand curve, and then

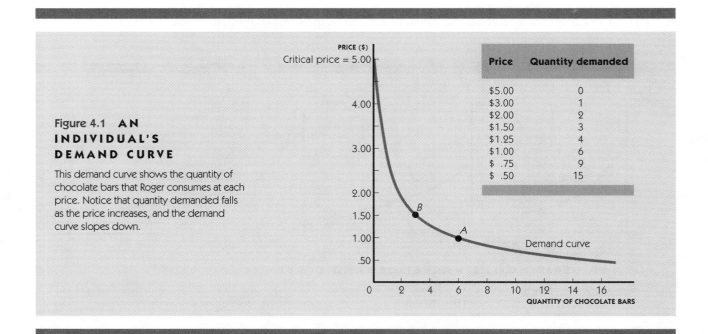

**Figure 4.1 AN INDIVIDUAL'S DEMAND CURVE**

This demand curve shows the quantity of chocolate bars that Roger consumes at each price. Notice that quantity demanded falls as the price increases, and the demand curve slopes down.

| Price | Quantity demanded |
|-------|-------------------|
| $5.00 | 0 |
| $3.00 | 1 |
| $2.00 | 2 |
| $1.50 | 3 |
| $1.25 | 4 |
| $1.00 | 6 |
| $ .75 | 9 |
| $ .50 | 15 |

read across to the vertical axis. Roger will buy 3 chocolate bars at a price of $1.50.

As the price of chocolate bars increases, the quantity demanded decreases. This can be seen from the numbers in Figure 4.1, and in the shape of its demand curve, which slopes downward from left to right. This relationship is typical of demand curves and makes common sense: the cheaper a good or service is (the lower down we look on the vertical axis), the more of it a person will buy (the farther right on the horizontal axis); the more expensive, the less a person will buy.

## THE MARKET DEMAND CURVE

Suppose there were a simple economy made up of two people, Roger and Jane. Figure 4.2 illustrates how to add up the demand curves of these two individuals to obtain a demand curve for the market as a whole. We "add" the demand curves horizontally by taking at each price the quantities demanded by Roger and by Jane and adding the two together. Thus, in the figure, at the price of $.75 Roger demands 9 chocolate bars and Jane demands 11 per week, so that the total market demand is 20 chocolate bars per week. The same principles apply no

matter how many people there are in the economy. The **market demand curve** gives the total quantity of the good that will be demanded per period at each price. The table in Figure 4.3 summarizes the information for our example of chocolate bars; it gives the total quantity of chocolate bars demanded by everybody in the economy at various prices. If we had a figure like Figure 4.1 for each person in the economy, we would construct the table in Figure 4.3 by adding up, at each price, the total quantity of chocolate bars purchased per week. Figure 4.3 tells us, for instance, that at a price of $3.00 per chocolate bar, the total market demand for chocolate bars is 1 million per week, and that lowering the price to $2.00 increases market demand to 3 million.

Figure 4.3 also depicts the same information in a graph. As with Figure 4.1, price lies along the vertical axis, but now the horizontal axis measures the quantity demanded each week by everyone in the economy. Joining the points in the figure together, we get the market demand curve. If we want to know what the total demand for chocolate bars will be when the price is $1.50 per chocolate bar, we look on the vertical axis at the price $1.50, find the corresponding point A along the demand curve, and read down to the horizontal axis; at that price, total demand is 4 million chocolate bars. If we want to know what the

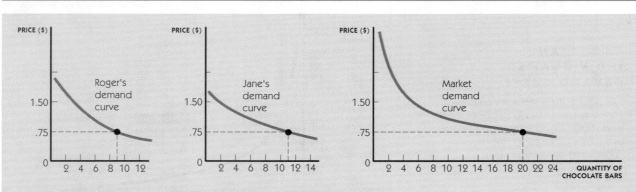

## Figure 4.2 DERIVING THE MARKET DEMAND CURVE

The market demand curve is constructed by adding up at each price the total of the quantities consumed by each individual. It shows what market demand would be if there were only two consumers. Actual market demand, as depicted in Figure 4.3, is much larger because there are many consumers.

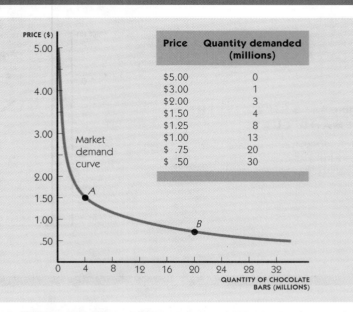

## Figure 4.3 THE MARKET DEMAND CURVE

The market demand curve shows the quantity of the good or service demanded by all consumers in the market at each price. The market demand curve is downward-sloping, for two reasons: at a higher price each consumer buys less, and at high enough prices some consumers decide not to buy at all—they exit the market.

| Price | Quantity demanded (millions) |
|-------|------------------------------|
| $5.00 | 0 |
| $3.00 | 1 |
| $2.00 | 3 |
| $1.50 | 4 |
| $1.25 | 8 |
| $1.00 | 13 |
| $ .75 | 20 |
| $ .50 | 30 |

price of chocolate bars will be when the demand equals 20 million, we find 20 million along the horizontal axis, look up to find the corresponding point *B* along the market demand curve, and read across to the vertical axis; the price at which 20 million chocolate bars are demanded is $.75.

Notice that just as the individual's demand decreases when the price of chocolate bars increases, so too when the price of chocolate bars increases, market demand decreases. Thus, the market demand curve also slopes downward from left to right. This general rule holds both because each individual's demand curve is downward-sloping and because as the price is increased, some individuals will decide to stop buying altogether. We have already examined the first of these reasons, but the second

deserves a closer look. In Figure 4.1, for example, Roger **exits the market**—consumes a quantity of zero—at the price of $5.00, at which his demand curve hits the vertical axis.

## SHIFTS IN DEMAND CURVES

A demand curve depicts the quantity demanded at various prices, when all other factors are held constant. When the price of a good increases, the quantity demanded of that good decreases, when everything else is held constant. But in the real world, everything is not held constant. Any changes other than the price of the good in question shift the whole demand curve—change the amount that will be demanded at

### DEMAND CURVE

The demand curve gives the quantity of the good demanded per stated time period at each price, holding all other determinants of demand constant.

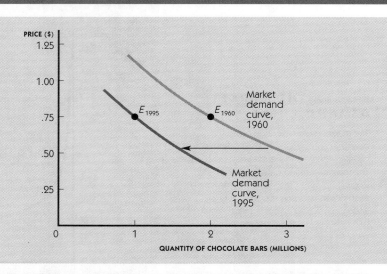

Figure 4.4 **SHIFTS IN THE DEMAND CURVE**

A leftwards shift in the demand curve means that a lesser amount will be demanded at every given market price.

each price. The shift in the demand curve for chocolate bars as Canadians have become more weight-conscious provides a good example. Figure 4.4 shows hypothetical demand curves for chocolate bars in 1960 and in 1995. We can see from the figure, for instance, that the demand for chocolate bars at a price of $.75 has decreased from 2 million chocolate bars per week (point $E_{1960}$, the original equilibrium) to 1 million (point $E_{1995}$), as people have reduced their purchase of chocolate bars.

## SOURCES OF SHIFTS IN DEMAND CURVES

Two of the factors that shift the demand curve—changes in income and in the price of other goods—are specifically economic factors. As an individual's income increases, she normally purchases more of any good or service. Thus, rising incomes shift the demand curve to the right, as illustrated in Figure 4.5. At each price, she consumes more of the good.

Figure 4.5 **A RIGHTWARDS SHIFT IN THE DEMAND CURVE**

If at each price there is an increase in the quantity demanded, then the demand curve will have shifted to the right, as depicted. An increase in income, an increase in the price of a substitute, or a decrease in the price of a complement can cause a rightwards shift in the demand curve.

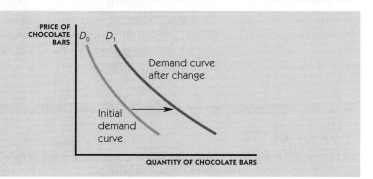

## CLOSE-UP: GASOLINE PRICES AND THE DEMAND FOR SMALL CARS

When demands for several products are intertwined, conditions affecting the price of one will affect the demand for the other. When gasoline prices in Canada increased in the 1970s the change affected the demand for small cars.

Actually, the price of gasoline soared twice in the 1970s, once when the Organization of Petroleum Exporting Countries (OPEC) shut off the flow of oil in 1973, and again when the Shah of Iran was driven from power in 1979, leading to a disruption of oil supplies. Between 1972 and 1981 gasoline prices rose almost 260 percent. How could people conserve on gasoline? Some might try to cut down on the number of trips they took, but the distance from home to office was not going to shrink for those who had to commute. One solution found by Canadian drivers was that when it came time to replace their old cars, they purchased smaller cars that offered better gas mileage.

Analysts classify car sales according to car size. In 1970, before the first rise in gas prices, 43.4 percent of the cars sold in Canada by North American manufacturers were full-size, 20.4 percent were compacts, and only 1.8 percent were subcompacts. By 1983 the proportions had shifted dramatically. In that year only 10.7 percent of the cars sold were full-size, while 22 percent were compacts and fully 33.6 percent were subcompacts.

The demand curve for any good such as cars assumes that the price of complementary goods, like gasoline, is fixed. The rise in gasoline prices caused the demand curve for small cars to shift out to the right and the demand curve for large cars to shift back to the left.

The reason for this is easy to see. Imagine that you drive 20,000 kilometres per year. A large car might require 16 litres per 100 kilometres, meaning you would have to buy some 3,200 litres of gasoline per year, while a small car might require only 8 litres per 100 kilometres, meaning you would only have to buy 1,600 litres of gas per year, half of what you did before. It is clear that the savings would be considerable over the lifetime of the car. If the price of gasoline were $.50 per litre, this saving of 1,600 litres would translate into a saving of $800 per year.

*Sources:* Statistics Canada, CANSIM Database 1996, Catalogue No. 62-004; Industry, Science and Technology Canada, *Statistical Review of the Canadian Automotive Industry (1988).*

Changes in the price of other goods, particularly closely related goods, will also shift the demand curve for a good. For example, when the price of margarine increases, some individuals will substitute butter. Butter and margarine are thus **substitutes.** When people choose between butter and margarine, one important factor is the relative price, that is, the ratio of the price of butter to the price of margarine. An increase in the price of butter and a decrease in the price of margarine both increase the relative price of butter. Thus, both induce individuals to substitute margarine for butter.

Chocolate bars and granola bars can also be considered substitutes, as the two goods satisfy a similar need. Thus, an increase in the price of granola bars makes chocolate bars relatively more attractive, and hence leads to a rightwards shift in the demand curve for chocolate bars. At each price, the demand for chocolate bars is greater. Two goods are substitutes if an increase in the price of one *increases* the demand for the other.

Sometimes, however, an increase in a price of other goods has just the opposite effect. Consider an individual who takes sugar in her coffee. In deciding on how much coffee to demand, she is concerned with the price of a cup of coffee *with* sugar. If sugar becomes more expensive, she will demand less coffee. For this person, sugar and coffee are **complements;** that is, an increase in the price of one *decreases* the demand for the other. A price increase of sugar shifts the demand curve of coffee to the left. At each price, the demand for coffee is less. Similarly a *decrease* in the price of sugar shifts the demand curve for coffee to the right.

Noneconomic factors can also shift market demand curves. The major ones are changes in tastes and in the composition of the population. The chocolate bar example is a change in taste. Other taste changes over the past decade in Canada include a shift from hard liquor to wine and from fatty meats to low-cholesterol foods. Each of these taste changes has shifted the whole demand curve of the goods in question.

Population changes that shift demand curves are often related to age. Young families with babies purchase disposable diapers. The demand for new houses and apartments is closely related to the number of new households, which in turn depends on the number of individuals of marriageable age. The Canadian population has been growing older, on average, both because life expectancies are increasing and because birthrates fell somewhat after the baby boom that followed World War II. So there has been a shift in demand away from diapers and new houses. Economists working for particular firms and industries spend considerable energy ascertaining population effects, called **demographic effects,** on the demand for the goods their firms sell.

Sometimes demand curves shift as the result of new information. The shifts in demand for alcohol and meat—and even more so for cigarettes—are related to improved consumer information about health risks.

Changes in the availability of credit also can shift demand curves for goods like cars and houses, which people typically buy with the help of loans. When banks reduce the money available for consumer loans, the demand curves for cars and houses shift.

Finally, what people think will happen in the future can shift demand curves. If people think they may become unemployed, they will reduce their spending. In this case, economists say that their demand curve depends on expectations.

## SHIFTS IN A DEMAND CURVE VERSUS MOVEMENTS ALONG A DEMAND CURVE

The distinction between changes that result from a *shift* in the demand curve and changes that result from a *movement along* the demand curve is crucial to understanding economics. A movement along a demand curve is simply the change in the quantity demanded as the price changes. Figure 4.6A illustrates a movement along the demand curve from point *A* to point *B; given a demand curve*, at lower prices, more is consumed. Figure 4.6B illustrates a shift in the demand curve to the right; *at a given price*, more is consumed. Quantity again increases from $Q_0$ to $Q_1$, but now the price stays the same.

In practice, both effects are often present. Thus, in panel C of Figure 4.6, the movement from point *A* to point *C*—where the quantity demanded has been reduced from $Q_0$ to $Q_2$—consists of two parts: a change in quantity demanded, resulting from a shift in the de-

---

### SOURCES OF SHIFTS IN MARKET DEMAND CURVES

A change in income

A change in the price of a substitute

A change in the price of a complement

A change in the composition of the population

A change in tastes

A change in information

A change in the availability of credit

A change in expectations

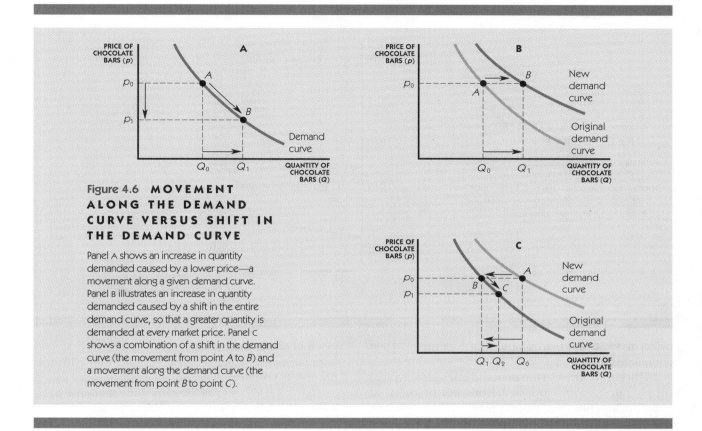

**Figure 4.6 MOVEMENT ALONG THE DEMAND CURVE VERSUS SHIFT IN THE DEMAND CURVE**

Panel A shows an increase in quantity demanded caused by a lower price—a movement along a given demand curve. Panel B illustrates an increase in quantity demanded caused by a shift in the entire demand curve, so that a greater quantity is demanded at every market price. Panel C shows a combination of a shift in the demand curve (the movement from point A to B) and a movement along the demand curve (the movement from point B to point C).

mand curve (the reduction in quantity from $Q_0$ to $Q_1$), and a movement along the demand curve as price changes (the increase in quantity from $Q_1$ to $Q_2$).

## SUPPLY

Economists use the concept of **supply** to describe the quantity of a good or service that a household or firm would like to sell at a particular price. "Supply" in economics refers to such seemingly disparate choices as the number of chocolate bars a firm wants to sell and the number of hours a worker is willing to work. As with demand, the first question

economists ask is, how does the quantity supplied change when price changes, keeping all other determinants of supply constant?

The table in Figure 4.7 shows the number of chocolate bars that the Melt-in-the-Mouth Chocolate Company would like to supply to the market at each price, per week. As the price rises, so does the quantity supplied. Below $1.00, the firm finds it unprofitable to produce. At $2.00 it would like to sell 85,000 chocolate bars per week. At $5.00 it would like to sell 100,000.

Figure 4.7 also depicts these points on a graph. The curve drawn by connecting the points is called the **supply curve.** It shows the quantity that Melt-in-the-Mouth will supply per week at each price, holding all other factors constant. As with the demand curve, we put the price on the vertical axis and the quantity supplied on the horizontal axis. Thus, we can read point A on the curve as indicating that at a

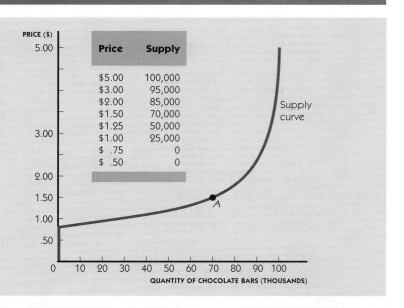

| Price | Supply |
|---|---|
| $5.00 | 100,000 |
| $3.00 | 95,000 |
| $2.00 | 85,000 |
| $1.50 | 70,000 |
| $1.25 | 50,000 |
| $1.00 | 25,000 |
| $ .75 | 0 |
| $ .50 | 0 |

### Figure 4.7 ONE FIRM'S SUPPLY CURVE

The supply curve shows the quantity of a good a firm is willing to produce at each price. Normally a firm is willing to produce more as the price increases, which is why the supply curve slopes upwards.

price of $1.50 the firm would like to supply 70,000 chocolate bars.

In direct contrast to the demand curve, the typical supply curve slopes upward from left to right; at higher prices firms will supply more. This is because higher prices yield suppliers higher profits—giving them an incentive to produce more.

## MARKET SUPPLY

The **market supply** of a good or service is simply the total quantity that all the firms in the economy are willing to supply per time period at a given price. Similarly, the market supply of labour is simply the total quantity of labour that all the households in the economy are willing to supply at a given wage. The table in Figure 4.8 tells us, for instance, that at a price of $2.00, firms will supply 7 million chocolate bars per week, while at a price of $.50, they will supply only 0.5 million.

Figure 4.8 also shows the same information graphically. The curve joining the points in the figure is the **market supply curve.** The market supply curve gives the total quantity of a good that firms are willing to produce at each price. Thus, we read point A on the market supply curve as showing that at a price of $.75, the firms in the economy would like to sell 2 million chocolate bars per week.

As the price of chocolate bars increases, the quantity supplied increases, other things remaining equal. The market supply curve slopes upwards from left to right for two reasons: at higher prices each firm in the market is willing to produce more, and at higher prices more firms are willing to enter the market to produce the good.

The market supply curve is calculated from the

## SUPPLY CURVE

The supply curve gives the quantity of the good or service supplied at each price all other factors remaining constant.

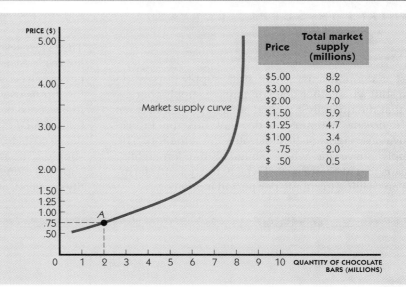

## Figure 4.8 THE MARKET SUPPLY CURVE

The market supply curve shows the quantity of a good or service all firms in the market are willing to supply at each price. The market supply curve is normally upward-sloping, both because each firm is willing to supply more of the good or service at a higher price and because higher prices entice new firms to produce.

| Price | Total market supply (millions) |
|---|---|
| $5.00 | 8.2 |
| $3.00 | 8.0 |
| $2.00 | 7.0 |
| $1.50 | 5.9 |
| $1.25 | 4.7 |
| $1.00 | 3.4 |
| $ .75 | 2.0 |
| $ .50 | 0.5 |

supply curves of the different firms in the same way that the market demand curve is calculated from the demand curves of the different households: at each price we add horizontally the quantities that each firm is willing to produce.

Figure 4.9 shows how this is done in a market with only two producers. At a price of $1.25, Melt-in-the-Mouth Chocolate produces 50,000 chocolate bars, while the Chocolates of Choice Company produces 40,000. So the market supply is 90,000 bars.

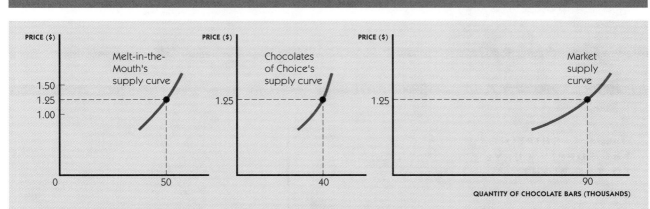

## Figure 4.9 DERIVING THE MARKET SUPPLY CURVE

The market supply curve is constructed by adding up the quantity that each of the firms in the economy is willing to supply at each price. It shows what market supply would be if there were only two producers. Actual market supply, as depicted in Figure 4.8, is much larger because there are many producers.

## SHIFTS IN SUPPLY CURVES

Just as demand curves can shift, supply curves too can shift when other determinants of supply change, so that the quantity supplied at each price increases or decreases. Suppose a drought hits the Prairie provinces. Figure 4.10 illustrates the situation. The supply curve for wheat shifts to the left, which means that at each price of wheat, the quantity farmers are willing to supply per period is smaller.

## SOURCES OF SHIFTS IN SUPPLY CURVES

There are several sources of shifts in market supply curves, just as in the case of the market demand curves already discussed. One is changing prices of the inputs used to produce a good. Figure 4.11 shows that as corn becomes less expensive, the supply curve for cornflakes shifts to the right. Producing cornflakes costs less, so at every price firms are willing to supply a greater quantity. That is why the quantity supplied along the curve $S_1$ is greater than the quantity supplied, at the same price, along the curve $S_0$.

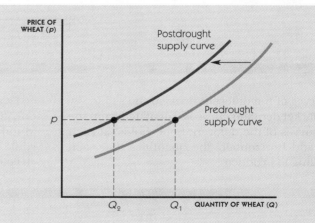

Figure 4.10 **SHIFTING THE SUPPLY CURVE TO THE LEFT**

A drought or other disaster (among other possible factors) will cause the supply curve to shift to the left, so that, at each price, a smaller quantity is supplied.

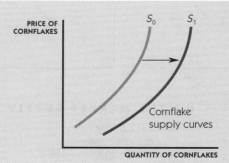

Figure 4.11 **SHIFTING THE SUPPLY CURVE TO THE RIGHT**

An improvement in technology or a reduction in input prices (among other possible factors) will cause the supply curve to shift to the right, so that, at each price, a larger quantity is supplied.

**USING ECONOMICS: THE DROUGHT OF 1988 AS A SUPPLY SHOCK**

For the Canadian prairies and the midwestern United States, 1988 brought one of the worst droughts ever recorded. Wheat production was down 40 percent in Canada and 10 percent in the United States; corn production fell by 24 percent in Canada and 35 percent in the United States; soybean production was down 9 percent in Canada and 20 percent in the United States; and oats and barley were down 13 percent in Canada and 40 percent in the United States.

From an economist's perspective, an unpredictable event like a severe drought is a good example of a shift in the supply curve. The drought reduced the amount of any crop that could be supplied at any given price, which means that the supply curve itself shifted to the left.

As an economist would predict, this shift in the supply curve led to higher prices for these farm products. To cite some examples from the Winnipeg Commodity Exchange, feed-wheat prices rose by almost 50 percent between 1987 and 1988, corn prices by 43 percent, and soy-

beans by 50 percent. Overall, crop prices rose by about 12 percent.

The drought also had a number of predictable side effects on substitute and complement goods. For example, higher prices in North America stimulated foreign agricultural production. Canadian farmers planted many more hectares in 1989, to make up for some of their lost production the previous year. Since much grain is fed to cattle, the higher price of grain led many farmers to slaughter their cattle sooner than they had originally planned. As a result, meat production rose slightly in 1988, and meat prices (adjusted for inflation) dropped slightly. Supermarket prices increased sharply for consumers in the middle of the summer; fruit and vegetable prices were up 5 percent in July 1988.

Despite these many side effects, the drought of 1988 had only a temporary effect on prices and quantities. Because of stockpiles of goods and the possibility of buying farm products from other nations, the agricultural system has enough flexibility to live through a bad year.

Another source of shifts is changes in technology. The technological improvements in the computer industry over the past two decades have led to a rightwards shift in the market supply curve. Yet another source of shifts is nature. The supply curve for agricultural goods may shift to the right or left depending on weather conditions, insect infestations, or animal diseases.

Reduction in the availability of credit may curtail firms' ability to borrow to obtain inputs needed for

**SOURCES OF SHIFTS IN MARKET SUPPLY CURVES**

A change in the prices of inputs

A change in technology

A change in the natural environment

A change in the availability of credit

A change in expectations

production, and this too will induce a leftwards shift in the supply curve. Finally, changed expectations can also lead to a shift in the supply curve. If firms believe that a new technology for making cars will become available in two years' time, this belief will discourage investment today and will lead to a temporary leftwards shift in the supply curve.

## SHIFTS IN A SUPPLY CURVE VERSUS MOVEMENTS ALONG A SUPPLY CURVE

Distinguishing between a movement *along* a curve and a *shift* in the curve itself is just as important for supply curves as it is for demand curves. In Figure 4.12A, the price of chocolate bars has gone up, with a corresponding increase in quantity supplied. Thus, there has been a movement along the supply curve.

By contrast, in Figure 4.12B, the supply curve has shifted to the right, perhaps because a new production technique has made it cheaper to produce chocolate bars. Now, even though the price does not change, the quantity supplied increases. The quantity supplied in the market can increase either because the price of the good has increased, so that for a *given supply curve* the quantity produced is higher, or because the supply curve has shifted, so that at a *given price* the quantity supplied has increased.

## LAW OF SUPPLY AND DEMAND

This chapter began with the assertion that supply and demand work together to determine the market price in competitive markets. Figure 4.13 puts a market supply curve and a market demand curve on the same graph to show how this happens. The price actually paid and received in the market will be determined by the intersection of the two curves. This point is labeled $E_0$, for equilibrium, and the corresponding price ($.75) and quantity (20 million) are called, respectively, the **equilibrium price** and the **equilibrium quantity.**

Since the term "equilibrium" recurs throughout the book, it is important to understand the concept clearly. Equilibrium describes a situation where there are no forces (reasons) for change. No one has an incentive to change the result—the price or quantity in the case of supply and demand.

Physicists also speak of equilibrium in describing a weight hanging from a spring. Two forces are working on the weight. Gravity is pulling it down; the spring is pulling it up. When the weight is at rest, it is in equilibrium, with the two forces just offsetting each other. If one pulls the weight down a little bit, the force of the spring will be greater than the force of gravity, and the weight will spring up. In the absence of any further intrusions, the weight will bob

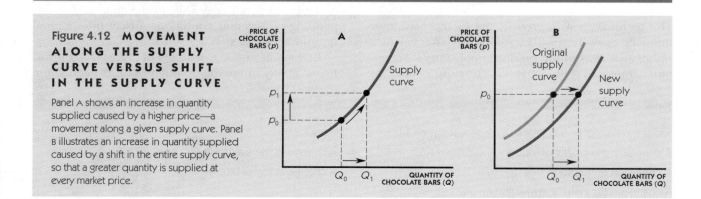

**Figure 4.12 MOVEMENT ALONG THE SUPPLY CURVE VERSUS SHIFT IN THE SUPPLY CURVE**

Panel A shows an increase in quantity supplied caused by a higher price—a movement along a given supply curve. Panel B illustrates an increase in quantity supplied caused by a shift in the entire supply curve, so that a greater quantity is supplied at every market price.

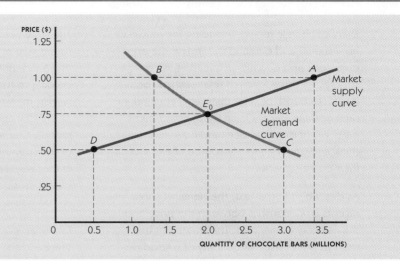

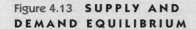

**Figure 4.13 SUPPLY AND DEMAND EQUILIBRIUM**

Equilibrium occurs at the intersection of the demand and supply curves, at point $E_0$. At any price above $E_0$, the quantity supplied will exceed the quantity demanded, the market will be out of equilibrium, and there will be excess supply. At any price below $E_0$, the quantity demanded will exceed the quantity supplied, the market will be out of equilibrium, and there will be excess demand.

back and forth and eventually reach its equilibrium position.

An economic equilibrium is established in the same way. At the equilibrium price, consumers get precisely the quantity of the good they are willing to buy at that price, and producers sell precisely the quantity they are willing to sell at that price. Neither producers nor consumers have any incentive to change.

But consider the price of $1.00 in Figure 4.13. There is no equilibrium quantity here. First find $1.00 on the vertical axis. Now look across to find point A on the supply curve, and read down to the horizontal axis; point A tells you that at a price of $1.00, firms want to supply 3.4 million chocolate bars. Now look at point B on the demand curve. Point B shows that at a price of $1.00, consumers only want to buy 1.3 million chocolate bars. Like the weight bobbing on a spring, however, this market will work its way back to equilibrium in the following way. At a price of $1.00 there is **excess supply** of 2.1 million chocolate bars. As producers discover that they cannot sell as much as they would like at this price, some of them will lower their prices slightly, hoping to take business from other producers. When one producer lowers prices, his competitors will have to respond, for fear that they will end up unable to sell their goods. As prices come down,

consumers will also buy more, and so on until the market reaches the equilibrium price and quantity.

Similarly, assume that the price is lower than $.75, say $.50. At the lower price, there is **excess demand:** individuals want to buy 3 million chocolate bars (point C), while firms only want to produce 0.5 million (point D). Consumers unable to purchase all they want will offer to pay a bit more; other consumers, afraid of having to do without, will match these higher bids or raise them. As prices start to increase, suppliers will also have a greater incentive to produce more. Again the market will tend toward the equilibrium point.

To repeat for emphasis: at equilibrium, no purchaser and no supplier has an incentive to change the price or quantity. In competitive market economies actual prices tend to be the equilibrium prices, at which demand equals supply. This is called the **law of supply and demand.** Note: this law does not mean that at every moment of time the price is precisely at the intersection of the demand and supply curves. As with the example of the weight and the spring, the market may bounce around a little bit when it is in the process of adjusting. What the law of supply and demand does say is that when a market is out of equilibrium, there are predictable forces for change.

**CLOSE-UP: THE STRUCTURE OF ECONOMIC MODELS**

Every economic model, including the model of how supply and demand determine the equilibrium price and quantity in a market, is constructed of three kinds of relationships: behavioural relationships, identities, and equilibrium relationships. Recognizing these component parts will help you understand how economists think and understand the source of many of their disagreements.

As described in the text, the demand curve represents a relationship between the price and the quantity demanded. The statement that normally as prices rise the quantity of a good demanded decreases is a description of how individuals behave. It is called a behavioural relationship. The supply curve for each firm is also a behavioural relationship.

Economists disagree over behavioural relationships in at least two ways. First, they may differ over the strength of the connection. For any given product, does a change in price lead to a large change in the quantity demanded or a small one? Second, economists may sometimes even disagree over the direction of the effect. There are some special cases where a higher price may actually lead to a *lower* quantity supplied.

The statement that the market demand is equal to the sum of the individual demands is an identity. An identity is a statement that is true according to the definition of the terms; in other words, market demand is *defined* to be the sum of the demands of all individuals. Similarly, it is an identity that market supply is equal to the sum of the supplies of all firms; the terms are defined in that way. Economists rarely disagree over identities, since disagreements over definitions are pointless.

Finally, an equilibrium relationship exists when there are no forces for change. In the supply-and-demand model, the equilibrium occurs when the quantity demanded is equal to the quantity supplied. An equilibrium relationship is not the same as an identity. It is possible for the economy to be out of equilibrium, at least for a time. Of course, being out of equilibrium implies that there are forces for change pushing towards equilibrium. But an identity must always hold true at all times, as a matter of definition.

Economists usually agree about what an equilibrium would look like, but they often differ on whether the forces pushing the markets towards equilibrium are strong or weak, and thus on whether the economy is fairly close to equilibrium or sometimes rather far from it.

## USING DEMAND AND SUPPLY CURVES

The concepts of demand and supply curves—and market equilibrium as the intersection of demand and supply curves—constitute the economist's basic model of demand and supply. This model has proved to be extremely useful. It helps explain why the price of one commodity is high and that of another is low. It also helps *predict* the consequences of certain changes. Its predictions can then be tested against

what actually happens. One of the reasons that the model is so useful is that it gives reasonably accurate predictions.

Figure 4.14 repeats the demand and supply curve for chocolate bars discussed earlier in the chapter. Now, however, assume that sugar becomes more expensive. As a result, at each price the amount firms are willing to supply is reduced. The supply curve shifts to the left, as in panel A. There will be a new equilibrium, at a higher price and a lower quantity of chocolate consumed.

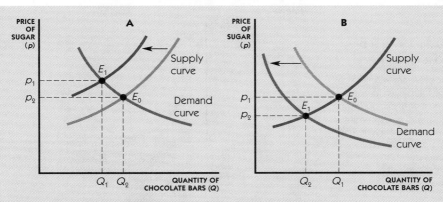

**Figure 4.14** **EFFECTS OF SHIFTS IN THE SUPPLY AND DEMAND CURVES FOR CHOCOLATE BARS**

An increase in the price of sugar results in firms supplying fewer chocolate bars at each price; the supply curve for chocolate bars shifts to the left, as in panel A. At the new equilibrium, $E_1$, there is a higher price and a lower quantity. If consumers become more health conscious, they may demand fewer chocolate bars at each price; the demand curve for chocolate bars shifts to the left, as in panel B. There will be a new equilibrium, $E_1$, at a higher price and a lower quantity of chocolate bars consumed.

Alternatively, assume that Canadians become more health-conscious, and as a result at each price fewer chocolate bars are consumed: the demand curve shifts to the left. Again, there will be a new equilibrium at a lower price and a lower quantity of chocolate bars consumed.

This illustrates how changes in observed prices can be related to shifts in either the demand or the supply curve. When the war in Kuwait interrupted the supply of oil from the Middle East in 1990, it caused a shift in the supply curve. The model predicted the result: an increase in the price of oil. This increase was the natural process of the law of supply and demand.

ing it to say, "Supply and demand." That prices are determined by the law of supply and demand is one of the most long-standing and widely held ideas of economists. It provides our fourth consensus point:

**4   Prices**

> *In competitive markets, prices are determined by the law of supply and demand. Shifts in the demand and supply curves lead to changes in the equilibrium price. Similar principles apply to the labour and capital markets. The price for labour is the wage, and the price for capital is the interest rate.*

## CONSENSUS ON THE DETERMINATION OF PRICES

The law of supply and demand plays such a prominent role in economics that there is a joke about teaching a parrot to be an economist simply by teaching

## PRICE, VALUE, AND COST

To an economist, price is the amount given in exchange for a good or service. In this sense, price is determined by the forces of supply and demand. Adam Smith, often thought of as the founder of

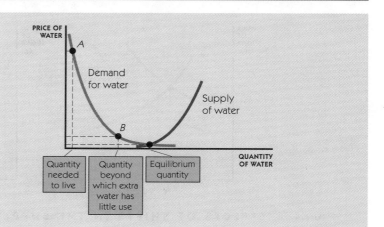

**Figure 4.15 SUPPLY AND DEMAND FOR WATER**

Point *A* shows that people are willing to pay a relatively high price for the first few units of water. But to the right of *B*, people have plenty of water already and are not willing to pay much for an additional amount. The price of water will be determined at the point where the supply curve crosses the demand curve. In most cases, the resulting price is extremely low.

modern economics, called our notion of price "value in exchange" and contrasted it to the notion of "value in use":

> The things which have the greatest value in use have frequently little or no value in exchange; and, on the contrary, those which have the greatest value in exchange have frequently little or no value in use. Nothing is more useful than water, but it will purchase scarce any thing; scarce any thing can be had in exchange for it. A diamond, on the contrary, has scarce any value in use; but a very great quantity of other goods may frequently be had in exchange for it.[1]

The law of supply and demand can help to explain the diamond-water paradox and many similar examples where "value in use" is very different from "value in exchange." Figure 4.15 presents a demand and a supply curve for water. Individuals are willing to pay a high price for the water they need to live, as illustrated by point *A*, on the demand curve. But above some quantity, *B*, people will pay almost nothing more for additional water. In most of the inhabited parts of the world water is readily available, so it gets supplied in plentiful quantities at low prices. Thus, the supply curve of water intersects the demand curve to the right of *B*, as in the figure; hence

the low equilibrium price. Of course, in the desert the water supply may be very limited and as a result the price will be very high.

To an economist the statements that the price of diamonds is high and the price of water is low are statements about supply-and-demand conditions. They say nothing about whether diamonds are "more important" or "better" than water. In Adam Smith's terms, they are not statements about value in use.

One way to think of the difference between the value in exchange versus the value in use is to distinguish between the *marginal* value of an object and its *total* value. The marginal value is the value of an additional unit of an object. An individual's demand curve can be thought of as a schedule of his marginal values, or marginal benefits. Thus, in Figure 4.1 Roger was willing to pay $3.00 for the first chocolate bar. That was the marginal value he attached to it. He was only willing to pay $2.00 for the second bar; it had a lower value to him. As the number of chocolate bars increased, the marginal value of each additional bar declined. His total value can be thought of as the sum of the values of all chocolate bars purchased. Thus, if he bought four chocolate bars, the total value he attached to them could be thought of as the sum of the marginal values of each ($3.00 + $2.00 + $1.50 + $1.25). Geometrically, the total value is like the area under his demand curve, while the marginal value is what he is willing to pay for the last

[1] *The Wealth of Nations* (1776), Book I, Chapter IV.

unit. Goods like water can have a high value in use but a low value in exchange if they are plentiful enough to more than satisfy basic requirements, so that their marginal value has become quite small even though their total value is large.

Just as economists take care to distinguish the words "price" and "value," they also distinguish the *price* of an object (what it sells for) from its *cost* (the expense of making the object). This is another crucial distinction in economics. The costs of producing a good affect the price at which firms are willing to supply that good. An increase in the costs of production will normally cause prices to rise. And in the competitive model, *in equilibrium,* the price of an ob-

ject will equal its cost of production (including the amount needed to pay a firm's owner to stay in business rather than seek some other form of employment). But there are important cases—as we shall see in later chapters—where price does not equal cost.

When we think of the competitive model, it is interesting to consider the case of a good in fixed supply, such as land. Normally, land is something that cannot be produced, so its cost of production can be considered infinite (though there are situations where land can be produced, as when the Netherlands filled in part of the sea to expand its usable land). Yet there is still an equilibrium price of land—where the demand for land is equal to its (fixed) supply.

## REVIEW AND PRACTICE

### SUMMARY

**1** An individual's demand curve gives the quantity demanded of a good or service per time period at each possible price. It normally slopes down, which means that the person demands a greater quantity of the good at lower prices and a lesser quantity at higher prices.

**2** The market demand curve gives the total quantity of a good or service demanded per time period by all individuals in an economy at each price. As the price rises the quantity demanded falls, both because each person demands less of the good and because some people exit the market.

**3** A firm's supply curve gives the amount of a good or service the firm is willing to supply per time period at each price. It is normally upward-sloping, which means that firms supply a greater quantity of the good at higher prices and a lesser quantity at lower prices.

**4** The market supply curve gives the total quantity of a good that all firms in the economy are willing to produce per time period at each price. As the price rises, the quantity supplied rises, both because each

firm supplies more of the good and because some additional firms enter the market.

**5** The law of supply and demand says that in competitive markets, the equilibrium price is that price at which quantity demanded equals quantity supplied. It is represented on a graph by the intersection of the demand and supply curves.

**6** A demand curve shows *only* the relationship between quantity demanded and price. Changes in tastes, in demographic factors, in income, in the prices of other goods, information, the availability of credit, or expectations are reflected in a shift of the entire demand curve.

**7** A supply curve shows *only* the relationship between quantity supplied and price. Changes in factors such as technology, the prices of inputs, the natural environment, expectations, or the availability of credit are reflected in a shift of the entire supply curve.

**8** It is important to distinguish movements along a demand curve from shifts in the demand curve, and movements along a supply curve from shifts in the supply curve.

## KEY TERMS

| | | | |
|---|---|---|---|
| demand curve | complement | market supply curve | excess demand |
| market demand curve | demographic effects | equilibrium price | law of supply and demand |
| substitute | supply curve | excess supply | |

## REVIEW QUESTIONS

**1** Why does an individual's demand curve normally slope down? Why does a market demand curve normally slope down?

**2** Why does a firm's supply curve normally slope up? Why does a market supply curve normally slope up?

**3** What is the significance of the point where supply and demand curves intersect?

**4** Explain why, if the price of a good is above the equilibrium price, the forces of supply and demand will tend to push the price towards equilibrium. Explain why, if the price of the good is below the equilibrium price, the market will tend to adjust towards equilibrium.

**5** Name some factors that could shift the demand curve out to the right.

**6** Name some factors that could shift the supply curve in to the left.

## PROBLEMS

**1** Imagine a company lunchroom that sells pizza by the slice. Using the following data, plot the points and graph the demand and supply curves. What is the equilibrium price and quantity? Find a price at which excess demand would exist and a price at which excess supply would exist, and plot them on your diagram.

| Price per Slice | Demand (Number of Slices per Week) | Supply (Number of Slices per Week) |
|---|---|---|
| $1 | 420 | 0 |
| $2 | 210 | 100 |
| $3 | 140 | 140 |
| $4 | 105 | 160 |
| $5 | 84 | 170 |

**2** Suppose a severe drought hit the sugarcane crop. Predict how this would affect the equilibrium price and quantity in the market for sugar and the market for honey. Draw supply and demand diagrams to illustrate your answers.

**3** Imagine that a new invention allows each mine worker to mine twice as much coal. Predict how this will affect the equilibrium price and quantity in the market for coal and the market for heating oil. Draw supply and demand diagrams to illustrate your answer.

**4** Canadians' tastes have shifted away from beef, towards chicken. Predict how this change affects the equilibrium price and quantity in the market for beef, the market for chicken, and the market for roadside hamburger stands. Draw supply and demand diagrams to illustrate your answer.

**5** During the 1970s the postwar baby boomers reached working age, and it became more acceptable for married women with children to work. Predict how this increase in the number of workers is likely to affect the equilibrium wage and quantity of employment. Draw supply and demand curves to illustrate your answer.

# USING DEMAND AND SUPPLY

T he concepts of demand and supply are among the most useful in economics. The demand and supply framework explains why dentists are paid more than lawyers, or why the income of unskilled workers has increased less than that of skilled workers. It can also be used to predict what the demand for condominiums or disposable diapers will be fifteen years from now, or what will happen if the government increases the tax on cigarettes. Not only can we predict that prices will change, we can predict by how much they will change.

This chapter has two purposes. The first is to develop some of the concepts required to make these kinds of predictions, and to illustrate how the demand and supply framework can be used in a variety of contexts.

The second is to look at what happens when governments interfere with the workings of competitive markets. Rents may seem too high for poor people to afford adequate housing. The price of wheat may seem unfairly low, not adequate to compensate farmers for their work. Political pressure constantly develops for government to intervene on behalf of the group that has been disadvantaged by the market—whether it be poor people, farmers, or oil companies, which ask for government help when the price of oil falls. The second part of this chapter traces the consequences of political interventions into the workings of some markets.

## KEY QUESTIONS

**1** What is meant by the concept of elasticity? Why does it play such an important role in predicting market outcomes?

**2** What happens when market outcomes are interfered with, as when the government imposes price floors and ceilings? Why do such interferences give rise to shortages and surpluses?

## SENSITIVITY TO PRICE CHANGES: THE PRICE ELASTICITY OF DEMAND

If tomorrow supermarkets across the country were to cut the price of bread or milk by 50 percent, the quantity demanded of these items would not change much. If stores offered the same reduction on premium ice cream, however, demand would increase

substantially. Why do price changes sometimes have small effects and at other times large ones? The answer lies in the shape of the demand and supply curves.

The demand for ice cream is more sensitive to price changes than is the demand for milk, and this is reflected in the shape of the demand curves, as illustrated in Figure 5.1. The demand curve for ice cream (panel A) is much flatter than the one for milk (panel B). When the demand curve is somewhat flat, a change in price, say from $2.00 a litre to $2.10, has

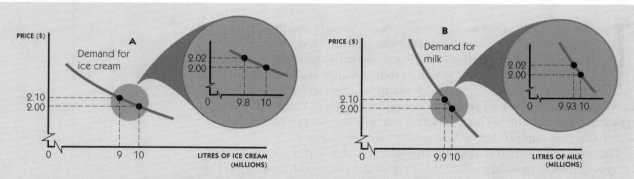

**Figure 5.1 ELASTIC VERSUS INELASTIC DEMAND CURVES**

Panel A shows a hypothetical demand curve for ice cream. Note that quantity demanded changes rapidly with fairly small price changes, indicating that demand for ice cream is elastic. The telescoped portion of the demand curve shows that a 1 percent rise in price leads to a 2 percent fall in quantity demanded. Panel B shows a hypothetical demand curve for

milk. Note that quantity demanded changes very little, regardless of changes in price, meaning that demand for milk is inelastic. The telescoped portion of the demand curve shows that a 1 percent rise in price leads to a .7 percent fall in quantity demanded.

a large effect on the quantity consumed. In panel A, the demand for ice cream decreases from 10 million litres at a price of $2.00 a litre to 9 million litres at a price of $2.10 per litre.

By contrast, when the demand curve is steep it means that a change in price has little effect on quantity. In panel B, the demand for milk decreases from 10 million litres at $2.00 per litre to 9.9 million litres at $2.10 per litre. But saying that the demand curve is steep or flat just pushes the question back a step: why are some demand curves steeper than others?

The answer is that though substitutes exist for almost every good or service, substitution will be more difficult for some goods and services than for others. When substitution is difficult, if the price of a good increases the quantity demanded will not decrease by much, and if the price falls the quantity demanded will not increase much. The typical consumer does not substitute milk for beer—or anything else—even if milk becomes a good deal cheaper.

On the other hand, when substitution is easy a fall in price may lead to a large increase in quantity demanded. For instance, there are many good substitutes for ice cream, including sherbets and frozen yogurts. The price decrease for ice cream means that these close substitutes have become relatively more expensive, and the demand for ice cream would thus increase significantly.

For many purposes, economists need to be precise about how steep or how flat the demand curve is. For precision they use the concept of the **price elasticity of demand**—the "price elasticity" or the "elasticity of demand," for short. The price elasticity of demand is defined as the absolute value of the percentage change in the quantity demanded divided by the percentage change in price. That is,

$$\text{elasticity of demand} = -\frac{\text{percent change in quantity demanded}}{\text{percent change in price}}.$$

The minus sign is included because when the price increases, quantities demanded are reduced, and vice versa. The minus sign makes the elasticity of demand a positive number. Thus, if the quantity de-

manded falls by 8 percent in response to a 2 percent increase in price, the elasticity of demand is 4.

It is easiest to calculate the elasticity of demand when there is just a 1 percent change in price. Then the elasticity of demand is just the percent change in the quantity demanded. In the telescoped portion of Figure 5.1A, we see that increasing the price of ice cream from $2.00 a litre to $2.02—a 1 percent increase in price—reduces the demand from 10 million litres to 9.8 million, a 2 percent decline. So the price elasticity of demand for ice cream is 2.

By contrast, assume that the price of milk increases from $2.00 a litre to $2.02 (again a 1 percent increase in price), as shown in the telescoped portion of Figure 5.1B. This reduces demand from 10 million litres per year to 9.93 million. Demand has gone down by .7 percent, so the price elasticity of demand is .7. Larger values for price elasticity indicate that demand is more sensitive to changes in price. Smaller values indicate that demand is less sensitive to price changes.

Why is elasticity defined in terms of percentage changes rather than in terms of the actual change in quantity demanded divided by a change in price (or the inverse of the slope of the demand curve)? The reason is that a percentage change is a unitless number, whereas the size of an actual change depends on the units in which quantities are measured. Thus, the change in quantity of milk demanded from a $1 change in price will depend upon whether quantities are measured in litres or millilitres, whereas the percentage change in quantity demanded will be independent of units of measurement.

## PRICE ELASTICITY AND REVENUES

The revenue received by a firm from selling a good is price times quantity. We write this in a simple equation. Letting $R$ denote revenues, $p$ price, and $Q$ quantity:

$$R = pQ.$$

This means that when price goes up by 1 percent, whether revenues go up or down depends on the magnitude of the decrease in quantity. If quantity

## PRICE ELASTICITY OF DEMAND

| Elasticity | Description | Effect on Quantity Demanded of 1% Increase in Price | Effect on Revenues of 1% Increase in Price |
|---|---|---|---|
| Zero | Perfectly inelastic (vertical demand curve) | Zero | Increased by 1% |
| Between 0 and 1 | Inelastic | Reduced by less than 1% | Increased by less than 1% |
| One | Unitary elasticity | Reduced by 1% | Unchanged |
| Greater than 1 | Elastic | Reduced by more than 1% | Reduced; the greater the elasticity, the more revenue is reduced |
| Infinite | Perfectly elastic (horizontal demand curve) | Reduced to zero | Reduced to zero |

decreases by more than 1 percent, then total revenues decrease; by less than 1 percent, they increase. We can express this result in terms of the concept of price elasticity.

Business firms must pay attention to the price elasticity of demand for their products. Suppose a cement producer, the only one in town, is considering a 1 percent increase. The firm hires an economist to estimate the elasticity of demand, so that the firm will know what will happen to sales when it raises its price. The economist tells the firm that its demand elasticity is 2. This means that if the price of cement rises by 1 percent, the quantity sold will decline by 2 percent.

The firm's executives will not be pleased by the findings. To see why, assume that initially the price of cement was $1,000 per tonne, and 100,000 tonnes were sold. To calculate revenues, you multiply the price times the quantity sold. So initially revenues were $1,000 × 100,000 = $100 million. With a 1 percent increase, the price will be $1,010. If the elasticity of demand is 2, then a 1 percent price increase results in a 2 percent decrease in the quantity sold. With a 2 percent quantity decrease, sales are now 98,000 tonnes. Revenues are down to $98.98 million ($1,010 × 98,000), just slightly over 1 percent. Because of the high elasticity, this cement firm's price *increase* leads to a *decrease* in revenues.

The price elasticity of demand works the same way for price decreases. Suppose the cement producer decided to decrease the price of cement 1 percent, to $990. With an elasticity of demand of 2, sales would then increase 2 percent, to 102,000 tonnes. Thus, revenues would *increase* to $100,980,000 ($990 × 102,000), that is, by a bit less than 1 percent. When the change in revenues more than offsets the change in prices, we say that the demand for that good is **relatively elastic,** or *sensitive* to price changes.

In the case where the price elasticity is **unity,** or 1, the decrease in the quantity demanded just offsets the increase in the price, so price increases have no effect on revenues. If the price elasticity is less than unity, then when the price of a good increases by 1 percent, the quantity demanded is reduced by less than 1 percent. Since there is not much reduction in demand, elasticities in the range between 0 and 1 mean that price increases will increase revenues. And price decreases will decrease revenues. We say the demand for that good is **relatively inelastic,** or *insensitive* to price changes.

### EXTREME CASES

There are two extreme cases that deserve attention. One is that of a flat demand curve, a curve that is perfectly horizontal. We say that such a demand curve is perfectly elastic, or has **infinite elasticity,** since even a slight increase in the price results in demand dropping to zero. The other case is that of a steep demand curve, a curve that is perfectly vertical. We say that such a demand curve is perfectly inelastic, or has **zero elasticity,** since no matter what the change in price, demand remains the same.

### PRICE ELASTICITIES IN THE CANADIAN ECONOMY

The elasticity of demand for most foods is low (an increase in price will not affect demand much). The elasticity of demand for most luxuries, such as perfume, ski trips, and Mercedes cars, is high (an increase in price will lead to much less demand). Table 5.1 gives one set of estimates of the elasticities of demand for broad commodity groups in Canada. The price elasticity of demand for food is .47, in contrast to the price elasticity for transportation, which is 1.37. These are for broad commodity groups. One might expect that for specific goods within these broad categories, the price elasticity of demand would be much higher. For example, the price elasticity of purchased meals or snack foods would be higher than that for food broadly defined. More generally, goods for which it is easy to find substitutes will have high price elasticities; goods for which substitutes cannot easily be found will have low price elasticities.

### Table 5.1 SOME PRICE ELASTICITIES IN THE CANADIAN ECONOMY

| Commodity Group | Elasticity |
| --- | --- |
| *Elastic demands* | |
| Household expenses | 1.28 |
| Transportation | 1.37 |
| *Inelastic demands* | |
| Tobacco and alcohol | .54 |
| Clothing | .52 |
| Food | .47 |
| Shelter | .38 |
| Miscellaneous | .67 |

*Source:* Alan Powell, "Post-War Consumption in Canada: A First Look at the Aggregates," *Canadian Journal of Economic and Political Science* 31 (November 1965): 559–65.

## CALCULATING PRICE ELASTICITIES

In practice, the data economists have for calculating elasticity seldom represent very small changes in prices. Rather, economists observe, say, an 8 percent change in quantity resulting from a 4 percent change in price. They calculate what is sometimes called the **arc elasticity** (to distinguish it from the **point elasticity,** referring to a *small* change) by the earlier formula:

$$\text{elasticity} = -\frac{\text{percentage change in quantity}}{\text{percentage change in price}}$$

which in this case is 2.

The percentage change in quantity is

$$\text{percentage change in quantity} = \frac{\text{change in quantity}}{\text{quantity}} \times 100 = \frac{\Delta Q}{Q} \times 100$$

where the symbol $\Delta$, the Greek letter delta, means "change in." Thus, $\Delta Q$ means "change in quantity." Similarly, if $\Delta p$ means change in price,

$$\text{percentage change in price} = \frac{\text{change in price}}{\text{price}} \times 100 = \frac{\Delta p}{p} \times 100.$$

Thus, the elasticity can be written

$$\text{elasticity} = -\frac{\Delta Q/Q \times 100}{\Delta p/p \times 100} = -\frac{\Delta Q}{\Delta p} \times \frac{p}{Q}.$$

This raises a slight technical problem. What values of $p$ and $Q$ do we use in calculating elasticities—the initial ones, the final ones, or values somewhere in between? If the change is small enough, it makes little difference. For large changes, however, it does make a difference. A common procedure is to use values of $p$ and $Q$ that are midway between the initial and final points.

### ELASTICITY AND SLOPE

The elasticity of a curve is often confused with its slope. The best way to see the distinction is to look at the **linear demand curve.** The linear demand curve is a straight line, depicted in Figure 5.2. Recall that when we draw the demand curve, we put price on the vertical axis and output on the horizontal axis. Thus, the quantity demanded is related to the price by the equation

$$Q = a - bp.$$

If $a = 100$ and $b = 2$, at a price of 1, $Q = 98$; at a price of 2, $Q = 96$; at a price of 3, $Q = 94$, and so forth.

The demand curve also gives the price at which a particular quantity of the good will be demanded. Thus, we can rewrite the equation to read

$$p = \frac{a}{b} - \frac{Q}{b},$$

so that (with $a = 100$, $b = 2$ as before), at $Q = 100$, $p = 1$; at $Q = 99$, $p = 1.5$; at $Q = 98$, $p = 2$.

Slope gives the change along the vertical axis per unit change along the horizontal axis:

$$slope = \frac{change\ in\ price}{change\ in\ quantity} = \frac{\Delta p}{\Delta Q}.$$

Equivalently, slope is the change in price for a unit change in quantity. In our example, as we change quantity by 1, price changes by $-\frac{1}{2}$. More generally, the slope of the linear demand equation above is $-\frac{1}{b}$.[1]

We can now rewrite the expression for elasticity as

$$elasticity = -\frac{\Delta Q/Q}{\Delta p/p} = -\frac{\Delta Q}{\Delta p} \times \frac{p}{Q}$$

$$= b \times \frac{p}{Q}$$

$$= -\frac{1}{slope} \times \frac{p}{Q}.$$

Everywhere along a linear demand curve the slope

[1] To see this, observe that at $Q + 1$, the price is

$$\frac{a}{b} - \frac{Q+1}{b}.$$

The change in price is

$$\frac{a}{b} - \frac{Q}{b} - \left(\frac{a}{b} - \frac{Q+1}{b}\right) = \frac{a}{b} - \frac{Q}{b} - \frac{a}{b} + \frac{Q+1}{b} = \frac{1}{b}.$$

is the same, but the elasticity is very high at low levels of output and very low at high levels of output.

The formula for elasticity has one other important implication, illustrated in Figure 5.3. Of two demand curves going through the same point, the flatter demand curve has the higher elasticity. At the point where they intersect, $p$ and $Q$ (and therefore $p/Q$) are the same. Only the slopes differ. The one with the smaller slope has the greater elasticity.

### SMALL VERSUS LARGE PRICE CHANGES

Often, economists are interested in what would happen if there were a large price change. For instance, if a 50 percent tax were imposed on cigarettes, what would happen to demand?

When price changes are small or moderate, we can *extrapolate*. That is, we can extend what we know to make conclusions beyond the range of what we know. For example, if a 1 percent change in price results in a 2 percent change in quantity, then a 3 percent change in price will probably result in an approximately 6 percent change in quantity.

With large price changes, however, such extrapolation becomes riskier. The reason is that *price elasticity is typically different at different points along the demand curve*. Thus, in the linear case considered above, the slope of the demand curve $(-\frac{1}{b})$ is constant. The elasticity $(bp/Q)$ will fall as one moves down the demand curve, since $p$ is falling while $Q$ is rising.

## THE DETERMINANTS OF THE ELASTICITY OF DEMAND

In our earlier discussion we noted one of the important determinants of the elasticity of demand: the availability of substitutes. There are two important determinants of the degree of substitutability: the quantity of the good consumed and the length of time it takes to make an adjustment.

When the price of a commodity is low and the consumption is high, a variety of substitutes exist. Figure 5.4 illustrates the case of aluminum. When the price of aluminum is low, it is used as a food wrap (aluminum foil), as containers for canned goods, and in airplane frames because it is lightweight. As the

## Figure 5.2 LINEAR DEMAND CURVE

The linear demand curve is a straight line; it is represented algebraically by the equation $Q = a - bp$. The slope of the demand curve is a constant. However, the elasticity varies with output. At low outputs (high prices) it is very high. At high outputs (low prices) it is very low.

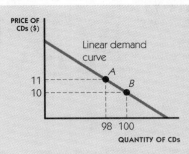

## Figure 5.3 COMPARING ELASTICITIES

If two demand curves intersect, at the point of intersection, the flatter demand curve has the greater price elasticity.

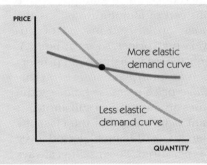

## Figure 5.4 CHANGING ELASTICITY ALONG A DEMAND CURVE

Near point $A$, where the price is high, the demand curve is quite steep and inelastic. In the area of the demand curve near $B$, the demand curve is very flat and elastic.

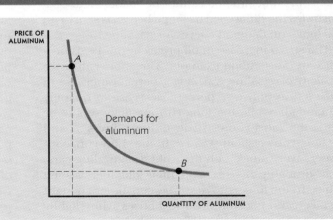

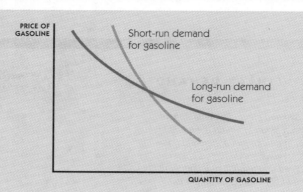

Figure 5.5 **ELASTICITY OF DEMAND OVER TIME**

Demand curves tend to be inelastic in the short run, when there is little time to adapt to price changes, but more elastic in the long run.

price increases, customers seek out substitutes. At first, substitutes are easy to find, and the demand for the product is greatly reduced. For example, plastic wrap can be used instead of aluminum foil. As the price rises still further, tin is used instead of aluminum for cans. At very high prices, say near point A, aluminum is used only where its lightweight properties are essential, such as in airplane frames. At this point it may take a *huge* price increase before some other material becomes an economical substitute.

A second important determinant of the elasticity of demand is the length of the time period over which responses are measured. Because it is always easier to find substitutes and to make other adjustments when you have a longer time to make them, the elasticity of demand is normally larger in the **long run**—in the period in which all adjustments can be made—than it is in the **short run,** when at least some adjustments cannot be made. Figure 5.5 illustrates the difference in shape between short-run and long-run demand curves for gasoline.

The sharp increase in oil prices in the 1970s provides an outstanding example. The short-run price elasticity of gasoline was .2 (a 1 percent increase in price led to only a .2 percent decrease in quantity demanded), while the long-run elasticity was .7 or more; the short-run elasticity of fuel oil was .2, and the long-run elasticity was 1.2. In the short run, consumers were stuck with their old gas-guzzling cars, their draughty houses, and their old fuel-wasting habits. In the long run, however, consumers bought smaller cars, became used to houses with slightly lower temperatures, installed better insulation in their homes, and turned to alternative energy

sources. The long-run demand curve was therefore much more elastic (flatter) than the short-run curve. Indeed, the long-run elasticity turned out to be much larger than anticipated.

How long is the long run? There is no simple answer. It will vary from product to product. In some cases adjustments can occur rapidly; in other cases they are very gradual. As old gas guzzlers wore out, they were replaced with fuel-efficient compact cars. As furnaces wore out, they were replaced with more efficient ones. New homes are now constructed with more insulation, so that gradually, over time, the fraction of houses that are well insulated is increasing.

## THE PRICE ELASTICITY OF SUPPLY

Supply curves normally slope upwards. As with demand curves, they are steep in some cases and flat in others. The degree of steepness reflects sensitivity to price changes. A steep supply curve, like the one for oil in Figure 5.6A, means that a large change in price generates only a small change in the quantity firms want to supply. A flatter curve, like the one for chicken in Figure 5.6B, means that a small change in price generates a large change in supply. Just as with demand, economists have developed a precise way of representing the sensitivity of supply to prices in a way that parallels the one already introduced. The **price elasticity of supply** is defined as the percentage change in quantity supplied divided by the percentage change in price (or the percentage change in

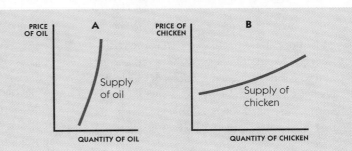

**Figure 5.6 DIFFERING ELASTICITIES OF SUPPLY**

Panel A shows a supply curve for oil. It is inelastic: quantity supplied increases only a small amount with a rise in price. Panel B shows a supply curve for chicken. It is elastic: quantity supplied increases substantially with a rise in price.

quantity supplied corresponding to a price change of 1 percent).

$$\text{Elasticity of supply} = \frac{\text{percentage change in quantity supplied}}{\text{percentage change in price}}.$$

The elasticity of supply of oil is low: an increase in the price of oil will not have a significant effect on the total supply. The amount of oil that has been discovered and can be extracted is relatively fixed. Though some wells can be exploited more intensively and some new wells can be brought into production, an increase in price will have proportionately little effect on the available supply. The supply of chicken, on the other hand, is much more responsive to price. Existing producers can increase their output readily, and new producers can easily enter the market.

As is the case with demand, if a 1 percent increase in price results in more than a 1 percent increase in supply, we say the supply curve is elastic. If a 1 percent increase in price results in less than a 1 percent increase in supply, the supply curve is inelastic. In the extreme case of a vertical supply curve—where the amount supplied does not depend at all on price—the curve is said to be perfectly inelastic, or to have *zero* elasticity, and in the extreme case of a horizontal supply curve, the curve is said to be perfectly elastic, or to have *infinite* elasticity.

Just as the demand elasticity differs at different points of the demand curve, so too does the supply elasticity differ at different points of the supply curve. Figure 5.7 shows a typical supply curve in manufacturing. An example might be ball bearings. At very low prices, plants are just covering their operating

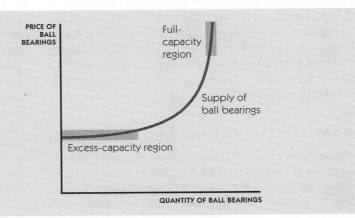

**Figure 5.7 CHANGING ELASTICITY ALONG A SUPPLY CURVE**

When output is low and many machines are idle, a small change in price can lead to a large increase in quantity produced, so the supply curve is flat and elastic. When output is high and all machines are working close to their limit, it takes a very large price change to induce even a small change in output; the supply curve is steep and inelastic.

### USING ECONOMICS: CALCULATING RESPONSES TO OIL PRICE CHANGES

As oil prices have fluctuated during the past decade, government analysts have repeatedly had to calculate the implications of those changes for oil consumption. If Canada consumes more oil, it will need to import more, and that in turn affects the balance of payments.

Assume prices of oil are expected to rise by 10 percent over the next two years. What will this do to the consumption of oil in Canada, if the elasticity of demand is .7? An elasticity of demand of .7 means that a 1 percent increase in price reduces demand by .7 percent. So a 10 percent increase in price will reduce demand by 7 percent. If the initial level of demand is 10 million barrels, demand will fall to 9.3 million.

What happens to total expenditures? If the initial price was $20 a barrel, total revenues initially were $0.2 billion. Now, with a price of $22 a barrel (a 10 percent increase from $20), they

have gone up to $22 × 9.3 million = $0.204 billion.

What happens to imports? Canada imports oil from abroad, and because the price of each barrel it imports has increased, it is worse off. But this is partly offset by the decreased use of oil. Assume Canada produces 5 million barrels, and that production remains unchanged. Initially, it imported 5 million, but now, it imports only 4.3 million. Canadian expenditures on imports actually fall: before the expenditures were 5 million × $20 = $0.1 billion; now they are 4.3 million × $22 = $94.6 million.

In the long run, the elasticity of demand is greater, so the reduction in consumption is larger. If the long-run elasticity is 1, then consumption falls to 9 million barrels, and expenditures remain unchanged. Imports fall to 4 million barrels, with a value of $88 million.

costs. Some plants are shut down; there is excess capacity in the industry. In this situation, a small increase in price elicits a large increase in supply. The supply curve is relatively flat (elastic). But eventually, all machines are being worked to full capacity throughout the day. In this situation, it may be hard to increase supply further, so that the supply curve becomes close to vertical (inelastic). In other words, however much the price increases, the supply will not change very much.

### SHORT RUN VERSUS LONG RUN

Economists distinguish between the responsiveness of supply to price in the short run and in the long run, just as they do with demand. The long-run supply elasticity is greater than the short-run. We define the short-run supply curve as the supply response *given the current stock of machines, buildings, and land*

*devoted to production.* The long-run supply curve assumes that firms can adjust the stock of machines, buildings, and land.

Farm crops are a typical example of a good whose supply in the short run is not very sensitive to changes in price; that is, the supply curve is steep (inelastic). After farmers have done their spring planting, they are committed to a certain level of production. If the price of their crop goes up, they cannot go back and plant more. If the price falls, they are stuck with the crop they have. In this case, the supply curve is relatively close to vertical, as illustrated by the steeper curve in Figure 5.8.

The long-run supply curve for many crops, in contrast, is very flat (elastic). A relatively small change in price can lead to a large change in the quantity supplied. A small increase in the price of soybeans relative to the price of wheat may induce many farmers to shift their planting from wheat and other crops to

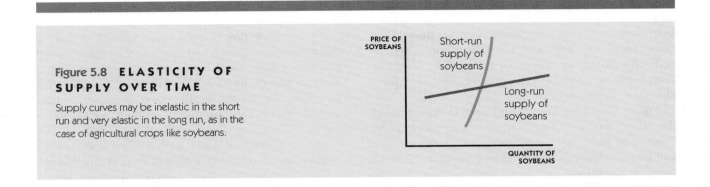

**Figure 5.8 ELASTICITY OF SUPPLY OVER TIME**

Supply curves may be inelastic in the short run and very elastic in the long run, as in the case of agricultural crops like soybeans.

soybeans, generating a large increase in the quantity of soybeans. This is illustrated in Figure 5.8 by the flatter curve.

Earlier, we noted the response of consumers to the marked increase in the price of oil in the 1970s. The long-run demand elasticity was much higher than the short-run. So too for supply. The higher prices drove firms, both in Canada and abroad in places like the United States, Mexico, and the North Sea off the coast of Great Britain, to explore for more oil. Though the alternative supplies could not be increased much in the short run (the short-run supply curve was inelastic, or steep), in the long run new supplies were found. Thus, the long-run supply elas-

ticity was much higher (the supply curve was flatter) than the short-run supply elasticity.

## IDENTIFYING PRICE AND QUANTITY ADJUSTMENTS

When the demand curve for a good such as wine shifts to the right—when, for instance, wine becomes more popular, so that at each price the demand is greater—there is an increase in both the equilibrium price of wine and the quantity demanded, or consumed. Similarly, when the supply curve for a good such as corn shifts to the left—say, because of a drought that hurt the year's crop, so that at each price farmers supply less—there is an increase in the equilibrium price of corn and a decrease in quantity. Knowing that the shifts in the demand or supply curve will lead to an adjustment in both price *and* quantity is helpful, but it is even more useful to know whether most of the impact of a change will be on price or on quantity. It is the price elasticity of both the demand and supply curves that determine how much adjustment occurs in the price relative to the quantity in response to shifts in demand or supply.

## PRICE ELASTICITY OF SUPPLY

| Elasticity | Description | Effect on Quantity Supplied of 1% Increase in Price |
|---|---|---|
| Zero | Perfectly inelastic (vertical supply curve) | Zero |
| Between 0 and 1 | Inelastic | Increased by less than 1% |
| One | Unitary elasticity | Increased by 1% |
| Greater than 1 | Elastic | Increased by more than 1% |
| Infinite | Perfectly elastic (horizontal supply curve) | Infinite increase |

## USING DEMAND AND SUPPLY ELASTICITIES

In Chapter 4 we saw how the law of supply and demand can be used to help explain changes in prices and to understand the consequences of, say, bad weather. The law of supply and demand, together with the concepts of demand and supply elasticity, help us be more precise in our predictions. They help us *quantify* the magnitudes of price and quantity changes as a result of, say, bad weather, which shifts the supply curve, or of increased consumer awareness of the health hazards of alcohol, which shifts the demand curve.

Figure 5.9 shows the typical range of outcomes. If the supply curve is highly elastic (approaching the horizontal, as in panel A), shifts in the demand curve will be reflected more in changes in quantity than in price. If the supply curve is *relatively* inelastic (approaching the vertical, as in panel B), shifts in the demand curve will be reflected more in changes in price than in quantity. If the demand curve is highly elastic (approaching the horizontal as in panel C), shifts in the supply curve will be reflected more in changes in quantity than in price. Finally, if the demand curve is *relatively* inelastic (approaching the vertical as in

panel D), shifts in the supply curve will be reflected more in changes in price than in quantity.

The extreme cases can be easily seen by extending the graphs in Figure 5.9. If one tilts the supply curve in panel A to be completely flat (perfectly elastic), a shift in the demand curve will have no effect on price. If one tilts the supply curve in panel B to be vertical (perfectly inelastic), a shift in the demand curve will have no effect on quantity.

Because demand and supply curves are likely to be less elastic (more vertical) in the short run than in the long run, shifts in the demand and supply curves are more likely to be reflected in price changes in the short run, but in quantity changes in the long run. In fact, price increases in the short run provide the signals to firms to increase their production. Therefore, short-run price increases can be thought of as responsible for the output increases that occur in the long run.

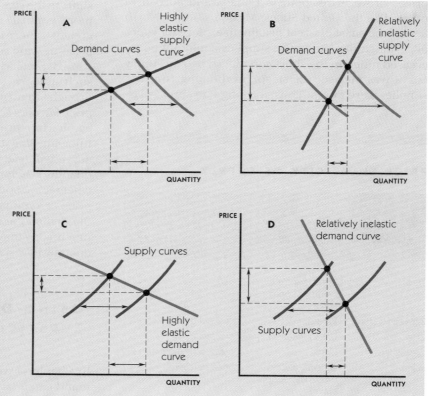

**Figure 5.9  ELASTICITY OF DEMAND AND SUPPLY CURVES: THE NORMAL CASES**

Normally, shifts in the demand curve will be reflected in changes in both price and quantity, as seen in panels A and B. When the supply curve is highly elastic, shifts in the demand curve will result mainly in changes in quantities; if it is relatively inelastic, shifts in the demand curve will result mainly in price changes. Likewise, shifts in the supply curve will be reflected in changes in both price and quantity, as seen in panels C and D. If the demand curve is highly elastic, shifts in the supply curve will result mainly in changes in quantities; if it is relatively inelastic, shifts in the supply curve will result mainly in price changes.

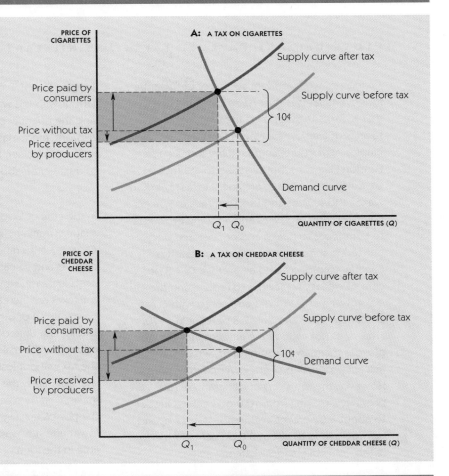

## Figure 5.10 PASSING ALONG A TAX TO CONSUMERS

A tax on the output of an industry shifts the supply curve up by the amount of the tax. Panel A shows that if the demand curve is relatively inelastic, as it is for cigarettes, then most of the tax will be passed on to consumers in higher prices. Panel B shows that if the demand curve is relatively elastic, as it is for cheddar cheese, then the tax cannot be passed along to consumers in higher prices, and must instead be absorbed by producers.

## TAX POLICY AND THE LAW OF SUPPLY AND DEMAND

Understanding the law of supply and demand is vital for many questions of public policy. One of the important ways economists use this law is in projecting the effect of taxes. Assume that the tax on a pack of cigarettes is increased by 10 cents, that the tax is imposed on cigarette retailers, and that all the companies try to pass on the cost increase to consumers by raising the price of a pack by 10 cents. At the higher price fewer cigarettes will be consumed, with the decrease in demand depending on the price elasticity of demand. With lower demand firms may reduce

their price; by how much depends on the price elasticity of supply. The new equilibrium is depicted in Figure 5.10A.

For firms to produce the same amount as before, they must receive 10 cents more per pack (which they pass on to the government). Thus, the supply curve is shifted up by 10 cents. Since the demand for cigarettes is relatively inelastic, this shift will result in a large increase in price and a relatively small decrease in quantity demanded.

When a tax on producers results in consumers paying a higher price, economists say the tax is "passed on" or "shifted" to consumers. The fact that the consumer bears the tax (even though it is collected from the producers) does not mean that the producers are "powerful" or have conspired together. It simply

# CLOSE-UP: ARE PAYROLL TAXES JOB KILLERS?

An increasingly important source of tax revenue for governments is the system of payroll taxes, that is, taxes that apply on the wages and salaries of employees. Payroll taxes include unemployment insurance premiums and Canada Pension Plan contributions paid to the federal government, as well as provincial taxes levied on wages and salaries and used to finance workers' compensation programs and, in some provinces, to contribute to health and/or postsecondary education spending. According to Statistics Canada, employers paid an average of 7.8 percent of wages and salaries to federal and provincial governments in 1993 compared with 6.7 percent in 1990 and only 2.3 percent in 1970. (This does not include the amount that the employees themselves contributed, which is a significant proportion of employer contributions.) However, the rates vary considerably across provinces, ranging from 10.0 percent in Quebec to about 8.0 percent in Ontario, Manitoba, and Newfoundland to about 5.8 percent in Alberta, British Columbia, and Saskatchewan.

Not surprisingly, business organizations such as the Canadian Chamber of Commerce view the increase in payroll taxes with some alarm. They argue that a payroll tax is a "tax on jobs" and as such discourages firms from hiring workers. Is that a justifiable concern? There are a number of reasons why we might be cautious in supposing that payroll taxes have killed jobs.

For one thing, the standard supply and demand analysis tells us that when a tax is imposed on a market, the market will respond by some combination of price increase and quantity reduction.

Imagine Figure 5.10 applying to the market for labour with the wage rate on the vertical axis and the quantity of labour on the horizontal axis. The more elastic the demand and supply curves for labour, the less will be the reduction in quantity of labour as a result of the tax, and vice versa.

In the case of labour markets, we might expect that the demand is highly elastic, given that Canadian firms must compete in international markets and so cannot afford to let their labour costs increase. However, although Canadian payroll taxes are increasing, they still remain well below those of other industrialized nations, including the United States and Western European countries. This makes it easier for firms to absorb the tax without losing their ability to compete. At the same time, the supply of labour may be quite inelastic. In these circumstances, a good part of the payroll tax might be absorbed in the form of lower after-tax wages for workers, and relatively little in the form of reduced employment.

In the end, the effect of payroll taxes on employment is an empirical question, one that economists are only now beginning to grapple with. A recent study by two economists from Lakehead University, Livio Di Matteo and Michael Shannon, estimated that a 1 percent increase in the payroll tax would cause employment to fall by .32 percent, resulting in over 40,000 lost jobs.

*Sources:* Bruce Little, "Quebec Payroll Taxes Highest," *The Globe and Mail,* September 22, 1995; Livio Di Matteo and Michael Shannon, "Payroll Taxation in Canada: An Overview," *Canadian Business Economics* (Summer 1995): 5–22.

reflects the system of supply and demand. Note, however, that the price did not rise the full 10 cents. Producers receive slightly lower after-tax prices and therefore bear a small fraction of the tax burden.

A tax imposed on a good or service for which the demand is very elastic leads to a different result. Assume, for instance, that the government decides to tax cheddar cheese (but no other cheeses). Since many cheeses are almost like cheddar, the demand curve for cheddar cheese is very elastic. In this case, as Figure 5.10B makes clear, most of the tax is absorbed by the producer, who receives (net of tax) a lower price. Production of cheddar cheese is reduced drastically as a consequence.

Which of these two cases applies can be important for tax policy. If the government is primarily interested in a tax as a source of revenue, it would prefer to apply the tax to goods that have inelastic demands. In Figure 5.10, tax revenues are indicated by the shaded areas. The less elastic the demand for the good being taxed, the larger the shaded area. But if the purpose of the tax is to discourage consumption of the good, the more elastic the demand, the more successful the measure will be, even though less tax revenue will be raised. Finally, if the government is concerned about the fairness of the tax, it may prefer not to tax heavily goods whose demands are inelastic because goods that are consumed proportionately more by low-income persons will have lower income elasticities of demand, and these are typically also goods with low price elasticities of demand.

## SHORTAGES AND SURPLUSES

The law of supply and demand works so well most of the time in a developed modern economy that everyone can take it for granted. If you are willing to pay the "market price"—the prevailing price of the good or service as determined by the intersection of demand and supply—you can obtain almost anything. Similarly, if a seller of a good or service is willing to charge no more than the market price, he can always sell what he wants to.

When the price is set so that demand equals supply—so that any individual can get as much as she wants at that price, and any supplier can sell the amount he wants at that price—economists say that the market **clears,** or is in equilibrium. But when the market does not clear, there are dramatic shortages or surpluses. To an economist, a **shortage** means that people would like to buy something, but they simply cannot find it for sale at the going price. A **surplus** means that sellers would like to sell their product, but they cannot sell as much of it as they would like at the going price. These cases where the market does not seem to be working are often the most forceful reminders of the importance of the law of supply and demand. The problem is that the "going price" is not the market equilibrium price.

Shortages and surpluses can be seen in Figure 5.11, the standard supply and demand diagram. In both

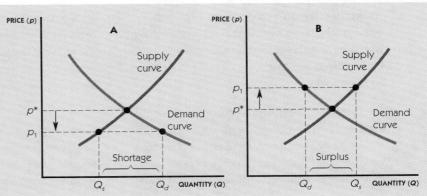

### Figure 5.11 SHORTAGES AND SURPLUSES

In panel A, the actual price $p_1$ is below the market-clearing price $p^*$. At a price of $p_1$, quantity demanded exceeds quantity supplied, and a shortage exists. In panel B, the actual price $p_1$ is above the equilibrium price $p^*$. In this case, quantity supplied exceeds quantity demanded, and there is a surplus, or glut, in the market.

For the past dozen years or so, Canadian smokers have faced skyrocketing prices for cigarettes and other tobacco products as a direct consequence of government tax policies. Cigarettes are subject to an impressive array of taxes at both the federal and provincial levels of government. At the federal level, these include a specific excise tax, an excise duty on domestically manufactured tobacco, and a customs duty on imports. As well, cigarettes are subject to the Goods and Services Tax (GST) applicable to all consumer products. The provinces collect a specific excise tax on cigarettes, and most of them include cigarettes in the provincial retail sales tax base. The combined efforts of provincial and federal governments have led to an increase in cigarette taxes of 250 percent in the past fifteen years.

Why do governments find tobacco taxes an attractive instrument of policy? Two reasons are usually given. One is that the demand for cigarettes is relatively inelastic, which makes the tax a reliable source of revenue. If the demand for a product is inelastic, the attempt by producers to pass the tax on to consumers will not cause much decline in demand, and the government will collect a great deal of additional revenue. The second reason is to discourage the purchase of cigarettes by Canadians, since smoking is viewed as being an activity with adverse health effects, at least some of which are borne by nonsmokers.

The relative effectiveness of the policy in meeting these two objectives clearly depends upon the elasticity of demand. If the demand is very inelastic, the tax is a good source of revenue but an ineffective instrument for discouraging smoking. On the other hand, if it is more elastic, it will succeed in discouraging demand but will raise relatively little revenue. The evidence is somewhat mixed. Empirical studies have shown that in the short run the elasticity of demand for cigarettes is around −0.3 (so a 10 percent increase in price would lead to a 3 percent decline in demand), while in the long run it is closer to −1.2. The higher elasticity in the long run suggests that it takes some time before smokers adjust to a price increase and reduce smoking, presumably owing to the addictive nature of the product. It has also been found that the elasticity is higher among the young than among the old. These results would suggest that cigarette taxes are more of an instrument for discouraging smoking than for raising revenues, at least in the long run. In fact, since the long-run elasticity is greater than unity, an increase in cigarette taxes should lead to a decline in tax revenues in the long run: a 10 percent increase in prices leads to a greater than 10 percent decline in sales.

Pushing cigarette taxes ever higher to restrict consumption, however, has led to an unforeseen problem, which detracts considerably from its perceived success and frustrates both objectives of cigarette tax policy. Since Canadian cigarette taxes have increased much more than those in the United States, the incentive to smuggle cigarettes into Canada from the United States for personal consumption or for resale has correspondingly increased.

Moreover, most Canadian cigarettes that have been exported to the United States free of tax are smuggled back in. Over the period 1985–91, exports of cigarettes to the United States

Increased over fivefold, and border seizures increased dramatically as well. The federal government responded in the spring of 1992 with a stiff export tax, but pressure from cigarette producers soon forced the government to reduce cigarette taxes drastically to remove the incentive for smuggling. Apparently there is a limit to

the extent to which Canada can increase its cigarette taxes significantly above those in the United States.

*Sources:* Editorial entitled "The Benefits and the Costs," *The Globe and Mail,* February 17, 1993; Informetrica, *Some Implications of Tobacco Taxation,* 1992.

panels A and B, the market equilibrium price is $p^*$. In panel A, the going price, $p_1$, is below $p^*$. At this price demand exceeds supply; you can see this by reading down to the horizontal axis. Demand is $Q_d$; supply is $Q_s$. The gap between the two points is the "shortage." With the shortage, consumers scramble to get the limited supply available at the going price.

In panel B, the going price, $p_1$, is above $p^*$. At this price demand is less than supply. Again we denote the demand by $Q_d$ and the supply by $Q_s$. There is a surplus in the market of $Q_s - Q_d$. Now sellers are scrambling to find buyers.

At various times and for various goods, markets have not cleared. There have been shortages of apartments in Toronto; farm surpluses have plagued both Western Europe and North America; in 1973 there was a shortage of gasoline, with cars lined up in long lines outside of gasoline stations. Unemployment is a type of surplus, when people who want to work find that they cannot sell their labour services at the going wage.

In some markets, like the stock market, the adjustment of prices to shifts in the demand and supply curves tends to be very rapid. In other cases, such as in the housing market, the adjustments tend to be sluggish. When price adjustments are sluggish, shortages or surpluses persist as prices adjust. For instance, houses tend not to sell quickly during periods of decreased demand, which translate only slowly into lower housing prices.

When the market is not adjusting quickly toward equilibrium, economists say that prices are **sticky.** Even in these cases, the analysis of market equilibrium is useful. It indicates the direction of the changes—if the equilibrium price exceeds the current price, prices will tend to rise. Moreover, the rate at which prices fall or rise is often related to the gap, at the going price, between the quantity demanded and the quantity supplied.

## INTERFERING WITH THE LAW OF SUPPLY AND DEMAND

The law of supply and demand, which governs how prices are set, can produce results that some individuals or groups do not like. For example, a reduced supply of oil may lead to a higher equilibrium price for oil. The higher price is not a malfunction of the law of supply and demand, but this is little comfort to those who use gasoline to power their cars and oil to heat their homes. Low demand for unskilled labour may lead to very low wages for unskilled workers. An increase in the demand for apartments in Vancouver leads, in the short run (with an inelastic supply), to an increase in rents—to the delight of landlords and the dismay of renters.

In each of these cases, pressure from those who did not like the outcome of market processes has led governments to act. The price of oil and natural gas was at one time regulated; minimum wage laws set a minimum limit on what employers can pay, even if the workers are willing to work for less; and rent control laws limit what landlords can charge. The concerns behind these interferences with the market are understandable, but the agitation for government action is based on two errors.

First, someone (or some group) was assigned blame for the change: the oil price rises were blamed on the oil companies, low wages on the employer, and rent increases on the landlord. As already explained, economists emphasize the role of anonymous market forces in determining these prices. After all, if landlords or oil companies are basically the same people today as they were last week, there must be some reason that they started charging different prices this week. Sometimes the price increase is the result of producers colluding to raise prices. This was the case in 1973, when the oil-exporting countries got together to raise the price of oil. The more common situation, however, is illustrated by the increase in the price of oil in August 1990, after Iraq's invasion of Kuwait. There was no collusion this time. The higher price simply reflected the anticipated reduction in the supply of oil. People rushed to buy, increasing short-term demand and pushing up the equilibrium price.

The second error was to forget that as powerful as governments may be, they can no more repeal the law of supply and demand than they can repeal the law of gravity. When they interfere with its working, the forces of supply and demand will not be balanced. There will either be excess supply or excess demand. Shortages and surpluses create problems of their own, often worse than the original problem the government was supposed to resolve.

Two straightforward examples of governments' overruling the law of supply and demand are **price ceilings,** which impose a maximum price that can be charged for a product, and **price floors,** which impose a minimum price. Rent control laws are price ceilings, and minimum wage laws are price floors. A closer look at each will help highlight the perils of interfering with the law of supply and demand.

## PRICE CEILINGS: THE CASE OF RENT CONTROL

Price ceilings—setting a maximum charge—are always tempting to governments because they seem an easy way to assure that everyone will be able to afford a particular product. Thus, in the last couple of decades in Canada, price ceilings have been set for a wide range of goods, from natural gas to oil to rental accommodation. In each case the result has been to create shortages at the controlled price. More people want to buy the product than there are products, because producers have no incentive to produce more of the good. Those who can buy at the cheaper price benefit; producers and those unable to buy suffer.

The effect of **rent control** laws—setting the maximum rent that a landlord can charge for a one-bedroom apartment, for example—is illustrated by Figure 5.12. In panel A, $R^*$ is the market equilibrium rental rate, at which the demand for housing equals the supply. However, the local government is concerned that at $R^*$, many poor people cannot afford housing in the city, so it imposes a law that says that rents may be no higher than $R_1$. At $R_1$, there is an excess demand for apartments. While the motives behind the government action may well have been praiseworthy, the government has created an artificial scarcity.

As with many government policies, there are some gainers and some losers. The gainers will be the households that happen to be lucky enough to have an apartment. Their rent will be lower than it otherwise would have been. Among the losers will be the owners of rental accommodation, who will receive lower rents and incomes than in the absence of rent controls. There are also the potential landlords who would otherwise have supplied rental accommodation at the market price, but are unable to cover costs at the controlled rent. Perhaps the most important losers are the households that are unable to find rental accommodation, given the limited supply. Among these will be low-income households, who are presumably the ones that the policy was meant to benefit.

The extent of the shortage created and the number of low-income households unable to find rental accommodation will depend upon the extent to which quantities demanded and supplied respond to the artificially lowered price. As we have seen, the less elastic the demands and supplies, the less will be the response of quantities to price changes. Thus, if demands and supplies were very inelastic, the amount of excess demand created will be small, and

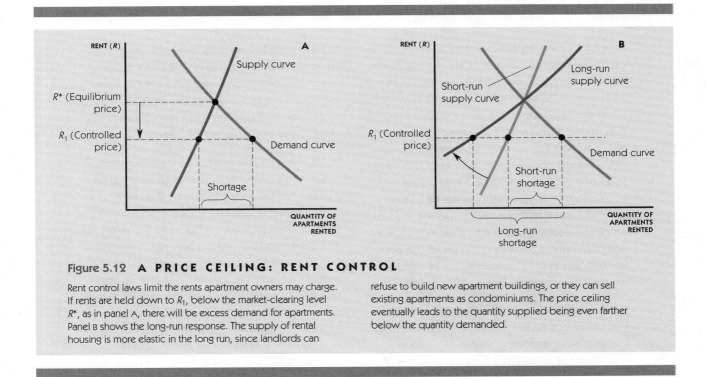

**Figure 5.12  A PRICE CEILING: RENT CONTROL**

Rent control laws limit the rents apartment owners may charge. If rents are held down to $R_1$, below the market-clearing level $R^*$, as in panel A, there will be excess demand for apartments. Panel B shows the long-run response. The supply of rental housing is more elastic in the long run, since landlords can refuse to build new apartment buildings, or they can sell existing apartments as condominiums. The price ceiling eventually leads to the quantity supplied being even farther below the quantity demanded.

the government may have accomplished what they set out to do with limited disruption to the market. In the short run, both demands and supplies are likely to be quite inelastic, so rent controls might be temporarily beneficial.

However, the problems caused by rent control are likely to be worse in the long run than in the short run, because long-run supply curves are more elastic than short-run supply curves. In the short run, the quantity of apartments does not change much. But in the long run, the quantity of apartments can decline for several reasons, as landlords try to minimize the losses from rent control. Apartments may be abandoned as they deteriorate; they can be converted to condominiums and sold instead of rented; and apartment owners may not wish to construct new ones if they cannot charge enough in rent to cover their costs. Figure 5.12B illustrates how the housing shortages under rent control will increase over time. As time goes by, more and more would-be residents will be unable to find rental housing in the market. Since renters tend to be poorer than those who can buy a home, a shortage of rental housing will tend to hurt the poor most.

## PRICE FLOORS: THE CASE OF THE MINIMUM WAGE

To many Canadians, it has long seemed fair that if you work full time fifty-two weeks a year at some job, you ought to earn enough to support yourself and a family. Yet there are some jobs, especially those demanding low skill levels, for which this may not be the case. In the absence of government intervention, the wage rates on such jobs might be so low as to leave the worker and the worker's family below the poverty line. The result is either that other members of the family are forced to go to work or all are forced to live in poverty. Given this possibility it is easy to see the source of the sentiment for

## Close-up: Rent Control in Ontario

Rent control was implemented by most provinces in Canada as part of the general policy of wage and price controls to fight inflation in 1974 and 1975. When inflation subsided, so did wage and price controls. In some places, however, rent control remained in effect. In Ontario the immediate impact of rent control was a decline in rental housing starts from 26,000 in 1973 to 15,000 in 1974 to 3,800 in 1975. The response to this decline in supply has been for governments to become increasingly involved as suppliers or subsidizers in the rental market. Given this subsidization and the social and political opposition to rent decontrol, rent control has become entrenched since 1974 in Ontario.

Although the rationale behind rent control is to give lower-income persons access to affordable housing, other economic classes often benefit most from the system. The decreased supply of rental units reduces the turnover rate and thus the availability of rental housing. The original occupiers of the regulated housing are the initial winners.

Contributing to this allocation problem is the existence of "key money." In 1985 in Toronto, a tenant occupying a one-bedroom apartment in a prime downtown location might be offered a $2,000 cash inducement to vacate ($5,000 for a two-bedroom apartment). In this manner, cheap rent-controlled housing was transferred to those who could afford to make key-money payments. The government's rent-control objectives were undermined, and a black market for rental housing was established.

Until 1986, rental units constructed after 1975 were not subject to rent control. Since middle- to upper-income persons could more easily gain access to the limited number of regulated units becoming available (through the black market), lower-income persons were left either to scramble for a place in the newer, uncontrolled, and more expensive units, or were forced into run-down areas or even onto the street.

In 1986 several changes to the Ontario system of rent control were enacted in order to enhance equity and efficiency. Landlords were allowed to cover maintenance costs in their yearly rent increases, thereby reducing the incentive to allow rent-controlled units to become run down. And, post-1975 construction was included in the rent-control scheme. Still, in 1987, the vacancy rate of rental units in Toronto was only 0.1 percent. In the early 1980s, the four western provinces and New Brunswick all removed the rent controls that had been in existence since the 1970s. Vacancy rates in 1987 for Vancouver, Edmonton, and St. John were 2.3 percent, 5.5 percent, and 5.4 percent, respectively.

It appears that rent controls have not been effective in providing low-cost housing to the poor. In addition to the effects on the rental market itself, there have also been effects on the owner-occupied housing market and on labour mobility. The severe shortage of rental housing is seen by some economists as a problem that only decontrol and a freely functioning market can solve.

Sources: Lawrence B. Smith, "An Economic Assessment of Rent Controls: The Ontario Experience," In Richard J. Arnott and Jack M. Mintz, eds., Rent Control: The International Experience (Kingston, Ontario: The John Deutsch Institute for the Study of Economic Policy, 1987), pp. 57–72; R. Andrew Muller, "Ontario's Options in the Light of the Canadian Experience with Decontrol," In Richard J. Arnott and Jack M. Mintz, eds., Policy Forum on Rent Controls in Ontario (Kingston, Ontario: The John Deutsch Institute for the Study of Economic Policy, 1987), pp. 21–38.

governments to interfere with the market and attempt to force firms to pay a decent wage. In Canada, all provinces and territories have enacted **minimum wages** at rates ranging from $4.75 in Newfoundland and Prince Edward Island to $6.85 in Ontario and $7.00 in British Columbia. Rates have tended to be raised periodically to keep pace with the cost of living, and have tended to be about half the average wage for all workers.

The minimum wage is an example of a price floor. While price ceilings are meant to help demanders (buyers), price floors are meant to help suppliers (sellers). With a price floor such as the minimum wage, buyers (employers) cannot pay less than the government-set minimum wage.

Price floors have predictable effects, too. The reasoning is simply the reverse of that for price ceilings. If the government attempts to raise the minimum wage higher than the equilibrium wage, the demand for workers will be reduced and the supply increased. There will be an excess supply of labour. Of course, those who are lucky enough to get a job will be better off at the higher wage than at the market equilibrium wage; but there are others who might have been employed at the lower market equilibrium wage who cannot find work and are worse off. These tend to be among the least skilled workers.

How much unemployment does the minimum wage create? That depends on the level at which the minimum wage is set and on the elasticity of demand and supply for labour. If the minimum wage is set low enough, then it has little effect, either on wages or on employment. Panel A of Figure 5.13 shows a market in which an equilibrium wage is above the minimum wage. A small increase in the minimum wage has no effect on either the wage rate or the employment level. With the current level of minimum wages, only very unskilled individuals are affected. Most other workers, even the unskilled, get paid more than the minimum wage.

Panel B of Figure 5.13 shows the case where the demand and supply for unskilled labour are very inelastic, so that wages can be increased significantly with little increase in unemployment. In Panel C, demand and supply for unskilled labour are both very elastic, and the minimum wage has been set

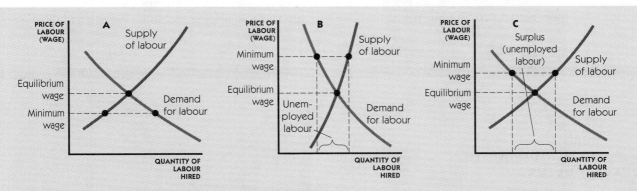

## Figure 5.13 EFFECTS OF MINIMUM WAGES

In panel A, the minimum wage is below the equilibrium wage. However, since the minimum wage is a price floor, there is nothing to stop the market from paying the higher equilibrium wage, and any increase in the minimum wage will have no effect so long as the minimum wage remains below the equilibrium wage. In panel B; an increase in the minimum wage will result in very little increase in unemployment, as the demand and supply curves for labour are inelastic. In panel C, the demand and supply curves are more elastic; the minimum wage is above the equilibrium wage, creating a large surplus of workers who would like to work but cannot find jobs. Increases in the minimum wage in this case will increase unemployment significantly.

significantly above the market equilibrium wage. As a result, substantial unemployment is generated by the minimum wage.

## QUANTITY CONTROLS: SUPPLY MANAGEMENT IN AGRICULTURE

Price ceilings and floors represent direct interference with market prices. Alternatively, governments can regulate quantities traded on markets, and thereby indirectly determine market prices. For example, if governments can restrict the quantity of a product supplied, this will artificially increase the market price. As with minimum prices, they may be tempted to do this to make suppliers better off.

An example of quantity controls is the system of **supply management** that has been used in some sectors of Canadian agriculture, such as the markets for milk, turkeys, chickens, and eggs. Under this system the government's regulatory agency controls the aggregate supply of all producers through the issuing of **quotas** denominated in units of the product. In order to produce, say, 1,000 turkeys, a producer must be allocated a quota of 1,000. Producers without a quota cannot produce. The quotas might initially have been allocated to producers in accordance with their actual production. However, once

issued, the quotas can be traded and have a market price.

The effect of quotas on the market for turkeys can be illustrated in Figure 5.14. The equilibrium price would have been $p_e$ and the equilibrium quantity $Q_e$. Suppose the government now sets the total number of quotas at $Q$. At this quantity, the price that consumers would pay would be $p$. If quotas could be freely sold and bought, they would naturally end up going to the producers who would value them most; those with the lowest costs of production. In terms of the supply curve, producers whose costs are $c$ or below would be the lowest-cost ones. They would be willing to pay at least $p-c$ for a quota to produce each turkey, since this is the difference between the selling price they would receive and the costs to the marginal producer. Producers whose costs were higher than $c$ would not pay $p-c$ for a quota, since that would entail their making a loss. Thus, the equilibrium price for the quota would be $p-c$, and the total value of quotas to produce turkeys in a given period would be given by the shaded area.

The use of quotas has some advantages over price floors as a way of assisting producers. For one thing, quotas avoid the excess supply induced by price floors. In the case of agricultural products, this excess supply is pure waste. For another, the fact that quotas are tradable implies that the most efficient producers

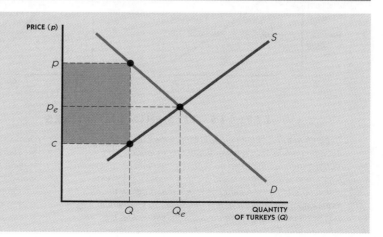

**Figure 5.14 QUOTAS IN AGRICULTURE**

If the government establishes a quota of $Q$ units of turkeys, the market price of turkeys will be $p$, and the value of the quota per period will be given by the shaded area between $p$ and $c$.

should be the ones who end up supplying the product, since the price of quotas will be bid up to force the higher-cost producers out of the market.

On the other hand, there are disadvantages of quotas. For one, since quotas involve artificially restricting the quantity and increasing the price, consumers are among the losers. For another, the output of the market is not allowed to settle at its most efficient level, that is, the level where the marginal benefit to consumers (i.e., the price) is equal to the marginal cost of supplying the product. Finally, since quotas are typically applicable not just to this year's production but to production in future years as well, the full benefit of a quota is much larger than that illustrated in the diagram. The latter only shows the value of the quota in one production period. If the quota lasts indefinitely, its value must include that of all future years as well. This can make the dollar value of a quota immense. Much of this value accrues to the producers lucky enough to be allocated a quota when the quota is first established. It does nothing to improve the incomes of new producers wishing to enter the industry in the future. They end up having to pay an enormous price for a quota to the existing owners. To that extent, it does nothing to assist those whom it was intended to benefit.

## ALTERNATIVE SOLUTIONS

Large changes in prices cause distress. It is natural to try to find scapegoats and to look to the government for a solution. Such situations call for compassion, and the economists' caution can seem coldhearted. But the fact remains that in competitive markets, the price changes are simply the impersonal workings of the law of supply and demand; without the price changes there will be shortages and surpluses. The examples of government attempts to interfere with the workings of supply and demand provide an important cautionary tale: one ignores the workings of the law of supply and demand only at one's peril. This does not mean, however, that the government should simply ignore the distress caused by large price and wage changes. It only means that government must take care in addressing the problems; price controls, including price ceilings and floors, are unlikely to be effective instruments.

Later chapters will discuss ways in which the government can address dissatisfaction with the consequences of the law of supply and demand—by making use of the power of the market rather than trying to fight against it. For example, if the government is concerned with low wages paid to unskilled workers, it can try to increase the demand for these workers. A shift to the right in the demand curve will increase the wages these workers receive. The government can do this either by subsidizing firms that hire unskilled workers or by providing more training to these workers and thus increasing their productivity.

If the government wants to increase the supply of housing to the poor, it can provide housing subsidies for the poor, which will elicit a greater supply. If government wants to conserve on the use of gasoline, it can impose a tax on gasoline. Noneconomists often object that these sorts of economic incentives have other distasteful consequences, and sometimes they do. But government policies that take account of the law of supply and demand will tend to be more effective, with fewer unfortunate side effects, than policies that ignore the predictable economic consequences that follow from disregarding the law of supply and demand.

# REVIEW AND PRACTICE

## SUMMARY

**1** The price elasticity of demand describes how sensitive the quantity demanded of a good is to changes in the price of the good. When demand is inelastic, an increase in the price has little effect on quantity demanded; when demand is elastic, an increase in the price has a large effect on quantity demanded.

**2** If price changes do not induce much change in demand, the demand curve is steep and is said to be inelastic, or insensitive to price changes. If the demand curve is rather flat, indicating that price changes induce large changes in demand, demand is said to be elastic, or sensitive to price changes. Demand for necessities is usually quite inelastic; demand for luxuries is elastic.

**3** The price elasticity of supply describes how sensitive the quantity supplied of a good is to changes in the price of the good.

**4** If price changes do not induce much change in supply, the supply curve is very steep and is said to be inelastic. If the supply curve is very flat, indicating that price changes cause large changes in supply, supply is said to be elastic.

**5** The extent to which a shift in the supply curve is reflected in price or quantity depends on the shape of the demand curve. The more elastic the demand, the more a given shift in the supply curve will be reflected in changes in equilibrium quantities and the less it will be reflected in changes in equilibrium prices. The more inelastic the demand, the more a given shift in the supply curve will be reflected in changes in equilibrium prices and the less it will be reflected in changes in equilibrium quantities.

**6** Likewise, the extent to which a shift in the demand curve is reflected in price or quantity depends on the shape of the supply curve.

**7** Demand and supply curves are likely to be more elastic in the long run than in the short run. Therefore a shift in the demand or supply curve is likely to have a larger price effect in the short run and a larger quantity effect in the long run.

**8** Elasticities can be used to predict to what extent consumer prices rise when a tax is imposed on a good. If the demand curve for a good is very inelastic, consumers in effect have to pay the tax. If the demand curve is very elastic, the quantities produced and the price received by producers are likely to decline considerably.

**9** Government regulations may prevent a market from moving toward its equilibrium price, leading to shortages or surpluses. Price ceilings lead to excess demand. Price floors lead to excess supply.

**10** Surpluses from price floors can be avoided by a system of quotas, but quotas benefit the select group of producers who are initially allocated the quotas.

## KEY TERMS

price elasticity of demand

price elasticity of supply

infinite elasticity of demand

infinite elasticity of supply

zero elasticity of demand

zero elasticity of supply

market clearing

sticky prices

price ceiling

price floor

short-run elasticity

long-run elasticity

quotas

## REVIEW QUESTIONS

**1** What is meant by the elasticity of demand and the elasticity of supply? Why do economists find these concepts useful?

**2** Is the slope of a perfectly elastic demand or supply curve horizontal or vertical? Is the slope of a perfectly inelastic demand or supply curve horizontal or vertical? Explain.

**3** If the elasticity of demand is unity, what happens to total revenue as the price increases? What if the demand for a product is very inelastic? What if it is very elastic?

**4** Under what condition will a shift in the demand curve result mainly in a change in quantity? in price?

**5** Under what condition will a shift in the supply curve result mainly in a change in price? in quantity?

**6** Why do the elasticities of demand and supply tend to change from the short run to the long run?

**7** Under what circumstances will a tax on a product be passed along to consumers?

**8** Why do price ceilings tend to lead to shortages? Why do price floors tend to lead to surpluses?

**9** What determines the market price of a quota?

## PROBLEMS

**1** Suppose the price elasticity of demand for gasoline is .2 in the short run and .7 in the long run. If the price of gasoline rises 28 percent, what effect on quantity demanded will this have in the short run? in the long run?

**2** Imagine that the short-run price elasticity of supply for a farmer's wheat is .3, while the long-run price elasticity is 2. If prices for wheat fall 30 percent, what are the short-run and long-run changes in quantity supplied? What are the short- and long-run changes in quantity supplied if prices rise by 15 percent? What happens to the farmer's revenues in each of these situations?

**3** Assume that the demand curve for hard liquor is highly inelastic and the supply curve for hard liquor is highly elastic. If the tastes of the drinking public shift away from hard liquor, will the effect be larger on price or on quantity? If the federal government decides to impose a tax on manufacturers of hard liquor, will the effects be larger on price or on quantity? What is the effect of an advertising program that succeeds in discouraging people from drinking? Draw diagrams to illustrate each of your answers.

**4** Imagine that wages (the price of labour) are sticky in the labour market, and that a supply of new workers enters that market. Will the market be in equilibrium in the short run? Why or why not? If not, explain the relationship you would expect to see between the quantity demanded and supplied, and draw a diagram to illustrate. Explain how sticky wages in the labour market affect unemployment.

**5** For each of the following markets, explain whether you would expect prices in that market to be relatively sticky or not:
    (a)  the stock market
    (b)  the market for autoworkers
    (c)  the housing market
    (d)  the market for cut flowers
    (e)  the market for pizza-delivery people

**6** Suppose a government wishes to ensure that its citizens can afford adequate housing. Consider three ways of pursuing that goal. One method is to pass a law requiring that all rents be cut by one quarter. A second method offers a subsidy to all builders of homes. A third provides a subsidy directly to renters equal to one quarter of the rent they pay. Predict what effect each of these proposals would have on the price and quantity of rental housing in the short run and the long run.

# PART TWO

# Full-Employment Macroeconomics

"Peace and prosperity" is the slogan on which many political candidates have run for office, and the failure to maintain prosperity has led to many a government's defeat. There is widespread belief among the citizenry that government is responsible for maintaining the economy at full employment with stable prices and for creating an economic environment in which growth can occur.

Although most economists agree with these sentiments, there are dissenting views. Some claim that the government has relatively little power to control most of the fluctuations in output and employment; some argue that, apart from isolated instances such as the Great Depression of the 1930s, neither inflation nor unemployment is a major *economic* problem (though they obviously remain political problems); and some believe that government has been as much a cause of the problems of unemployment, inflation, and slow growth as part of their solution. We will explore these various interpretations in greater depth in the chapters that follow.

The problems of unemployment, inflation, and growth relate to the performance of the entire economy. Earlier in the book, we learned how the law of supply and demand operates in the market for oranges, apples, or other goods. At any one time, one industry may be doing well, another poorly. Yet to understand the forces that determine how well the economy as a whole is doing, we want to see beyond the vagaries that affect any particular industry. This is the domain of macroeconomics. Macroeconomics focuses not on the output of single products like orange juice or peanut butter, nor on the demand for masons or bricklayers or computer programmers. Rather, it is concerned with the characteristics of an entire economy, such as the overall level of output, the total level of employment, and the stability of the overall level of prices. What accounts for the "diseases" that sometimes affect the economy—the episodes of massive unemployment, rising prices, or economic stagnation—and what can the government do, both to prevent the onset of these diseases and to cure them once they have occurred?

Macroeconomic *theory* is concerned with what determines the level of employment and output as well as the rate of inflation and the overall growth rate of the economy, while macroeconomic *policy* focuses on what government can do to stimulate employment, prevent inflation, and increase the economy's growth rate.

We begin our study of macroeconomics in Chapter 6 by learning the major statistics used to assess the state of the economy: the rates of unemployment, inflation, and growth. Chapter 8 builds on the microeconomic analysis of Chapter 7 to construct an *aggregate* model of the economy. Paralleling our earlier discussions, we focus on the labour, product, and capital markets. We see how the demand and supply for labour determine the real wage and how the real wage changes in response to shifts in either of these curves. We then see how the price level and the interest rate are determined in the product and capital markets. In this basic aggregate model, we assume full employment. The rate of growth is determined, in part, by the level of investment that emerges from the market equilibrium. And changes in the price level (and the rate of inflation) are determined by changes in the money supply.

International trade plays an important role in the Canadian economy. Exports make up close to one third of the output of the economy, and Canada has been borrowing billions of dollars from abroad annually. Clearly, international economic relations affect both the product and capital markets, as Chapter 8 also discusses.

In the last few years, two of the most frequently discussed issues of the Canadian economy have been the current-account deficit and the soaring fiscal deficit—the huge excess of federal expenditures over taxes, reaching almost 5 percent of the economy's output in 1992. Chapter 9 uses the full-employment model of Chapter 8 to address these and several other important questions. It shows, for instance, that to a large extent the current-account deficit is a *consequence* of the fiscal deficit and that another consequence of the fiscal deficit is slower economic growth.

# 6

# MACROECONOMIC GOALS AND MEASURES

J ust as doctors take a patient's temperature to help determine just how sick the patient is, economists use statistics to get a quantitative measure of the economy's performance. This chapter introduces the major statistics that summarize the overall condition of the economy. In studying these measures, economists look for patterns. Are good years regularly followed by lean years? Does inflation usually accompany high employment levels? If they find patterns, they analyze them.

This chapter also discusses problems of measurement that affect almost every economic variable. It often means little when the rate of unemployment or inflation changes by a few tenths of a percent, just as there is rarely cause for alarm when a person's temperature changes by a tenth of a degree. But over time the statistics describing the economy may change more dramatically. When unemployment statistics show an increase from 5 percent to 10 percent—a change from 1 out of 20 workers without jobs to 1 out of 10— few would doubt that there has been a sizable increase in unemployment.

The sections below discuss unemployment, inflation, and growth, and explain how each is measured.

KEY QUESTIONS

**1** What are the main objectives of macroeconomic policy?

**2** How are unemployment, output, growth, and inflation measured?

**3** What are some of the central problems in measuring these variables?

## THE THREE MACROECONOMIC ILLS

Chapter 1 characterized the economy in terms of a set of interconnected labour, product, and capital markets. The circular flow diagram shows firms obtaining labour and capital from households and using it to produce goods, which are then sold to households, who buy the goods with the income they earn providing labour and capital to firms. Given these interconnections, it is not surprising that problems in one part of the economy may be manifested in other parts. The "symptoms" in one part may indicate disease elsewhere in the system.

Later chapters will enable us to understand the entire system. Here we focus on the symptoms, each of which is most closely associated with a particular part of the system.

In the 1993 federal election, the Liberals under Jean Chrétien campaigned on a slogan of "Jobs, Jobs, Jobs" and won handily. The Canadian economy seemed stuck in a prolonged slowdown. The **unemployment rate,** the percentage of willing workers unable to find a job, seemed stuck at around 10 percent since the recession of the early 1980s, and that was high by historical standards. Moreover, many existing workers faced the threat of displacement as the economy adjusted to increased competitive pressures from abroad, and anxiety was especially rife among young people entering the work force for the first time. As we have learned, the basic competitive model says that when the economy is in equilibrium, there is full employment of all resources. But in the early 1990s, a significant part of our most important resources—our human resources—was idle. Demand did not equal supply in the labour market.

A few years earlier, policy makers had worried about another problem: **inflation,** or rising prices. These price increases were moderate by historical standards—about 5 percent a year. But policy makers feared that if left unchecked, the inflation rate would grow. At the beginning of the 1980s, inflation had hit double-digit levels (12.9 percent in 1981). Still, the Canadian experience had been tame compared to that in some other countries. In Ukraine, the inflation rate recently hit 10,000 percent a year! Demand and supply of goods in the product market was not in equilibrium at a stable price level. Instead, prices continued to increase.

Although we may focus on unemployment or inflation at any given moment, the real long-run concern is living standards. By the early 1970s, average Canadians not only expected their children to enjoy better living standards, but also expected their own incomes to rise continually over time—a pattern that had held true for more than a century. But things started unraveling around 1973. Average family incomes stagnated, and incomes at the lower part of the income distribution fell, sometimes dramatically. The problem was inadequate **economic growth,** due partly to insufficient amounts of money going from the capital market to fund new investments and new innovations.

These three ills—unemployment, inflation, and lack of growth—are the diseases that our macroeconomic doctors are constantly trying to cure, with varying degrees of success.

## GROWTH

For generations, Canadians had simply taken for granted that each generation would be better off than the previous one. Wages were increasing, and

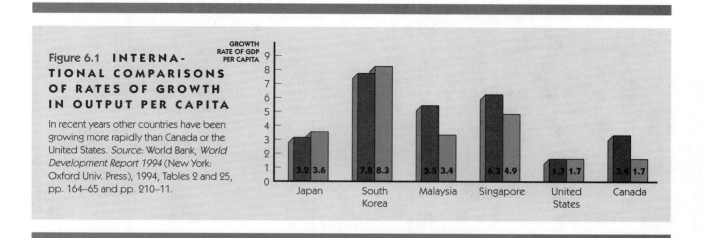

**Figure 6.1 INTERNATIONAL COMPARISONS OF RATES OF GROWTH IN OUTPUT PER CAPITA**

In recent years other countries have been growing more rapidly than Canada or the United States. *Source:* World Bank, *World Development Report 1994* (New York: Oxford Univ. Press), 1994, Tables 2 and 25, pp. 164–65 and pp. 210–11.

GROWTH RATE OF GDP PER CAPITA

| | Japan | South Korea | Malaysia | Singapore | United States | Canada |
|---|---|---|---|---|---|---|
| | 3.2 3.6 | 7.8 8.3 | 5.5 3.4 | 6.3 4.9 | 1.7 1.7 | 3.4 1.7 |

each successive generation could enjoy both higher incomes and more leisure than the previous one. Growth in Canada was rapid in the first half of the twentieth century, owing to the discovery and exploitation of natural resources and westward expansion fueled by high levels of immigration. The resource-based growth spread into the manufacturing sectors as well, largely financed by foreign investment. Compared to most European and Asian countries, rates of growth were high. The continued increases in productivity, measured as output per hour, provided the basis for continued increases in standards of living. There was a widely held feeling among Canadians that "the future belonged to Canada." The benefits of high growth were spread among all segments of society, including the poorest, by a combination of rising wages and the institution of many social programmes.

Beginning around 1973, doubts arose concerning these expectations. The rate of increase in productivity growth slowed down: from around 4 percent per year from 1960 to 1973, to about 1 percent by 1993. These changes were reflected in stagnation in real wages—wages adjusted for the effects of increasing prices. In fact, average real wages in the manufacturing sector have been virtually stagnant since the late 1970s.

A country's annual growth rate is the rate of change of its total output over the year. In comparing growth rates across countries—as well as comparing growth rates within the same country over time—we have to adjust for differences in population. To make such comparisons we measure individual output, or **output per capita.** To calculate output per capita simply divide the total output by the population. As Figure 6.1 shows, Japan and several other countries experienced far more rapid growth in output than Canada and the United States. For years, North Americans could take comfort in the idea that they were simply catching up. But by the 1980s, in some industries productivity in Japan exceeded that in North America. Particularly worrisome for Canada is that our growth rate declined by one half from the 1970s to the 1980s.

## MEASURING OUTPUT

The output of the economy consists of millions of different goods. We could report how much of each good the economy produced: 1,362,478 hammers, 473,562,382 potatoes, 7,875,342 wristwatches, and so forth. Such data may be useful for some purposes, but they do not provide us with the information we want. If next year the output of hammers goes up by 5 percent, the output of potatoes goes down by 2 percent, and the output of wristwatches rises by 7 percent, has total output gone up or down? And by how much?

We need a single number that summarizes the

**USING ECONOMICS: CALCULATING REAL GDP**

Earlier we distinguished between real and nominal GDP. Now we can demonstrate the calculation for real GDP.

Between 1993 and 1994 nominal GDP rose from $712,855 million to $750,053 million, but the rate of change in the general price level for all goods and services (the GDP deflator) went up from 126.9 to 128.0, taking 1986 as a base year. What was the percentage increase in real GDP?

Nominal GDP increased by 5.2 percent ($100 \times \left[ \frac{750,053}{712,855} - 1 \right]$), and the price level increased by .9 percent ($100 \times \left[ \frac{128}{126.9} - 1 \right]$).

Percent change in real GDP = Percent change in nominal GDP − Percent change in price level

| 4.3 | = | 5.2 | − | .9 |

output of the economy. But how do we add up the hammers, potatoes, wristwatches, and millions of other products produced in the economy? We do this by adding the money value of all the final goods and services (those that are not used to make other goods and services) produced and arriving at a single number that encapsulates the production of the economy. This number is called the **gross domestic product,** or **GDP.** It is the standard measure of the output of an economy, and sums up the total money value of the goods and services produced by the residents of a nation during a specified period. GDP includes everything from buttons to air travel, and from haircuts to barrels of oil. It makes no difference whether the production takes place in the public or private sector, or whether the goods and services are purchased by households or by government.[1]

There is one problem with using money as a measure of output. The value of a dollar changes over time. Chocolate bars, books, movie tickets, hammers—all cost more today than they did ten years

ago. Another way of saying this is that a dollar does not buy as much now as it did ten years ago. We do not want to be misled into believing that the output is higher when in fact only the price level has risen.

To keep the comparisons of different years straight, economists adjust GDP for changes in the average level of prices. Unadjusted GDP is known as **nominal GDP.** The term **real GDP** is used for inflation-adjusted GDP figures, which are truer year-to-year measures of what the economy actually produces. To calculate real GDP, economists take the nominal value of GDP—the money value of all the goods and services produced in the economy—and divide it by a measure of the price level. Thus, real GDP is defined by the equation

$$\text{real GDP} = \frac{\text{nominal GDP}}{\text{price level}}.$$

If nominal GDP has risen 3 percent in the past year but inflation has also increased prices by 3 percent, then real GDP is unchanged. If nominal GDP has risen 3 percent in the past year but prices have increased by 6 percent, real GDP has actually decreased. Later in the chapter, we will see how to adjust for changes in the price level.

[1] We use prices not only because they are a convenient way of making comparisons, but also because prices reflect how consumers value different goods. If the price of an orange is twice that of an apple, it means an orange is worth twice as much (at the margin) as an apple.

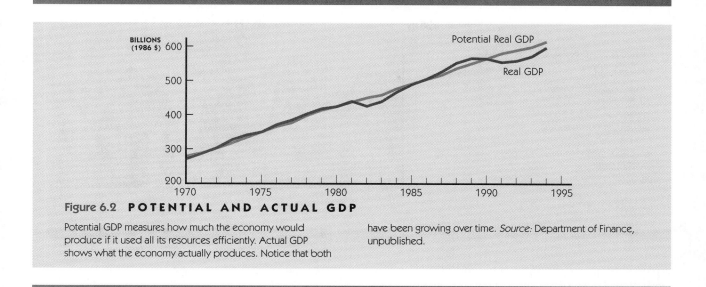

**Figure 6.2  POTENTIAL AND ACTUAL GDP**

Potential GDP measures how much the economy would produce if it used all its resources efficiently. Actual GDP shows what the economy actually produces. Notice that both have been growing over time. *Source:* Department of Finance, unpublished.

## POTENTIAL GDP

GDP measures how much the economy actually produces. But the economy is generally capable of producing more than it actually does. Another measure, **potential GDP,** indicates what the economy *could* produce if labour and machines were used fully to their capacity.

Figure 6.2 shows how potential (real) GDP and actual (real) GDP have increased over the past quarter century.[2] Output does not grow smoothly, and there have been periods in which actual output has been far below potential output. The jagged progression in the figure shows the effect of short-term fluctuations around an upwards trend. Sometimes these fluctuations represent only a slowdown in the rate of growth; sometimes output actually falls. The dips in real GDP from 1981 to 1982 and from 1990 to 1991 represent periods when Canada's economic output actually declined. Strong upwards fluctuations are called **booms,** and downwards ones are called **recessions.** Severe downturns are referred to as **depressions.** The last depression, called the Great Depression because of its length and depth, began in 1929. The economy did not fully recover from it until World War II. There is no technical definition of a boom, but there is one of a recession; a recession is said to have occurred when GDP falls for at least two consecutive quarters. (For statistical purposes, the year is divided into quarters.)

The economy's fluctuations are sometimes referred to as **business cycles** but the term "cycle" suggests a degree of regularity that is not really present: though it is true that every so often the economy has a downturn, the time between one **trough,** the bottom of a recession, and another, or one **peak,** the top of a boom, and another is highly variable, from just a couple of years, to as many as eight. Indeed, the likelihood of a downturn in the economy after, say, five years from the previous trough is no

[2] Figure 6.2 shows actual GDP exceeding potential GDP in a few years. How is this possible, if potential GDP really measures what the economy *could* produce? The answer is that the estimates of potential GDP are based on assumptions about "normal" levels of unemployment and on the fact that even when the economy is quite strong, some capacity is not fully utilized. In fact, for short spurts of time, such as when a country goes to war, actual GDP can exceed estimates of potential GDP by a considerable amount.

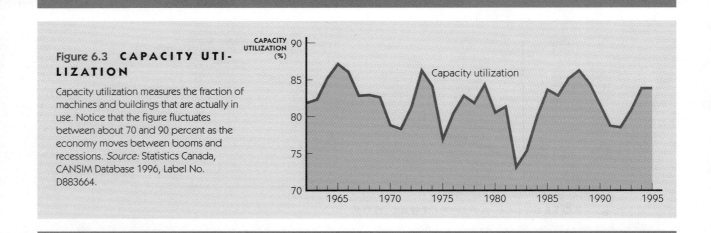

**Figure 6.3 CAPACITY UTILIZATION**

Capacity utilization measures the fraction of machines and buildings that are actually in use. Notice that the figure fluctuates between about 70 and 90 percent as the economy moves between booms and recessions. *Source:* Statistics Canada, CANSIM Database 1996, Label No. D883664.

greater than, say, three years from the previous trough, and even using sophisticated statistical models, economists find it difficult to predict the next turning point in the economy.

In recessions the economy operates well below its potential. Unemployment is high and a large fraction of machines remain idle. Figure 6.3 shows the percentage of Canada's industrial capacity that was utilized for the past several decades. The figures vary from slightly more than 70 percent of industrial capacity in a recession to almost 90 percent of industrial capacity in a boom. The economy never shows a 100 percent capacity-utilization rate because some machines are being repaired and maintained, while others are idle because they are not suited for the economy's current structure. Low capacity utilization—like unemployment of workers—represents a waste of scarce economic resources.

## MEASURING GDP: THE VALUE OF OUTPUT

There are three approaches to measuring GDP (whether real or nominal), all of which yield the same result. Two concentrate on output data. The third—relying on the fact that the value of all output becomes income to someone—uses income figures to obtain a measure of output.

### THE FINAL GOODS APPROACH

On the face of it, measuring GDP is a straightforward task, albeit massive. One gathers together the dollar values of all goods and services sold in a country, and then adds them up. Unfortunately, matters are not this simple, because it is first necessary to distinguish between final goods and intermediate goods. Final goods are those that are sold to consumers—like automobiles, books, bread, and shoes. Intermediate goods are those that are used to produce outputs—such as coal when it is used to make steel, or apples when they are used to make applesauce. A good such as an apple can be either a final or an intermediate good, depending on how it is used. The **final goods approach** to GDP adds up the total dollar value of goods and services produced, categorized by their ultimate users.

The reason it is so important to distinguish between final and intermediate goods is that the value of final goods *includes* the value of the intermediate goods that went into making them. When Ford Canada sells a car for $20,000, that figure may include $400 worth of Uniroyal tires. It would be double counting to list in GDP the revenues of both the car maker and the tire producer. Likewise for the steel, plastic, and other components that go into the car. In fact, cases where some intermediate goods are used to produce other intermediate goods could even lead to triple or quadruple counting.

One way of calculating the value of the final goods of the economy is to consider where those goods go. There are four possibilities. Some final goods are consumed by individuals—we call this aggregate **consumption,** and we include all consumption goods and services, regardless of where they are produced. Some are used by firms to build buildings and make machines—this is called aggregate **investment;** again, we include all investment goods, regardless of where they are produced. Some are purchased by government, and are called **government spending.** And some of the goods, called **exports,** go abroad. If we didn't import (buy from abroad) any goods, then GDP would simply consist of goods that went for private consumption, private investment, to the government, or for export. But not all the consumption or investment or what the government purchases is produced at home. To account for imports when we calculate GDP we have to subtract the amount imported. Thus,

$$GDP = C + I + G + X - M$$

where $C$ = consumption, $I$ = investment, $G$ = government purchases, $X$ = exports, and $M$ = imports. The difference between exports and imports is referred to as **net exports.** Thus, GDP equals consumption plus investment plus government expenditures plus net exports.

### THE VALUE-ADDED APPROACH

A second way to calculate the value of GDP is to study the intermediate goods and services directly. The production of most items occurs in several stages. Consider the automobile. At one stage in its production, iron ore, coal, and limestone are mined. At a second stage, these raw materials are shipped to a steel mill. At a third stage a steel company combines these ingredients to make steel. Finally, the steel and other inputs, such as rubber and plastics, are combined by the automobile firm to make a car. The difference in value between what the automaker pays for intermediate goods and what it receives for the finished cars is called the firm's **value added.**

$$\text{Value added} = \text{firm's revenues} - \text{cost of intermediate goods.}$$

GDP can be measured by calculating the value added at each stage of production.

GDP = sum of value added of all firms.

### THE INCOME APPROACH

The third method used to calculate GDP involves measuring the income generated by selling products, rather than the value of the products themselves. This is known as the **income approach.** Firms do five things with their revenues. They pay for labour, they pay interest, they buy intermediate goods, they pay indirect taxes such as excise taxes, and what is left over they enjoy as profits.

$$\text{Revenues} = \text{wages} + \text{interest payments} + \text{cost of intermediate inputs} + \text{indirect taxes} + \text{profits.}$$

But we already know that the firm's value added is its revenue minus the cost of intermediate goods. Therefore, value added = wages + interest payments + indirect taxes + profits. And since the value of GDP is equal to the sum of the value added of all firms, GDP must also equal the sum of the value of all wage payments, interest payments, indirect taxes, and profits for all firms:

$$\text{GDP} = \text{wages} + \text{interest payments} + \text{indirect taxes} + \text{profits.}$$

People receive income from wages, from capital, and from profits of the firms they own or own shares in. Thus, the right-hand side of this identity is the total income of all individuals plus government revenue from indirect taxes. This is an extremely important result, one economists uses frequently, so it is worth highlighting: *aggregate output equals aggregate income.*

***Differences between Individual Incomes and National Income*** The notion of income used above to calculate GDP differs slightly from the way individuals commonly perceive income, and it is important to be aware of the distinction.

First, people are likely to include in their view of income any capital gains they earn. Capital gains are

Gross domestic product is a way of adding up the value of the millions of goods and services produced in an economy. But creating that single number requires making difficult decisions. Here are some of the problems:

*Measuring Quality Changes*   A tomato today is very similar to a tomato fifty years ago, but an automobile today is very different from one even twenty years ago. With some products, quality (and price) changes almost every year.

GDP statisticians try to make adjustments for changes in quality. For example, when antipollution devices were first required in automobiles in the early 1970s, the price of cars rose. Statisticians decided that the increased cost was a quality improvement and effectively adding to real output, since consumers were buying a "better" car.

*Measuring Government Services*   The standard GDP calculation measures price and quantity at the point of sale. But what about goods that are not sold, at least not directly?

One important category of such goods is government-produced services. Imagine that provincial government bureaucrats become more efficient and are able to process automobile registrations faster. This might mean that the province can hire fewer workers to do the same job. But GDP statistics simply reflect the number of hours worked by government officials, not the actual value of what they produce. If the government becomes more efficient, measured GDP might go down, even though actual output—the number of registrations—increases.

*Measuring Nonmarketed Goods*   Nonmarketed goods and services, like housework done by family members, present similar problems. The statistics underestimate the true level of production in the economy, because they ignore such economic activity. If one spouse stays at home and cleans and cooks, that is not measured in GDP. However, if that spouse leaves home to take a job and hires someone else to do the cleaning and cooking, then both the spouse and the housekeeper are measured in GDP.

*The Magnitude of Statistical Problems*   How important are these difficulties in measurement? One indication may be obtained from estimates of the value of household work in Canada. Since household work does not involve any market transactions, its economic value cannot be measured directly using wage payments. Instead, studies of the value of work done in the household obtain indirect measures by one of two methods.

The first, called the *replacement cost* method, estimates the value of household work by using the hourly wage rates for specific forms of household work that are performed as paid jobs. Examples include food preparation, cleaning, child care, and the like. This method assumes that household work and market replacements are equally productive. The second, called the *opportunity cost* method, assumes that paid work is given up when one chooses to do household work. It uses average hourly employment earnings to evaluate household work.

The value of household work in 1992 was estimated by Statistics Canada to be 41.4 percent of GDP when the replacement cost method was used and 30.6 percent of GDP when the opportunity cost method was used. These numbers have been declining gradually over the past thirty years as the participation rate of married women in the labour force has increased. Whichever measure you prefer, this reflects the fact that a significant amount of productive work is being done outside the market.

*Source:* William Chandler, "The Value of Household Work in Canada, 1992," *Canadian Economic Observer*, April 1994, pp. 3.1–3.9.

increases in the value of assets, and accordingly do not represent production (output) in any way. The national income accounts used to calculate GDP, which are designed to focus on the production of goods and services, do not include capital gains.

Second, profits that are retained by a firm are included in national income, but individuals may not perceive these retained profits as part of their own income. Again, this is because the GDP accounts measure the value of production, and profits are part of the value of production, whether those profits are actually distributed to shareholders or retained by firms.

## COMPARISON OF THE FINAL GOODS AND INCOME APPROACHES

Earlier we learned how to break down the output of the economy into four categories—consumption, investment, government expenditures, and net exports. We break down the income of the economy into three categories: payments to workers, consisting mainly of wages; payments to owners of capital, including profits, interest, and rents; and indirect taxes. As Table 6.1 shows, the value of GDP is the same, whether calculated in output or income terms: in 1994, Canadian GDP was approximately $750 billion.

## Table 6.1 TWO APPROACHES TO CANADIAN GDP, 1994 (IN $ BILLIONS)

| Final outputs | | Income | |
|---|---|---|---|
| Consumption | 453 | Employee compensation | 410 |
| Investment | 142 | Profits, rents, interest | 245 |
| Government expenditures | 151 | Indirect taxes | 94 |
| Exports | 249 | | |
| Imports | −244 | | |
| Error | −1 | Error | 1 |
| Total | 750 | Total | 750 |

*Source:* Statistics Canada, CANSIM Database 1996, Matrices 6701 and 6702.

That the value of output is equal to the value of income—that GDP measured either way is identical—is no accident. What each firm receives from selling its goods must go back somewhere else into the economy—as wages, profits, interest, or taxes. The income to households flows back in turn either to firms—as consumption goods and services households purchase or as savings, which eventually are used to purchase plant and equipment by firms—or to government, in the form of taxes or newly issued government bonds. Similarly, the money spent by the government must have come from somewhere else in the economy—either from households or corporations in the form of taxes, or through borrowing.

## ALTERNATIVE MEASURES OF OUTPUT

In an economy like Canada's, a substantial proportion of our purchases and sales are with foreigners. Different ways of taking account of this lead to different measures of output. Since GDP includes exports but excludes imports, it is a measure of all goods and services produced by Canadians, regardless of where they are eventually used. Quite naturally, this has been the standard measure of output used in Canada as well as in most European countries. But until 1991 the United States, for which international trade has been far less important, used **gross national product (GNP)** as its main statistical measure of output. GNP includes imports and excludes exports.

The basic difference between GDP and GNP is that GNP includes income that residents of a country receive from abroad (wages, returns on investment, interest payments), but excludes similar payments made by residents of a country to those abroad. By contrast, GDP ignores income received from or paid overseas. Thus, in the example of Table 6.1, the category of profits, rents, and interest includes all such amounts earned in Canada, regardless of whether they accrue to Canadians or foreigners. Similarly, on the final outputs side, exports are included and imports deducted. Imports must be deducted, since consumption, investment, and government expenditure measures will include in them some imported goods.

The treatment of machines and other capital goods (buildings) is another problem in measuring national output. Machines wear out, and worn-out machines are a cost of production that should be balanced against total output.

Consider a firm that has a machine worth $1,000 and uses that machine, with $600 of labour, to produce $2,000 worth of output. Furthermore, assume that at the end of the year the machine is completely worn out. The firm then has a *net* output of $400: $2,000 minus the labour costs *and* minus the value of the machine that has worn out.

The reduction in the value of the machine is called the machine's **depreciation.** Since machines wear out at all sorts of different rates, accounting for how much the machines in the economy have depreciated is an extremely difficult problem. The GDP figures take the easy road and make no allowance for depreciation. The term "gross" in "gross domestic product" should serve as a reminder that the statistic covers all production. Economists sometimes use a separate measure that includes the effects of depreciation, called **net domestic product (NDP),** which subtracts an estimate of the value of depreciation from GDP:

NDP = GDP – depreciation.

The problem is that economists have little confidence in the estimates of depreciation. For this reason they usually use the GDP figure as the measure of the economy's output. Since GDP, GNP, and NDP go up and down together, for most purposes, it does not much matter which one you use as long as you are consistent.

## UNEMPLOYMENT

Increasing living standards is the central economic goal over the long run, but when the economy goes into a downturn, unemployment becomes a source of immediate concern. To an economist, unemployment represents an underutilization of resources. People who are willing and able to work are not being productively employed. To the unemployed individuals and their families, unemployment represents economic hardship and changes in their way of life. If a person is unemployed for a long time, he will be unable to meet his current expenses—like utilities and rent—and will have to move to cheaper housing and reduce other aspects of his standard of living.

Unemployment not only costs individuals their pay-cheques, but also can deal a powerful blow to their self-respect. Unemployed workers in today's urban Canada cannot fall back on farming or living off the land as they might have done in earlier times. Instead, they and their families may be forced to choose between poverty and the bitter taste of government or private charity. Many of these families break up under the strain.

Unemployment presents different problems for each age group of workers. For the young, having a job is necessary for developing job skills, whether they are technical skills or such basic work prerequisites as punctuality and responsibility. For them persistent unemployment not only wastes valuable human resources today but also reduces the future productivity of the labour force. Furthermore, young people who remain unemployed for an extended period are especially prone to becoming alienated from society and turning to antisocial activities such as crime and drugs.

For the middle-aged or elderly worker, losing a job poses different problems. Despite prohibitions against age discrimination in the Charter of Rights and Freedoms, employers are often hesitant to hire an older worker. They may fear she is more likely to become sick or disabled than a younger person is. They may worry about being able to "teach old dogs new tricks." If older workers are unemployed for long periods of time, they may have lost some of their skills. Even if the unemployed older worker succeeds in getting a job, it often entails reduced wages and lower status than in her previous job and may make less than full use of her skills. The toll of such changes is a heavy burden of stress on the newly reemployed worker and her family.

In addition to these personal losses, unemployment poses heavy costs for communities. If people in a town are thrown out of work—say, because a big employer closes down or decides to move—everyone else in town is likely to suffer as well, since there will be fewer dollars circulating to buy everything from cars and houses to gasoline and groceries. As more unemployment results in fewer people paying local taxes, the quality of schools, libraries, parks, and police can be threatened.

Unemployment may also reinforce racial or ethnic tensions in society as a whole. The unemployment rate for aboriginal persons is more than twice that of whites, and that for blacks is almost as high. The differential is even higher for younger persons. Even among white groups, those of different ethnic backgrounds have quite different unemployment rates. For example, according to the 1986 census, the unemployment rate of persons of French origins was 11.77 percent, compared with 8.06 percent for those from other Western European backgrounds.

Unemployment thus represents a tragedy for the individual and the family, a source of dislocation and stress for a community, and a waste of productive resources for society as a whole.

## THE MAGNITUDE OF THE PROBLEM

The Canadian economy is what happens when 13 million people get up and go to work. A neat shorthand description, but not quite complete. Living in the midst of those who have jobs is a fluctuating group of hundreds of thousands of healthy people who do not. During the recession year of 1991, 1.3 million people were out of a job, and one fourth of those people were out of work for 15 weeks or more. From the standpoint of the economy as a whole, the unused potential production of workers who cannot find jobs is a major loss. A simple calculation, based on the difference in the unemployment rate in 1982–85 and the average rate in the surrounding years, puts the loss in GDP from the high unemployment of the early 1980s at roughly $15 billion per year, for a per capita loss of about $800. That means that every man, woman, and child in Canada would have had on average an additional $800 to spend if the extra unemployed workers had been gainfully employed.

## UNEMPLOYMENT STATISTICS

In Canada, unemployment data are collected by Statistics Canada, which surveys a representative mix of households and asks each whether a member of the household is currently seeking employment. The unemployment rate is the ratio of the number seeking employment to the total labour force. If there are 12 million Canadians employed and 1 million say they are looking for a job but cannot find one, then the total labour force is 13 million, and the

$$\text{unemployment rate} = \frac{\text{number unemployed}}{\text{labour force}}$$

$$= \frac{\text{number unemployed}}{\text{number employed} + \text{number unemployed}}$$

$$= \frac{1 \text{ million}}{12 \text{ million} + 1 \text{ million}} = 7.7 \text{ percent}.$$

Figure 6.4 plots the unemployment rate for Canada since 1966. The figure illustrates two facts. First, unemployment is persistent. Second, the level of unemployment can fluctuate dramatically. In the worst days of the Great Depression, almost one fifth of the Canadian labour force was unemployed. As recently as March 1983, the unemployment rate reached 13.9 percent. The level of unemployment in the late 1980s, at about 8 percent, while much lower than that of the early 1980s, is still higher than the rate that prevailed in the mid-1960s, around 3 percent. In the early 1990s, unemployment rates have again reached double-digit levels.

Unemployment in Canada has often been much worse than in the United States (Figure 6.5), but it has been comparable to that elsewhere in the world. In European countries, unemployment reached over 10 percent during much of the 1980s, and in many developing countries over 20 percent.

## PROBLEMS WITH THE UNEMPLOYMENT STATISTICS

Some economists believe that the Statistics Canada unemployment survey provides too high an estimate of the true unemployment rate. Some suggest that the number of households reporting an unemployed

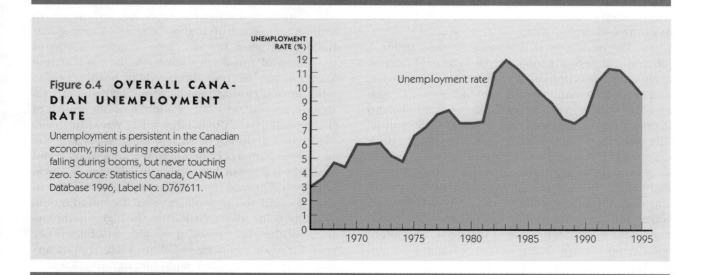

**Figure 6.4 OVERALL CANADIAN UNEMPLOYMENT RATE**

Unemployment is persistent in the Canadian economy, rising during recessions and falling during booms, but never touching zero. *Source:* Statistics Canada, CANSIM Database 1996, Label No. D767611.

Figure 6.5 **INTERNATIONAL UNEMPLOYMENT COMPARISONS**

The Canadian unemployment rate is comparable to that of Western European countries; over the past decade it has been much higher than that in the United States. *Source: Economic Report of the President (1995),* Table B-111.

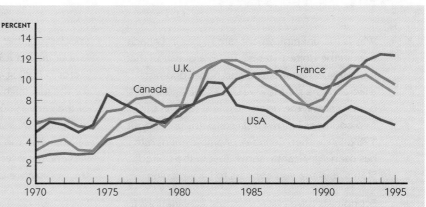

worker depends on who is asked. If the mother of a teenager is asked, she may report that her son is seeking a job, but the teenager may not view himself as actively seeking employment. Others believe the survey's estimate is too low. Some workers who want jobs may have abandoned hope of finding a job. They are referred to as **discouraged workers.** The statistics will not count them as unemployed, and thus will provide an underestimate of the number who would choose to work if a job were available. The fraction of the working-age population that is employed or seeking employment is called the **labour force participation rate.** Because of discouraged workers, the labour force participation rate tends to decline in recessions.

Despite these ambiguities, when the unemployment rate increases by more than a trivial amount, it is safe to conclude that the economy has slowed down. Some individuals have been laid off and have not found new jobs, and firms may have slowed down the pace at which they hire new workers.

## FORMS OF UNEMPLOYMENT

Economists distinguish among different kinds of unemployment. Right before Christmas there is a huge demand for retail salespeople to work in department stores and shopping malls across the country. In many parts of the country, construction slows down in the winter because of the climate. Also because of weather, tourism often increases in the summer, and so does the number of jobs that cater to tourists. The supply of labour also increases in the summer, as high school and university students enter the labour force on a temporary basis. Unemployment that varies with the season is called **seasonal unemployment.** Since these movements in employment and unemployment reflect normal seasonal patterns, the unemployment rate you see reported on the news is adjusted according to the average amount of seasonal unemployment. These adjustments are called seasonal adjustments. Thus, if the average unadjusted unemployment rate is normally .4 percent higher in the summer than at other times, the seasonally adjusted unemployment rate for July will be the measured unemployment rate minus .4 percent.

While workers in construction, agriculture, and tourism regularly face seasonal unemployment, other workers become unemployed only as part of a normal transition from one job to another. This kind of unemployment is referred to as **frictional unemployment.** If people could move from job to job instantaneously, there would be no frictional unemployment. In a dynamic economy such as Canada's, with some industries growing and others declining, there will always be movements from one job to

## CLOSE-UP: THE UNEMPLOYMENT RATE GAP BETWEEN CANADA AND THE UNITED STATES

Why is the unemployment rate higher in Canada than in the United States? This is a question that has intrigued economists and noneconomists alike over the past few years. As the figure below shows, the unemployment rates in the two countries followed similar paths until about 1982. Since then Canada's unemployment rate has risen significantly above that in the United States, and the gap appears to be widening.

Economists have offered several explanations for this deviation. Some of these focus on the demand side of the labour market, arguing that willing workers in Canada find it more difficult to land a job than do those in the United States. One reason might be that the Canadian labour market, because it is so much smaller than the American market, is too "thin" to allow for as high a proportion of good matches between the unemployed and potential employers. This might explain the existence of a gap, but it does not explain why it only arose in the 1980s. One possibility might be that jobs are becoming more

specialized, and that the overall size of the labour market is becoming a more important factor in finding a good match. Another reason for the gap might be the fact that the recessions of the early 1980s and 1990s were more severe in Canada, thus leading to more unemployment. Again, while this may explain some temporary divergence, it is less satisfactory in accounting for the persistence of the gap.

Still others have argued that the higher levels of unemployment in Canada are a result of problems on the supply side of the labour market, due primarily to government policies. Higher minimum wage levels in Canada may explain some of the difference. Also, beginning in 1971 unemployment insurance benefits in Canada were made increasingly more generous and linked to the prevailing unemployment rate. This induces people to stay unemployed longer as they search for better matches. This disincentive effect should become less important given the recent changes in unemployment insurance in-

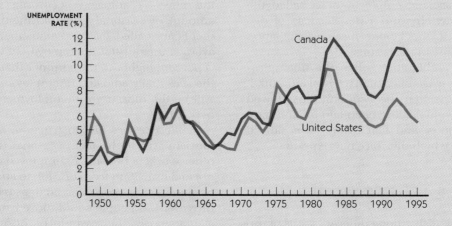

volving decreasing benefits and longer periods of work needed to qualify. If so, we should see the gap narrowing in the near future.

Recently it has been discovered that part of the gap in jobless rates is due simply to a discrepancy in the way unemployment is measured in the two countries. In Canada, if jobless people say they are searching for work yet do nothing more than read want ads, they are counted as being officially unemployed. In the United States, such "passive" job seekers are counted as being out of the labour force altogether, and therefore are not treated as unemployed. Statistics Canada has estimated that this difference accounts for almost one fifth of the difference in unemployment rates.

Sorting out the importance of these and possibly other reasons for the emergence of the unemployment gap is a topic of intense research. It is also of immense policy importance. The appropriate government policy response to addressing the gap clearly hinges on what is causing the gap in the first place.

*Sources:* Statistics Canada, CANSIM Database, 1996, Matrix 2075; U.S. Bureau of Labor Statistics, 1996, Series ID 21000000; Statistics Canada, *Historical Statistics of Canada,* 2nd ed., Ottawa, 1983; "Gap in Jobless Rate Still a Puzzle," *The Globe and Mail,* Feb. 12, 1996, pp. B1, B5.

another, and hence there will always be frictional unemployment.

Most bouts of unemployment are short-lived; the average person who loses a job is out of work for only three months. However, about 10 percent of the jobless have been unemployed for more than six months. This kind of long-term unemployment often results from structural factors in the economy, and is called **structural unemployment.** Substantial structural unemployment is quite often found side by side with job vacancies, because the unemployed lack the skills required for the newly created jobs. For example, there may be vacancies for computer programmers, while construction workers are unemployed. By the same token, there may be job shortages in those parts of the economy that are expanding (as in the West) and unemployment in areas that are suffering decline (as in southern Ontario during the period of decline in demand for North American cars).

The final kind of unemployment is the unemployment that increases when the economy goes into a slowdown and decreases when the economy goes into a boom. This is called **cyclical unemployment,** and is the fundamental concern of this part of the book. Government policy is particularly targeted towards reducing both the frequency and magnitude of this kind of unemployment, by reducing the frequency and magnitude of the recessions that give rise to it. Government also seeks to reduce its impact, by providing unemployment insurance for those temporarily thrown out of work.

## INFLATION

In the 1920s, the years of silent pictures, a movie ticket cost a nickel. By the late 1940s, in the heyday of Hollywood, the price was up to $.50. By the 1960s, the price of a movie was $2.00, and now it is about $8.00. This steady price rise is no anomaly. Most other goods have undergone similar increases over time. This increase in the general level of prices is called inflation. While unemployment tends to be concentrated in certain groups within the population, *everyone* of affected by inflation. Thus, it is not surprising that when inflation becomes high, it almost always rises to the top of the political agenda.

It is not inflation if the price of only one good goes

up. It *is* inflation if the prices of *most* goods go up. The **inflation rate** is the rate at which the *general level* of prices increases.

## MEASURING INFLATION

If the prices of all goods rose by the same proportion, say by 5 percent, over a period of a year, measuring inflation would be easy: the rate of inflation for that year would be 5 percent. The difficulties arise from the fact that the prices of different goods rise at different rates, and some goods even decline in price. Over the past twenty years, while the price of fruit has increased by 241 percent, the price of gasoline by 261 percent, and the price of health care by 242 percent, the price of computers has declined by over 90 percent! To determine the change in the overall price level, economists calculate the *average* percentage increase in prices. But since some goods loom much larger in the typical consumer's budget than others, this calculation must reflect the relative purchases of different goods. A change in the price of housing, for example, is much more important than a change in the price of pencils. If the price of pencils goes down by 5 percent but the price of housing goes up by 5 percent, the overall measure of the price level should go up.

Economists have a straightforward way of reflecting the differing importance of different goods. They ask, what would it cost consumers to purchase the same bundle of goods this year that they bought last year? If, for example, it cost $22,000 in 1996 to buy what it cost consumers only $20,000 to purchase in 1995, we say that prices, *on average,* have risen by 10 percent. Such results are frequently expressed in the form of a **price index,** which, for ease of comparison, measures the price level in any given year relative to a common base year.

The price index for the base year is, by definition, 100. The price index for any other year is calculated by taking the ratio of the price level in that year to the price level in the base year and multiplying it by 100. For example, if 1995 is our base year and we want to know the price index for 1996, we first calculate the ratio of the cost of a certain bundle of goods in 1996 ($22,000) to the cost of the same bundle of goods in 1995 ($20,000), which is 1.1. The price index in 1996 is therefore $1.1 \times 100 = 110$. The index of 110, using 1995 as a base, means that prices are 10 percent higher, on average, in 1996 than in 1995.

There are several different price indices, each using a different bundle of goods. To track the movement of prices that are important to Canadian households, the government collects price data on the bundle of goods that represents how the average Canadian household spends its income. This index is called the **consumer price index,** or CPI. To determine this bundle, the government, through Statistics Canada, conducts a Family Expenditure Survey, which is updated once a decade or so.

Other price indices are calculated using different market baskets. One such measure is the **industrial products price index,** which measures the average level of prices of goods sold by producers. This index is useful because it gives us an inkling of what will happen to consumer prices in the near future. Usually, if producers are receiving higher prices from wholesalers, in a short while retailers will have to charge higher prices. This will be reflected in a higher consumer price index.

Earlier in the chapter we observed that real GDP is nominal GDP divided by the price level. The price index we use for calculating real GDP is called the GDP deflator. It represents a comparison between what it costs to buy the total mix of final goods and services produced in the economy today and what it would cost using base year prices. It differs from the CPI in one significant way. While the latter uses a bundle of goods and services in the amounts purchased by an average consumer in the base year, the GDP deflator uses the bundle of goods and services produced by the economy in the current year. The GDP deflator for 1996 is the cost of the goods and services produced by the economy in 1996 divided by the cost of those same goods and services at 1986 prices. Calculating real GDP by dividing nominal GDP by the GDP deflator gives the real value of GDP today using base year prices.

This approach encounters a problem when relative prices change dramatically. If the price of computers should fall rapidly as the output of computers increases—as happened over the past two decades—then real output, using prices of an earlier

## USING ECONOMICS: CALCULATING THE CONSUMER PRICE INDEX

Encapsulating the movements of masses of prices into an index provides an easy way to look at price trends over time. Suppose that in 1986 it took $1,000 to buy a basket of goods purchased by the average Canadian family in a month. Assume that in 1996 it cost $1,340 to buy the same basket. Then the price index for 1996 is just a ratio of the cost in 1996 to the cost in the base year 1986, times 100. That is,

CPI for 1996 = 1,340/1,000 × 100 = 134.

The advantage of an index is that once we have an index number for any year, we can compare

it with any other year. The CPI for 1973 was 36, and for 1993 it was 130. Between those years, the index rose by 94, so the increase was

100 × 94/36 = 261 percent.

On average, prices rose by 261 percent from 1973 to 1993.

The figure below shows the level of the consumer price index from 1900 to the present, using 1983 as the base year.

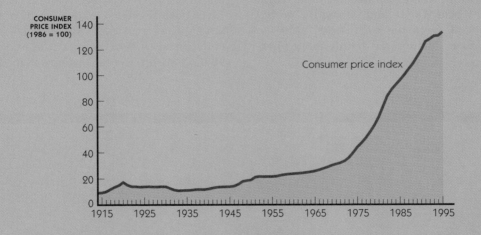

CONSUMER PRICE INDEX (1986 = 100)

Consumer price index

base year such as 1986, will look like it is increasing very rapidly. When the base year is changed—as is done periodically—the growth rate of the economy will appear to diminish suddenly. Of course, the growth rate of the economy did not really diminish; our yardstick just distorted the picture.

One way to mitigate this distortion is to calculate real GDP using a chain price index. Statistics Canada provides such a measure alongside the GDP price

deflator. The chain price index measures the change in prices between two consecutive periods using as weights the composition of goods and services produced in the first of the two periods. The change in price occurring over several consecutive periods is then the sum of the changes in each of the periods. Chain price indices for GDP are reported by Statistics Canada for two different reweighting periods, the year and the quarter. The price index calculated using a chain price index tends to be slightly higher than the GDP deflator. For example, the GDP deflator for 1995 was 127.6 (relative to a 1986 base year), while the chain price index reweighted annually was 129.6. So real GDP calculated using the chain price index as the price level would be slightly lower than it would be using the GDP deflator.

## THE CANADIAN EXPERIENCE WITH INFLATION

As we have learned, the inflation rate is the percentage increase in the price level from one year to the next. Figure 6.6 shows the inflation rate for Canada since 1915. Three interesting features stand out.

First, the inflation rate was relatively low for most of the period, with three exceptions: around World War I, around World War II, and during the period 1973–1982. Indeed, from the early 1920s until the early 1960s, average inflation ran at only about 1 percent per year.

Second, prices can actually come down. During the recession that followed World War I, prices fell by more than 25 percent, and in the Great Depression of the 1930s by more than 20 percent. It may seem hard to believe in an era when inflation seems the ever-present threat, but at the end of the nineteenth century, the concern was **deflation,** which is a steady decline of the price level. Borrowers at that time who were in debt and had not anticipated the fall in prices found that the real value of the dollars they had to pay back was worth far more than that of the dollars that they had borrowed. They were as upset about this as investors (lenders) are today when inflation makes the value of the dollars they get back from an investment or loan worth less than the value of the dollars they originally put in.

Finally, while prices on average have been stable and there have even been periods of price decline, there have also been a few periods of high inflation, when prices increased rapidly. The most notable recent episode was in the late 1970s and early 1980s. In 1981 alone, prices rose by more than 12 percent.

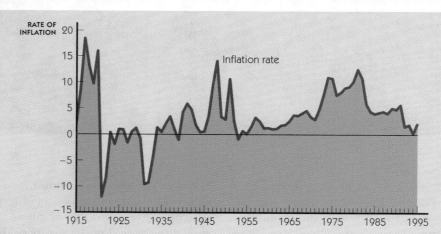

**Figure 6.6 THE INFLATION RATE, 1915–95**

The inflation rate is the percentage increase in the price level in a given year. Notice that inflation was low through most of the early part of this century (although high during World Wars I and II), rose sharply in the 1970s and early 1980s, and then fell somewhat in the later 1980s. *Source:* Statistics Canada, CANSIM Database, 1996, Label No. P700000.

## THE IMPORTANCE OF INFLATION

In modern economies, much has been done to ease the pain of inflation. For workers, rising levels of prices are usually accompanied by higher wages, and if a worker faces higher prices but has commensurately more money in her pocket, she is just as well off. Likewise, the Canadian government has taken steps to adjust the income of retirees to changes in the price level. Most significant, Old Age Security payments and other transfer programmes are now "indexed," that is, adjusted, to keep up with changes in the cost of living.

Why, then, does fighting inflation rank so high as a priority in economic policy? There seem to be three answers.

The first is that some groups still suffer. Anyone whose income does not adjust fully is made worse off by increases in the price level. Second, when the rate of inflation suddenly increases, those who have lent money find that the dollars they are being paid back with are worth less. Thus, creditors (those who lend money) are worse off, while debtors are better off. When the inflation rate varies, both borrowing and lending become riskier.

Third, many feel that something is fundamentally wrong with the economy when what cost $1 five years ago costs $2 today. Sometimes these observers are right. Inflation can reflect gross errors in government economic policy, such as spending that is far in excess of revenues, or excessive provision of credit. But frequently inflation gets the blame when something else is the underlying problem. The steep increase in oil prices in 1973 set off a worldwide inflationary spiral. With eastern Canadians paying more to the oil-exporting countries, that part of the country was, in a sense, poorer. Someone had to take a cut. Furthermore, the worldwide economic downturn set off by the 1973 oil price rise made the cut that had to be taken that much larger. Thus, workers' real wages fell. They blamed inflation for their declining standard of living. But inflation was not really the culprit—higher oil prices were.

As the economy has adapted to inflation, economists have increasingly debated about how concerned we should be about moderate rates of inflation—the 3 to 6 percent inflation that has occurred regularly during the past few decades. They worry that the cures for moderate inflation may be worse than the disease. Still, most economists think that double-digit inflation levels, at the very least, are symptomatic of some kind of malfunction in the economy. Certainly there is a consensus that the kinds of rapid inflation experienced in Israel and some Latin American countries are extremely disruptive to their economies.

## CONNECTING THE THREE MAJOR VARIABLES

Often the three major macroeconomic variables move together. For example, when the economy is in a recession, as it was in 1992, unemployment tends to be higher, inflation tends to be lower, and growth comes to a standstill. These connections make sense. After all, when the economy is suffering tough times, businesses reduce their output, lay off workers, and do not hire new workers. In addition, businesses that are having a hard time selling products in a competitive market are less likely to raise prices.

## FLOWS AND STOCKS

GDP, GNP, and NDP are all measures of output *per year*. Rate measurements such as these are called **flow statistics.** When a news report says, "The quarterly GDP statistic, just released, shows that GDP was $700 billion per year," it does not mean that $700 billion of goods and services was produced during the quarter. Rather, it means that $175 billion was produced during the quarter, so that if that rate of production was maintained for a whole year, the total value of goods and services would be $700 billion.

Flow statistics need to be contrasted with **stock statistics,** which measure an item at a single point in time. Among the most important stocks is the capital stock, the total value of all the buildings and machines that underlie the productive potential of the economy.

The relationships between stocks and flows are simple. The stock of capital at the end of 1996 con-

Price indices have increasingly come to play an important role in economic life, in spite of the dry technical flavour that seems to pervade them. Payments to the elderly under the Old Age Security and Canada Pension Plan systems increase with a cost-of-living index, the consumer price index (CPI). The tax brackets, personal exemptions, and tax credits under the income tax system are all adjusted by a factor based on the CPI.

It has long been recognized that the price index used by the federal government for adjusting both benefits and tax brackets is seriously flawed: it overstates the rate of inflation—increases in the cost of living—by up to 3 percent a year. If the CPI *overstates* increases in the cost of living, then indexing payments to the elderly to reflect fully changes in the CPI will cause the real value of the payments to increase in times of inflation. Similarly, fully indexing tax brackets, credits, and exemptions to the CPI will cause real inflation-adjusted tax revenues to decrease. Both distortions will increase the real budget deficit of the federal government—the first by increasing the real outlays, the second by reducing the real receipts of the government.

The upward bias stems from three problems. The first is the "fixed basket problem." Price indices are generally calculated by comparing how much it costs to purchase a particular market basket of goods that represents an average consumers' expenditure pattern. But expenditure patterns change steadily over time, while the market basket is revised only infrequently. As people buy more of the goods that have become relatively less expensive, and less of the goods that have become relatively more expen-

sive, the index increasingly overweights goods whose prices are rising.

The second major problem is "quality adjustments." New products that can do new and better things than older products constantly enter the market. To compare the prices of the new products with the old, some quality adjustment must be made. If the price goes up by 10 percent but the product lives longer and does what it is supposed to do better, in a real sense the price increase is less than 10 percent and may even be a price reduction. The quality adjustments may sometimes be easy: one machine can do what two machines did before. But usually the comparisons are difficult. If we measure quality of computers by calculations per minute, memory, and disk storage, the rate of decrease in computer prices is phenomenal. But even this does not fully reflect the quality improvement. We can do things with the computer now that were unimaginable twenty-five years ago at any price. And how do we treat a new drug that cures a disease that was previously incurable? Statistics Canada tries to make adjustments for quality. But the consensus is that these adjustments are imperfect and do not offset this second source of overestimation in the inflation rate.

The third problem is technical, having to do with the way the data are collected and the details of the calculation. For example, if 20 percent of the stores are offering a 50 percent discount on an item selling for $100, the average price, *weighted by the number of stores,* is $.2 \times \$50 + .8 \times \$100 = \$90$. But if these discount stores sell 50 percent of the items, then the average price, *weighted by sales,* is really $.5 \times \$50 + .5 \times \$100 = \$75$. Insufficient weight given to the prices of discounted sales at which purchases actually occur results in another upward bias.

The federal government recognized these problems long ago. Beginning in 1986, the inflation factor used to index the tax brackets, exemptions, and credits in the income tax system was reduced from the full change in the CPI to the change in the CPI less 3 percent. In years like 1994 and 1995, when the inflation rate was less than 3 percent, no indexation had to be done. But when the government tried to apply the same logic to Old Age Security benefits, the public outcry was so great that they abandoned the attempt.

sists of the stock of capital at the end of 1995 plus or minus the flows into or out of this stock during 1996. Investment is the flow into the capital stock. Depreciation is the flow out of the capital stock.

Similarly, we can look at the *number* of unemployed individuals as a stock. This number at the end of 1996 consists of the number at the end of 1995 plus or minus the flows into or out of the unemployment pool during 1996. Layoffs, firings, resignations, and new entry into the labour force can be thought of as flows into the unemployment pool; new hires represent flows out of the unemployment pool.

# REVIEW AND PRACTICE

## SUMMARY

**1** The three central macroeconomic policy objectives of the government are low unemployment, low inflation, and high growth. Macroeconomics studies how these aggregate variables change as a result of household and business behaviour, and how government policy may affect them.

**2** Gross domestic product (GDP) is the typical way of measuring national output. Real GDP adjusts GDP for changes in the price level.

**3** GDP can be calculated in three ways: the final goods approach, which adds the value of all final goods produced in the economy; the value-added approach, which adds the difference between firms' revenues and costs of intermediate goods; and the income approach, which adds together all income received by those in the economy. All three methods give the same answer.

**4** Productivity—real GDP per hour worked—has not been increasing as rapidly in Canada in the last two decades as it did earlier. This is reflected in stagnating real average wages, and real wages of the less skilled are actually declining.

**5** Unemployment imposes costs both on individuals and on society as a whole, which loses what the unemployed workers could have contributed and ends up supporting them in other ways.

**6** Seasonal unemployment occurs regularly depending on the season; for example, construction is seasonal in areas with harsh winters. Frictional unemployment results from people being in transition between one job and another. Structural unemployment refers to the unemployment generated as the structure of the economy changes, with the new jobs being created having requirements different from the old jobs being lost. Cyclical unemployment increases or decreases with the level of economic activity.

**7** The inflation rate is the percentage increase in the price level from one year to the next. Canadian inflation was low through most of the early part of this century, rose sharply in the 1970s and early 1980s, and then fell somewhat in the later 1980s and early 1990s. In different countries at different times, inflation has sometimes been very high, with prices increasing by factors of tens or hundreds in a given year.

**8** The amount of inflation between two years is measured by the percentage change in the amount it would cost to buy a given basket of goods in those years. Different baskets define different price indices, such as the consumer price index, the producer price index, and the GDP deflator.

**9** Economists seek to understand why many macroeconomic variables seem to move together. For example, in a boom, unemployment tends to fall, inflation tends to rise, and productivity tends to rise. In a recession, the reverse happens.

## KEY TERMS

discouraged workers

labour force participation rate

inflation rate

deflation

gross domestic product (GDP)

nominal and real GDP

potential GDP

boom

recession

depression

gross national product (GNP)

net domestic product (NDP)

productivity, or GDP capita

seasonal unemployment

frictional unemployment

structural unemployment

cyclical unemployment

consumer price index (CPI)

GDP deflator

## REVIEW QUESTIONS

**1** What are the three main goals of macroeconomic policy?

**2** What is the difference between nominal GDP, real GDP, and potential GDP?

**3** What is the difference between the final outputs approach to measuring GDP, the value-added approach, and the income approach?

**4** What is the difference between GDP, GNP, and NDP?

**5** What has happened in the last two decades to the rate of change of productivity? to average real wages? to wages of the least skilled?

**6** What is the difference between frictional unemployment, seasonal unemployment, and structural unemployment?

**7** When there is a reduction in the number of hours worked in the economy, is this normally shared equally by all workers? Are workers in some groups more impacted by increased unemployment than those in other groups?

**8** When the prices of different goods change at different rates, how do we measure the rate of inflation?

**9** Are all groups of people affected equally by inflation? Why or why not?

## PROBLEMS

**1** Which would you expect to fall fastest in a recession, real GDP or potential GDP? Could potential GDP rise while real GDP fell?

**2** Explain how these two factors would have different effects on real GDP per capita and real GDP per hour worked:
  (a)  people working longer weeks
  (b)  a larger proportion of adults holding jobs

**3** Geoffrey spends his allowance on three items: chocolate candy, magazines, and renting VCR movies. He is currently receiving an allowance of $30 per month, which he is using to rent 4 movies at $2 apiece, buy 10 chocolate bars at $1 apiece, and purchase 4 magazines at $3 apiece. Calculate a Geoffrey price index (GPI) for this basket of goods, with the current price level equal to 100, in the following cases.
  (a)  The price of movies rises to $3.
  (b)  The price of movies rises to $3, and the price of chocolate bars falls by $.20.
  (c)  The price of movies rises to $3, the price of chocolate bars falls by $.20, and the price of magazines rises to $4.

**4** An increase in the consumer price index will often affect different groups in different ways. Think about how different groups will purchase items like housing, travel, or education in the CPI basket, and explain why they will be affected differently by increases in the overall CPI. How would you calculate an "urban CPI" or a "rural CPI"?

**5** Given the information below about the Canadian economy, how much did real GDP grow between 1965 and 1975? between 1975 and 1985?

|      | Nominal GDP (billions) | Consumer price index |
|------|------------------------|----------------------|
| 1965 | $ 58                   | 26.1                 |
| 1970 | $ 89                   | 31.0                 |
| 1975 | $172                   | 46.0                 |
| 1980 | $310                   | 70.5                 |
| 1985 | $478                   | 97.8                 |
| 1990 | $668                   | 121.8                |

**6** Much of this chapter has discussed how economists adjust the data to find what they want to know—for example, by adjusting for inflation or dividing by the population level. What adjustments might you suggest for analyzing education expenditures? Old Age Security payments?

**7** Firms typically do not fire workers quickly as the economy goes into a recession—at least not in proportion to the reduction in their output. How might you expect output per worker and output per hour to move over the business cycle?

# 7

# MICROFOUNDATIONS

C hapter 6 took up the key objectives of macroeconomic policy—growth, full employment, and stable prices—and the way success in reaching each of these objectives is gauged. In Chapter 8, we begin to look specifically at what determines such aggregate variables as the economy's output and employment levels. The behaviour of these macroeconomic variables is determined by the actions of the millions of households and firms that make up the economy. Accordingly, an understanding of macroeconomics begins with microeconomics. Earlier chapters discussed how prices are determined in competitive markets by the intersection of demand and supply curves (for goods, for labour, and for loans). This chapter rounds out that discussion.

First, we look at how households and firms interact in product, labour, and capital markets. We then survey the economy as a whole, from the perspective of the basic competitive model first introduced in Chapter 2. However, many economists believe that the basic competitive model provides an incomplete description of the economy. Most important, the model assumes that in every market, demand equals supply. When applied to the

**1** How are the demand and supply curves for goods and services derived? for labour? for capital?

**2** How does the basic competitive model provide answers to the questions of what will be produced and in what quantities, how it will be produced, and for whom it will be produced?

**3** How are the various parts of the economy tied together?

**4** What are the most important limitations of the basic competitive model? Why may markets by themselves not result in economic efficiency?

labour market, this assumption means that there is no unemployment. Since one of the main concerns in macroeconomics is what determines the unemployment rate and why there are periods in which it seems to be persistently high, we must go beyond the basic competitive model. Accordingly, the final section of this chapter points out the discrepancies between modern economies and the basic competitive model. This lays the groundwork for the analysis of such central macroeconomic phenomena as unemployment and economic instability, to which we turn in Part Three.

## HOUSEHOLDS IN THE BASIC COMPETITIVE MODEL

In the basic competitive model, rational households interact with profit-maximizing firms in competitive markets. The supply and demand curves introduced in Chapter 4 give us a framework for analyzing this interaction. Here and in the next section we explore the determinants of the demand and supply curves— why they have the shapes they do, and what causes the curves to shift. This section takes the perspective of households, and the next one gives the firm's viewpoint. The principles developed here will be applied to each of the markets that make up the economy: product, labour, and capital. After looking at the decisions of households and firms, we will look at the market equilibrium, how firms and households interact in all three markets, and the implications for the economy as a whole of these interactions.

## THE HOUSEHOLD'S CONSUMPTION DECISION

As we saw in Chapter 2, individuals face a budget constraint. They have a certain amount of money to spend; they can only consume more of one good by consuming less of another. The trade-off is given by relative prices. If the price of apples is twice that of oranges, by giving up one apple, an individual can get two oranges.

Chapter 4 suggested that normally demand curves are downward-sloping, as shown in Figure 7.1; that is, as the price rises, people consume less of a good. There are two reasons for this. First, as the price of apples increases, apples become less attractive relative to oranges and other goods. To get one more apple, Alfred must give up more oranges, so Alfred substitutes oranges and other fruits for apples. The reduction in demand resulting from the change in the relative price—the fact that to get one more apple, Alfred must give up more oranges—is called the **substitution effect.**

Second, if Alfred spends all or even part of his income on apples, he is worse off when the price of apples increases. He simply cannot buy what he bought before. He is, in this sense, poorer, just as he would be if his income had been reduced. If we define **real income** as what an individual's income will buy (rather than simply the money received), Alfred's real income has been reduced. When this happens, he spends less on almost every good.[1] The reduction

---

[1] There are some exceptions. A good for which the demand decreases as income increases is said to be *inferior,* while goods for which demand increases as income increases are said to be *normal.*

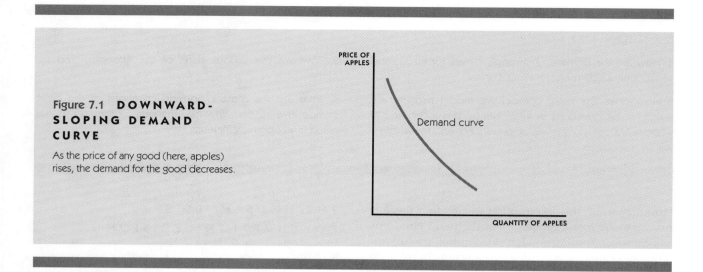

**Figure 7.1 DOWNWARD-SLOPING DEMAND CURVE**

As the price of any good (here, apples) rises, the demand for the good decreases.

in Alfred's demand for apples resulting from the reduction in real income is called the **income effect.** Both the income and substitution effects lead Alfred to demand fewer apples when the price increases. This is why the demand curve for apples is depicted as downward-sloping: at higher prices, fewer apples are demanded.

Chapter 4 identified a number of factors, such as income, tastes, and demographics, that affect the market demand curve. Most important, demand in one market is affected by prices determined in other markets. For instance, the price of oranges will have an effect on the demand for apples. On a broader level, the intertwining of markets is a central feature of macroeconomic analysis; for instance, an increase in wages, as a result of a shift in the demand or supply curves of labour, increases the income individuals have to spend, and thus affects the demand curve for each and every good.

## THE HOUSEHOLD'S SAVING DECISION

The same kind of analysis applies to Alfred's decision about how much to save. We can think of a decision about how much to save as a decision about how much to consume now and how much to consume in the future. Assuming that Alfred has a fixed income, if he reduces his consumption, he has money left over, which he saves. He takes this savings and puts it in the bank or invests it some other way and receives a return of $r$, the interest rate. If $r$ is 10 percent, then for every dollar of reduced consumption today, he gets $1.10 in the future. Thus, $1.10 is the *relative* price of consumption today versus consumption in the future.

What is the effect of an increase in the interest rate? If Alfred saves nothing—he takes his current income and simply consumes it—then the interest

## SUBSTITUTION AND INCOME EFFECTS

Substitution effect: The reduction in demand resulting from the change in the relative price; the individual substitutes less expensive products for more expensive ones.

Income effect: The reduction in demand resulting from the reduction in real income that occurs when the price of any good rises.

## USING ECONOMICS: INCOME ELASTICITIES

In Chapter 5 we introduced the concept of price elasticity: the percentage change in demand from a 1 percent increase in price. Economists use an analogous concept, income elasticity, to quantify income effects: the income elasticity is the percentage change in demand from a 1 percent increase in income.

As an economy grows, it will normally import more goods. Governments often want to know by how much imports will be rising. The answer is provided by the income elasticity of demand for the imported goods. In Canada many imports consist of luxury goods, for which the income elasticity is large; this means that a 1 percent increase in income may lead to a greater than 1 percent increase in imports. If Canadian incomes increase from $600 billion to $630 billion—by 5 percent—imports are $200 billion, and the income elasticity of imported goods is 1.2, then imports will be expected to rise by 6 percent, or by $12 billion. If foreigners' income is expected to rise by only 3 percent and Canadian exports are $300 billion, and if the foreign income elasticity for imports is slightly smaller, say, 1, then as a result of foreigners' increased income, they will buy $9 billion more Canadian goods (3 percent × $300 billion × income elasticity of demand, 1). Under these circumstances, the trade surplus—the gap between exports and imports—will be expected to fall by $3 billion ($9 billion more exports − $12 billion more imports).

rate has no effect. If he does save, he has more to consume in the future. He is better off. When an individual's income goes down, she normally consumes less of all goods. When Alfred is better off, he normally consumes more of every good; this means, in our example, that he consumes more now and more in the future. This is the income effect of higher interest rates. Alfred consumes more now, which implies that he saves less.

On the other hand, an increase in the interest rate means that for each dollar of consumption Alfred gives up today, he gets more consumption in the future; the trade-off has changed. This is the substitution effect, and the substitution effect of higher interest rates leads Alfred to consume less today and more in the future. Thus, an increase in the interest rate has an income effect leading to lower savings and a substitution effect leading to more savings. The net effect is ambiguous, though most studies indicate that on average, the substitution effect slightly outweighs the income effect: savings increases slightly. Figure 7.2 shows the supply of savings as a slightly upward-sloping curve.

### EXPECTATIONS

To an economist, a decision about whether to consume today or consume five years from now is just like a decision about whether to consume apples or oranges. Alfred looks at his preferences and his opportunity set, and especially the trade-offs. The trade-offs are given by relative prices—here determined by the interest rate. But there is one important difference. In making his decisions about the future, Alfred must form expectations: how much he will want to set aside for the future may depend upon what he expects his future wage will be, or what the price of his favourite goods will be.

### INVESTING

Having decided how much to save, Alfred now faces a new problem: what to do with his savings. He has a number of choices. For instance, he could put his money in a bank account. Alternatively, he could buy a certificate of deposit, which is a promise from the bank to pay him in, say, six months or a year a

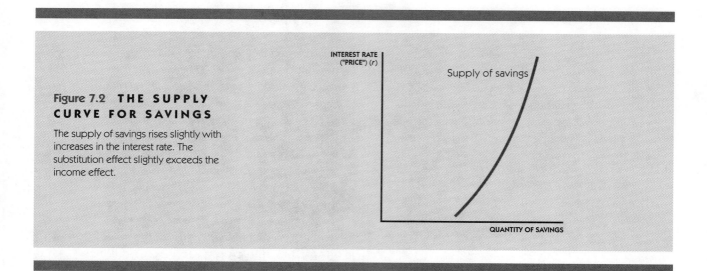

**Figure 7.2 THE SUPPLY CURVE FOR SAVINGS**

The supply of savings rises slightly with increases in the interest rate. The substitution effect slightly exceeds the income effect.

specified interest plus the money he invested, his principal. Other options include corporate stocks and corporate or government bonds. In evaluating his alternatives, Alfred looks at several characteristics of each asset: the **expected return** (what he expects to get on average), the risk, the tax advantages, and how costly it would be for him to sell the asset quickly, should he need to do so (technically called the **liquidity**).

In taking his investment decisions, again expectations play a key role. If Alfred believes that a new smog-reducing technology will make living in Toronto much more attractive in ten years' time, he will believe that the price of land will increase ten years from now. But if land is expected to have a high value ten years from now, it will have a high value nine years from now—since if it did not, investors would recognize that by buying the land cheaply and holding it for just one year, they would make an enormous capital gain. But, reasoning backwards, if land is expected to have a high value nine years from now, it will have a high value eight years from now. The upshot: an event which is believed to have a large effect increasing values ten years from now will be reflected in the price *today*. The demand for assets today—and thus the price today—reflects expectations of events that will affect uses in the future, and hence demands in the future. Just as different markets within the economy are linked together today, so are markets linked together over time.

Risk arises whenever there is uncertainty about the returns. If an oil company is successful and finds oil, investing in the company can yield huge returns. But if it does not find oil, not only may there be no returns, even the amount invested will not be recovered. High-tech companies are similarly engaged in risky research ventures: if their research pays off, investors will be repaid many times what they invested. But in many cases, their research does not pay off, or someone else beats them to the patent office. Then, investors lose everything they have invested. Some stocks are less risky—food businesses tend to do well no matter how well the economy is doing. There is little downside risk, but neither is there the great upside potential of the high-tech companies.

## THE HOUSEHOLD'S LABOUR SUPPLY DECISION

We can use the same basic reasoning that we have employed to analyze the demand for apples and savings to discuss how much Alfred decides to work. Of course, in some jobs Alfred may have no choice; if he wants to work for Grinding Grinders, he may have to work a 60-hour week, while if he wants to work for Easy Riding Stables, his work week may be only 30 hours. But the number of hours he wants to work will affect which job he chooses; and economists believe

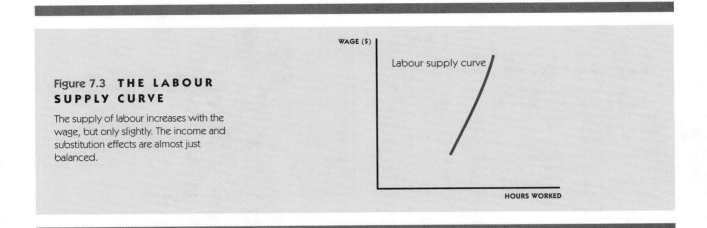

**Figure 7.3 THE LABOUR SUPPLY CURVE**

The supply of labour increases with the wage, but only slightly. The income and substitution effects are almost just balanced.

that by and large, employers respond to preferences of workers. If workers on average want shorter work weeks, then over time, work weeks will get shorter. In fact, the work week is considerably shorter today than it was at the beginning of the century.

The question is, what determines how much Alfred would like to work? Again, we need to look at Alfred's opportunity set. If he works less, his income will be lower; he will not be able to consume as much as he otherwise could. In taking his decision, he looks at the trade-off, the benefit of the extra leisure and the cost of the reduced amount of goods he can buy. This trade-off is given by the wage he receives. The wage is the price of labour. The **real wage** is the nominal wage divided by the average price of the goods a person buys (as reflected, for instance, in the consumer price index). Thus, the real wage tells us how much extra consumption Alfred can have if he works an hour more.

What happens when real wages increase? Again, there is an income effect. Alfred is better off and so would like to consume more of every good; viewing leisure as a "good," he wants more leisure—that is, he wants to work less. On the other hand, the higher wage has changed the trade-off. For every hour of leisure he gives up, he now gets, for example, $20 of extra consumption rather than $10. The substitution effect causes him to want to work more. Again, the net effect is ambiguous. Most studies show that the income and substitution effects are almost precisely balanced, so that the labour supply curve appears to be fairly steep, as depicted in Figure 7.3.

## FIRMS IN THE BASIC COMPETITIVE MODEL

Competitive firms maximize their profits.[2] Profits are just revenues minus costs. Revenues are the price of a good times the quantity sold of the good. The firm in the basic competitive model believes that it has no effect on price—it takes the market price as given. For instance, any wheat farmer believes that the price of wheat will be unaffected by the amount of wheat he sells.

### THE FIRM'S SUPPLY DECISION

In deciding how much to produce, the firm in the competitive model compares the extra revenue it receives from producing one more unit of output—the price—with the extra cost, which is called the **marginal cost.** When price exceeds marginal cost, the firm gains more than the increased costs; it pays to expand output. By contrast, if marginal cost exceeds price, it pays to contract output. What the firm does is produce at the level where price equals marginal cost. This is the profit-maximizing level of output.

[2] Alternatively, we can describe firms as maximizing their market value; to do that, they must maximize their profits. They may, of course, be willing to give up some profits today if they think profits in the future will be increased by enough to compensate.

## Figure 7.4 THE FIRM'S REVENUE AND COST CURVES

In competitive markets, a firm's total revenues increase in proportion to the output sold. Its total costs also increase with output. Profits are the difference between the two. They are maximized at Q*, where the slope of the total revenue curve—which equals the price—and the slope of the total cost curve are the same. The slope of the total cost curve is the marginal cost.

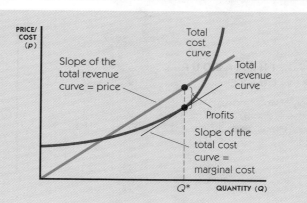

Here is another way of looking at the firm's decision. Figure 7.4 shows the firm's total costs of producing each level of output. Total costs increase as the firm produces more. The figure also shows the company's total revenue curve. The firm's profit at any level of output is simply the difference between the two at that level of output. The slope of the total revenue curve measures the increase in revenues when output increases by a unit, called the **marginal revenue.** In competitive markets, a firm's total revenue increases in proportion to output. The total revenue curve is thus a straight line through the origin, with a slope equal to the market price: marginal revenue equals price. The slope of the total cost curve is the marginal cost. As long as marginal revenue is higher than marginal cost, profits are increasing. Profits are maximized when the two curves have the same slope—when marginal revenue (price) equals marginal cost.

We learn more about the firm's production decision by looking more closely at its costs. The firm's **average costs,** total costs divided by output, are shown in Figure 7.5. The average cost curve is U-shaped. It heads downwards at low levels of output because there are certain costs a firm must pay just to remain in operation. It has to pay rent, pay its top management, and so forth. These are referred to as **fixed** or **overhead costs.** If these were the *only* costs, then average costs would decline rapidly as output increases. There are other costs, however,

called **variable costs,** and these not only increase, but often increase faster than output, at least beyond a certain point. In the short run, the firm cannot immediately expand the number of machines and workers. To produce more, it has to work two or three shifts, and must work its machines and workers at full speed. This is expensive. Thus, its average costs start to increase. This explains why the typical firm has a U-shaped average cost curve.

Figure 7.5 also shows the firm's marginal costs. In the figure, marginal costs are initially relatively flat. If the firm wishes to expand production, it simply hires more workers and buys more raw materials. But as we just saw, after some point it becomes more expensive to produce an extra unit. Marginal costs start to increase. Eventually the firm may find that it simply cannot increase its output beyond a certain level. The marginal cost curve in the figure intersects the average cost curve at its lowest price. This is no accident. When marginal costs—the costs of producing an extra unit—exceed the average costs, the marginal costs are pulling up the average, so average costs are rising. When marginal costs are below average costs, marginal costs are pulling down the average, so average costs are falling.

Once we understand the average cost curve, we can add an important qualification to the statement above that the firm in the competitive model produces at the point where price equals marginal cost. It does so only *so long as it covers costs*—that is, so

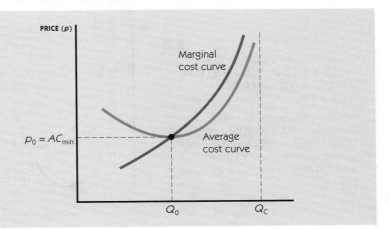

## Figure 7.5 THE FIRM'S AVERAGE COST CURVE

The typical firm faces a U-shaped average cost curve. Marginal costs increase with output. The marginal cost curve intersects the average cost curve at the bottom of the U-shaped average cost curve. The output at this point is denoted by $Q_0$, and the average cost by $AC_{min}$. The maximum output the firm can produce is $Q_c$. It is prohibitively expensive to produce beyond this point.

long as price equals or exceeds average costs. If price is below average costs, the firm shuts down. Thus, the firm's supply curve is its marginal cost curve in the region where price exceeds minimum average costs; otherwise, the firm supplies zero.

### THE MARKET SUPPLY CURVE

The collection of firms making the same product is called an **industry.** The industry or market supply curve, as we saw in Chapter 4, is obtained by adding up the supply curves of all the firms in the industry. Figure 7.6 shows a typical shape, with a horizontal portion at price $p_0$ and an upward-sloping portion beyond that. In the figure, the industry simply cannot produce at an output beyond $Q_c^M$; this point is referred to as the total **capacity** of the industry.

The reason that the market supply curve has this shape can be seen if we return to the U-shaped cost

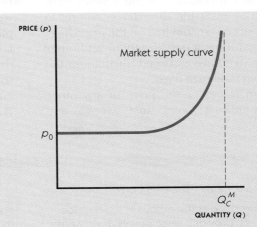

## Figure 7.6 THE MARKET SUPPLY CURVE

The figure illustrates a typical shape, with a horizontal portion at price $p_0$ and an upward-sloping portion beyond that. There is some total capacity of the industry: it simply cannot produce at output beyond $Q_c^M$.

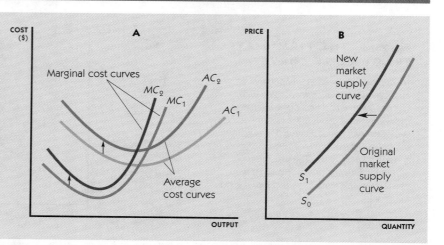

**Figure 7.7 EFFECTS OF INCREASED WAGES ON COST AND SUPPLY CURVES**

In panel A, an increase in wages or the price of any other input shifts all the cost curves upwards. Here, the effects on the average and marginal cost curves are shown. As a result, the market supply curve shifts, as in panel B.

curves illustrated in Figure 7.5. Assume all firms have the same average cost curves, with minimum average cost equal to $AC_{min}$ and the corresponding output equal to $Q_0$. Then, when the price is $p_0 = AC_{min}$, each firm is indifferent between not operating and operating at $Q_0$. If there are $N$ firms, then industry output at price $p_0$ is somewhere between 0, when all shut down, and $N \times Q_0$, when all operate. Above $p_0$, the market supply is the sum of the amounts supplied by each of the firms, all of which will be operating.

***The Effect of Wage Increases on the Market Supply Curve*** The amount the industry is willing to supply depends, of course, not just on the price it receives but on what it must pay for labour and other inputs. Implicitly, we have assumed throughout the analysis so far that those are fixed.

An increase in wages or the price of any other input shifts *all* of the cost curves—total, average, and

marginal—upwards. Figure 7.7, panel A, illustrates the effects on average and marginal costs. As a result, the supply curve of the industry shifts, as depicted in panel B.

## THE FIRM'S DEMAND FOR LABOUR AND CAPITAL

The firm's production decision is intimately tied to its demand for labour. At each level of wages and prices, we can calculate the amount firms are willing to supply. But we can also calculate their demand for labour. As the wage increases at a given price level, firms' demand for labour will decrease, for two reasons. First, the upwards shift in the marginal cost curve means that firms will wish to produce less. With lower levels of production, they will demand

**THE FIRM'S SUPPLY DECISION**

Competitive firms produce at the output at which price equals marginal costs, provided price equals or exceeds average costs. If price is below average costs, the firm shuts down.

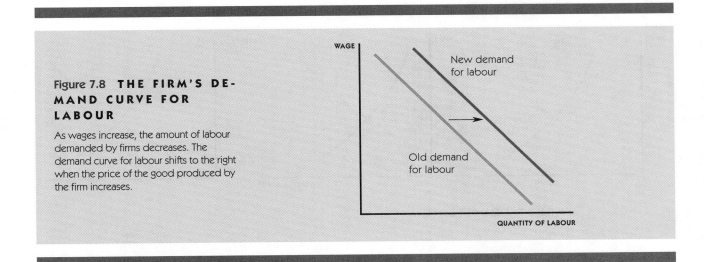

**Figure 7.8 THE FIRM'S DEMAND CURVE FOR LABOUR**

As wages increase, the amount of labour demanded by firms decreases. The demand curve for labour shifts to the right when the price of the good produced by the firm increases.

less labour. But in addition, if wages increase, labour becomes more expensive relative to other inputs. Firms will thus substitute, where possible, other inputs for labour. In some cases this may be easy; for instance, some industries can use more machines, or more expensive machines that require fewer workers to run them. In other cases it is more difficult.

We can immediately extend this analysis to the industry, and then to the whole economy: as wages increase (at fixed prices), the total amount of labour demanded by all firms together—the market demand for labour—decreases.

Figure 7.8 shows a firm's demand curve for labour, which is downward-sloping. It is drawn under the assumption of a given price of output. If the price of output increases, firms will want to produce more; and at the higher level of output, they will want more labour. The demand curve for labour will shift to the right, as depicted in the figure.

Exactly the same kind of analysis applies to the demand for capital.[3] As the interest rate—the price of using capital—increases, firms' demand for capital

decreases; each firm produces less and each firm substitutes other inputs, such as labour, for capital, which has become more expensive.

## MARKET EQUILIBRIUM IN THE BASIC COMPETITIVE MODEL

Now that we have analyzed the behaviour of firms and households, we need to put these results together to analyze equilibrium in each of the major markets of the economy.

### THE LABOUR MARKET

Figure 7.9, panel A, shows the demand and supply curves for labour, taking prices and interest rates as given. We find the demand curve for labour through the analysis of the behaviour of the firm, as described above, and the supply curve of labour through an analysis of the household's labour supply decision. The intersection gives the equilibrium wage. When the demand for labour equals the supply of labour, we say that the labour market **clears.** By definition, in the basic competitive model there is no unemployment, since the wage is set at the level at which the demand for labour equals the supply.

---

[3] Recall the discussion of Chapter 1, which pointed out that the term "capital" is used in two different ways: it refers to capital goods—plant and equipment—and to the funds used to purchase these capital goods. Here, we are referring to the latter, to the supply of funds made available to firms by households and to the demand for funds by firms to finance their investment.

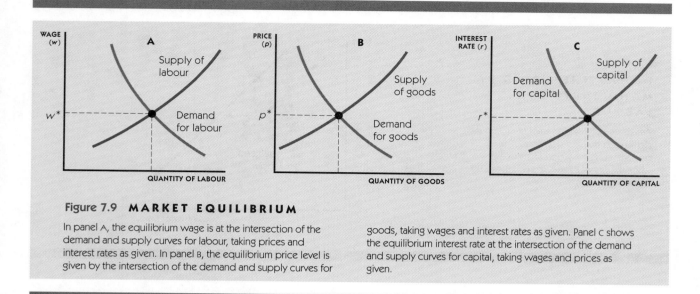

**Figure 7.9 MARKET EQUILIBRIUM**

In panel A, the equilibrium wage is at the intersection of the demand and supply curves for labour, taking prices and interest rates as given. In panel B, the equilibrium price level is given by the intersection of the demand and supply curves for goods, taking wages and interest rates as given. Panel C shows the equilibrium interest rate at the intersection of the demand and supply curves for capital, taking wages and prices as given.

## THE PRODUCT MARKET

Figure 7.9, panel B, shows the demand and supply curves for goods, taking wages and interest rates as given. The demand curve is derived from the household's consumption decision, and the supply curve, from the firm's production decision. This aggregate view of the product market incorporates demand and supply curves for each of the many products produced in the economy, and closer inspection would reveal a myriad of product markets. The intersection of the demand and supply curves for any individual good gives its equilibrium price, as we saw in Chapter 4. When we talk about the product market as a whole, with an aggregate demand and supply curve, we say that the intersection of the demand and supply curves gives the equilibrium price level.

## THE CAPITAL MARKET

Figure 7.9, panel C, shows the demand and supply curves for capital, derived from the supply of savings by households and the demand for funds by firms to finance new investment. As we saw earlier, we can think of the interest rate as the price of borrowing; higher interest rates mean that households have to give up more future consumption if they wish to increase current consumption by a dollar. The intersection of the demand and supply curves gives the equilibrium interest rate.

## GENERAL EQUILIBRIUM

The **general equilibrium** of the economy is the situation in which *all* markets are in equilibrium, or all markets clear: the demand for each good equals its supply, the demand for each kind of labour equals its supply, and the demand for capital equals its supply. We call such a situation an equilibrium because when all markets clear, there is no incentive for prices—including the price of labour (the wage) and the price of capital (the interest rate)—in any market to change.

## THE INTERRELATEDNESS OF MARKETS

It is important to recognize that all markets are interrelated: what goes on in one market may have repercussions throughout the economy. Consider a tax that firms must pay on each worker hired. Figure

## Figure 7.10 EFFECT OF A TAX ON LABOUR

The tax means that the wage received by a worker is less than the cost of labour to the firm, which includes the tax. As a result of the tax, the wage received by the worker normally goes down, and the total cost of labour to the firm normally goes up. These are, however, only the initial effects. These wage changes give rise to changes in the product and capital markets, and the resulting changes in interest rates and prices have reverberations back on the demand and supply curves for labour, and hence on the equilibrium wage rate.

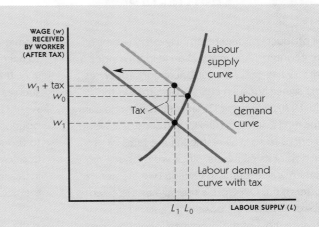

7.10 shows the initial effect of the tax. The tax means that the wage received by a worker is less than the cost of labour to the firm, which includes both the wage and tax. At each wage received by the worker, $w$, the cost of the worker to the firm has gone up (to $w_1 + t$), so the demand for labour decreases. The demand curve shifts to the left. As the figure illustrates, the wage received by the worker accordingly goes down, from $w_0$ to $w_1$, and the total cost of the worker to the firm, $w_1 + t$, goes up. But this is not the end of the story.

Lower wages received by households result in their demanding fewer goods; the demand curve for each product shifts to the left. Higher wages paid by firms result in firms' being willing to supply less output at any given price; the supply curve for each product shifts to the left. Output is reduced, and normally the price will change.

If the price level increases, this will have ramifications back on the labour market. At higher prices, households' real wages—the extra goods workers can buy as a result of working an hour more—will be lower, and they will be willing to supply less labour. At higher prices, firms will, at each wage, be willing to produce more, and hence will demand more labour. The wage rate—both the wage paid by firms and the wage received by workers—will thus increase. We then need to trace the effect of this wage increase back on the product market.

The labour market is not the only market to be disturbed. The capital market will also be affected. As firms expand or contract production, they will demand more or less capital. As wages increase, firms will substitute capital for labour, since labour has become relatively more expensive. Accordingly, the demand curve for capital shifts. At the same time, if

## GENERAL EQUILIBRIUM

The general equilibrium of the economy occurs when all markets clear. The demand for labour equals the supply; the demand for each good equals its supply; and the demand for capital equals the supply.

All markets are interrelated; disturbances to one market have consequences for the equilibrium in other markets.

## CLOSE-UP: THE NATIONAL ENERGY PROGRAMME AND GENERAL EQUILIBRIUM

Oil products permeate virtually every sector of the economy. Any major change in their price inevitably has general equilibrium consequences. One significant such change occurred in the mid-1970s when the Organization of Petroleum Exporting Countries (OPEC) cartel caused world oil prices to soar by restricting the rates of production of its members. Since we produce more oil than we consume in Canada (we are net exporters), the OPEC price rise might have been expected to have a positive effect. However, because most of the producers of oil are concentrated in Alberta while the users are spread across the country, the gains were expected to be concentrated in Alberta.

In an effort to shield the users from the higher prices and to spread the benefits around the country, the federal government introduced the National Energy Programme (NEP) in 1980. The NEP restricted the price of oil in Canada to well below the world price. This was partly accomplished by a tax imposed on exports sold from western Canada to foreigners, and by a subsidy paid on imports coming into eastern Canada. The federal government also imposed a tax on the production of oil, effectively reducing the ability of the Alberta government to do so. Finally, tax incentives were offered to encourage production by Canadian-owned firms in the oil industry.

To the extent that the NEP was successful both at keeping domestic oil prices lower than they would otherwise have been and at spreading the revenues from selling Canadian oil abroad at the higher world price across the country, certain general equilibrium consequences could be avoided. For one thing, if the windfall profits

from the OPEC oil price rise had been allowed to accrue to Alberta firms and the Alberta treasury, that province could offer fiscal benefits such as lower taxes and better services that would attract labour and capital out of neighbouring provinces. The NEP was partly intended to reduce this so-called "fiscally induced migration" by sharing the revenues from the oil price increase across the country as well as reducing the size of the price increase.

Quite apart from that were the ramifications that a large oil price rise would have had for industries in other parts of the country. A major study conducted for Transport Canada in 1982 found that the NEP could be important for the survival of Maritime producers who export to central Canada and the United States. For some Maritime goods the energy cost of transportation is a large component of the product price. In the case of New Brunswick green lumber, the cost of trucking diesel fuel accounted for 4.8 percent of the product price in 1982. This cost was not nearly as high for the competing firms in Ontario, Quebec, and the northern states in the United States where the Maritime products were sold. More generally, it was estimated that rising energy prices could have a "significant negative impact on the competitive position" of Maritime producers of canned fruits and vegetables as well as lumber. (Less sensitive to energy prices were the canned and frozen fish industries, since oil inputs make up a much smaller proportion of their costs.) In a general equilibrium sense, then, the NEP was seen to benefit seemingly remote Maritime sectors by keeping energy prices low.

Of course, in attempting to address the unequal regional impact of the rise in oil prices by keep-

*Sources:* Edward A. Carmichael and J. K. Stewart, *Lessons from the National Energy Program,* (Toronto: C. D. Howe Institute, 1983); E. H. M. Jagoe and A. D. Fiander, *Assessment of the Impact of the NEP on the Long-Haul Freight Movements from the Maritime Provinces,* for Transport Canada Strategic Planning, Group Project No. 59-86, June 1982.

ing them artificially low, the government prevented market economic forces from taking their natural course. As is often the case, objectives of fairness can be accomplished only with a cost in terms of economic efficiency.

workers' income is reduced, they are likely to reduce their savings, so the supply curve of capital also shifts. As the demand and supply curves of capital shift, the interest rate changes, and this too has effects, both on the product market (since households' incomes and firms' cost curves are thereby affected) and on the labour market (for the same reasons).

The process continues. Eventually the economy settles down to a new equilibrium. General equilibrium analysis takes all of these interactions into account.

## CIRCULAR FLOWS

The relationships among the various parts of the economy are sometimes illustrated by means of a **circular flow** diagram. Households buy goods and services from firms. Households supply labour and capital to firms. The income individuals receive, whether in the form of wages or the return on their savings, is spent to buy the goods that firms produce.

Figure 7.11 depicts this circular flow for a simplified economy in which there are no savings and therefore no capital, no government, and no foreign trade. Firms hire labour from households and sell goods and services to households. The income they receive from selling their products goes to pay their workers, and anything left over is paid out to households as profits.

A circular flow can be analyzed from any starting point, but let's start on the upper arrow, at point A, moving from left to right. Consumers pay money to firms to buy their goods and services, and this money then flows back through the firms to households at B in the form of wages, rents on land, and profits. Not only is the circular flow diagram useful in keeping track of how funds flow through the economy, it also enables us to focus on certain balance conditions, which must always be satisfied. Thus, in the figure,

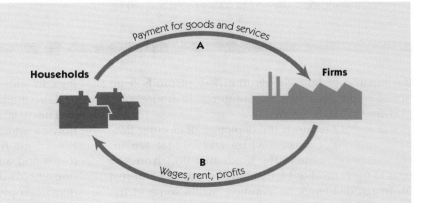

**Figure 7.11 A SIMPLE CIRCULAR FLOW DIAGRAM**

In this simple circular flow diagram, only labour and product markets and only the household and firm sectors are represented. It can be analyzed from any starting point. For example, funds flow from households to firms in the form of purchases of goods and services. Funds flow from firms to households in the form of payments for the labour of workers and profits paid to owners.

Payment for goods and services

A

Households

Firms

B

Wages, rent, profits

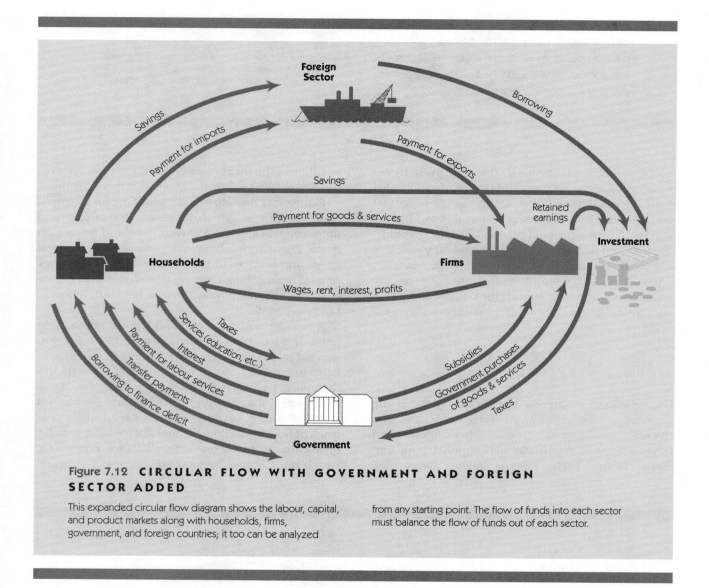

**Figure 7.12 CIRCULAR FLOW WITH GOVERNMENT AND FOREIGN SECTOR ADDED**

This expanded circular flow diagram shows the labour, capital, and product markets along with households, firms, government, and foreign countries; it too can be analyzed from any starting point. The flow of funds into each sector must balance the flow of funds out of each sector.

the income of households (the flow of funds from firms) must equal the expenditures of households (the flow of funds to firms).

Figure 7.12 expands the depiction of circular flow in several ways. First, savings and capital are included. Here, some of the funds that flow from the firm to the household are a return on capital (interest on loans, dividends on equities), while some of the funds that flow from the household to the firm are savings, which go to purchase machines and build-

ings. In addition, firms retain some of their earnings and use them to finance investment.

The diagram is expanded further to include funds flowing into and out of the government. Now households and firms have both additional sources of funds and additional places where funds go. Some households receive money from the government (like unemployment insurance from the federal government and welfare payments from the provinces); some sell their labour services to the government rather than private firms; and some receive interest on loans to the government (government bonds). And there is now an important additional outflow: part of household income goes to the government, in the form of taxes. Similarly, firms have additional sources of inflow in the sales of goods and services they make to the government and in government subsidies to firms, and an additional outflow in the taxes they must pay to the government.

Just as the flow of funds into and out of households and firms must balance, the flow of funds into the government must balance the flow of funds out.[4] Funds go out as purchases of goods and services from firms, purchases of labour services from households, and payments of interest to households on the government debt. Funds also go out as direct flows to households, for unemployment insurance, welfare payments, and so forth (called "transfer payments" in the diagram), and to firms as subsidies. Funds flow into the government from taxes on both households and firms. When there is a deficit—when the government spends more than it collects in taxes—as there has been in recent years, funds go into the government as borrowings from households. The government finances the difference between what it spends and what it raises in taxes by borrowing (in our diagram, from households).

Figure 7.12 also includes the flow to and from foreign countries. Firms sell goods to foreigners (exports) and borrow funds from foreigners. Households buy goods from foreigners (imports) and invest funds in foreign firms. Again, there must be a balance in the flow of funds: Canadian exports plus what the country borrows and receives as investment income from abroad (the flow of funds from abroad) must equal its imports plus what it lends and pays as investment income abroad (the flow of funds to other countries).[5]

[4] We ignore here the possibility that the government can simply pay for what it obtains by printing money. In Canada, the government always finances any shortfall in revenue by borrowing.

[5] This condition will play an important role in the discussion of Chapter 9. It can be put another way: the difference between Canadian imports and exports must equal the net flow of funds from abroad (the difference between what the country borrows from abroad and what it lends, net of investment income received less that paid).

The flow of funds diagram is useful as a way of keeping track of the various relationships in the economy. The various balance conditions that make up the diagram are basically identities. Identities, as we know, are statements that are always true; they follow from the basic definitions of the concepts involved. Household income, for example, must equal expenditures on goods plus savings (the flow of funds to firms).

The interconnections and balance conditions making up circular flow analysis are the same as those that arise in the competitive equilibrium model discussed earlier in the chapter. Even if the economy were not competitive, however, the interrelationships and balance conditions of the circular flow diagram would still be true. The circular flow diagram is useful, for it reminds us that whether the economy is competitive or not, if one element of a balance changes, some other element *must* change.

Let's put the circular flow diagram to work. Consider an increase in the personal income tax, such as occurred in 1992 under the Conservatives. The flow of funds into the government was increased. The circular flow diagram reminds us that if flows in and out are to remain balanced, then either some other flow into the government must be reduced or some flow out of the government must be increased. That is, either some other tax must be reduced, government borrowing must decrease, or government expenditures must increase. In this instance, the intent was to reduce government borrowing.

## THE ROLE OF GOVERNMENT

In the basic competitive model, we ignored government, arguing that before we can understand what government does, we must first understand how markets *without government* function. But the government is important. In Canada today, expenditures by all levels of government are over 48 percent of GDP. This compares with about 20 percent in 1939, immediately before World War II. The figure for the United States is 36 percent, and in the industrialized countries overall it is 40 percent. Some of these expenditures include pure transfers of money rather than expenditures on goods and services. Government expenditures on goods and services are about 20 percent of GDP; about one fifth of the output produced in the economy is used by the government.

What is the rationale for all of this government activity? What does the government do? What *should* the government do? In recent years the last question has been at the centre of extensive political debate, with one side claiming that the government has extended its reach beyond what it *should* be doing, the other side arguing that there is an important role for government, though to be sure government should improve how it does what it does.

## THE EFFICIENCY OF MARKETS

Behind this debate is one of the most fundamental ideas in economics: competitive markets are efficient. Firms have an incentive to lower costs to the minimum level possible, and to produce the goods that consumers want. As we saw in Chapter 4, prices guide firms in their production decisions and households in their consumption decisions.

Adam Smith argued that in competitive economies, the public interest is best served by individuals pursuing their own self-interest. As he put it:

> Man has almost constant occasion for the help of his brethren, and it is in vain for him to expect it from their benevolence only. He will be more likely to prevail if he can interest their self-love in his favor, and show them that it is for their own advantage to do for him what he requires of them. . . . It is not from the benevolence of the butcher, the brewer, or the baker, that we expect our dinner, but from their regard to their own interest. We . . . never talk to them of our own necessities but of their advantages.[6]

Smith's insight was that individuals work hardest to help the overall economic production of society when their efforts help themselves. He argued that an "obvious and simple system of liberty" provided the greatest opportunities for people to help themselves and thus, by extension, to create the greatest wealth for a society.

[6] Adam Smith, *The Wealth of Nations* (1776), Book I, Chapter IV.

Smith used the metaphor of the **"invisible hand"** to describe how self-interest led to social good: "He intends only his own gain, and he is in this as in many other cases led by an invisible hand to promote an end which was no part of his intention. . . . By pursuing his own interest he frequently promotes that of the society more effectually than when he really intends to promote it."

Economics has progressed considerably since Adam Smith's day, but his fundamental argument still has great appeal. Competitive markets ensure that the economy operates along its production possibilities curve: given the economy's inputs, more of one good can be produced only by decreasing production of other goods. Competitive markets produce the goods that consumers want: production simultaneously takes into account the trade-offs individuals are willing to make (how many apples they are willing to give up to get one more orange) and the trade-offs the production possibilities curve gives the economy (how many apples have to be given up to get one more orange).

Moreover, competitive markets ensure that goods get to the "right" people: As we saw in Chapter 3, if individuals do not like the particular mix of goods they have, they can trade; exchange will continue until no further mutually advantageous trades are feasible.

As a result, in competitive markets, no one can be made better off without someone else being made worse off. An economy with this property is said to be **Pareto-efficient,** a concept named after the great Italian economist Vilfredo Pareto.

## LIMITATIONS OF THE BASIC COMPETITIVE MODEL

While the basic model provides a good starting point for economic analysis, under some circumstances it may not provide a good description of the economy. In this book we will be particularly concerned with the problem of unemployment. Periodically the economy is plagued with high levels of unemployment. In the Great Depression, which began in 1929, unemployment in Canada reached almost 20 percent, and in the United States it reached 25 percent.

Ireland in recent years has faced unemployment rates of 20 percent, and Spain, rates of 15 percent or more. With so many people unable to find a job for so long, the assumption that all markets—including the labour market—are clearing seems, at least at times, inappropriate.

In the remaining chapters of this book, we will spend considerable time understanding the causes of large-scale unemployment and related macroeconomic market failures. Many of the explanations for unemployment are related to other ways in which market economies differ from the assumptions of the competitive equilibrium model. The remaining pages of this chapter take up the most important of these differences.

## IMPERFECTIONS OF COMPETITION

The basic competitive model begins with the assumption that there are so many buyers and sellers in each market that each firm and each individual believes that it has no effect on the equilibrium price. We say that firms and households are **price-takers.** In particular, the amount produced by any firm has a negligible effect on the market price.

In many markets, firms do seem to have an effect on the price. They are **price-makers.** This is true of many of the goods we buy—from automobiles to film, brand-name cereals, beer, and soft drinks. The production decision of a price-maker determines the price it receives; alternatively, such a firm picks a price, and the price it picks determines how much it can sell. The difference between the price-taking firms of the basic competitive model and the price-making firms of imperfect competition can be represented by the demand curves they face. With perfect competition, firms face a horizontal demand curve. They can sell as much as they want at the going market price. With imperfect competition, firms face a downward-sloping demand curve.

The basic rule for determining how much firms produce is still that firms produce more if the extra (or marginal) revenue of producing one more unit exceeds the marginal cost. Profit maximizing entails setting marginal revenue equal to marginal cost. The important difference between perfect and imperfect competition is that with its downward-sloping demand curve, if the imperfectly competitive firm increases its output, price falls. The extra revenue the firm receives (its marginal revenue) is less than the price at which it sells the last unit, because in order to sell that last unit, the firm had to lower the price on all the other units it sold.

Thus, in Figure 7.13, the marginal revenue curve is below the demand curve, and the equilibrium output is that at which marginal revenue equals mar-

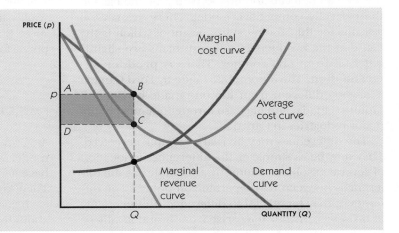

**Figure 7.13 IMPERFECT COMPETITION**

In markets with a single firm or sufficiently few firms that there is imperfect competition, firms face downward-sloping demand curves. They set marginal revenue equal to marginal cost. Profits are the difference between price and average costs times the quantity produced, the area ABCD.

ginal cost. The profits per unit sold are the difference between the price and average costs. Total profits are shown in the figure as the rectangle *ABCD*, the difference between price and average costs times the quantity produced.

The extreme case of imperfect competition is no competition. A firm that faces no competitors is called a **monopolist.** There are relatively few industries with only one firm. At one time, Kodak was a virtual monopolist in the photographic film industry, as was Inco in the nickel industry.

When there are a few firms in an industry, it is called an **oligopoly.** The analysis of oligopolies is complicated by the fact that the extra revenue a firm receives from selling an extra unit depends in part on how the company's rivals react. Firms must consider rivals' possible reactions when they take decisions such as whether to produce more or to advertise more.

In between oligopolies and perfect competition is a situation called **monopolistic competition,** where there are sufficiently many firms that no firm worries about the reactions of rivals to any action it takes. At the same time, however, there are sufficiently few firms that each one faces a downward-sloping demand curve for its product. With monopolistic competition, barriers to entry (such as the cost of entering a market) are low enough that profits may be driven to zero, but still firms are not price-takers.

In most markets in modern economies, competition is not perfect. A firm that raises its price does not lose all of its customers, as would be the case in the perfectly competitive model. There are several reasons for this, the most important of which is the fact that the products of different firms are slightly different from one another. There is **product differentiation.** The automobile made by Ford Canada is slightly different from the one made by General Motors Canada, and likewise throughout most of the major industries in Canada.

The differences may be real or simply perceived. They may be as simple as the differences in location of several gasoline stations, or as complex as the differences between two separate computers. The differences may be related to differences in the quality of products, or they may arise from brand loyalty or firm reputations. As will be discussed briefly later in this chapter, developing new and better products,

different from those produced by other firms, is one of the main ways in which firms compete in modern economies. In the basic competitive model, however, firms only compete on price.

In labour markets competition is also often limited. In many industries workers do not compete actively against one another but rather work together, through unions. Together, they threaten to refuse to work for a firm unless the firm raises its wages; they use their market power to extract higher wages by threatening a strike. Of course, their market power is limited to the extent that the employer may turn to nonunion workers. However, that option has been curtailed in British Columbia, Ontario, and Quebec, all of which have passed legislation outlawing the hiring of replacement workers.

For the present purposes, it is important to note that the ability of unions to extract higher wages depends on the ability of firms to pay higher wages. When a firm has profits resulting from monopoly power, then it can pay higher wages. When the firm operates in a highly competitive industry, if it pays higher wages, it cannot compensate by charging higher prices.

The growth in union membership began to level off in 1975. In fact, within the private sector there has been a marked decline; the major area of growth of unionization is among public employees. Part of this decline is attributed to the increased competition faced by such traditionally highly unionized sectors as automobiles and steel. These sectors have grown smaller, some claim, partly as a result of the high wages the unions have won for their workers. In most European countries, however, unions remain powerful and play a major role in setting wages.

## IMPERFECT INFORMATION

An important assumption of the basic competitive model is that households are well informed. They have good information about the products they buy. They know the prices at which they can acquire each good at each store. They have good information about the firms in which they invest. Similarly, firms have good information about potential employees. Firms know each worker's abilities. They can costlessly monitor what workers are doing and ensure that they do as they are told. It is clear that these assumptions are not quite correct; households and firms both face limited or, as economists say, **imperfect information.** This fact has important implications for how each of the markets in the economy functions.

In the product market, imperfect information provides an additional reason why each firm faces a downward-sloping demand curve. If firm A lowers its prices below that of its rival, firm B, it does not instantly garner for itself all of B's customers. Customers may not know that firm A has lowered its prices; even if they do, they may not be sure that the product being sold by A, or the services it provides in conjunction with the product, are of the same quality as the product sold by B. Thus, imperfect information leads to imperfect competition.

In the labour market, a firm must spend considerable resources trying to screen various applicants, to find out which are best suited for the firm. Even then it will not be perfectly successful. Some of the workers it hires will turn out to be unsuitable. Thus, in many jobs, hiring and training workers is extremely costly. Firms often find that by paying higher wages, they can get a larger and better-quality applicant pool from which to choose workers, and the workers they hire are less likely to quit.

Also, firms spend considerable energy in trying to motivate workers. They realize that low morale leads to low productivity. They may provide economic incentives for hard work: the carrot, higher pay or increased promotion possibilities with better performance, and the stick, the threat of being sacked for bad performance. The theory that by paying workers higher wages one can obtain a higher-quality labour force, one that works harder and quits less frequently, is called the **efficiency-wage theory,** and will be discussed more extensively in Chapter 17.

Just as managers may have trouble getting workers to do what they want, owners of the firms may have trouble getting their managers to act in the interests of the owners. The owners would, of course, like the managers simply to maximize profits or the market value of the firm. Because the typical shareholder has her wealth spread out among many firms, she may not care much about the risks incurred by the firm. That is why she simply wants the firm to maximize its profit or market value, and profit-maximizing firms are one of the assumptions of the basic competitive model.

But the shareholders do not themselves take the decisions concerning what the firm does. They must rely on those who manage the firm, and the managers may not do what is in the interests of the shareholders—they may not maximize profits or market value. For instance, a manager's welfare is closely tied with that of the firm. If the firm goes bankrupt, he has a good chance of being out of a job, and other firms may be reluctant to hire him; even if the firm does not go bankrupt, if it does badly, the manager's pay is likely to suffer. Therefore, managers may take too few risks. Another possibility is that they may use their position to enhance their life-style rather than the profits of the firm; they may use corporate jets not to improve productivity but perhaps to fly around to vacation spots also owned by the firm.

There are, in fact, some checks on managerial discretion. A manager who does not take actions that maximize the value of the firm under her charge may find that her firm is threatened with a takeover. Or shareholders may revolt and elect a board that fires the management. But both of these checks provide only imperfect discipline.

Finally, information problems have a major effect on how capital markets work. Take the example of a firm that wishes to borrow money. Normally, you might think that if some potential borrower cannot obtain all the funds he wants at the going interest rate, all he needs to do is offer to pay a higher interest rate. Lenders would prefer to receive the higher interest rate, and it would seem that no one is precluded from the market. But this does not seem to work, and for a simple reason. Lenders worry that if they charge a higher interest rate, their expected returns will actually decrease because the chance of default will increase. At higher interest rates, safer investors find that it does not pay to borrow. A disproportionate number of those willing to borrow at high rates are high-flyers—people who are undertaking high-risk projects that if successful will yield high returns, more than enough to cover the interest charge, but if unsuccessful will simply go bankrupt, leaving the lender "holding the bag."

Thus, the relationship between expected returns to the lender and the interest rate charged may look

Canada spent about $3,200 per person on health care in 1992. This was about 20 percent more per person than Germany spent; 32 percent more than Sweden; 36 percent more than Japan; and whopping 100 percent more than the United Kingdom. Only the United States spent more. Moreover, health care expenditures are the most rapidly growing component of government expenditures in Canada. In 1994, health care expenditures by governments in Canada (mainly provincial governments) were twice as high as they were ten years earlier. They had grown from 12.5 percent of total government expenditures to 13.5 percent in just five years. The containment of health care expenditures has become one of the policy priorities of the decade.

Why have health costs increased so rapidly? Economists have offered several explanations, many of which focus on the incentives that exist in the system for using and financing health care, the absence of competitive pressures for economizing, and the role of imperfect information in the provision of health care.

Sick people do not usually act as cautious self-interested consumers, carefully shopping around for different medical care providers and balancing the marginal benefits of various treatments. Most people have incomplete information about what is wrong with them, what treatment might help, and what medical actions are really needed. Moreover, under our system of publicly provided health care, a patient has little reason to care about costs. Her attitude might be that if a trip to the doctor might help, it is worth a try. Unlike with the markets for other goods and services, prices are not used as a rationing device for consumers.

Uncertain information about what health care is truly necessary presents another problem, this one to do with health care professionals. Under our fee-for-service system, doctors are paid for the amount of care they provide, the number of tests they run, and the number of procedures they perform. When patients have both full insurance and incomplete information, they are unlikely to question whether another test or procedure is really necessary. Health care professionals are trained to look after a patient's health. So they face strong economic and professional pressures to try everything, rather than weighing costs of treatment with potential benefits.

If adverse incentives are the problem, it is natural to look for ways in which the system can be changed so as to correct them. Several suggestions have been made. One is simply to institute user fees on patients for the use of health services. Detractors argue that this may have little deterrent effect since it is really the doctor rather than the patient who determines how many services are used. Furthermore, user fees will make health care less accessible to those least able to afford it. Another suggestion is to put doctors on salaries instead of paying them fees for each service performed. After all, other health care workers, such as nurses, are salaried, not to mention other public-sector professionals such as professors and judges. While this would reduce the incentive for doctors to overuse health services, it might also reduce their incentive to take on additional patients and to perform time-consuming procedures.

A more wide-ranging reform would involve changing not only the compensation scheme for doctors but also the organization through which doctors deliver their services. Today many doctors operate their own practices individually. The proposal is that groups of doctors would join together in health maintenance organizations

(HMOs) and provide a wide range of medical services to their patients. Patients would be free to join the HMO of their choice, and the HMO would be obliged to accept all patients who selected it. The HMO would receive a specific sum of money per patient (referred to as a "capitation fee") and would be responsible for providing comprehensive health care to each patient. The HMO would pay the health care professionals in their own organization in a manner of their choice. This could be by salary or fee-for-service or some combination of the two.

The use of the HMO for delivering health care is intended to introduce into the system incentives for cost effectiveness as well as competitive pressures. Since patients would be free to shop around, HMOs would effectively compete with each other for patients and would be induced to offer the best mix of services they could. The fact that the payment per patient in the HMO is fixed implies that the HMO would have an incentive to economize on the use of health services. And since each HMO would have to compete for health care professionals, each would be induced to offer a good working environment with adequate facilities.

The HMO concept is not without difficulties, however. Since the HMO would be obliged to provide services to all patients who choose to join it, there is obviously an advantage to attracting those patients who are less likely to have serious health problems. The HMO might try to do this by putting more effort into providing the sorts of services that attract the healthier elements of the population. It might be difficult for the government to preclude this "cream skimming" through regulation.

These and other options will undoubtedly be considered as governments try to contain rising health costs.

---

like the curve in Figure 7.14. In this case, there is an optimal interest rate, $r^*$, at which the bank's expected return is maximized. If at that interest rate the demand for funds exceeds the supply, lenders will not be willing to lend at a higher interest rate, because they know that their expected returns will actually be lower if they do so. In this situation, economists say there is **credit rationing.** Some borrowers are rationed in the amount of credit they can obtain. The capital market does not clear.

---

### Figure 7.14  EXPECTED RETURNS FROM LENDING

Increasing the interest rate charged may actually lead to lower expected returns, as the best risks decide not to apply for loans and those who do borrow undertake riskier projects.

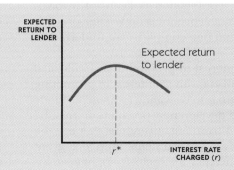

## MISSING MARKETS

The basic competitive model assumes that there are competitive markets for all goods and services; the only reason a market for a good might not exist is if demand is zero at the minimum cost of producing it. In fact, many markets are missing; among the most important of these are the markets that would provide insurance against the various risks that households and firms face. As a result, government has stepped in to provide a variety of insurance programmes, partly because the private sector did not, at least not at the time the programs were initiated.

## TECHNOLOGICAL CHANGE

The basic competitive model proceeds under the assumption that every firm has a given technology, a given way of converting inputs into outputs. There is a given array of products that are produced. In fact, the development of new products and less expensive ways of producing old products is an essential part of modern industrial economies; the fact that modern economies do these things so well is often cited as one of their greatest virtues.

Because the basic competitive model ignores technological change, it cannot address fundamental issues: Why has productivity increased less rapidly in recent years? Why does productivity seem to increase faster in some countries than in others?

Moreover, there is a limited number of firms in sectors of the economy in which technological change is important. Each faces a downward-sloping demand curve. It is a price-maker, not a price-taker. These are the characteristics of imperfect competition. Nevertheless, competition is keen—it involves the race to develop new products and better production methods, so that one company can undercut its rivals.

Government's interest in promoting technological progress often conflicts with its interest in promoting competition. If a firm is to be willing to spend its funds to do research and develop new products, it must be able to get a return from any inventions that are the fruit of that research. Governments therefore grant patents, giving an inventor the exclusive right to an invention for a period of twenty years. The losses from the reduction in competition for this limited period are thought to be outweighed by the gains from the spur to innovation that the patent provides.

Even with a good patent system, there may be insufficient spur to innovation. Firms seldom capture all the benefits that accrue from their inventive activity. Other firms see what they have done, learn from it, and use it as a basis for producing still better products. Customers benefit. Innovation in the computer industry has made faster and faster computers available at lower and lower prices. And in the long run, workers benefit as well, as the improved technology becomes reflected in higher wages. Economists say there are **externalities** associated with innovation.

## EXTERNALITIES

Externalities occur when the actions of a household or firm generate benefits or costs to other households or firms without compensation. For example, a factory that releases toxic fumes into the air generates a negative externality for those who breathe the air. Innovations, on the other hand, are often thought to produce positive externalities. Whenever there are externalities, markets will not be efficient, since people will not take into account either all the benefits or all the costs of their actions.

## ADJUSTMENTS

The basic competitive model focuses on the *equilibrium* of the economy, the state of the economy in which there are no forces for change, where the supply for each good equals the demand—that is, where all markets clear.

Of course, the economy is always changing. One year the price of oil may rise as a war in the Middle East reduces the supply. Another year exports may decline as foreign customers face an economic downturn. Technological progress in the Japanese car industry may have a direct and obvious impact on North American producers and customers. There is a constant need for prices—including the price of labour (the wage) and the price of capital (the interest rate)—to change. Earlier we saw how what happens in one market can, and normally will, have repercussions in other markets.

Imagine that the economy is initially in an equilibrium and then is disturbed, say by a large increase in the price of imported oil. The task of finding the new equilibrium prices for the millions of other goods and services in the economy is an extraordinarily difficult one. The adjustments do not occur overnight; in some cases, they may take weeks, months, perhaps stretch out to years. Meanwhile, some markets may not be in equilibrium: demand may not equal supply (markets may not clear).

## INCOME DISTRIBUTION

Even if all the conditions of the basic competitive model were satisfied, this would only mean that the economy was efficient. The resulting distribution of income might be totally unacceptable. Those with few skills might receive a wage that is below what they need to survive.

Behind the macroeconomic objectives of stable prices, full employment, and high growth lie other concerns, including the distribution of income. To a large extent, the goals may be complementary. Reducing unemployment is of particular benefit to the poor, since lack of jobs is one of the main causes of poverty. Eliminating those market failures that give rise to unemployment will at the same time make the distribution of income more equitable.

Though high rates of growth generally are thought to benefit everyone, this presumption has come to be questioned. Many of the benefits of the long economic expansion that began in 1983 seem to have gone to those in the upper part of the income distribution. Real wages of the unskilled remain unchanged, or actually lower. This experience has convinced many that the government needs to take a more active stance, not only in preventing unemployment, but in ensuring that the fruits of growth will be shared by all.

## GOVERNMENT FAILURES

Whenever there is a market failure, there is a *potential* role for government. But government, like markets, often departs from the ideal: governments are subject to imperfections of information. They often do not fully anticipate all the consequences of their actions. Thus, they did not fully anticipate the devastating effects that superhighways had on urban centres, which was to facilitate the flight to the suburbs.

Nor did they anticipate the extent to which reforms in mental institution policies would lead to homelessness in cities. They often do not fully anticipate private-sector responses to government actions. For instance, a few years ago the government waged an aggressive campaign against cigarette smoking. Among the measures taken was a significant increase in the excise tax on cigarettes. This caused the price of cigarettes in Canada to be much higher than in the United States. This price differential made it more attractive for persons to engage in the smuggling of cigarettes across the border for illegal resale in Canada at lower prices, including Canadian cigarettes previously exported to the United States free of tax. It has been suggested that in some border areas at least one quarter of the cigarettes purchased by consumers were smuggled, thereby defeating partly the purpose of the excise tax on cigarettes.

Both bureaucrats and politicians are motivated at least in part by private incentives, which may lead them to take actions that are not in the public interest. The political process itself encourages politicians to think more about how votes will be affected by their actions than about any broader concept of public interest.

As a result of increased recognition of these "government failures," there is increased interest in ascertaining how they can be reduced, by, say, more extensive use of performance measures and by encouraging more competition within the public sector and between the public and private sectors. In certain areas, such as the postal service, productivity in the public sector has increased rapidly.

Today, when they consider the proper role of government in the economy, economists ask not only whether there is a market failure, but also whether government—in view of its limitations—is likely to remedy those market failures.

## THE BASIC MODEL COMPARED WITH THE REAL WORLD: A SUMMARY

If the real world matched up to the assumptions of the basic model of perfectly competitive markets, then markets could be given free rein. They would

## The Basic Model versus the Real World

| The basic model | The real world |
| --- | --- |
| 1 All markets are competitive. | 1 Most markets are *not* characterized by the degree of competition envisioned in the basic model. |
| 2 Technological know-how is fixed and cannot change. | 2 Technological change is a central part of competition in modern industrial economies. |
| 3 Firms, consumers, and any other market participants have easy access to information that is relevant to the markets in which they participate. | 3 Good information may be impossible to come by, and in most cases is costly to obtain. In many markets, buyers of products know less than the sellers. |
| 4 Sellers bear the full and complete costs of bringing goods to market, and buyers reap the full benefit. | 4 Externalities mean that market transactions may not accurately account for costs and benefits and the private market provides an inadequate supply of public goods. |
| 5 All desired markets exist. | 5 Some markets may not exist, even though goods or services in that market might be provided at a cost consumers would be willing to pay. |
| 6 There is no involuntary unemployment. | 6 There is involuntary unemployment. Adjustments may be slow, so that even if markets eventually clear, unemployment may persist for extended periods of time. |
| 7 Competitive markets provide an efficient allocation of resources. | 7 Efficiency is not enough. The income distribution generated by the market may be socially unacceptable. |

supply efficient outcomes. If an outcome seemed inequitable, society simply would redistribute initial wealth and let markets take care of the rest.

In the two centuries since Adam Smith first enunciated the view that markets ensure economic efficiency, economists have investigated the model with great care. Nothing they have discovered has shaken their belief that markets are, by and large, the most efficient way to coordinate an economy. However, they have found significant departures between modern economies and the competitive model. Few would go so far as to condemn the model totally for its flaws; its insights are simply too powerful. Rather, most economists use the basic competitive model as the starting point for building a richer, more complete model that recognizes the following qualifications.

1. Most markets are not as competitive as those envisioned by the basic model.

2. The basic model simply ignores technological change. It tells us about the striving for efficiency that occurs as consumers and firms meet in competitive markets, but it assumes that all firms operate with a given technology. Competition in the basic model is over price, yet in the real world, the primary focus of competition is the development of new and better products and the improvements in production, transportation, and marketing that allow products to be brought to customers at lower costs and thus at a lower price. This competition takes place not between the multitude of small producers envisaged in the basic competitive model, but often between industrial giants like Du Pont and Dow Chemical, and between the industrial giants and upstarts, like IBM and a slew of small computer firms that eventually took away a major share of the computer market. Changes in technology lie behind economic growth, and growth is one of the principal concerns of macroeconomics.

3. The individuals and firms envisioned in the basic model have easy and inexpensive access to the information they need in order to operate in any market they enter. Buyers know what they are buying, whether it is stocks or bonds, a house, a car, or a refrigerator. Firms know perfectly the productivity of

each worker they hire, and when a worker goes to work for a firm, he knows precisely what is expected of him in return for his promised pay.

We have already encountered instances in which information problems are important and may fundamentally affect how markets work. In the following chapters we will see other instances in which imperfect information and the other market imperfections to which imperfect information gives rise help to explain a variety of macroeconomic phenomena. We will see, for instance, in Chapter 17 how lack of information about the quality of people applying for jobs may make firms worry that if they lower the wages they pay, they will obtain a lower-quality work force. In Chapter 16, we will see that lack of information about the consequences of changing prices may result in prices being rigid, which partly explains the slow adjustment of the economy to equilibrium.

4. The basic model assumes that the costs of bringing a good to the market accrue fully and completely to the seller, and that the benefits of consuming a good go fully and completely to the buyer. Earlier in this chapter, however, we encountered the possibility of externalities, which are extra costs or benefits that do not figure in the market calculation.

5. The basic model answers the question "What goods will be produced, and in what quantities?" by assuming that all desired goods that *can* be brought to market *will* be brought to market. Trees that bloom in gold coins and tablets that guarantee an eternal youth are out of the question. But if customers want to buy green hair colouring, cancer-causing tobacco prod-

ucts, or life insurance policies overladen with extras, then producers can be expected to supply such goods. There are, however, some products consumers would like to buy but cannot that are so similar to existing products that we can expect they *could* be supplied. The most obvious example, already given, is the firm that wants to borrow money but cannot, even at high interest rates.

Imperfections in the capital market—the inability to obtain funds—play an important role in economic fluctuations, as we shall see. When firms cannot obtain funds to produce or to invest, production, investment, and employment all suffer. And, as in the recession that began in 1990, firms often attribute cutbacks in production and investment to an inability to obtain funds.

6. In the basic model, all markets hover at or near equilibrium. They clear: supply meets demand at the market price. Decades of evidence, however, suggest that labour markets often do not clear. Workers sometimes want to supply their labour services at the market wage, but cannot do so. The Great Depression of the 1930s is the most dramatic example of large-scale unemployment. During that period, unemployment rates rose to nearly 20 percent of those willing and able to work.

7. Even if markets are efficient, the way they allocate resources may appear to be socially unacceptable; there may be massive pockets of poverty, or other social needs may remain unmet. Income distribution is a major concern of modern societies and their governments.

## REVIEW AND PRACTICE

### SUMMARY

**1** An increase in the price of a good reduces a person's demand for that good, both because of the income effect—the higher price makes the individual worse off, and because she is worse off, she reduces her consumption—and because of the substitution effect—the good is now more expensive *relative* to other goods, so she substitutes other goods.

**2** An increase in the interest rate has an ambiguous effect on savings and current consumption. The income effect leads to more current consumption (reduced savings), but the substitution effects leads to less current consumption. The net effect on savings is probably slightly positive.

**3** An increase in the wage rate has an ambiguous effect on labour supply. Individuals are better off, and so the income effect leads to more leisure (less work). But the substitution effect—the increased consumption from working an additional hour—leads to more work. In practice, the two effects probably just offset each other.

**4** The typical firm has a U-shaped average cost curve. It produces at the level where price equals marginal cost, so long as price equals or exceeds average costs. The market supply curve is found by adding the supply curves of each of the firms in an industry. The typical shape is relatively horizontal when output is very low, but close to vertical as capacity is reached.

**5** General equilibrium analysis stresses that all markets are interrelated. Equilibrium occurs when demand equals supply for every good and service and every input; the labour, capital, and product markets clear.

**6** The circular flow diagram shows the flow of funds among the various parts of the economy.

**7** Under certain ideal conditions, competitive markets are Pareto-efficient: no one can be made better off without making someone else worse off. The economy operates along its production possibilities schedule, produces the goods individuals want, and ensures that goods are allocated efficiently among individuals.

**8** There are some important limitations to the basic competitive model, which explains why markets sometimes fail to produce efficient outcomes. Among these are imperfections of competition, imperfections of information, and externalities. Competitive markets may also spend too little on developing new technologies, may be slow in adjusting to new situations, and may fail to distribute income in an egalitarian way.

## KEY TERMS

| | | | |
|---|---|---|---|
| substitution effect | average costs | circular flow | monopolistic competition |
| real income | fixed or overhead costs | invisible hand | product differentiation |
| income effect | variable costs | Pareto efficiency | imperfect information |
| expected return | industry | price-takers | efficiency-wage theory |
| liquidity | capacity | price-makers | |
| marginal cost | market clearing | monopoly | |
| marginal revenue | general equilibrium | oligopoly | |

## REVIEW QUESTIONS

**1** Use the concepts of income and substitution effects to explain why demand curves for goods are normally downward-sloping. Why may increases in the interest rate not lead to much more savings? Why may increases in the wage rate not lead to a much greater amount of work done?

**2** What are some of the important factors individuals take into account in deciding how to invest their savings?

**3** Why are average cost curves often U-shaped?

**4** How is the level of output of a firm determined? What is the effect of an increase in wages on the market supply curve?

**5** Why is the demand curve for labour by firms downward-sloping?

**6** Why may what happens in one market have effects on other markets? Illustrate with an example.

**7** What is a circular flow diagram, and what do we learn from it?

**8** How is output determined in a monopoly? What are some forms that imperfect competition takes?

**9** What are the most important reasons that competitive markets may not yield efficient outcomes?

**10** Describe various aspects of the efficiency of competitive markets? What is meant by Pareto efficiency?

## PROBLEMS

**1** Assume that Alfred has $10,000, which he can either consume today or save and consume next year. If the interest rate is 10 percent, how much can he consume next year if he consumes nothing now? Draw a budget constraint, with "Consumption today" on the horizontal axis and "Consumption next year" on the vertical. Show how the budget constraint shifts if the interest rate increases to 20 percent. Use the budget constraint diagram to discuss the income and substitution effects of the increase in the interest rate.

**2** Assume now that Alfred has no income this year, but next year will come into an inheritance of $11,000. The bank is willing to lend money to Alfred at a 10 percent interest rate. Draw his budget constraint. Show how the budget constraint shifts if the interest rate the bank charges increases to 20 percent. Why can you be certain that as a result of the higher interest rate, his consumption this year will go down? (Hint: Explain why the income and substitution effects now both work in the same direction.)

**3** If Alfred saves an extra dollar today and invests it at 7 percent interest, how much extra consumption can he have in thirty years' time?

**4** Draw Alfred's budget constraint between leisure and consumption, assuming he can work 2,000 hours a year and his wage is $10 an hour. Show how his budget constraint changes if his wage increases to $15 an hour. Use the diagram to discuss income and substitution effects.

**5** Use demand and supply diagrams for the labour, product, and capital markets to trace out the effects of immigrant workers. Look first at the labour market—what does the increase in the supply of labour do to the equilibrium wage? Explain how the resulting lower wage will shift the demand and supply curves for goods and for capital. Describe how these changes in prices and interest rates will affect the demand and supply curves for labour.

**6** Use the extended circular flow diagram, with the foreign sector included, to trace out the possible consequences of the following:
   (a) a law requiring that businesses raise the wages of their employees
   (b) a decision by consumers to import more and save less
   (c) an increase in government expenditure financed by a corporate income tax
   (d) an increase in government expenditure without an accompanying increase in taxes

**7** For each of the programmes listed below, discuss what market failures might be given as reasons for implementing the programme:
   (a) automobile safety belt requirements
   (b) regulations on automobile pollution
   (c) unemployment insurance
   (d) Medicare (free health care)
   (e) workers' compensation (insurance for workers injured on the job)
   (f) federal deposit insurance
   (g) federally insured mortgages
   (h) law requiring lenders to disclose the true rate of interest they are charging on loans (truth-in-lending law)
   (i) National Meteorological Service
   (j) urban renewal

# CHAPTER 8

# THE FULL-EMPLOYMENT MODEL

If we look at history in decades, the market economy creates jobs for almost all who seek them. In the 1980s the Canadian labour force increased by 2.3 million people, and the number of people employed increased by the same amount. But sometimes the markets fail, as is evident when one out of ten, one out of six, or even (during the Great Depression) one out of five job seekers cannot find jobs. Yet—so far at least—every period in which the market fails to create enough jobs for those who seek them is followed by a period in which the economy catches up. Thus, while the number of persons employed actually fell by 247,000 from 1990 to 1991, in the two years from 1993 until 1995 employment rose by half a million workers.

The economic theories in the next part of the book explain why there are important episodes in which markets fail to create enough jobs and what the government can do about them. In this part of the book, we will see how the economy works in the long run—when it creates jobs at a pace that matches new entries into the labour force. We focus on the aggregate behaviour of the economy—on movements in such macroeconomic variables as output and wages—when resources are fully employed. We show how

## KEY QUESTIONS

**1** In an economy operating at full employment, what determines the real wage, the level of output, and investment?

**2** How is the economy affected by government expenditures and international trade? When government increases its expenditures but raises taxes to pay for the increased

expenditures, what happens to investment? How might the answer differ between a country like Canada, which relies heavily on international trade, and a country like the United States?

**3** How are the markets in the economy interlinked?

competitive markets, when they work well, help explain the vitality of the Canadian economy. No government official calculates where to place the 600,000 new workers who are expected to enter the labour force between 1996 and the year 2000. Indeed, if anyone from the prime minister on down had been asked where all the new labour force entrants would find jobs in the 1993–94 growth spurt, no one would have known the precise answer, though they could have pointed to particular parts of the economy that would be the most likely source of job growth. But on the basis of past experience they would have said that somehow, somewhere, the economy would create the jobs. The economic theories that we explore in this and the following chapters help explain how this comes about.

## MACROECONOMIC EQUILIBRIUM

The model we employ here is the basic competitive model from earlier chapters. In it, large numbers of households and firms interact in the labour, product, and capital markets. Households supply labour to firms, which use the labour to produce goods and which compensate workers by paying them wages. Households also save, and those savings finance firms' investments—the plant and equipment that firms need to produce. For the use of their funds, households receive interest and dividends from firms. With the income they earn from working and the return they earn from their savings, households buy the products that firms produce.

Two key lessons emerged from the basic competitive model. First, all markets are interrelated. What goes on in one market has an impact on others. The demand for labour depends on the level of output (the product market) and the level of output depends on the price determined on the labour market, the wage rate. Second, wages, interest rates, and prices adjust to equate demand and supply. In this part of the book we continue to focus on product, labour, and capital markets, and to assume that the adjustments in wages, interest rates, and prices are sufficiently rapid that for practical purposes all markets are always in equilibrium—that is, they all clear, with demand equalling supply. This assumption is not only a convenient starting point, but gives us powerful insights into some of the basic macroeconomic questions. We began the chapter with the observation that *somehow* the economy creates jobs for the thousands of new entrants into the labour force each year. It has managed to do this without any government official or private individual managing the process. The magic of the market, the adjustment of wages and prices equilibrating the labour market, guides this process. The model we present here explains how this happens.

The analysis here differs in one important way from the kind of microeconomic analysis of earlier chapters. In macroeconomics, we focus on aggregates, on total output, rather than on the output of individual products. We focus on total employment, and on average prices, which we refer to as the price level. We also proceed as if there is a single representative good being produced by a single representative kind of labour. We can picture the economy *as if* all firms produced the same commodity and all workers were identical. In looking at these aggregates, we

## CLOSE-UP: THE BIRTH OF THE MICRO-MACRO SPLIT

Today even noneconomists have heard the terms "microeconomics" and "macroeconomics." But economists actually began thinking in those terms only in the 1930s, when the global economy suffered the collapse that became known as the Great Depression. In Canada, the economy shrank 43 percent from 1929 to 1933; the unemployment rate hit almost 20 percent in 1933. Attention focused on the factors that determined aggregate variables like the unemployment rate and GDP.

John Maynard Keynes expressed the general idea when he wrote in 1936: "The division of Economics . . . is, I suggest, between the Theory of the Individual Industry or Firm and of the rewards and the distribution of a given quantity of resources on the one hand, and the Theory of Output and Employment *as a whole* on the other hand."

The first known written use of the words "microeconomic" and "macroeconomic" is by P. de

Wolff, a little-known economist at the Netherlands Statistical Institute. In a 1941 article, De Wolff wrote: "The micro-economic interpretation refers to the relation . . . for a single person or family. The macro-economic interpretation is derived from the corresponding relation . . . *for a large group of persons or families (social strata, nations, etc.)*."

In the 1960s and 1970s, many economists became concerned that macroeconomic thinking had strayed too far from its microeconomic roots. Interestingly, some of the most important economic work of the last 20 years, which will be described in the following chapters, has sought to break down that wall and explain how rational, well-informed consumers and profit-maximizing firms can combine in a way that sometimes creates unemployment, inflation, or fluctuations in growth.

*Source:* Hal R. Varian, "Microeconomics," in John Eatwell, Murray Milgate, and Peter Newman, eds., *The New Palgrave: A Dictionary of Economics* (1987), 461–63.

---

ignore the richness of the microeconomic detail we dealt with earlier. Hidden behind an increase in the price level are a myriad of changes in relative prices. Some prices have gone up faster than this average, some have gone up more slowly, some may even have decreased. The basic premise of macroeconomics is that we can say a great deal about the aggregates without inquiring into these details.

## THE LABOUR MARKET

The working assumption in the basic competitive model is that all markets clear. In the labour market, the fact that the demand for labour equals the supply implies that there is full employment. No worker

who wishes to get a job for which she is qualified at the going market wage will fail to get one. Adjustments in wages ensure that this will occur.

The assumption of *zero* unemployment, while it is clearly unrealistic, is a useful simplification, particularly for studying changes in the economy in periods in which unemployment is relatively low, or for comparing the economy at different periods in which unemployment was low, such as 1980 and 1989. In fact, when economists talk about full employment, they do not literally mean zero unemployment. As we saw in Chapter 6, there will always be some workers who will be temporarily not working because they are changing jobs—either searching for a better job or looking for a new employer because of structural changes in the economy—or because they are in seasonal industries. Nonetheless, the case of zero unemployment serves as a useful benchmark in much the same way as the perfectly competitive model does.

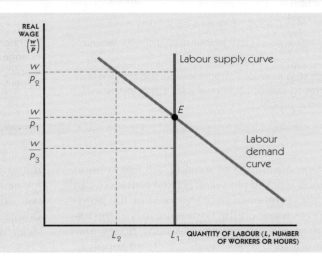

## Figure 8.1 EQUILIBRIUM IN THE LABOUR MARKET

Equilibrium in the labour market is at the intersection of the aggregate demand and supply curves for labour. If the wage is above $w_1$, where demand equals supply, there will be unemployment, putting pressure on wages to fall as workers compete to offer their services. Below $w_1$, there will be excess demand for labour, which will put pressure on wages to rise.

In thinking about the aggregate labour market, the relationship between wages ($w$) and the price level ($P$) is very important. Economists distinguish between real and nominal wages. The real wage, as we learned in Chapter 7, is the nominal wage adjusted for increases in the price level. Dividing the nominal wage by the price level gives us the real wage, or $w/P$. This means that if wages and the price level change together, the real wage will remain the same. Suppose that nominal wages and the price level both increase by 2 percent in the course of a year. The real wage would be exactly the same as it was at the beginning of the year, because the increase in the nominal wage would be offset by a proportional increase in prices. Alternatively, if the price level is held constant, changes in the nominal wage represent changes in the real wage, and if the nominal wage is held constant while the price level increases or decreases, the real wage will fall or rise.

Figure 8.1 shows the aggregate labour market, with the real wage ($w/P$) on the vertical axis, the quantity of labour ($L$) on the horizontal axis, and the aggregate demand and supply curves for labour. With a given set of machines and technology, the aggregate demand for labour depends on the wages firms must pay, the prices firms receive for the goods they produce, and the prices they have to pay for other inputs, including raw materials and machines. Holding the prices of goods and inputs constant, the aggregate demand curve traces out the quantity of labour demanded by firms at different wages. At lower wages, the quantity of labour demanded is greater. There are two reasons for this. First, as wages fall relative to the cost of machines, it pays firms to substitute workers for machines. Second, as the wage falls, labour becomes relatively less expensive compared with the price of the goods it produces (so at the old level of employment, the value of the marginal product of the last unit of labour hired would exceed the wage), and again employers will hire more workers. Thus, the demand curve for labour slopes down, as shown in the diagram.

The figure also shows an aggregate labour supply curve. To simplify matters, we assume that labour supply is inelastic[1]. That is, individuals are either in the labour force, working a full forty-hour work week, or they are not. They do not enter and exit the market as wages go up and down, nor do they reduce or increase the hours they work in response to such

---

[1] Recall the definition of elasticity from Chapter 5: the percentage change in quantity divided by the percentage change in price. Thus, an inelastic labour supply means that a 1 percent increase in price results in a small percentage increase in supply. A perfectly inelastic labour supply curve is vertical: that means the labour supply does not change at all when wages increase.

## LABOUR MARKET EQUILIBRIUM

Real wages adjust to equate labour demand with labour supply.

A rightwards shift in labour supply lowers the real wage, inducing firms to create additional jobs equal to the increased labour supply.

Technological change or new investment induces changes in the real wage, so that all workers remain fully employed. The real wage adjusts to equate supply and demand.

changes. One advantage of making the assumption that the hours worked per week is fixed is that we can put *either* the number of hours worked or the number of workers hired on the horizontal axis of the figure. The demand and supply of labour hours (per week) is simply forty times the demand and supply of workers.

Basic supply-and-demand analysis implies that market equilibrium should occur at the intersection of the demand and supply curves, point $E$. The reason for this is simple: if the wage happens to be above the equilibrium wage $w_1/P$, say, at $w_2/P$, the demand for labour will be $L_2$, much less than the supply, $L_1$. There will be an excess supply of workers. Those without jobs but who want jobs will offer to work for less than the going wage, bidding down the wages of those already working. The process of competition will lead to lower wages, until eventually de-

mand again equals supply. Likewise, if the wage is lower than $w_1/P$, say at $w_3/P$, firms in the economy will demand more labour than is supplied. Competing with one another for scarce labour services, they will bid the wage up to $w_1/P$.

## SHIFTS IN THE DEMAND AND SUPPLY OF LABOUR

With the basic competitive model, clear predictions can be made of the consequences of shifts in the demand and supply of labour. Consider first shifts in the supply curve of labour. This can occur as more young people reach working age than old people retire, or because of new immigrants, or because of social changes that lead more women to join the labour force. Figure 8.2 shows the increase in the

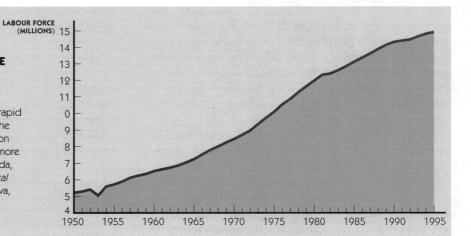

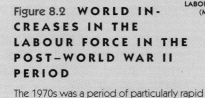

**Figure 8.2 WORLD IN-CREASES IN THE LABOUR FORCE IN THE POST–WORLD WAR II PERIOD**

The 1970s was a period of particularly rapid expansion, as baby boomers entered the labour force and the female participation rate rose. The workforce increased by more than 3.5 million. *Source:* Statistics Canada, CANSIM Database, 1996; ibid., *Historical Statistics of Canada,* Series D137, Ottawa, 1983.

Figure 8.3 **EFFECTS OF A SHIFT IN THE SUPPLY OF LABOUR**

A shift of the supply curve to the right leads to a fall in real wages.

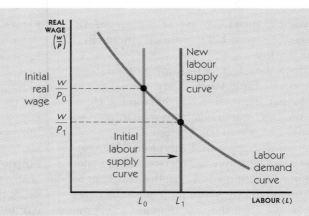

labour force over the last 45 years. In particular, it shows a rapid expansion in the 1970s as the baby boomers (those born shortly after World War II) entered the labour force and the fraction of women in the labour force increased. The consequences of such a large shift in the labour supply curve are depicted in Figure 8.3. The supply curve, here depicted as vertical, shifts to the right. The equilibrium real wage falls. The economy responds to the lower wages by creating more jobs. The wages (the price of

labour) tell firms that labour is less scarce, in a sense, than it was before, and so they should economize less in the use of labour.

Consider now the effects of a shift in the demand curve for labour. First consider the case of a decrease in investment leading to a reduction in the quantity of machines available for use by workers. This reduces the productivity of workers, thereby shifting the demand curve for labour to the left, as depicted in panel A of Figure 8.4. For a given real

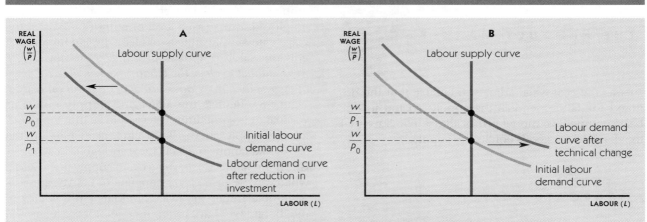

Figure 8.4 **EFFECTS OF CHANGES IN INVESTMENT AND TECHNOLOGY**

New investment or technological change shifts the demand curve for labour. Panel A shows a reduction in investment. Workers have fewer machines to work with, and the demand curve for labour shifts to the left, lowering equilibrium real wages. Panel B shows an increase in technology. The demand curve shifts to the right, as workers' marginal productivity increases, leading to higher equilibrium real wages.

wage firms want to hire fewer workers than before. The real wage rate must fall to restore equilibrium in the labour market.

Panel B depicts the effects of technological progress on the demand for labour. Workers are more productive and the labour demand curve shifts to the right. In this case, the real wage rises from $w_0/P$ to $w_1/P$ so that the labour market is in equilibrium.

These examples suggest that increases in investment and technology imply an increase in the demand for labour represented by a rightwards shift in the labour demand curve. Although this is in general true, it may be the case that the demand for some types of labour, especially unskilled labour, actually declines with investment in new machines and technology, while the demand for high-skill workers increases. In this case the labour market is really made up of two markets: skilled and unskilled workers. An increase in investment or technology may shift the demand for skilled workers out as in panel B, but shift the demand for unskilled workers in as in panel A. This represents one of the cases where merely studying the market for all labour is not sufficient to understand an interesting macroeconomic phenomenon—the increase in wage inequality based on skill levels.

## THE PRODUCT MARKET

Just as the real wage adjusts to ensure that the demand for labour equals the supply, so too in our basic competitive model prices adjust to ensure that the demand for goods equals the supply.

### AGGREGATE SUPPLY

At any point in time, the economy has a certain capital stock—a set of machines and buildings that together with labour and materials produces output. If more workers are hired, output increases. The relationship between employment and output is called the **short-run production function,** depicted in

Figure 8.5. There are diminishing returns. As more workers are hired, output goes up, but at a diminishing rate. The most productive machines are used first; if more labour is put to work, it is assigned to older and less productive machines.

We have been assuming that there was a fixed supply of labour. With this fixed supply of labour, the economy has a certain productive **capacity,** also referred to as the potential GDP, or the **full-employment level of output.** This level of output is also referred to as the **aggregate supply.** It represents the amount of goods and services that firms would be willing to supply given their plant and equipment, assuming wages and prices are flexible and adjust so that everyone is fully employed.

Output can occasionally exceed "capacity": for short spurts, as during wars, output can be increased further by deferring maintenance, running machines three shifts, and so forth.

Even with a fixed stock of machines, if the labour supply increases the capacity of the economy increases. This is a movement *along the short-run production function.* Figure 8.5 shows that if employment increases from $L_f$ to $L_f'$, then output increases from $Y_f$ to $Y_f'$.

Note that the level of aggregate supply is determined by the labour supply. Whatever the price level of output might be, real wages will adjust in the full-employment model to ensure that all workers are employed. If the price level of output increases, the wage rate simply adjusts to clear the labour market and the same output is produced. That is, *if real wages adjust to clear the labour market, then the level of aggregate supply does not depend at all on prices.* Figure 8.6 depicts the **aggregate supply curve** as vertical. It is sometimes referred to as the "long-run" labour supply curve, "long run" used here in the sense that labour markets have enough time to clear. Given the labour force, aggregate supply is the same whatever the price level happens to be. We address what determines the price level later in this part of the book. We have seen that an increase in the labour force leads to a shift in the aggregate supply curve to the right, as depicted.[2]

[2] Later we will see how technical change and investment shift the short-run production function out, and even with a fixed labour supply, also shift the aggregate supply curve to the right.

## Figure 8.5 SHORT-RUN PRODUCTION FUNCTION

In the short run, with given technology and a given set of plant and equipment, as more labour is employed, output increases but with diminishing returns, because each successive increase in input results in smaller increases in output. $L_f$ is the full-employment level of employment, so $Y_f$ is the full-employment level of output. An increase in the labour supply to $L_f'$ generates a movement along the short-run production function; the full-employment level of output will increase to $Y_f'$.

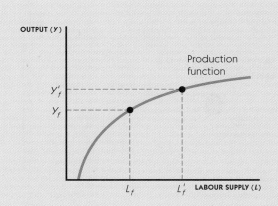

## Figure 8.6 AGGREGATE SUPPLY CURVE

If real wages adjust to clear the market, the aggregate supply curve is vertical. If the labour force grows, the aggregate supply curve shifts to the right.

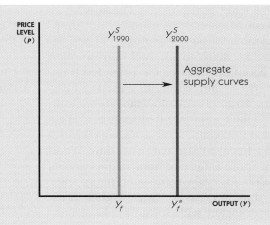

## AGGREGATE DEMAND AND EQUILIBRIUM OUTPUT

Aggregate demand is the sum total of the goods and services demanded by all the households, firms, and governments in the economy—plus foreigners wish-ing to buy the country's goods and services. In Chapter 6, we divided aggregate output into four components: consumption, investment, government expenditures, and (net) exports. Analyses of aggregate demand thus focus on identifying the demand for each of these components.

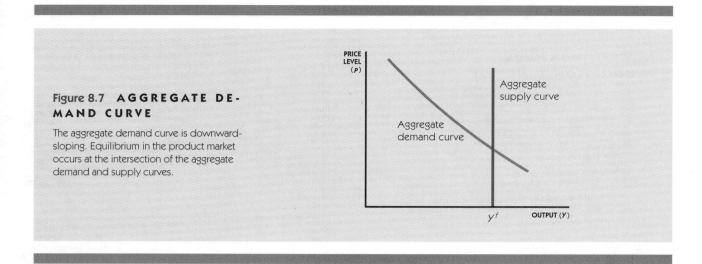

**Figure 8.7  AGGREGATE DEMAND CURVE**

The aggregate demand curve is downward-sloping. Equilibrium in the product market occurs at the intersection of the aggregate demand and supply curves.

The aggregate demand curve gives the quantity of goods and services demanded at each price level. The aggregate demand curve has the shape of the demand curves encountered in Part One; in particular, it is downward-sloping, as depicted in Figure 8.7. The reason for this can be seen by focusing on consumption, which accounts for 60 percent of aggregate demand. Households' demand for *real* consumption (taking into account changes in the price level) depends on their *real* wealth. When they are wealthier, they purchase more goods. An important part of individuals' wealth is their money and other financial assets denominated in dollars, such as Canada Savings Bonds promising to pay $100 in ten years' time. When the price level increases, the *real* value of these assets decreases. Households real wealth—and hence their consumption—thus decreases. Thus, higher price levels will be associated with lower levels of consumption and lower levels of aggregate demand, as depicted in the figure.[3]

The equilibrium, the intersection of the aggregate demand and supply curves, determines the price level and output. Since we know that in equilibrium demand equals supply and supply is fixed at $Y_f$, equilibrium output equals $Y_f$.

[3] Later in the chapter, we shall see that there are other reasons that the aggregate demand curve may have the shape depicted.

## THE CAPITAL MARKET

We turn now to the capital market. Equilibrium in the capital market requires that savings, the supply of funds, equal investment, the demand for funds. Our analysis of each builds on the microfoundations developed in Chapter 7.

### SAVINGS

The most important determinants of savings are income and interest rates. Each year, families have to decide how much of their income to spend on current consumption and how much to save for future consumption, for retirement, for emergencies, to pay for their children's postsecondary education, to buy a new car or a new home. On average, families with higher incomes spend more *and* save more. Of course, what is relevant is how much income households have to spend; this is called their **disposable income,** their income after taxes. When government increases taxes, it reduces disposable income, and when disposable income is reduced, household savings are reduced.

In this chapter we assume that the stock of plant

In equilibrium, output is equal to the full-employment level of output, that is, the output that can be generated by the available labour force working with the given set of plant and equipment.

Increases in the labour supply (rightwards shifts in the labour supply curve), increases in the stock of plant and equipment as a result of net investment, and technological change all increase the full-employment level of output.

and equipment as well as the labour supply are givens. With wages and prices adjusting to ensure that the labour market clears, aggregate output is fixed. We now make use of an important result from Chapter 6: we saw there that national income equals aggregate output. The money that gets paid for purchasing goods has to go into somebody's pockets, and thus becomes somebody's income. Thus, if aggregate output is given so is aggregate income. Here, we also assume that taxes are fixed, so that with aggregate income given, so is aggregate disposable income.

With taxes fixed, our focus is on the interest rate, which is the return on savings. Figure 8.8 shows two different possibilities. In panel A, savings increases significantly with the interest rate, whereas in panel B, savings responds only slightly to changes in the interest rate. Empirical studies suggest that savings are *slightly* sensitive to interest rates, that is, the savings curve is *almost* vertical—it looks more like panel B than panel A.

But doesn't a higher interest rate provide greater incentives to save? The answer is yes, but there is another effect: at higher interest rates, individuals do not need to put aside today as much as they otherwise would for their retirement or to buy a home. At higher interest rates, savers are better off. Individuals who are better off consume more and save less. We refer to this as the income effect, in contrast to the "incentive" effect, or substitution effect. The two effects pull in opposite directions, and on balance tend to offset each other. That is why savings is not very sensitive to the interest rate.

Of course, when individuals look at the return to savings, they take into account inflation—the fact that a dollar in the future may buy less than a dollar today. Thus, the relevant interest rate for savings is the *real* interest rate, which is just the nominal interest rate minus the rate of inflation. If the nominal interest rate is 10 percent and the rate of inflation is 4 percent, then the real interest rate is 6 percent. As in

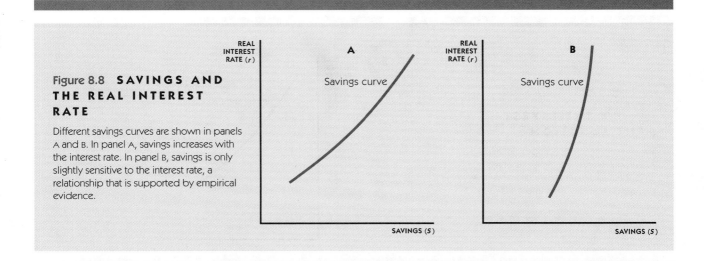

**Figure 8.8 SAVINGS AND THE REAL INTEREST RATE**

Different savings curves are shown in panels A and B. In panel A, savings increases with the interest rate. In panel B, savings is only slightly sensitive to the interest rate, a relationship that is supported by empirical evidence.

the macroeconomic analysis of the labour and product markets, here we ignore the differences among the various interest rates at play in the economy. We refer to the interest rate in general in the macroeconomic analysis of savings and investment.

## INVESTMENT

Economists use the word "investment" in two different ways. Households think of the stocks and bonds they buy as investments; these are **financial investments.** These financial investments provide the funds for firms to use to buy capital goods—machines and buildings. The purchases of new machines and buildings represent firms' investments, referred to as **capital investments.** In macroeconomics, when we refer to investments it is to capital, not financial, investments.

Firms invest in order to increase their capacity to produce goods and services. They expect the revenues from the sales of these extra products to cover the cost of the investment as well as the cost of additional workers and raw materials required to increase production, leaving them with a profit. Thus, one determinant of investment is firms' **expectations** about the future, which we assume for now to be fixed.

We focus instead on the other key determinant of investment, the interest rate. Many firms borrow to finance their investment. The cost of these funds—what they have to pay the bank or other creditors for using the funds—is the interest rate. The higher the interest rate, the fewer the investment projects that are profitable—the fewer the projects that, after the bank has been paid back the interest, will yield a return to the investing firm sufficient to compensate it for the risk its owners undertake. Even if the firm is flush with cash, the interest rate matters. The interest rate then becomes the opportunity cost of the firm's money, what it could have obtained if, instead of making the investment, it had simply decided to lend the money to the government or some other firm.

The **investment function** gives the level of real investment at each value of the real interest rate. The investment function slopes downwards to the right: investment increases as the real interest rate decreases. This is depicted in Figure 8.9, which shows the real interest rate on the vertical axis and the real investment level on the horizontal axis.

There is another way of seeing why the interest rate matters: while the firm puts out money today to buy machines, the returns it receives, in increased profits, do not occur until the future. A dollar received in the future is not worth as much as a dollar today, because of the time value of money: a dollar today could have been put in the bank and earned interest; if the interest rate is 7 percent, in ten years

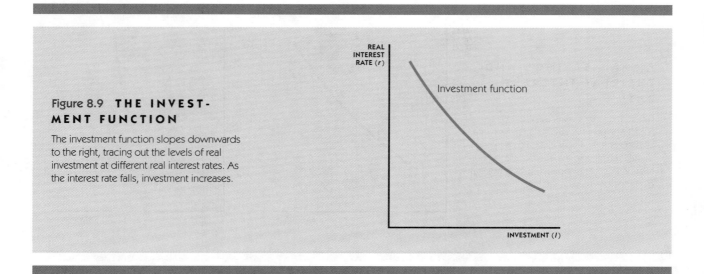

Figure 8.9 **THE INVEST-MENT FUNCTION**

The investment function slopes downwards to the right, tracing out the levels of real investment at different real interest rates. As the interest rate falls, investment increases.

## CAPITAL MARKET EQUILIBRIUM

In equilibrium, savings equals investment.

Increases in savings (shifts to the right in the savings schedule) lead to lower real interest rates and higher levels of investment.

Shifts to the right in the investment schedule lead to higher real interest rates, but unchanged or higher levels of investment.

the dollar will have doubled to $2. We thus say that the **present discounted value** of $2 ten years from now is a dollar today. (The present discounted value of a dollar in the future is what someone would be willing to pay today for that dollar.) An increase in the interest rate *reduces* the present discounted value of future dollars. At a 14 percent interest rate, a dollar put in the bank today has doubled to $2 in five years and quadrupled to $4 in ten years. Thus, a dollar in ten years is worth only a quarter, while at 7 percent it is worth fifty cents. An investment is undertaken if the present discounted value of expected

profits is more than the cost; with an increase in the interest rate, fewer investments meet this criterion. The aggregate level of investment thus decreases.

## EQUILIBRIUM IN THE CAPITAL MARKET

The equilibrium real interest rate is the rate at which savings equals investment, depicted in Figure 8.10. We have also shown there the effect of an increased demand for investment at each real interest

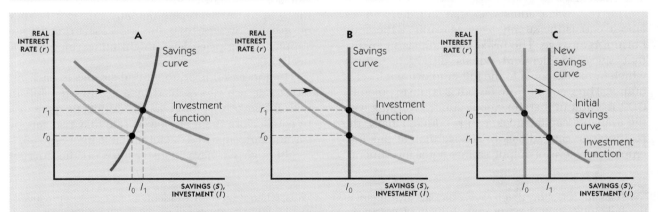

### Figure 8.10 EQUILIBRIUM IN THE CAPITAL MARKET

Equilibrium requires that the demand for funds, or investment, equal the supply, savings. The level of desired investment decreases as the real interest rate increases.

Panel A. Savings increase slightly with increases in the real interest rate. Panels B and C. Savings are not interest-sensitive, so the savings curve is a vertical straight line. The equilibrium level of investment is simply equal to the full-employment level of savings.

A shift in the investment function so that at every real

interest rate the demand for investment is increased is depicted in panels A and B. In panel A, investment is increased from $I^*$ to $I_1^*$, whereas in panel B, with inelastic savings, the only effect is to increase the real interest rate from $r^*$ to $r_1^*$, leaving investment and savings unchanged. Panel C shows a rightward shift in the savings curve. The level of savings increases at each real interest rate, resulting in a decrease of the real interest rate from $r_0$ to $r_1$, and an increase in investment from $I_0$ to $I_1$.

rate. In panel A, both the equilibrium real interest rate and the equilibrium level of savings and investment are increased, while in panel B, only the real interest rate is changed. Because savings are not sensitive to the real interest rate in the latter case, and savings must equal investment, investment remains unchanged. By contrast, a rightward shift in the savings curve, so that at every real interest rate savings increases, results in a reduction in the real interest rate and an increse in investments. This is shown in panel C. Because the savings curve is almost vertical, the major impact of a shift in the savings curve is a change in investment.

## THE GENERAL EQUILIBRIUM

We can now describe the general equilibrium of the economy, the real wage, price level, and real interest rate at which the labour, product, and capital markets all clear:

The real wage adjusts so that the demand for labour equals the supply. This determines the equilibrium real wage. The price level adjusts to ensure that aggregate demand equals aggregate supply, which in turn is equal to the full-employment level of output. Thus, equilibrium output is equal to potential GDP, the output that the labour supply, working with the available capital stock, can produce. Finally, the real interest rate adjusts to ensure that, at this full-employment level of output, savings equal investment.[4]

## USING THE GENERAL EQUILIBRIUM MODEL

The general equilibrium model is useful because it allows us to understand the effects of various changes in the economy—from the market in which they originate to all the other markets in the economy.

Consider the effect of the introduction of personal computers to the economy. The marginal product of workers increases, causing a shift in the demand curve for labour to the right. The equilibrium real wage increases, as shown in Figure 8.11, panel A.

Given the greater productivity of workers and the fixed labour supply, full-employment output increases as shown by a rightwards shift in the aggregate supply curve (panel B). Aggregate demand may rise because of an increase in investment (at every value of the real interest rate) as firms take advantage of the available profit opportunities opened up by the new computer technology. At the same time, the increase in income leads to increases in consumption and in savings at each interest rate. If aggregate demand rises by the same amount as aggregate supply, the price level is unchanged. Of course, the shift in the aggregate demand curve at $P_0$ may be greater or less than the increase in aggregate supply, so the price level might either increase or decrease.

The increased investment and savings at each interest rate are represented by a rightwards shift in both the investment and savings functions (panel C). In equilibrium the real interest rate may rise, fall, or stay the same (panel C depicts a stable interest rate).

Although we have focused here on the current

---

[4] We can, in fact, show that if savings equals investment at the full-employment level of output, then aggregate demand equals aggregate supply at that level of output.

In our simplified model with no government and no foreign trade, there are two sources of aggregate demand, investment and consumption:

$$Y_d = C + I.$$

Since national output *always* equals national income, full-employment output, $Y_f$, equals full-employment income, and full-employment incomes are either saved or consumed:

$$Y_f = C + S.$$

Thus, when desired investment, as reflected in the investment schedule, equals full-employment savings,

$$I = S^d,$$

where we use the superscript to remind us that this is the "desired" level of savings, then from the second equation,

$$I = Y_f - C.$$

Substituting the fourth equation back into the first equation gives

$$Y_d = C + I = C + Y_f - C = Y_f,$$

aggregate demand equals full-employment output, the aggregate supply. There is equilibrium in the product market.

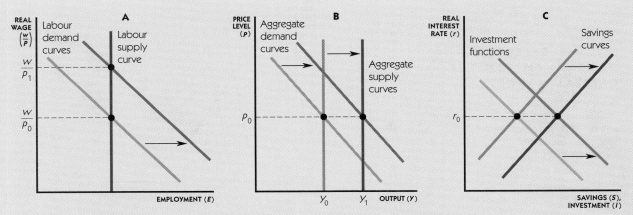

**Figure 8.11 EFFECTS OF INTRODUCING PERSONAL COMPUTERS INTO THE ECONOMY**

Panel A depicts the labour market. Personal computers increase the marginal product of workers, resulting in a rightward shift of the labour demand curve and an increase in the equilibrium real wage from $w_0/P$ to $w_1/P$. Panel B depicts the product market. With the increased productivity of workers, the aggregate supply curve shifts to the right. Output increases from $Y_0$ to $Y_1$. If aggregate demand increases owing to an increase in investment and an increase in consumption from higher incomes, the aggregate demand curve will shift to the right. If the increase in aggregate demand is the same as the increase in aggregate supply, the price level will remain at $P_0$. Panel C depicts the capital market. Investment increases as firms purchase computers, and savings increase as a result of increased income. Both the investment and savings curves shift to the right. There may be no net effect on the interest rate, as shown here.

effects of these changes, there are important future effects. In the future, there will be more plant and equipment. The economy's future capacity ($Y_f$) will increase. Thus, not only are all markets linked today, but markets today are also linked with markets in the future.

## GOVERNMENT

Introducing government into the analysis potentially affects all markets, depending upon the nature of the intervention. To simplify matters, let us suppose that government expenditures take the form of purchases of goods and services produced in the private sector. In practice, of course, some government expenditures involve hiring labour to produce public goods and services within the public sector. To the extent that this is true, our analysis would have to be slightly modified, but the overall effect on output, employment, and investment would not alter. Given that gov-

ernment expenditures take the form of purchases of goods and services from the private sector, they add to aggregate demand. At the same time, the taxes imposed to finance government expenditures reduce disposable income and thus subtract from aggregate demand.

Focusing on the capital market makes the effects of government on general equilibrium clear. In Figure 8.12, the reduction in disposable income from taxes shifts the savings curve to the left, reducing equilibrium savings, from $S_0$ to $S_1$. With an unchanged investment schedule, the equilibrium interest rate rises and the equilibrium investment level falls.

Government also affects the composition of output. Figure 8.13 shows how an increase in government expenditure matched with an increase in taxes changes the composition of output. The total size of the pie is unchanged; we assume that the economy remains at full employment. Thus, the effect of government is simply to change how the pie is divided. Investment and consumption are both lowered—or

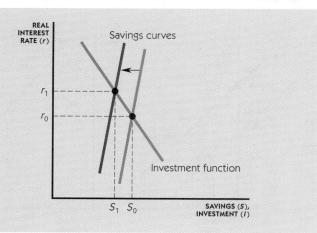

## Figure 8.12 EFFECTS OF GOVERNMENT ON THE CAPITAL MARKET

Government taxes reduce disposable income and savings, resulting in a leftwards shift of the savings curve. The equilibrium interest rate rises from $r_0$, to $r_1$, and the investment level falls.

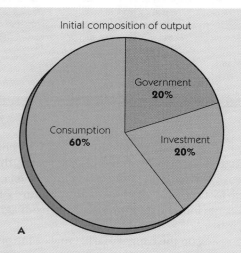

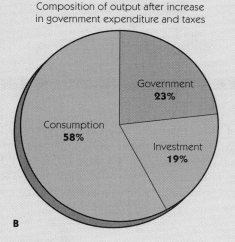

## Figure 8.13 EFFECT OF AN EQUAL INCREASE IN GOVERNMENT EXPENDITURES AND TAXES ON THE COMPOSITION OF OUTPUT

An increase in government expenditure financed by an increase in taxes leads to a decrease in consumption and investment. Government expenditure is said to "crowd out" private expenditure.

**crowded out**—to make room for increased government expenditures. Even if government increases taxes by an amount to pay fully for the increased expenditure—in our example, by 3 percent of GDP—consumption is reduced by less, as individuals adjust in part by reducing savings.

## THE MONEY SUPPLY

Government may also play a role in the economy by changing the amount of money in circulation. This is done through monetary policy, a subject we will consider later in the book. For now, it is important to

**USING ECONOMICS: QUANTIFYING IMPACTS ON INVESTMENT OF INCREASED GOVERNMENT EXPENDITURES MATCHED BY INCREASED TAXES**

Increased government expenditures, even when matched by increased taxes, "crowd out" private investment. It is easy to quantify the effect. Assume the government increases government expenditure by $10 billion and increases taxes on individuals by $10 billion. With higher taxes, individuals have a lower income, and so—at any interest rate—they save less. For simplicity, assume that for each extra hundred dollars of after-tax income, individuals save ten dollars. Thus, the increased $10 billion of taxes reduces savings by $1 billion. For simplicity, assume that the savings is completely inelastic, that is, the savings curve is

a vertical straight line. Then, if savings equals investment, and savings is reduced by $1 billion, so is investment. In the new equilibrium, aggregate output is unchanged (at the full-employment level); government expenditures are increased by $10 billion, offset by a reduction of consumption of $9 billion and of investment by $1 billion.

If savings has a slight positive elasticity, then as interest rates rise, there will be increased savings. Thus, investment will be reduced less and consumption more than if savings is totally insensitive to the interest rate.

understand the consequences of changes in the money supply for the full-employment model.

By and large, economists agree that in a full-employment economy, money affects the price level, but little else. In particular, it does not affect the quantity of goods produced or the number of workers employed. We can use an imaginative example to understand the point. Suppose that the entire supply of money in the economy was instantaneously increased by a multiple of ten. In effect, we have tacked a zero onto the money supply. Dollar bills are now worth $10; five-dollar bills are now worth $50; ten-dollar bills are now worth $100; your chequing account of $250 dollars is now worth $2,500, and so on. Stores, acting perfectly efficiently, and knowing that the money supply has multiplied by ten, would increase their prices tenfold. Thus, the actual amount of goods and services produced and consumed would be the same; there would be no real effect. The only difference would be the numbers on the bills, bank statements, and price tags.

The lesson is more general: an increase in the supply of money accompanied by a proportionate increase in the price level has no real effects on the economy. When changing the money supply has no real effects we say that money is *neutral*. If the econ-

omy is at full employment and prices are perfectly flexible, prices will increase proportionally with the money supply. Thus, the **neutrality of money** is a basic property of the full-employment model. We can see this by tracing through the effects of an increase in the money supply in the product, labour, and capital markets, as shown in Figure 8.14.

Panel A of Figure 8.14 shows the aggregate supply and aggregate demand curves. An increase in the money supply represents an increase in money balances held by the public, so private wealth increases. This results in a rightwards shift of the aggregate demand curve. The price level increases from $P_0$ to $P_1$, but the equilibrium level of output remains at $Y_0$.

In panel B we see the aggregate supply and aggregate demand curves for labour. In the labour market the increase in the price level will be matched by an increase in the nominal wage, from $w_0$ to $w_1$, so that the real wage remains at its original level, $w_0/P_0 = w_1/P_1$. At this real wage, the demand for labour continues to equal its supply. Thus, the effect on the labour market of an increase in the price level is simply a proportionate increase in the nominal wage. There are no real effects—the equilibrium real wage $w/P_0$ and the equilibrium level of employment $L_0$ are not affected.

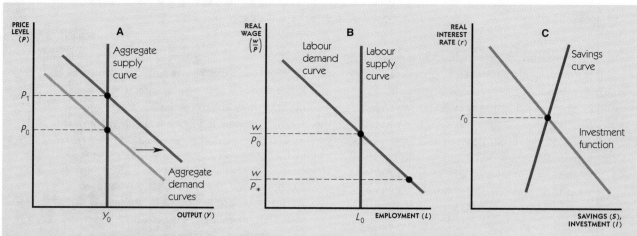

**Figure 8.14  EFFECT OF AN INCREASE IN THE MONEY SUPPLY ON THE THREE MAJOR MARKETS**

An increase in the money supply shifts the aggregate demand curve upwards, causing the price level to rise, as in panel A. In panel B, equilibrium in the labour market is restored by the nominal wage increasing in proportion to prices so that the real wage is unchanged. The real interest rate is unaffected by a once-over change in the price level.

In the capital market, real savings and investment both depend on the real interest rate, which is not affected by the increase in the price level. Accordingly, in panel C, neither the savings curve nor the investment function shifts. At each interest rate, *nominal* savings and investment would increase by an amount exactly proportional to the increase in the money supply. Why? Because households and firms must increase the dollar amount of savings and investment in order to maintain the value of savings and investment relative to the higher price level. But panel C shows the levels of *real* savings and investment at each real interest rate. The equilibrium real interest rate, $r_0$, remains the same. The overall result once again displays the neutrality of money because there are no real effects in the capital market. Only the *nominal* levels of savings and investment change in proportion to the change in the price level.

It is important to note that this discussion involves a once-over increase in the money supply rather than a continuing one. This means that the price level increases one time only; there is no ongoing in-

flation. Since there is no inflation, the nominal and the real interest rate are the same thing. As we will see later in the book, if the money supply increases continuously, the inflation rate will be positive and the nominal interest rate will exceed the real one. In the full-employment economy, money will still be neutral. The real interest rate will be unaffected by inflation, and the level of real investment and savings will not change.

The neutrality of money highlights the important distinction economists make between real and nominal phenomena. As we have seen here and in earlier chapters, in referring to nominal variables such as nominal GDP and nominal wages, we mean the current money value of those variables, that is, the value *without* adjustments for changes in the price level. As this example shows, our full-employment model with flexible prices makes a perfect distinction between real and nominal phenomena. Relationships between real variables—which are the focus of the model—are completely independent of changes in nominal variables.

While the neutrality of money is a basic property

of our full-employment model with flexible prices, it is important to keep in mind the limitations of the model. If price increases themselves had literally no consequences, inflation would not be a matter of much concern. But, as we learned in Chapter 6, it is a concern. Later chapters will explore the more complicated effects of increases in the money supply when the economy is not at full employment and prices are not perfectly flexible.

## INTERNATIONAL TRADE AND CAPITAL FLOWS

Participation in international markets introduces more fundamental changes into the analysis. It affects the product market because net exports are one of the four key components of aggregate demand. More important, it introduces an additional source of funds for financing investment. The savings schedule depicted so far is the *domestic* source of funds. If investment, the demand for funds, exceeds domestic savings, firms can borrow abroad.

The transactions that Canadians engage in with residents of other countries represent a small proportion of total world transactions. So Canada as a whole is a price taker on world goods and capital markets. We are referred to as a **small open economy.** This means that Canada faces an essentially

horizontal supply of funds on world markets at a given real interest rate, as depicted in Figure 8.15. If Canada pays a higher interest rate than that paid in other countries, those with capital divert their funds to Canada. If we pay less than the interest rate available in other countries—adjusted, of course, for risk—we can obtain no capital. In this sense our capital market is a small open one. But it's a small open capital market in another sense. Those who have capital in Canada can take their funds and invest them abroad. If Canadian firms pay a lower interest rate than that paid abroad, even Canadian investors will not invest their funds at home. For a small open economy, *the interest rate is determined by the international capital market*. Effectively, such a country takes the interest rate as fixed. This in turn means that the level of investment is fixed, at $I^*$ in Figure 8.15. A shortfall between the level of savings, $S_0$, and that level of investment is funded by borrowing from abroad, by the quantity $B_0$ in the figure. A reduction in the amount of savings to $S_1$ increases the amount of foreign borrowing to $B_1$ but leaves investment unaffected.

This result contrasts markedly with our earlier result for a closed economy, one in which there was no foreign borrowing or lending. There, we noted that lower savings (a shift to the left in the savings curve) results in less investment. There is a similar contrast in the effect of an increase in government expenditure matched by an increase in taxes. In a

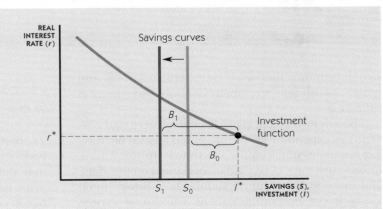

**Figure 8.15 SUPPLY OF SAVINGS IN A SMALL OPEN ECONOMY**

In a small open economy the real interest rate, $r^*$, is determined by the international capital market. Investment is fixed at $I^*$. If domestic savings equal $S_0$, the shortfall, $B_0$, is made up by borrowing from abroad. A reduction in savings to $S_1$ leads to increased borrowing ($B_1$).

## POLICY PERSPECTIVE: A GLOBAL CAPITAL SHORTAGE?

No sooner had the world economy begun showing signs of the recovery from the worldwide recession of the early 1990s than the newspapers sounded a new alarm: a global capital shortage.

Of course, economists are reluctant to refer to "shortages," because they recognize that prices —or in this case, interest rates—adjust to demand and supply. What was really worrying people was the possibility that the world's savings curve was shifting left and the world's investment curve was shifting right—and the combination was driving up real interest rates. The reason for the anxiety was not hard to see. In the 1990s, real interest rates in Canada have averaged about 6 percent, far higher than the average real interest rates that had prevailed over the first nine decades of the century, between .5 percent and 1.5 percent.

Moreover, several factors suggested that the situation might not be simply a temporary aberration. First, national savings rates in the countries of the Organization for Economic Cooperation and Development (OECD) were all down significantly from what they had been a decade or so earlier, by about 4 percent of GDP on average. Second, Eastern Europe and Russia represented a vast area of potential investment that was at

last opening up to the world's capital market, and the reforms required to make these economies more hospitable to foreign investment were occurring, albeit at a slower pace than had been anticipated. Third, many less developed countries that had previously discouraged foreign investment were now actively seeking it. While these "emerging markets" remained small on the scale of the world capital market, they represented an enormous potential increase in demand. Some of the fastest-growing countries, like Singapore and China, have managed to sustain savings rates roughly commensurate with their high investment rates (exceeding 25 percent of GDP). But in South Asia and Latin America, investment demand could easily exceed savings by a substantial amount.

It is too soon to tell whether the higher real interest rates are to remain a feature of the world's capital market in coming decades. If so, Canadian firms will have to pay higher real interest rates. Higher real interest rates in turn will imply lower levels of investment. Unless they can use technological change and new business practices to sufficiently offset the decreased level of investment, we can expect a slowing down of the rate of increase in productivity.

---

closed economy increased taxes reduce savings and hence, investment. In a open economy, investment is unchanged.

Though investment is unaffected by increased government expenditures, the increased foreign borrowing has consequences for the future. In the future, interest will have to be paid to foreigners on this debt, and this will lower future standards of living, much as the lower level of investment would have. (These effects will be discussed at greater length in the next chapter.)

## IS CANADA A PRICE-TAKER ON WORLD CAPITAL MARKETS?

There is no doubt that Canada's proportion of worldwide capital market transactions is very small. But that does not necessarily mean that Canada is a price-taker. Although capital flows quite freely between countries, the world capital market is far from fully integrated. Individuals know more about what is going on in their own country than what is going on

## OPEN ECONOMY INVESTMENT

Canada is essentially a small open economy. In a small open economy, the real interest rate is determined internationally and is unaffected by Canadian savings and in-

vestment. Reductions in the Canadian savings rate are reflected fully in increases in borrowing from abroad. The level of investment is unaffected.

abroad. Foreign investors may require a slightly higher rate of return on investments in Canada to compensate them for this increased risk. Small firms in Canada find it a lot easier to get bank loans from Canadian banks than from, say, American ones. In recent years, with the greater flow of information, the magnitude of this risk premium—the extra they must earn—has decreased, but it is still positive.

The result is that to attract more and more funds from abroad, real interest rates offered in Canada might have to rise. If Canada's savings rate were to fall, the increased demand for borrowing from abroad would cause the real interest rate to rise. In turn, this would cause investment to fall, unlike in a small open economy. However, the fall in investment would be much less than if the economy were closed to world markets.

Whether or not Canada really is a price-taker in capital markets is an empirical question. Most economists think that we are at least approximately so, that is, changes in our demand for borrowing from abroad have a small enough impact on real interest rates to be ignored when analyzing macroeconomic issues. In much of what follows, we assume that Canada is a small open economy.

## CONSENSUS IN MACROECONOMICS

Macroeconomic issues are often front and centre in newspapers and nightly newscasts on television. There is good reason for this. As we learned in Chapter 6, the macroeconomic problems of unemployment, slow growth, and inflation have substantial, widespread consequences. With modest productivity gains, the concern is with slow economic growth; when the unemployment rate increases, the focus is

on impending recession; when the consumer price index goes up faster, attention shifts to inflation. These problems, and the ways to address them, are often hotly debated, giving rise to controversy. In this context, the views of economists often appear to be contradictory, and the old saw about how any two economists will give you three opinions may seem true. But in fact, there is remarkable consensus among economists about basic macroeconomic principles.

In this chapter we encounter our fifth and sixth points of consensus:

**5 The Effects of Government Expenditures at Full Employment**

*When the economy is at full employment and the economy is closed, increases in government expenditures must come at the expense of private consumption and/or investment. Even when matched with increases in taxes, such increases crowd out private investment, since the increased taxes will normally lead to a reduction in savings. If the economy is open, government expenditures lead to increased foreign borrowing, since the fall in savings is not matched by a fall in investment.*

**6 The Neutrality of Money**

*At full employment, an increase in the money supply only leads to a proportionate increase in prices and wages, with no real consequences.*

## LOOKING FORWARD

This chapter has used the basic competitive model to analyze the full-employment macroeconomic equilibrium of the economy. We have seen how real wages adjust to ensure that the demand for labour

# CLOSE-UP: IS CANADA A SMALL OPEN ECONOMY?

The presumption that Canada is a price-taker on international capital markets seems on the surface to be a natural one. After all, financial capital is highly mobile across borders, so differences between interest rates across countries should not persist. And Canada's international transactions make up a relatively small proportion of those on world capital markets.

Yet, as the accompanying figure shows, aggregate investment and aggregate savings tend to move together. When investment rises, savings tend to rise as well; when investment falls, so does savings. This would seem to contradict the small-open-economy assumption. Canadian capital markets do not have to clear, so savings should be able to move independently of investment. Changes in investment in Canada need not be financed by changes in domestic savings. They can be financed by capital inflows. Similarly, changes in Canadian savings need not go towards investment projects in Canada. It can be used to buy foreign assets.

The fact that Canadian savings and investment tend to move together turns out to be something that has been observed for other countries as well, and has led some economists to question the suitability of the small-open-economy assumption. Obviously, there is a lot at stake, since the way the economy responds to changes in, say, government expenditure policies depends upon whether or not the domestic interest rate responds.

But is the observed correlation between savings and investment in an open economy really incompatible with the economy being a price-taker in world capital markets? One way to reconcile the observed correlation is to recognize that savings and investment may both be responding to some common determinant besides the interest rate. For example, if productivity improves in Canada, this will make investment more attractive, causing the investment demand curve to shift to the right. More investment will be undertaken at the given interest rate. The same productivity shock will cause Canadian GDP to rise, and some of that increase will certainly lead to higher savings. Thus, the savings curve will also shift to the right and savings will rise. Conversely, if costs of production were to rise, for example because energy prices

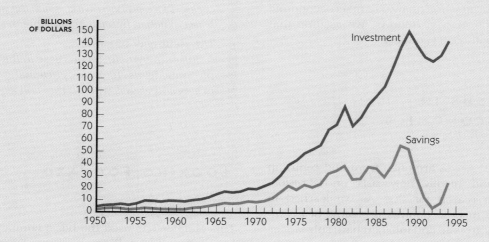

BILLIONS OF DOLLARS

rise, domestic investment will become less profitable at the going interest rate and will fall. This will result in a lower GDP which in turn will leave Canadians with less income. Savings will fall. These movements in savings and investment happen independently of any changes in interest rates and so

are quite compatible with the small open economy assumption.

*Sources:* Statistics Canada, CANSIM Database, 1996; M. Feldstein and C. Horioka, "Domestic Saving and International Capital Flows," *The Economic Journal* 90 (June 1980): 314–29.

always equals the supply, even in the face of changes in technology and new investments that might replace workers. We have seen how prices and interest rates adjust, say, in the face of shifts in the demand for investment so that the economy continues to produce at its productive capacity and so that savings continues to equal investment at the full-employment level of output.

In the long run, wages, prices, and interest rates do adjust in much the manner described here. In the short run, however, they may not. If they did adjust instantaneously, then the model presented here would be a good description not only of how the economy in the long run is able to create enough new jobs to match the increase in supply, but also of the economy in the short run. But wages and prices in particular may be *sticky*, that is, fail to adjust to the market-clearing levels. This has profound implications for how the economy behaves in the short run, as we shall see in the following two parts. First, however, we take a closer look at some of the important implications of our full-employment model.

## REVIEW AND PRACTICE

### SUMMARY

**1** Macroeconomic equilibrium focuses on equilibrium levels of aggregates: employment, output, and investment. In a full-employment competitive equilibrium, each is determined by equating demand and supply. Full employment is attained as a result of flexible wages and prices.

**2** The real wage equates the demand for labour to the supply. Increases in the labour supply are reflected in lower real wages, which induce firms to create additional jobs to match the increased supply.

**3** The full-employment level of output is the level of output that the economy can produce with its given stock of plant and equipment, when labour is fully employed. It will increase with increases in the labour supply.

**4** The price level adjusts to equate aggregate demand to aggregate supply.

**5** The real interest rate, which takes account of inflation, equates investment and savings. The desired level of investment decreases with increases in the real interest rate. Savings depends on disposable income and the real interest rate. With flexible wages and prices, labour is fully employed, so output is always at the full-employment level. Since aggregate output equals national income, if taxes are fixed, disposable income will be fixed. Savings increases slightly with increases in the real interest rate.

**6** In a closed economy, government expenditures, when paid for by increases in taxes, crowds out consumption and investment. In a small open economy like Canada, investment is unchanged and foreign borrowing increases.

**7** Decreases in savings (shifts to the left in the savings curve) lead to reduced investment in a closed economy, and to increased foreign borrowing in a small open economy.

**8** All the markets in the economy are interlinked. Changes in one market have effects on all other markets.

**9** In a full-employment economy with perfectly flexible wages and prices, money is neutral: increases in the money supply are simply reflected in increases in prices.

## KEY TERMS

real wage

disposable income

investment function

short-run production function

full-employment level of output

aggregate supply curve

expectations

crowding out

neutrality of money

small open economy

## REVIEW QUESTIONS

**1** How do competitive markets with flexible wages and prices ensure that labour is always fully employed? What induces firms to create just the right number of additional jobs to match an increase in the number of workers?

**2** Describe the effects of changes in labour supply (shifts in the labour supply curve) on equilibrium real wages and potential GDP (full-employment level of output).

**3** What determines the economy's productive capacity or aggregate supply or potential GDP? How does aggregate supply increase when labour supply increases?

**4** What is the aggregate demand curve? Why is it downward-sloping? Why is the aggregate supply curve vertical? What determines the price level?

**5** What is the investment schedule? Why does investment decrease when the real interest rate increases? What role do expectations play in investment?

**6** What determines the level of savings? Explain why, if taxes are fixed, disposable income in a full-employment economy is fixed. Explain why savings may not be very sensitive to the real rate of interest.

**7** How is the equilibrium rate of interest determined?

**8** How do government expenditures matched by taxes affect the market equilibrium?

**9** What difference does it make whether the economy is closed or open? Illustrate by examining the effects of an increase in government expenditure.

**10** How does the Canadian economy differ from a closed economy? from a larger economy such as the United States?

## PROBLEMS

**1** In the text, we assumed that the labour supply did not depend on the real wage. Assume that at higher real wages more individuals wish to work and trace through how each of the steps in the analysis has to be changed. Show the equilibrium in the labour market. What happens to real wages, employment, GDP, and savings if the labour supply curve shifts to the right?

**2** An increase in capital resulting from an increase in investment allows a given number of workers to produce more. Show the effect on the short-run production function and the full-employment level of output. It may be the case that while the short-run production function shifts upward, its slope becomes flatter at some levels of employment (output). What does this imply for the aggregate demand curve for labour? Is it possible that the equilibrium real wage could actually fall?

**3** In Chapter 7 we learned that firms hire workers up to the point where the wage equals the value of the marginal product of labour, the price times the extra output that an extra worker produces. Explain why the slope of the short-run production function is the marginal product of labour. Explain why, with diminishing returns, an increase in the real wage leads to a lower level of demand for labour. Draw an example of a shift outward in the short-run production function caused, say, by technological change, which causes at any real wage the demand for labour to decrease; to increase.

**4** Explain how income and substitution effects offset each other in the supply curve of labour; in the supply curve for savings.

**5** Trace through how the effects of a change in one market, such as an increase in the supply of labour, has effects on other markets. How was it possible for there to be a large increase in the labour supply, such as occurred during the 1970s and 1980s, and yet for real wages to change relatively little?

**6** Trace through the effects on an increase in taxes without a corresponding increase in government expenditures, or an increase in government expenditures without a corresponding increase in taxes.

**7** What are some of the reasons that even in an open economy investment and savings might be highly correlated?

**8** "Even if, in an open economy, a decrease in savings does not decrease investment, decreased savings still means that future generations will be worse off." Discuss.

**9** Consider a closed economy initially in equilibrium with $40 billion savings (investment) and a real interest rate of 4 percent. Households save 10 percent of their $400 billion income. The government imposes a $10 billion additional tax on households, used to finance $10 billion additional government expenditures. If the interest elasticity of savings is zero, while a 10 percent increase in the real interest rate (from 4 to 4.4 percent) decreases investment by 2.6 percent, what is the new equilibrium level of investment, savings, and the real interest rate? Show that if the interest elasticity of savings is .1 (so an increase of the interest rate to 4.4 percent generates $.4 billion in increased savings), the new equilibrium entails the real interest rate rising by 7 percent, to 4.28 percent. What happens to investment in this case?

# 9

# USING THE FULL-EMPLOYMENT MODEL

T he federal budget deficit ballooned during the 1980s and was transformed from a problem that mainly interested economists and political pundits into one squarely in the national spotlight. By the 1993 federal election, public opinion polls were persistently ranking the huge deficits among the central problems facing the country. In this chapter we use the model developed in Chapter 8 to elucidate the consequences of the deficit. Another problem that rose to prominence in the latter half of the 1980s was the deficit in the **current account** of the balance of payments, which is the net exports of goods and services minus the net inflow of investment income and transfers from abroad. A modest current-account surplus in 1984 turned into a deficit that reached almost $30 billion by 1991; of this, about $7 billion was due to a deficit in goods and services trade, and the rest was due to a net outflow in investment income. The full-employment model can help us to understand the

## KEY QUESTIONS

**1** What are the consequences of the huge fiscal deficits of the 1980s?

**2** What gave rise to the huge current-account deficits of the late 1980s and 1990s? What are their consequences?

**3** How do deficits affect economic growth? What are some other policies that can help promote growth?

**4** What difference does it make for policy if the economy is a small open one?

current-account deficit, and how it might be affected by various policies.

In Chapter 6 we described the three fundamental economic problems of growth, unemployment, and inflation. By assumption, the full-employment model of Chapter 8 cannot shed light directly on the problem of unemployment (though in the next chapter we will explain how unemployment can result from a simple change in one of the critical assumptions of that model). In the last chapter we saw how the full-employment model provides us with useful insights into inflation—with the price level increasing in proportion to the money supply. In this chapter, we show how the full-employment model provides us with useful insights into the problem of growth.

## THE GOVERNMENT BUDGET DEFICIT

When the government spends more than it receives in taxes and other revenues in any given year, it has a **budget,** or **fiscal, deficit.** It must borrow to finance that deficit. Government spending rose during the 1980s from 21.3 percent of GDP in 1981 to 23.1 percent of GDP in 1991. But taxes failed to rise to match this boost in spending, and as a result the government had to borrow increasingly large sums of money. Figure 9.1 shows the resulting explosion in the federal budget deficit.

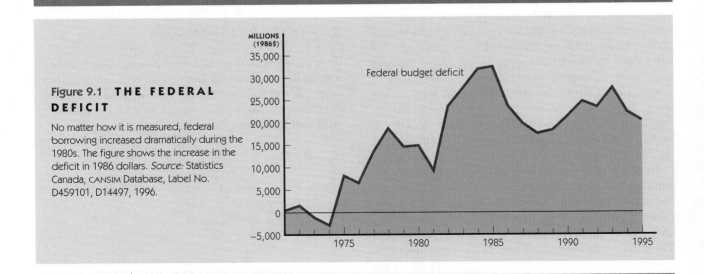

**Figure 9.1 THE FEDERAL DEFICIT**

No matter how it is measured, federal borrowing increased dramatically during the 1980s. The figure shows the increase in the deficit in 1986 dollars. *Source:* Statistics Canada, CANSIM Database, Label No. D459101, D14497, 1996.

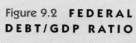

## Figure 9.2 FEDERAL DEBT/GDP RATIO

The federal debt fell dramatically after World War II, continued to fall until the mid-1970s, and then began to rise rapidly as federal budget deficits persisted. *Source:* Statistics Canada, CANSIM Database, Label No. D469409, D10000, 1996.

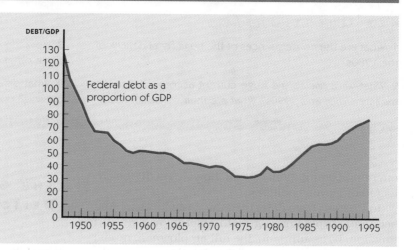

From 1976 to 1993, the federal deficit (in 1986 dollars) more than quadrupled, from $6.5 billion to $27.7 billion. These represented the first major deficits in times other than during wars or serious depressions. The **federal debt** is the cumulative amount that the government owes. Figure 9.2 puts the resulting federal debt in context, by measuring it as a percentage of GDP. The debt/GDP ratio fell from 1.27 at the end of World War II to under a third by the mid-1970s. As federal budget deficits have persisted, the debt as a percentage of GDP rose dramatically, to 75% by 1994. When provincial government debt is included, the debt-to-GDP ratio rises to almost 1.0, roughly $24,000 for every man, woman, and child in Canada.

Compared with other western countries, Canada does not fare very well. As Figure 9.3 shows, Canada's deficit and debt as a proportion of GDP are higher than those of most European countries, as well as Japan and the United States.

In Chapter 20 we will discuss at greater length some of the political and economic events that gave rise to the deficit, as well as the debates about precisely how deleterious the deficit is for the economy's well-being. Here, we use the model of Chapter 8 to give us a *qualitative* picture of the consequences.

In Chapter 8 we discussed the effects of an increase in government expenditures matched with an increase in taxes. Here, we look at the effect of an increase in government expenditures not matched with an increase in taxes. (The same results hold for a decrease in taxes unmatched with a decrease in expenditures.) Our earlier analysis identified the openness of the economy as a critical determinant. We examine the two extreme cases, a closed economy and a small open economy, remembering that the Canadian economy lies between these extremes but is closer to the latter.

## A CLOSED ECONOMY

In a closed economy, if the government increases its expenditures without increasing taxes, it must borrow the difference.[1] In this case private savings, $S_p$, has to go for two purposes—to finance the deficit, $D$, and to finance investment, $I$:

$$S_p = D + I.$$

Alternatively, we can think of the deficit as *negative public savings:*

$$D = -S_g.$$

---

[1] It used to be that some governments simply printed money to pay for the difference. Today, within developed countries, printing money for this purpose is more the exception than the rule.

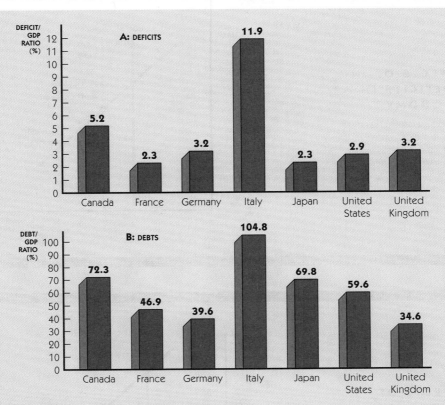

**Figure 9.3** **INTERNATIONAL COMPARISONS**

Canada has had higher deficit/GDP and debt/GDP ratios than the United States, Japan, and most European countries. Data are for 1990; deficits are cyclically adjusted. *Source:* L. Bartolini, et al., "Fiscal Restructuring in the Group of Seven," International Monetary Fund Working Paper, 1995.

From this perspective, we can rewrite the first equation as

$$S_p - D = I$$

or

$$S = S_p + S_g = I.$$

National savings, $S$, consisting of private (household and business) savings ($S_p$) plus government savings ($S_g$) equals investment.

In Figure 9.4, the increased deficit is reflected as a shift to the left of the savings curve, decreasing the equilibrium level of investment and increasing the equilibrium real interest rate. Because investment is lower, output and living standards in the future will be lower.

## A SMALL OPEN ECONOMY

The difference between an open economy and a closed economy is that when national savings are reduced in an open economy the country can turn to other countries to finance its investment. Figure 9.5 shows the increased deficit reducing national savings and shifting the savings curve to the left. The

## Figure 9.4 EFFECTS OF INCREASED DEFICITS IN A CLOSED ECONOMY

Increased deficits reduce *national* savings. With a leftward shift in the savings curve, the equilibrium level of interest rates is higher and the equilibrium level of investment is lower.

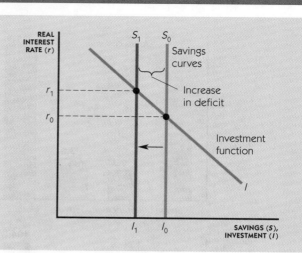

## Figure 9.5 EFFECTS OF INCREASED DEFICITS IN AN OPEN ECONOMY

Increased deficits shift the national savings curve to the left. Investment is unaffected, but foreign borrowing increases.

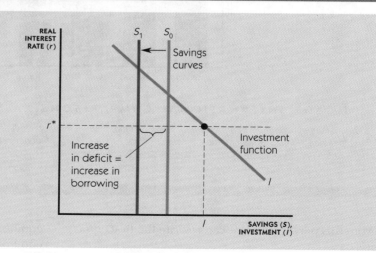

leftward shift leaves investment unchanged; it is determined simply by the international real interest rate. But it increases borrowing from abroad, so that in future years the country will be poorer, as it will have to pay interest on this indebtedness. Once again, living standards in the future are lower than they would have been in the absence of the deficit.

If we look at who has bought the additional bonds the government has been issuing in recent years, we note that some but not all of the higher deficit has been financed by foreigners. But the consequences are equally or even more disturbing if foreigners do not *directly* finance the deficit. The government can increase foreign debt directly by borrowing directly

## CLOSE-UP: THE PUBLIC VEIL

Current consumption may depend not only on today's income, but also on income that is expected to be received in the future. This has potentially profound implications for the ability of the government to use deficit policies to influence consumer spending.

If the government increases its budget deficit by, say, cutting taxes but keeping public spending unchanged, the deficit it creates is a liability for future taxpayers. In the future, taxes will have to be increased to pay interest and to repay the debt. If individuals have their taxes reduced this year but know they will have to pay for it with higher taxes in the future, their lifetime income will remain unchanged. In that case, a tax cut while keeping public expenditures fixed will have no effect on aggregate consumption, and therefore on aggregate demand.

The view that it makes *no* difference to current consumption whether the government finances a given level of expenditures by taxes or borrowing—that the two are perfectly equivalent—is called the Ricardian equivalence view, after David Ricardo, the nineteenth-century English economist who also discovered the principle of comparative advantage. Ricardo actually described the theory, then discarded it as impractical in the real world. In recent years, the view has been resurrected.

The theory of Ricardian equivalence suggests that, contrary to the view illustrated in Figures 9.4 and 9.5, deficit financing has no effect on the national savings curve. The increase in public dissaving resulting from a government deficit would be completely offset by an increase in private savings as households set aside funds that they or their heirs will have to pay as higher taxes in the future. Thus, deficits will lead to neither decreased investment, as in Figure 9.4, nor increased foreign borrowing, as in Figure 9.5.

Evidence seems to suggest that Ricardian equivalence does not hold in practice. The huge increases in government borrowing in the 1980s did not give rise to appreciably higher private savings levels. The reasons why the theory does not hold are not completely understood, but they are summarized by the idea of the "public veil." If rational individuals could see through the public veil—that is, if they could look at government borrowing, forecast the future tax liabilities of themselves and their heirs, and act accordingly—then Ricardian equivalence would hold. But people do not seem to behave that way.

Some economists say that this is because most people simply spend most of what they earn and do not adjust to whether the government is saving more or less. Other economists argue that even if taxes do need to be raised in the future, there is some uncertainty about when this will happen and who will pay at that time. If the burden of repaying can be passed on to future generations, as seems likely, and if parents do not fully adjust bequests to their heirs to reflect this, then the tax reduction does not represent an increase in the current generation's lifetime wealth, and accordingly aggregate consumption should rise for this generation.

Many governments around the world, including federal and provincial governments in Canada, are striving to reduce their budget deficits. The immediate goal of such deficit cutting is to reduce government borrowing, thereby freeing up savings for domestic investment and possibly reducing interest rates by reducing the "risk premium" associated with lending to highly indebted governments. Both of these effects will lead to more economic growth, ideally more than enough to offset any reduction in growth brought about by the lower government spending and/or higher taxes. A longer-term objective is to reduce the debt burden of the government (lowering the debt/GDP ratio), thus allowing a larger fraction of tax revenues to be spent on programmes, rather than being used to service—pay interest on—the accumulated debt. Achieving the first objective, lowering interest rates and spurring growth, will obviously help achieve the second.

Governments have access to two fiscal policy tools to cut a budget deficit: increase its tax revenues or reduce its expenditures, or some combination of these two. If it is simply the size of the deficit that is affecting interest rates, inhibiting economic growth, and increasing the debt/GDP ratio, then it should not matter how a government reduces its deficit, just that it does.

But some evidence is emerging that the approach a government takes to deficit reduction does matter to its success in achieving its goals. A study comparing fiscal policy changes over the last thirty years in countries belonging to the Organization for Economic Cooperation and Development (OECD) has reached some sugges-

tive conclusions. First, it seems that faster deficit reduction plans—those that pursue a very "tight" fiscal policy—are more successful at lowering the debt/GDP ratio than slower deficit reduction plans. Apparently capital markets are more impressed (and reward governments with greater reductions in interest rates) with policies that are intended to work quickly, especially within the current government's mandate, and are therefore less likely to be reversed. It also seems to matter how the deficit reduction is pursued. In those plans that were successful in lowering the debt/GDP ratio, about half of the deficit reduction came from cuts to welfare payments and the government's wage bill. Those that relied on other spending cuts or on tax increases were not successful. Again, capital markets seem to view such cuts as being a better predictor of a lasting commitment to deficit reduction than they do an increase in taxes.

In all the successful episodes economic growth was quite high, so some might argue that the successful governments were really just lucky. On the other hand, since one of the objectives of any deficit reduction programme is to spur growth, one might make the counterargument that the successful governments made their "good luck."

Debates such as this suggest that the evidence must be viewed cautiously. Nonetheless, the implications for policy are suggestive. An aggressive approach to deficit reduction that relies heavily on spending cuts, like the programmes instituted by the Klein government in Alberta and the Harris government in Ontario, is more likely to be successful at reducing the debt-to-

GDP ratio than a more timid approach. In fact, one could argue that in the case of Alberta it already has been, since the first budget surplus and resulting debt pay-down occurred a year ahead of schedule. The more gradualist approach of the Chrétien federal government might be less likely to succeed if one went by the past experiences in the OECD countries.

*Source:* "It's Not What You Do. . . ," *The Economist,* January 20, 1996, p. 80.

from abroad, or it can increase foreign debt indirectly by sopping up available domestic savings so that Canadians no longer have the money to invest in Canadian businesses and foreigners come in to fill the gap. Some economists have described the latter situation by saying that government borrowing can "crowd in" foreign investment.

## THE CURRENT-ACCOUNT DEFICIT

A deficit or surplus on the current account is the aggregate of a variety of types of transactions between Canadians and foreigners. One component is the merchandise-trade balance, the difference between imports and exports of goods. Another is the net import of services, including such things as travel, insurance, and transportation costs. Yet another is the balance of investment income, such as interest and dividends paid to foreigners and received from foreign sources. A final component is net transfers to

and from foreigners. This includes such things as remittances sent home by persons who have immigrated to Canada and inheritances received from or sent abroad. The movements in the components of the current account since 1960 are shown in Figure 9.6. Historically, the merchandise-trade balance has typically been in a surplus position, while the services-trade and investment-income accounts have been in deficit. After having risen to record levels in the mid-1980s, the surplus on the trade account gradually deteriorated until recently. It has increased substantially beginning in 1993. This deterioration was matched by a substantial erosion of the services-trade and, especially, the investment-income accounts. Overall, the current account has been in a deficit position almost continuously since 1960, but in the past decade the size of the deficit has increased dramatically.

The current-account deficit on the balance of payments and the budget deficit of the government have moved together. This is no accident, for the two are in fact closely related. The reason for this we already noted: in an open economy, an increase in government expenditure not matched by an increase in taxes (or a decrease in taxes not matched

## EFFECTS OF BUDGET DEFICITS

### Closed Economy

An increase in government expenditures not accompanied by an increase in taxes (or a decrease in government expenditures not accompanied by a corresponding decrease in taxes) results in higher interest rates and decreased investment.

### Open Economy

In a small open economy, budget deficits result in increased foreign borrowing; interest rates and investment remain unchanged.

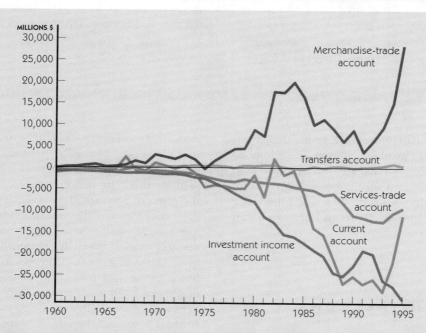

**Figure 9.6 COMPONENTS OF CANADA'S CURRENT-ACCOUNT DEFICIT**

Though the merchandise-trade account had been in surplus, the size of the surplus has been declining until very recently. At the same time, the deficits in the services-trade account and the investment-income account have increased, leading to an increase in the overall current-account deficit. *Source:* Statistics Canada, CANSIM Database, 1996.

by a reduction in government expenditures) results in an increased deficit and increased foreign borrowing. We will now see why increased foreign borrowing implies an increase in the current-account deficit.

## CAPITAL FLOWS

To see the relationship, we first need to see the links between trade and investment-income flows and capital flows. Let's trace what happens when a Canadian buys a German car. It seems like a simple matter: he pays Canadian dollars to his dealer. His dealer buys the car for dollars from an importer. The importer buys the car from the German manufacturer, who wants to be paid in German marks. For

the importer, this is no problem: he goes to a bank, perhaps in Germany, and exchanges his dollars for marks. But the bank won't just hold those dollars. It will sell them, either to someone wanting to purchase Canadian products or to someone wanting to invest in a dollar-denominated asset. The same story will apply when Canadians purchase services supplied by foreign firms or pay interest or dividends to foreigners on Canadian assets they own. Thus, every dollar paid to a foreigner whether for goods or services or as investment income eventually comes back, either to pay Canadians for similar items or to purchase an investment in Canada. By the same token, every dollar used by Canadians to purchase investments abroad must also come back to Canada as purchases by foreigners.

We call the money coming into Canada to buy investments, to be deposited in Canadian financial institutions, to buy Canadian government bonds, or to lend to Canadians for any reason—including buying a German car—**capital inflows.** Canadian dollars going to other countries for similar purposes are called **capital outflows.** For most purposes, we are interested in **net capital inflows,** the inflows minus the outflows.

As we have seen, every dollar a Canadian spends to buy a foreign good or service or to pay investment income to foreigners eventually comes back, either to buy Canadian goods and services, as investment income to Canadians on the assets they own abroad, or to buy an asset in Canada. We can express this relation by a simple equation:

Current payments by Canadians = current receipts by Canadians + net capital inflows.

Subtracting current receipts from both sides of this equation, we obtain:

Current payments by Canadians − current receipts by Canadians = net capital inflows.

On the left-hand side is the current-account deficit, and on the right-hand side, net capital inflows are defined to be the **capital-account surplus.** Thus, the basic balance-of-payments identity can be written:

Current-account deficit = capital-account surplus.

Thus, a current-account deficit and a capital-account surplus (net inflow of foreign capital) are two ways of saying the same thing. This can be put yet another way: the only way that Canadian consumers and businesses can spend more abroad than they receive from abroad is if foreigners are willing to make up the difference by lending to or investing in Canada.

In a world of multilateral trade, the accounts between any particular country and Canada do not have to balance. Assume that Japan and the United States are in current-account balance and the United States and Canada are in current-account balance, but Japanese investors like to put their money into the United States and Americans like to

invest in Canada. The United States has zero net capital inflows, with a positive capital inflow from Japan offset by a capital outflow to Canada. In this situation, the Canadian current-account deficit with Japan is offset by a capital inflow from the United States. But what must be true for any country is that total current payments to all foreigners minus total current receipts from all foreigners (the current-account deficit) must equal all capital inflows (the capital-account surplus).

The basic balance-of-payments identity can describe a capital outflow as well as a capital inflow. In the 1950s, the United States had a substantial current-account surplus, as the country exported more than it imported. There was a net capital outflow from America, which gradually accumulated. Japan is now in a similar situation, with a capital-account deficit and a current-account surplus.

## EXCHANGE RATES

If a country borrows more (or less) from abroad, the **exchange rate** ensures that the current account of the balance of payments adjusts. The exchange rate tells how much of one currency must be exchanged for a given amount of another. For instance, in October 1995, one dollar could be exchanged for approximately 75 yen. Exchange rates may change rapidly. In 1992 a dollar was worth 100 yen. At the beginning of 1995, a dollar was worth only 71 yen. It then fell to only about 61 yen in April: a fall in value of 14 percent in three months. When the dollar has become less valuable relative to the yen, we say it has **depreciated** in value; the yen has become more valuable—its value has **appreciated**.

The exchange rate is thus a price—the relative price of two currencies. Like any price, the exchange rate is determined by the laws of supply and demand. For simplicity, let us continue to focus on the exchange rate between the dollar and the yen, ignoring the fact that in the world trading system, all exchange markets are interlinked. Figure 9.7 depicts the market for dollars in terms of the exchange rate with the yen. The exchange rate in yen per dollar is on the vertical axis, and the quantity of Canadian dollars is on the horizontal axis. The supply curve for dollars represents the quantity of dollars supplied

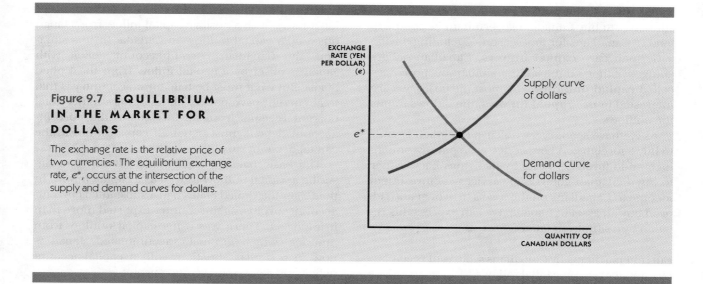

**Figure 9.7 EQUILIBRIUM IN THE MARKET FOR DOLLARS**

The exchange rate is the relative price of two currencies. The equilibrium exchange rate, $e^*$, occurs at the intersection of the supply and demand curves for dollars.

by Canadians to purchase Japanese goods and to make investments in Japan. At higher exchange rates—when a dollar buys more yen—Canadians will supply higher quantities of dollars. The supply curve for dollars thus slopes upwards to the right. The demand curve for dollars represents the dollars demanded by the Japanese to purchase Canadian products and to make investments in Canada. At higher exchange rates—when it takes more yen to buy one dollar—the Japanese demand lower quantities of dollars, resulting in a demand curve that slopes downwards to the right. The equilibrium exchange rate, $e^*$, lies at the intersection of the supply and demand curves for dollars.

Now we can see how the exchange rate connects the flow of capital and goods and services between countries. We continue with the case of Canada and Japan. Suppose Canada wants to borrow more from Japan. Higher Canadian interest rates will attract more Japanese investment to Canada. Japanese demand for dollars increases at each exchange rate, shifting the demand curve for dollars to the right, as depicted in Figure 9.8. The higher interest rates will also make Japanese investments relatively less attractive to Canadian investors, who will therefore increase their investments at home. Canadians will be willing to supply fewer dollars at each exchange rate,

shifting the supply curve for dollars to the left. These shifts in the supply and demand curves for dollars cause the exchange rate to rise from $e_0$ to $e_1$—the dollar appreciates and the yen depreciates.[2] Since the dollar can now buy more Japanese products, Canadian imports increase (Japanese exports increase). Changes in the exchange rate thus ensure that the current-account deficit moves in tandem with foreign borrowing.

## THE SAVINGS-INVESTMENT IDENTITY

The relationship between the fiscal deficit and the current account deficit can be seen another way using the savings and investment identity:

Private (household and business) savings + capital flows (borrowing) from abroad = investment in machines and equipment + government budget deficit.

Private savings and capital flows from abroad can be

[2] Later, in Chapter 16, we shall see that matters are somewhat more complicated. Investors have to take into account expectations concerning changes in the exchange rates as well.

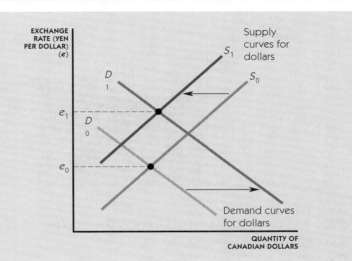

Figure 9.8 **EXCHANGE-RATE EFFECTS OF INCREASED FOREIGN BORROWING**

The equilibrium exchange rate is $e_0$ before the increase in Canadian borrowing from Japan. Higher interest rates in Canada attract Japanese investment to Canada, shifting the demand curve for Canadian dollars to the right. At the same time, Canadian domestic investing is increased, represented by a shift to the left of the supply curve for dollars. The exchange rate rises from $e_0$ to $e_1$. At the higher exchange rate, the dollar buys more yen, so Canadian imports of Japanese products increase.

thought of as the "sources" of funds, and investment and budget deficits can be thought of as the uses of funds. A slightly different approach is to think of the fiscal deficit as dissaving, or negative savings. When a household spends less than its income it is saving, and when it spends more than its income it is dissaving, and it is the same with government. The savings-investment identity can thus be rewritten:

Private savings + government savings + capital flows from abroad = investment.

The savings-investment identity says that if there is an increase in the budget deficit and if private savings and investment are unchanged, capital flows from abroad must increase and foreigners must end up holding more Canadian assets. But the identity does not specify which assets they will hold. It does not say, for example, that the link between the current-account deficit and the fiscal deficit is that foreign investors are buying Canadian government bonds. That may be true, but it is only part of the story. Foreign investors may be buying Canadian companies, and Canadians may be holding Canadian government bonds.

## WHY CURRENT-ACCOUNT DEFICITS ARE A PROBLEM

Borrowing from abroad is not necessarily bad, any more than borrowing in general is necessarily bad. Throughout its history Canada has borrowed heavily

**BASIC TRADE IDENTITIES**

capital inflows = current account deficit

investment = private savings + government savings + capital inflows

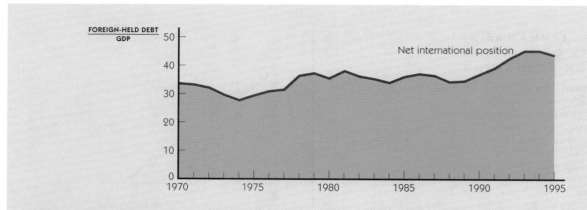

**Figure 9.9 CANADA'S INTERNATIONAL INDEBTEDNESS INCREASES**

Though Canada has always been a net borrower in international capital markets, the extent of indebtedness increased dramatically in the 1980s. *Source:* Statistics Canada, CANSIM Database, Label No. D65219, D10000, 1996.

from abroad. Eventually, one would expect that to be reversed. A typical pattern would be that in the early stages of development, countries borrow, use the money to build up their economies, and repay the loans with a portion of their economic gains. More mature economies, on the other hand, typically lend capital.

To some extent this has happened in Canada. For most of the 1980s, direct investment by Canadians abroad exceeded foreign direct investment in Canada. However, this has been more than offset by the rapid escalation of other forms of borrowing from abroad, reflected in the current-account deficit. When the government borrows year after year the cumulative budget deficits lead to a high level of government debt, and when the country borrows from abroad year after year, the cumulative current-account deficits (cumulative capital inflows) also lead to a high level of debt to foreigners.

The effect of the large current-account deficits of the 1980s was to cause the level of Canadian indebtedness to foreigners to escalate rapidly. Figure 9.9 shows the extent of this increase. The level of indebtedness—the value of all of Canada's assets abroad

plus what others owe it minus the value of all assets within Canada owned by foreigners minus what it owes others—virtually tripled between 1978 and 1990.[3] The effect of this has been to increase the amount of interest and dividend payments to foreigners each year. This is reflected in the rapid deterioration in the investment-income part of the current account.

The consequences for the nation are little different from those you would experience if you borrowed a large amount from the bank. In the future, unless you used the borrowed funds to make an investment that yielded a return at least equal to the interest you had to pay, you would be unable to consume as much as you would otherwise, because you must pay the bank interest as well as the principal. Consider this rough calculation: if the nation's debt

---

[3] One has to be careful about interpreting the figures. Critics of such figures point out that many of the assets that Canada owns abroad have greatly increased in value since it obtained those assets, but the data do not adequately reflect these increases. Still, there is little doubt about the general picture—there is a definite deterioration in Canada's net investment position.

## LONG-RUN CONSEQUENCES OF PERSISTENT CURRENT ACCOUNT DEFICITS

*Increased foreign indebtedness,* leading eventually to *increased interest and dividend payments abroad,* and if foreign borrowing is not used to finance investments which yield returns sufficient to pay the increased interest and dividend payments, *lower living standards.*

to foreign investors reaches $300 billion by the year 2000 and the average rate of interest is 6 percent, the interest payments alone work out to over $600 for every man, woman, and child in Canada *every year.*

## USING THE BASIC MODEL TO ANALYZE THE CURRENT-ACCOUNT DEFICIT

The full-employment model can be used both to provide insights into the origins of the current-account deficit and to think about policies that might reduce it. As we have seen, an increase in the deficit—a decrease in national savings—in an open economy leads to more foreign borrowing (a capital-account surplus). And increased foreign borrowing leads to an increased current-account deficit. Exchange rates adjust to accommodate the current-account deficit.

To reduce the current-account deficit, we can either shift the aggregate savings curve to the right or the investment function to the left. (See Figure 9.10.) The latter obviously is not very desirable—it means that the economy will be less productive in the future. That is why attention has focused on shifting

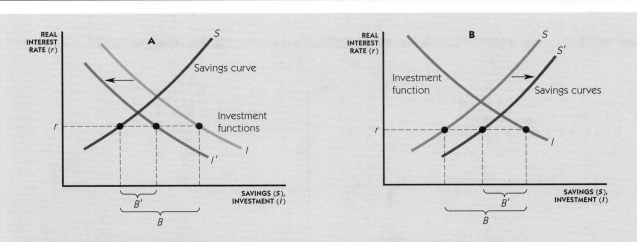

### Figure 9.10 **POLICIES TO REDUCE THE CURRENT-ACCOUNT DEFICIT**

The current-account deficit can be reduced either by shifting the investment function to the left (panel A) or the savings function to the right (panel B). In either case, the capital inflow (capital-account surplus) falls from *B* to *B'*.

**REDUCING THE CURRENT ACCOUNT DEFICIT**

increase private savings

reduce the fiscal deficit

reduce investment

the aggregate savings curve. There are two ways to do this: either increase government savings (reduce the government budget deficit) or increase private savings.

## GROWTH

The full-employment model can also be used to analyze policies that might promote economic growth. There are three keys to increased growth: (1) a more productive labour force, which results from improved education and training; (2) more and better capital, which results from increased investment in plant and equipment and investment in **infrastructure,** such as roads and airports; and (3) technological progress, partially the result of public and private expenditures on research and development. Expenditures in all three categories are referred to as **investments,** which are expenditures made today whose benefits come in the future. Investments in people are often called **human capital investments.** All three of these investments shift future short-run production functions out, as depicted in Figure 9.11, so that the level of output that can be obtained at any level of employment is increased.

In a closed economy, there are basically two ways to increase investment: shift either the investment function or the savings function to the right.

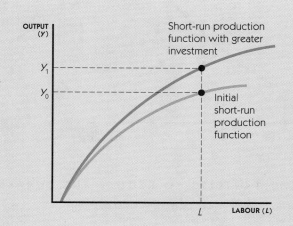

**Figure 9.11 INCREASING THE ECONOMY'S PRODUCTIVE POTENTIAL**

Improved education and training, the result of investments in people, more and better capital, the result of investments in plant and equipment, and improved technology, the result of investments in research and development and technology, all shift the short-run production function out, so that the level of output produced by any level of employment is increased.

## Figure 9.12 EFFECT OF INVESTMENT TAX CREDIT: CLOSED ECONOMY

An investment tax credit shifts the investment schedule to the right, resulting in a higher equilibrium interest rate and more investment. The higher level of investment increases the rate of growth, at least in the short run.

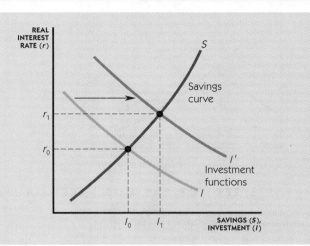

## STIMULATING INVESTMENT

Governments have used tax policy as a way of shifting the investment function, as illustrated in Figure 9.12. With an **investment tax credit,** firms can subtract a fraction of the cost of the investment from their taxes, so that in effect the government is paying part of the cost of the machine. With a 10 percent investment tax credit, a machine costing $100 results in a reduction in tax payments of $10, so the net cost of the machine is only $90. Naturally, this will encourage the firm to invest more.

Another way that the government encourages investment through the tax system is through **accelerated depreciation.** When a firm buys a machine that lasts, say, 10 years, it is allowed to deduct 10 percent of the cost of the machine each year, to reflect the fact that over time, the machine is becoming worth less and less. The deduction is called a **depreciation allowance** or a **capital cost allowance.**

Between 1972 and 1988, firms using machinery and equipment in manufacturing and processing were allowed to "accelerate" the machines' depreciation. They were able to deduct half of the value of the machine in each of the first two years of its use, despite the fact that they might use the machine for, say, ten years or more. This meant that taxes they

paid in the first two years were lower. A dollar today is worth far more than a dollar three years from now so that accelerating depreciation means that the present discounted value of the tax reductions associated with depreciation allowances is greatly increased. This makes investments more attractive, shifting the investment function to the right.

## STIMULATING SAVINGS

The government has also tried a variety of ways of shifting the savings function, again largely by providing tax preferences, including especially Registered Retirement Savings Plans (RRSPs) and Registered Pension Plans (RPPs), which allow taxpayers to deduct savings for retirement from their taxable incomes and defer taxes on them until retirement. RRSPs may have been successful in encouraging savings, not so much because of the extra incentives they provide, but because of the advertising that banks did to recruit new RRSP accounts. Critics of RRSPs argue, however, that even if RRSPs have succeeded in increasing *private* savings, the net effect on national savings is negative. Any tax preference, RRSPs included, means that the government loses tax revenues, and the lost tax revenue contributes to

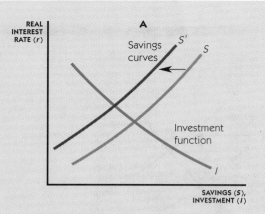 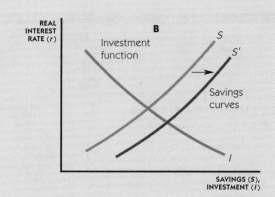

**Figure 9.13  EFFECT OF SAVINGS INCENTIVES: CLOSED ECONOMY**

RRSPs increase the incentive for households to save, but the tax preferences mean a loss of government revenues, and hence an increased deficit. In panel A, private savings increase by an insufficient amount to offset the increased deficit, so that the aggregate savings curve shifts to the left. Investment is actually

lowered. In panel B, the increased private savings more than offset the increased deficit; the aggregate savings curve shifts to the right, leading to lower interest rates, increased investment, and higher growth.

the budget deficit. And the deficit, we have seen, is equivalent to *negative* government savings. If the lost tax revenue exceeds the increased private savings, national savings actually decreases. How much private savings increases with low taxes depends on the **interest elasticity of savings:** if the after-tax interest rate, which is what savers care about, is increased by 1 percent, by what percentage does savings increase? Most estimates suggest that savings is *relatively inelastic*: even if an individual faces a 40 percent marginal tax rate, lowering the tax rate to zero, thus increasing the after-tax return substantially, will not cause the individual to increase his savings much. The reason is simple: if he is saving for his retirement, the amount he has to save, to provide any level of retirement income, will be reduced as the after-tax interest rate increases.[4] If savings is

relatively inelastic, then the increase in private savings is insufficient to offset the increased deficit, and national savings is reduced. Panels A and B of Figure 9.13 illustrate the two possible cases.

## REDUCING THE GOVERNMENT BUDGET DEFICIT

We saw earlier that reducing the budget deficit is equivalent to shifting the aggregate savings curve to the right. But we need to emphasize that the net effect on growth depends on *how* the deficit is cut. In Figure 9.14 we illustrate a case where deficit reduction actually leads to lower growth. As we saw earlier, the shift in the aggregate savings curve to the right leads to lower interest rates and increased *private* investment. This shifts the economy's future short-run production function out to *OP'*. But if the government reduces the deficit by cutting back on productive public investments such as research, investments in education, or infrastructure, the future short-run production function shifts in, to *OP''*—

[4] Higher interest rates mean that savers are better off. Because they are better off, they consume more today. This is called the *income effect*. At the same time, a higher after-tax interest rate increases the incentive to save; this is called the *substitution effect*—for every dollar of consumption forgone today, the individual can consume more dollars of consumption in the future. The income and substitution effects largely offset each other.

## Figure 9.14 EFFECT OF DEFICIT REDUCTION ON ECONOMIC GROWTH

The lower deficit shifts the aggregate savings curve to the right, leading to lower interest rates and higher investment. This shifts the future short-run production function out, from *OP* to *OP′*. But if the deficit reduction is accomplished by cutting back productive public investments, the effect of these lower investments is to shift the short-run production function in. It is possible that the net effect may actually be to lower future output, as illustrated by the curve *OP″*.

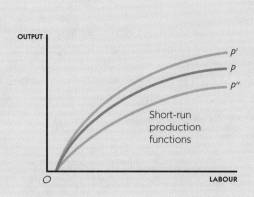

below where it was before the deficit reduction. A dollar of deficit reduction does not, in general, result in an increase of private investment by a dollar (because the investment function is upward-sloping[5]), so that even if public investment is *less* productive than private investment, deficit reduction attained through reducing investment can lower economic growth. And there is evidence that public investments in education, research, and infrastructure may actually yield higher marginal returns than private investment.

## OPEN ECONOMY

In an open economy, there is no close link between savings and investment, since the country can always borrow to finance its investment. For a small open economy, which we can take Canada to be, with a perfectly elastic supply of funds at the international interest rate $r^*$, the level of investment is determined by that interest rate.

If a small open economy wishes to increase its growth rate, it focuses its attention on shifting its in-

vestment function; changes in the savings curve only affect the amount it borrows abroad—though, as we have seen, this will have important consequences for the economy's future well-being.

## CONSENSUS IN MACROECONOMICS

From this chapter emerges a seventh point of consensus in macroeconomics:

### 7 Growth

*Increases in standards of living require increases in productivity; increases in productivity require expenditures on research and development, investments in new technology, plant, equipment, and infrastructure, and increases in the skills of the labour force.*

In a closed economy, investment can be increased either by shifting the investment curve to the right (such as by an investment tax credit) or the savings curve to the right (such as by preferential tax

---

[5] Only if the investment function were a horizontal straight line would a shift in the savings curve to the right by a dollar result in an increase in investment by a dollar.

## USING ECONOMICS: ESTIMATING THE EFFECT OF DEFICIT REDUCTION

In 1995, there seemed to be general agreement among all political parties that the federal and provincial budget deficits should be reduced. Still, there seemed to be some disagreement about the best way of doing this. Some, like the federal Liberal government, would rely entirely on expenditure cuts. Others, like the Ontario Conservative government, wanted even deeper cuts in expenditures that would finance large tax cuts. What can one say about the effects of these alternative programmes on economic growth?

Consider first a programme that entails $20 billion in government expenditure cuts, a quarter of which, $5 billion, comes from cuts in government investment. Assume the economy manages to remain at full employment and there are no tax cuts, so consumption remains unchanged. National savings increases by the amount of the cut in government expenditures, since this represents a decline in the deficit and therefore an increase in public savings. Historical experience suggests that the $20 billion increase in national savings will result in $10 billion in increased private investment. With consumption unchanged, government expenditures decreased by $20 billion and investment increased by $10 billion. For the economy to remain at full employment, net exports must increase by $10 billion. Exchange rates must change to accommodate the increase in net exports. A private investment increase of $10 billion offset by a reduction of $5 billion in

public investment means that aggregate investment increases by $5 billion per year. The $5 billion dollars per year for ten years yields at the end of the decade $50 billion more capital accumulated, which at a return of approximately 7 percent means that national income will be $3.5 billion greater than it otherwise would have been. In that case, GDP in ten years is estimated to be approximately .35 percent higher than it otherwise would have been—$1 trillion—representing an increase in the expected growth rate from an annual 2.5 percent to 2.8 percent.

Alternatively, assume that the plan had an extra $5 billion annually of tax cuts, financed half by cuts on investments. The extra $5 billion in tax cuts—because they are fully financed by expenditure cuts—leaves public savings unchanged, but since households' disposable income has increased by the amount of the tax cut, their savings increases. Typically, an increase in household income of $5 billion yields an increase in savings of around $.5 billion. An increase in national savings of $.5 billion generates an extra $.25 billion in private investment. Thus, aggregate investment is reduced by $2.25 billion as a result of the tax cut programme, the reduction in public investment of $2.5 billion less the extra investment generated. Thus, almost half of the gain in growth from the original deficit reduction package is lost with the tax cuts, which are partially financed by reductions in public investment.

treatment). Some preferential tax treatments, such as RRSPs, may actually lower national savings, since the induced private savings may be less than the increased government budget deficit. Similarly, in a closed economy deficit reduction will result in increased private investment, but if the deficit reduction is attained through reducing public investment, future output and living standards may actually be reduced.

In an open economy, investment can only be increased by shifting the investment curve to the right. Increased savings only leads to reduced borrowing from abroad.

# REVIEW AND PRACTICE

## SUMMARY

**1** The early 1980s were marked by a surge in the size of government budget deficits, leading to marked increases in the debt/GDP ratio. The government response has been to sharply curtail government expenditures.

**2** In a closed economy, increases in the fiscal deficit lead to lower private investment and increased interest rates. The net effect of reductions in the deficit depends on how it is done: if generated by reductions in public investment, growth is likely to be reduced, since the increased private investment is unlikely to be sufficient to offset the reduced public investment.

**3** In a small open economy, increases in the deficit have no effect on investment but do lead to increased foreign indebtedness and larger current-account deficits. Cumulative increases in foreign indebtedness will make future citizens worse off, as they have to pay interest on the foreign indebtedness.

**4** The large increases in the current-account deficit that began in the 1980s were largely explained by the large increases in the fiscal deficit, which began at that time. Policy options to reduce the Canadian current-account deficit and foreign borrowing (capital-account surplus) include decreasing investment (a bad idea for long-term growth), increasing household and business savings (a good idea if the government could induce it), or reducing the government budget deficit.

**5** The savings-investment identity for an open economy says that the sum of private savings, capital flows from abroad, and government savings is equal to investment. This identity implies that a change in any one factor must also involve offsetting changes in other factors.

**6** Increases in investments in human capital, plant and equipment, infrastructure, and improved technology all shift the short-run production function out, increasing the full-employment output of the economy and the economy's rate of growth. Investment can be stimulated either through investment tax credits or accelerated depreciation, or, in a closed economy, by increasing the rate of savings through tax preferences. Because of a low interest elasticity of savings, tax preferences may not be very effective.

## KEY TERMS

budget deficit

current-account deficit

capital flows (capital outflow, inflow)

exchange rate

appreciate

depreciate

investment tax credit

depreciation allowance

accelerated depreciation

interest elasticity of savings

infrastructure

## REVIEW QUESTIONS

**1** What happened to the size of the budget deficits in the 1980s? What are some of the alternative ways of describing these changes? What is the relationship between the deficit and the level of the debt? Why might the deficit/GDP ratio or the debt/GDP ratio be a more meaningful number than the dollar value of the deficit or the debt, by itself?

**2** What are the consequences of an increased fiscal deficit for private investment?

**3** Why do the consequences for growth of deficit reduction depend on whether the deficit reduction is accomplished by cutting government investment, by cutting government consumption expenditures, or by raising taxes?

**4** What happened to the current-account deficit during the 1980s? How did the foreign indebtedness of the Canadian economy change during the 1980s? What is the relationship between these two changes?

**5** What is the relationship between the current-account deficit and an inflow of foreign capital?

**6** What is the relationship between the current-account deficit and the fiscal deficit?

**7** What is the exchange rate? How is it determined? What role does the exchange rate play in ensuring that current-account deficits are offset by capital-account surpluses, and vice versa?

**8** What is the balance-of-payments identity?

**9** What is the savings-investment identity for an open economy?

**10** What is the effect of an increase in the supply of savings in a full-employment economy?

**11** How may government stimulate investment and savings?

## PROBLEMS

**1** Suppose a certain country has private savings of 6 percent of GDP, foreign borrowing of 1 percent of GDP, and a balanced budget. What is its level of investment? If the budget deficit is 1.5 percent of GDP, how does your answer change?

**2** Why does it make a difference if a country borrows abroad to finance the expansion of its railroads, or to finance increased public pension benefits for the elderly?

**3** Assume investments in human capital yield a return of 15 percent, private investments yield a total return of 10 percent, and public investments in research yield a return of 25 percent. Assume the government budget deficit is $10 billion per year, and the government wishes to eliminate it. What will be the impact on economic growth of a deficit reduction package which consists of reducing health expenditures by $5 billion, education expenditures by $4 billion, and research expenditures by $1 billion?

**4** The primary fiscal deficit is defined as the difference between government expenditures *excluding interest payments* and tax revenues; it represents what the deficit would have been had the government not inherited any debt. Discuss why the concept of a primary deficit may or may not be useful or relevant.

**5** If the economy is growing at 5.5 percent per year, and the debt/GDP ratio is 60 percent, what is the critical value of the deficit/GDP ratio, such that if the deficit/GDP ratio exceeds that number, the debt/GDP ratio will increase, and if the deficit/GDP ratio falls short of that number, it decreases. (This is a mildly hard exercise.)

**6** Canadian foreign indebtedness is greater than that of Mexico. But does this necessarily mean that Canada has a larger debt problem than Mexico? Why or why not? Can you think of a situation in which an individual with debts of larger value than another person's may actually have less of a debt problem than the other person?

**7** If Parliament were to pass a law prohibiting foreigners from buying Canadian Treasury bills, would this prevent government borrowing from leading to capital inflows? Discuss.

**8** Japan had large trade surpluses during the 1980s. Would this cause Japan to be a borrower or a lender in international capital markets?

**9** If a nation borrowed $5 billion from abroad one year and its imports were worth $80 billion, what would be the value of its exports? How does your answer change if, instead of borrowing, the nation lent $10 billion abroad?

**10** Since other countries benefit from exporting their products to Canada, why should the Canadian government not charge them for the privilege of selling in Canada?

# PART THREE

# Unemployment

# Macroeconomics

art Two explored full-employment macroeconomics. The basic assumption there was that the economy operates as envisioned in the basic competitive model: prices, wages, and interest rates adjust quickly and fully to ensure that all markets clear. Most important, the demand for labour equals the supply of labour. The assumption may be unrealistic, but the model is instructive. We saw how deficits crowd out investment and increase foreign borrowing, and we got to look more closely at economic growth.

The full-employment model needs to be revised to address two further, fundamental macroeconomic phenomena: unemployment and inflation. In this part, we take up unemployment, reserving inflation for Part Four. Over the long run, as we have seen, the economy has managed to create jobs to keep pace with the increasing number of workers. But in the short run, mismatches between demand and supply not only give rise to public outcries, but are among the most important determinants of the fate of elected officials. Today government is viewed as having the responsibility for keeping the economy on an even keel, which means avoiding the pitfalls of excessive unemployment.

Here, in Part Three, we examine the problem of maintaining the economy at full employment. The most fundamental difference in our analysis in this part of the book is that we drop the assumption that wages and prices instantaneously adjust to clear all markets. For simplicity, we will assume that they do not adjust at all, that they are fixed. In Part Four, we will take up the in-between case, exploring how wages and prices adjust, and why they often change so slowly.

Chapter 10 provides an overview of the macroeconomics of unemployment and introduces some of the basic concepts. The next two chapters focus on the product market. Chapter 11 looks at aggregate demand, which determines the level of aggregate output in situations of unemployment. Chapter 12 looks more closely at two of the most important components of aggregate demand, consumption and investment.

Chapters 13–15 focus on the capital market and the links between that market and the product market. We begin with a discussion of money, in Chapter 13. Chapter 14 discusses monetary theory—how changes in the supply of money and the availability of credit affect the level of economic activity, and how the Bank of Canada changes the supply of money and credit availability. Chapter 15 puts together the entire unemployment model with fixed prices and wages, focusing on how fiscal and monetary policy can be used to restore the economy to full employment. To reach a better understanding of the roles these two alternative policy instruments play, Chapter 15 contrasts both their consequences and the difficulties that are faced in using them effectively.

# CHAPTER 10

# OVERVIEW OF UNEMPLOYMENT MACROECONOMICS

P eople worry about jobs. They worry about layoffs. If they are laid off, they worry about how long it will take to get another job. In all market economies, there is some unemployment. In a dynamic economy, some firms and industries are shrinking—jobs are being lost—at the same time that new jobs are being created. It takes time for individuals to switch from one job to another. But at times, as we saw in Chapter 6, the unemployment rate becomes very high. Labour markets do not clear: the demand for labour is much less than the supply. In such situations, governments take it as their responsibility to reduce the unemployment rate—not necessarily to zero, but at least to a low level.

We have seen how all markets of the economy are interlinked. The labour market is linked to the product market and the product market to the capital market. The labour market is particularly sensitive to changes in the product market: if output goes down, so too will the demand for labour. If real wages adjust too slowly, there will be unemployment. In this chapter we do not ask why they adjust slowly; that is a question we will discuss in Part Four. We focus instead on the consequences. After a few words about

## KEY QUESTIONS

**1** How do economists analyze what determines levels of aggregate output and employment in the short run, when wages and prices are fixed?

**2** What causes shifts in the aggregate demand and supply for labour? Why may unemployment result if wages fail to adjust in response to these shifts?

**3** What is the aggregate demand curve? What happens when the price level is fixed at a level at which aggregate

demand is less than aggregate supply? What are the consequences of a shift in the aggregate demand curve in these circumstances?

**4** How can we use aggregate demand curves to interpret some of the major macroeconomic episodes of the past fifty years?

the nature of macroeconomic models, we discuss the labour market, then the product market, and finally the capital market. The chapter closes by applying the framework to discuss recent macroeconomic events.

## MORE ABOUT MACROECONOMIC MODELS

In Part Two we developed the full-employment macroeconomic model. The critical assumption made in Part Two was that wages and prices adjust so that all markets, including the labour market, clear: there is no unemployment. The basic way in which this part differs from Part Two is that here we are concerned about the problem of unemployment. The basic explanation for unemployment is that wages do not adjust quickly enough to shifts in either the demand or supply curve for labour, so that *at least for a while, and sometimes for extended periods of time*, the demand for labour at market wages and prices may be less than the supply. In this part of the book, to simplify matters, we assume that wages and prices are fixed: they do not adjust at all. Economists say that such wages and prices are **rigid.** The results are much the same as they would be if they adjusted slowly in the direction required by market clearing, but too slowly to ensure that the demand and supply for, say, labour were equated.

While some prices, such as those on the stock market and those determined by daily auctioning, adjust quickly, others, wages in particular, adjust slowly. Unions often sign three-year contracts, and even nonunionized firms let workers know their wages at the beginning of the year and are reluctant to lower wages quickly in response to either the availability of cheaper labour elsewhere or a decrease in the demand for their products. At the lower end, minimum wage laws prevent employers from reducing wages. Over the last 15 years, many European countries have had much higher rates of unemployment than countries in North America, and this is widely attributed, in part at least, to their greater wage rigidity.

The fact that slow adjustments can lead to persistent unemployment is one of the reasons that macroeconomists focus so much on dynamics—how, and in particular, how fast things change. In Part Four we will describe the dynamics of the economy, focusing in particular on price and wage adjustments. We will analyze how and how fast the economy adjusts.

This part of the book focuses on the short run, a time span that ranges from a week or a month up to a few years. Although investment is occurring in the economy, we assume the net change in the capital stock to be so small in the short time horizons upon which we focus that it can be ignored. Except when we focus explicitly upon *changes* in government actions, we will also assume that tax rates, levels of expenditures, and the money supply are all fixed.

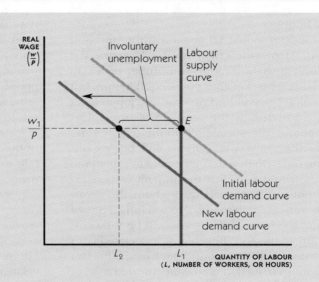

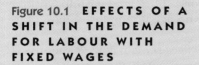

Figure 10.1 **EFFECTS OF A SHIFT IN THE DEMAND FOR LABOUR WITH FIXED WAGES**

Equilibrium in the labour market is at the intersection of the aggregate demand and supply curves for labour. If the demand for labour decreases and the wage is fixed, employed labour decreases from $L_1$ to $L_2$.

## THE LABOUR MARKET

Since unemployment is our key concern in this part of the book, our discussion naturally begins with the labour market. In Chapter 8, we described equilibrium in the labour market as the intersection of the aggregate demand and supply curves for labour. Both depended on real wages (nominal wages divided by the price level). We are assuming that prices are fixed, so any changes in real wages reflect changes in nominal wages.

In the earlier discussion of the labour market we simplified the analysis in two ways. We assumed that each worker supplied exactly 40 hours of labour, no more and no less, per week, and that real wages did not affect aggregate supply.[1] Thus, the aggregate labour supply curve was vertical. Wages were flexible, so that they adjusted to equate demand and supply, at $w_1/P$ in Figure 10.1.

[1] The fact that each worker works 40 hours means that we can put on the horizontal axis either the number of workers or the number of hours worked.

But what happens if wages do not adjust quickly? Assume that for some reason the demand curve for labour suddenly shifts to the left, so that at each wage, fewer workers are demanded. At the old equilibrium wage, $w_1/P$, the supply for labour exceeds the demand. However, if the wage is stuck at the original level, $w_1/P$—above the wage at which the demand for labour equals the supply—firms will still only hire the amount demanded. More workers will be willing to work than can get jobs at that wage. Those without jobs will be involuntarily unemployed. In Figure 10.1 the demand for labour will only be $L_2$, while the supply is $L_1$. The distance between these two points measures the amount of **involuntary unemployment.** At this high wage, the supply of labour exceeds the demand.

Involuntary unemployment arising from reductions in the demand for labour combined with wage rigidity would be much less of a social problem if the impact could be spread over the entire population. Even if the demand for labour were reduced by 10 percent and wages did not fall, the consequences would be limited if each worker worked 10 percent fewer hours. The problem in that case would be

**underemployment.** Each person in the economy might work only 36 hours per week, when she wished to work 40 hours.

In the modern industrial economy, the problem is different. Most workers continue to work the same, or only a slightly reduced, number of hours when the labour market goes out of equilibrium, but an unfortunate few will find no full-time job at all at the going wage. This is the problem of unemployment. Whenever the supply of labour exceeds the demand at the going wage, there will be "rationing"—some individuals will not be able to sell all the labour they would like. But the impact of this rationing is not evenly spread throughout the economy: some workers will manage to sell little if any of their labour services, while others will be fully employed. Many of the social problems associated with a reduced demand for labour result from the fact that the economic burden is so concentrated.

The analysis is little different if we assume an upward-sloping rather than vertical labour supply curve. This would mean that workers change the number of hours they work in response to wage changes, supplying less labour at lower wages and more labour at higher wages. Consider Figure 10.2, which shows an upward-sloping labour supply curve and a labour demand curve that shifts to the left, from $LD_1$ to $LD_2$. The initial equilibrium entails a wage of $w_1/P$ and employment of $L_1$. Now suppose there is a reduction in labour demand, represented by the leftward shift of the labour demand curve. If wages adjusted quickly, there would be a new equilibrium, with wages at $w_2/P$ and a lower level of employment at $L_2$. In this case, the reduction in employment is referred to as **voluntary unemployment.** At the lower wage, $w_2/P$, fewer people wish to work; those who wish to work have jobs, and those who are unemployed have chosen not to work.

By contrast, if wages remain at $w_1/P$ after the shift of the labour demand curve, then employed labour falls to $L_3$. At this wage, the number willing to work is much higher: it remains at $L_1$. The workers who cannot get jobs represent involuntary unemployment. They are willing and able to work at the going wage, $w_1/P$, but simply cannot find jobs.

Most economists believe that the labour supply curve, while not perfectly inelastic (or vertical), is relatively inelastic, and that much of the responsiveness comes from decisions to participate in the labour force (rather than in the desired number of hours worked per week). Moreover, as we have noted, when demand for labour is less than the supply, the shortfall usually takes the form mostly of reduction in employed workers, rather than hours worked per worker. For simplicity, in the following analysis we shall assume that the hours worked per worker are fixed, and reductions in the demand for labour hours are translated directly into reductions in employment.

Figure 10.2 **THE EFFECTS OF A SHIFT IN THE DEMAND FOR LABOUR WITH FIXED WAGES AND ELASTIC LABOUR SUPPLY**

If wages do not fall when the demand for labour shifts to the left, unemployment results.

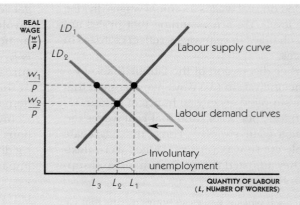

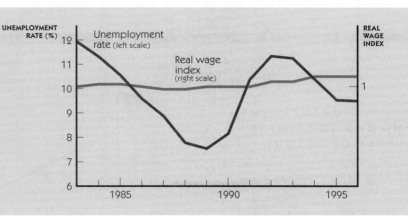

**Figure 10.3 REAL WAGES AND UNEMPLOYMENT**

During the period 1976–94 the unemployment rate fluctuated between 7.2 and 11.9 percent. The real wage was almost constant. *Sources:* Statistics Canada, CANSIM Database, 1996, Matrixes 1402, 2075, 2301, 3701; ibid., *Historical Statistics of Canada* (Ottawa, 1983).

## UNEMPLOYMENT AND WAGE RIGIDITIES

If we look at data on real wages—the wage adjusted for changes in the price level—we see that wages vary little with economic conditions. Figure 10.3 plots the real wage and unemployment rate during 1976–94. During that period the unemployment rate fluctuated between 7.2 and 11.9 percent, yet the real wage was almost constant. Even in the Great Depression, with massive unemployment, real wages did not fall, or fell very little.

Given the relatively small changes in real wages, the magnitude of the changes in unemployment cannot be explained by movements along a fixed, steep labour supply curve. Then how can we account for such large changes in unemployment?

There are but two possibilities. One is that the labour market always remains in equilibrium. This would imply that the labour supply curve shifts dramatically in a way that just offsets shifts in the labour demand curve so that in spite of large variations in employment, real wages remained unchanged. Few economists accept this account. Even if there were sudden, dramatic shifts in the labour supply curve, it is hard to believe that these would occur in just the right amount to offset shifts in the labour demand curve.

Economists have focused their attention on the other possible explanation: at least at times, demand for labour is less than supply, and the labour market

is not in equilibrium. How does such a situation arise? First there is a shift in the demand curve for labour, as illustrated in Figures 10.1 and 10.2. Such shifts can occur fairly rapidly, mainly because of changes in output. Second, real wages fail to fall enough to restore equilibrium (where demand for labour equals supply), resulting in involuntary unemployment. Because there is widespread agreement over this explanation, we may present it as our eighth point of consensus:

### 8 Unemployment

*Unemployment is typically generated by shifts in the aggregate demand curve for labour when real wages fail to adjust. The shifts in the aggregate labour demand curve usually arise from changes in aggregate output.*

To understand unemployment we must understand what causes changes in output. Thus, we now turn to the product market. Later, in Part Four, we will return to another basic issue of unemployment: What causes real wages to adjust slowly?

## UNEMPLOYMENT AND THE AGGREGATE SUPPLY OF LABOUR

While most unemployment arises from sudden leftward shifts in the demand curve for labour, occasionally large rightward shifts in the supply curve for

### Figure 10.4 UNEMPLOYMENT AND THE AGGREGATE SUPPLY OF LABOUR

Unemployment may arise from rightward shifts of the aggregate supply curve for labour, when wages fail to adjust. The initial equilibrium wage is $w_0/P$, at the intersection of the aggregate demand curve for labour and the initial aggregate supply curve for labour ($LS_0$). The aggregate supply curve for labour then shifts from $LS_0$ to $LS_1$. The real wage remains at $w_0/P$, where the quantity of labour demanded, $L_0$, is less than the quantity of labour supplied, $L_1$, resulting in unemployment ($L_1 - L_0$).

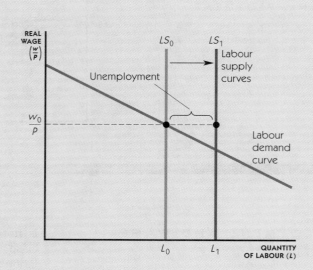

labour can also give rise to unemployment, as illustrated in Figure 10.4. Normally, aggregate labour supply changes only slowly, such as through demographic changes or changes in participation rates. But there are circumstances in which aggregate supply can shift dramatically in a short span of time. For instance, in the early 1990s, Israel was faced with a flood of Jewish immigrants from Russia, which increased its labour force by more than 10 percent. In the short run, real wages did not adjust quickly enough, and unemployment rose. Remarkably, within five years the unemployment rate was back down—though the adjustment seems to have been more through a compensating shift in the aggregate demand curve for labour than a lowering of the real wage. Another instance of potentially rapid shifts in the labour supply curve is associated with changes in tax or unemployment insurance provisions, which might induce a smaller or larger fraction of the population to join the labour force—though in practice such changes appear to take place more gradually. In regionally diverse countries, like Canada, large changes in interregional migration can cause rapid changes in labour supply in some regions. With fixed real wages, unemployment will rise in the regions to which the migrants are moving.

## BASIC ISSUES IN THE ANALYSIS OF UNEMPLOYMENT

**1** What causes shifts in the demand curve for labour?

**2** What causes shifts in the supply curve of labour?

**3** Why do wages fail to adjust?

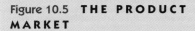

## Figure 10.5 THE PRODUCT MARKET

The full-employment level of output, $Y_s$, is given by the vertical aggregate supply curve. The aggregate demand curve intersects the aggregate supply curve at the price level $P_0$. Full-employment equilibrium is at point $E$, the intersection of the aggregate demand and supply curves.

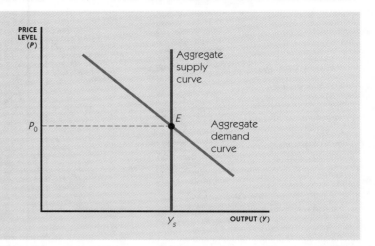

# THE PRODUCT MARKET IN THE SHORT RUN

Just as the demand and supply curves for labour were the basic tools for analyzing the labour market, the aggregate supply and demand curves for goods provide the framework for analyzing the product market. Recall the graph of the product market from Chapter 8. Redrawn here as Figure 10.5, it shows the vertical aggregate supply curve and the downward-sloping aggregate demand curve intersecting at point $E$. As we know from Chapter 8, the aggregate supply curve defines the economy's full-employment level of output, denoted as $Y_s$. At point $E$ the economy is at full employment at the price level $P_0$.

As with wages in our short-run analysis of the labour market, we assume that prices are fixed in the short-run analysis of the product market. In the short run, prices change little in response to movements of the aggregate demand and supply curves. For instance, automobile manufacturers typically change their prices only when new models come out. There are costs associated with changing prices, such as those of printing new catalogues and price lists, and risks—if a firm raises its price and its rival does not, it might price itself out of the market and

lose customers. While there are a few markets, such as the stock market or the market for gold, in which prices adjust to shifts in the demand and supply curves on a daily or faster basis, for most goods and services, whether sold by producers, wholesalers, or retailers, there is considerable price rigidity.

Consider what happens in the short run if aggregate demand shifts to the left, as depicted in Figure 10.6. At price level $P_0$, firms will produce only the quantity that they can sell, the quantity $Y_1$, below the full-employment level of output. One result of the reduced output will be a decrease in the demand for labour. Because of fixed wages in the labour market, this results in involuntary unemployment. Eventually prices and wages may adjust and if the aggregate demand curve remains in its new position ($AD_1$), the economy may move down the aggregate demand curve towards the future full-employment equilibrium, $E_f$. But this process of adjustment is beyond the scope of our concern here. In the short run, a period that may span a year or more, the economy will be stuck at $P_0$, with output below capacity and involuntary unemployment.

Another scenario is also possible, as illustrated in Figure 10.7. At price level $P_0$, demand exceeds supply, output is limited by aggregate supply ($Y_s$), and there is upward pressure on prices, anticipating the economy's eventual movement up the aggregate

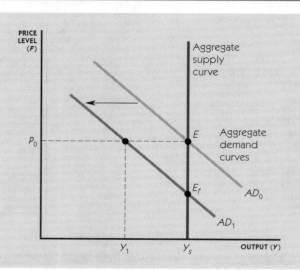

### Figure 10.6 OUTPUT BELOW CAPACITY

With the price level fixed at $P_0$, if the aggregate demand curve shifts to the left, the economy will fall below the full-employment level of output, $Y_s$. Output will be given by the aggregate demand curve at $P_0$, the level of output $Y_1$. Eventually if aggregate demand remains $AD_1$, the economy will move down the aggregate demand curve towards the future full-employment equilibrium, $E_f$.

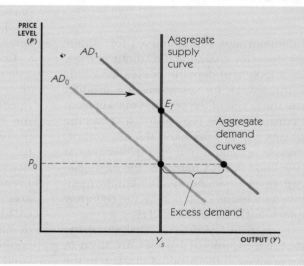

### Figure 10.7 EXCESS DEMAND

If the aggregate demand curve shifts to the right (from $AD_0$ to $AD_1$) beyond the full-employment level of output at $P_0$, aggregate demand will exceed the economy's capacity to produce. There will be excess demand and upward pressure on prices. Eventually, the economy will move up the aggregate supply curve towards the future full-employment equilibrium at $E_f$.

supply curve towards the future full-employment equilibrium, $E_f$. Under such circumstances the problem is not unemployment but inflation, a subject we will consider in detail in later chapters. For now, the point to remember is that inflation be-comes a concern when aggregate demand exceeds aggregate supply at a given price level; unemployment is the opposite problem, when demand at a given price level is less than the full-employment supply, $Y_s$. A general principle applies here: with prices fixed at a given level, if demand and supply are not equal, the *short* side of the market (whichever side is smaller) determines the actual level of short-run output.

## THE ECONOMY BELOW CAPACITY

The economy may fall below the full-employment level of output for any number of reasons. Anything that decreases the demand at a given price level for consumption, investment, government expenditures, or net exports can give rise to a leftward shift in the aggregate demand curve, bringing the economy to a level of output below the full-employment level. For instance, an economic downturn in the United States, Japan, or Europe will decrease their demand for Canadian goods, decreasing our exports to them at any price level. Or, if businesses lose confidence in the future, they will be less willing to invest. Such unexpected shifts in the aggregate demand curve are referred to as **demand shocks.**

Occasionally, excess capacity can be caused by shifts in the supply schedule as when a wave of immigration brings additional workers faster than the economy can absorb them, or improvements in technology increase the economy's productive capacity. When such shifts are sudden and unanticipated, they are referred to as **supply shocks.**

However it gets there, when the economy falls below the full-employment level of output, the options for policy makers are clear: either wait for the economy to adjust to a new full-employment equilibrium, or take action to shift the aggregate demand curve to the right, reestablishing the full-employment level of output at the existing price level. Policy makers have tended to take action. As the British economist John Maynard Keynes once said: "In the long run, we are all dead." That the economy will resume full employment in the long run offers little solace to the unemployed. Figure 10.8 depicts the economy beginning at a level of output below capacity at $Y_0$. By shifting the aggregate demand curve to the right, the economy can be brought to the full-employment level of output, or at least closer to it—and faster than if markets were allowed to adjust on their own.

Anything that increases the demand at a given price level for consumption, investment, government expenditures, or net exports may lead to a rightward shift in the aggregate demand curve. One option for government is to increase its expenditures. For instance, if defence expenditures are increased, aggregate demand at each price level increases, shifting the aggregate demand curve to the right. With excess capacity in the economy, this results in increased output.

Increasing government expenditures in response to involuntary unemployment is an act of **fiscal policy,** an area of great concern in discussions of

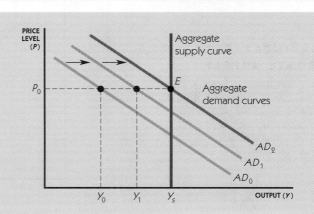

### Figure 10.8 ATTAINING FULL EMPLOYMENT

At price level $P_0$, if the government can shift the aggregate demand curve enough to the right, the economy can be moved to operate at full capacity. When the aggregate demand curve shifts from $AD_0$ to $AD_1$, output increases from $Y_0$ to $Y_1$. At $AD_2$, the economy attains the full-employment equilibrium at $P_0$.

macroeconomic policy. Fiscal policy is concerned with changes in government expenditures and taxes, directed at improving macroeconomic performance, including increasing output when there is excess capacity. Economists sometimes refer to a government effort to stimulate the economy through fiscal policy as a **fiscal stimulus.**

## THE SUPPLY SIDE OF THE PRODUCT MARKET

So far we have focused on the demand side of the market, and shifts in aggregate demand. What effect do increases in aggregate supply have on involuntary unemployment, when the economy is below capacity?

Increased capacity of the economy may result from new investment or new technology. This shifts $Y_s$ to the right. Figure 10.9 shows a rightward shift of the aggregate supply curve when the economy is initially below capacity at the price level $P_0$. The result is simply an increase in the amount by which aggregate supply exceeds aggregate demand at $P_0$. There is no effect on output, and thus no decrease in unemployment.

On the other hand, when there is excess demand

for goods (see Figure 10.7), an increase in aggregate supply will reduce the magnitude of the excess demand for goods, and thus the magnitude of the inflationary pressures. This was part of the rationale for the "supply-side" policies of the early 1980s, in which lower taxes were supposed to lead to increased labour supply and increased investment. The aggregate supply curve would shift to the right, reducing inflationary pressures.

## THREE MORE POINTS OF CONSENSUS

The important results of this analysis of aggregate demand and supply can be summarized in our ninth, tenth, and eleventh points of consensus in macroeconomics.

### 9  Stimulating the Economy when It Is Below Capacity

*When the economy has excess capacity, an increase in aggregate demand results in an increase in aggregate output, with relatively little effect on prices.*

The increase in aggregate demand can, of course, come from any source: an increase in consumption

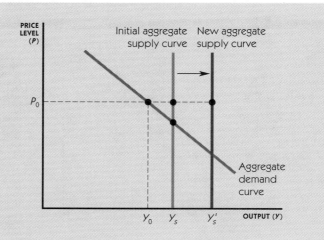

**Figure 10.9  INCREASING AGGREGATE SUPPLY**

At the current price level $P_0$, aggregate demand is less than $Y_s$, so that an increase in the economy's productive capacity has no effect on output, but increases the downward pressure on prices.

PRICE LEVEL ($P$)

Initial aggregate supply curve    New aggregate supply curve

$P_0$

Aggregate demand curve

$Y_0$  $Y_s$  $Y_s'$    OUTPUT ($Y$)

by households, expenditure by government, investment by firms, or net exports.

## 10  The Effect of Overstimulating the Economy

*When the economy is close to capacity, with most machines and workers fully employed, then a further increase in the demand for goods and services results in upward pressure on prices and has little effect on output.*

## 11  Supply-Side Effects when There Is Excess Capacity

*When the economy has excess capacity, increases in capacity have little effect on output.*

## LINKS WITH THE CAPITAL MARKET

We have now discussed the labour and product markets, two of the three central markets of the economy. These are both linked to the capital market in important ways.

In the capital market, interest rates are influenced by **monetary policy**—the actions of the **Bank of Canada,** which is the public agency responsible for controlling the money supply and interest rates. As we will see in Chapters 14 and 15, actions taken by the Bank can cause interest rates to rise and fall to some extent, though given the openness of the Canadian economy to international capital markets, the extent may be limited and of short duration. Changes in interest rates have important consequences for the product and labour markets. Consider first the product market. Low interest rates may encourage home construction and investment, leading to a higher demand for goods and a higher level of output. If the Bank of Canada detects a lull in economic activity, it may choose to lower the interest rate. Figure 10.10 shows the effect of lower interest rates on the product market. There is a rightward shift of the aggregate demand curve, where the economy is initially operating with excess capacity. The shift in the aggregate demand curve leads to an increase in aggregate output. We could then trace through the effects to the labour market: higher aggregate output leads to a higher level of employment.

On the other hand, if the Bank of Canada is worried that the inflation rate is about to increase, it typically takes action that raises the interest rate. One

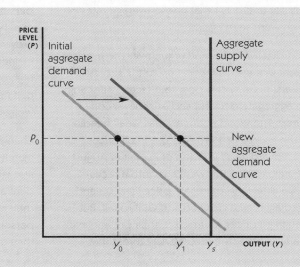

**Figure 10.10  THE LINK BETWEEN THE CAPITAL MARKET AND THE PRODUCT MARKET**

Lower interest rates lead to increased investment. This in turn leads to a rightward shift in the aggregate demand curve. If the economy is initially operating with excess capacity, aggregate output increases.

## CLOSE-UP: TRACING THE RECESSION AND RECOVERY OF THE EARLY 1990S THROUGH THE THREE AGGREGATE MARKETS

Any major macroeconomic event will have ramifications in the aggregate product, labour, and capital markets. The recession of 1990–92 and the subsequent economic recovery offer a good example.

Since the 1970s, economic growth has been in the range of 2 or 3 percent annually, measured in real terms. In 1989 it was 2.3 percent. But in the first and second quarters of 1990, the rate of real annual GDP growth was less than 1 percent. Then matters really went downhill. In the third quarter, real GDP *fell* by .4 percent. Over the next four quarters, real GDP fell at annual rates of 2.0, 3.5, 2.2, and 1.5 percent. Although the economy began growing again in the first quarter of 1992, the increases were small. Even in the first quarter of 1993, real GDP was smaller than it had been in the first quarter of 1990. The recession was technically over—the shrinkage of the economy had stopped—but people certainly did not feel a return to robust economic health. Indeed, it was only in late 1993 that growth rates of 2 to 3 percent were evident and it was not until 1994 that above-average rates of growth were seen again.

Economists will study and argue over the precise sequence of events leading up to the recession for years, but it seems clear that factors affecting both aggregate demand and price level contributed. The world economy was weak heading into the middle of 1990. The rise in oil prices that followed Iraq's invasion of Kuwait in August 1990 helped turn this weakness into a recession. It shifted the aggregate price level up and caused aggregate demand and GDP to fall. But although oil prices returned to their prewar level by early in 1991, the recessionary threat that

they had posed had plunged consumers and businesses into a downward spiral, where low confidence in the future led to reduced spending in Canada and abroad—a shift in the aggregate demand curve. The reduced spending in turn shrank the economy, confirming the gloomy expectations. The recovery really only took hold after several quarters of economic growth had taken place in the United States and a decline in the value of the Canadian dollar had led to large increases in Canadian exports. This outward shift of the aggregate demand curve increased GDP.

The slowdown in the product market reduced the demand for labour, moving the economy away from full employment. Canadian employment peaked in April 1990, when 13.2 million Canadians held jobs, but then sank to 12.8 million by April 1992. The sluggish recovery in early 1992 prevented the number of jobs from declining still further, but since businesses could not be sure whether the recovery was for real, they were not ready to hire many more workers. This persisted until employment began to grow in mid-1993. However, the labour force had also grown, leading to unemployment rates that remained persistently high. From a recessionary high of 11.9 percent the unemployment rate had fallen to just over 9 percent in early 1996, well above the prerecession low of 7.1 percent.

Changes in aggregate capital markets were intimately linked to these changes in the product and labour markets. As people grew less confident about their jobs and the economic future, their savings increased sharply. Total Canadian personal savings in 1990 were 25 percent higher than the levels in the late 1980s. Similar rises in savings were observed in the United States, our major trading partner. These high savings rates persisted well into 1995.

Higher savings rates meant that consumers were not buying as much. Businesses, seeing their sales falling, hesitated to invest. Banks, concerned about the ability of borrowers to repay, were reluctant to lend. The low levels of consumer spending and business investment at home and in the United States contributed to the economy's doldrums. Interest rates began falling as inflationary pressures eased in the recession. By mid-1992, the prime rate offered by the banks and the 90-day Treasury bill rate had dropped to about half of their 1990 levels. Mortgage rates had also fallen significantly. But in tough economic times, like late 1990 and 1991, even these low borrowing rates were not enough to persuade people to buy new homes or businesses to invest in new plant and equipment—at least not to an extent to restore economic prosperity in short order. It would take several years to reverse these trends.

*Source:* Statistics Canada, CANSIM Database 1996, various series.

key indicator used by the Bank in determining monetary policy is the tightness of the labour market. When the unemployment rate gets "too low" (in the view of policy makers)—to a level which cannot be sustained without a buildup of inflationary pressures—they tend to raise the interest rate. A situation with inflationary pressure is typically one where, at the current price level, aggregate demand exceeds the economy's full-employment level of output, as was depicted earlier, in Figure 10.7. A higher interest rate dampens the level of aggregate demand: at each price, the quantity of investment that firms wish to make is reduced, so that the aggregate demand curve shifts to the left. If the Bank's assessment of the economic situation is correct, the leftward movement of the aggregate demand curve simply decreases the upward pressure on prices without having much effect on output. But if the Bank increases interest rates too far, this will shift the aggregate demand curve too much to the left, so that aggregate demand at the current price level $P_0$ will be less than $Y_s$: output will fall and unemployment will increase.

We have assumed that the Bank of Canada can, in fact, influence the interest rate. As we stressed in Chapter 8, the Canadian economy might actually be a small open one with very little influence over interest rates. In these circumstances, attempts by the Bank of Canada acting alone to increase interest rates will induce large inflows of capital from abroad, thereby preventing the interest rate from rising. The Bank's actions will still affect aggregate demand, but via a different avenue. Large inflows of capital will cause the value of the Canadian dollar to appreciate, which in turn will make imports cheaper for Canadians and our exports more expensive to foreigners. Net exports, which is one of the components of aggregate demand, will fall and this will be appropriate if the Bank wants to dampen inflationary pressures arising from excessive aggregate demand. On the other hand, if several countries face situations of aggregate excess demand at the same time and respond by taking the same sort of restrictive monetary actions simultaneously, international interest rates will fall.

We have thus come full circle: all the markets of the economy are interconnected. So too are all the major policy concerns. The Bank of Canada may stimulate the economy by cutting the interest rate and/or causing the value of the Canadian dollar to fall. On the other hand, aggressive action to contain inflation by restraining the economy—by raising the interest rate and the value of the dollar—discourages investment and net exports, and may lead to lower growth. If the Bank acts *excessively aggressively,* it may overshoot, lowering output and inducing unemployment. Rather than just curtailing inflation, it may actually push the economy into a recession. Later chapters will pursue these links, as well as the trade-offs for policy makers.

### INTERDEPENDENCIES AMONG MARKETS

Changes in the capital market—such as lower interest rates or a depreciation of the Canadian dollar—have direct impacts on the product market, shifting the aggregate demand curve.

Changes in the product market—such as increased aggregate demand—have impacts on the labour market, shifting the demand curve for labour.

## MACROECONOMIC LESSONS FROM THE POSTWAR PERIOD

Macroeconomic consensus has been developed in part through a series of hard-learned lessons in the decades following World War II. In the brief historical sketches that follow, this consensus is used to highlight some of the major policy discussions of the period.

### FISCAL EXPANSION IN THE 1960S

In 1962, Canada was emerging from a two-year recession. Real GDP was growing at the rate of 6.8 percent and unemployment was falling. The federal budgets of 1963 and 1964 raised taxes and effectively erased the budget deficit. However, even though real GDP growth remained well above 6 percent in 1965, the government chose to adopt an expansionary fiscal policy. Following the lead of the Kennedy administration in the United States two years earlier, taxes were cut. This made sense in the United States, since in 1963 its unemployment rate was stuck at a relatively high level and its budget was in surplus. The policy of shifting the aggregate demand curve to the right by lowering taxes was successful in the sense that it led to increased output and reduced unemployment without increasing prices. This was because the U.S. economy was operating with excess capacity, as in panel A of Figure 10.11.

But when the tax cuts were introduced in Canada, the economy was already operating at near capacity. The price level was that at which aggregate demand equalled aggregate supply, as shown in panel B of Figure 10.11. The expansionary policy that shifted

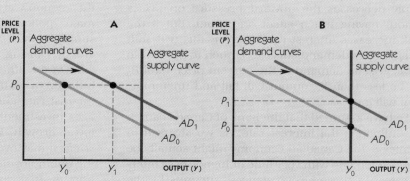

**Figure 10.11 EXPANSIONARY POLICY IN THE 1960S**

In response to high unemployment in the United States, the Kennedy administration cut taxes and shifted the aggregate demand curve to the right. Since the U.S. economy was operating below capacity, the result was an increase in output from $Y_0$ to $Y_1$ (panel A). Panel B shows the result when the Canadian government followed suit. Since the economy was already operating at capacity, the price level rose from $P_0$ to $P_1$ with no increase in output.

the aggregate demand curve to the right resulted in an increase in prices with little effect on output or employment. The inflation that resulted was to persist throughout the 1960s.

Inflationary pressures did emerge in the United States in the late 1960s. The U.S. economy was now operating with high employment along its aggregate supply curve, but was faced with the need to undertake large government expenditures, partly to fight the Vietnam War. President Johnson was unwilling to raise taxes to pay for these expenditures, with the result that aggregate demand shifted to the right and caused inflation. Given the interdependencies of the Canadian and American economies, some of the high demand in the United States spilled over into Canada and increased our levels of output and inflation further.

In response, the 1966 budget reduced government expenditures and raised taxes with the expected result that output growth slowed down moderately. The government quickly reacted in 1967 with further expansionary fiscal policy. This was an overreaction, since further inflation was induced and remained a problem for the rest of the 1960s. Once again restrictive policies had to be undertaken to combat inflation. Whereas real GDP over the 1960s had averaged 5.2 percent, the anti-inflation policies of the latter half of the decade reduced it to 2.5 per-

cent by 1970. Given a decade of high growth and inflation, unemployment was low for most of the 1960s.

## THE RECESSION OF 1980–81

By 1981 there was a widespread view that something had to be done to stop inflation in both Canada and the United States, which was high and appeared to be increasing. The Bank of Canada and its counterpart in the United States, the Federal Reserve Board (the "Fed"), are generally given credit for stopping inflation, though in the process their actions caused the worst recession in the postwar period and marked the beginning of the rapid run-up of government debt in Canada. The Bank and the Fed took strong actions to tighten the availability of credit and to raise interest rates. By 1981, interest rates reached record levels in excess of 20 percent before inflation was deemed defeated. (How a central bank implements policies to reduce the availability of credit, and the broader impact of such measures will be the subject of Chapters 14 and 15.) As a result of the Bank's actions, firms cut back their investments and households cut back their purchases of items like cars and houses. Thus, the aggregate demand curve shifted to the left, as shown in Figure 10.12, and the

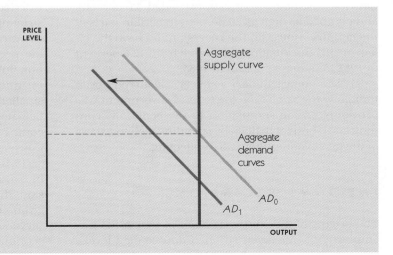

### Figure 10.12 MONETARY POLICY CONTROLS INFLATION BUT CAUSES A RECESSION

Beginning in the late 1970s and early 1980s, the Bank of Canada, concerned about runaway inflation, acted to restrict credit and thus consumption and investment. The resulting leftward shift in the aggregate demand curve caused a major recession. The effects were so strong that they more than offset the increased expansionary effects from the 1981 tax cut. The downward price pressures did, however, serve to reduce the pace of inflation.

**POLICY PERSPECTIVE:
THE ROLE OF ECONOMIC DATA**

Because it takes time for policy changes to have an effect, policy makers would like to have a crystal ball. If they knew in advance that the economy was going to go into recession in six months if no action was taken, they could take some action now. But policy makers not only don't have a crystal ball to see into the future, they often don't even know precisely where things stand today or even how things stood yesterday. It takes time to produce reliable economic data that indicate the strength of the economy. The most rapidly produced data are for employment and unemployment, which are reported monthly; estimates of output are reported quarterly. But regardless of how often reporting takes place, the numbers when they first become available are preliminary and subject to large adjustments and corrections.

An example of this can be seen when looking at the onset of the recession of the early 1990s. In late 1990, Statistics Canada reported that annual growth rates of real GDP had been 2.2 percent, 1.6 percent, and .5 percent, respectively, in the first three quarters of the year. By late 1991, these estimates had been revised down, to 1.4 percent, 1.0 percent, and .5 percent. We now know that the true figures were 1.0 percent, .4 percent, and −.4 percent. Technically, the recession had begun by the third quarter of 1990 and the government and central bank policy makers did not even know it in December of 1991— over a full year later! Although it is difficult to assess what these policy makers might have done differently had they known the true state of the economy, it is clear that better and more timely data would help them make better informed and more timely decisions.

*Sources:* Statistics Canada, *Canadian Economic Observer*, December 1990 and December 1991; Statistics Canada, CANSIM Database 1996, Label No. D20463.

economy was thrown into a major recession. The national unemployment rate exceeded 11 percent, and climbed as high as 20 percent in certain parts of the country. However, the recession did have the effect of curbing inflation, which fell from 12.5 percent in 1981 to under 4 percent in 1985.

These contractionary effects occurred even though *at the same time* the federal government was providing strong stimulation to the economy, running large budget deficits by spending well in excess of the tax revenues they were collecting.

## THE 1991 RECESSION

The origins of the 1991 recession, in which the unemployment rate again reached double-digit levels, remain somewhat controversial. The standard interpretation is that inflation increased gradually from 1988 to 1991. As the Bank again became increasingly worried about inflation, it stepped on the brakes, restricting credit and raising interest rates. The large leftward shift in the aggregate demand curve had the predictable effect of lowering equilibrium output. But when the Bank subsequently loosened interest rates to restart the economy, the impacts were smaller and took longer to take effect than it had anticipated. The slow recovery is often thought to have contributed to the massive defeat of the Mulroney Conservative government in 1993.

Two factors complicate this story. The Gulf War, in January 1991, almost coincided with the recession; the sudden increase in oil prices is sometimes given credit for stalling out the economy. Most observers, however, note that the slowdown of the economy had actually set in slightly before. Still, the economic disruption of the war may have contributed to the downturn.

**USING ECONOMICS: QUANTIFYING LINKS BETWEEN LABOUR AND PRODUCT MARKETS**

Government-policy economists need to know more than just that an increase in output will translate into an increase in employment. They need to know something about the quantitative relationship: If they succeed in reducing unemployment by 1 percentage point, say from 10 percent to 9 percent, how much will output increase? If they succeed in reducing interest rates by 1 percentage point, say from 6 percent to 5 percent, how much will output increase? In making their calculations, they often use simple rules of thumb, based on historical experience. The most famous of these is called Okun's law, after the American economist Arthur Okun. Okun's law gives the percentage increase in output associated with a one-percentage point decrease in the unemployment rate. It is currently estimated to be about 2 for Canada. Thus, lowering the unemployment rate from 10 percent to 9 percent will increase output by 2 percent.

In light of this calculation, in early 1996 there was widespread support for the view that the Bank of Canada should lower interest rates, given the absence of any inflationary pressures. This would stimulate economic growth. At the

beginning of 1996, the unemployment rate stood at 9.5 percent. If lower interest rates succeeded in lowering unemployment to 9 percent, then, according to Okun's law, output would increase by approximately 1 percent over what it otherwise would have been. Given that the economy had been forecast to grow at about 3 percent for the year, this represented a substantial increase in the growth rate *for that year.*

Okun's law can also be used in reverse. In early 1993, the unemployment rate stood at 11.2 percent. Policy makers might want to know how much output would have to increase in order to get the unemployment rate down to 10 percent. Okun's law gave them an answer: it would have to grow by about 2.4 percent *more* than the amount by which output would have increased simply from the increase in productivity and the increase in employment that would result from the increased labour force with a *fixed* unemployment rate. With GDP at the time of approximately $700 billion, this meant that aggregate demand would have to be increased by approximately $16.8 billion.

Second, since the early 1980s the federal government had been running a large budget deficit, averaging over $20 billion annually. By 1990, the cumulative effect of this was to start causing a rapid rise in the stock of debt—the debt as a percentage of GDP, referred to as the **debt/GDP ratio,** rose from 36 percent in 1980 to 70 percent in 1992. The high interest rates were in fact exacerbating the problem, given that interest payments on the debt had become roughly the size of the deficit itself. Financial markets were beginning to become anxious about the problem, and this was alleged to have driven interest rates even higher than they otherwise would have been. The response of the federal government was to

embark on a programme of expenditure control, which served to shift the aggregate demand curve further to the left. This contributed to the difficulty the economy had in moving out of the recession.

## DEFICIT REDUCTION VERSUS JOB CREATION

The final episode we will discuss is the drama that has played out since the Liberal government of Jean Chrétien took office in 1993. The Liberals won the election on a platform that promised both job creation and deficit reduction. The budgets of 1995 and 1996 put in place very significant expenditure reductions without changing tax rates. Some economists were worried: expenditure cuts serve to reduce aggregate demand. Potentially, that could have made the economic downturn even worse. But there were two other effects.

The first was that the lower demand for borrowing by the government (and the anticipated decrease in future years) may have itself stimulated demand. Reducing the demand for loans puts downward pressure on interest rates. To the extent that interest rates actually fell, investment was stimulated. Furthermore, even if interest rates were prevented from falling by the openness of international capital markets, this would be reflected in an outward flow of capital resulting in a fall in the value of the Canadian dollar. Net exports would increase. According to either case, the lower demand for borrowing by the government caused a shift to the right in aggregate demand.

The second effect was that at the same time as the Canadian government was engaging in expenditure reduction, the American economy was taking off as a result of lower interest rates there. High demand in the United States naturally spilled over into Canada, resulting in a strong demand for Canadian exports. Overall, despite the loss in public-sector employment as a result of expenditure restraint, job creation in the private sector was strong enough to cause the unemployment rate to fall from 11.2 percent in 1993 to 9.5 percent two years later.

## REVIEW AND PRACTICE

### SUMMARY

**1** Unemployment macroeconomics assumes that wages and prices are fixed in the short run.

**2** To explain unemployment, we need to explain why the aggregate labour market does not clear. If real wages do not adjust to shifts in the aggregate supply and demand curves for labour, and either the demand curve for labour shifts to the left or the supply curve for labour shifts to the right, then the quantity of labour supplied will exceed the quantity demanded at the prevailing wage, and there will be involuntary unemployment.

**3** The demand curve for labour shifts because of a fall in the production of goods by firms, as a result of a decrease in the demand for their products.

**4** In the product market, if aggregate demand at a given price level is less than the economy's full-employment output (capacity), output will be limited by aggregate demand. Shifting the aggregate demand curve to the right will increase output and employment, and may restore the economy to full employment.

**5** If, at a given price level, aggregate demand exceeds aggregate supply, output will be limited by aggregate supply, and there will be upward pressure on prices.

**6** All markets in the economy are interrelated. Thus, disturbances in the product market have consequences for the labour market, and disturbances in the capital market have consequences for the product market. For instance, when there is involuntary unemployment, lower interest rates may result in increased investment, increasing output and employment. Or, in a small open economy, an increase in the demand for borrowing by the government will cause the value of the Canadian dollar to rise. Net exports will fall, reducing output and employment.

## KEY TERMS

rigid prices and wages

voluntary unemployment

involuntary
unemployment

underemployment

demand shocks

supply shocks

fiscal policy

fiscal stimulus

monetary policy

Bank of Canada

## REVIEW QUESTIONS

**1** If the labour market always cleared, would there be any unemployment? What does it mean for the labour market not to clear?

**2** If the labour market always cleared, could there be variations in the level of employment?

**3** What inferences do you draw from the following two facts?
(a) The labour supply curve is relatively inelastic.
(b) Large variations in employment coexist with relatively small variations in real wages.

**4** What might shift the aggregate demand curve for labour?

**5** If prices are rigid, and at a level *above* that at which aggregate demand equals supply, what will be the level of output? What will happen if the aggregate demand curve shifts to the left? To the right? If the aggregate supply curve shifts to the left? To the right?

**6** If prices are rigid, and at a level *below* that at which aggregate demand equals supply, what will be the level of output? What will happen if the aggregate demand curve shifts to the left? To the right? If the aggregate supply curve shifts to the left? To the right?

**7** What are some of the ways in which the various markets of the economy are interlinked?

**8** Use the aggregate demand and supply curve framework to describe some of the major macro-economic episodes of the postwar period.

## PROBLEMS

**1** In the 1970s, a large number of new workers entered the Canadian economy from two main sources. The baby boom generation grew to adulthood and the proportion of women working increased substantially. If wages adjust, what effect will these factors have on the equilibrium level of wages and quantity of labour? If wages do not adjust, how does your answer change? In which case will unemployment exist? Draw a diagram to explain your answer.

**2** Soon after Iraq invaded Kuwait in August 1990, many firms feared that a recession would occur. They began cutting back on production and employment. If wages adjust, what effect will this cutback have on the equilibrium level of wages and employment? If wages do not adjust, how does your answer change? In which case will unemployment exist?

**3** During the 1980s, government spending and budget deficits rose dramatically in Canada. This had the effect of shifting the aggregate demand curve to the right. What effect would you expect this change to have on the equilibrium level of prices and national output? Draw a diagram to illustrate your answer.

**4** In early 1995, Mexico faced a financial crisis, which led to a major economic downturn in that country. Under the North American Free Trade Agreement, Canadian products can be sold freely on Mexican markets. If nothing else had happened, what effect would you expect the financial crisis to have on the aggregate demand curve in Canada and on the level of national output in the short run, at a given price level?

**5** In the early 1990s, there was a massive wave of Russian immigrants into Israel. Yet, within a few years, unemployment returned to normal levels and real wages had not fallen. Using aggregate demand and supply curves for goods and labour, explain how this could have occurred. (Hint: new immigrants generate additional demand for goods as well as additional supplies of labour.)

**6** While for the most part, macroeconomics focuses on aggregate employment, ignoring distinctions among different categories of workers, it sometimes focuses on broad categories, such as skilled and unskilled workers. Assume, for simplicity, that there are just these two categories, and that for the most part, they cannot be substituted for each other.

(a) Draw demand and supply curves for skilled and unskilled workers, marking the initial equilibrium in each market.

(b) Assume now that there is a technological change which increases the demand for skilled labour at each wage, while it shifts the demand curve for unskilled labour to the left. If wages do not adjust, can there be vacancies of one type of labour at the same time there is unemployment of another type?

# CHAPTER 11

# AGGREGATE DEMAND

In Chapter 10 we learned that the major cause of unemployment is a shift in the demand curve for labour without a commensurate fall in the real wage. We also learned that the major cause of a shift in the demand curve for labour is a reduction in aggregate output. Thus, to understand events in the labour market, we must understand the product market: What determines the level of output and its changes?

In this and the following chapter we will answer that question, focusing on the circumstances where supply imposes no constraints, that is, where there is excess capacity of machines and unemployment of labour. In this simple scenario, output is determined entirely by aggregate demand.

This chapter explains what determines the level of aggregate demand at any particular set of wages and prices, what causes changes in aggregate demand, and why output can be so volatile.

## KEY QUESTIONS

**1** When the economy has excess capacity, what determines the aggregate level of output?

**2** What are the components of aggregate expenditures?

**3** How do consumption and imports increase with income?

**4** Why, if investment or government expenditures or exports increase by a dollar, does aggregate output increase by more than a dollar? What determines the amount by which it increases?

## INCOME-EXPENDITURE ANALYSIS

Let us return for a moment to the aggregate demand and supply framework that we introduced in Chapter 10, focusing on a situation where the economy has a large excess capacity. Figure 11.1 shows the aggregate demand and supply curves, and with the price level $P_0$ such that there is a large excess supply: at $P_0$, aggregate demand is much less than the economy's capacity to produce. In this situation, a shift in the aggregate demand curve, from $AD_0$ to, say, $AD_1$ leads to an increase in aggregate output, from $Y_0$ to $Y_1$.

But what determines the level of aggregate demand at each price level? And what determines changes in this level of demand? Recall the four components of aggregate output and demand: consumption, investment, government expenditures, and net

exports. Aggregate demand at any price level is just the sum of consumption, investment, government expenditures, and net exports "demanded" at that price level. We can think of this "demand" as the expenditures in four parts of the economy: household expenditures on consumer goods, firms' expenditures on investment goods, government expenditures on public goods and services, and foreigners' expenditures on net exports.

The key to solving for the *equilibrium* level of output and the equilibrium level of aggregate demand is the **aggregate-expenditures schedule.** The term "aggregate expenditures" refers to the total of expenditures on consumption, investment, government goods and services, and net exports. The aggregate-expenditures schedule traces out the relationship, at a fixed price level, between aggregate expenditures and national income—the aggregate income of everyone in the economy. It is depicted in Figure 11.2, where the vertical axis indicates aggregate ex-

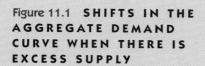

**Figure 11.1 SHIFTS IN THE AGGREGATE DEMAND CURVE WHEN THERE IS EXCESS SUPPLY**

When the economy has excess capacity, changes in aggregate demand result in different levels of output at the fixed price level, $P_0$.

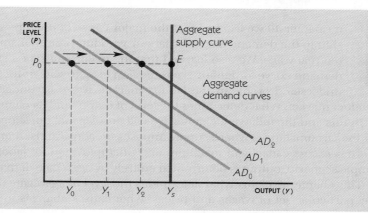

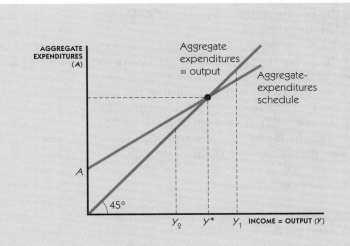

**Figure 11.2  THE AGGREGATE-EXPENDITURES SCHEDULE AND INCOME-EXPENDITURE ANALYSIS**

The aggregate-expenditures schedule gives the sum of consumption, investment, government expenditures, and net exports at each level of national income. Aggregate expenditures increase with income. Equilibrium occurs at the intersection of the aggregate-expenditures schedule and the 45-degree line. At outputs greater than $Y^*$, such as $Y_1$, output exceeds aggregate expenditures. Goods that are being produced are not being sold; there are unintended inventory accumulations. The reverse is true for outputs less than $Y^*$.

penditures and the horizontal axis indicates national income.

The aggregate-expenditures schedule has three critical properties. First, it is upward-sloping: as national income goes up, so do aggregate expenditures. Changes in other variables, like interest rates, tax rates, and exchange rates, cause the aggregate-expenditures schedule to shift up or down, and they may even change the slope.

Second, as income increases by a dollar, aggregate expenditures increase by less than a dollar. The reason for this is that consumers save some of their increased income. Figure 11.2 also shows a line through the origin at a 45-degree angle. The slope of this line is unity. All along this line, a one-dollar change in the vertical axis is matched by a one-dollar change in the horizontal axis. Since aggregate expenditures increase less than dollar for dollar with increased income, the aggregate expenditures schedule is flatter than the 45-degree line.

Third, even if national income were zero, aggregate expenditures would remain positive. This is reflected in the fact that the aggregate-expenditures schedule intercepts the vertical axis at a positive level, point A. (We will discuss the reasons for this later in the chapter.)

The facts that (a) the aggregate-expenditures schedule is flatter than the 45-degree line through the origin and (b) aggregate expenditures are positive, even when income is zero, imply that the aggregate-expenditures schedule intersects the 45-degree line, as seen in the figure.

What is the relationship between the aggregate-expenditures schedule and the aggregate demand schedule discussed in the last chapter? The aggregate-expenditures schedule shows expenditures, at each level of income, given the price level; the aggregate demand curve shows aggregate demand (or expenditures) at each level of price, given that the level of income is at its short-run equilibrium level. This brings us to our central question: What determines the short-run equilibrium level of output when there is excess capacity. We need two more concepts for our analysis besides the aggregate-expenditures schedule.

## THE NATIONAL INCOME-OUTPUT IDENTITY

National income is equal to national output (as shown in Chapter 8). This reflects the fact that when a good is purchased, the money that is paid must eventually wind up as someone's income: as wages of workers in the firm that produced the good or of workers who produced the intermediate goods that were used in the production of the final good; as interest payments in the pockets of those who have lent the firm money; as profits, in the pockets of the owners of the firm; or as tax revenues to the government. For simplicity, we will assume that the residents of the country neither receive money (net) from abroad nor pay money (net) abroad, so GNP and GDP coincide. If $Y$ is used to represent national income, this identity can be written

GDP = national income = $Y$.

This identity is our second necessary concept. It allows us to interpret the horizontal axis in Figure 11.2 in two different ways. We can say the aggregate-expenditures schedule gives the level of expenditures at each level of national *income*. We can also say it gives the level of expenditures at each level of national *output*.

## EQUILIBRIUM OUTPUT

Normally, firms produce only what they believe they can sell. This means that the total output produced by all firms will equal the total demand for output. This is our third necessary concept, and it can be put another way: in equilibrium, aggregate expenditures, which we denote by $AE$, must equal aggregate output (GDP). Since aggregate output equals national income ($Y$), we have the simple equation

$AE$ = GDP = $Y$.

In Figure 11.2, the line at a 45-degree angle through the origin is labeled "Aggregate expenditures = output." The line traces all points where the vertical axis (aggregate expenditures) equals the horizontal axis (national income, which equals aggregate output).

Equilibrium lies at the point on the aggregate-expenditures schedule that also satisfies the aggregate-expenditures-equal-output condition. That is, equilibrium occurs at the intersection of the aggregate-expenditures schedule and the 45-degree line.

The corresponding equilibrium value of aggregate output is denoted by $Y^*$.

The analysis that determines equilibrium output by relating income (output) to aggregate expenditures is called **income-expenditure analysis.** We can see that $Y^*$ is the equilibrium in two different ways. The first way is to note that it is the only point that satisfies the two conditions for equilibrium. In equilibrium, everything produced must be purchased. Thus, aggregate expenditures must be equal to national output (income), as represented by the 45-degree line. In equilibrium, the level of aggregate expenditures must also be what households, firms, and government want to spend in total at that level of national income, given by the aggregate-expenditures schedule.

The second way is to consider what happens at a level of income $Y_1$, in excess of $Y^*$. At that point, the aggregate-expenditures schedule lies below the 45-degree line. What households, firms, and government would like to spend at that level of national income, as reflected in the aggregate-expenditures schedule, is less than national income (output). More goods are being produced than individuals want to buy. Some of the goods, like strawberries, cannot be stored. They simply spoil. The goods that can be stored go into inventories.

Economists distinguish between **planned inventories** and **unplanned inventories.** Firms choose to have some inventory on hand because it makes business more efficient. Planned inventories are considered an investment, and their buildup is therefore counted as part of investment spending in the aggregate-expenditures schedule. Unplanned inventories are simply goods that firms are producing but cannot sell. At output level $Y_1$, firms find that unplanned inventories are piling up—they are producing goods that cannot be sold, which are either spoiling or increasing inventories beyond the desired level. Firms respond by cutting back production until they reach $Y^*$. At $Y_2$, the aggregate-expenditures schedule lies above the 45-degree line. Households, firms, and government are spending more than national income, or output. In other words, they are purchasing more than the economy is producing. This is possible because firms can sell out of inventories. As planned inventories are depleted, firms increase production until equilibrium is restored, when output (income) again is equal to $Y^*$.

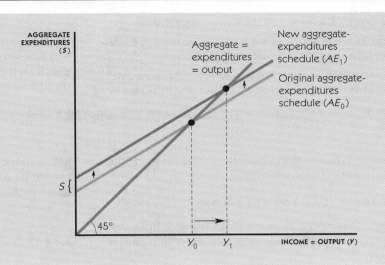

**Figure 11.3 EFFECT OF A SHIFT IN THE AGGREGATE-EXPENDITURES SCHEDULE**

An upward shift in the aggregate-expenditures schedule results in an increase in the equilibrium level of output. The magnitude of the increase in equilibrium output from a given upward shift in the aggregate-expenditures schedule is greater than the magnitude of the upward shift; $Y_1 - Y_0$ exceeds $S$, the magnitude of the shift.

## SHIFTS IN THE AGGREGATE-EXPENDITURES SCHEDULE

The aggregate-expenditures schedule can shift through a variety of changes in the economy that lead households, firms, and government to decide, *at each level of income*, to spend more or less. Figure 11.3 shows what happens if the level of aggregate expendi-

tures increases at each level of national income by the amount $S$. The new aggregate-expenditures schedule is denoted by $AE_1$. The equilibrium output increases from $Y_0$ to $Y_1$, *which is greater than the amount S*. How much greater depends on the slope of the aggregate-expenditures schedule. In Figure 11.4, the aggregate-expenditures schedule shifts up by the same amount it did in Figure 11.3, but the aggregate-expenditures

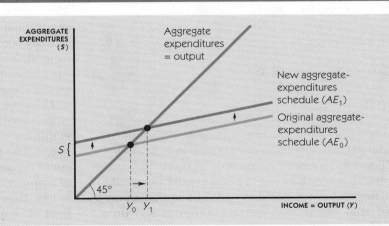

**Figure 11.4 THE IMPORTANCE OF THE SLOPE OF THE AGGREGATE-EXPENDITURES SCHEDULE**

The flatter the aggregate-expenditures schedule, the smaller the magnitude of the increase in output resulting from a given upward shift in the schedule.

## INCOME-EXPENDITURE ANALYSIS

**1** Equilibrium output is at the point where the aggregate-expenditures schedule equals output (income).

**2** Upward shifts in the aggregate-expenditures schedule result in increases in equilibrium output. The increases in equilibrium output are larger than the initial shift in the aggregate-expenditures schedule. How much larger depends on the slope of the aggregate-expenditures schedule: the steeper the slope, the greater the increase.

schedule is flatter. Consequently, the increase in equilibrium output is much smaller.

### MATHEMATICAL FORMULATION

We can describe the equilibrium using simple algebra. The aggregate-expenditures equation can be written:

$$AE = b + cY,$$

where $b$ is the vertical intercept of the aggregate-expenditures schedule (the value of $AE$ when $Y = 0$) and $c$ is the slope of the aggregate-expenditures schedule (an increase in $Y$ of $1 increases $AE$ by $$c$). The fact that the slope is less than 45 degrees implies that $c$ is between 0 and 1. Equilibrium requires aggregate-expenditures to equal income—which, under our simplifying assumptions, equals $Y$:

$$AE = Y.$$

Substituting the value of $AE$ above yields

$$Y = b + cY,$$

which can be solved for $Y$:

$$Y = b/(1 - c).$$

An upward shift in the aggregate-expenditures schedule corresponds to an increase in $b$, say to $b + 1$. Then $Y$ increases by an amount $1/(1 - c)$.

Since $c$ is less than 1, $1/(1 - c)$ is greater than 1. If $c = .9$, then $1 - c = .1$, and $1/(1 - c) = 10$, so that an upward shift in the aggregate-expenditures schedule by $1 increases GDP by $10.

The property that an upward shift of the aggregate-expenditures schedule causes a multiple increase in equilibrium GDP is called the multiplier. Later in the chapter we will take a closer look at it.

## A LOOK FORWARD

We have just learned two of the central principles of macroeconomics: (1) shifts in the aggregate-expenditures schedule determine changes in the equilibrium output of the economy, and (2) the magnitude of those changes is greater than the magnitude of the shift up or down in the aggregate-expenditures schedule and increases with the slope of the aggregate-expenditures schedule. The remainder of this chapter explores the implications of these principles. Two questions are addressed.

The first question is: What determines the slope of the aggregate-expenditures schedule, the extent to which aggregate expenditures increase as income increases? As we have seen, the flatter that schedule (the smaller its slope), the smaller the increase in output from any upward shift in the schedule. The second question is: What causes shifts in the aggregate-expenditures schedule? And what, if anything, can the government do to shift the schedule? The possibilities for government are an important issue. In the last chapter we saw that unemployment is created when there is a shift in the demand curve for labour without a corresponding downward adjustment of wages. The primary reason for a shift in the demand curve for labour is a change in the equilibrium level of output. When output is low, the demand for labour is low. If government can increase the equilibrium level of output by somehow shifting the aggregate-expenditures schedule, then it can increase the level of employment.

To answer these questions, we need to take a closer look at each of the four components of aggregate expenditures: (1) consumption of goods and services, such as food, television sets, or haircuts, all of which are purchased by consumers; (2) investment in capital goods, machines or buildings that are bought by firms to help them produce goods; (3) government purchases, both goods and services bought for current use (public consumption) and goods and services like buildings and roads, bought for the future benefits they generate (public investment); and (4) net exports. We say net exports because we have to subtract those goods and services bought by Canadian households, businesses, and government that are produced abroad—imports—and that have already been included in consumption, investment, and government expenditures.

Using *AE* for aggregate expenditures, *C* for consumption spending, *I* for investment spending, *G* for government spending, and *E* for net exports, we can set out the components of aggregate expenditures in equation form:

$$AE = C + I + G + E.$$

This equation is nothing more than a definition. It says that consumption spending, investment spending, government spending, and net exports add up to aggregate expenditures. Net exports is sometimes written as $X - M$, where *X* stands for exports and *M* for imports. These symbols represent enormous numbers for the Canadian economy. In 1994, *AE* was $750 billion, of which *C* was $453 billion, *I* was $142 billion, *G* was $150 billion, *X* was $249 billion, and *M* was $244 billion.

We now take a brief look at each of these categories.

## CONSUMPTION

The most important determinant of consumption is income. On average, families with higher incomes spend more. Table 11.1 shows the relationship between consumption and income for a hypothetical family. The same information is depicted graphically

**Table 11.1 RELATIONSHIP BETWEEN INCOME AND CONSUMPTION**

| Income | Consumption |
|--------|-------------|
| $ 5,000 | $ 6,000 |
| 10,000 | 10,500 |
| 20,000 | 19,500 |
| 30,000 | 28,500 |

in Figure 11.5, panel A, where the amount of consumption is given along the vertical axis and income along the horizontal axis. The upward slope of the line indicates that consumption for this family increases as income does. The relationship between a household's consumption and its income is called its **consumption function.** Every family has different consumption patterns because the tastes and circumstances of families differ, but the pattern shown in Table 11.1 is typical.

Aggregate consumption is the sum of the consumption of all the households in the economy. Just as when a typical family's income rises its consumption increases, when the total income of the economy rises, aggregate consumption increases. For purposes of macroeconomics, it is the **aggregate consumption function,** the relationship between aggregate consumption and aggregate income, that is of importance. And the measure of income that is important is disposable income, or what people have after paying taxes. The relationship between aggregate consumption and aggregate income is given in Table 11.2, and the aggregate consumption function is depicted graphically in Figure 11.5, panel B.

## THE MARGINAL PROPENSITY TO CONSUME

The amount by which consumption increases when disposable income increases by a dollar is called the **marginal propensity to consume** (*MPC*). For Canada as a whole, the marginal propensity to consume

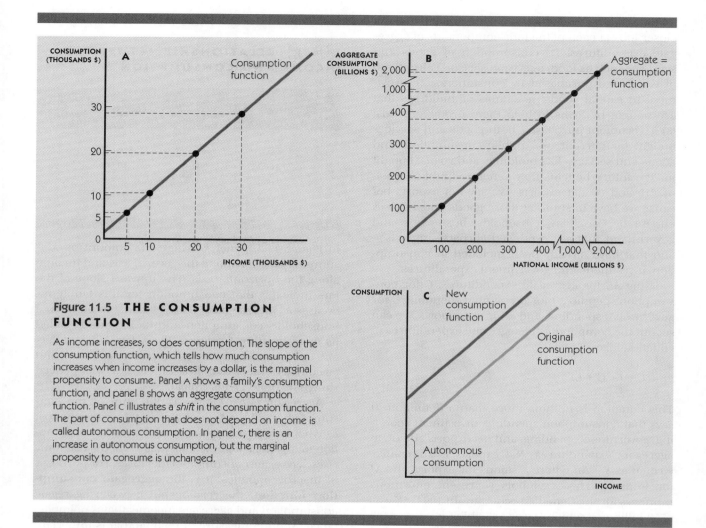

**Figure 11.5 THE CONSUMPTION FUNCTION**

As income increases, so does consumption. The slope of the consumption function, which tells how much consumption increases when income increases by a dollar, is the marginal propensity to consume. Panel A shows a family's consumption function, and panel B shows an aggregate consumption function. Panel C illustrates a *shift* in the consumption function. The part of consumption that does not depend on income is called autonomous consumption. In panel C, there is an increase in autonomous consumption, but the marginal propensity to consume is unchanged.

in the postwar period has been somewhere between .85 and .90. That is, of each extra dollar of income households receive, they spend on average between 85 and 90 percent.[1] If aggregate income increases by $10 billion, then aggregate consumption will increase by between $8.5 and $9.0 billion. In the hypothetical consumption function illustrated in Figure 11.5, panel B, the marginal propensity to consume is .9: when disposable income goes up by $10 billion,

[1] In the late 1970s, consumption was sometimes as high as 95 percent of household income. More recently, consumption has been somewhat lower. These statistics give the *average* ratio of consumption to disposable income. The *marginal* propensity to consume is somewhat smaller.

aggregate consumption goes up by $9 billion.

The slope of the aggregate consumption function conveys important information. It tells us by how much aggregate consumption (measured along the vertical axis) rises with an increase of a dollar of aggregate disposable income (horizontal axis). In other words, the slope of the aggregate consumption function is the marginal propensity to consume. In panels A and B of Figure 11.5, the fact that consumption increases as income rises is reflected in the upward slope of the consumption function, and the marginal propensity to consume is equal to this slope. Flatter slopes would illustrate lower marginal propensities to consume.

**Table 11.2 AGGREGATE CONSUMPTION AND NATIONAL INCOME (billions of dollars)**

| Disposable income | Consumption (C) |
| --- | --- |
| $ 100 | $ 105 |
| 200 | 195 |
| 300 | 285 |
| 400 | 375 |
| 650 | 600 |
| 1,000 | 915 |
| 2,000 | 1,815 |

Figure 11.5, panel C, shows a shift in the consumption function. The intercept with the vertical axis—the level of consumption that would prevail even if disposable income were zero—is increased. This part of consumption, which does not depend on the level of income, is sometimes called **autonomous consumption.**[2] With the shift depicted in the figure, the marginal propensity to consume remains unchanged: the slope of the consumption function is the same. Sometimes both autonomous consumption and the marginal propensity to consume change. In the late 1970s, the level of autonomous consumption and the marginal propensity to consume both appeared to be higher than in previous decades.

As usual, we have to be careful to distinguish between changes in consumption that result from *movements along a consumption function*—the increase in consumption that results from higher incomes—and changes in consumption that result from a *shift in the consumption function*. Chapter 12 will discuss some of the factors that lead to shifts in the consumption function.

The consumption function can be written mathematically as

$$C = a + mY_d,$$

[2] People can consume even when their income is zero by using up savings.

where $C$ is consumption, $a$ is the level of autonomous consumption, $m$ is the marginal propensity to consume (the extra amount spent on consumption when disposable income increases by a dollar), and $Y_d$ is disposable income, income after paying taxes.

## THE MARGINAL PROPENSITY TO SAVE

Individuals have to either spend or save each extra dollar of disposable income, so savings and consumption are mirror images of each other. The equation income = consumption plus savings tells us that when disposable income rises by a dollar, if aggregate consumption increases by 90 cents, aggregate savings increases by 10 cents. The higher level of savings stemming from an extra dollar of income is called the **marginal propensity to save** (*MPS*). This is the counterpart to the marginal propensity to consume, and the two must always sum to 1:

marginal propensity to save + marginal propensity to consume = 1.

The high marginal propensity to consume today means that there is a low marginal propensity to save. Thirty-five years ago, the marginal propensity to consume was even larger than it is today, between .9 and .95; of each extra dollar of disposable income, between 90 and 95 cents was spent on consumption. By the same token, the marginal propensity to save was smaller; between 5 and 10 cents of each extra dollar of disposable income went into savings.

## INVESTMENT

We now turn to the second major component of GDP, investment. Investment varies greatly from year to year, and, as we learned in Chapter 8, depends on the level of interest rates. Now, however, our focus is on the income-expenditure schedule, the relationship between aggregate demand and national income. We assume the level of investment is unrelated to the level of income this year. This assumption is made largely

**USING ECONOMICS: CALCULATING EQUILIBRIUM OUTPUT**

Equilibrium output can be calculated as follows. Since

$$C = a + mY$$

and

$$AE = C + I = a + mY + I,$$

and since in equilibrium, aggregate expenditures equal income,

$$AE = Y,$$

we have

$$Y = a + mY + I,$$

or

$$Y = \frac{a + I}{1 - m}.$$

As a numerical example, let $a = \$200$ billion, $I = \$100$ billion, and $m = .75$. When we substitute all these, we get $Y = \$1{,}200$ billion.

to simplify the analysis, but it also reflects the view that investment is primarily determined by firms' estimates of the economic prospects over the future. Accordingly, investment levels are not greatly affected by what happens this year and, in particular, by the level of national income. We can now analyze equilibrium output in a simplified economy with no government and foreign trade. Aggregate expenditures thus consist only of consumption and investment.

Table 11.3 combines the information from Table 11.2 with a fixed level of investment, $50 billion. Because we have assumed away government—both taxes and expenditures—disposable income is the same as national income. The table shows the level of aggregate expenditures for various levels of national income. Aggregate expenditures consist of the sum of consumption and investment, shown in the fourth column of the table and plotted in Figure 11.6.

**Table 11.3 SOME COMPONENTS OF AGGREGATE EXPENDITURES**
**(billions of dollars)**

| Disposable income ($Y_d$) | Consumption expenditures ($C$) | Investment spending ($I$) | Total aggregate expenditures |
|---|---|---|---|
| $ 100 | $ 105 | $50 | $ 155 |
| 200 | 195 | 50 | 245 |
| 300 | 285 | 50 | 335 |
| 400 | 375 | 50 | 425 |
| 650 | 600 | 50 | 650 |
| 1,000 | 915 | 50 | 965 |
| 2,000 | 1,815 | 50 | 1,865 |

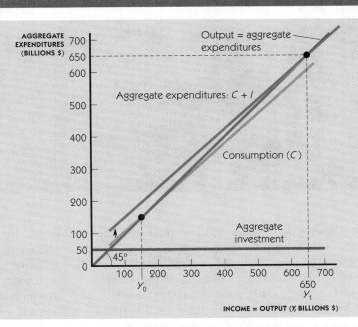

### Figure 11.6 A BEGINNING VIEW OF OUTPUT DETERMINATION: CONSUMPTION PLUS INVESTMENT

Investment is fixed, so the aggregate-expenditures schedule is a fixed amount above the consumption function alone. The slope of $C + I$ is the same as that of the consumption function; it is just the marginal propensity to consume.

Because we assume investment does not depend on current income, the slope of the upper line in the figure is exactly the same as the slope of the consumption function: as income increases, aggregate expenditures increase by the same amount that consumption does, that is, by the marginal propensity to consume. The slope of the aggregate-expenditures schedule is still the marginal propensity to consume. The equilibrium—the intersection of the aggregate-expenditures schedule and the 45-degree line—is at $Y_1$ ($650 billion).

## THE MULTIPLIER

One of the fundamental insights of income-expenditure analysis is that factors shifting the aggregate-expenditures schedule will have a compound effect on output. Consider, for instance, an upward shift in the aggregate-expenditures schedule induced by an increase in investment of $1 billion. We continue to assume that the marginal propensity to consume is .9. The first-round effect of the extra investment spending, shown in Table 11.4, is straightforward:

### Table 11.4 EFFECTS OF AN INCREASE IN INVESTMENT OF $1 BILLION (millions of dollars)

| | |
|---|---:|
| First round | $ 1,000 |
| Second round | 900 |
| Third round | 810 |
| Fourth round | 729 |
| Fifth round | 656 |
| Sixth round | 590 |
| Seventh round | 531 |
| Eighth round | 478 |
| Ninth round | 430 |
| Tenth round | 387 |
| Eleventh round | 349 |
| Sum of twelfth and successive rounds | $ 3,140 |
| Total increase | $10,000 |

## USING ECONOMICS: CALCULATING THE MULTIPLIER

Earlier, we showed that

$$Y = \frac{a + I}{1 - m}.$$

To see the multiplier, assume that $I$ increases by a dollar. Now,

$$Y_1 = \frac{a + I + 1}{1 - m}.$$

$Y_1 - Y$, the change in $Y$, is found by subtraction:

$$Y_1 - Y = \frac{1}{1 - m}.$$

The smaller $m$, the marginal propensity to consume, the flatter the aggregate-expenditures schedule, and the smaller the multiplier. If $m = .9$, the multiplier is 10. If $m = .8$, the multiplier is 5.

output increases by $1 billion as firms purchase capital goods. This is only the beginning, however. The value of this increased output is distributed to the members of the economy as income, in the form of either higher wages, higher interest payments, or higher profits that become income to the firms' owners. Given that the marginal propensity to consume is .9, this will lead consumption demand to increase by .9 × $1 billion = $900 million. This second-round effect creates a $900 million increase in output and thus income, which in turn brings on a third-round increase of consumption of .9 × $900 million = $810 million. In the next round, output is increased by .9 × $810 million, then by .9 times that amount, then by .9 times that amount, and so on. In this example, when all the increases are totalled, a $1 billion increase in investment will lead to a $10 billion rise in equilibrium output.

Unfortunately, the multiplier process also works in reverse. Just as an increase in investment leads to a multiple increase in national output, a decrease in investment leads to a multiple decrease in national output. In our example, with an $MPC$ of .9, if investment decreases by $1 billion, national output will decrease by $10 billion. The relationship between any change in investment expenditures and the resulting eventual change in national output is called the investment multiplier, or just **multiplier** for short. (An increase in government expenditures or net exports has a similar multiplier effect, as we will see shortly.)

In our simple model, with no trade and no government, the multiplier has a simple mathematical form: $1/(1 - MPC)$. As we learned earlier, any income an individual does not consume is saved, and an increase of income by a dollar must be spent either on consumption or on savings. Therefore,

$1 - MPC = MPS$, the marginal propensity to save.

This result allows us to rewrite the basic formula for the multiplier:

$$\text{multiplier} = \frac{1}{1 - MPC} = \frac{1}{MPS}.$$

In other words the multiplier is the reciprocal of the marginal propensity to save. If the marginal propensity to consume is .9, the marginal propensity to save is $1 - .9 = .1$, and the multiplier is 10.

## THE MULTIPLIER

An increase in investment leads to an increase in output that is a multiple of the original increase.

The multiplier equals $1/(1 - MPC)$, or $1/MPS$.

When we add government, the equation for aggregate expenditures becomes

$$AE = C + I + G$$
$$= a + mY_d + I + G,$$

where $Y_d$ is disposable income. For simplicity, we assume that a given fraction, $t$, of income is paid in taxes, so

$$Y_d = Y(1 - t).$$

Hence, in equilibrium, with aggregate expenditures equalling income,

$$AE = Y = a + mY(1 - t) + I + G$$

or

$$Y = \frac{a + I + G}{1 - m(1 - t)}.$$

Hence,

$$\text{multiplier} = \frac{1}{1 - m(1 - t)}.$$

If $m = .8$, $t = .25$, the multiplier = 2.5. By contrast, the multiplier without taxes is 5, twice as large. The reason is simple. Without taxes every dollar of extra income translates into 80 cents of extra expenditure. With taxes, when income goes up by a dollar, consumption increases by only $.8 (1 - .25) = 60$ cents.

## THE EFFECTS OF GOVERNMENT

The basic operation of the multiplier is unchanged when government is included in the analysis. Changes in government expenditure lead, through a multiplier, to larger changes in equilibrium output. But, as we will see, the effects of government change the size of the multiplier.

Government serves as a double-edged sword in the macroeconomy: its spending increases aggregate expenditures at the same time that its taxes reduce the amount of people's income. Let us take taxes first. Since consumption depends on individuals' disposable income—the amount of income they have available to spend after paying taxes—government taxes also reduce consumption.

Total income equals total output, denoted by $Y$. Disposable income is simply total income minus taxes, $T$:

disposable income $= Y - T$.

Taxes do two things. First, since at each level of national income disposable income is lower with taxes, consumption is lower. Taxes shift the aggregate-expenditures schedule down. Second, when taxes increase with income, the multiplier is lower (the slope of the aggregate-expenditures schedule is smaller). This is because taxes typically go up with income. When total income increases by a dollar, consumption increases by less than it otherwise would, since a fraction of the increased income goes to government.

Without taxes, when investment goes up by a dollar, income rises by a dollar, which leads to an increase in consumption determined by the marginal propensity to consume. This increase in consumption then sets off the next round of increases in national income. If, when income goes up by a dollar, government tax collections increase by 40 cents, then disposable income increases by only 60 cents. So the increase in consumption with taxes is 40 percent smaller than it is without. In other words, the consumption function is flatter, as shown in panel A of Figure 11.7. Because the slope of the aggregate consumption function is flatter, the slope of the aggregate-expenditures schedule is flatter, as

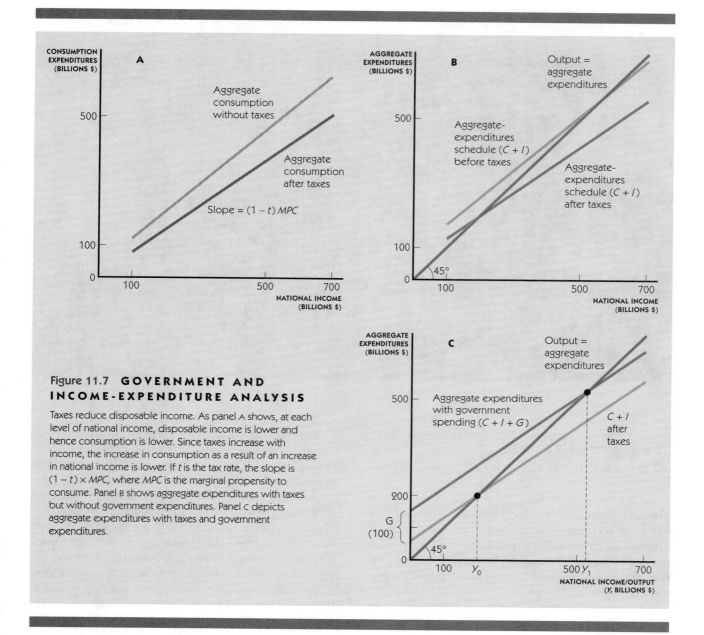

**Figure 11.7 GOVERNMENT AND INCOME-EXPENDITURE ANALYSIS**

Taxes reduce disposable income. As panel A shows, at each level of national income, disposable income is lower and hence consumption is lower. Since taxes increase with income, the increase in consumption as a result of an increase in national income is lower. If $t$ is the tax rate, the slope is $(1 - t) \times MPC$, where $MPC$ is the marginal propensity to consume. Panel B shows aggregate expenditures with taxes but without government expenditures. Panel C depicts aggregate expenditures with taxes and government expenditures.

illustrated in panel B. And because the slope of the aggregate-expenditures schedule is flatter, the multiplier is smaller.

How about government spending? The answer to this question would be simpler if government's expenditures moved in lockstep with its revenues. However, the government can spend more than it raises in taxes, by borrowing. When annual government expenditures exceed tax revenues, there is a **deficit,** as discussed in Chapter 8.[3] There is considerable debate about the effects of deficits, as discussed in that chapter. Here we make the simplifying assumption that the deficit itself (as opposed to the spending imbalance that created the deficit) has no *direct* effect on either consumption or investment.

[3] When annual government expenditures are less than tax revenues, there is a *surplus*.

We also assume that government expenditures do not increase automatically with the level of income; they are assumed to be fixed, say at $100 billion. Thus, while taxes shift the aggregate-expenditures schedule down and flatten it, government expenditures shift the aggregate-expenditures schedule up by the amount of those expenditures, as shown in panel C of Figure 11.7. In this panel, the upward shifts in the aggregate-expenditures schedule from government expenditures have been superimposed on the downward shifts in the aggregate-expenditures schedule from taxes depicted in panel B. Note that the contributions of investment, *I* (which are still assumed to be $50 billion), and government expenditures, *G*, raise the schedule but do not change its slope. The slope in panel C is the same as in panel B. Equilibrium again occurs at the intersection of the aggregate-expenditures schedule and the 45-degree line. Government expenditures can have a powerful effect in stimulating the economy. But if the economy is in a serious recession, the government may have to increase expenditures a great deal to raise output to the full-employment level.

## THE EFFECTS OF INTERNATIONAL TRADE

The analysis so far has ignored the important role of international trade. This is appropriate for a **closed economy,** an economy that neither exports nor im-

ports, but not for an **open economy,** one actively engaged in international trade. Canada, like most other industrialized nations, is very much an open economy.

International trade can have powerful effects on national output. To begin with, exports expand the market for domestic goods. In recent years, Canada has exported goods and services amounting to about 33 percent of national output. This is comparable to countries in the European Union. Larger, more self-sufficient economies export a much smaller proportion of their output: 11 percent for the United States and 12 percent for Japan.

But just as exports expand the market for domestic goods, imports decrease it. What matters for aggregate expenditures is net exports, and in recent years these have declined sharply in Canada. Net exports dropped from 3.5 percent of GDP in 1984 to less than 1 percent in 1986. By 1989, they actually became negative. That is to say, imports exceeded exports. By 1991, net exports amounted to negative 1 percent of GDP. This deterioration in net exports reflected mainly a decline in export growth; the growth rate of imports has stayed at historic levels. More recently, exports have shot up so that net exports in 1995 were 2.5 percent of GDP. These dramatic changes in net exports are illustrated in Figure 11.8.

### IMPORTS

When households' incomes rise, households buy not only more Canadian-made consumer goods but

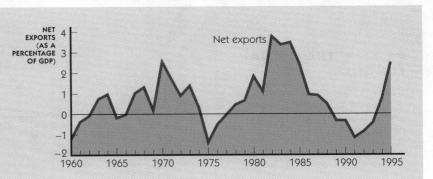

**Figure 11.8 CANADIAN NET EXPORTS SINCE 1960**

Canadian net exports have alternated between being negative and positive. For most of the 1980s they were positive, before turning negative in 1989. By 1994, they had turned positive again. *Source:* Statistics Canada, CANSIM Database 1996, Labels D10000, D10323, D10326.

## Table 11.5 IMPORTS AND DISPOSABLE INCOME (billions of dollars)

| Disposable income | Imports |
|---|---|
| $ 100 | $ 25 |
| 200 | 50 |
| 300 | 75 |
| 400 | 100 |
| 500 | 125 |
| 1,000 | 250 |
| 2,000 | 500 |

also more goods from abroad. We can illustrate an **import function** in much the same way that we illustrated a consumption function. (We have assumed investment and government expenditures to be fixed here, so for now there is no schedule relating either of these to income.) The import function shows the levels of imports corresponding to different levels of income. Table 11.5 shows hypothetical levels of imports for different levels of income. For simplicity, we assume that imports are bought by consumers and that, accordingly, it is disposable income that determines their level. The import function is depicted in Figure 11.9.

Imports increase with income. The **marginal propensity to import** gives the amount of each extra dollar of disposable income spent on imports. If the marginal propensity to import is .25, then if income goes up by $1,000, imports go up by .25 × $1,000 = $250. In Figure 11.9, the marginal propensity to import is given by the slope of the import function.

### EXPORTS

What foreigners buy from Canada depends on the income of foreigners and not directly on income in Canada. Exports may also depend on other factors, such as the marketing effort of Canadian firms and the prices of Canadian goods relative to those of foreign goods. Our focus here is to determine output in Canada. For simplicity, we assume that these other factors are fixed and do not depend on what happens in Canada. In particular, we assume that foreigners' incomes do not depend significantly on incomes in Canada. Hence, the level of exports is taken as fixed at $100 billion.

Exports minus imports (net exports) are sometimes referred to as the **balance of trade.** Net exports at each level of national income are given in Table 11.6. At very low levels of income, net exports are positive: exports exceed imports. As income increases, imports increase and exports remain unchanged. Eventually imports exceed exports; the balance of trade becomes negative.

Trade, like taxes, has the effect of flattening the

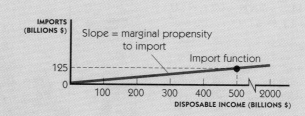

### Figure 11.9 THE IMPORT FUNCTION

Imports increase steadily as disposable income rises. The slope of the import function is determined by the marginal propensity to import.

**Table 11.6   NET EXPORTS** (billions of dollars)

| Disposable income | Exports | Imports | E (exports – imports) |
|---|---|---|---|
| $ 100 | $100 | $ 25 | $ 75 |
| 200 | 100 | 50 | 50 |
| 300 | 100 | 75 | 25 |
| 400 | 100 | 100 | 0 |
| 500 | 100 | 125 | –25 |
| 1,000 | 100 | 250 | –150 |
| 2,000 | 100 | 500 | –400 |

aggregate-expenditures schedule. This is because as income increases, some of it goes to buy foreign goods rather than domestically produced goods. Hence, aggregate expenditures—spending for goods produced within the country—increase by a smaller amount. In a closed economy, when income increases by a dollar, aggregate expenditures increase by the marginal propensity to consume. In an open economy, when income increases by a dollar, aggre-

gate expenditures increase by the marginal propensity to consume *minus* the marginal propensity to import. The difference between the two can be thought of as the marginal propensity to consume domestically produced goods.

This can be seen in Table 11.7, which shows, for different levels of national income, the level of disposable income, consumption, investment, government expenditures, and net exports. Every time

**Table 11.7   AGGREGATE-EXPENDITURES SCHEDULE** (billions of dollars)*

| National income | Disposable income | Consumption | Investment | Government | Net exports | Aggregate expenditures |
|---|---|---|---|---|---|---|
| $ 167 | $ 100 | $ 105 | $50 | $100 | $ 75 | $ 330 |
| 333 | 200 | 195 | 50 | 100 | 50 | 395 |
| 500 | 300 | 285 | 50 | 100 | 25 | 460 |
| 667 | 400 | 375 | 50 | 100 | 0 | 525 |
| 1,667 | 1,000 | 915 | 50 | 100 | –150 | 915 |
| 3,333 | 2,000 | 1,815 | 50 | 100 | –400 | 1,565 |

*The numbers in the table are constructed under the following assumptions: a tax rate of .4, a marginal propensity to consume of .9, and a marginal propensity to import of .25.

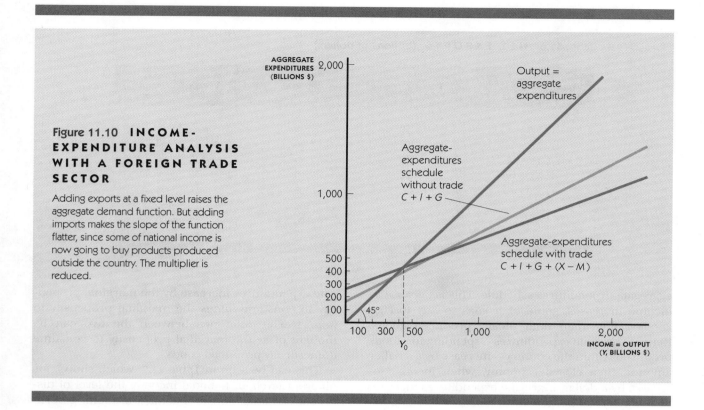

**Figure 11.10 INCOME-EXPENDITURE ANALYSIS WITH A FOREIGN TRADE SECTOR**

Adding exports at a fixed level raises the aggregate demand function. But adding imports makes the slope of the function flatter, since some of national income is now going to buy products produced outside the country. The multiplier is reduced.

aggregate income increases by $167 billion, disposable income increases by only $100 billion; and while consumption increases by $90 billion, net exports *fall* (because imports increase) by $25 billion, so the net increase in aggregate expenditures is only $65 billion. In a closed economy with government, aggregate expenditures would have increased by $90 billion.

At an income of $667 billion (a disposable income of $400 billion), net exports are zero. At higher levels of income, net exports are negative. At lower levels, they are positive. Thus, trade increases aggregate expenditures at lower levels of national income, and decreases aggregate expenditures at higher levels of national income. At low levels of income, the stimulation provided by exports more than offsets the losses from imports; at higher levels of income just the opposite happens.

In Figure 11.10, the income-expenditure analysis

diagram is again used to show how the level of output is determined. As before, the equilibrium condition that output equals aggregate expenditures, $Y = AE$, is represented by the 45-degree line. The aggregate-expenditures schedule now sums all of its components: $C + I + G + (X - M)$. The slope of this line is even flatter than in Figure 11.7, panel C. This is because, as income increases, net exports—one of the components of aggregate expenditures—actually decrease. Equilibrium again occurs at the intersection of the aggregate-expenditures schedule and the 45-degree line, the output level $Y_0$ in the figure.

We know that whenever the aggregate-expenditures schedule is flattened, the multiplier is lowered. To see precisely how this works in the case of trade, think again about how the multiplier works through various rounds in the economy. The first-round effect of the increase in investment is augmented by the second-round effect of the rise in consumption

USING ECONOMICS: PUTTING INTERNATIONAL TRADE INTO THE EQUATION

When we add trade, aggregate expenditures are given by

$$AE = C + I + G + X - M.$$

Imports are now related to disposable income by the import function

$$M = mpi \times Y_d,$$

where $mpi$ is the marginal propensity to import; exports are assumed to be fixed. Hence, aggregate expenditures are

$$AE = a + mY(1 - t) + I + G + X - mpi(1 - t)Y.$$

Since aggregate expenditures equal income, in equilibrium

$$y = \frac{a + I + G + X}{1 - (1 - t)(m - mpi)},$$

so the multiplier is

$$\frac{1}{1 - (1 - t)(m - mpi)}.$$

If $t = .25$, $m = .8$, $mpi = .3$, then the multiplier is

$$\frac{1}{1 - .75(.8 - .3)} = \frac{1}{.625} = 1.6,$$

much smaller than in the absence of trade (2.5).

---

induced by the higher income of those producing the investment goods. This is augmented by the third-round effect of the increase in consumption induced by the higher income of those involved in producing the second round. And so on. But now, when investment rises by $100 million, the second-round effect is only the increase in consumption of domestically produced goods. If the marginal propensity to consume is .9, the tax rate is .4, and the marginal propensity to import is .25, the increase in *domestically produced* consumption goods is $39 million (not $54 million, as it would be without trade, or $90 million, as it would be without taxes or trade).[4] Not only is the second-round effect smaller. The third-round effect is also smaller. The increase of $39 million in the second round leads to increased consumption of

domestically produced goods of $15.2 million in the third round.

If more of the income generated on each successive round is not spent on goods produced within the country, as is the case here, the multiplier will be smaller. When income generated in one round of production is not used to buy more goods produced within the country, economists say there are **leakages.** In a closed economy there are two types of leakage: savings and taxes. In an open economy there are three types of leakage: savings, taxes, and imports.

## BACK TO THE AGGREGATE DEMAND CURVES

We began the chapter with an aggregate demand and supply schedule. The objective of this chapter was to show how at any price level, aggregate demand—and

[4] Of the $100 million, the government takes 40 percent, leaving households with $60 million. Households consume 90 percent of this amount, but 25 percent of their income is spent on imports; the implication is that 65 percent of their income is spent on domestically produced consumer goods (.65 × $60 million = $39 million).

One lesson the multiplier teaches is that critics should take a second look before condemning government efforts to stimulate the economy as "too small." After all, if the multiplier is large enough, a seemingly small policy change may have enough muscle to boost the economy significantly.

But an expansionary policy may not work as vigourously in one part of the country as in another. This is because the magnitude of the multiplier, and thus the effectiveness of fiscal policy, differs, depending on the propensity to consume rather than save, the proportion of income paid in taxes, and the propensity to import.

Though it is doubtful whether Canadians in different regions have noticeably different consumption or saving habits at a given point in time, the size of the multiplier can be very different. For one thing, tax rates can differ significantly across provinces. For example, personal disposable income as a proportion of gross provincial product (GPP) is roughly 60 percent in Nova Scotia compared with 70 percent in Manitoba. This indicates that the proportion of income paid as taxes is higher in Nova Scotia. This directly affects the multiplier; the multiplier is smaller in Nova Scotia, so a given amount of provincial government spending in Nova Scotia has less impact there than is the case in Manitoba.

Perhaps more important, the marginal propensity to import into a province is likely to differ considerably across provinces. Some provinces are likely to be more "open" than others in the sense that they rely more on trade with nonresidents, including both foreigners and those in other provinces. As we have seen, a larger marginal propensity to import gives rise to larger leakages of spending from the economy in question and a smaller multiplier. For example, imports into Ontario make up about 65 percent of its GPP, while for British Columbia this proportion is more like 50 percent. This may seem a bit surprising, since one would expect more populous provinces to be more self-sufficient than others. On the other hand, Ontario's population is more concentrated near major U.S. manufacturing areas. In any case, as a consequence the multiplier is much smaller in Ontario than in British Columbia, so a given amount of provincial government expenditure will be less stimulating.

Of course, the multiplier in both British Columbia and Ontario is, by the same reasoning, smaller than the multiplier for all of Canada. This implies that a dollar's worth of federal government spending will have a greater effect on aggregate demand throughout Canada than a dollar's worth of Ontario government spending will have in Ontario. Thus, it is more difficult for Ontario to pursue fiscal policy to affect its level of GPP than for the federal government to do so with GDP in mind. Only if all provinces were to coordinate their fiscal policies would the impact through the multiplier be the same as at the federal level.

*Sources:* Statistics Canada, CANSIM Database 1996; John Whalley and Irene Trela, *Regional Aspects of Confederation* (Toronto: University of Toronto Press, 1986), pp. 116–17.

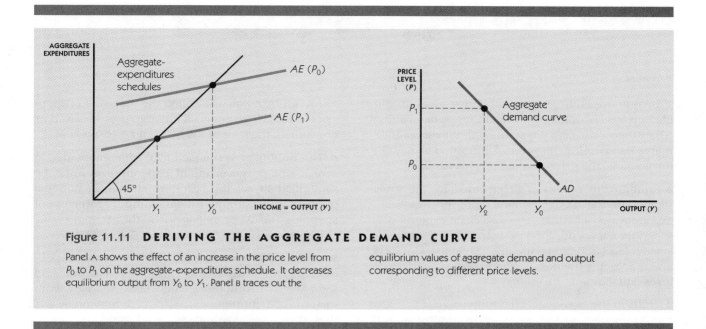

**Figure 11.11  DERIVING THE AGGREGATE DEMAND CURVE**

Panel A shows the effect of an increase in the price level from $P_0$ to $P_1$ on the aggregate-expenditures schedule. It decreases equilibrium output from $Y_0$ to $Y_1$. Panel B traces out the equilibrium values of aggregate demand and output corresponding to different price levels.

equilibrium output, when there is excess capacity—is determined. We can use the analysis to *derive* the aggregate demand curve simply by asking what happens to aggregate demand, and equilibrium output, when the price level changes. To answer that question, all we have to ascertain is *how the aggregate-expenditures schedule shifts when the price level increases or decreases.* For instance, we suggested in Chapter 8 that when the price level rises, *at each level of income* consumers will consume less, since the real value of their bank balances will have decreased. We also suggested that if *current* price levels are lower relative to fixed beliefs about *future* price levels, then households may *substitute* current consumption (which has become relatively cheap) for future consumption. In either case, the aggregate-expenditures schedule shifts down, as depicted in Figure 11.11, and equilibrium output falls. Thus, while $Y_0$ is the point on the aggregate demand schedule corresponding to $P_0$, $Y_1$ is the point on the aggregate demand schedule corresponding to $P_1$. Later chapters will explore more carefully how changes in the price level shift the aggregate-expenditures schedule.

## LIMITATIONS OF THE INCOME-EXPENDITURE APPROACH

In this chapter we have analyzed the determination of national output by focusing exclusively on the aggregate-expenditures schedule, which underlies the aggregate demand curve. But what happened to aggregate supply? Isn't that important too?

Recall that aggregate demand rules the roost when there is excess capacity. That is, changes in aggregate demand alone determine what happens to national output when there are idle machines and workers that could be put to work if only there were sufficient demand to purchase the goods they produce.

Often there is excess capacity in the economy, and then the approach taken here, ignoring capacity constraints, makes perfect sense. There are other times, however, when the economy is working close to capacity. Then aggregate supply has to be brought into the picture—as was done in Chapter 8.

# REVIEW AND PRACTICE

## SUMMARY

**1** Income-expenditure analysis shows how the equilibrium level of output in the economy is determined when there is excess capacity, so that aggregate demand determines the level of output. Throughout the analysis, the price level is taken as fixed.

**2** Equilibrium output is determined by the intersection of the 45-degree line and the aggregate-expenditures schedule. The aggregate-expenditures schedule shows the level of aggregate expenditures at each level of national income, while the 45-degree line represents the points where aggregate expenditures equal output (income).

**3** Shifts in the aggregate-expenditures schedule give rise to changes in the equilibrium level of output. The magnitude of the increase in output resulting from an upward shift in the aggregate-expenditures schedule depends on the slope of the schedule. Much of macroeconomic analysis focuses on what determines the slope of the aggregate-expenditures schedule, what causes shifts in the schedule, and how government can shift the schedule.

**4** Aggregate expenditures are the sum of consumption, investment, government expenditures, and net exports. Net exports are the difference between exports and imports.

**5** Consumption increases as disposable income increases, and the relationship between income and consumption is called the consumption function. The amount by which consumption increases when disposable income increases by a dollar is called the marginal propensity to consume (*MPC*). The amount by which savings increases when disposable income

increases by a dollar is called the marginal propensity to save (*MPS*). Since all income must be saved or consumed, the sum of the *MPC* and *MPS* must be 1.

**6** The multiplier is the factor by which a change in investment or government expenditures must be multiplied to get the resulting change in national output. In a simple model without government spending, taxes, or net exports, the multiplier for changes in investment is $1/(1 - MPC)$, or $1/MPS$.

**7** Government spending increases aggregate expenditures, and taxes reduce disposable income and therefore consumption. When taxes increase with income, consumption increases with income by less than it otherwise would, since a fraction of the increased income goes to government. The aggregate-expenditures schedule is flatter, and the multiplier is smaller.

**8** Exports increase aggregate demand, and imports reduce aggregate demand. Imports increase with income, but exports are determined by factors in other countries. Trade flattens the aggregate-expenditures schedule, because as income increases some of it goes to buy foreign rather than domestic goods. As a result, the multiplier is smaller.

**9** The aggregate-expenditures schedule is used to derive the equilibrium level of output at each price level, assuming that there is excess capacity in the economy. As the price level increases, the aggregate-expenditures schedule shifts down. The aggregate demand curve then traces out the equilibrium level of output at each price level.

## KEY TERMS

aggregate-expenditures schedule

income-expenditure analysis

planned and unplanned inventories

consumption function

marginal propensity to consume

autonomous consumption

marginal propensity to save

multiplier

closed economy

open economy

import function

marginal propensity to import

## REVIEW QUESTIONS

**1** What is the aggregate-expenditures schedule? What are the components of aggregate expenditures?

**2** How is the equilibrium level of output determined? Why are points on the aggregate-expenditures schedule above the 45-degree line not sustainable? Why are points on the aggregate-expenditures schedule below the 45-degree line not sustainable?

**3** What is a consumption function? What determines its slope? What is an import function? What determines its slope?

**4** What is the consequence of a shift in the aggregate-expenditures schedule? Give examples of what might give rise to such a shift.

**5** Illustrate the difference between a change in consumption resulting from an increase in income with a given consumption function and a change in consumption resulting from a shift in the consumption function.

**6** Why is the sum of the marginal propensity to save and the marginal propensity to consume always 1?

**7** Show that the magnitude of the effect of a given shift in the aggregate-expenditures schedule on equilibrium output depends on the slope of the aggregate-expenditures schedule. What determines the slope of the aggregate-expenditures schedule? How is it affected by taxes? by imports?

**8** How can changes of a certain amount in the level of investment or government spending have a larger effect on national output? What is the multiplier?

**9** What is the relationship between the aggregate-expenditures schedule and the aggregate demand curve? How does the aggregate-expenditures schedule shift when the price level increases? How can the aggregate demand curve be derived?

## PROBLEMS

**1** In the economy of Consumerland, national income and consumption are related in this way:

| National income | $1,500 | $1,600 | $1,700 | $1,800 | $1,900 |
|---|---|---|---|---|---|
| Consumption | $1,325 | $1,420 | $1,515 | $1,610 | $1,705 |

Calculate national savings at each level of national income. What is the marginal propensity to consume in Consumerland? What is the marginal propensity to save? If national income rose to 2,000, what do you predict consumption and savings would be?

**2** To the economy of Consumerland add the fact that investment will be $180 at every level of output. Graph the consumption function and the aggregate-expenditures schedule for this simple economy. What determines the slope of the aggregate-expenditures schedule? What is the equilibrium?

**3** Calculate the first four rounds of the multiplier effect for an increase of $10 billion in investment spending in each of the following cases:

(a) a simple consumption and investment economy where the *MPC* is .9

(b) an economy with government but no foreign trade, where the *MPC* is .9 and the tax rate is .3

(c) an economy with an *MPC* of .9, a tax rate of .3, and a marginal propensity to import of .1

**4** If, at each level of disposable income, savings increases, what does this imply about what has happened to the consumption function? What will be the consequences for the equilibrium level of output?

**5** Use the income-expenditure analysis diagram to explain why a lower level of investment, government spending, and net exports all have similar effects on the equilibrium level of output.

**6** In a more stable economy, where national output is less vulnerable to small changes in, say, exports, government policy is less effective (changes in government expenditures do not do much to stimulate the economy); in a less stable economy, government policy is more effective. Explain why there is a trade-off between the stability of the economy and the power of government policy.

# 12 *

# CONSUMPTION AND INVESTMENT

N ow that we have developed the overall framework of income-expenditure analysis, we take a closer look at two of the components of aggregate expenditures, consumption and investment. Examining them will help us understand both why the level of economic activity fluctuates and what policies the government might pursue to reduce those fluctuations or to stimulate the economy.

* This chapter may be skipped or taken up after subsequent chapters without loss of continuity.

## KEY QUESTIONS

**1** Why may current consumption not be very dependent on current income, and what implications does this have for the use of tax policy to stimulate the economy?

**2** What other factors determine the level of aggregate consumption?

**3** What are "consumer durables," and why are expenditures on them so volatile?

**4** What are the major determinants of the level of investment? What role do variations in real interest rates and the availability of credit play? What role is played by expectations and changes in the willingness to bear risk?

**5** Why is the variability in investment and expenditures on consumer durables so important?

## CONSUMPTION

According to the consumption function presented in Chapter 11, the demand for goods and services by households is determined by the level of disposable income. As disposable income goes up, so does consumption. Knowing this year's disposable income, then, an economist can use the consumption function to predict this year's consumption spending.

This simple consumption function, often referred to as the Keynesian consumption function, is a good starting point for a discussion of the relationship between consumption and disposable income, as shown in Figure 12.1. Income varies from year to year, and so does consumption. If they moved in lockstep as the simple consumption function predicts, a straight line could be drawn through all the points in the figure. The relationship is remarkably close to the linear relationship predicted by the theories. Still, economists have sought to develop even better predictors of consumption.

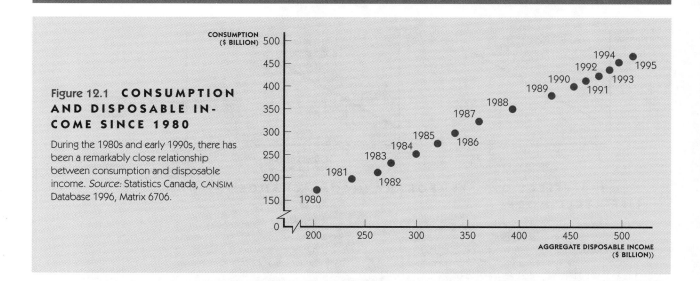

Figure 12.1 **CONSUMPTION AND DISPOSABLE INCOME SINCE 1980**

During the 1980s and early 1990s, there has been a remarkably close relationship between consumption and disposable income. *Source:* Statistics Canada, CANSIM Database 1996, Matrix 6706.

## FUTURE-ORIENTED CONSUMPTION FUNCTIONS

In the decades after Keynes's time, many economists questioned his notion that current consumption depends primarily on current income. They argued that individuals, in making consumption decisions, look at total income over their lifetime, averaging good years with bad, and recognizing that income typically increases with work experience.

The Nobel laureate Franco Modigliani, for one, emphasized that people save for retirement. He called this motive **life-cycle savings,** to convey the notion that individuals will save during their working years so they will not have to curtail their consumption after they retire. Milton Friedman, also a Nobel laureate, emphasized how the future affects consumption today by pointing out that people save in good years to carry them through bad years. His view is called the **permanent-income hypothesis.** Permanent income is a person's average income over her lifetime. Friedman stressed that consumption depends not so much on current income as on total lifetime income, averaging good years with bad. Whereas Modigliani emphasized the role of savings in smoothing consumption between working and retirement years, Friedman emphasized its role in smoothing consumption between good and bad years. Underlying both views is the notion that people like their consumption patterns to be stable.

These future-oriented theories of savings and consumption yield consequences that differ from the basic Keynesian theory that consumption simply depends on this year's income. Consider an individual who happens to get a windfall gain in income one year—perhaps he wins $1 million in a provincial lottery. If the marginal propensity to consume is .9, the Keynesian consumption function predicts that he will consume $900,000 of his winnings that year. The future-oriented consumption theories suggest that the lucky winner will spread the extra income over a lifetime of consumption. Similarly, if the government temporarily lowers taxes for one year, the future-oriented consumption theories predict that a taxpayer will not dramatically increase consumption in that year but will spread over his lifetime the extra consumption that the one-year tax reduction allows. Thus, they suggest that *temporary* tax changes will be much less effective in stimulating consumption than the Keynesian model predicts.

Figure 12.2 compares the future-oriented consumption function and the Keynesian consumption function for the household. Suppose a household

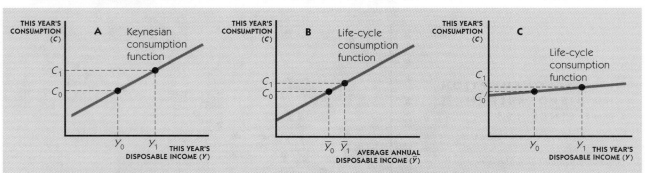

Figure 12.2 **EFFECT OF A TEMPORARY INCOME CHANGE IN THE LIFE-CYCLE MODEL**

With the Keynesian consumption function, panel A, a temporary change in income results in a large change in consumption. In the life-cycle model, panel B, a temporary change in income has only a small effect on average annual income over a lifetime, and thus leads to only a small change in consumption. Panel C shows how the life-cycle model predicts that consumption will react in response to *this year's income.* Since consumption does not change by much, the life-cycle consumption function is very flat.

Figure 12.3 **THE LIFE-CYCLE MODEL AND DETERMINING NATIONAL OUTPUT**

Since changes in today's income have much weaker effects on current consumption in the life-cycle model, the aggregate-expenditures schedule is much flatter, which implies that the multiplier is lower.

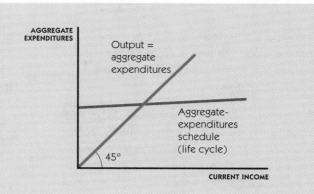

were to have a one-time increase in its disposable income. If consumption responds according to the Keynesian consumption function, it will increase from $C_0$ to $C_1$ as shown in panel A.

The future-oriented theories predict that consumption will not change very much. We can see this in two different ways. Panel B shows consumption depending on average disposable income over a person's lifetime. Now the change in this year's income from $Y_0$ to $Y_1$ has little effect on average disposable income ($Y_0$, $Y_1$), and hence little effect on consumption. Panel C puts this year's disposable income on the horizontal axis, as does panel A. The difference between the lines in panels A and C is the difference between Keynes's views and those of the future-oriented theorists. In the latter view, consumption is not very sensitive to current disposable income, which is why the line is so flat.

The principle that consumption depends not just on income this year but also on longer-run considerations holds at the aggregate level as well. Figure 12.3 shows the implications of future-oriented theories for aggregate expenditures and the determination of equilibrium output. Since the relationship between changes in today's income and changes in consumption is weaker than in the Keynesian model, the aggregate-expenditures schedule is now much flatter; in other words, increases in current income lead to relatively small changes in consumption and aggregate expenditures. This in turn has strong implications for the multiplier. An increase

in, say, investment, which shifts the aggregate-expenditures schedule up, increases equilibrium output by an amount only slightly greater than the original increase in investment. The multiplier is very small.

## WEALTH AND CAPITAL GAINS

The future-oriented consumption theories suggest not only that current income is relatively unimportant in determining consumption but also that variables ignored by Keynes may be important. For instance, wealthier people consume more (at each level of current income). Since consumption is related to wealth, changes in consumption will be affected by changes in wealth.

The distinction between income and wealth as a determinant of consumption is important. It corresponds to the distinction between flows and stocks. Flows are measured as rates. Both income and consumption are flow variables. They are measured as dollars *per year*. Wealth is a stock variable.[1] It is measured simply by the total value ("dollars") of one's assets. Future-oriented theories emphasize that there is no reason why an individual's current consumption should be related to his current income. What he consumes should be related to how well off he is, and

[1] Other stock variables in macroeconomics include capital stock and the public debt; other flow variables include investment and government expenditures.

## CLOSE-UP: AN EMPIRICAL PUZZLE AND AN INGENIOUS THEORY— FRIEDMAN'S PERMANENT-INCOME HYPOTHESIS

The genesis of Milton Friedman's permanent-income hypothesis was an empirical puzzle. The story of how he solved it illustrates insightful economic analysis at work.

When economists plotted aggregate disposable personal income in various years with the corresponding level of aggregate consumption, they obtained something like panel A of the figure. These data suggested a consumption function in which consumption increases roughly proportionately with income. But when economists plotted the consumption of different income groups against their current income for any particular year, they obtained something more like panel B. This suggests a consumption function in which consumption increases less than proportionately with income. The problem Friedman set for himself was how to reconcile the data.

His ingenious solution was to say that consumption is related to people's long-term or "normal" income, what he called their permanent income. Friedman observed that people with low incomes included a disproportionate number who were having unusually bad years. And correspondingly, those with very high incomes included a disproportionate number having unusually good years. Those having a bad year did not reduce their consumption proportionately; those having a particularly good year did not increase their consumption proportionately. Friedman was thus able to explain how, over time, aggregate consumption could rise in proportion to income for the population as a whole even though the consumption of any particular household increased less than proportionately with current income.

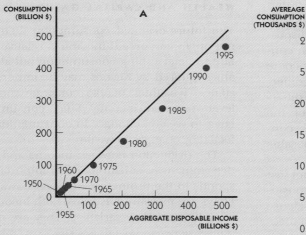
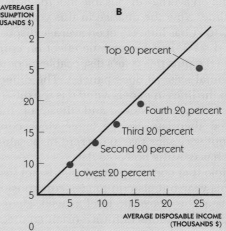

## CONSUMPTION FUNCTIONS

Panel A shows that as income has increased over time, consumption has increased almost in proportion. Panel B illustrates the fact that individuals with higher income increase their consumption somewhat less than proportionately, especially at the highest income levels. *Sources:* Statistics Canada, CANSIM Database 1996, Matrix 6706; Statistics Canada, *Family Expenditure in Canada,* 1992, Catalogue No. 62-555.

Another U.S. economist, Robert Hall, has pointed out an unsettling consequence of the permanent-income hypothesis. If the level of consumption a person chooses depends on permanent income, which incorporates all information about what future *expected* income will be, changes in consumption are related only to *unexpected* changes. By definition, unexpected changes are random and unpredictable. Thus, the permanent-income theory predicts that changes in consumption are largely random and unpredictable—not good news for economists trying to understand and forecast such patterns.

that is better measured by his wealth.[2] Capital gains, or changes in the value of assets, change an individual's wealth. Thus, these theories predict that when stock or real estate prices rise in value and people expect this change to last for a long time, individuals who own these assets will increase their level of consumption. They will do so because their overall wealth has grown, even if they do not immediately receive any income from the increase in value.

There is some evidence to support this view. Many economists believe that the stock market crash of 1929, which preceded the Great Depression, contributed to that Depression by generating a downward shift in the consumption function. On the other hand, when share prices on the Toronto Stock Exchange fell by over 22 percent on a single day in October 1987, consumption did not decline sharply in the way one might have expected: people responded only slightly to this capital loss. One reason for this is that individuals respond to changes in wealth only slowly, and in 1987 their consumption had not yet fully responded to the increases in stock market prices that had occurred during the preceding few years. A prolonged and persistent decline in the stock market might have an extremely depressing effect on consumption.

## RECONCILING CONSUMPTION THEORY WITH FACTS

The permanent-income and life-cycle hypotheses contain large elements of truth. Families do save for their retirement, so life-cycle considerations are important.

[2] Future-oriented theories take an expansive view of what should be included in wealth: they include *human capital*, the present discounted value of future wage income. (See Chapter 8 for a definition of present discounted value.)

And households do smooth their consumption between good years and bad, so permanent-income considerations are relevant. Even so, household consumption appears to be more dependent on current income than either theory would suggest. There are two reasons for this, durable goods and credit rationing. Each plays an important role in consumption.

### DURABLE GOODS

Goods such as cars, refrigerators, and furniture are called **durable goods.** Purchasing a durable good is like an investment decision, because such goods are bought for the services they render over a number of years. Decisions to postpone purchasing a durable good have quite different consequences than decisions not to buy food or some other nondurable. If you do not buy strawberries today, you will have to do without them. But not buying a durable does not mean you will do without the durable, but that you will have to make do with the services provided by an older durable. The costs of postponing the purchase of a new car are often relatively low; you can make do with an old car a little bit longer. However, the benefits of postponing the purchase may be significant.

Given these considerations, it should be no surprise that purchases of durable goods vary a great deal, not only from year to year but also relative to income. Figure 12.4 traces the purchases of durables as a percentage of disposable income during the postwar period. These fluctuations in purchases of durables, together with the variations in investment, seem to account for much of the variation in economic activity over the business cycle. Variations in the *services provided by durable goods*—and hence in true consumption—are much smaller.

Thus, when a household's income is temporarily low, rather than borrowing to maintain a steady pat-

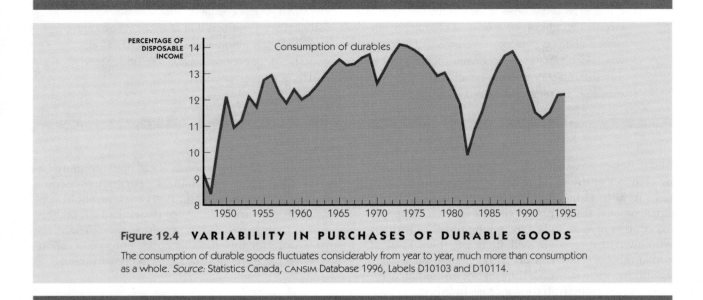

**Figure 12.4  VARIABILITY IN PURCHASES OF DURABLE GOODS**

The consumption of durable goods fluctuates considerably from year to year, much more than consumption as a whole. *Source:* Statistics Canada, CANSIM Database 1996, Labels D10103 and D10114.

tern of purchases of durables, the household simply postpones the purchase of a durable good. This makes aggregate expenditures depend critically on current income.

## CREDIT RATIONING

Empirical studies show that even nondurable consumption expenditures seem more dependent on current income than the future-oriented theories suggest. These theories, in particular the permanent-income hypothesis, assume that when an individual has a bad year, he can maintain his consumption at a steady level: either the household has a large stock of savings to draw on while its income is temporarily low, or the household can easily borrow.

For many people neither of these conditions is true. Most individuals, even in Canada, have few liquid assets upon which to draw. They may have considerable savings tied up in a pension scheme, but they cannot draw upon these until they retire. They may have some equity in their houses, but the last thing they want to do is sell their home. Moreover, it is precisely in times of need, when a person is unemployed or a business is doing badly, that banks are least forthcoming with funds. (As the saying goes, banks only lend to those who don't need the money!)

**Credit rationing** occurs when people are unable to obtain funds at the market rate of interest, because of the risks associated with lending to them. Many people are credit-rationed. For those who have no assets and are credit-rationed, cutting back on consumption when income declines is not a matter of choice. For these individuals, consumption depends heavily on current income.

If people were not credit-rationed, short-term unemployment would not be as important a problem as it appears to be. The suffering caused by temporary layoffs would be much less. To see why, we need to look again at the concept of total wealth. Assume that Evan will work for forty years, that his initial salary is $25,000 per year, that his salary in real terms increases 5 percent per year, and that 5 percent is the real rate of interest. Then the present discounted value of his lifetime earnings is $1 million. This is his wealth, assuming that he has no unexpected windfall, no inheritance from his great-aunt, and no other assets. Imagine that Evan loses his job and is unemployed for half a year. At first glance, that looks like a personal calamity. But upon closer inspection, we see that it represents a loss of only a bit more than 1 percent of his lifetime wealth.

If Evan could borrow six months' pay, he would have no trouble paying it back, and the period without work would be no tragedy—his life-style would be constrained, but insignificantly. Since he would have to cut expenditures by only a bit more than 1 percent, cutting out a few movies, a fancy restaurant meal or two, and a few other activities would do the trick. However, for most people, losing a job for half a year would in fact be a major disaster—not because of the reduction in total lifetime wealth, but because most individuals face important constraints on the amount they can borrow. Without a job, they cannot obtain loans, except possibly at very high interest rates. Because of these credit constraints, for most lower- and many middle-income individuals the traditional Keynesian consumption function is all too relevant. When their current income is reduced, their consumption is perforce reduced.

## MACROECONOMIC IMPLICATIONS OF CONSUMPTION THEORIES

The alternative theories of consumption we have explored so far have two sets of macroeconomic implications. First, the future-oriented theories of consumption, in arguing that consumption does not depend heavily on current income, maintain that the aggregate-expenditures schedule is flat, and consequently, as we saw in Chapter 11, the multiplier is low. This is both good and bad news for the economy. It is good news because a small multiplier means that decreases in the level of investment lead to much smaller decreases in the level of national income than they would if the multiplier were large. It is bad news because it means that government efforts to stimulate the economy through temporary reduction in taxes—or to dampen an overheated economy through temporary increases in taxes—will be less effective than if the multiplier were larger.

Second, by identifying other determinants of consumption, future-oriented theories help explain why the ratio of consumption to disposable income may shift from year to year. Expectations concerning future economic conditions, changes in the availability of credit, or variations in the price of houses or shares of stock are among the factors that can give rise to such shifts in the consumption function. These shifts in turn give rise to larger variations in the equilibrium level of national output. Indeed, they help explain how a slight downturn in economic activity can become magnified. With a downturn, consumers may lose confidence in the future. They worry about layoffs and cut back on purchases of durables. At the same time, banks, nervous about the ability of borrowers to repay loans should the downturn worsen, become more restrictive. Even those adventurous souls willing to buy a new car in the face of the uncertain future may find it difficult to find a bank willing to lend to them. The net effect is a downward shift in the consumption function, exacerbating the initial decline in national income.

### DETERMINANTS OF CONSUMPTION

1 Keynesian consumption function: Stresses the dependence of consumption on current disposable income

2 Future-oriented consumption theories: Stress the dependence of consumption on total lifetime wealth and the role of savings in smoothing consumption

  a Life-cycle theory: Stresses the importance of savings for retirement

  b Permanent-income theory: Stresses the role of savings in smoothing consumption between good and bad years

  c Implications

    i Consumption not very dependent on current income: small multipliers

    ii Consumption sensitive to capital gains and losses

3 Explanations of why consumption seems to be more dependent on current income than future-oriented theories predict

  a Durable goods

  b Credit constraints

With unemployment rates stubbornly high and with the economy in an economic downturn, governments in Canada have gambled on fiscal stimulation as a way of increasing consumer demand. The Harris Conservative government elected in Ontario in 1995 was swept into office with their so-called Common Sense Revolution, part of which involved a rapid reduction in income tax rates. The hope was that the response of consumers would kick-start the economy without at the same time making an already bad provincial budget deficit worse.

The tax cut would put more money in the hands of consumers. Will they spend it and create the additional demand needed? If consumption depended only on income currently received, the answer would be yes. A reduction in the tax rate would increase disposable income and consumers would spend a proportion of that, where the proportion is the marginal propensity to consume. But matters may not be as simple as that. There are a couple of reasons why con-

sumers may not spend much of the money a tax cut would put in their hands.

First, given the combination of a relatively sluggish economy and high interest rates in recent years, many consumers have accumulated relatively high levels of personal debt to finance past spending. Part of the increase in after-tax income might be expected to go to repaying part of that debt rather than to new consumption. Second, some consumers might adopt a more future-oriented view, as suggested by the life-cycle and permanent-income theories of consumption. If they are unsure how long the reduced tax rates will last, they may regard the increase in after-tax income as temporary. If so, some of it will be set aside for future consumption.

Given the uncertainty about the response of consumers to a sudden tax cut, it is easy to see why some economists regarded the Harris tax cuts as a gamble. If the gamble is lost, the government ends up with much less tax revenue and few extra jobs created.

# INVESTMENT

Variations in the level of investment are probably the principal cause of variations in aggregate expenditures, and hence in national output. Just how volatile investment is can be seen in Figure 12.5. In recent years, investment has varied from 16 to 23 percent of GDP.

The investment spending relevant for aggregate expenditures includes three broad categories. The first is firms' purchases of new capital goods, which includes buildings, machines, automobiles, cash registers, and desks that firms use: these make up the **plant and equipment** portion of overall investment. Second, firms also invest in **inventories** as they store their output in anticipation of sales or store the raw materials they will need to produce more goods. The third investment category consists of households' purchases of new homes. The purchases of previously owned capital goods or houses do not count, because they do not increase output. (Households' fi-

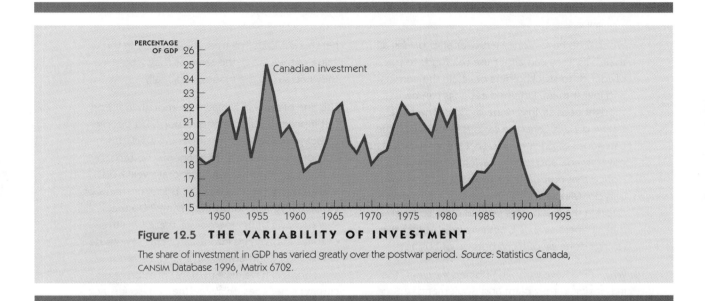

**Figure 12.5 THE VARIABILITY OF INVESTMENT**

The share of investment in GDP has varied greatly over the postwar period. *Source:* Statistics Canada, CANSIM Database 1996, Matrix 6702.

nancial investments such as stocks and bonds are a related but different concept. Usually when an individual buys, say, a share of stock, she buys it from someone else. She makes an investment, but someone else makes a "disinvestment." There is simply a change in who owns the economy's assets. There is, however, a close relationship between investment in new capital goods and the capital market in general: when firms issue new shares or borrow funds by issuing bonds, they procure the resources with which to purchase new capital goods. In this way, financial investments and capital investments, which concern us here, are closely linked.)

We restrict our focus in this discussion to business investment, which includes two of our three major investment categories: plant and equipment, and inventories. The third major investment category, consumers' demand for new housing, is best analyzed as a very long-lived durable good, using the principles governing the demand for durable goods developed earlier in this chapter.

Three questions concern us here. What determines the level of business investment? Why is it so variable? And how does government influence it? We focus first on plant and equipment investment and then on inventory investment.

## INVESTMENT IN PLANT AND EQUIPMENT

To undertake an investment, firms must believe that the expected future returns will be large enough to compensate them for the risks of the investment. Moreover, firms are aware that a dollar in the future is worth less than a dollar today—if they have a dollar this year, they can put it in the bank and get back the dollar with interest next year. As the interest rate rises, future dollars are worth less relative to today's dollars—the present value of a dollar to be received in the future has fallen. (The concept of present value was introduced in Chapter 8.) The present value of the future returns on all potential investment projects will fall. That means there will be fewer projects with future returns large enough to offset forgone interest. To put it another way, think of the firm as having to borrow the money for the investment project. Higher interest rates increase the cost of undertaking the project. Fewer projects will have a sufficiently high return to pay these higher interest costs. Thus, *higher interest rates lead to lower levels of investment.* The relationship between interest rates and investment is the **investment schedule** we introduced in Chapter 8, and is depicted as the

## CLOSE-UP: THE CORPORATE VEIL

When firms have money left over after paying all their bills, they can either use the funds to pay dividends to stockholders or retain the earnings and invest them. Retained earnings can be thought of as savings done by firms. The table below divides Canadian savings in 1995 into the categories of private (personal and corporate), government, and foreign savings in Canada. Notice that corporations save more than individuals do. (Much of personal savings is also done through the businesses people own, so much so that business savings is actually much larger than savings done by persons outside of business.)

When firms save through retained earnings, they may invest in new plant and equipment, reduce their indebtedness, or buy government securities and those of other firms. But in each case, the future profits of the firm should be higher as it receives a return from this investment, and anticipation of these higher profits should raise the price of shares of stock in the firm. Strictly ratio-

nal shareholders will treat this increase in the value of their stock the same as they would if they had saved the money personally.

This line of analysis is plausible enough in theory, but it poses a number of questions. Do people in fact perceive what is happening inside the corporation? In the term economists often use, do they see through the "corporate veil"? Do shareholders react so that the prices of shares of stock fully reflect corporate savings? Do the shareholders then incorporate these wealth changes and savings into their overall savings decisions? Recent theories have emphasized that shareholders have imperfect information concerning what goes on inside the firm, so it is not surprising that they have only blurry vision through the corporate veil.

The extent to which individuals see through the corporate veil is important, because it affects the size of the multiplier. Assume that the gov-

## SAVINGS BY SECTOR IN 1995

|  |  | % of total savings |
| --- | --- | --- |
| Gross personal savings | $ 64 billion | 44 |
| Gross corporate savings | $ 86 billion | 60 |
| Gross private savings | $150 billion | 104 |
| Gross government savings | –$ 15 billion | –10 |
| Foreign savings in Canada | $ 9 billion | 6 |
| Gross savings | $144 billion | 100 |

*Source:* Statistics Canada, CANSIM Database 1996, Matrix 6705.

ernment is successful in stimulating investment. But assume also that firms finance that investment by increasing their retained earnings, forgoing an increase in dividends. If people do not see through the corporate veil, they may only perceive that their dividends have not increased, without fully realizing that the corporation is putting their money into productive investments. If the low dividends lead individuals to reduce their consumption from what it otherwise would have been, then the total increase in aggregate demand resulting from the increase in investment will be much smaller than predicted by traditional Keynesian theory.

downward-sloping curve in Figure 12.6. Of course, what matters for investment is the *real interest rate,* the cost of funds taking into account the effect of inflation. If the nominal interest rate increases but future prices increase in an offsetting way, firms' investments will be unaffected. (The real interest rate is the nominal interest rate minus the rate of inflation.) And, of course, what matters for long-term investments is the long-term real interest rate over the period of the investment.

## EXPECTATIONS AND RISK

Perhaps the hardest part of a firm's investment decision is predicting future returns. In some cases, there are **technological risks**—the firm may be using a new technology that could prove unreliable. In most cases, there are **market risks**—will there be a market for the product? At what price will it sell?

What wage will workers demand in the future? What will be the price of electricity and other inputs? The firm has no crystal ball: it has to make an educated guess, recognizing that there is uncertainty.

Typically, firms insist on being compensated for bearing the risks associated with uncertainty. There are three major determinants of the amount that firms require to compensate them for the risks they face: the magnitude of the risks, their ability to share the risks, and their willingness to bear the risks. When the economy goes into a recession, typically firms perceive that the risks of investing are greater. The primary way that firms "share" risks is through the stock market. In companies whose shares are widely held, large numbers of shareholders can own shares in the company. They can reduce their risk by diversifying the portfolio of shares they hold. If they hold small amounts of many different shares, the risks associated with the loss from any one share are

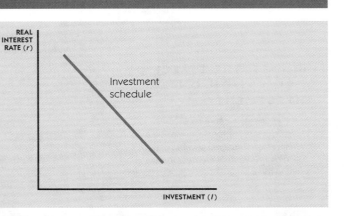

Figure 12.6 **THE INVEST-MENT SCHEDULE**

The level of investment increases as the real interest rate falls, and vice versa.

offset by the possibility of gains from other shares. When the stock market is booming, firms find it easy to issue new shares and thus to spread risks more widely. Finally, the ability and willingness of firms to bear risks depends on their own financial strength. If their net worth has been eroded by a series of losses, and if they have had to borrow to remain afloat, their ability and willingness to bear risks will be reduced.

### AVAILABILITY OF FUNDS

There is one more important determinant of investment. The analysis so far has assumed that firms can borrow funds, if they wish to, at the market rate of interest. Particularly in economic downturns, many firms *claim* they cannot borrow as much as they would like. When they cannot borrow, they must resort to using retained earnings—their profits, less what they pay out to shareholders in dividends—to finance their investment. For instance, in the 1992 economic downturn, many builders claimed that they could not obtain funds to continue their construction activities. Banks simply would not lend to them. At that time, many banks had been badly hurt by high defaults. With their capital eroded, they were less willing to bear the risks of lending. However, some banks, and many economists, argued that the issue was not banks' unwillingness to make loans. The problem was a shortage of good borrowers and an unwillingness of many borrowers to pay an inter-

est rate commensurate with the bank's perceptions of the riskiness of the loan.

### RECESSIONS

As the economy goes into a recession, typically the investment schedule shifts to the left, as depicted in Figure 12.7: expectations of profits decrease, risks appear larger, the ability to share risks is decreased, and the ability and willingness to bear risks is reduced. Moreover, firms that are not able to borrow and have to use retained earnings to finance investment have fewer funds available for investment. And banks—their capital base eroded from higher defaults and with a perception of a greater risk of default for new loans—may be less willing to make loans. Under these circumstances, even large changes in real interest rates may be unable to generate much additional investment.

## A LOOK AT THE DATA

There is considerable evidence that lowering the interest rate does stimulate investment. Some kinds of investment, such as in machinery and equipment, seem to be more interest-sensitive than others. Panel A of Figure 12.8 shows the correlation between investment and real interest rates over the postwar period. It shows that when real interest rates rise, as in the early 1980s, investment as a percentage of GDP

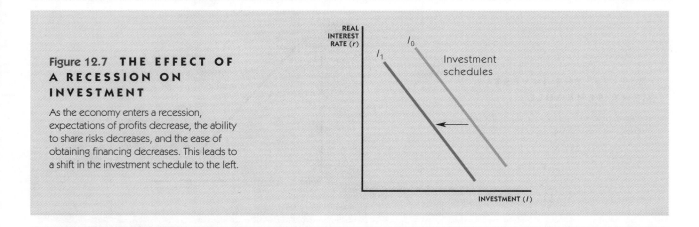

**Figure 12.7 THE EFFECT OF A RECESSION ON INVESTMENT**

As the economy enters a recession, expectations of profits decrease, the ability to share risks decreases, and the ease of obtaining financing decreases. This leads to a shift in the investment schedule to the left.

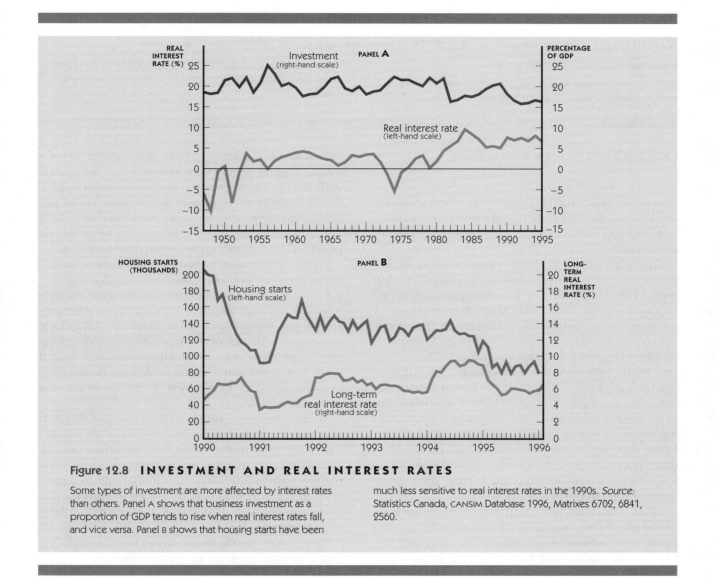

**Figure 12.8** **INVESTMENT AND REAL INTEREST RATES**

Some types of investment are more affected by interest rates than others. Panel A shows that business investment as a proportion of GDP tends to rise when real interest rates fall, and vice versa. Panel B shows that housing starts have been much less sensitive to real interest rates in the 1990s. *Source:* Statistics Canada, CANSIM Database 1996, Matrixes 6702, 6841, 2560.

declines. Similarly, investment rises when real interest rates fall, as was the case in the mid-1980s. On the other hand, panel B shows that housing starts seem not to be so sensitive to real interest rates, at least this was the case during the 1990s.

Interest rates are an important determinant of investment, but they are not the only determinant. As we have seen, changes in expectations, perceptions of risk, and willingness to bear risk may all shift the investment schedule. Indeed, in certain periods of time, much of the variation in investment appears to

be related to variables other than the real interest rate. For example, in panel A, the level of real interest rates in the late 1980s and early 1990s tended on average to be higher than in the 1960s, yet real investment (relative to GDP) was not relatively low.

We can also understand why business investment can be volatile: changes in expectations, availability of funds, firm net worth, as well as interest rates can affect investment. Indeed, Keynes thought that firms' investment decisions were so unpredictable as to be based on "animal spirits."

## WHY INVESTMENT MAY BE LOW IN RECESSIONS

Expectations of future profits are low.

Banks' unwillingness to lend and low firm profits make it impossible for firms to finance investment projects.

Perceptions of greater risk and lower ability to bear risk make banks less willing to lend and firms less willing to invest.

## INVENTORY INVESTMENT

One of the most volatile components of investment is inventories, the materials that are being held in storage awaiting either use in production or sale to customers.

Inventories are typically very large. In 1995, for example, the value of inventories in the manufacturing sector was 145 percent of total monthly shipments. In other words, for every $100 of manufactured goods sold each month there was almost $150 worth of goods in storage.

There is a cost to holding inventories. If firms borrow funds to finance their inventories, planning to pay back the loans after selling the inventoried products, they must pay interest on these funds while the products remain unsold. If a company finances the inventories itself, it faces an opportunity cost. The funds that pay for the inventory could be used for other purposes. Beyond the cost of the inventory itself, storage space costs money, as does spoilage or deterioration in the process of storage.

Given the costs, why do firms hold so much in inventories? One reason is that inventories on the input side facilitate production. This is called the **production-facilitating function** of inventories. For instance, it is very costly for a printing plant to run out of paper and have workers and machines standing idle until more arrives. On the output side, customers often rely upon the producer to supply the good to them when they need it. To do that, the producer must maintain inventories sufficient to meet anticipated sales. If there are delays in fulfilling an order, the customer may well turn elsewhere.

Inventories also enable firms to save money by producing at a steady rate. It is expensive to let sales dictate the level of production. There would be too much variation from day to day or even month to month. Workers and machines might be left idle or

forced to work overtime. Thus, firms prefer to set a steady level of production, which, when combined with the unsteady demand for their products, produces inventory. To smooth production, firms put goods into inventories in slack periods and take them out of inventories in peak times. This is called the **production-smoothing function** of inventories.

In the production-facilitating explanation, inventories are positively correlated with the level of output and aggregate expenditures: inventories increase when the level of output is high. In the production-smoothing explanation, inventories are negatively correlated with aggregate expenditures: they go up when expenditures go down. The combination would seem to suggest that inventories reduce fluctuations in national output, by allowing firms to keep an even level of production.

In fact, however, rather than serving to dampen business fluctuations, inventories seem to exacerbate them. Inventories vary far more than output, and as was mentioned earlier, they seem to be a major contributing factor to fluctuations in aggregate expenditures. This is true even for inventories of consumer goods, which should play a particularly smoothing role.

One reason for the variability of investment in inventories may again be the risk-averse behaviour of firms and the availability of credit. When the economy enters a recession, firms often find that their net worth is decreased. They are less willing to make any kind of investment, including inventory investment. Where possible, they would like to "disinvest," or convert their assets back into cash. By far, the easiest kind of disinvestment is to sell off inventories. When a business faces credit rationing, it may be forced to sell its inventories to raise the requisite capital. And even if it is not yet forced to sell off its inventories, it may fear future credit rationing and, in anticipation, seek to reduce its inventories.

Often, as the economy goes into a recession, inven-

## CLOSE-UP: JUST-IN-TIME INVENTORY MANAGEMENT

CAMI of Ingersoll, Ontario, is one of three Japanese automobile plants in Canada. It was established in 1986 as a joint venture between Suzuki Motor Corporation, Japan, and General Motors of Canada Limited. CAMI's plant was built in a needlelike shape, called a *nagare* design. *Nagare* is a Japanese term meaning "flowing like a river." The reason? It is a "just-in-time" or *kanban* manufacturing system. Instead of delivering goods from factories to warehouses, where goods are kept until they are sent out as orders come in, the company tries to produce only *after* receiving an order. The needlelike shape facilitates this by allowing delivery ports all along the assembly line so that suppliers can ship goods several times a day to a dock directly adjacent to the appropriate spot on the line—a key part of a just-in-time manufacturing system.

The just-in-time inventory system was pioneered by Toyota in 1972. The idea was to hold inventories to a bare minimum by providing inputs only when they were immediately needed. Toyota, like many large manufacturers, faced a basic inventory dilemma. On the one hand, running out of some input to production could shut down a factory. On the other hand, keeping large stockpiles around meant paying for them in advance and maintaining a large storage area. Besides, some products do not keep especially well if stored for too long.

In a just-in-time inventory system, many small deliveries of materials are made throughout a working day, rather than a few large deliveries that need to be stored for days or weeks. The goal is to have supplies arrive just in time to be used, rather than go into storage. At CAMI each box of inventory parts comes with a kanban card, inserted by the inventory department. Team leaders file the cards in colour-coordinated slots on a kanban board. Inventory workers travel the length of the needlelike plant to collect them. The number of cards filed indicates if a part is running low and should be reordered from the supplier.

Besides saving on the costs of carrying inventory, just-in-time systems seem to help companies modernize in many other ways. *The Economist* magazine described it this way: "A favourite analogy is with water in a river. When the level of water falls, rocks start to appear. The rocks can be removed rather than hit." In other words, carrying big inventories can allow a company to cover up a variety of other organizational problems. Thinking about how to organize matters so inventories do not stand around or accumulate can be a powerful tool for thinking about the overall efficiency of the organization.

If just-in-time systems were widely adopted across the entire economy, the overall stability of the economy would tend to be enhanced. When sales dip, a business with large inventories may cut off purchases of inputs altogether for a time, depleting inventories. A business with just-in-time inventories will reduce purchases only a little, and will cut production just by the amount of the reduction in sales.

*Sources: The Economist,* April 25, 1987; Richard J. Schonberger, "The Transfer of Japanese Manufacturing Management Approaches to U.S. Industry," *Academy of Management Review* 7 (1982): 479–87; "Bringing JIT's Benefits to the Bottom Line," *Traffic Management,* November 1991, p. 57; *The Globe and Mail, Report on Business Magazine,* March 1992, pp. 20–21.

## WAYS OF STIMULATING INVESTMENT

**1** Increasing business confidence: Government demonstrates a commitment to maintaining high levels of employment and output.

**2** Lowering the cost of investment: Subsidies to investment through the tax system.

**3** Increasing the availability of credit or making it available on more attractive terms: Monetary policy or direct government lending programmes.

tories build up "involuntarily." Retail stores make orders on the basis of higher expected sales. When the sales fail to materialize, the store winds up holding the unsold merchandise as "inventory." This unintended inventory accumulation can feed back quickly into reduced orders from the factory. And when factory orders get reduced, the factories wind up holding larger inventories than expected. They have based their production plans on a certain level of deliveries to stores, and when the orders are not realized, factory inventories build up. This in turn leads quickly to a cutback in production. The resulting cutback in production is referred to as an **inventory correction,** as firms try to restore inventories to their "normal" size relative to sales. Cyclical variability induced by inventories are called **inventory cycles.**

## POLICIES TO STIMULATE INVESTMENT

The government cannot control all of the determinants of investment, but it has a variety of instruments that may affect it. If the business community is convinced of the government's commitment to economic stability, businessmen may perceive less risk and be more willing to invest. But predicting, let alone controlling, the psychology of business executives is at best a tricky business.

Temporary tax changes like the investment tax credit are more reliable than predictions of the psychological climate, but they are a cumbersome tool, requiring action by Parliament. Temporary tax changes may also distort how resources are allocated, though the macroeconomic gains, in higher levels of output, may well be worth the microeconomic losses from these distortions.

For the most part, however, the government relies on monetary policy, which affects both the availability of credit and the terms on which firms can borrow. Firms raise funds through the capital market. How and when the government, through monetary authorities, affects the capital market (interest rates and availability of credit) are important, complex questions that we will explore in the next three chapters. For now, it is worth noting once again the interrelationships among all the pieces of the macroeconomic puzzle. What goes on in the product market (the determination of the equilibrium level of output) affects the labour market (the level of unemployment in the economy), and what goes on in the capital market (interest rates and the availability of credit) affects investment and thus the product market.

## REVIEW AND PRACTICE

### SUMMARY

**1** The Keynesian consumption function stresses the importance of current disposable income in determining consumption. In contrast, the life-cycle hypothesis says that people save during their working lives so that they can spend after retirement. The permanent-income hypothesis argues that people save in good years to offset the bad years.

**2** In the Keynesian consumption function, the government could manipulate this year's consumption by changing this year's tax rate. In the future-oriented theories, temporary tax reductions would have a limited effect in stimulating consumption, since people are considering a longer horizon than this year for their consumption decisions.

**3** Both the life-cycle and permanent-income models predict that consumption will depend on lifetime wealth, and that capital gains will therefore affect consumption.

**4** Household consumption appears to be more dependent on current income than either the life-cycle or permanent-income theory suggests. Consumers can easily postpone the purchase of durables when current income falls. Also, limitations on ability to borrow (credit rationing) may keep the consumption of many people with little savings close to their current income.

**5** Future-oriented theories of consumption suggest that the aggregate-expenditures schedule is flat and the multiplier is low.

**6** Variations in the level of investment are probably the principal reason for variations in total aggregate expenditures. The three main categories of investment are firms' purchases of plant and equipment, firms' increase or decrease of inventories, and households' purchases of new homes.

**7** Historically, short-term variations in real interest rates have often proved to be only one factor in explaining variations in investment.

**8** The availability of funds is an important determinant of variations in investment. Most firms finance much of their investment out of retained earnings.

**9** Firms will be induced to invest if they anticipate that demand for their products will rise, or if the price of the investment project goes down—for instance, because of favourable tax treatment.

**10** In an economic downturn, firms are less willing to bear risk, and this contributes to a downturn in investment.

## Key Terms

| | | | |
|---|---|---|---|
| life-cycle savings | durable goods | inventories | technological risks |
| permanent-income hypothesis | credit rationing | investment schedule | market risks |
| | plant and equipment | | |

## Review Questions

**1** What is the difference between the Keynesian model of consumption, the life-cycle model, and the permanent-income model?

**2** Why do the life-cycle and permanent-income hypotheses predict that temporary tax changes will have little effect on current consumption?

**3** What factors affect consumer expenditures on durables? Why are these expenditures so volatile?

**4** How will the existence of credit rationing make consumption more dependent on current income than the future-oriented consumption theories would suggest?

**5** What are the possible sources of funds for firms that wish to invest? Which is used most often? which least often?

**6** Why does an investment tax credit stimulate investment?

**7** How might changes in perceptions of economic risk affect investment levels?

**8** Why might firms' willingness to bear risk decrease in a recession?

**9** What are the costs and benefits to the firm of holding inventories? Why might inventory investment be as volatile as it is?

## PROBLEMS

**1** Under which theory of consumption would a temporary tax cut have the largest effect on consumption? Under which theory would a permanent rise in Old Age Security benefits have the largest effect on consumption? Under which theory would permanently higher unemployment insurance benefits have the largest effect on consumption? Explain.

**2** Which theory of consumption predicts that aggregate savings will depend on the proportion of retired and young people in the population? What is the relationship? Which theories predict that consumption will not be very affected by whether the economy is in a boom or recession? Why?

**3** If the government made it easier for people to borrow money, perhaps by enacting programmes to help them get loans, would you expect consumption behaviour to become more or less sensitive to current income? Why?

**4** How would you predict that a crash in the stock market would affect the relationship between consumption and income? How would you predict that rapidly rising prices for homes would affect the relationship between consumption and income? Draw shifts in the consumption function to illustrate. How do your predictions differ depending on whether the consumer is a Keynesian, life-cycle, or permanent-income consumer?

**5** A company that expects the long-term real interest rate to be 3 percent is considering a list of projects. Each project costs $10,000, but they vary in the amount of time they will take to pay off, and in how much they will pay off. The first will pay $12,000 in two years; the second, $12,500 in three years; the third, $13,000 in four years. Which projects are worth doing? If the expected interest rate was 5 percent, does your answer change? You may assume that prices are stable.

**6** Take the projects in problem #5 and reevaluate them, this time assuming that inflation is at 4 percent per year and the payoffs are in nominal dollars at the time they occur. Are the projects still worth doing?

**7** Draw a diagram to show how investment is affected in each of the following situations.
(a) The government passes an investment tax credit.
(b) Businesses believe the economic future looks healthier than they had previously thought.
(c) The government reduces the real interest rate.

**8** Imagine that the government raises personal income taxes, but also enacts an investment tax credit for a corresponding amount. Describe under what circumstances this combination of policies would be most effective in stimulating aggregate demand. Consider differing theories of consumption, and the choice between permanent and temporary changes in the tax system.

**9** Explain how a purchase of a durable good is like an investment. How might an increase in the interest rate or a change in credit availability affect the demand for durables?

## APPENDIX: THE INVESTMENT-SAVINGS IDENTITY

We typically think of savings and investment together. Saving is a virtue—"A penny saved is a penny earned"—and so is investment. Increased investment enhances the future productivity of the economy. It has frequently been suggested that the Canadian government should encourage savings, the presumption being that savings are automatically converted into investment.

When a closed economy is operating along its production possibilities curve, with all resources fully utilized, increased savings—reduced consumption—mean that more capital goods can be produced. Then savings and investment will move together. But when the economy is operating below its production possibilities curve, increased savings—reduced consumption—may simply push the economy further below that curve.

In *open* economies, savings and investment do not have to change together even when the economy is on its production possibilities curve. This is because the economy can undertake investment, even when there is little domestic saving, by borrowing from abroad.

The income-expenditure analysis of Chapter 11 focused on the relationship between aggregate expenditures and income. Equilibrium occurs when aggregate expenditures equal national income. An alternative way of describing how national output is determined focuses on savings and investment. We look at a simple model first, in which disposable income equals national income. For this to be the case, we assume that taxes are zero and all of a firm's profits are paid out as dividends. To simplify further, we assume there are no government savings or dissavings, or any flow of funds from abroad. Later we will relax these assumptions to get a fuller picture.

That individuals can either spend their income today or save it is true by definition:

income = consumption + savings.

With no government purchases or net exports, we know from the components of aggregate expenditures that firms can produce only two kinds of goods: consumer goods and investment goods. Thus, output, $Y$, can be broken into its two components:

$Y$ = consumption + investment.

These two identities can be combined to form a new one. Since the value of national output equals national income,

$Y$ = income,

we can use the right-hand side of the first two equations to get

consumption + savings = consumption + investment.

Subtracting consumption from both sides of this equation yields

savings = investment.

One way to understand this identity is to think of firms as producing a certain amount of goods, the value of which is just equal to the income of the individuals in the economy (because everything firms take in they pay out as income to someone). The income that is not consumed is, by definition, saved. On the output side, firms either sell the goods they produce or put them into inventory for sale in future years. Some of the inventory buildup is planned, because businesses need inventories to survive. Some of it is unplanned—businesses may be surprised by an economic downturn that spoils their sales projections. Both intended and unintended inventory buildups are considered investment. Thus, the goods that are not consumed are, by definition, invested.

This identity (savings equals investment) can be transformed into an equation determining national output, once it is recognized that in equilibrium firms will cut back production if there is unintended inventory accumulation. Because firms will cut back, in equilibrium the amount companies invest is the amount they wish to invest (including inventories), given current market conditions. The equilibrium condition, then, is that

investment = desired investment.

Now switch over to the savings side of the identity. The consumption function presented earlier tells how much people wish to consume at each level of income. But since what is not consumed is saved, the consumption function can be transformed into a savings function, giving the level of savings at each level of income. Savings is income minus consumption:

savings = income − consumption.

Figure 12.9 shows the savings function. The slope of this curve, the amount by which savings increases with income, is the marginal propensity to save, which is 1 minus the marginal propensity to consume.

Since savings must equal investment, and in equilibrium investment must equal desired investment, then in equilibrium

savings = desired investment.

The figure shows a fixed level of desired investment,

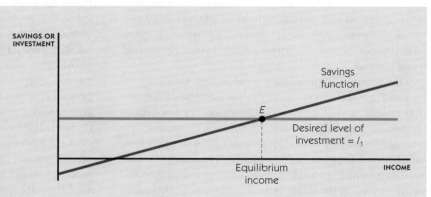

**Figure 12.9 THE SAVINGS FUNCTION AND NATIONAL INCOME**

As income increases, the amount individuals desire to save increases. The amount by which savings increases as the result of a $1 increase in income—the slope of the savings function—is called the marginal propensity to save. In equilibrium, savings equals desired investment. Thus, equilibrium occurs at the intersection of the savings function and the level of investment.

$I_1$. Desired investment is horizontal because investment is assumed to be unaffected by the level of income. Equilibrium occurs at the intersection of the desired investment curve and the saving curve, point $E$.

As with income-expenditure analysis, savings-investment analysis shows how an increase in investment leads to an increase in output that is a multiple of itself. Figure 12.10 shows that as investment shifts up from $I_1$ to $I_2$, the equilibrium shifts from $E_1$ to $E_2$, and output increases from $Y_1$ to $Y_2$. The change in investment, $\Delta I$, is again smaller than the change in

output. This should not surprise us, since income-expenditure analysis and savings-investment analysis are two ways of looking at the same thing.

## THE PARADOX OF THRIFT

We can use a similar diagram to illustrate what may seem to be a paradoxical result. When the economy's resources are not fully employed, an increase in thrift—the level of savings at each level of income—may have no effect at all on the equilibrium

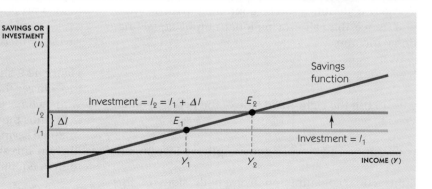

**Figure 12.10 USING THE SAVINGS-INVESTMENT DIAGRAM**

A shift in investment from $I_1$ to $I_2$ leads to an increase in output from $Y_1$ to $Y_2$; the increase in output is a multiple of the original increase in investment.

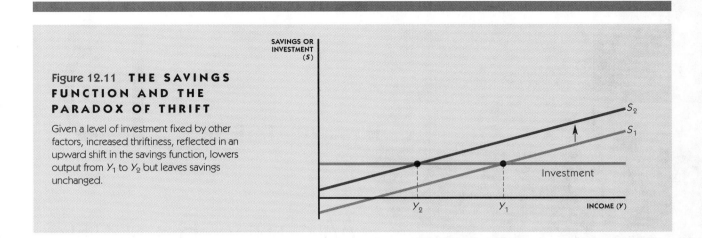

**Figure 12.11 THE SAVINGS FUNCTION AND THE PARADOX OF THRIFT**

Given a level of investment fixed by other factors, increased thriftiness, reflected in an upward shift in the savings function, lowers output from $Y_1$ to $Y_2$ but leaves savings unchanged.

level of savings or investment. The only effect of greater thrift is to lower national income and output. Figure 12.11 shows the effect of an upward shift in the savings function—at each level of income, savings are higher. But in equilibrium, savings equal investment. With investment fixed, savings, in equilibrium, must also be the same. To attain that level of savings (equal to the level of investment), income must be lowered from $Y_1$ to $Y_2$.

## GOVERNMENT SAVINGS, BUSINESS SAVINGS, AND BORROWING FROM ABROAD

What happens when government purchases and net exports are allowed to enter the picture? Again, savings equal investment. Now, however, there are three additional sources of investment funds, along with the household savings we have considered so far (denoted by the symbol $S_h$). Funds can be obtained from abroad ($S_x$) or from the government ($S_g$). Just as household savings are the difference between the household's income and its consumption, government savings are the difference between its

income (tax revenues) and its expenditures. In recent years, government savings have been negative—the government has been spending more than its income. Finally, businesses save, too, when their receipts exceed what they pay out as wages, taxes, interest, and dividends,[3] and these savings ($S_b$) are another source of investment funds. Thus,

$$S_b + S_h + S_g + S_x = I.$$

We frequently combine business and household savings together, as private savings ($S_p$):

$$S_p = S_h + S_b.$$

The new savings-investment identity is

$$S_p + S_g + S_x = I.$$

Investment must equal the sum of private savings, government savings, and borrowing from abroad.

[3] Additions to inventory are included in the firm's books as if they were sales; the firm records a "profit" even though there is no cash to show for it. This profit is saved, and is reflected in statistics on business savings.

# MONEY, BANKING, AND CREDIT

S ome say money is the root of all evil. Some say money makes the world go 'round. Actually, money does not *do* anything, in and of itself. The economy is made up of real people working with real machines to make goods that satisfy needs directly. Money for the most part is just paper and a ledger mark in a bank account. It satisfies needs only indirectly, when it is spent.

In Chapter 8 we encountered the principle of money neutrality. At full employment, an increase in the money supply only leads to a proportionate increase in prices and wages, with no real consequences. Yet controlling the supply of money is considered such an important function of government that failure to exercise that control has been blamed not only for inflations but also for depressions. In the short run, the economy may deviate significantly from full employment, and under such conditions monetary policy may affect output and employment substantially.

We have emphasized that all markets are interlinked. Fluctuations in aggregate output cause fluctuations in employment. Changes in aggregate output can be traced to changes in the level of aggregate demand, which in

## KEY QUESTIONS

**1** What *is* money? What economic functions does it serve?

**2** What is meant by the money supply, and how is it measured?

**3** What institutions in our economy are responsible for controlling the money supply and determining monetary policy?

**4** How do modern economies create money through the banking system? How do monetary authorities affect the creation of money and the availability of credit? In other words, how do they affect the supply of money and credit?

---

turn can be related to changes in the level of investment and net exports. Investment depends on interest rates and other aspects of the capital market. Net exports depend upon the value of the exchange rate, which is heavily influenced by the flow of funds in the capital market.

So it is to the capital market that we now turn. We will see in this and the next two chapters how government can through monetary policy affect interest rates, the exchange rate, and the availability of credit, and thus the levels of investment and net exports in the short term. This chapter will explain what money is, what it does, and why it is so important. The following two chapters will show how, why, and when monetary policy affects the level of economic activity.

## MONEY IS WHAT MONEY DOES

We use the term "money" to mean much more than just currency and coins. When someone asks how much money you make, he means what is your income. When someone says, "He has a lot of money," she means he is wealthy, not that he has stashed away lots of currency. When someone accuses corporations of being "interested only in making money," she means they are interested only in making profits.

Economists define money by the functions it serves, and we must look at these functions before we can develop a formal definition of money.

## MONEY AS A MEDIUM OF EXCHANGE

Money's first function is to facilitate trade—the exchange of goods or services for mutual benefit. This is called the **medium of exchange** function of money. Trade that occurs without money is called **barter.** Barter involves a direct exchange of one good or service for another. Two families agree to take turns baby-sitting for each other, or a doctor and a lawyer agree to trade consultations. Nations sometimes sign treaties phrased in barter terms. For example, a certain amount of oil might be traded for a certain amount of machinery or weapons.

Barter works best in simple economies. One can imagine an old-style farmer bartering with the blacksmith, the tailor, the grocer, and the doctor in his small town. For simple barter to work, however, there must be a **double coincidence of wants:** one individual must have what the other wants, and vice versa. Henry has potatoes and wants shoes, Joshua has an extra pair of shoes and wants potatoes. Bartering can make them both happier. But if Henry has firewood and Joshua does not need any of that, then bartering for Joshua's shoes requires one or both of them to go searching for more people in the hope of making a multilateral exchange. Money provides a way to make multilateral exchange much simpler. Henry sells his firewood to someone else for money and uses the money to buy Joshua's shoes. The convenience of money becomes even clearer when one considers the billions of exchanges that take place in a modern economy.

Any easily transportable and storable good can, in principle, be used as a medium of exchange. A wide variety of items have served that function. Indeed, the choice of an item as "money" can be thought of as a social convention. The reason you accept money in payment for what you sell is that others will accept it for things you want to buy. Different cultures have used a variety of items as money. North American Indians used wampum, and the early settlers used beaver pelts. South Sea Islanders used cowrie shells. In World War II prisoner-of-war camps, cigarettes served as a medium of exchange.

For a long time, gold was the major medium of exchange. However, the value of a gold coin depends on its weight and purity, as well as on the supply and demand for gold in the gold market. It would be expensive to weigh and verify the quality of gold every time you engaged in a transaction. So one of the functions of governments, right up until the twentieth century, was to mint gold coins, certifying their weight and quality. Criminals have profited by shaving the edges off gold coins. The ridges on Canadian dimes and quarters are a carryover from coins developed to deter this practice.

Today all the developed countries of the world use paper bills as well as metal coins for currency. However, most business transactions use not currency but cheques drawn on banks, credit cards whose balances are paid with cheques, or funds wired from one bank to another. Economists consider chequing account balances to be money, just as currency is, because they are accepted as payment at most places and thus serve the medium of exchange function. Since most people have much more money in their chequing accounts than they do in their wallets, it should be evident that the economists' measure of the money supply is much larger than the amount of coins and other currency in circulation.

## MONEY AS A STORE OF VALUE

People will be willing to exchange what they have for money only if they believe they can later exchange the money for the goods or services they want. Thus, for money to serve its role as a medium of exchange, it must hold its value, at least for a short while. This function is known as the **store of value** function of money. There was a time when governments feared that paper money by itself would not be accepted in the future and so paper money was not as good

a store of value as gold. People had confidence in paper dollars only because they were backed by gold (if you wished, you used to be able actually to exchange your paper dollars for gold).

Today, however, all major economies have **fiat money**—money that has value only because the government says it has value and because people are willing to accept it in exchange for goods. The five-dollar bill in your pocket answers this need for security with its simple message: "This note is legal tender." The fact that bills are legal tender means that if you owe someone $100, you have fully discharged that debt if you give her a hundred-dollar bill.

There are many other stores of value. Gold, which is no longer "money" because it no longer serves as a medium of exchange, nevertheless continues to serve as a store of value. In India people hold much of their savings in the form of gold. Land, corporate stocks and bonds, oil and minerals—all are stores of value. None of them is perfectly safe, in the sense that you cannot be precisely sure what they can be exchanged for in the future. But currency, chequing account balances, and other forms of money are not a perfectly safe store of value either. If prices change, then what you can buy with the dollars in your pocket or bank account will also change.

## MONEY AS A UNIT OF ACCOUNT

In performing its roles as a medium of exchange and a store of value, money serves a third purpose. It is a way of measuring the relative values of different goods. This is the **unit of account** function of money. Money provides a simple and convenient yardstick for measuring relative market values. If a banana costs 25 cents and a peach 50 cents, then a peach is worth twice as much as a banana. A person who wishes to trade bananas for peaches can do so at the rate of two bananas for one peach.

Imagine how difficult it would be for firms to keep track of how well they were doing without such a yardstick. The ledgers might describe how many of each item the firm bought or sold. But the fact that the firm sold more items than it purchased would tell you nothing about how well that firm was doing. You need to know the value of what the firm sells relative to the value of what it purchases. Money provides the unit of account, the means by which the firm and others take these measurements.

## CLOSE-UP: A GLOSSARY OF FINANCIAL TERMS

One of the problems in defining money is the wide variety of assets that are not directly used as a medium of exchange but can be readily converted into something that could be so used. Should they be included in the money supply? There is no right or wrong answer. Below are definitions of ten terms, some of which were defined in earlier chapters. Each of these assets serves, in progressively less satisfactory ways, the function of money.

| | |
|---|---|
| Currency and coins | Five-, ten-, twenty-, fifty-dollar bills, and pennies, nickels, dimes, quarters, and one- and two-dollar coins. |
| Traveller's cheques | Cheques issued by a bank or firm, such as American Express, which you can convert into currency on demand and are widely accepted. |
| Demand deposits or chequing accounts | Deposits that you can withdraw upon demand (convert into currency) by writing a cheque. |
| Personal savings deposits | Deposits that technically you can withdraw only upon notice; in practice, banks allow withdrawal upon demand, without notice. |
| Personal fixed-term deposits | Deposits that are held in specialized forms (for example, Registered Retirement Savings Plans or Quebec Stock Savings Plans), which can offer a higher rate of return or tax advantages and are often designed as personal pension funds and have a penalty for early withdrawal. |
| Certificates of deposit | Money deposited for a fixed period of time (usually six months to five years), with a penalty for early withdrawal. |
| Nonpersonal notice deposits | Deposits that require the depositor to give notice before withdrawing or transferring funds, and that bear higher interest rates than personal savings or demand deposits. |
| Nonpersonal fixed-term deposits | Similar to nonpersonal notice deposits, except deposited for a fixed term with a penalty for early withdrawal. |
| Mutual funds in financial institutions | Shares in an investment pool managed by a financial institution comprising such assets as Treasury bills and corporate and public shares and bonds. Some financial institutions allow you to convert your shares by writing a cheque. |
| Eurodollars | U.S. dollar bank accounts in banks in Europe. |

We are now ready for the economic definition of **money.** Money is anything that is generally accepted as a medium of exchange, a store of value, and a unit of account. In other words, money is what money does.

## MEASURING THE MONEY SUPPLY

The quantity of money is called the **money supply**, a stock variable like the capital stock. Most of the other variables discussed in this chapter are stock variables as well, but they have important effects on the flow variables (like the level of economic activity, measured as dollars *per year*).

What exactly should be included in the money supply? A variety of items serve some but not all of the functions of money. For example, the chips issued in casinos for gambling serve as a medium of exchange inside the casino and perhaps even in some nearby stores and restaurants. But no place outside the casino is obligated to take them; they are neither a generally accepted medium of exchange nor a unit of account.

The economists' measure of money begins with the currency and coins that we carry around. Economists then expand the measure of money to include other items that serve the three functions of money. Chequing accounts, or **demand deposits,** are included in the money supply, as are some other forms of accounts in banks and other financial institutions. But what are the limits? There is a continuum that runs from items that everyone would agree should be called money to items that can work as money in many circumstances to items that can occasionally work as money to items that would never be considered money.

Economists have developed several measures of the money supply to account for different points on the continuum. The narrowest measure, called **M1,** is the total of currency outside the banks and demand deposits held in banks. M1 is currency plus items that can be treated like currency through the banking system. At the beginning of 1996, M1 in Canada totalled $60 billion.

A broader measure, **M2,** includes everything that is in M1 plus some items that are *almost* perfect substitutes for M1. Personal savings deposits, daily interest chequing accounts (which combine the features of chequing and savings accounts), and nonpersonal notice deposits are included in M2. At the beginning of 1996, M2 totalled $386 billion.

The common characteristic of assets in M2 is that they are very *liquid,* or easily convertible into M1. You cannot just tell a store that the money it requires is in your savings account. But if you have funds in your savings account it is not hard to turn them into something the store will accept. You can transfer funds from your savings account into your chequing account, or withdraw them as currency.

A third level of money, **M3,** includes everything that is in M2 (and thus everything that is in M1) plus nonpersonal fixed-term deposits and foreign currency deposits. M3 is just about as liquid as M2. At the beginning of 1996, M3 totalled $477 billion.

In recent years, many other financial institutions have begun to take on some of the traditional roles of banks, including offering both chequing and savings account privileges. This has been a consequence of the rapid change in communications technology as well as the lessening of regulation of financial institutions. Since deposits in these nonbank financial institutions fulfill many of the same functions as bank deposits, it is useful to include them in the definition of the money supply. This is done by using an alternative way of expanding M2, referred to as **M2+.** M2+ includes everything in M2 plus deposits in the so-called **near banks.** Near banks include such deposit-taking institutions as trust and mortgage loan companies, credit unions, and caisses populaires, and are discussed further below. At the beginning of 1996, M2+ totalled $617 billion.

The Bank of Canada regularly publishes the size of M1, M2, M3, and M2+. Figure 13.1 shows the relative magnitude of the four different measures of the money supply, while Figure 13.2 shows that during the past decade different measures have grown at different rates.

Recent changes in financial institutions such as the growth of mutual funds and the more extensive use of credit cards have made it even more difficult to determine what to include in the money supply. For instance, some asset-trading intermediaries (brokerage firms) such as investment dealers or mutual funds now provide cheque-writing privileges. This makes the investments in these firms as liquid as regular demand deposits, and thus complicates the choice of the appropriate money supply definition.

## MONEY AND CREDIT

One of the key properties of money, as noted, is that it is a medium of exchange. However, many transactions today do not entail the use of any of the measures presented so far: M1, M2, M3, or M2+. They involve credit, not money. In selling a suit of clothes or a piece of furniture or a car, stores often do not receive money. They receive, rather, a promise from you to pay money in the future. Credit is clearly tied

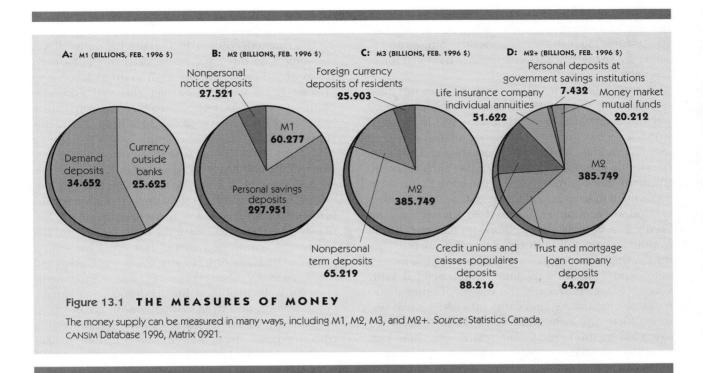

**Figure 13.1  THE MEASURES OF MONEY**

The money supply can be measured in many ways, including M1, M2, M3, and M2+. *Source:* Statistics Canada, CANSIM Database 1996, Matrix 0921.

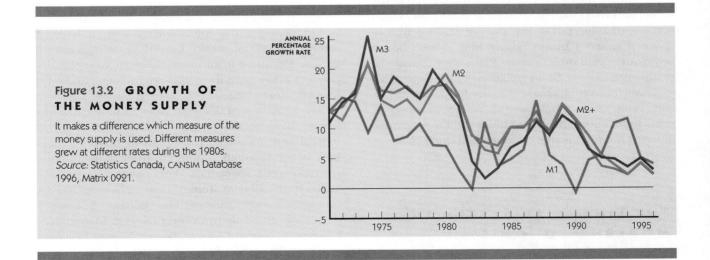

**Figure 13.2  GROWTH OF THE MONEY SUPPLY**

It makes a difference which measure of the money supply is used. Different measures grew at different rates during the 1980s. *Source:* Statistics Canada, CANSIM Database 1996, Matrix 0921.

to money: what you owe the store is measured in dollars. You want something today, and you will have the money for it tomorrow. The store wants you to buy today and is willing to wait until tomorrow or next week for the money. There is a mutually advan-tageous trade. But because the exchange is not *simultaneous,* the store must rely on your promise.

Promises, the saying goes, are made to be broken. But if they are broken too often, stores will not be able to trust buyers, and credit exchanges will not occur. There is therefore an incentive for the development of institutions, such as banks, to ascertain who is most likely to keep economic promises and to help ensure that once such a promise has been made it is kept.

When banks are involved, the store does not need to believe the word of the shopper. Rather, the shopper must convince the bank that he will in fact pay. Consider a car purchase. Suppose a bank agrees to give Luke a loan, and he then buys the car. If he later breaks his promise and does not pay back the loan, the car dealer is protected. It is the bank that tries to force Luke to keep his commitment.

Modern economies have relied increasingly on credit as a basis of transactions. Banks have a long tradition of extending **lines of credit** to firms. This means that a bank agrees to lend a business money automatically (up to some limit), as it is needed. With Visa and MasterCard and the variety of other international credit cards that came into widespread use in the 1970s and 1980s, lines of credit have also been extended to millions of consumers, who now can purchase goods even when they have no currency or chequing account balances on hand. Today individuals can also easily get credit based on the equity in their houses, the difference between the value of the house and what they owe on their mortgage, which is the loan taken out to buy the house. This type of credit is called a **home equity loan.** When house prices increased rapidly in the 1980s, they provided a ready source of credit for millions of home owners.

These innovations make it easier for people to obtain credit. But they have also altered the way economists think about the role of money in the economy, blurring definitions that once seemed quite clear.

## THE FINANCIAL SYSTEM IN MODERN ECONOMIES

Broadly speaking, a country's **financial system** includes all institutions involved in moving savings from households and firms whose income exceeds their expenditures and transferring it to other households and firms who would like to spend more than their income allows. Here we take a closer look at the most important of these institutions.

The financial system in Canada not only allows consumers to buy cars, televisions, and VCRs even when they do not have the cash to do so but it also enables firms to invest in factories and new machines. Sometimes money goes directly from, say, a household doing some saving to a firm that needs some additional cash. For example, when Ben buys a new bond from Bell Canada that promises to pay a fixed amount in 90 or 180 days (or in 5 or 15 years), he is lending money directly to Bell Canada.

But most of the funds flow through **financial intermediaries.** These are firms that stand in between the savers, who have the extra funds, and the borrowers, who need them. The most important group of financial intermediaries is the banks, but there are many other groups of financial intermediaries as well, including life insurance companies, credit unions, and trust companies. All are engaged in looking over potential borrowers, ascertaining who are good risks, and monitoring their investments and loans. The intermediaries take "deposits" from consumers and invest them. By putting the funds into many different investments, they diversify and thus reduce the risk. One investment might turn sour, but it is unlikely that many will. This diversification provides the intermediary with a level of safety it could not obtain if it put all its eggs in one basket. Financial institutions differ in who the depositors are, where the funds are invested, and who owns the institutions.

The functions of different types of financial institutions have been kept quite separate by restrictive federal and provincial regulation in financial markets, which resulted in different types of institutions with different specialties. The result was the so-called **four-pillar system** of financial institutions: it recognized four functions and assigned one function each to four types of financial institutions. Unsecured lending was to be performed by chartered banks and credit unions/caisses populaires; corporate trusteeship, by trust companies; securities underwriting and brokerage, by investment dealers; and insurance, by life or property and casualty insurance companies. These restrictions were meant not only to limit the power of banks but also to enhance their security by restricting their participation

## CLOSE-UP: A GLOSSARY OF FINANCIAL INTERMEDIARIES

A variety of financial intermediaries take funds from the public and lend them to borrowers or otherwise invest the funds. The principal legal differences between these institutions relate to the kinds of loans or investments they make.

| | |
|---|---|
| Chartered banks | Banks chartered by the federal government under the Bank Act to receive deposits and make loans. |
| Insurance companies | Companies that collect premiums from policy holders from which insurance payments are made. They invest in mortgage loans, bonds, and shares. |
| Trust and mortgage loan companies | Firms that receive deposits and make mostly mortgage loans. Trust companies also administer trusteed pension plans on behalf of employees and employers. |
| Credit unions and caisses populaires | Cooperative (not-for-profit) institutions, originally formed by an occupational group or union, that take deposits or issue shares to members and make loans to members. |
| Mutual funds | Financial intermediaries that take funds from a group of investors and invest them. They issue shares to invest in a diverse portfolio of common and preferred shares, bonds, and mortgages. They may specialize in one type of financial asset; for instance there are bond mutual funds and stock mutual funds. |
| Sales finance and consumer loan companies | Companies that issue short-term paper and bonds and lend to firms and consumers needing short-term credit. |
| Investment companies | Companies that issue shares in order to buy long term into other companies; they may be specialized, for example, venture-capital companies that lend to promising young firms. |
| Investment dealers | Retail agents for purchasing financial assets. Some (such as brokerage firms) operate cash-management accounts that enable people to place stocks, bonds, and other assets into a single account, against which they can write cheques. |

in the risky trading of stocks. But in recent years, these restrictions have come under attack as limiting competition in the financial sector. A process of deregulation has begun. Not only are the traditional functions of banks being undertaken by other financial institutions, but also the banks are moving into areas such as dealing in securities that previously were restricted to other institutions.

## THE CENTRAL BANKING SYSTEM

Just as there is a continuum of ways of defining money, from currency and demand deposits to nonpersonal notice deposits, that serve in varying degrees the functions of money, so, too, is there a continuum of financial institutions, or near banks, that perform in varying ways some or many of the functions that banks perform. For instance, trust companies accept deposits and make loans today in a way that is almost identical to that of banks. Near banks play an important role in our financial system. Their actions affect the supply of money (particularly money in the broader definitions, such as M2, M3, and M2+). For simplicity, the discussion here focuses on chartered banks and the narrower definition of money, M1. Traditionally banks have been the most important source of capital for businesses and the focus of government attempts to control the level of investment and hence the level of economic activity.

Governments have two objectives in their involvement with the bank portion of the financial system. The first is to protect customers: when banks go bankrupt, depositors stand to lose their life's savings. The typical saver is not in a position to audit a bank's books to see whether it is really sound. Many banks closed during the Depression of the 1930s, leaving thousands destitute. Today banks are more tightly regulated. In addition, depositors are insured by government agencies, which limits their losses should a bankruptcy occur.

The second objective of government involvement in the banking system is to influence key financial variables such as the amount of money and credit in the economy, the interest rate, and the exchange rate, so as to stabilize the level of economic activity. We have seen the important intermediary role that the banking system plays in taking funds from savers and providing them to investors. By its actions the government can affect the amount of funds flowing through the banking system to investors and this helps determine the interest rate and the exchange rate, which in turn influence the level of economic activity. Sharp declines in investment or net exports can throw the economy into recession; sharp increases can set off an inflationary spiral.

## THE CENTRAL BANK

Different economies have developed a variety of institutions and laws for accomplishing these twin objectives of safeguarding the banking system and influencing key financial market variables. The most important institution in each country is its **central bank.** The central bank is the bank from which other banks can borrow. But it is more than a banker's bank. It is also responsible for stabilizing the level of

economic activity by controlling the money supply and the availability of credit, and for regulating the banking system to ensure its financial health.

In Canada, the central bank is the **Bank of Canada,** established by the Bank of Canada Act of 1934. The Bank is managed by a Board of Directors consisting of the governor, the senior deputy governor, twelve directors, and the deputy minister of finance, who is nonvoting. The directors are appointed by the minister of finance for three-year terms. The directors in turn appoint the governor and senior deputy governor for seven-year terms. The conduct of monetary policy is the responsibility of the governor, along with the senior deputy governor, with final approval formally resting with the minister of finance. In practice, the governor has a large degree of independence in the exercise of authority.

The structure of the Bank of Canada is quite different from that of the Federal Reserve, which is the central bank in the United States. The Federal Reserve is organized on a more regional basis and consists of a Board of Governors (the Federal Reserve Board), which supervises a system of twelve regional Federal Reserve banks. The latter monitors the operations of six thousand member banks, very few of which operate on a nationwide basis. The Canadian system is much more centralized. The main chartered banks themselves tend to be national in scope, each with a large number of branches across the country. Ours is referred to as a **branch banking system,** in contrast to the **unitary banking system** of the United States. The Bank of Canada also operates as a single national entity. In recent years there has been some pressure for more explicitly regional input into the central banking structure. Persons in some regions have felt that the priorities of monetary policy were being set with central Canada's interests most in mind. Most suggestions for change do not go so far as to propose moving to a Federal Reserve–like system in Canada. Typically they call for more explicit regional representation on the Bank's Board of Directors.

## CONTROLLING THE MONEY SUPPLY

The main function of the Bank of Canada is to control the supply of money in the banking system. It is able to do this both by influencing the amount of currency in circulation and by influencing the amount of deposits held in the chartered banks. (Recall that the money supply measure M1 consists of currency and demand deposits.) The ability of the Bank to affect the amount of deposits held in the chartered banks arises from the fact that the banks maintain deposits at the Bank of Canada. As we shall see later, there is a relationship between the amount of deposits that the public holds in the banking system and the deposits the banks hold in the Bank of Canada. The Bank is able to influence the deposits held by the banks in the Bank of Canada by engaging in various financial transactions with the banking system, called **settlement balance management,** whose purpose is to move funds between the Bank of Canada and the chartered banks. Some of these involve **open-market operations**—the purchase or sale of government bonds or Treasury bills by the Bank from the financial market. Others arise because the federal government holds its operating accounts both in the chartered banks and in the Bank of Canada. As the manager of the government's accounts, the Bank can determine how they are divided between accounts in the banks and accounts in the Bank of Canada. At a stroke of a pen the Bank can transfer funds between the federal government's accounts in the chartered banks and its accounts in the Bank. A **drawdown** involves transferring funds from the government's accounts in one or more of the banks to a government account in the Bank of Canada. This results in the chartered bank's reducing its deposits in the Bank of Canada to reimburse the Bank for the funds withdrawn. Conversely, a **redeposit** is a transfer of funds from a government account in the Bank of Canada to a government account in one of the chartered banks, causing chartered bank deposits in the Bank of Canada to rise. Later in this chapter we shall see exactly how these cash-management transactions translate into changes in the money supply.

## REGULATING BANKS

The other primary objective of the central bank is to ensure the financial soundness of banks. The Canadian branch banking system is dominated by a few large banks, which manage most of the deposits and control most of the assets of the banking system. The chartered banks have 60 percent of the chequable deposits and 73 percent of the total assets held by financial institutions in Canada. By contrast, trust and mortgage loan companies have 6 percent of the assets and the credit unions and caisses populaires have 8 percent.

According to the Bank Act, to open its doors a bank must obtain a federal charter. A charter gives a financial institution the right to call itself a bank and to make an unlimited quantity of unsecured business and personal loans. There are two types of charters. Schedule I charters are granted only to domestically owned banks with a large number of shareholders, of which there are eight. Schedule II charters are those whose share ownership is concentrated. There are close to sixty schedule II banks, almost all of them subsidiaries of foreign banks. In the future they will include subsidiaries of nonbank financial institutions. They face somewhat more restrictions than schedule I banks.

Chartered banks face a number of regulations and restrictions. Banks have to keep accounts, called **settlement balances,** at the Bank of Canada. These are used for cheque-clearing purposes. Each day thousands of cheques written on an account in one bank will be deposited in another. At the end of the day, when all the cheques have been added up, some of the banks will end up owing others money. They settle these differences by transferring funds from the clearing balances held in the Bank of Canada. The banks are supervised by the superintendent of financial institutions and must report weekly to the Bank of Canada. The banks face certain restrictions on their lending practices and asset holdings. For example, they cannot acquire more than 10 percent ownership of nonfinancial companies, and their holdings of real estate and shares cannot exceed 70 percent of the value of their shareholders' equity for each type and 100 percent for both combined.

Deposits in the banks are insured by the Canada Deposit Insurance Corporation (CDIC) for up to $60,000 per depositor. In return, banks must abide by certain restrictions imposed by the CDIC. The banks also belong to the Canadian Payments Association (CPA), which operates an automated clearing and settlement mechanism for clearing cheques written against one bank that are deposited in another. Other financial institutions such as credit unions and caisses populaires and trust and mortgage loan

# POLICY PERSPECTIVE:
## SHOULD THE BANK OF CANADA ACT BE REFORMED?

Since the formation of the Bank of Canada in the mid-thirties, its mandate and organizational structure have remained largely unchanged. In fact, there has been only one major amendment to the Bank of Canada Act, that of 1967 establishing the right of the minister of finance to issue written directives to the governor, a right that has yet to be exercised. Many would argue that the Bank's mandate, accountability, and governance are badly adapted to the 1990s, given the changes in economic climate as well as the growing importance and needs of regions outside central Canada. Moreover, given that control of Bank policy is in the hands of the governor and a small group of senior officials, there is some feeling that the Bank lacks "legitimacy" and is unresponsive to regional needs.

In recognition of this, in 1991 the federal government proposed a major set of reforms to the Bank of Canada Act. The proposed reforms accompanied a wide-ranging package of proposed changes to the Constitution designed mainly to achieve a lasting agreement with the Quebec government but also to enhance the effectiveness with which the Canadian economic union operated.

The intention of the reforms was to reestablish legitimacy while at the same time respecting the Bank's independence. The proposed changes included four main elements.

*The Bank's Mandate*   The Bank's mandate is currently fairly broad: to protect the external value of currency and to help stabilize the business cycle. The proposed amendment would limit the Bank's mandate to achieving and maintaining price stability. Some monetary policy experts, such as Peter Howitt of the University of Western

Ontario, do not agree with this proposal. Howitt argues that while price stability might be rightly considered to be the long-run objective of the Bank, monetary policy does affect more than the price level in the short run. The mandate of the Bank should be broad enough to take account of the short-run effects of monetary policy on real activity as well as the long-run effects on price stability. Others, like David Laidler, also of the University of Western Ontario, favour the federal proposal, but believe that the Bank must also aim at price-level predictability. Laidler would go one step further by recommending a quantitative goal for permissible price-level increases. The premise of this argument is that the conduct of monetary policy should be based more on "rules" than on "discretion." The exercise of discretion in monetary policy is said to be as likely to be destabilizing as stabilizing, given the unpredictability of the policy effects and the lags involved before the measures take effect.

*The Appointment of Directors*   The Board of Directors consists of twelve directors from "diversified occupations" appointed for three-year terms by the minister of finance; a governor and a senior deputy governor appointed for seven-year terms; and the deputy minister of finance. In practice, the Board of Directors has little influence over monetary policy; the operations of the Bank are in the hands of the governor, senior deputy governor, and the Bank's professional staff. The proposal is to amend the act to ensure regional representation on the Board of Directors by requiring the federal government to consult with provincial and territorial governments before appointing directors. Laidler argues that this proposal may only result in an imbalance in representation (for example, by giving Prince

Edward Island and Ontario equal membership) without improving the effectiveness of the Board of Directors. He recommends enhancing the Board of Directors' legitimacy by removing the "diversified occupations" requirement from the act so that more monetary policy experts can serve, and by making the position of directors full time, well paid, and of a longer term.

*Ratification by the Senate*   The appointment of the governor would be ratified by the Senate, which, under the constitutional reform proposals, would be an elected one. This proposal is intended to improve the legitimacy of the governor and thus of the Bank itself.

*Regional Consultative Panels*   The last reform is to create regional consultative panels so as to ensure that perspectives from all across the country are brought to bear on monetary policy. In these panels, the regional and provincial eco-

nomic situations would be reviewed, and the reports from the meetings of regional consultative panels would be published as part of the minutes of the Bank of Canada's Board of Directors.

When the federal government sat down with the provincial and territorial governments in 1992 and negotiated a package of constitutional reforms (the so-called Charlottetown Accord), reform of the Bank of Canada Act was dropped from consideration. Whether it will regain urgency in the future remains to be seen.

*Sources:* David Laidler, *How Shall We Govern the Governor? A Critique of the Governance of the Bank of Canada* (Toronto: C. D. Howe Institute, 1990); Peter Howitt, "Reform of the Bank of Canada and Harmonization of Macroeconomic Policies," in R. W. Boadway and D. D. Purvis, eds., *Policy Forum on the Economic Aspects of the Federal Government's Constitutional Proposals* (Kingston: John Deutsch Institute for Economic Policy, Queen's University, 1991), pp. 39–59; *Canadian Federalism and Economic Union: Partnership for Prosperity* (Ottawa: Minister of Supply and Services, 1991).

companies (the latter two are federally or provincially licensed rather than chartered) are also members of the CPA and are able to have their deposits insured by the CDIC.

Thus, the chartered banks are subject to a variety of regulations. The superintendent of financial institutions, the Bank of Canada and the CDIC all share the job of supervision. In spite of this system, the major bankruptcies in 1985 of Canadian Commercial Bank and Northlands Bank raised questions about the adequacy of bank regulation.

## CREATING MONEY IN MODERN ECONOMIES

In order to understand how the Bank of Canada goes about its task of controlling the money supply, we need to know more about how a bank runs its busi-

ness, particularly how banks create deposits, or money. The money supply of today is created not by a mint or printing press but largely by the banking system. When you put money into the bank, the bank does not simply take the currency down to its vault, put it into a little slot marked with your name, and keep it there until you are ready to take it out. Instead, banks realize that not all their thousands of depositors will withdraw their money on any given day. Some will come by next week, some in two weeks, some not for a year or more. In the meantime, the bank can lend out the money deposited in its vault and charge interest. The more money the bank can persuade people to deposit, the more can be lent out and thus the more money the bank will earn. To attract depositors, the bank pays interest on its deposits, effectively passing on (after taking its cut) the interest earned on its loans.

How much can safely be lent out? Money retained by a bank in case those who have deposited money want it back is called its **reserves.** How much needs to be kept as reserves? Should the bank keep reserves of 5 percent of deposits? 20 percent of deposits? The less it keeps as reserves, the more money it can earn, but the greater the possibility that it will not have enough funds on hand if a large number of depositors want their deposits back at the same time. To understand how these reserves work and how they affect the supply of money and credit available in the economy, we need to take a close look at the typical bank's balance sheet.

## A BANK'S BALANCE SHEET

Bankers see the world backwards. Where else would loans be called "assets" and deposits be called "liabilities"? This is the perspective shown on a bank's **balance sheet.** Like any firm's balance sheet, it describes the bank's **assets** and **liabilities.** Assets are what the firm owns, including what is owed to it by others. That is why the bank's loans appear as assets on its balance sheet. Liabilities are what it owes to others. We can think of the bank's depositors as having loaned money to the bank. They can get their money back when they wish. That is why deposits are treated by the bank as liabilities.

Table 13.1 shows the balance sheet of Maple Leaf Bank. Its assets are divided into three categories: loans outstanding, government bonds, and reserves, including cash in the vault. Least secure are the loans outstanding. These consist of loans to business firms, real estate loans (mortgages), car loans, house-

remodelling loans, and so on. Government bonds are more secure than loans to households or firms. Most banks' holdings of government bonds are typically concentrated in Treasury bills (or T-bills), short-term bonds maturing in thirty, sixty, or ninety days after the date of issue.[1] Most secure are the banks' reserves. These are held in two forms: deposits, or clearing deposits, held at the "banker's bank," the Bank of Canada, and the cash in the vault. The amount of reserves the banks choose to hold is of crucial importance for determining the amount of deposits in the banking system and thus the money supply.

On any given day, thousands of a bank's customers will be engaging in transactions involving their deposits in the bank. Some will be reducing their deposits by writing cheques or making withdrawals; others will be depositing cheques or cash into their accounts. On balance, the bank may end up having to pay out funds at the end of the day or it may be a net recipient. It does not know in advance. In Chapter 7 we explained that the amount of money people need to set aside for a rainy day depends in part on how easily they can borrow and at what cost. The same is true for banks. They can borrow to meet any shortfall of reserves, but the higher the interest rate, the more costly it is for them to be left short of funds and the more reserves they will want to hold. Banks can borrow either from the financial markets or from the Bank of Canada. Borrowing from financial markets to meet day-to-day shortfalls of reserves involves short-term borrowing. Banks do so on what is referred to as the **overnight market,** the market specializing in one-day (overnight) loans. The price of borrowing on the overnight market is referred to as the **overnight interest rate.** The alternative is to borrow from the Bank of Canada, where they are charged the **bank rate,** the rate of interest charged by the Bank of Canada to the chartered banks. Most of the banks' borrowing for short-term cash management is on the overnight market, since the bank rate is typically higher than the overnight interest rate.

The upshot is that the banks determine how many reserves of cash and clearing balances to hold

## Table 13.1 MAPLE LEAF BANK'S BALANCE SHEET

| Assets ($ millions) | | Liabilities ($ millions) | |
| --- | --- | --- | --- |
| Loans outstanding | 56 | Deposits | 60 |
| Government bonds | 6 | | |
| Reserves | 3 | Net worth | 5 |
| Total | 65 | Total | 65 |

[1] Long-term bonds are volatile in price, because their price changes with changes in interest rates. Banks typically hold short-term government bonds because the risk of such changes over a relatively short period of time is low, and banks wish to avoid risk.

on the basis of what they think they need for meeting possible shortfalls of funds on days when their customers are drawing down their deposits overall, and of what the cost of borrowing happens to be, the interest rate on overnight funds. The banks are also somewhat constrained by the Bank Act as to the amount of reserves they must hold as deposits in the Bank of Canada. Each bank's holdings of clearing balances must average at least zero over each month.[2] These clearing balances earn no interest so banks would prefer not to hold too many of them. But if banks hold too few reserves, they face the possibility that not only will a shortfall cause them to have to borrow to meet their cash requirements, but they will also have to hold extra reserves to ensure that their average monthly holdings are at least zero. In practice, the banks do hold significant amounts of reserves. Table 13.2 shows the holding of reserves by the chartered banks as a whole for a typical month. It indicates that in the month of July 1995, banks held reserves of almost 4 percent of their nonterm deposits, deposits that could be withdrawn without notice. The system of banking in which banks hold a fraction of the amount of their deposits as reserves is called the **fractional reserve system.**

The liability side of Maple Leaf Bank's balance sheet consists of two items: deposits and net worth. Deposits are what the bank owes to its customers; net worth is what it "owes" to its shareholders. Deposits can take on a variety of forms: these include chequing accounts, which are technically known as demand deposits, and the variety of forms of savings accounts, which are technically known as time deposits. The bank's net worth is the difference between the value of its assets and the value of its liabilities. If the bank's assets were sold and its depositors paid off, what remained would be the net worth of the bank.

---

[2] Prior to 1992, the Bank Act imposed reserve requirements on the banks. Banks had to hold 10 percent of their demand deposits as reserves (cash and deposits in the Bank of Canada). The Bank Act of 1992 phased out reserve requirements, partly because as near banks competed more and more with banks for deposits, the banks argued that they were placed at a competitive disadvantage by reserve requirements that are not imposed on the near banks. Now the level of reserves held by banks is determined mainly by what the banks regard as prudent, given that it is costly for the bank to borrow if it runs short of cash.

**Table 13.2 RESERVES OF THE CHARTERED BANKS AS OF JULY 1995**

| | $ Millions | |
|---|---|---|
| Reserves (cash and deposits in the Bank of Canada) | | 3,799 |
| Chequing deposits in the banks | 56,110 | |
| Nonchequable savings deposits | 44,305 | |
| Total nonterm deposits | | 100,415 |
| Reserves as percentage of deposits | | 3.8% |

*Source: Bank of Canada Review*, Autumn 1995, Tables C1 and C2.

Since net worth is *defined* as the difference between the value of the liabilities and the value of the assets, it should be clear that the numbers on both sides of the balance sheet should balance.

## HOW BANKS CREATE MONEY

As we have seen, the coins and currency manufactured by the Royal Canadian Mint are a relatively small part of the money supply. Who creates the rest of the money? Banks do.

To see how banks create money, let's consider all the Canadian banks as one huge superbank. Assume that this bank decides that its reserves will be kept at 10 percent of deposits. Now suppose that a multibillionaire deposits $1 billion in currency in his account.

The bank reasons as follows. It wants to keep a reserve-to-deposit ratio of 1:10 and has a long line of loan applicants. When the bank makes a loan, it credits the borrower with funds in her chequing account; it does not actually give her currency. It does this by placing an entry into its books on both the left- and right-hand side of the ledger: there is a loan on the asset side and a deposit on the liability side. If it makes $9 billion worth of loans, its liabilities will have gone up $10 billion (the $1 billion originally deposited by the multibillionaire plus the $9 billion worth of loans). On the asset side, the bank takes the $1 billion in currency to the Bank of Canada and is credited with the amount in its clearing balances, so that it now has $1 billion in reserves. Thus, its reserves have increased by $1 billion, its deposits by $10 billion; it has satisfied its desired reserve holdings.

We can reach the same result by a slower route, as shown in Table 13.3. The bank might reason, now that its deposits have gone up by $1 billion, that it must keep $100 million of it in the Bank of Canada as a reserve. But it can lend out the remaining $900 million (.9 × $1 billion). This is the first-round balance sheet that appears in the table. Deposits have increased $1 billion, loans have increased $.9 billion, and reserves have increased $.1 billion.

For simplicity, let's assume that the loan is all made to one customer: Desktop Publishing borrows $900 million so that it can purchase new computers from Computer Canada. When Desktop pays $900 million for the computers, Computer Canada deposits the money in its account. Thus, the loan of $900 million is reflected in the addition of $900 million in deposits. This is shown on the right-hand side of the second-round balance sheet in the table, where deposits have now risen from $101 billion to $101.9 billion.

But with the $900 million additional deposits, the bank is allowed to increase its lending by .9 × $900 million, or $810 million, putting $90 million into reserves. These changes are shown in the left-hand side of the second-round balance sheet. Assume that all $810 million is lent out to various companies, each of which uses the money to purchase new goods. In each case, some other firm will sell its goods and will put these new funds into the superbank. As a result, new deposits at the superbank will again grow by $810 million. As the third round begins, deposits are once again increased.

But the bank is still not in equilibrium. Because of the increase in deposits of $810 million, it can lend out .9 × $810 million = $729 million. And so the process continues. Notice that on each round, the increase in deposits is smaller than in the previous round. In the second round, the increase in deposits was $900 million, in the third round $810 million, and so on. The after-deposit equilibrium balance sheet in the last part of the table shows that the bank has increased its deposits by ten times the original deposit ($100 billion to $110 billion) and increased

its lending by nine times the original deposit ($91 billion to $100 billion). The $1 billion injection into the banking system has turned into a $10 billion increase in the money supply.

In the new situation, the banking system is in equilibrium. Its reserves of $11 billion are precisely equal to 10 percent of its $110 billion deposit. It cannot lend out any more without violating its desired **reserve ratio.**

In this way, any new deposit into the banking system results in a multiple expansion of the number of deposits. This is the "miracle" of the fractional reserve system. Deposits increase by a factor of 1/reserve ratio. In the superbank example, the desired reserve ratio was 10 percent; 1/reserve ratio is 1/.1, or 10. If the desired reserve ratio had been 5 percent, deposits would have increased by 1/.05, or 20. Note that as the deposits increased, so did the supply of outstanding loans.

In this example, there were no "leakages" outside the system: no one decided to hold currency rather than put her money back into the bank. Whenever sellers were paid, they put what they received into the bank. With leakages, the increase in deposits and thus the increase in money will be smaller. In the real world, these leakages are large; the ratio of M1 to reserves is around 15, much smaller than the reciprocal of the reserve ratio reported in Table 13.2. Nevertheless, the increase in bank reserves will lead to some multiple increase in the money supply. This relationship between the change in reserves and the final change in deposits is called the **money multiplier.**[3]

### MONEY MULTIPLIERS WITH MANY BANKS

The money multiplier works just as well when there is more than one bank involved. Assume that Desktop Publishing and Computer Canada have their bank accounts in separate banks, Prairie Bank and Maritime Bank. When Desktop Publishing writes a cheque for $900 million to Computer Canada, $900 million is transferred from Prairie Bank to Maritime

---

[3] This multiplier should not be confused with the multiplier introduced in Chapter 9. That multiplier showed that an increase in investment or government expenditures leads to a multiple increase in the equilibrium level of aggregate expenditures. There are clearly some similarities in the way we go about calculating these multipliers.

## Table 13.3 SUPERBANK BALANCE SHEET

| Before-deposit equilibrium | | | |
|---|---|---|---|
| **Assets** | | **Liabilities** | |
| Loans outstanding | $ 91 billion | Deposits | $100 billion |
| Government bonds | 2 billion | | |
| Reserves | 10 billion | Net worth | 3 billion |
| Total | 103 billion | Total | 103 billion |

| First round (Add $1 billion deposits, $.9 billion loans) | | | |
|---|---|---|---|
| **Assets** | | **Liabilities** | |
| Loans outstanding | $ 91.9 billion | Deposits | $101 billion |
| Government bonds | 2.0 billion | | |
| Reserves | 10.1 billion | Net worth | 3 billion |
| Total | 104.0 billion | Total | 104 billion |

| Second round (Add $.9 billion deposits, $.81 billion loans to previous round*) | | | |
|---|---|---|---|
| **Assets** | | **Liabilities** | |
| Loans outstanding | $ 92.71 billion | Deposits | $101.9 billion |
| Government bonds | 2.00 billion | | |
| Reserves | 10.19 billion | Net worth | 3.0 billion |
| Total | 104.90 billion | Total | 104.9 billion |

| Third round (Add $.81 billion deposits, $.73 billion loans to previous round*) | | | |
|---|---|---|---|
| **Assets** | | **Liabilities** | |
| Loans outstanding | $ 93.44 billion | Deposits | $102.71 billion |
| Government bonds | 2.00 billion | | |
| Reserves | 10.27 billion | Net worth | 3.00 billion |
| Total | 105.71 billion | Total | 105.71 billion |

| After-deposit equilibrium (Add $10 billion new deposits, $9 billion new loans to original equilibrium) | | | |
|---|---|---|---|
| **Assets** | | **Liabilities** | |
| Loans outstanding | $100 billion | Deposits | $110 billion |
| Government bonds | 2 billion | | |
| Reserves | 11 billion | Net worth | 3 billion |
| Total | 113 billion | Total | 113 billion |

*In each subsequent round, new deposits equal new loans of the previous round; new loans equal .9 × new deposits.

We have seen that today most money is created within the banking system, but this has not always been the case. When money consisted primarily of gold and silver, the money supply was determined by accidents of fate: the discovery of new sources of these metals. The discovery of the New World, for instance, with its stocks of gold and silver, greatly increased the money supply of Europe in the sixteenth and seventeenth centuries.

With the advent of fiat money, expansion of the money supply was a government decision: How fast should the printing presses be run? When the government's revenues fell short of its expenditures and it could not borrow or found borrowing to be too expensive, it paid for expenditures with newly printed money.

In the early days of colonization and settlement of Canada, money consisted of various gold and silver coins, referred to as "specie." Much of it was sent by the imperial government to pay for both the military and the civil administration. Other coins, such as Spanish and American silver dollars, French louis d'or, and johannes from Portugal, were acquired in trade.

The system worked reasonably well in normal times. But sometimes cash-flow crises occurred when the coin sent from the imperial government in Europe to the colonial government arrived late or was insufficient to meet extraordinary expenditure requirements, especially during times of war. Two episodes illustrate the problem, one under the French regime and one under the British.

In 1685, the government of the colony of New France did not receive its supply of silver coin from France until September. In order to finance

expenditures such as supplies and soldiers' wages within the colony, the government was forced to be inventive—it issued cut-up playing cards bearing the signatures of senior administrators. These were declared legal tender and redeemable in coin or bills once the shipment came in from France. This playing-card monetary regime was eventually accepted by the colonials, who developed confidence in the government's promise to redeem the cards and who recognized the convenience and the advantages of the system. The money was light, easy to produce, and less costly than shipping coin. It was also reliable, and it stayed within the colony as it was useless elsewhere. The paper money was supposed to be backed by coins that arrived from France each autumn, but confidence in it was lost when, during the war with the English between 1749 and 1759, more paper money was issued than could be redeemed. When the British took Quebec in 1759, they promptly removed the French paper money from circulation, leaving coins as the only currency.

The British colonial government was reluctant to issue monetary notes, as it viewed the playing-card episode in New France as a failure. But the specie system was unable to cope with the demand for funds to finance its expenditures in the War of 1812. Britain was preoccupied with Napoleon in Europe and could not afford to send to Canada adequate funds to cover soldiers' wages, munitions, and fortifications. The result was a cash-flow crisis in British North America.

At the time, the colonial government did not have seigniorage powers (the power to mint money). Its budget was decided overseas, and the monies were shipped as the imperial government saw fit. Domestic and international capital markets were unsophisticated and were not accessible for borrowing as they are today. The response of Sir Isaac Brock, the colonial administrator and commander of the British forces against the Americans in the War of 1812, was to issue paper money referred to as "army bills" to pay for the war. The money was issued in various denominations, redeemable in coin at the government's discretion. An interest rate of 4 percent was paid on bills of $25 and over. The war was short, so the government did not overextend itself, but redeemed the army bills in 1814 at full value plus interest. The experiment was considered a success, since the funds crisis had been resolved and the notes had served as a convenient temporary medium of exchange. Confidence was restored in paper money, paving the way for its issue by the commercial banks shortly after the war ended.

The convenience of note issuance motivated the government to allow private banks to issue their own bank notes, convertible into gold coin. Two of the first to do so, around 1820, were the Bank of Montreal and the Bank of Nova Scotia. Private banks enjoyed sovereignty, as they profited greatly from the practice. The government finally introduced Dominion Notes in 1867. Private bank notes were convertible either into Dominion Notes or directly into specie, and Dominion Notes were convertible into specie.

Convertibility of notes to gold was suspended during World War I, but the gold standard did not break down until 1929. During the years of the Great Depression (1929–33), Canada, along with most of the nations in the international system, experienced serious deflation. Lenders like deflation: they prefer to be paid back with dollars that are worth more than they were at the time the loan was made. By the same token, debtors dislike deflation, for it means they have to pay off their loans with money that is worth more. Thus farmers and others who are in debt are often at odds with the banks to which they owe money. In deflationary times, this conflict is often resolved in the debtors' favour by printing money and inflating the economy, even when the government cannot afford to convert its entire money supply into its existing stock of gold. Such was the situation during the Great Depression, after the final breakdown of the gold standard in 1929.

*Sources:* H. H. Binhammer, *Money, Banking and the Canadian Financial System,* 5th ed. (Scarborough, Ontario: Nelson Canada, 1988); Norman E. Cameron, *Money, Financial Markets and Economic Activity,* 2nd ed. (Don Mills, Ontario: Addison-Wesley, 1992).

Bank. Once that $900 million had been transferred, Maritime Bank will find that it can lend more than it could previously. As a result of the $900 million increase in deposits, it can lend .9 × $900 = $810 million. Suppose it lends the $810 million to the New Telephone Company, which uses the money to buy a machine for making telephones from Equipment Manufacturing. If Equipment Manufacturing has its bank account at Pacific Bank, after Equipment Manufacturing has been paid, Pacific Bank will find that because its deposits have increased by $810 million, it can lend .9 × $810 = $729 million. The process continues, until the new equilibrium is identical to the one described earlier in the superbank example, where there is a $10 billion increase in the money supply. The banking system as a whole will have expanded the money supply by a multiple of the initial deposit, equal to 1/reserve ratio.

It should be clear that when there are many banks, no individual bank can create multiple deposits. Individual banks may not even be aware of the role they play in the process of multiple-deposit creation; all they see is that their reserves have increased and that therefore they are able to make more loans.

The process of multiple-deposit creation may

## MONEY MULTIPLIER

An increase in reserves leads to an increase in total deposits by a multiple of the original increase.

seem somewhat like a magician pulling rabbits out of a hat: it seems to make something out of nothing. But it is, in fact, a real physical process. Deposits are created by making entries in records; today electronic impulses create records on computer tapes. The rules of deposit creation are rules specifying when you may make certain entries in the books. It is these rules—in particular, the fractional reserve ratio adopted by the banks—that give rise to the system's ability to create multiple deposits.

## THE FOUR INSTRUMENTS OF MONETARY POLICY

Most changes in the money supply are not the result of someone depositing a billion dollars of currency in a bank. Instead, they are the result of actions by the Bank of Canada, which influences the amount of reserves in the banks with the aim of changing the supply of money and credit. By such action the Bank affects the level of economic activity. The connections between the actions the Bank takes and their effect on the level of economic activity are the subjects of the next two chapters. Here, our concern is simply with the supply of money and credit. Money and credit, as we have seen, represent two sides of a bank's balance sheet. When deposits (money) increase, either bank loans (credit) or bank holdings of government debt must increase. Frequently both will. Though ultimately our concern will be with bank lending, bank lending is not directly under the control of the Bank of Canada, so the Bank must affect bank lending through the money supply. The Bank has various policy instruments with which it can affect the money supply and the availability of credit: drawdowns and redeposits, open-market operations, setting the bank rate, and moral suasion.

## DRAWDOWNS AND REDEPOSITS

The Bank of Canada can affect the money supply through changing the amount of reserves held by the banks. The most direct way to do that is by using drawdowns or redeposits. As we have mentioned, the Bank manages the federal government's accounts and decides in particular how to divide them between accounts in the banks and accounts with itself. If the Bank wishes to increase the level of reserves in the banks, it can transfer funds from a government account in the Bank of Canada to an account in one of the banks—a redeposit procedure. To pay for the money withdrawn on the government's behalf, the Bank increases the reserve deposits of the bank in the Bank of Canada (its clearing balance). This increase in bank reserves allows the bank to increase its loans, and the money multiplier goes to work. If the banks prefer to hold reserves of 5 percent of deposits, a redeposit of $10 million will ultimately generate new deposits of $200 million ($10 million/.05). Loans from the banking system will rise by $190 million.

Conversely, if the Bank wants to reduce the money supply and quantity of bank loans, it engages in a drawdown. It transfers government of Canada deposits from the banking system to itself. The banks must pay for the withdrawn deposit by reducing their clearing balances at the Bank of Canada. This will cause them to lower their loans, and the money multiplier then takes over in the banking system as a whole. Deposits fall by a multiple of the drawdown, and loans fall accordingly.

The use of drawdowns and redeposits is the main means by which the Bank of Canada influences bank reserves on a day-to-day basis. Ultimately, the objective is to influence the money supply and availability of credit. But in the end, the way in which the banks respond to changes in reserves is up to them, and that may be unpredictable. They may respond to an increase in reserves partly by increasing their reserve ratios rather than by expanding their loans to maintain their previous reserve ratio. For example, consider Superbank which currently holds 10 percent of its deposits as reserves. If the Bank of Canada increases its reserves by $100 million, rather than lending out $90 million and keeping $10 million as reserves, Superbank may lend out only $80 million, thereby causing its reserve ratio to rise. Given this uncertainty about how the banks will respond to changes in their reserves, the Bank may wish to employ some of the other instruments available to it.

## OPEN-MARKET OPERATIONS

One of the other instruments the Bank can use is open-market operations. As we have seen, open-market operations involve the Bank of Canada's entering financial markets directly to buy or sell government debt, either long-term debt (bonds) or short-term debt (Treasury bills). Imagine the Bank buys $1 million of Treasury bills from wealthy Joe Brown (or a thousand different Joe Brown families), paying him with a $1 million cheque payable by the Bank. Joe Brown takes the cheque down to his bank, Maple Leaf Bank, which credits his account with $1 million. Maple Leaf Bank then presents the cheque to the Bank of Canada, which credits the bank's reserve account with $1 million. Maple Leaf Bank now has $1 million of new deposits and $1 million in new reserves. Assuming that it prefers to hold only 5 percent of its deposits as reserves, it now lends out an additional $950,000. Once again, the money multiplier goes to work, as that loan gets deposited back in the banking system, making possible a second set of new loans, and so on. The total expansion of the money supply will be equal to a multiple of the initial $1 million increase in deposits. And credit—the amount of outstanding loans—has also increased by a multiple of the initial increase in deposits. Precisely the opposite occurs if the Bank sells Treasury bills on the open market. The purchaser of the T-bills will write a cheque against his account in a bank. When the Bank receives the cheque, it will be cleared by the bank by drawing down their reserve balances at the Bank of Canada. A multiple reduction of bank deposits and loans will ensue.

The purchase of T-bills from Joe Brown by the Bank of Canada has a quite different effect from a purchase of the same securities by a private citizen, Jill White. In the latter case, Jill White's deposit account goes down by $1 million, and Joe Brown's deposit account goes up by $1 million. The funds available in the system as a whole remain unchanged. The money multiplier goes to work only when the funds enter from "outside," and in particular from the Bank of Canada.

From the point of view of its effect on the reserves in the banking system, open-market purchases of T-bills by the Bank of Canada are equivalent to redeposits of government balances into the banks, and open-market sales are equivalent to a drawdown of government deposits from the banking system. Why does the Bank engage in both sorts of operations? One reason is that, by simply changing bank reserves, there is no guarantee that banks will want to change the credit they make available by as much as the Bank of Canada would like. Intervening on the market for short-term assets, including the overnight market, will allow the Bank to have some influence on short-term market interest rates. Open-market purchases of short-term assets will not only add reserves to the banking system but will also put downward pressure on interest rates, thereby not only causing the demand for credit to rise but also reducing the cost to the banks of running short of clearing balance reserves. Thus, the banks will be less willing to hold reserves and more inclined to expand their loans. A given increase in bank reserves will therefore give rise to greater lending by the banks. For this reason, the Bank often uses open-market operations in short-term assets to supplement drawdowns and redeposits when it wants to change the quantity of loans and deposits in the economy.

The Bank of Canada can conduct open-market operations using any type of government security, from long-run bonds to shorter-term assets like Treasury bills. In practice, the Bank engages in open-market operations in securities of different maturity for different reasons. While it tends to use purchases and sales of short-term securities as a supplement to drawdowns and redeposits as a way of getting more credit into the financial system in response to short-term needs, it uses open-market operations in government bonds with longer-term objectives in mind. For example, purchases or sales of government bonds are used for ensuring that the growth of the money supply over time is appropriate, given how the economy is developing.

## THE BANK RATE

A third possible instrument of monetary policy is a change in the bank rate. As explained earlier in this chapter, the Bank of Canada is called the banker's bank because it holds banks' deposits and banks can borrow from it. The interest rate the banks pay when they borrow directly from the Bank of Canada is called the bank rate. The higher the bank rate, the more expensive it is for the banks to borrow from the Bank of Canada in the event that they lose deposits. It might be expected that if the Bank of Canada raises the bank rate, banks would wish to increase their reserve-to-deposit ratio so as to reduce the chances that they would have to borrow from the bank. Moreover, they would likely want to charge higher interest rates to their customers. Thus, the amount of loans in the economy should fall.

In fact, banks infrequently borrow from the Bank of Canada. When they are short of reserves, the banks tend to borrow directly from the financial market, especially the overnight market. The reason is that the Bank of Canada typically sets the bank rate above the overnight interest rate. The bank rate therefore does not serve as a constraint on the

banks. Its role in monetary policy is a less direct one. The Bank of Canada uses changes in the bank rate to signal its intentions to the financial markets. An increase in the bank rate is a signal that the Bank intends to follow a more restrictive monetary policy, relying on drawdowns and/or open-market sales to reduce credit and put upward pressure on the short-term interest rate.

## MORAL SUASION

One final instrument that can be used by the Bank of Canada to influence monetary policy is referred to as **moral suasion.** In fact, moral suasion has little to do with morality as such. It is simply a term referring to the Bank of Canada's ability to persuade the banks to take certain actions that the Bank thinks would further the objectives of monetary policy at a given point in time. Moral suasion is possible because there are a relatively small number of banks in Canada, the banks are constantly in communication with the Bank of Canada, and the Bank of Canada wields a certain amount of implicit authority over the banks because of its role as a regulator and the fact that it can ultimately engage in open-market operations to achieve its objectives.

The object of the moral suasion can take a variety of forms. At one extreme it may simply involve the Bank of Canada's discussing with the banks its current monetary policy objectives. At the other, the Bank may wish the banks to take some specific action, such as changing the composition or size of their liabilities (deposits), or restricting some forms

---

### INSTRUMENTS OF MONETARY POLICY AVAILABLE TO THE BANK OF CANADA

**1** Drawdowns and redeposits: By transferring government of Canada accounts between itself and the chartered banks, the Bank can directly change the amount of reserves in the banking system and thus the money supply.

**2** Open-market operations: By buying and selling government securities, the Bank of Canada also changes the supply of reserves and thus the money supply. This can also affect interest rates in the economy.

**3** Bank rate changes: By changing the bank rate, the Bank signals its intent to financial markets; a higher bank rate indicates that the Bank wants to pursue a restrictive monetary policy, and vice versa.

**4** Moral suasion: By communicating directly to the banks, the Bank elicits their cooperation in achieving monetary policy objectives.

of lending. Given that moral suasion is not done publicly, it is not easy to assess how important or successful it has been in the past. Some have suggested that it is more important now than in the recent past because banks no longer have to maintain fixed reserve requirements, but instead are simply monitored by the Bank of Canada.

## SELECTING THE APPROPRIATE INSTRUMENT

Of the four instruments, drawdowns and redeposits, and open-market operations are the most effective. Changes in bank rates and moral suasion are viewed as blunt tools compared with the fine-tuning that open-market operations make possible. Changes in the bank rate, however, are used only to announce major shifts in monetary policy. Such changes can be quite effective in signalling tighter credit (changes in monetary policy that entail higher interest rates and reduced credit availability) or looser credit (changes in monetary policy that have the reverse effect). For instance, banks, foreseeing a tightening of credit, may cut back their lending, and firms may postpone investment plans.

## THE STABILITY OF THE CANADIAN BANKING SYSTEM

The fractional reserve system explains how banks create money, and it also explains how banks can get into trouble without the Bank of Canada. Even before the advent of the Bank of Canada, well-managed banks kept reserves equal to some average expectation of day-to-day needs. A bank could get into trouble in a hurry if one day's needs exceeded its reserves.

If (for good reasons or bad) many depositors lose confidence in a bank at the same time, they will attempt to withdraw their funds all at once. The bank simply will not have the money available, since most of the money will have been lent out in loans that cannot be called in instantaneously. This situation is called a **bank run.** Bank runs were common in nineteenth-century America, often depicted in the old Western movies, where customers in a small town would line up at the bank while it paid out what reserves it had on a first-come, first-served basis until there was no money left. Such a run could quickly drive even a healthy bank out of business. If a rumour spread that a bank was in trouble and a few savers ran to the bank to clean out their accounts, then other investors would feel they were foolish not to run down to the bank themselves and withdraw their deposits. One vicious rumour could result in a healthy bank's shutting down; the panic could set off a run on other banks, thus destabilizing the banking system and the whole local economy.

## THREE LEVELS OF PROTECTION OF THE BANKING SYSTEM

Bank runs and panics have periodically afflicted the banking system. They have been much more prevalent in the United States than in Canada, largely because of the branch banking system that exists in Canada. Large banks with many branches are able to share reserves and pool each other's risks more readily. Nonetheless, bank failures can occur, and when they do they can be quite traumatic both for the depositors and for the economy as a whole. As mentioned, one of the reasons why the Bank of Canada was set up was to make them less likely. There are three levels of protection.

First, the Bank of Canada acts as a "lender of last resort." If a bank faces a run, it can turn to the Bank to borrow funds to tide it over. Knowing that the bank can meet its obligations means that there is no need to run to the bank. In fact, the banks rarely have to resort to loans from the Bank of Canada. However, if another serious depression came along, that safeguard would always exist. The safeguard can only be effective as long as each bank's assets exceed its liabilities—as long as it is solvent. The objective of the next two levels of protection is to ensure that banks are in fact solvent.

The second level of protection is provided by the owners of the bank. Most banks are started by investors who put up a certain amount of money in exchange for a share of ownership. The net worth of the firm—the difference between the bank's assets and its liabilities—is this initial investment, augmented or decreased over time by the bank's profits or losses. If the bank makes bad investment decisions, then these shareholders can be forced to bear the cost. This cushion provided by shareholders not only protects depositors, it also encourages the bank to be more prudent in its loans. If the bank makes bad loans, the owners risk their entire investment. But if the owners' net worth in the bank is too small, the owners may see themselves in a "Heads I win, tails you lose" situation. If risky investments turn out well, the extra profits accrue to the bank; if they turn out badly, the bank goes bankrupt, but since the owners had little at stake, they have little to lose. To protect against this danger, the government through the Bank Act requires banks to maintain certain ratios of net worth to assets. These are called **capital adequacy requirements.** Capital adequacy requirements protect against insolvency; they mean that if the bank invests badly and many of its loans default, the bank will still be able to pay back its depositors. By contrast, reserves and the ability to borrow from the Bank protect against illiquidity; they ensure that if depositors want cash, they can get it.

As a third and final backstop, the banks are required to insure each depositor for up to $60,000 with the Canada Deposit Insurance Corporation (CDIC). In fact, the CDIC insures all deposit-taking institutions in Canada. Since deposits are guaranteed by the CDIC, depositors fearing the collapse of a financial institution have no need to rush to it. The deposit insurance thus not only protects depositors but also has an enormous impact in increasing the stability of the banking system. The effectiveness of deposit insurance lies in the fact of its existence: the threat against which it insures is much less likely to occur. It is as if life insurance somehow prolonged life.

Deposit insurance has an offsetting disadvantage, however. Depositors no longer have any incentive to monitor financial institutions, to make sure that they are investing funds safely. Regardless of what the institution does with depositors' funds, the funds are protected. Thus, to the extent that capital adequacy requirements fail to provide financial institutions with appropriate incentives to make good loans, regulators must assume the full responsibility of ensuring the safety and soundness of financial institutions.

Chapter 14 takes a closer look at the relations between monetary policy, the financial position of banks, money and credit, and the level of economic activity.

## REVIEW AND PRACTICE

### SUMMARY

**1** Money is anything that is generally accepted in a given society as a medium of exchange, store of value, and unit of account.

**2** There are many ways of measuring the money supply, which have names like M1, M2, M3, and M2+. All include both currency and chequing accounts. They differ in what they include as assets that are close substitutes to currency and chequing accounts.

**3** A buyer does not need money to purchase a good, at least not right away, if the seller or a financial institution is willing to extend credit.

**4** Financial intermediaries, which include banks, trust and mortgage loan companies, credit unions and caisses populaires, insurance companies, and others, all have in common that they form the link between savers who have extra funds and borrowers who desire extra funds.

**5** Government is involved with the banking industry for two reasons. First, by regulating the activities banks can undertake and providing deposit insurance, government seeks to protect depositors and ensure the stability of the financial system. Second, by influencing the willingness of banks to make loans, government attempts to influence the level of investment and overall economic activity.

**6** By making loans, banks can create an increase in the supply of money that is a multiple of an initial increase in the banks' deposits. If every bank lent all the money it could while maintaining its existing reserve ratio and every dollar lent were spent to buy goods from other firms that deposited the cheque in their account, the money multiplier would be a fraction: 1/the reserve ratio chosen by the banks. In practice, the money multiplier could be considerably smaller than that fraction, because banks may not lend as much as their existing reserve ratio would allow.

**7** The Bank of Canada can affect the money supply by transferring federal government deposits between itself and the banks (drawdowns and redeposits) or by open-market operations. It can also influence the behaviour of banks by moral suasion and by changing the bank rate.

**8** Bank runs are rare because the Bank of Canada acts as a lender of last resort, because capital adequacy requirements are imposed on banks, and because deposits are insured by the Canada Deposit Insurance Corporation. However, the structure of deposit insurance can encourage financial institutions to take more risks than they might otherwise.

## KEY TERMS

| | | | |
|---|---|---|---|
| medium of exchange | demand deposits | unitary banking | money multiplier |
| double coincidence of wants | M1, M2, M3, M2+ | settlement balances | reserve ratio |
| | near banks | drawdown | bank rate |
| store of value | financial intermediaries | redeposit | moral suasion |
| unit of account | central bank | open-market operations | capital adequacy requirements |
| money | branch banking | reserves | |

## REVIEW QUESTIONS

**1** What are the three characteristics that define money?

**2** What are the differences between M1, M2, M3, and M2+?

**3** When consumers or businesses desire to make a large purchase, are they limited to spending only as much as the M1 money that they have on hand? Explain.

**4** What is the Bank of Canada?

**5** What are the two main reasons for government involvement in the banking system?

**6** In what ways can the Bank of Canada reduce the money supply?

**7** What has the government done to make bank runs less likely?

## PROBLEMS

**1** Identify which of money's three traits each of the following assets possesses, and which traits the asset does not possess:
  (a) a house
  (b) a day pass for an amusement park
  (c) German marks held by a resident of Montreal
  (d) a painting
  (e) gold

**2** How might bank depositors be protected by legal prohibitions on banks' entering businesses like insurance, or selling and investing in stocks or venture capital? What are the possible costs and benefits of such prohibitions for depositors and for the government?

**3** Down Home Trust Company has the following assets and liabilities: $6 million in government bonds and reserves; $40 million in deposits; $36 million in outstanding loans. Draw up a balance sheet for the company. What is its net worth?

**4** What factors might affect the value of a bank's loan portfolio? If these factors are changing, explain how this would complicate the job of a bank examiner trying to ascertain the bank's net worth. Why would the bank examiner be concerned about the value of the net worth?

**5** While gardening in his backyard, Lucky Bob finds a mason jar containing $100,000 in currency. After he deposits the money in his lucky bank, where the reserve ratio is .05, how much will the money supply eventually increase?

**6** Why is it that if the Bank of Canada sells government bonds the money supply changes, but if a big company sells government bonds (to anyone other than the Bank) the money supply does not change?

**7** "So long as the Bank of Canada stands ready to lend to any bank with a positive net worth, requiring banks to maintain a minimum ratio of reserves to deposits is unnecessary. What underlies the stability of the banking system is the central bank's role as a lender of last resort, combined with policies aimed at ensuring the financial viability of the banks—for instance, the net worth requirements." Comment.

# 14

# MONETARY
# THEORY

I n Chapter 13 we saw the close link between the creation of money and the availability of credit (loans). This chapter explains why the money supply and the availability of credit are important to the economy. Knowing this, we can understand monetary policy, the collection of measures aimed at affecting the money supply and the availability of credit.

Changes in the money supply and in the availability of credit are really two sides of the same coin. We begin by looking at the direct effects of the Bank of Canada's activities on the money supply, then turn to its effects on credit availability.

## KEY QUESTIONS

**1** What determines the demand for money? How and why does it depend on the interest rate and the level of income?

**2** How is the demand for money equilibrated to the supply of money?

**3** What are the consequences of changes in the supply of money when prices are fixed? When does a change in the supply of money lead to a change in real output? When does it largely lead to a change in the amount of money that individuals are willing to hold?

**4** What are the channels through which monetary policy affects the economy? What role is played by changes in the real interest rate? the availability of credit? the exchange rate?

## MONEY SUPPLY AND ECONOMIC ACTIVITY

In this chapter we continue with our assumption that the price level is fixed. (Recall that if prices are completely flexible, changes in the money supply elicit proportionate changes in the price level, leaving the real stock of money unchanged.) When prices are fixed, if the Bank of Canada increases the money supply, there are only two possible results. First, people who get the additional money could just hold on to it. Their bank balances would grow, but nothing would happen to the rest of the economy. In this case, monetary policy will be relatively ineffective—an outcome that is most likely when the economy is in a deep recession. Second, those who get the additional money could spend it. If the economy has excess capacity and prices are fixed, this spending will increase aggregate expenditures. Incomes and output will increase.

What actually happens when the money supply is increased is some combination of changed holdings of money and changed output. One of the purposes of this chapter is to understand the circumstances under which each of these effects predominates.

In Chapter 13, we learned several different ways of measuring the money supply—M1, M2, M3, and M2+. For much of our discussion of money we do not have to be precise about which definition we have in mind. But it is natural to focus our attention on M1, for two reasons. First, M1 is the supply of money most directly under the control of the Bank. It is through the banking system that monetary policy has its most direct impact. M2 and M3 include such items as money market mutual fund balances which are not directly related to the banking system. Second, our primary focus here is on money's role as a medium of exchange. Money facilitates transactions. M1, which includes chequing accounts and currency, is the definition of money most directly related to its use as a medium of exchange.

Within M1, we will often focus on the portion most directly under the Bank's control: demand deposits and other chequing account deposits. This is also appropriate because they are the most important components of M1, accounting for about 60 percent of the M1 total.

### THE VELOCITY OF MONEY

The speed with which money circulates in the economy, its **velocity,** is as important to monetary policy as the money supply itself. In a bustling city, where money changes hands quickly, a given money supply supports many more transactions than in a depressed city where people do not make exchanges as often. If individuals as a whole keep money under the mattress for weeks after they have been paid, money may circulate very slowly. The velocity of money is formally defined as the ratio of nominal GDP to the money supply. If $Y$ represents the quantity of final goods and services produced in the economy and $P$ is a weighted average of their prices (the price level), $PY$ is equal to

## USING ECONOMICS: CALCULATING VELOCITY

To see how velocity is calculated, use the identity velocity, $V$ = nominal income, $PY$ divided by the money supply, $M$, and assume that $PY$ = $600 billion per year and $M$ = $100 billion. In this case, $V$ is 6 per year. If producing one dollar of output required only one transaction, the average dollar would have to circulate six times every year to produce output (income) of $600 billion. If $M$ were only $50 billion, every dollar would have to circulate twelve times per year (a velocity of 12) or twice as fast, for a national output (income) of $600 billion.

nominal GDP (which, as we know, equals aggregate income). Using the symbol $V$ to denote velocity and $M$ as the money supply, we get

$$V = PY/M.$$

Let's use the velocity equation to look at what happens when the money supply increases. If $M$ increases, and the price level is fixed, either $V$ must be lowered, or $Y$ must increase. This matches the possible consequences of an increase in the money supply with which we began the chapter. Either individuals may hold the extra money, which would decrease velocity, or the amount bought, $Y$, may increase.

The essential problem of monetary theory is to understand when each of these outcomes will result. When the *only* effect is on money holdings, monetary policy is completely ineffective in stimulating aggregate output and employment. But if there is *some* effect on output as well, then monetary policy can be a useful instrument in stimulating the economy. It may take a large dose of the medicine—a large increase in the money supply—to achieve any desired goal, but it can be done. To answer the question of when individuals will tend to hold any additional supply of money rather than spend it, we have to understand the determinants of the demand for money.

## THE DEMAND FOR MONEY

The velocity of money depends on how willing people are to hold, or keep, money. Because currency is an asset that bears no interest, it is like a hot potato—there are strong incentives to pass it along.

Preferring to earn interest, people have an incentive to exchange currency for either goods or an interest-bearing asset like a Treasury bill. The only reason to hold currency is its convenience. You can buy groceries with currency, but not with a T-bill, unless you convert your T-bill back to currency, which incurs transaction costs.

### THE EFFECT OF INTEREST RATES

People's willingness to hold money is a result of their balancing the benefits of holding money—the convenience—against the *opportunity cost*, the forgone interest, which could have been earned if the money in your chequing account or in your pocket had been invested in some other asset. If chequing deposits pay interest of 0 percent and very short-term government bonds (Treasury bills) pay 4 percent, then the cost of holding money is 4 percent per year. Today some chequing accounts pay interest, so the opportunity cost of holding funds in them is lower than it used to be. Nevertheless, the difference between the interest paid on chequing accounts and the return to other assets of similar risk deters people from holding money. We focus on the interest rate paid on T-bills for a simple reason: they are just as safe as money. The only difference is that T-bills yield a higher interest rate, but money is better as a medium of exchange.

The demand for money is much like the demand for any other good: it depends on the price. The nominal interest rate ($i$) the individual could have earned on a government bond can be thought of as the price of money, since it measures the opportunity cost of holding money. As the nominal interest

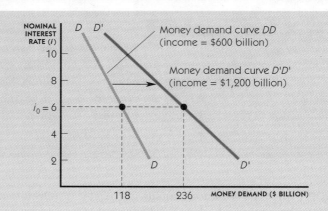

### Figure 14.1 DEMAND CURVE FOR MONEY

The quantity demanded of money falls as the opportunity cost of holding funds—that is, the nominal interest rate—increases. An increase in income causes a shift in the money demand function from $DD$ to $D'D'$.

rate rises, the amount of money demanded declines, as shown in Figure 14.1.

### THE EFFECT OF INCOME

The benefits of holding money are related to money's use as a medium of exchange. The more transactions people engage in, the more money they will want to hold. The demand for money arising from its use in facilitating transactions is called the **transactions demand for money.** This demand for money rises with *nominal* income: higher incomes mean that the value of goods bought will be greater, which implies that the value of transactions will be greater. In fact, the demand for money increases proportionately with the nominal value of output, $PY$: if prices double, then—other things being equal—people will need to have twice the amount of money to engage in the same transactions. This is illustrated in Table 14.1, which shows a hypothetical example. Figure 14.1 shows that an increase in income shifts the demand curve to the right. With an income level of $600 billion, the demand for money is given by the curve on the left. The table and figure illustrate the two basic properties of the demand for money. It decreases as the interest rate rises, and it increases at a fixed interest rate in proportion to income. Doubling the income level to $1,200 billion at any fixed interest rate shifts the demand curve for money out.

In equilibrium and if for the moment we assume that the economy is not a small open one, the interest

### Table 14.1 DEMAND FOR MONEY

| Nominal interest rate | Money demand for income of | |
|---|---|---|
| | $600 billion | $1,200 billion |
| | ($ billions) | |
| 2% | $124 | $248 |
| 4% | 121 | 242 |
| 6% | 118 | 236 |
| 8% | 115 | 230 |
| 10% | 112 | 224 |

rate adjusts to make the demand for money equal the supply. Figure 14.2 shows supply curves for money as well as a demand curve. The supply of money is controlled by the government (the Bank of Canada), through the instruments described in Chapter 13. The amount of money the Bank makes available does not depend at all on the interest rate. That is why the supply curves are vertical. The equilibrium interest rate with money supply $M_0$ is $i_0$.

The principles described in this section—that the nominal interest rate is the opportunity cost of holding money, that the demand for money decreases

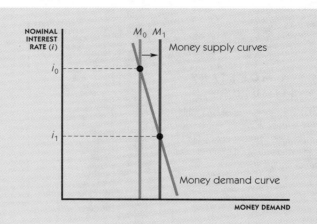

**Figure 14.2 EQUILIBRIUM INTEREST RATES**

The interest rate adjusts to make the demand for money equal the supply. In this diagram, a government-induced shift in the supply of money from $M_0$ to $M_1$ has a large effect on the interest rate, since the demand for money is relatively inelastic with respect to the interest rate.

as the interest rate rises, and that the interest rate is determined to equate the demand and supply of money—are together sometimes called **Keynesian monetary theory** or, sometimes, **traditional monetary theory.** Keynes used this theory to explain how monetary policy works when it works, and why it sometimes does not work. To do this, he traced out the effects of a change in the supply of money on the interest rate, the effects of a change in the interest rate on investment, and the effects of a change in investment on the level of national income.

The Keynesian theory was developed in an era when much less attention was devoted to international financial markets. It relied on the ability of monetary policy to influence domestic interest rates. However, as we have seen in Chapter 8, a highly open economy like ours may face an interest rate that is determined on international capital markets. In these circumstances, a change in the money supply will not affect the interest rate. Instead, it will cause the value of the Canadian dollar to change. Nonetheless, the implications for national income are unchanged; only the channels through which the changes occur will differ. In the case where changes in the money supply affect the interest rate, the investment component of aggregate demand will be affected. In the case where the exchange rate is affected, net exports will be changed. More generally, some combination of the two may occur. Let us begin by taking a closer look at each of the steps in

the analysis for the traditional case, where changes in the money supply primarily affect the interest rate. Later in this chapter we return to the situation in which much of the effect of monetary policy occurs through exchange rate changes.

## HOW MONETARY POLICY MAY AFFECT THE ECONOMY THROUGH CHANGING INTEREST RATES

Figure 14.2 can also be used to show how changes in the money supply can lead to changes in the interest rate. Initially, the money supply is at $M_0$ and the equilibrium interest rate is $i_0$. When the government increases the money supply to $M_1$, the interest rate falls to $i_1$. In the figure, the demand for money is relatively inelastic, so that an increase in the supply of money at a given level of income causes a large decrease in the interest rate. If the price level is fixed, as we assume it is in this chapter, the inflation rate is zero and the nominal interest rate $i$ is also the real interest rate $r$. As the interest rate falls, investment rises. As investment spending increases, income (which is the same as output) rises via the multiplier.

The increase in investment shifts the aggregate-expenditures schedule up, as depicted in Figure 14.3,

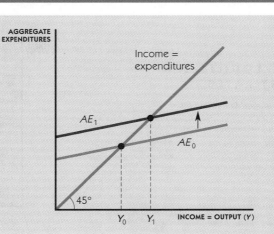

**Figure 14.3 A MONETARY POLICY STIMULUS**

An increase in the money supply may shift the aggregate-expenditures schedule up, because of increased investment by firms, leading to an increased equilibrium output. A similar effect occurs at each price level.

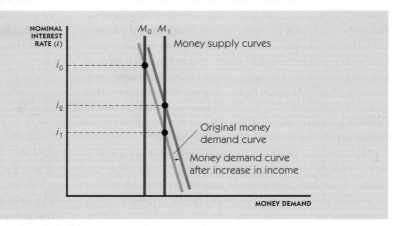

**Figure 14.4 SECOND-ROUND EFFECTS OF AN INCREASED MONEY SUPPLY**

In the first round, the increased money supply led to lower interest rates (Figure 14.2), which led in turn to higher levels of national income (Figure 14.3). This higher level of income now shifts the money demand curve up, since the demand for money at each interest rate is higher. The equilibrium interest rate is $i_2$.

and results in a higher equilibrium level of output. Output increases from $Y_0$ to $Y_1$.

When income increases, the money demand curve shifts to the right, as shown in Figure 14.4. Thus, the eventual equilibrium attained will involve a smaller decrease in the rate of interest than $i_1$. The new equilibrium interest rate will lie somewhere between $i_0$ and $i_1$: in the figure, it is $i_2$.

We can trace out the consequences for equilibrium in the product market at $r_2$: panel A of Figure 14.5 shows the level of investment, $I_2$, when the inter-

est rate is $r_2$, while panel B shows the aggregate-expenditures schedule when investment is equal to $I_2$, and the equilibrium level of output $Y_2$.

The aggregate-expenditures schedule assumes a particular price level. A similar effect occurs at each price. In Chapter 11 we showed how to derive the aggregate demand curve by tracing out the intersection of the aggregate-expenditures schedule with the 45-degree line *at each price level*. Since at each price level, the equilibrium level of output is higher, the aggregate demand curve has shifted to the right, as

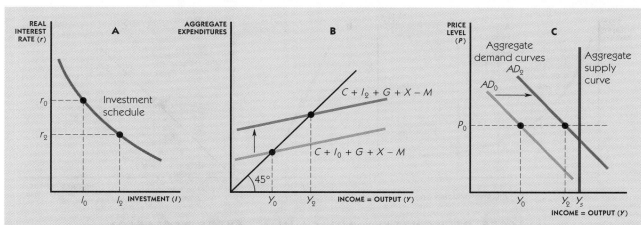

Figure 14.5  **TRACING OUT THE FULL EFFECTS OF AN INCREASE IN THE MONEY SUPPLY**

An increase in the money supply leads to a lower interest rate. Panel A shows that the lower interest rate leads to increased investment. Panel B shows that the increased investment shifts the aggregate-expenditures schedule up, leading to a higher equilibrium output *at each price level.* Panel C shows that as a result, the aggregate demand curve shifts to the right.

depicted in panel C. In this chapter, we are focusing on situations where price is fixed and there is excess capacity, such as occurs when the aggregate demand curve intersects the aggregate supply curve along the horizontal portion of the aggregate supply curve. We see clearly in panel C how the shift in the aggregate demand curve translates into an increase in aggregate output from $Y_0$ to $Y_2$.

The results of this section lead us to our twelfth point of consensus in economics:

**12  Using Monetary Policy to Stimulate the Economy**

*When there is excess capacity and prices are rigid, increasing the money supply stimulates the economy, leading to higher levels of output.*

While there is consensus on the conclusion that monetary policy can stimulate the economy, there is far less agreement about two other issues: the *quantitative effects*—the amount by which any given change in the money supply increases output—and how it does it, that is, the *channels* through which monetary policy exerts its effects.

## WHAT DETERMINES THE EFFECTIVENESS OF MONETARY POLICY?

There are three principal determinants of how much an increase in the money supply increases output via changes in the interest rate: (1) the elasticity of the demand for money, (2) the sensitivity of investment to the interest rate, and (3) the size of the multiplier.

Increasing the money supply will be less effective in increasing output when the demand for money is relatively elastic (when the money demand curve is relatively flat). When the demand for money is relatively elastic, an increase in the money supply has little effect on interest rates—interest rates decrease only slightly. *Other things being equal,* when the interest rate decreases little, there is only a small increase in investment, resulting in a small increase in GDP (see Figure 14.6, panel A).

Increasing the money supply will be less effective in increasing output when investment is not very sensitive to the interest rate (is inelastic). In this case

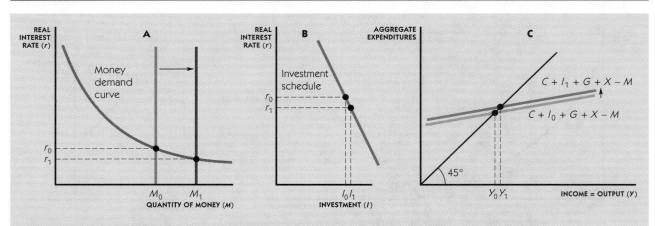

**Figure 14.6 EFFECTS OF MONETARY POLICY IN A SEVERE RECESSION**

Panel A shows that if the demand curve for money is flat, an increase in the money supply has little effect on interest rates. Panel B shows that if the investment schedule is steep, a decrease in interest rates has little effect on investment. Panel C shows that if the aggregate-expenditures schedule is not very steep, an increase in investment causes aggregate output to increase relatively little.

a decrease in the interest rate resulting from an increase in the money supply will have little effect on investment, and therefore GDP (Figure 14.6, panel B).

An increase in investment has less of an effect on output when the multiplier is small. For any given increase in investment, the smaller the multiplier, the smaller the increase in GDP. Thus, an increase in the money supply will result in a smaller increase in output when the multiplier is smaller. And, as we saw in Chapter 11, the multiplier is smaller if (1) the marginal propensity to save is large, (2) tax rates are large, or (3) the marginal propensity to import is large. In these circumstances, the increase in investment causes only a small increase in $Y$ as in panel C of Figure 14.6.

Many economists, following Keynes, argue that when the economy is in a deep recession, monetary policy is relatively ineffective. They believe that the demand curve for money appears as in Figure 14.6: at least at low interest rates it is relatively flat. As a result, *monetary authorities have a hard time driving the interest rate down further.* Exacerbating the problem facing monetary authorities is the fact that in severe recessions, prices may start to fall. In the Great

Depression, prices fell by more than 20 percent. In the economic downturn in Japan in 1994 and 1995, prices fell. What investors care about is *real interest rates:* the difference between the nominal interest rates and the rate of inflation. If the nominal interest rate falls but the rate of inflation falls more, real interest rates rise. With falling prices, real interest rates exceed the nominal interest rates. If prices are falling at 10 percent a year, then even a zero nominal interest rate corresponds to a 10 percent real interest rate—by historical standards, an extremely high real interest rate.

Moreover, given investor pessimism about economic prospects, it takes a large fall in interest rates to induce firms to invest much more. Since by definition, in a recession there is considerable excess capacity, the marginal return from extra investment is close to zero. New machines simply add to excess capacity, not to profits. Only if the new machines are much better than the old (using so much less labour that the savings in labour more than offset the additional capital costs) or if they are designed to make a new product, will it pay firms to make additional investments. Moreover, a lengthy period of losses will

### TRADITIONAL MONETARY THEORY

The nominal interest rate is the opportunity cost of holding money.

The demand for money decreases as the interest rate rises.

The interest rate equates the demand and supply for money.

### TRADITIONAL THEORY OF MONETARY POLICY

*When* monetary policy is effective in generating increased output, it is because the policy induces a lower interest rate.

Monetary policy is ineffective in deep recessions, because

**1** The money demand curve is elastic, so changes in the money supply induce only small changes in interest rates; and

**2** Even large changes in the interest rate induce little change in investment and hence in aggregate demand.

deplete a firm's cash reserves and increase its indebtedness. Facing the threat of bankruptcy, it will be reluctant to undertake additional new investments, even if it could persuade banks to lend it money. As a result of these negative factors, as the economy goes into a recession the investment schedule will not only shift down but also will become relatively inelastic; thus, lower interest rates have only a small effect in inducing additional investment (see panel B, Figure 14.6).

Since increasing the money supply has a small effect on interest rates and the decrease in interest rates has only a small effect on investment, increasing the money supply has a small effect on output, as illustrated in panel C.

Some economists have described the ineffectiveness of monetary policy in deep recessions by saying that it is like pushing on a string. While economists differ in their judgments about how deep a recession has to become before monetary policy becomes relatively ineffective, they agree on the basic principle. This brings us to our thirteenth point of consensus in economics:

**13 Monetary Policy in a Deep Recession**

> *When the economy is in a deep recession, monetary policy is relatively ineffective in stimulating the economy to recover.*

Some advocates of monetary policy claim, however, that all that matters is that there be some effect of monetary policy. A weak effect for a given percent-

age change in the money supply simply means that monetary authorities have to take more aggressive actions, by increasing the money supply by a larger percentage.

### MONETARISM

While there is broad agreement on the two consensus points in this chapter and in the box above, some economists—called **monetarists**—argue that the *only* effect of monetary policy is on the price level. They believe that the basic assumption underlying this chapter—that prices are fixed—is simply wrong. They argue that prices are flexible, even in the short run. Thus, *all* that happens when the money supply increases is that the price level changes with no changes in output or employment. In fact they believe that prices move approximately in proportion to the change in the money supply. They believe that the full-employment model discussed in Chapter 8 applies at all times. Some monetarists believe that even if there is unemployment and output is below the economy's capacity, increases in the money supply are still mostly reflected in changes in the price level.

To see how monetarists arrive at this conclusion, we need to return to the equation of exchange. The equation of exchange, as presented, was a *definition* of velocity. But they make one additional assumption—velocity is constant. Thus

$$M\bar{V} = PY$$

where the bar over the $V$ reminds us that it is fixed. If $Y$ is assumed fixed (say, at its full-employment level), then increases in $M$ get translated into proportionate increases in $P$.

This equation also gives us a simple rule for the expansion of the money supply. If we want prices to be stable, and real income is increasing at, say, 2 percent a year, then the money supply should increase at 2 percent a year. Monetarists believe that monetary policy should focus on the monetary aggregates (the measures of the money supply) and that money supply should increase in proportion to increases in real output. Doing this will lead to stable prices.

These are the *conclusions* of the monetarists. They can, however, be simply related to the traditional monetary theory. Monetarists believe that the demand for money is just proportional to nominal output (income). It does not depend on the interest rate. Note the contrast with traditional Keynesian theory. While Keynes assumed that in deep recessions the demand curve for money was almost horizontal (the elasticity was very large), monetarists assume that the demand curve is vertical: demand does not depend on the interest rate.

$$M_d = kY^m.$$

That is, the demand for money, $M_d$, equals a constant, $k$, times nominal income (output), $Y^m$. Since money demand equals money supply,

$$M_d = M_s,$$

increasing money supply increases nominal aggregate output (income) proportionately. Furthermore, since nominal income is the price level $P$ times the real output, $Y$,

$$Y^m = PY,$$

if $Y$ is *fixed*, then increasing nominal output (income) $Y^m$ leads to an equi-proportionate increase in the price level. In other words, if money supply doubles, in equilibrium, money demand must double. Money demand can only double if nominal aggregate output (income) doubles, and nominal aggregate output (income) can double only if the price level doubles.

Thus, the assumption that the demand for money does not depend on the interest rate is equivalent to the assumption that velocity ($PY/M$) is constant; and the theory that holds that because velocity is constant, increases in the money supply are reflected simply in proportionate increases in income is called the **quantity theory of money.** While there have been long periods for which velocity has been nearly constant, in recent years it has changed, and often in ways that are hard to predict, as Figures 14.7 and 14.8 illustrate.

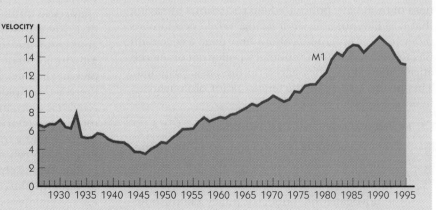

**Figure 14.7 CHANGING VELOCITY: VELOCITY SINCE 1926**

Velocity declined considerably in the Great Depression and increased fairly steadily after World War II until 1980. The trend changed dramatically after 1980. *Sources:* Statistics Canada, CANSIM Database 1996, Matrixes 6702 and 0921; M. C. Urquhart, ed., *Historical Statistics of Canada* (Toronto: Macmillan Company of Canada, 1965), pp. 113, 230.

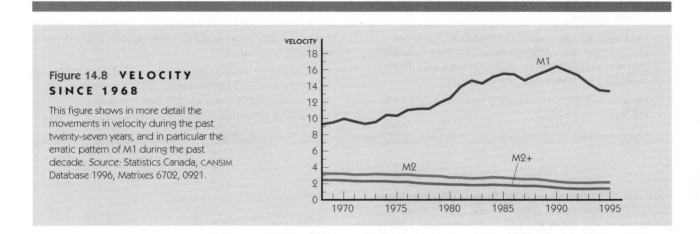

**Figure 14.8 VELOCITY SINCE 1968**

This figure shows in more detail the movements in velocity during the past twenty-seven years, and in particular the erratic pattern of M1 during the past decade. *Source:* Statistics Canada, CANSIM Database 1996, Matrixes 6702, 0921.

## CRITICISMS OF THE TRADITIONAL THEORY OF THE DEMAND FOR MONEY

In traditional, or Keynesian, monetary theory, the mechanism by which monetary policy affects the economy is simple: when the government increases the supply of money, interest rates must fall in order for the demand for money to equal the supply. Lower interest rates induce more investment and consumer purchases of durables, stimulating aggregate demand. In recent years, changes in the financial system have led to a reexamination of this theory. In particular, economists have raised several questions concerning the demand function for money underlying the theory. Some questions focus on the relationship between the demand for money and income, others on the effect of interest rates on the demand for money.

### THE RELATIONSHIP BETWEEN MONEY AND INCOME

Earlier we saw that what particularly distinguishes money from other assets such as government Treasury bills is its role as a medium of exchange in facilitating transactions. The traditional monetary theory implies that the higher people's income, the more money they will want to hold. In other words, there is a simple relationship between the volume of transactions and the level of income. This would be the case if most transactions were directly related to output—employers paying wages and buying goods from suppliers, customers buying goods from firms, and so on.

But in fact, in terms of their dollar value, most transactions are for exchanges of financial assets, not the purchase of goods and services. One individual thinks Canadian Pacific stock is going to go down, so he sells his shares. Another person thinks it is going up, and so she buys shares. The volume of these financial transactions has virtually no direct bearing on national output and income. Moreover, the *ratio* of these transactions to national income may change markedly with economic conditions. When there is greater uncertainty and change, there may be more such exchanges, as people take differing views of what the future holds and as individual circumstances change rapidly.

In the longer run, a number of other factors affect the relationship between money and income. For instance, not all transactions require payment by cash or cheque; today most transactions are made with credit. You need neither have money in a bank account nor currency in your pocket to buy a car or a vacation in Banff, so long as you can get credit. You can pay with a credit card or write a cheque against

---

### CRITICISMS OF TRADITIONAL MONETARY THEORY

There is no simple relationship between the demand for money and income.

> Most transactions involve not goods and services (output) but the exchange of assets. The connection between transactions related to output and those related to exchange may not be stable.

> Transactions do not necessarily need money; credit will suffice.

Changes in technology have allowed more extensive use of credit and make possible much higher velocities.

There is no simple relationship between real interest rates and the money supply.

> Today most money takes the form of demand deposits and is interest-bearing. Thus, the opportunity cost of holding money is low and is not directly related to the interest rate.

---

your trust company account line. Of course, some kinds of transactions are still not easily done with credit. In most cities for example, you still have to pay for taxis with cash. But in Australia, taxis accept Visa, MasterCard, and American Express. The transactions that require money at the point of sale represent a relatively small and shrinking proportion of all transactions in the modern economy.

Indeed, technology has altered the whole idea of the velocity of money. With electronic fund transfers, in which computers can transfer funds from bank to bank or from account to account almost instantaneously, the velocity of circulation can become extremely high, even close to infinite for a few moments.

## THE RELATIONSHIP BETWEEN INTEREST RATES AND THE DEMAND FOR MONEY

This brings us to the second set of criticisms of the traditional theory of the demand for money: most money, as we have seen, is in the form of demand deposits, and today—unlike fifty years ago, when Keynesian monetary theory was first formulated—demand deposits often bear interest. Thus, the opportunity cost of holding "money" is not the interest rate, but the *difference* between the return on, say, a government bond and the interest paid on demand deposits. That difference is generally small and relates primarily to the bank's cost of running the chequing account. The existence of interest-bearing chequing accounts calls into question the extent to which the demand for money will rise or fall in response to changes in interest rates.

## OTHER CRITICISMS OF TRADITIONAL MONETARY THEORY

Traditional monetary theory assumed that changing the money supply affected the economy through changes in *real* interest rates. Yet there have been long periods in which real interest rates have varied very little. More recently, nominal interest rates move up or down with inflation, so variations in real interest rates are still far smaller than variations in nominal interest rates. Monetary policy seems to have effects far greater than would be indicated by the relatively small variations in real interest rates.

## ALTERNATIVE MECHANISMS

Traditional monetary theory has thus been questioned on two fronts—both the theory of demand for money, which underlies it, and the role of interest rates. But monetary policy *does* seem to matter. There are several alternative mechanisms through which monetary policy exercises its influence.

### CREDIT AVAILABILITY

One channel is through **credit availability.** In Chapter 13, we looked at the two sides of the bank's balance sheet—its deposits (the money supply) and its assets, which include loans. Various actions of the Bank of Canada both reduce deposits (the money supply) and the supply of available loans. Figure 14.9 shows the demand and supply of "credit." Restrictive monetary policy has the effect of reducing banks' supply of loans, which shifts the loan supply curve to the left and increases the equilibrium interest rate at which credit is made available.

At times banks may ration the amount of credit they make available. Typically they do not simply lend to anyone willing to borrow at the interest rates they charge. At times, they may not extend loans to all those deemed "credit-worthy" who would like loans. They could, of course, raise the interest rate charged; but they may worry that by doing so, the best risks—those most likely to repay the loan—will go else-

where, or decide it is not worth borrowing at such interest rates. As with other prices, if interest rates remain fixed, then a shift in the loan supply curve has an even larger effect than when interest rates adjust, as Figure 14.10 illustrates.

Even when credit is not being rationed, banks respond to a situation of tighter credit by adjusting terms of the loan contract other than the interest rate: for instance, they may require more collateral.

In any case, the shift in the availability of credit (the shift of the loan supply curve to the left) results in lower investment, either because interest rates are higher, making it less attractive to undertake investments, because other terms of the loan contract

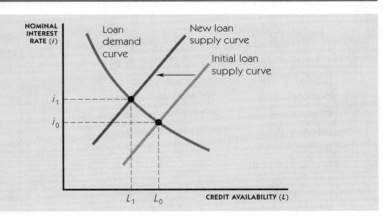

**Figure 14.9 MONETARY POLICY AND THE MARKET FOR CREDIT**

Restrictive monetary policy reduces the supply of credit by banks causing the supply curve to shift to the left and the interest rate to rise from $r_0$ to $r_1$. The amount of loans falls from $L_0$ to $L_1$.

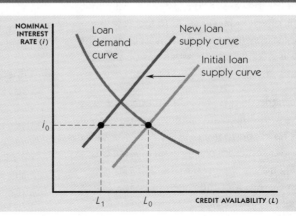

**Figure 14.10 MONETARY POLICY UNDER CREDIT RATIONING**

If banks are reluctant to raise interest rates, restrictive monetary policy will reduce the supply of loans, but not the demand. Loans fall from $L_0$ to $L_1$. With an excess demand for loans, banks will allocate them by rationing.

How much independence should the central bank have in pursuing monetary policy? At one extreme, the central bank may be given a clear mandate, like controlling inflation, and then be given the authority to pursue that goal with minimal political interference. At the other extreme, the central bank may be subject to considerable political control and thus come under pressure to stimulate the economy, even if it means allowing greater inflationary pressure.

Germany and Switzerland have exceptionally independent central banks. In Germany, the law explicitly states that the central bank has the "assigned task of preserving monetary stability" and "shall be independent of instructions from the federal government." Perhaps not surprisingly, both countries have had relatively low rates of inflation—about 3.5 percent since 1975. The flip side is that monetary policy is not often used to stimulate the economy in the face of an economic downturn.

In the United Kingdom and Italy, the central banks are subject to more political control. In the United Kingdom, the Bank of England is by law subordinate to the Treasury Department and must make short-term loans to the Treasury whenever they are requested. As a result, the Bank is often under pressure to increase the money supply and stimulate the economy. The average inflation rate in Britain has been over 12 percent since 1975.

Canada, the United States, and Japan are countries with intermediate systems, whose central banks have considerable independence but are still under some political pressure. A famous sparring match occurred in the late 1950s between Governor of the Bank of Canada James Coyne and Finance Minister Donald Fleming.

Coyne refused to go along with the expansionary policies advocated by the government, and the government responded by introducing a bill declaring the position of governor vacant. Though the bill never passed, Coyne resigned anyway. As a result of the "Coyne Affair," a mechanism of consultation and directive was developed which was ultimately put into the Bank of Canada Act in 1967. Under the mechanism, the governor and the minister of finance consult regularly on monetary policy. In the event of disagreement, the act empowers the minister of finance to issue a written directive overriding the Bank's monetary policy decisions for a fixed period of time. The directive power gives the government ultimate responsibility for monetary policy, but in the absence of a directive the Bank has immediate responsibility. No directive has ever been issued, though if one were issued, a likely outcome would be the resignation of the governor.

Whether the central bank should be less accountable to the government is an ongoing political issue. Many observers believe that the questions of monetary policy are better kept out of the political process. The goals of monetary policy, especially price stability and the maintenance of the value of the currency, are longer-term goals that do not necessarily coincide with the four-year terms of office of most politicians.

Other believe that in a democracy, any matter of such importance to the functioning of the economy should be controlled by Parliament. That is, the central bank should be accountable in some way to the elected representatives of the people and should have some reasonably clear responsibilities. They worry that the Bank may reflect too strongly the views of bankers and the business community, especially those in central Canada.

are adjusted to make borrowing less attractive, or because funds required to undertake investments simply are not available.

## PORTFOLIO EFFECTS

An alternative channel by which monetary policy may affect the economy is through the price of shares and long-term bonds. At lower *nominal* interest rates, the value of long-term bonds increases. People feel wealthier, and because they feel wealthier, they consume more. Moreover, because bonds yield lower returns, investors turn to stocks. As the demand for stocks increases, their price rises. Higher stock prices lead to increased consumption and also to increased investment: at the higher stock price, more firms believe that it is a good time to issue new shares, to raise additional capital, to finance new investments.

## MONETARY POLICY IN AN OPEN ECONOMY

So far, we have assumed that changes in the money supply have their initial effect on the interest rate. But in today's open, international economy, perhaps the most important way monetary policy affects the level of economic activity is through the exchange rate: increasing the money supply, which puts downward pressure on domestic interest rates, leads to an outflow of capital and to a depreciation of the Canadian dollar—a fall in the number of, say, yen that can be obtained for a dollar. This makes Canadian goods more attractive abroad, and foreign goods less attractive here, and thus increases exports and decreases imports. For instance, between January and April 1995 the exchange rate between the dollar and the yen fell from 71 yen to the dollar to 61 yen to the dollar. Thus, to a Japanese consumer, a $100 Canadian shirt fell in price by 14 percent, from 7,100 yen to 6,100 yen $(1,000 \div 7,100 \times 100\% = 14\%)$. And to a Canadian consumer, the price of Japanese goods increased by 16.5 percent. A computer that sold in Japan for 100,000 yen and thus cost $1,408 in Canada would now cost Canadians $1,640 $(232 \div 1,408 \times 100\% = 16.5\%)$. (In practice, the changes were somewhat less dramatic, since in the short run, exporters and importers "absorb" some of the variation in exchange rates.)

As exports increase and imports decrease, *net* exports increase. As Figure 14.11 illustrates, an increase in net exports leads to an increase in aggregate output. In this section, we explain in more detail how monetary policy affects the exchange rate. We begin with a review of what determines the exchange rate.

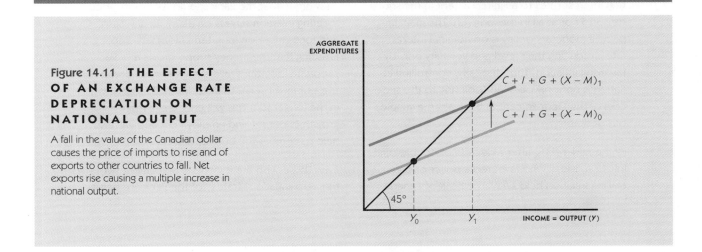

Figure 14.11 **THE EFFECT OF AN EXCHANGE RATE DEPRECIATION ON NATIONAL OUTPUT**

A fall in the value of the Canadian dollar causes the price of imports to rise and of exports to other countries to fall. Net exports rise causing a multiple increase in national output.

## CLOSE-UP: WHAT IS THE APPROPRIATE GOAL FOR MONETARY POLICY?

The way monetary policy should be conducted is a matter of constant debate, although the substance of the debate shifts with the times. The current debate is between those who see price stability, the absence of inflation, as the primary objective of the Bank of Canada and those who view employment and economic growth as also being relevant for monetary policy. This has overshadowed an earlier debate concerning whether the Bank should exercise discretion in its policy at all or follow a simple "monetary rule" that would tie increases in the money supply to growth of GDP.

Those who argue that monetary policy should concentrate on low inflation as its primary objective say that price stability is a prerequisite to full employment and an efficient economy. A stable price level reduces uncertainty about the economy and also lowers nominal interest rates. This in turn leads to higher industrial investment and a higher demand for consumer durables. Moreover, globalization and innovations in financial markets has meant increased volatility of capital flows. Central banks in highly open economies such as Canada can only influence real interest rates to a limited extent in the short run, and not at all in the long run. The main impact of monetary policy is on nominal interest rates, reducing their level and volatility only by lowering inflation. Thus, they say, controlling inflation is not only possible (pointing to the success of the German central bank as an example) but desirable.

By the mid-1980s, after a decade of double-digit inflation, those who favoured a policy of controlling inflation held sway. The Bank of Canada announced that it would pursue a "zero-inflation policy," a policy designed to keep inflation between 0 and 2 percent on an annual basis. This approach has been in place ever since.

But detractors argue that the zero-inflation policy is responsible for the low levels of growth experienced by the Canadian economy in recent years. The Bank currently pursues its zero-inflation policy by adopting restrictive monetary policy to increase short-term interest rates whenever it feels that inflationary pressures are building, for example, in response to a depreciation in the Canadian dollar or to indications that output is approaching full-employment level. Increases in short-term interest rates decrease both investment and net exports, lowering aggregate demand and thus national income. Critics argue that, by pursuing the zero-inflation goal, the Bank is at least partly responsible for the high government deficits of recent years. Higher interest rates increase the cost of servicing the public debt, leading to still higher budget deficits. The lower the inflation target, the more often the Bank must intervene to increase interest rates, and the more forceful must that intervention be. They argue that the Bank should worry less about meeting inflation targets on a day-to-day basis and focus more on long-term monetary stability. Ensuring that the money supply grows at an appropriate long-term rate is not only less disruptive but might serve to keep interest rates down in the longer run. This will encourage more growth in output and employment and will also help to combat the budget deficit.

Even those who are in general agreement with the zero-inflation strategy of the Bank are beginning to question its tactics. They argue that the Bank has too often overreacted and undershot its inflation target (inflation has been close to the lower end of the 0–2 percent target range), and that this has led to slow growth and high unemployment. They say that the Bank has established its reputation for being committed to price stability and therefore need not respond to every fleeting fear of inflation. While this fear may have been warranted when the Bank first began its quest for price stability, they say, it is less so now, so the Bank can take a longer-term view of its policy.

*Sources:* Richard G. Lipsey (ed.), *Zero Inflation: the Goal of Price Stability,* (Toronto, C. D. Howe Institute, 1990); Robert C. York (ed.), *Taking Aim: The Debate on Zero Inflation,* (Toronto, C. D. Howe Institute, 1990); Pierre Fortin, "A Strategy for Deficit Control Through Faster Growth," *Canadian Business Economics,* Volume 3, Fall 1994, 3–26; Kenneth J. Boessenkool, David E. W. Laidler, and William B. P. Robson, *Devils in the Details: Improving the Tactics of Recent Canadian Monetary Policy,* C. D. Howe Institute, Commentary No. 79, April 1996.

## HOW MONETARY POLICY AFFECTS EXCHANGE RATES

In Chapter 9 we saw that exchange rates—for example, the yen-dollar exchange rate—are determined by the intersection of the demand and supply curves for dollars. The demand for dollars is determined in turn by Japan's demand for Canadian goods and services and Japan's desire to invest in Canada. Similarly, the supply of dollars is determined by Canadian demand for Japanese goods and services and Canadians' desire to invest in Japan.

When the Bank of Canada increases the money supply, it causes the interest rate to fall. Foreigners find it less attractive to invest in Canada and Canadians find it more attractive to invest abroad. This shifts the demand curve for dollars to the left and the supply curve of dollars to the right, as in Figure 14.12. The net result is a depreciation in the exchange rate—and an increase in exports and a decrease in imports.

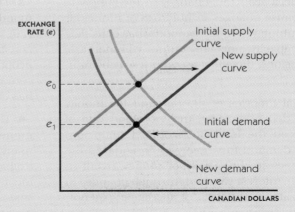

### Figure 14.12 MONETARY POLICY AND THE EXCHANGE RATE

Expansionary monetary policy causes the demand for Canadian dollars to fall as foreigners reduce investment in Canada, and the supply of dollars to rise as Canadians invest more abroad. The exchange rate depreciates.

If the economy is a small open one, *all* of the influence of monetary policy will work through changes in the exchange rate and its effect on net exports. That is because the interest rate in Canada is determined by that prevailing on international capital markets. Any pressure for interest rates to rise caused by a reduction in the money supply will cause enough capital to flow into the Canadian economy to prevent the rise. This leaves changes in the exchange rate as the sole avenue by which monetary policy works. Aggregate demand stimulation will come from changes in net exports, not from investment. As discussed in Chapter 8, whether Canada is truly a price taker on international capital markets is a matter for dispute. Still, given the importance of international capital markets to the Canadian economy, it seems quite likely that much of the effect of monetary policy would work through exchange rate rather than interest rate changes.

## THE EFFECTIVENESS OF TRADITIONAL CHANNELS OF MONETARY POLICY

Thus, although there is a new channel, exchange rates, through which monetary policy exercises its influence, some of the other channels may in fact be much weaker in an open economy. We saw that one of the ways monetary policy exercises its influence is by reducing the availability of credit. But if Canadian firms can borrow abroad, then restricting credit from Canadian banks simply induces borrowers to seek funds elsewhere. To be sure, not everyone has access to foreign banks. But hundreds of multinational firms do. And if enough of these firms switch their borrowing abroad, it frees up Canadian banks to continue their lending to those who do not have access to foreign banks.

## REVIEW AND PRACTICE

### SUMMARY

**1** Theories concerning the effect of monetary policy on the economy focus on two sides of the banks' balance sheet, on money and on credit.

**2** When prices are fixed, changes in the supply of money can cause changes in holdings of money or changes in output. When the economy has considerable excess capacity, normally output will increase; in deep recessions, the effect on output may be minimal.

**3** Traditional theories of the demand for money focus on its dependence on the (nominal) rate of interest and on the level of income. Equilibrium requires the demand for money to be equal to the supply. Changes in the supply of money result in changes in the interest rate and, through changes in the interest rate, in the level of aggregate expenditures and equilibrium output.

**4** Traditional theories also posit that in severe recessions, the interest elasticity of the demand for money may be high and the interest elasticity of investment is low, so monetary policy may be relatively ineffective.

**5** The quantity theory of money holds that the demand for money does not depend on the interest rate, and accordingly that the velocity of money is constant. Increases in money supply then result in proportionate increases in national income. In recent years, velocity has not only not been constant; it has changed in relatively unpredictable ways.

**6** There are many difficulties with the traditional monetary theory. Nowadays, money is not used for many transactions, and many transactions involve exchanges of assets, which have little to do with income generation. Changes in technology and the structure of the economy may alter the money-income relationship. Most money bears interest, and the opportunity cost is only the difference between the interest rate it pays and the interest rate on government Treasury bills.

**7** Portfolio theories stress the effect of changes in monetary policy on the demand and supply of various assets (including money) and the resulting effect on prices of assets.

**8** Credit availability theories stress the effects of monetary policy on the availability of credit (the supply of loans) by banks.

**9** In an open economy, monetary policy is likely to have a smaller effect on interest rates and credit availability than it otherwise would. If the Bank of Canada attempts to restrict credit or raise interest rates, Canadian firms can borrow from abroad.

**10** In an open economy, monetary policy has effects on exchange rates: a reduction in the money supply leading to higher interest rates leads to an appreciation of the dollar, a decrease in exports, and an increase in imports.

**11** In a small open economy, all of the effect of monetary policy works through the exchange rate and none through interest rates. Changes in aggregate demand can be attributed to changes in net exports rather than to investment.

## KEY TERMS

velocity

transactions demand for money

Keynesian monetary theory

traditional monetary theory

monetarism

quantity theory of money

credit availability

portfolio effects

## REVIEW QUESTIONS

**1** What might happen in response to a change in the money supply?

**2** Why does demand for money fall as the interest rate rises? What is the opportunity cost of holding money that pays interest (such as demand deposits)?

**3** What might cause changes in the relationship between the demand for money and income besides changes in the interest rate?

**4** Why might changes in the money supply not lead to increases in the level of investment in a severe recession?

**5** What assumptions are involved in the quantity theory of money? What conclusion can be drawn on the basis of those assumptions? What is the evidence concerning the constancy of the velocity of circulation?

**6** What are alternative mechanisms by which portfolio theories suggest that monetary policy affects the economy? Describe how monetary policy might affect investment or consumption, *even if monetary policy had little effect on interest rates.*

**7** How do exchange rate changes affect equilibrium levels of output?

**8** How does monetary policy affect equilibrium exchange rates?

**9** How does the fact that an economy is open affect monetary policy?

## PROBLEMS

**1** If GDP is $600 billion and the money supply is $40 billion, what is velocity? How does your answer change if GDP rises to $700 billion while the money supply remains the same? If GDP remains at $600 billion while the money supply increases to $50 billion, how does velocity change?

**2** Graph the money demand curve from the following data, with quantity of money demanded given in billions of dollars.

| Interest rate | 7% | 8% | 9% | 10% | 11% | 12% |
|---|---|---|---|---|---|---|
| Money demand | 45 | 44 | 43 | 42 | 41 | 40.5 |

How do changes in national income affect the demand curve?

**3** Using money supply and demand diagrams, explain how the elasticity of the money demand curve determines whether monetary policy can have a substantial effect on the interest rate.

**4** Explain how the elasticity of investment with respect to interest rates determines whether monetary policy can have a substantial effect on aggregate demand.

**5** Explain how each of the following might affect the demand for money:
   (a) interest is paid on chequing accounts
   (b) credit cards become more readily available
   (c) electronic fund transfers become common
Would the changes in the demand for money necessarily reduce the ability of the Bank of Canada to use monetary policy to influence the economy?

**6** How might an increase in national income affect the exchange rate? Before 1971 exchange rates were fixed by the government, and the government bought and sold dollars in order to maintain the set rate. Contrast the effects of an increase in investment on equilibrium output, assuming the exchange rate is fixed, and the effects if exchange rates are *flexible*, so are allowed to vary freely to equilibrate demand and supply.

**7** Describe the impact on the Japanese economy of the appreciation of yen relative to the dollar, using the aggregate-expenditures schedule.

**8** Explain whether each of the following changes would tend to appreciate or depreciate the Canadian dollar, using supply and demand curves for the foreign exchange market to illustrate your answers:
   (a) higher interest rates in Japan
   (b) faster economic growth in Germany
   (c) a higher Canadian rate of inflation
   (d) a tight Canadian monetary policy
   (e) an expansionary Canadian fiscal policy

**9** Suppose that at the start of 1991, a Canadian investor put $10,000 into a one-year German investment. If the exchange rate was 1.5 marks per dollar, how much was this in marks? Over the course of the year, the German investment paid 10 percent interest. But when the investor switched back to dollars at the end of the year, the exchange rate was now 2 marks per dollar. Did the change in exchange rates cause the investor to earn more or less money? How much? How does your analysis change if the mark had fallen to 1 per dollar?

## APPENDIX: AN ALGEBRAIC DERIVATION OF EQUILIBRIUM IN THE MONEY MARKET

The money demand equation can be written

$$M_d = M_d(r, Y^m),$$

where $M_d$ is the demand for money and $Y^m = PY$, the value of national income. If $M_s$ is the money supply, then the equilibrium condition that the demand for money equals the supply can be written

$$M_s = M_d(r, Y^m). \qquad \text{[a]}$$

From Chapter 11, we know that

$$Y^m = C + I + G + (X - M),$$

where $I$ (investment) depends on the interest rate, $r$, and $G$ (government expenditures), $X$ (exports), and $M$ (imports) is assumed to be fixed. If consumption is just $(1 - s)$ times income, $Y^m$, then

$$Y^m = (1 - s)Y^m + I(r) + G + (X - M),$$

or

$$Y^m = [I(r) + G + (X - M)]/s. \qquad \text{[b]}$$

Equations [a] and [b] provide us two equations in two unknowns, $r$ and $Y^m$. The solution gives us the equilibrium income and interest rate. An increase in the money supply results in a new solution, with a lower interest rate and a higher level of national income.

# CHAPTER 15

# FISCAL AND
# MONETARY
# POLICY

There are three principal objectives of monetary and fiscal policy: maintaining full employment, promoting economic growth, and maintaining price stability. In Chapters 8 and 9, we saw that when the economy is at full employment, government policy can have significant effects on the growth rate, by affecting the level of investment. At full employment there is a fixed-size pie, and government actions affect how that pie is divided. But when there is unemployment and resources are not fully utilized, government actions can affect both the size of the pie and how it is divided. Even if a smaller share of national output goes to investment, if national output is increased enough, the level of investment will actually increase, and long-run growth will be promoted.

This chapter pulls together the insights of earlier chapters of this part to see how fiscal and monetary policy may be used to stimulate the economy and promote economic growth. We will compare the effects of monetary and fiscal policy, and analyze several issues that arise in the application of policy today. Later chapters will explore how fiscal and monetary policy relate to the problem of maintaining price stability.

## KEY QUESTIONS

**1** What difference does it make whether we use monetary or fiscal policy to help the economy get out of a recession?

**2** What are the economic effects of an increase in government expenditure accompanied by an increase in taxes of the same amount?

**3** What might be the consequences of balanced-budget legislation on economic stability?

## FISCAL POLICY

In Chapter 10 we defined fiscal policy as efforts to improve macroeconomic performance through changes in government expenditures and taxes. Faced with output below the full-employment level, policy makers may help restore the economy to full employment through an increase in government expenditures or a reduction in taxes. Recall our aggregate-expenditures diagram from Chapter 11. An increase in government expenditures shifts the aggregate-expenditures schedule up, as shown in panel A of Figure 15.1. Equilibrium output at each price level increases, and the aggregate demand schedule shifts to the right, as illustrated in

panel B of Figure 15.1. A tax cut puts more money in the pockets of consumers, leading to an increase in consumption. This shifts the aggregate-expenditures schedule up (panel A of Figure 15.1) and results in a rightward shift of the aggregate demand curve (panel B of Figure 15.1). Either way, the economy is brought closer to the full-employment level of output.

## IS IT WORTH INCURRING A DEFICIT TO GET OUT OF A RECESSION?

The problem with an increase in government expenditures or a tax cut is that both increase the deficit. This raises a major concern: even if the fiscal stimulus makes us better off now, future generations are

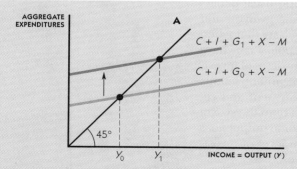
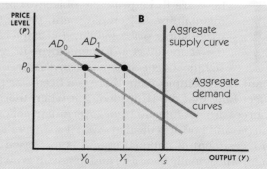

**Figure 15.1 EFFECT OF INCREASED GOVERNMENT EXPENDITURES**

Increased government expenditures shift the aggregate-expenditures schedule up, increasing the equilibrium level of output at each price level. Hence the aggregate demand schedule shifts to the right by an amount equal to the

multiplier times the increase in government expenditures. At the initial fixed price level, $P_0$, equilibrium output increases by the amount of the shift—the multiplier times the increase in government expenditures.

## USING ECONOMICS: JOB CREATION

In 1995 the unemployment rate stood at 9.5 percent, and there were 1.425 million persons unemployed. How much stimulation of aggregate demand would be required to cut unemployment by one percentage point? One percent of the labour force is 150,000 workers.

*Step 1.* Calculate the total increase in national output needed to create 150,000 jobs. To do this, we need to know the relationship between increases in national output (GDP) and job creation. Assume one new job is associated with an increase in GDP of $50,000. Thus,

Increase in GDP needed = $50,000 per job ×
150,000 jobs
= $7.5 billion.

*Step 2.* Calculate the increase in aggregate demand needed to generate this increase in GDP. To do this, we need to know the multiplier, which we take to be 2. Thus,

*Aggregate demand would have to shift upward by $3.75 billion.*

This corresponds to an increase in government expenditures of 3 percent of 1995 federal government expenditures.

saddled with debt. Doesn't that make them worse off? If government expands its investment—in infrastructure, human capital, or research—future generations may actually be better off, provided the return on those investments exceeds the interest rate. Estimated returns in many of these areas are very high. Most estimates put the return on investment in research in excess of 20 percent, and estimates of the return on investment in education greatly exceed the interest rate.

But even if increased expenditures are spent on consumption, the outcome may be favourable. Assume the government spends $1 billion in public consumption goods. As a result of the multiplier, the net increase in current income (consumption) is much higher. If the multiplier is 2, national income increases by $2 billion. At some future date—say in the next boom—the increased indebtedness has to be paid off, with interest. But there is only $1 billion in increased indebtedness. The trade-off between an increase in national income today of $2 billion, with a reduction in consumption in the future to repay

$1 billion (plus interest) in indebtedness, seems a favourable one. Indeed, the trade-off may be more favourable still, if the government has borrowed money from its own citizens. In this case, the government will simply impose a tax on some individuals, in order to repay those who purchased bonds to finance the original expenditure. Then there would be a transfer of resources from taxpayers to bondholders, but no reduction in aggregate consumption.

The trade-off from a debt-financed fiscal stimulus may be less favourable if the repayment of the extra debt takes a long time. The government's dissaving soaks up savings that would have been available for investment. The capital stock of the economy is thus smaller, and as a result, so is future national income, making future generations worse off.

The trade-off is also less favourable if the extra debt is financed through borrowing from abroad. In this case, the future tax revenues to pay for the stimulus will (in sum or in part) be transferred to foreigners. Future generations will accordingly be worse off.

## FISCAL POLICY UNDER FISCAL CONSTRAINTS

In recent years, as governments in many countries have run huge deficits, increasing government expenditures in a recession to stimulate the economy has often seemed politically impossible. In Canada, Parliament and most provincial legislatures would be extremely reluctant to undertake expenditure programmes financed by additional borrowing. And, in the United States, Congress now abides by a self-imposed constraint that it will not increase expenditures over agreed-upon levels unless there is an agreement to increase taxes by a corresponding amount. Similarly, the Maastricht Treaty, under which the countries of the European Union are supposed to form a common currency, calls for them to reduce their deficits to 3 percent of GDP by 1997. To achieve this goal requires cutting back on expenditures or raising taxes, but will leave little room for increasing expenditures or lowering taxes to stimulate the economy. In such situations, the government has no choice but to rely on monetary policy.

## BALANCED-BUDGET MULTIPLIERS

What happens if government matches increased expenditures with increased taxes? The **balanced-budget multiplier** is the increase in GDP from a dollar increase in government expenditures matched by a dollar increase in taxes when the economy is operating with excess capacity and the price level is fixed. The increased taxes reduce disposable income, and thus private consumption. This largely but not completely offsets the expansionary effect of the increased government expenditures. To see why it only partially offsets the expansionary effect, recall that a one-dollar reduction in disposable income only reduces consumption by the marginal propensity to consume times one dollar.

Suppose that an increase in government expenditures of $1 billion is matched by an equal increase in taxes (ignoring, for simplicity, the dependence of taxes on income, and ignoring exports and imports). The first-round net effect is

$1 billion − MPC × $1 billion = (1 − MPC) × $1 billion,

where MPC is the marginal propensity to consume. The multiplier, as we know from Chapter 11, is

$$\frac{1}{1 - \text{MPC}},$$

so the net effect is

$$\frac{1}{1 - \text{MPC}} \times (1 - \text{MPC}) \times \$1 \text{ billion} = \$1 \text{ billion}.$$

Thus, while the initial effect on aggregate demand of an increase in government expenditure is the full amount of the spending, the initial effect of a tax increase is only that amount multiplied by the marginal propensity to consume. So a spending increase accompanied by a tax increase of equal size will cause aggregate expenditures in the economy to rise initially by some fraction of the government expenditure increase. That will then be subject to a multiplier effect of the usual sort. In fact, in the special case where the tax increase does not itself affect the size of the multiplier, the net effect of a balanced-budget increase in government expenditures and taxation is that national income rises precisely by the amount of the increased government expenditure (rather than a multiple of that amount, as would be the case if taxes were not raised). The balanced-budget multiplier is unity.

Figure 15.2 shows the result of this "balanced-budget" increase in government expenditures. In panel A, the increase in government expenditures from $G_0$ to $G_1$ causes the aggregate-expenditures curve to shift up from $AE(G_0, T_0)$ to $AE(G_1, T_0)$. Then the tax increase from $T_0$ to $T_1$ causes the aggregate-expenditures curve to fall back to $AE(G_1, T_1)$. Total output rises by the same amount as government expenditures ($Y_1 - Y_0 = G_1 - G_0$). In panel B, the aggregate demand schedule shifts to the right by the amount of the increase in government expenditures. In effect, the multiplier is just unity.

## MONETARY POLICY

In earlier chapters we have seen how monetary policy can stimulate the economy. An increase in the money supply leads to lower interest rates and in-

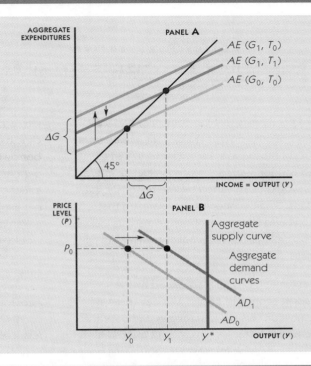

## Figure 15.2 EFFECT OF A BALANCED-BUDGET INCREASE IN GOVERN-MENT EXPENDITURES AND TAXES

An increase in government expenditures causes the aggregate-expenditures curve to rise from $AE(G_0, T_0)$ to $AE(G_1, T_0)$ in panel A. A rise in taxes by the same amount causes aggregate expenditures to fall to $AE(G_1, T_1)$. National income rises by the amount of government expenditures. In panel B, the aggregate demand schedule shifts from $AD_0$ to $AD_1$, an amount just equal to government expenditures.

creased credit availability, stimulating investment. This shifts the aggregate-expenditures schedule up and the aggregate demand schedule out, so that at any price level, aggregate output increases (see Figure 15.3). As we saw in Chapter 14, an additional mecha-

nism is at play in an open economy: as interest rates fall, exchange rates decrease, consequently, exports increase and imports decrease. Thus, net exports increase, and again, the aggregate-expenditures schedule shifts up.

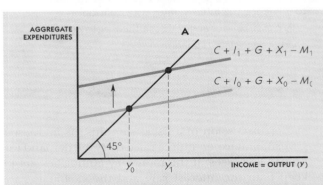

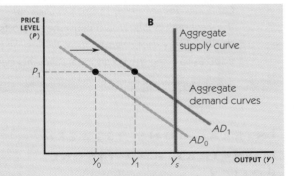

## Figure 15.3 THE EFFECT OF MONETARY POLICY

An increase in the money supply leads to lower interest rates and increased credit availability, stimulating investment. Panel A. This shifts the aggregate-expenditures schedule up. Panel B.

The aggregate demand schedule shifts out, so that at any price level, aggregate output increases.

Open economies, like Canada's, may find their policy options constrained by competition from the rest of the world. For example, in a small open economy any attempt to influence interest rates would be thwarted by international capital markets. Some economists have argued that openness to international capital markets makes it impossible to use fiscal policy to stimulate aggregate demand.

The argument, originally advanced by the Canadian economist Robert Mundell (now at Columbia University), is as follows: Suppose the government increases government expenditures and finances these increases by borrowing from the capital market. If the economy is a small open one, the increased borrowing cannot cause the interest rate to rise, so there would be no change in domestic savings or investment. The financing of the new borrowing must come entirely from abroad. But increasing borrowing from abroad would put pressure on the exchange rate—the proceeds of the borrowing would be converted into Canadian dollars by the government, causing the value of the Canadian dollar to rise. The rise in the value of the Canadian dollar would cause net exports to decline. Net exports would have to decline by enough to bring the balance of payments back into equilibrium. That is, they would have to decline by an amount equal to the amount initially borrowed to finance increased government expenditures. Ultimately, there would be no net effect on aggregate demand. The decrease in net exports would just offset the increase in government expenditures, and investment would remain unchanged! In other words, fiscal policy would be completely ineffective in stimulating aggregate demand.

According to this argument, governments of countries with small open economies would be restricted to using monetary policy for macroeconomic purposes. An expansionary monetary policy would stimulate aggregate demand by inducing an increase in net exports, while investment and government expenditures would remain unchanged.

The extent to which this sequence of events applies to Canada is disputable. While our economy is highly open, it may not literally be a small open economy. We may yet have some effect on our interest rate. Nonetheless, our limited ability to influence the interest rate would undoubtedly constrain our ability to use fiscal policy to change aggregate demand.

## INTERACTIONS BETWEEN MONETARY AND FISCAL POLICY

So far, we have treated monetary and fiscal policy as if they were two distinct policies. In fact, there are important interactions between them. Consider the earlier discussion of a fiscal stimulus. As increased government expenditures raise GDP, the demand for money increases. If the monetary authorities act to keep both the interest rate and the exchange rate fixed, investment and the net export schedule will be unchanged. Economists refer to this as an **accommodative monetary policy,** one that complements the objectives of fiscal policies, in this case by increasing the money supply so as to maintain the interest rate and exchange rate at their old levels. This means the fiscal stimulus will not be diminished by reduced investment or net exports, which would occur if interest rates were allowed to rise or the exchange rate to appreciate.

## DIFFERENCES BETWEEN MONETARY AND FISCAL POLICY

There are major differences between monetary and fiscal policy, in their effects on the composition of output, their efficacy, and the lags with which their effects are felt.

## EFFECTS ON THE COMPOSITION OF OUTPUT

Assume first that we could use either monetary or fiscal policy to stimulate the economy to the same extent. If we use monetary policy, to the extent that we lower interest rates, investment is stimulated. Thus, future levels of income will be higher. In these circumstances governments can use monetary policy to pursue both a high-growth and a full-employment strategy. If governments use fiscal policy, with a fixed money supply, as incomes increase, interest rates rise so that the demand for money remains equal to the supply. Unless the monetary authorities assume an accommodative policy, investment is actually discouraged. Figure 15.4 contrasts the composition of GDP under alternative policies. While both fiscal and monetary policy may be able to restore the economy

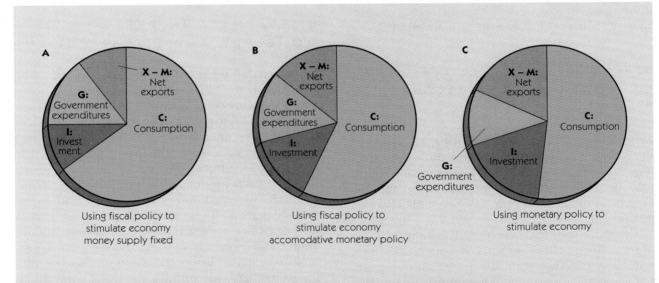

**Figure 15.4 COMPARISON OF THE EFFECT OF MONETARY AND FISCAL POLICIES**

As long as a country has some influence over its interest rate, the share of investment is highest when monetary policy alone is used to restore full employment, and lowest when monetary authorities keep the money supply constant and increased government expenditures alone are used to restore full employment.

to full employment, they have different effects on future economic growth.

But these differences become less clear the closer the economy is to a small open one. If the country faces a fixed interest rate on international capital markets, monetary policy affects net exports through the exchange rate rather than investment. Moreover, fiscal policy in the absence of accommodating monetary policy will not discourage investment. In the case of a small open economy, fiscal and monetary policies have similar effects on economic growth.

These differences also become less clear when we consider how government expenditures are spent. A substantial portion of government expenditures—in recent years, approximately 15 percent—go for physical investments, such as the construction of roads and buildings. Further, large amounts are devoted to investment in people (human capital) and technology, both of which serve to increase economic growth. If the government stimulates the economy by increasing public investment rather than lowering interest rates and stimulating private investment, the impact on growth will depend on the relative rates of return of these two forms of investment.

## DIFFERENCES IN THE EFFICACY OF MONETARY AND FISCAL POLICY

Recall Consensus Point 13 from Chapter 14: when the economy is in a deep recession, monetary policy may be ineffective. Increases in the money supply may have little effect on interest rates, and decreases in the interest rate may have little effect on investment.

Questions have also been raised about the efficacy of some fiscal policies. In some circumstances, a tax reduction may not stimulate much consumption. Consumers—worried about the future and thinking that the tax reduction may not be permanent—save the additional funds.[1] But if the economy has been

[1] Chapter 12 analyzes in more detail these future-oriented consumption decisions. Individuals base their consumption not on their current income but on their lifetime or permanent incomes, and a one-time once-and-for-all tax reduction has little effect on an individual's lifetime or permanent income.

in an extended downturn, leaving many individuals credit-constrained, even temporary tax cuts are likely to be effective at increasing consumption.

Many economists worry that increased deficits—tax cuts not matched by expenditure cuts, or expenditure increases not matched by tax increases—themselves dampen the economy. Since the government will have to turn to capital markets to finance the deficit, some private investment will be crowded out. The net impact of fiscal policy must take this into account: if increased deficit-financed government expenditures crowd out an equivalent amount of private investment, there will be no stimulative effect. In an economy as open as Canada's, this crowding-out effect is not likely to be so dramatic. Still, there may be some offsetting effects through changes in the exchange rate, but because imports and exports adjust so slowly—sometimes taking up to two years to adjust fully—the offsetting effects may not reduce much the efficacy of fiscal policy in the very short run.

## DIFFERENCES IN THE LAGS OF MONETARY AND FISCAL POLICY

Monetary and fiscal policy also differ in the speed with which they can take effect. Monetary policy stimulates the economy in part by lowering interest rates and increasing investment in equipment and housing. Even after firms see a decrease in interest rates, it may take some time before they place new orders for investment, and before the capital goods industry starts producing the newly ordered items. Similarly, though lower interest rates lead to increased demand for housing in the long run, it takes a while before plans are drawn up, permits are obtained, and construction starts. Typically, it takes six months or longer before the effects of monetary policy are realized. By contrast, increased government expenditures or reduced taxes have a direct and immediate effect in increasing incomes.

There is another important source of delay: governments must decide to take action. They must see that the economy is in a downturn, and that some kind of stimulus is needed. These lags in taking action are often significant. The lags of government decision making have been offset by the action of

When the Liberals under Jean Chrétien came to office in the fall of 1993, they faced two economic challenges: the huge deficits that had begun accruing in the early 1980s and had persisted since then had soared to 5.9 percent of GDP, and the economy remained in a prolonged slowdown, with an unemployment rate in excess of 11 percent. These two problems seemed to call for contradictory policies: increased deficits might stimulate the economy but exacerbate the deficit problem. The Chrétien government chose to embark on a long-run deficit-reduction programme, relying primarily on expenditure reductions—a policy that should have exacerbated the economic downturn. Yet the unemployment rate fell to 9.5 percent by 1995, and the government claimed that its economic policies had helped turn the economy around. Did the economic policies fuel the recovery or hinder it?

The episode demonstrates the complex relationships among monetary policy, expectations, and fiscal policy, as well as the potential importance of timing. The government tried to structure the deficit-reduction package so that expenditure cuts were phased in beginning only in 1995. It was believed that this would give the economy time to adjust and that, further, by then with government policies in place, there would be an economic recovery that could better withstand the cuts.

It was believed that the overall deficit-reduction package would restore confidence in the econ-omy, confidence that matters were being taken under control. With smaller future deficits, there would be less federal debt competing for funds with private investment. Investors would anticipate this; hence long-term interest rates would fall, even if the Bank of Canada did nothing. The lower long-term interest rates would help stimulate the economy. (Long-term interest rates did fall, though whether this was because of the deficit reduction or for other reasons remains hotly debated.) The Bank, in turn, recognizing that the economy was less likely to become overheated as a result of excessive fiscal deficits, would maintain an easier monetary policy than it otherwise would. Investment would be stimulated, and so would exports as the downward pressure on interest rates caused a depreciation of the Canadian dollar.

The hope of the government was that lower short-term interest rates induced by the Bank and lower long-term interest rates induced by increased investor confidence would more than offset the direct depressing effects of fiscal policy. The economy did indeed recover. While most economists believe that eventually the economy would have recovered in any case, most also think that the reduction in the deficit probably ensured that the recovery occurred faster and more strongly than otherwise would have happened.

**automatic stabilizers,** expenditures that automatically increase or taxes that automatically decrease when economic conditions worsen. Such measures avoid the lags inherent in time-consuming analysis, legislative decision making, and implementation.

The economy has a number of these automatic stabilizers. Expenditures on unemployment insurance and welfare automatically go up in an economic downturn. So do education and training expenditures, as more individuals delay entering the labour market to search for a job. Similarly, the income tax functions as an automatic stabilizer; the fact that the tax system is progressive enhances its role as an automatic stabilizer. A progressive tax system is one in which higher-income individuals pay a larger fraction of their income in taxes. As an individual's income increases, she moves into a higher tax bracket, and her average tax rate increases. Thus, when the total income (output) of the economy increases, average tax rates increase, and taxes as a fraction of GDP increase. Conversely, when the economy goes into a downturn, tax revenues decline even if the tax rate stays constant. But with a progressive tax system, they decline even more, since the average tax rate declines.

Automatic stabilizers can be very effective when countercyclical policy is called for: they stimulate the economy when it is entering a downturn and reduce aggregate demand when it is heating up. However, in other circumstances they can be disadvantageous. In the 1970s the economy experienced high unemployment together with high inflation, a condition known as **stagflation.** Nominal GDP continued to rise even as real GDP was stuck. The progressivity of the tax system meant that the average tax rate increased, exacerbating the economic downturn. Much of this effect was removed when the tax system was indexed for inflation in 1973—the tax brackets and the various exemptions were increased with the change in the consumer price index each year. Another example: The rate of unemployment has been persistently higher than historical averages in the past two decades, averaging over 10 percent since the beginning of the 1980s, compared with less than 6 percent in the 1960s and early 1970s. Even at the top of the business cycle, the unemployment rate has not fallen much below 8 percent. The result has been an auto-

matically higher level of government spending on such things as unemployment insurance and welfare, which has contributed to the buildup of government debt.

## CONSEQUENCES OF BALANCED-BUDGET LEGISLATION

Many people have thought that it is irresponsible for governments to run a deficit, reasoning that, like a business, governments cannot permanently run at a loss.[2] The huge deficits of the 1980s brought the issue to a head: there were strong political movements, especially in some provinces, to enact legislation requiring a balanced budget. Much of the impetus for this came from the United States, where many states have balanced-budget requirements as part of their constitutions. At the federal level, a proposal to amend the U.S. Constitution to require a balanced budget actually passed the House of Representatives in 1995, but failed by one vote to achieve the required two-thirds majority in the Senate.

One problem with **balanced-budget legislation** is that it would preclude automatic stabilizers from working. As we have seen, in economic downturns, automatic stabilizers typically result in expenditures increasing and revenues falling, leading to deficits. But under a balanced-budget requirement, the government would be forced to *destabilize* the economy and either raise taxes or cut expenditures as the economy went into a recession, when just the opposite medicine is required. The experience of the American states that have balanced-budget requirements supports this view. Evidence shows that typically, in economic booms their expenditures increase, reinforcing the boom, and in economic downturns they decrease, reinforcing the downturn.

With fiscal policy no longer being used to stabilize the economy—or worse, contributing to its instabil-

[2] The economic consequences of fiscal budget deficits are complicated, and will be discussed at greater length in Chapter 20.

ity—the burden of stabilization is put squarely on the shoulders of the monetary authorities. This means that interest rates and the exchange rate would have to fluctuate more than they otherwise would, causing greater expansions and contractions in the interest- and trade-sensitive sectors (housing, durable goods, plant and equipment and manufacturing). Since the lags in monetary policy, the time between when an action is undertaken and its effects are fully felt, are long and variable (typically six months or more), the economy itself will exhibit greater variability. And there are times when monetary policy is relatively ineffective in stimulating the economy—i.e., when the response of the economy to lowered interest rates is small, or smaller than anticipated—such as during the Great Depression and in the economic downturn of 1991. In such situations, the economic downturn will last longer and may be deeper than it would be if stronger automatic stabilizers were in place.

One proposal for reducing these destabilizing effects involves not balancing the actual budget but setting to zero the **full-employment deficit,** which is what the deficit would have been had the economy been operating at full employment. The full-employment deficit takes into account the changes in expenditures and revenues resulting from the current economic conditions. In a recession the full-employment deficit is smaller than the actual deficit. Most economists believe that the government is fiscally responsible so long as there is no full-employment deficit. Many argue that if there is to be legislation regarding a balanced budget, it should be written in terms of the full-employment deficit.

## PROVINCIAL AND LOCAL GOVERNMENTS

Though the discussion of fiscal policy has focused on the taxes and expenditures of the federal government, over one half of Canadian government expenditures are at the provincial and local levels. These expenditures and the taxes that finance them are governed by quite different considerations from those that prevail at the national level. The provinces do not see stabilizing the economy and maintaining full employment as their responsibility. They often find it difficult (or at least politically inopportune) to raise tax rates in bad times. When the economy goes into a recession, they find their revenues reduced and may respond by reducing their expenditures. This would in effect cut back on the fiscal stimulus at just the time it is most needed. The situation is identical to that of a balanced-budget reduction in government expenditures, whose outcome is reduced national output.

The ability of the provinces to adopt countercyclical fiscal policies is further restricted by the fact that many provincial debt loads have grown to unmanageable proportions. Total provincial debt is about one half of the federal debt. This is partly a result of rapidly increasing expenditure requirements in the areas of education and health care, and partly a result of reductions in the rate of growth of federal-provincial transfers. The provinces are left with relatively little room to maneuver in terms of affecting aggregate demand. It has also meant that attempts of the federal government to control the level of debt held by the public sector can only be partially

---

### BALANCED BUDGETS AND STABILIZATION POLICY

**1** An increase in government expenditure matched by an increase in tax revenues is expansionary.

**2** Automatic stabilizers increase expenditures and reduce taxes automatically as the economy goes into a recession. Standard versions of balanced-budget legislation would preclude the use of automatic stabilizers as well as elimi-

nate the possibility of discretionary fiscal policy to stabilize the economy.

**3** In practice, balanced-budget legislation would likely destabilize the economy, and force the entire burden of stabilization onto monetary policy.

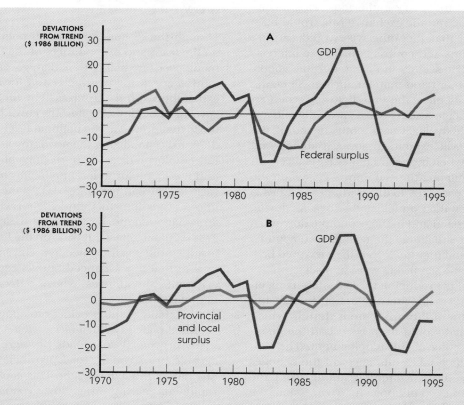

**Figure 15.5** GOVERNMENT BUDGET SURPLUSES OVER THE BUSINESS CYCLE 1970–95

Panel A shows how the federal budget surplus and GDP change relative to their long-term trends. The surplus is higher during booms and lower during recessions, thus contributing to the stability of the economy. Panel B shows that the same phenomenon also applies to provincial and local budget surpluses combined. *Source:* Statistics Canada, CANSIM Database 1996, Matrixes 2711–13, 6702, and 6841.

successful. Recent attempts to reduce the debt by restricting transfers to the provinces has resulted in the provinces' simply increasing their debt. Provinces find it as difficult to reduce their deficits as the federal government.

Given these constraints on the ability to pursue discretionary fiscal policy at the provincial level, it is interesting to observe how provincial and local budget surpluses vary over the business cycle. If these surpluses tended to be lower during booms, that would be evidence that provincial-local fiscal policy was procyclical, or destabilizing. That is, it would be providing stimulus when the economy needed a reduction in aggregate demand, and vice versa. Figure 15.5 compares how the provincial-local budget surplus behaves over the business cycle compared with the federal budget surplus. Panel A shows how both GDP and the federal budget surplus

## Close-up: Fiscal and Monetary Policy in the European Union

As a step towards the eventual goal of establishing a common currency in Western Europe, the countries of the European Union (EU) are currently preparing their economies to join the newly formed European Monetary Union (EMU). Under the terms of the Maastricht Treaty (1991), those nations that meet certain targets with regard to their governmental budget deficits, rates of inflation, and debt/GDP ratios will be eligible to join the EMU. Although a new currency and its associated central bank will not be created initially, countries will fix their exchange rates with regard to each other, so a British pound will always be worth the same number of German marks, and holding marks or pounds will be equivalent. This should bring about stability in European financial markets and enhance the workings of the pan-European common market. But the move to the EMU will also have implications for the use of traditional macroeconomic policies by member countries.

Joining the EMU effectively compels member nations to adopt a common monetary policy. Interest and inflation rates in each country will be determined by the requirement to maintain fixed currency exchange rates with respect to other European countries, and this will preclude the use of an independent monetary policy to influence aggregate demand. To illustrate this suppose the central bank of France attempted to pursue a more expansionary monetary policy than the rest of the EMU. Expansion of the French money supply would begin to lower French interest rates. This would cause an outflow of capital as investors sought the higher returns available in the rest of Europe. Individuals and companies would sell their holdings of

French francs and purchase other EMU currencies. But the increase in the supply of French francs would drive down the value of the franc against the other EMU currencies. To prevent this from occurring and to keep the exchange rate at its agreed-upon level the central bank of France would have to purchase the increased supply of francs. This would, of course, remove francs from circulation, defeating the original intent of an expansionary monetary policy.

Other aspects of the European Union also limit the ability of national governments to pursue their own fiscal policy. A common market in goods and services, the free flow of labour and capital, and national treatment of all European companies with regard to bidding on government contracts restrict the ability of a single nation to stimulate its economy using expansionary fiscal policy. Suppose the government of a small nation like Belgium increased its spending in an effort to increase its GDP. Because the Belgian government must treat all European firms identically regardless of their nationality, much of the initial increase in spending would go towards the purchasing of goods and services produced by French, German, British, and other European companies with only part of the business going to Belgian firms. Further, given the open markets in goods and services, subsequent spending created by the initial stimulus would also be spread among Belgium's trading partners. The expansionary effect would thus be diluted across the whole of the common market.

The nations of Europe have decided that the benefits of economic union (the free trade aspects of the common market and the stability provided by a common monetary system) outweigh the cost of losing these policy options. This is very similar to the position faced by provincial governments in federal nations like Canada. Given the common currency and the existence of a single central bank, individual provinces are clearly precluded from pursuing an independent monetary policy. Although some interprovincial barriers exist, the common-market aspects of confederation severely limit the ability of provinces to pursue their own fiscal policy. Recent history in Ontario provides evidence of this. In the early 1990s the New Democratic Party government of Bob Rae increased spending in an effort to fight a severe recession, with little measurable effect on provincial GDP or unemployment. More recently, Mike Harris's Conservative government adopted a plan of vigourous personal tax cuts as a way of increasing consumer spending and boosting economic activity in Ontario. Critics argued that the stimulative effect of these tax cuts would be spread across the country and would not be limited to the province.

differ from their long-run trend lines over the past 25 years. As can be seen, GDP and the federal budget surplus tend to fluctuate around the long-run trend together. That is, the federal fiscal stimulus provided through the federal budget is countercyclical, which is a desirable state of affairs. Panel B shows that the combined provincial-local fiscal stimulus is also countercyclical, despite the constraints that provinces and their municipalities may have in conducting discretionary fiscal policy. Apparently, automatic stabilizers implicit in their budgets are relatively strong.

## REVIEW AND PRACTICE

### SUMMARY

**1** Increasing government expenditure without increasing taxes stimulates the economy but generates a deficit. If the government spends the funds on investments that yield returns in excess of the interest rate, then increased government expenditure can make the economy stronger both today and in the future.

**2** Increases in government expenditure matched by increases in taxes can still stimulate the economy, but there will be no multiplier effects.

**3** Monetary policy stimulates the economy by increasing investment and net exports. Thus, stimulating the economy through monetary policy has a more positive effect on economic growth than doing so through fiscal policy, unless the increased government expenditures are spent on investments. In deep recessions, however, monetary policy may not be very effective.

**4** The lags associated with monetary policy may be longer than those associated with fiscal policy.

**5** Automatic stabilizers help to stabilize the economy, without any active decisions by policy makers.

**6** Most balanced-budget legislation would circumscribe the operation of automatic stabilizers and thus serve to destabilize the economy. All the burden of stabilization would be placed on monetary policy.

## KEY TERMS

balanced-budget
multiplier

accommodative mone-
tary policy

automatic stabilizers

stagflation

balanced-budget
legislation

full-employment deficit

## REVIEW QUESTIONS

**1** How does an increase in government expenditure shift the aggregate-expenditures schedule and the aggregate demand curve? How does monetary policy shift the aggregate-expenditures schedule and the aggregate demand curve?

**2** If the economy is in a recession, describe the trade-off between today and the future associated with an increase in government expenditures. How is the trade-off affected by what the government spends its increased expenditures on? If the government spends the funds on investments that yield high returns, is there still a trade-off? Even if the government spends the funds on public consumption, why might the trade-off still appear attractive?

**3** What is the effect of an increase in government expenditure matched by an increase in taxes?

**4** Compare the effects of monetary and fiscal policy on the level of investment and the composition of output.

**5** What other factor(s) are important in the choice between monetary and fiscal policy?

**6** What effect might balanced-budget legislation have on the stability of the economy?

**7** What are automatic stabilizers, and why are they important?

## PROBLEMS

**1** Show how a decrease in the price level leads to an increase in aggregate demand and equilibrium output if money supply remains unchanged and there is excess capacity in the economy.
>   (a) First, use the demand and supply curves for money to show the effect on interest rates.
>   (b) Then use the investment function to show the effect on investments.
>   (c) Then use the aggregate-expenditures schedule to show the effect on equilibrium output.

**2** Show the differences in the effect of an increase in government expenditures when monetary authorities (a) keep the money supply constant, and (b) expand the money supply to keep the interest rate constant. Trace out the effects on (a) the demand and supply curves for money and the equilibrium interest rate; (b) the levels of investment and net exports; (c) the aggregate-expenditures schedule and the equilibrium level of output at any fixed price; and (d) the aggregate demand schedule.

**3** Assume you are in charge of monetary policy. The economy is $6 billion below capacity, or 1 percent of its $600 billion capacity. (a) You are told the government does not plan to increase government expenditures or change tax rates at all. How much must you increase the money supply? Assume: the economy is a closed one; money demand has an interest elasticity of .8, an income elasticity of 1; investment elasticity is .8 and investment amounts to 10 percent of GDP ($54 billion); and the multiplier is 2. (b) In some countries, such as the United Kingdom, the monetary authorities are more directly under control of the government than in Canada. Assume the government says that it plans to increase government expenditures to restore full employment, but it wants the monetary authorities to keep interest rates constant. By how much must they increase the money supply? (Use the same assumptions as in part a.) Assuming the multiplier is 2, by how much must government expenditure be increased? (c) Now assume the monetary authorities are independent, and have announced that they will not change the money supply. By how much will interest rates rise if the government is successful in restoring the economy to full employment? How will that affect investment? What does this imply for the required magnitude of increase in government expenditure? Discuss how your answer might change if the economy were an open one.

**4** When individuals become wealthier they consume more. If prices fall, the *real value* of wealth which is denominated in monetary terms—like money and government bonds—increases. Would you expect this effect to be large or small?

Assume government bonds and money represent 10 percent of national wealth, and that an increase in real wealth of 10 percent leads to a .6 percent increase in consumption. Assume consumption represents 90 percent of GDP and the multiplier is 2. Assume prices fall by 5 percent. By approximately what percent will GDP increase? Assume the economy is 10 percent below capacity. How long would it take the economy to be restored to full employment if prices continued to fall at the rate of 5 percent per year?

**5** A closed economy is $6 billion below capacity, or 1 percent of its $600 billion capacity. The government contemplates stimulating the economy by alternative policies. Assume the multiplier is 2, and that investment is completely interest inelastic. Calculate the required increase in government expenditures. Calculate the required increase in government expenditures if the government increases taxes in tandem. Can monetary policy be used to stimulate the economy?

**6** Consider the extreme case where the individuals and firms within a country can borrow (or lend) abroad as much as desired at a fixed real interest rate. Can monetary authorities affect the level of real investment? Assume that as the monetary authori-

ties try to raise interest rates, funds flow in from abroad; as they flow in, they bid up the exchange rate. Trace through the effects of: (a) the increased demand for Canadian dollars by foreign investors wishing to invest in Canada on the exchange rate; (b) the exchange rate on the aggregate-expenditures schedule and on GDP.

**7** Several European countries are scheduled to form a European Monetary Union (EMU), in which they would have a single currency. Effectively, this means that exchange rates between the countries would be fixed, and there would be a single interest rate for all the countries. The governments have agreed that certain criteria must be met to join the EMU. These include reducing the fiscal deficit as a share of GDP to below 3 percent. What might be the macroeconomic effects of this deficit reduction (a) if each country's monetary authorities do not adjust interest rates? (b) if interest rates are reduced? Why might the simultaneous reduction of deficits by all the countries lead to a larger reduction in output than if only one country reduced its deficit, if interest rates do not fall? Use diagrams to illustrate your answer.

**8** Assume that after the European Monetary Union is established, interest rates will be the same in all countries within the Union. Assume that unemployment in one country within the Union, say France, increases. What can the government do to restore full employment?

Contrast what might be done about unemployment in France within the European Monetary Union with what might be done about unemployment in Quebec. In what ways will the situations be similar? How will they differ?

**9** Compare the effects on longer-term economic growth of using monetary rather than fiscal policy to stimulate an economy when capital flows freely internationally with the effects within a closed economy.

# PART FOUR

# THE DYNAMICS OF ADJUSTMENT

So far, we have discussed two of the three key macroeconomic problems: growth and unemployment. We now turn to the third, *inflation.* What causes it? Why is it a problem? What can government do about it?

This part of the book does more, however, than just round out our discussion of the three key macroeconomic problems. It also describes and explains the *dynamics of wage and price adjustments.* Part Two focused on full-employment economies; Part Three, on economies with unemployment. We emphasized that the key distinction between the two were assumptions about adjustments. In Part Two, we assumed that wages and prices adjusted quickly, so the labour market was always in equilibrium. In Part Three, we assumed that wages and prices were fixed. It was as if we were looking at a snapshot of the economy before the dynamic process unfolded. We recognized that when the demand for labour was lower than the supply at current wages, or when the demand for goods was lower than the supply at the current price level, there were pressures for wages and prices to fall. But we also recognized that adjustments do not occur instantaneously. Similarly, we recognized that the economy's resources were fully employed and, if the aggregate demand curve shifted to the right, there would be excess demand for goods at the going price level, which would create upward price pressure. But, again, we recognized that prices do not adjust instantaneously.

The fact that wages and prices do not adjust instantaneously—that they are sticky—means that after any disturbance there will be at least a period during which demand does not equal supply. If demand is lower than supply, output is limited by aggregate demand, so that an increase in aggregate demand—say, as a result of increased government expenditure—increases output and employment.

Understanding why unemployment persists and why prices may rise, not just once but year after year, entails understanding the dynamics of adjustment. In this part, we will *describe* observed regularities in wage and price adjustments and *explain* both the consequences of these observed patterns and the sources of wage and price stickiness.

Part Four consists of three chapters. Chapter 16 provides the basic description of wage and price dynamics. It explains the major determinants of the rate of inflation. Chapter 17 takes a closer look at the labour market to see why wages in particular often exhibit rigidities. Finally, Chapter 18 brings together the insights of Parts Two, Three, and Four to discuss some of the central policy issues in macroeconomics and the controversies surrounding them. Should the government intervene? And if so, what is the most effective form of intervention? What are the costs of inflation? Are there trade-offs between inflation and unemployment?

# CHAPTER 16

# INFLATION: WAGE AND PRICE DYNAMICS

I t is an axiom of political rhetoric that inflation is bad. Popular sentiment runs so strongly against inflation that it is usually taken for
granted that the government should do something about it. But if the
government is to do something about it, we have to know what
causes it. How do economists predict what the inflation rate will be
next year? How do we explain why some countries have higher inflation
rates than others? Or why Canada has a lower inflation rate today than it
did fifteen years ago?

   If inflation is so disliked, why don't governments simply get rid of it? The
answer is that normally, inflation can be reduced only at a cost: if the unemployment rate is allowed to increase, and vice versa. In this chapter we in-
quire into the trade-off between inflation and unemployment, and how the
terms of this trade-off can be changed. Many economists believe that in the
long run, there is no trade-off and that attempting to reduce unemployment
to too low a level is a chimera: not only does inflation increase, but it increases at a faster and faster rate, until inflation, not unemployment, becomes viewed as the central economic problem. This chapter explains these
critical debates which underlie so much of current policy discussions.

## KEY QUESTIONS

**1** What are the "costs" of inflation? Why does it make a difference whether inflation is anticipated or not? How can the costs be ameliorated?

**2** What is the trade-off between inflation and unemployment? How do expectations about inflation affect the level of inflation associated with any level of unemployment?

**3** Why might inflation accelerate if the unemployment rate is kept at too low a level? How do these considerations affect government policies?

**4** How do labour market factors and government policies affect this critical unemployment rate?

**5** Why is it that once inflation starts, it tends to persist? What role does the interlinking of product and labour markets play in this perpetuation of inflation?

**6** What role does monetary policy play in initiating or perpetuating inflation?

**7** What are some of the reasons for wage and price rigidities?

# THE COSTS OF INFLATION

We identified growth, unemployment, and inflation as the three key macroeconomic problems. In Part Two we discussed issues of growth, and in Part Three we discussed issues of unemployment. Here we focus on inflation and the relationship between inflation and unemployment. The costs of unemployment are apparent: not only is there a loss in output, but the misery of those who cannot get gainful employment is palpable. The costs of inflation are more subtle, and over the years have been greatly ameliorated.

People sense there is something wrong with the economy when there is high inflation. Workers worry that their pay-cheques will not keep pace with increases in the price level, and their living standards will be eroded. Investors worry that the dollars that they get paid back will be worth less than the dollars they invested, and that they may not have enough to live comfortably in their old age.

When inflation is anticipated, many of its economic costs disappear. For example, workers who know that prices will be rising by 10 percent this year may negotiate wages that rise fast enough to offset the inflation. Lenders know that the dollars that they will be repaid will be worth less than the dollars that they lent, and take that into account when they set the interest rate they charge or decide whether to make the loan.

But even when inflation is not perfectly anticipated, workers and investors can immunize themselves against the effects of inflation by having wages and returns *indexed* to inflation. When wages are perfectly indexed, a 1 percent increase in the price level (1 percent inflation rate) results in a 1 percent increase in wages. Such automatic indexing provisions are referred to as **cost-of-living adjustments** (COLAs). A worker with a COLA is relatively immune to the effects of inflation. Contracts containing COLAs became common in the late 1970s and early 1980s, a period of high inflation. As inflation fears have subsided in recent years, COLAs have become less prevalent.

For many years, Old Age Security payments to the elderly have been indexed to the rate of inflation. The tax brackets and tax credits in the income tax system have also been indexed, but at 3 percent under the actual rate of inflation. The Canadian government, like those in the United Kingdom and New Zealand, sells indexed government bonds so that savers can put aside money knowing that the returns will not be adversely affected by inflation. All these things ease the economic costs of inflation throughout the economy.

## CLOSE-UP: HYPERINFLATION IN GERMANY IN THE 1920s

Following World War I, Germany was required by the victorious Allied nations to make substantial "reparation" payments. But the sheer size of the reparations, combined with the wartime devastation of German industry, made payment nearly impossible. John Maynard Keynes, then an economic adviser to the British government, was among those who warned that the reparations were too large. To finance some of Germany's financial obligations, the German government started simply printing money.

The resulting increases in both the amount of circulating currency and the price level can be seen in the figure. From January 1922 to November 1923, the average price level increased by a factor of almost 10 billion.* People made desperate attempts to spend their currency as soon as they received it, since the value of currency was declining so rapidly. One story

* Thomas Sargent, "The Ends of Four Big Inflations," in Robert Hall, ed., *Inflation* (Chicago: University of Chicago Press, 1982), pp. 74–75.

often told by Keynes was how Germans would buy two beers at once, even though one was likely to get warm, for fear that otherwise, when it came time to buy the second beer, the price would have risen.

At an annual inflation rate of 100 percent, money loses half its value every year. If you save $100 today, in five years it will have buying power equal to only 3 current dollars. It is possible for nominal interest rates to adjust even to very high inflation rates. But when those high inflation rates fluctuate in unanticipated ways, the effects can be disastrous.

Periods of hyperinflation create a massive redistribution of wealth. If an individual is smart or lucky enough to hold assets in a form such as foreign funds or land, then the hyperinflation will do little to reduce that person's actual wealth. Those who cannot avail themselves of these "inflation-proof" assets will see their wealth fall.

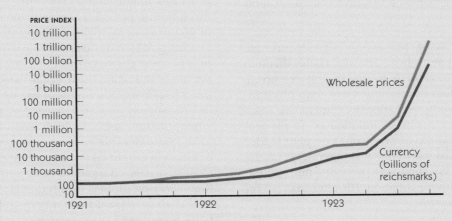

## THE GERMAN HYPERINFLATION

Inflation in Germany during the 1920s reached levels that may seem unbelievably high. At the end of 1923, prices were 10 billion times higher than they had been two years earlier.

## WHO SUFFERS FROM INFLATION?

While indexing softens the effects of inflation, the extent of indexing is far from complete. So who suffers today from inflation? Many people may suffer a little, since indexing does not fully protect them, but some are more likely to suffer than others. Among the groups most imperfectly protected are lenders, taxpayers, and holders of currency.

**Lenders**   Since most loans are not fully indexed to inflation, increases in inflation mean that the dollars that lenders receive back from borrowers are worth less than the ones they lent out. Many people put a large part of their savings for their retirement into bonds or other fixed-income securities. These people will suffer if an inflationary bout comes between them and their nest eggs. The extent to which they will suffer depends in large measure on whether the price changes were anticipated. After World War II, many people bought bonds yielding a 3 or 4 percent annual return. They did not anticipate much inflation. When inflation reached double-digit levels in the late 1970s, the rate of interest they received did not even come close to compensating them for the reduced value of the dollar they had invested. In real terms, they received a negative return on their savings.

**Taxpayers**   Our tax system is only partially indexed, and inflation frequently hurts investors badly through the tax system. All returns to investment are taxed, including those that do nothing more than offset inflation. Consequently, real after-tax returns are often negative. Consider a rate of inflation of 10 percent and an asset that yields a return of 12 percent before tax. If the individual has to pay a 33 percent tax on the return, his after-tax yield is 9 percent—not enough to compensate him for inflation. His after-tax real return is minus 1 percent.

**Holders of Currency**   Inflation also makes it expensive for people to hold currency because as they hold it, the currency loses its value. Currency facilitates a variety of transactions, and inflation interferes with the efficiency of the economy by discour-aging the holding of currency. The fact that inflation takes away the value of money means that inflation acts as a tax on holding money. Economists refer to this distortionary effect as an **inflation tax.**

This distortion is not as important in modern economies, for chequing accounts are frequently used instead of cash, and chequing accounts typically pay interest. As the rate of inflation increases, the interest rate paid on chequing accounts normally increases as well. Even in Argentina in the 1970s, when prices were rising at 800 percent a month, bank accounts yielded more than 800 percent a month. Still, poorer individuals who do not have chequing accounts and therefore must hold much of what little wealth they have in the form of currency are adversely affected.

**The Economy**   There are two costs of inflation to the economy as a whole. The first has to do with relative prices. Because price increases are never perfectly coordinated, increases in the rate of inflation lead to a greater variability of relative prices. If the shoe industry makes price adjustments only every three months, then in the third month, right before its price increase, shoes may be relatively cheap, while right after the price increase shoes may be relatively expensive. On the other hand, the prices of groceries might change continually throughout the three-month period. Therefore, the ratio of the price of groceries to the price of shoes will continually be changing. When the average rate of inflation is only 2 or 3 percent per year, this does not cause much of a problem. But when the average rate of inflation is 10 percent per month, inflation causes real distortions in how society allocates its resources. In particular, when inflation gets very high, economies tend to allocate considerable resources to avoiding the costs of inflation and to taking advantage of the discrepancies in prices charged by different sellers. Rather than carrying money, which quickly erodes in value, they rush to deposit their money in interest-bearing bank accounts.

The second economywide cost of inflation arises from the risk and uncertainty that inflation generates. If there were perfect indexing, the uncertainty about the rate of inflation would be unimportant. But as indexing is not perfect, the resulting uncertainty makes it difficult to plan. Lenders cannot charge interest that takes fully into account the fact that the dollars paid back will be worth less than the dollars lent. People saving for their retirements cannot know what to put aside. Business firms borrowing money are uncertain about the price they will receive for the goods they produce. Firms are also hurt when they build wage increases into multiyear contracts to reflect **anticipated inflation.** If for any reason a firm finds that the prices it can charge increase less rapidly than anticipated in the contract, the employer suffers.

## MISPERCEIVED COSTS OF INFLATION

We have discussed two significant costs of inflation, but much of the aversion to inflation comes from a variety of forms of misperceptions. If a poll were conducted asking people whether they were hurt or helped by inflation, most would say they were hurt. Much of this is simply misperception. People "feel" price increases much more vividly than they do the corresponding income increases. They "feel" the higher interest rates they have to pay on loans more than they do the decrease in the value of the dollars with which they repay lenders. A closer look at who benefits and who loses from unanticipated inflation suggests that there are probably more gainers than there are losers. This is simply because there are probably more debtors than lenders, and debtors benefit from unanticipated inflation.

In many inflationary episodes, many individuals not only *feel* worse off, they *are* worse off—but inflation itself is not the culprit. The oil price increases of 1973 set off a widespread inflation in Canada. The higher price of oil also made eastern Canada poorer than it had previously been, because it was an oil importer. Someone's standard of living had to be cut, and inflation did the cutting. Frequently those whose incomes were cut—unskilled workers, whose wages did not keep pace with prices—cited as the *cause* of their lower incomes the inflation that accompanied the oil price increases. However, generalized price inflation was only a symptom. The underlying cause of that particular inflation, and of the reduced real incomes, was a sharp rise in the price of oil.

It is clear that the costs of inflation are different, and undoubtedly lower, than they were before indexing was so extensive. Today economists do not agree on how seriously to take inflation. There is considerable evidence that high rates of inflation have strongly adverse effects on economic performance, but there is little evidence that there are any significant adverse effects from the moderate rates of inflation that Canada has experienced in recent years. Indeed, a small amount of inflation may be an aid to efficient resource allocation. Relative prices of different goods are continuously changing in any economy. If the rate of inflation is zero, changing relative prices means that some prices should rise and others should fall. Firms might find it difficult to lower prices, for example, because that might require lowering wages, which may be hard because of contracts or minimum wage laws. If so, the needed relative price changes would be hard to achieve with zero inflation, but might be feasible if a low level of inflation existed so that prices did not have to fall to allow relative prices to adjust.

## COSTS OF INFLATION, ACTUAL AND PERCEIVED

Real costs

Variability in relative prices

Increased uncertainty

Misperceptions

Failing to recognize offsetting increases in income

Blaming losses in real income that occur during inflationary episodes but are caused by other factors on inflation

## INFLATION AND UNEMPLOYMENT

There is some debate about the *magnitude* of the costs of inflation, but there is no debate on the fact that there *are* costs. If there were no costs involved in reducing inflation, governments would do so. But lower inflation can typically be obtained only at the cost of higher unemployment. In this section, we analyze the relationship between inflation and unemployment.

### FLEXIBLE VERSUS FIXED PRICES

In Parts Two and Three of the book we examined two different models of the economy, the full-employment and unemployment models. These models are based on opposite assumptions about prices and wages. The full-employment model assumes that prices and wages are perfectly flexible. The unemployment model assumes that prices and wages are fixed. The full-employment model gives us a useful picture of the economy in the long run. Eventually, prices and wages do adjust so that the economy returns to the full-employment level of output. The unemployment model is a closer picture of the economy in the very short run, in which prices and wages adjust very little, if at all. Our objective

now is to understand the middle ground between the very short run of the unemployment model (with fixed wages and prices) and the long run of the full-employment model.

In the fixed wage and price model, if at the current price level, $P_0$, aggregate demand exceeds aggregate supply, there is upward price pressure, as illustrated in Figure 16.1 by the aggregate demand curve, $AD_2$. The case we focused on in Part Three was one where at the current price level aggregate demand fell short of aggregate supply, as illustrated by the aggregate demand curve, $AD_1$.

As we know, in this situation output is limited by aggregate demand, $Y_1$. When the economy is below the full-employment level of output ($Y_s$), policy makers may attempt to shift the aggregate demand curve to the right, increasing output and reducing unemployment. But if the aggregate demand curve is shifted too far to the right, upward price pressure is injected into the economy, and inflation rears its head. On the other hand, if the initial situation is represented by $AD_2$, upward price pressure may be diminished by leftward shifts of the aggregate demand curve. If this is taken to extremes, the level of output may fall below the full-employment level.

The problems of inflation and unemployment lie on opposite sides of the aggregate supply curve. When aggregate demand exceeds aggregate supply, the economy experiences inflation (rising prices) as it moves to the future equilibrium level. On the other

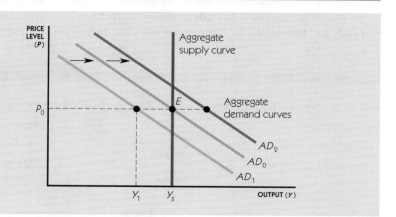

### Figure 16.1 SHORT-RUN EQUILIBRIUM

When aggregate demand is less than aggregate supply ($Y_s$) at the current price level, output will be limited by aggregate demand ($Y_1$), and there will be involuntary unemployment. When aggregate supply is less than aggregate demand at the current price level, output will be limited by aggregate supply and there will be upward price pressure.

hand, when aggregate demand is less than aggregate supply, unemployment becomes the problem. In both cases, the size of the effects on the rates of inflation and unemployment will depend on the size of the gap between aggregate supply and aggregate demand; the larger the gap, the larger the effect. This interconnection between inflation and unemployment is the key to understanding the dynamics of adjustment, the middle ground between the full-employment and unemployment models we have studied thus far.

The challenge for economists and policy makers is threefold: (1) to determine the state of the economy at any given time, (2) to determine how policy can change the state of the economy favourably, and (3) to determine how inflation and unemployment are likely to change in the future. Two of the key factors they look at in assessing the state of the economy are the unemployment rate—a measure of the "tightness" of the labour market—and the rate of change of wages. Economists and policy makers also

examine conditions in the product and capital markets, but for various reasons unemployment and wages give an especially good snapshot of where the economy is and where inflation is heading.

## THE PHILLIPS CURVE

The framework for thinking about the rate of change of wages is the same as that used for thinking about the rate of change of prices. Just as the greater the gap between demand and supply, the more "pressure" there is for price to increase and so the faster will be the rate of increase of price, so too in the labour market: the "tighter" the labour market, the faster we expect the price of labour—wages—to rise. This kind of relationship has been verified in a number of labour markets in a number of instances, as illustrated in Figure 16.2. The relationship is called the Phillips curve after A. W. Phillips, a New Zealander teaching in England in the 1950s.

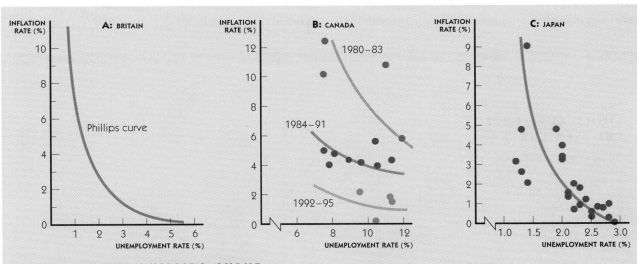

**Figure 16.2 THE PHILLIPS CURVE**

The Phillips curve shows that as the unemployment rate falls, the inflation rate rises. Panel A shows the curve A. W. Phillips actually plotted in 1958 for the British economy. Panel B depicts the Phillips curve relationship for Canadian data in the early 1980s, the late 1980s, and the early 1990s. Panel C gives the Phillips curve for Japan for 1970–95. *Sources: Economic Report of the President* (1995), Tables B-40, B-63, B-110, B-111; Statistics Canada, CANSIM Database 1996, Matrixes 2074, 7440.

The different panels of Figure 16.2 show Phillips curves for different countries and periods. In every case the unemployment rate at which inflation is zero is positive. There are several reasons for this. In the economy, not every worker is qualified to do every job. There may be unemployment of autoworkers and excess demand for computer programmers. If wages respond upwards to excess demand more strongly than they respond downwards to excess supply, average wages will be rising even when the excess demand for one type of labour equals the excess supply of the other. Similarly, there may be unemployment in Saint John and vacancies in Oshawa. But unemployed shipbuilders in Saint John cannot simply walk into jobs making automobiles in Oshawa. By the same token, there will always be some workers moving between jobs; in Chapter 6 we referred to this as frictional unemployment.

## THE EXPECTATIONS-AUGMENTED PHILLIPS CURVE

In the 1970s, the stable relationship between unemployment and inflation seemed to disappear. The economy experienced high unemployment with high inflation. There was a simple explanation for this: the rate at which wages increase at any level of unemployment depends on expectations concerning inflation. If workers expect prices to be rising, they will demand offsetting wage increases; and employers will be willing to grant those higher wage increases, because they believe that they will be able to sell what they produce at higher prices.

Inflationary expectations ran high in the 1970s, with the result that higher rates of inflation coexisted with higher unemployment. This is represented diagramatically in Figure 16.3. The Phillips curve shifts up, incorporating the inflationary expectations. Because it accounts for inflationary expectations, the newly positioned Phillips curve is called the **expectations-augmented Phillips curve.** The Phillips curve shifted up successively during the 1970s, until it stabilized in the early 1980s, and then fell back again in the late 1980s. But how can the Phillips curve be stable for long periods of time, yet be subject to changes such as those of the 1970s? The answer is that the Phillips curve stabilizes during periods when actual inflation equals expected inflation. This occurs at a special level of unemployment sometimes called the **natural rate of unemployment,** indicated by $U^*$ in Figure 16.3.

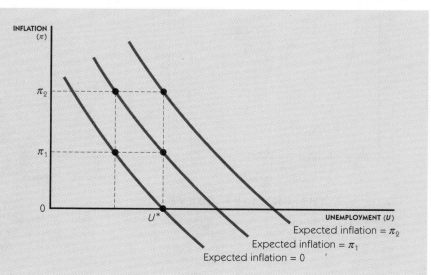

### Figure 16.3 THE EXPECTATIONS-AUGMENTED PHILLIPS CURVE

The position of the Phillips curve depends on inflationary expectations. Increased expectations concerning inflation shifts the Phillips curve up. $U^*$ is the non-accelerating-inflation rate of unemployment, the NAIRU, the rate of unemployment at which inflation is just equal to inflationary expectations. At lower unemployment rates, inflation exceeds inflationary expectations, and eventually the Phillips curve shifts up still more. At higher unemployment rates, inflation is less than the expectations concerning inflation, and the Phillips curve shifts down.

To better understand the role of the natural rate of unemployment, consider that expectations about inflation are affected both by recent experience and the changes in policy and economic conditions people expect. Take the simple case where expectations are simply adaptive, that is, they respond (or adapt) to recent experience. Assume the economy was initially in a situation where prices had been stable for an extended period of time. Given this historical experience, workers expect zero inflation. In Figure 16.3 the Phillips curve is the lowest curve. Suppose the government reduces unemployment below the rate $U^*$, where inflation equals expected inflation, and keeps it at the lower rate. This induces an increase in the inflation rate. As the inflation rate increases, the expectations-augmented Phillips curve shifts up, so that higher rates of inflation coexist at each level of unemployment. If the government continues to maintain the unemployment rate below $U^*$, this will fuel higher expected inflation, resulting in another upward shift of the expectations-augmented Phillips curve. Thus, if the government attempts to maintain the unemployment rate below the natural rate, the inflation rate will continue to increase. As expectations adapt to each successive increase in the inflation rate, inflation increases still more. Accordingly, today, the natural rate is generally known as the **non-accelerating-inflation rate of unemployment,** or NAIRU for short.

An economy cannot *permanently* lower its unemployment rate below the NAIRU without facing faster and faster inflation. This has emerged as one of the central points of consensus among macroeconomists around the world today, and is our fourteenth consensus point.

## 14 The Trade-off between Inflation and Unemployment

*When the unemployment rate remains below the NAIRU the rate of inflation increases; when it remains above the NAIRU it decreases. An economy cannot permanently lower its unemployment rate below the NAIRU without facing ever-increasing rates of inflation.*

An important consequence of this consensus is an emerging consensus on policy: the government should not push the unemployment rate below the NAIRU.

A key issue is how fast the expectations-augmented Phillips curve shifts up when the unemployment rate is below the NAIRU. The answer depends in part on the economy's recent inflationary experience: if inflation has been high and volatile, everyone will be sensitized to inflation, inflationary expectations may respond quickly, and the expectations-augmented Phillips curve shifts quickly. Recent experience in Canada, where inflation has been low and stable, suggests a rather sluggish response: if the unemployment rate is kept below the NAIRU by 2 percentage points for one year, then the inflation rate will increase by 1 percentage point. Conversely, to bring the inflation rate down by 1 percentage point requires keeping the unemployment rate *above* the NAIRU by 2 percentage points for one year (or by 4 percentage points for six months). The amount by which the unemployment rate must be kept above the NAIRU for one year to bring down inflation by 1 percentage point is called the **sacrifice ratio.** In 1995, the sacrifice ratio for Canada was believed to be about 2.

## SHIFTS IN THE NAIRU

But while the *concept* of the NAIRU is now well accepted, economists do differ in their estimate of what the critical level of unemployment is below which inflation begins. This is because the NAIRU itself may vary over time. In the early 1970s, most economists thought the NAIRU was around 5–6 percent. As unemployment rose precipitously during the late 1970s and early 1980s, many economists thought the NAIRU had risen to the 7.5–8.5 percent range. It seemed stuck there well into the 1990s. There is now some evidence that the NAIRU is beginning to decline in the second half of the 1990s.[1] Some economists remained cautious, however, worried that inflation would rear its head, but only with a lag. Today, few economists believe that the evidence is strong enough to suggest a precise number for the NAIRU; the best that can be done is to suggest a range of plausible values.

[1] See, for example, the evidence cited in Pierre Fortin, "A Strategy for Deficit Control Through Faster Growth," *Canadian Business Economics* 3 (Fall 1994): 3–26.

Some of the changes in the NAIRU are predictable. Earlier we noted that there were several factors that contributed to the fact that the NAIRU was positive, that is, with expectations of, say, zero inflation, the unemployment rate at which actual inflation would be zero was positive. There would always be some frictional unemployment, people moving from job to job. Such movement is more common among new entrants into the labour force. In the late 1970s, there were many new entrants, as the baby boomers reached working age and as more women entered the labour force for the first time. In addition, the liberalization of the unemployment insurance system in the early 1970s reduced the costs of time spent searching for new jobs, since the amount of benefits received during the job search were larger and lasted longer. This increased the NAIRU. In the 1990s, these trends have begun to reverse themselves. The baby boom peaked, and gov-

ernments began tightening up on unemployment insurance and welfare payments, which partially accounts for the decline in the NAIRU. Similarly, competitive pressures have increased, and private-sector unionization has decreased, so that wages more frequently fall, and are slower to rise. This too has helped lower the NAIRU.

## THE LONG-RUN PHILLIPS CURVE

The relationship between unemployment and the inflation rate *in the long run* is called the long-run Phillips curve (Figure 16.4). The long-run Phillips curve is vertical at the level of unemployment that we have identified as the NAIRU. But there is still a short-term trade-off. In the short term, the economy may be able to obtain lower unemployment at the price of higher inflation.

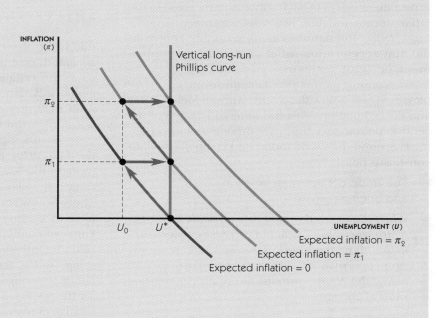

### Figure 16.4 VERTICAL LONG-RUN PHILLIPS CURVE

Assume that initially there is no inflation and that the government decides to "buy" less unemployment by allowing increased inflation. It expands the money supply, inducing an inflation rate of $\pi_1$. For a short while, unemployment is reduced to $U_0$, but then the inflationary expectations shift the expectations-augmented Phillips curve up, so that at $\pi_1$, unemployment increases back to $U^*$. If the government again attempts to lower the unemployment rate below $U^*$, it can do so only by allowing inflation to increase further, to $\pi_2$. But this raises the Phillips curve yet again. If the government kept inflation fixed at $\pi_2$, unemployment would rise again to $U^*$. Only by allowing the inflation rate to continue to accelerate can an unemployment rate below $U^*$ be sustained. The only unemployment rate that can be sustained with a fixed rate of inflation is $U^*$: the long-run Phillips curve is vertical.

## INFLATION AND UNEMPLOYMENT: BASIC CONCEPTS

*Phillips Curve*   Relationship between inflation and unemployment: the lower the unemployment rate, the higher the inflation rate.

*Inflation Expectations–Augmented Phillips Curve*   The level of inflation associated with any level of unemployment depends on expectations concerning inflation; the higher inflationary expectations are, the higher the level of inflation associated with any level of unemployment. As inflationary expectations increase, the inflation expectations–augmented Phillips curve shifts up.

*NAIRU*   The NAIRU (non-accelerating-inflation rate of unemployment) is the unemployment rate at which inflation remains constant. It is positive. If the unemployment rate remains below the NAIRU level, the rate of inflation will continue to azerate. To reduce the rate of inflation requires keeping the unemployment rate below the NAIRU for an extended period of time.

*Long-Run Phillips Curve*   The relationship between inflation and unemployment in the long run, with full adjustment of inflationary expectations. It is generally believed to be vertical.

## RATIONAL EXPECTATIONS

In the example given above, the expectations-augmented Phillips curve shifts up gradually over time, as market participants experience higher inflation rates and build those expectations into their wage bargains. It is assumed that their expectations *adapt* to what they actually experience.

In path-breaking work done in the 1970s that earned him the Nobel Prize in 1995, the American economist Robert Lucas suggested that the upward shift in the expectations-augmented Phillips curve could occur much more rapidly. Market participants did not have to wait until inflation actually occurred to build it into their expectations. They could *rationally anticipate* it. If, for instance, the government tried to stimulate the economy by expanding the money supply, firms and workers would rationally expect that prices would increase, and they would build that expectation into their behaviour. These expectations, based on an understanding of the structure of the economy, are referred to as **rational expectations.**

There was one very strong implication of rational expectations. Assume the government announced it was going to keep the unemployment rate below the NAIRU by expanding the money supply. Workers and firms would anticipate the increased inflation, and this would instantaneously shift up the expectations-augmented Phillips curve. Indeed, if the impact of

the faster expansion of the money supply was fully anticipated, prices would rise proportionately; there would be no increase in the "real" money supply, and hence no effect on the level of economic activity. In this case the vertical long-run Phillips curve applies even in a relatively short span of time, possibly even less than a year.

How quickly expectations adjust depends on economic circumstances. When inflation has been stable for an extended period of time, households and firms are likely to take the inflation rate as given. They will change expectations only gradually. But in economies that have experienced high and variable inflation, households and firms realize the importance of forming as accurate predictions of inflation as possible, and in that case, expectations are more likely to be highly responsive to changes in government policy.

There is one curious aspect of highly responsive expectations. While they imply that there is little scope for the government to reduce unemployment below the NAIRU level without inflation increasing very rapidly, there may also be little cost to the government's reducing the inflation rate. If firms and households believe that the government will reduce the inflation rate, inflationary expectations can be brought down almost overnight, with the consequent downward shift in the inflation expectations–augmented Phillips curve. The trick, of course, is for the government to convince others that it will succeed in getting the inflation rate down. It may be difficult to establish such credibility, and the "price" may be high—running the economy at a high unemployment rate over an extended period of time.

## INFLATION AND AGGREGATE DEMAND AND SUPPLY ANALYSIS

The previous section focused on the labour market—on unemployment—and described how the level of unemployment combines with inflationary expectations to determine the rate of inflation. Because wages and prices move in tandem, when we study the determinants of wage inflation we are in fact studying the determinants of overall inflation. In this section we take a closer look at the linkage between labour and product markets. This will enable us to see more closely the relationship between the dynamic analysis that we have just described, focusing on the rate of change of wages and prices, and the static analyses of Parts Two and Three, which used the tools of the aggregate supply and demand curves.

### AGGREGATE SUPPLY

We begin by concentrating on the product market, on aggregate demand and supply. In earlier chapters we described the economy's potential GDP, $Y_s$—the amount of output it could produce using the available labour supply and stock of plant and equipment. For simplicity, we assumed that the labour supply was inelastic. As a result, changes in the price level did not draw more people into the labour force, and thus the economy's potential output was not sensitive to the price level.

Another way of thinking of the economy's aggregate supply is that it is the level of output that would be produced if wages and prices were perfectly flexible, so that labour was always fully employed. Because of this assumption that wages and prices

can adjust fully to ensure full employment, economists sometimes call this vertical aggregate supply curve the **long-run aggregate supply curve.**[2]

Firms may not be willing to hire all the available workers if the price they receive for the goods is low *relative* to the wages they pay workers. The **short-run aggregate supply curve** assumes that wages are fixed—they do not fall to ensure that there is full employment. It asks, how much are firms willing to supply at each price level, given the level of wages? Typically, it has the shape depicted in Figure 16.5. The curve has three parts. If there is excess capacity, then there can be large increases in output with little or no increase in the price level—the horizontal portion. If the economy is using all of its resources fully, then no increase in the price level can elicit an increase in output—the vertical portion. And in between, there is an upward-sloping portion, where higher prices can coax producers to work their machines harder.

The relationship between the vertical portion of the short-run aggregate supply curve, the long-run (vertical) aggregate supply curve, and the NAIRU requires some discussion. In the short run, as we saw in Chapter 6, the economy can operate at more than 100 percent of capacity, as maintenance on machines is deferred. Moreover, for short periods of time, workers may be induced to work overtime. And workers who would not be regarded as suitable for permanent employment may be hired temporarily from the pool of unemployed workers who are searching for jobs. Firms would be willing to hire them given the relatively high price level relative to wage rates.

But it is not possible in the long run to defer main-

---

[2] Some economists think of the long-run aggregate supply curve as depicting the level which firms are willing to supply when the price level changes, and wages change commensurately. Firms' demand for labour depends on the *real wage*, the wage divided by the price level. Thus, if when the price level falls, wages fall in tandem, leaving the real wage unchanged, the demand for labour will remain unchanged. The long-run aggregate supply curve is thus vertical. The position of the aggregate supply curve then depends on the *level* at which the real wage is fixed. Here, we assume that the real wage is at the level at which labour is fully employed, so the vertical long-run aggregate supply curve corresponds to the economy's potential output.

## Figure 16.5 SHORT-RUN AGGREGATE SUPPLY CURVE

The short-run aggregate supply curve gives the level of output that will be produced at each price level, given a particular level of wages. By contrast, the long-run aggregate supply curve gives the level of output that will be produced when wages are flexible, and labour and capital are working at what might be viewed as a "normal" level of full capacity. Because for short periods of time capital and labour can work beyond this level, short-run aggregate supply will exceed long-run aggregate supply when prices are high.

The short-run aggregate supply curve has three portions: a flat portion where there is a large amount of excess capacity, a vertical portion where there is no spare capacity, and an upward-sloping portion in between.

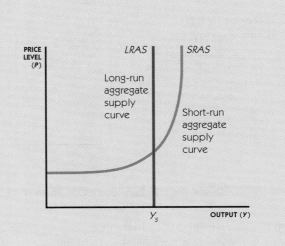

tenance or to induce workers to work, say, additional shifts. To the extent that one can work workers and machines "overtime," the vertical portion of the short-run aggregate supply curve lies to the right of the long-run aggregate supply curve, as depicted in Figure 16.5. The position of the long-run aggregate supply curve represents the normal "capacity" of the economy. When the economy is operating beyond normal full capacity, there will be upward pressure on prices, and when it is operating below full capac-

ity, there will be downward pressure on prices. Thus, the output of the long-run aggregate supply curve is that corresponding to the NAIRU; at that unemployment rate, the inflation rate is neither increasing nor decreasing.

### SHORT-RUN EQUILIBRIUM

We can now see how equilibrium output (in the short run) depends on the price level (Figure 16.6,

### SHORT-RUN OUTPUT DETERMINATION

When the price level fails to adjust to equate aggregate demand and aggregate supply, the short side of the market dominates.

**1** If at the given price level aggregate demand is less than aggregate supply, the actual output will be given by aggregate demand.

**2** If at the given price level aggregate supply is less than aggregate demand, the actual output will be given by aggregate supply.

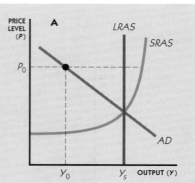

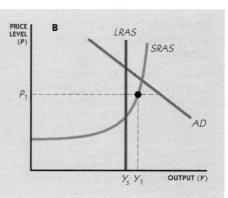

**Figure 16.6 SHORT-RUN OUTPUT DETERMINATION**

At $P_0$ in panel A, aggregate demand is less than aggregate supply. Output equals $Y_0$. In panel B, at the current price, $P_1$, the short-run aggregate supply exceeds the long-run aggregate supply, but aggregate demand is larger still. Output is determined by the short-run aggregate supply curve.

panel A). When the price level is very high, aggregate demand is less than aggregate supply—the familiar case of Part Three. Firms only produce what they can sell. Output is equal to aggregate demand, $Y_0$.

Panel B illustrates a case where at the current price, $P_1$, the short-run aggregate supply exceeds the long-run aggregate supply, but aggregate demand is larger still. Output is determined by the short-run aggregate supply curve, $Y_1$.

There is a general principle here: it is always the "short side" of the market—whichever is smallest, aggregate demand or aggregate supply—that determines output.

## SHIFTS IN AGGREGATE DEMAND CURVES

We can use this framework to show the consequences of shifts in the aggregate demand curves on inflationary pressures in the short run. There are three situations. Panel A of Figure 16.7 shows the aggregate demand curve initially intersecting the short-run aggregate supply curve along the horizontal portion of the aggregate supply curve. The initial price level is $P_0$ and the initial output is $Y_0$. (Recall that the short-run aggregate supply curve is drawn for a given wage rate.) There is large excess capacity. A rightward shift in the aggregate demand curve leads to a new equilibrium output, $Y_1$. At $Y_1$ there is no ex-

cess demand for goods. There is no upward price pressure. Because there is so much excess capacity, the increase in aggregate demand has not resulted in any inflationary pressure.

Panel B shows the aggregate demand curve initially intersecting the short-run aggregate supply curve along the vertical portion of the aggregate supply curve. We assume initially the price is $P_0$, so again, in the initial situation, aggregate demand just equals aggregate supply. Now, however, a rightward shift in the aggregate demand curve leads to no change in aggregate output—after all, the economy is already operating at full capacity. But there is large upward pressure on prices. Inflation that starts with a rightwards shift in the aggregate demand curve is referred to as **demand-pull inflation.**

The situation depicted in panel B occurred in 1965. At the time, the economies of both Canada and the United States were operating at close to capacity. President Johnson was faced with the need to undertake large government expenditures to fight the Vietnam War and to fight the so-called War on Poverty at home. But he was unwilling to raise taxes to pay for them. As a result, aggregate demand in the United States shifted to the right and caused inflation. Given the interdependencies of the Canadian and American economies, some of the high demand in the United States spilled over to Canada through a higher demand for our exports.

Panel C shows the aggregate demand curve ini-

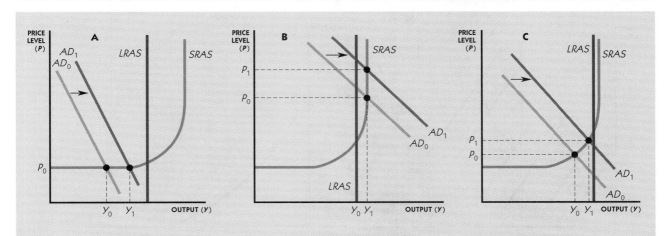

### Figure 16.7  SHIFTS IN THE AGGREGATE DEMAND CURVE

Panel A. The initial equilibrium is along the horizontal portion of the short-run aggregate supply curve, so that rightward shifts in the aggregate demand curve lead to increased output but to no upward price pressure. Panel B. The initial equilibrium is along the vertical portion of the short-run aggregate supply curve, so that rightward shifts in the aggregate demand curve lead to no increased output, but to considerable upward price pressure. Panel C. The initial equilibrium is along the upward-sloping portion of the short-run aggregate supply curve. Rightward shifts in the aggregate demand curve lead to upward pressures on prices. If nothing else changed, eventually equilibrium would be restored with aggregate demand equaling aggregate supply at $P_1$, with output higher than before.

tially intersecting the short-run aggregate supply curve along the upward-sloping portion of the aggregate supply curve. Again, we assume initially the price is $P_0$, where aggregate demand equals aggregate supply. Again, a rightward shift in the aggregate demand curve gives rise to upward price pressure, but now, as the price level increases, output actually increases, since the aggregate supply curve (in this region) is upward-sloping. At the given wage rate, the higher price level induces firms to expand their output by hiring more workers from the pool of unemployed or having their existing workers work overtime. Thus, the extent to which the shift in the aggregate demand curve gets reflected in increased prices or increased output depends on the slope of the short-run aggregate supply curve at the initial equilibrium: when it is horizontal, output increases and there is no price pressure; when it is vertical,

output cannot increase but there are large upward pressures on price; and when it is upward-sloping, output increases *and* there is upward price pressure. This "static" picture translates into the shape of the Phillips curve as it is typically depicted, as in Figure 16.8. When the unemployment rate is high, a given rightward shift in the aggregate demand curve (increasing aggregate demand at a given price level by, say, 1 percent) results in a large reduction in the unemployment rate and very little increase in the rate of inflation (the movement from A to B). Whereas when the unemployment rate is low, a rightward shift in the aggregate demand curve by the same amount results in a small reduction in the unemployment rate and a large increase in the rate of inflation (the movement from E to F); in between, the changes in the unemployment and inflation rates are "moderate" (the movement from C to D).

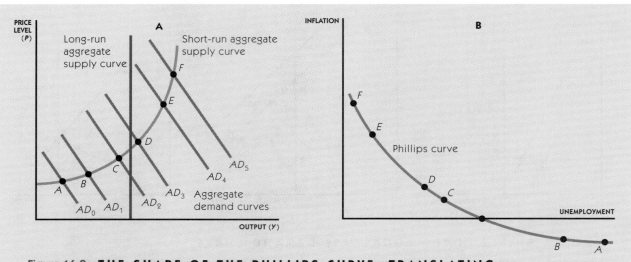

**Figure 16.8 THE SHAPE OF THE PHILLIPS CURVE: TRANSLATING STATIC SHIFTS IN THE AGGREGATE DEMAND CURVE INTO MOVEMENTS ALONG THE PHILLIPS CURVE**

When there is large excess capacity—when the unemployment rate is high—shifts in the aggregate demand curve result in large reductions in the unemployment rate and small increases in the inflation rate, the movement from *A* to *B*. When unemployment is very low, shifts in the aggregate demand curve result in small reductions in the unemployment rate and large increases in the inflation rate, the movement from *E* to *F*. In between, shifts in the aggregate demand curve result in moderate reductions in the unemployment rate and in the inflation rate, the movement from *C* to *D*.

## SHIFTS IN THE AGGREGATE SUPPLY CURVE

The short-run aggregate supply curve shows how aggregate output varies in the short run with changes in the price level, given the wage rate and other costs and given the capacity of the economy. Changes in any of the given factors will cause the curve to shift. An increase in capacity (say, because of additional investment) causes it to shift to the right. A decline in costs (say, a fall in the cost of imported inputs because of an appreciation of the dollar) causes the curve to shift down. Panel A of Figure 16.9 shows the combined effect of an increase in capacity and a decline in costs. The result is that at the old price level, there is excess supply and downward pressure on the price level and the wage rate.

An increase in the price of an important input, such as the huge increase in the price of oil that occurred in 1973 discussed below, represents an upward shift in the short-run aggregate supply curve as illustrated in panel B of Figure 16.9. The result was excess demand and pressure for increases in the price level. An increase in the wage rate would have the same effect.

Inflation that started as a result of this upward shift in the supply schedule (generated by an increase in costs of production) is called **cost-push inflation.** The Organization of Petroleum Exporting Countries (OPEC), consisting mainly of nations in the Middle East, decided in 1973 to impose an embargo on the shipment of oil to certain Western nations, including Canada and the United States. Even after the embargo was lifted, OPEC continued to restrict production, so that the price of oil rose dramatically, by

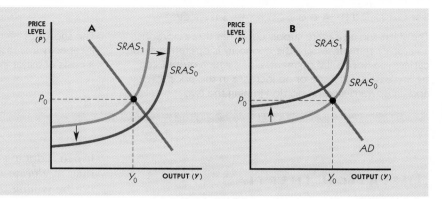

**Figure 16.9 SHIFTS IN THE AGGREGATE SUPPLY CURVE**

Increases in capacity and decreases in cost shift the aggregate supply curve down and out as in panel A, and lead to downward price pressure at the original price level, $P_0$. Panel B shows how the short-run aggregate supply curve shifts up as a result of an increase in the cost of major inputs, such as oil.

45 percent in real terms. For the Canadian economy as a whole, the higher oil prices raised costs of production. The result can be viewed as an upward shift in the short-run aggregate supply curve.

The timing could not have been worse. As we saw earlier, the massive increase in government expenditures in the United States to fight the Vietnam War had ignited inflation there, and that had spilled over into Canada as both net exports and the price of imported goods rose. As the Vietnam War wound down, the reduced government expenditures in the United States would have led to a reduction in net exports

from Canada and a leftward shift in our aggregate demand curve, resulting in downward price pressure. But the upward shift in the short-run aggregate supply curve more than offset this effect, and the economy had **stagflation**—inflation went up as unemployment went up, as illustrated in Figure 16.10. Thus, the inflationary episode that had begun with a rightward shift in the aggregate demand curve as a result of the increase in net exports induced by the Vietnam War was carried forward with an upward shift in the aggregate supply curve as a result of the oil embargo.

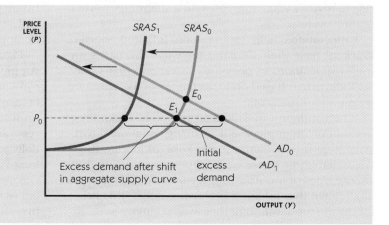

**Figure 16.10 THE OIL PRICE SHOCK AND THE END OF THE VIETNAM WAR**

The end of the Vietnam War resulted in a decline in net exports from Canada and shifted the aggregate demand curve to the left, from $AD_0$ to $AD_1$. If nothing else had happened, this would have put downward pressure on prices. But at the same time, the oil price shock shifted the short-run aggregate supply curve up, from $SRAS_0$ to $SRAS_1$. At the old price $P_0$, output was reduced, while upward price pressure persisted.

## SHORT-RUN AGGREGATE SUPPLY

The short-run aggregate supply curve has three portions: a vertical segment, where the economy is operating at full capacity; a horizontal segment, along which output can be increased with little or no increase in the price level; and an upward-sloping portion joining the two.

The short-run aggregate supply curve can shift to the right if capacity increases; or it can shift upward or downward if costs of major inputs such as oil increase or decrease.

# INFLATION INERTIA

Earlier in the chapter, we described how if the unemployment rate remains at the NAIRU level, inflation will simply continue at a given rate. This tendency of inflation to persist is referred to as **inflation inertia.** Inflation inertia occurs because higher wages lead to higher prices (and expectations of higher prices), which in turn lead to higher wages. At the higher prices, firms are willing to pay, and workers demand, higher wages. And at higher wages, consumers are willing to pay, and firms demand, higher prices.

It makes little difference how inflation is started, whether through a shift in the aggregate demand curve that gives rise to demand-pull inflation or through a shift in the aggregate supply curve that gives rise to cost-push inflation. Once started, wage increases give rise to price increases, which give rise to further wage increases, in a seemingly never-ending cycle.

Expectations help to maintain inflation inertia. Workers base their demand for wage increases on their *expectations* of price increases; and firms may set their prices based on *expectations* of increases in wages and other costs.

When inflation inertia is strong, it can take long periods of unemployment to bring inflation down. With high unemployment, workers' moderate their wage demands; lower wage demands translate into slower rates of increase in prices; as workers gradually realize that inflation is slowing down, this reinforces the moderation of their wage demands.

Sometimes, however, inflation can be stopped quickly by reversing expectations. If the government puts into place policies that are thought to be effec-

tive in reducing inflation, then, for instance, workers may moderate their wage demands and firms will not be willing to grant increased wages, since they do not anticipate that they will be able to get higher prices for the products they sell.

## MONETARY POLICY

Inflation is the continual increase in the prices of goods and services. Year after year, it takes more money to buy a Coke or rent a house. Thus, inflation is often viewed as essentially a monetary phenomenon. And in Part Two, where we assumed that prices were perfectly flexible, we saw that this was the case. Increases in the money supply translated into increases in the price level, with no real effect on the economy. On the other hand, in Part Three, where we assumed that prices were perfectly rigid, by assumption monetary policy did not have an *immediate* effect on inflation, but it did have an effect on output. In this part, which bridges the discussion between perfectly flexible and perfectly rigid prices, we will see that in general monetary policy has an effect on both output and inflation.

Figure 16.11 shows that an increase in the money supply shifts the aggregate demand curve to the right. (In Chapter 15 we saw how this happens: an increase in the money supply puts downward pressure on interest rates and the exchange rate, causing investment and net exports to rise.) Assume that initially aggregate demand equalled both short-run and long-run aggregate supply, and that initially there was no inflation. The shift in the aggregate demand curve leads at the current price level to upward price pressure, and, as we have seen, this upward price pressure gradually translates into higher prices. With higher prices, output increases along the short-run aggregate supply curve. As output increases, so does

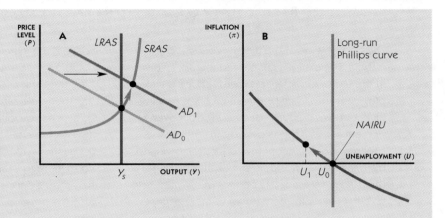

**Figure 16.11 EXCESSIVELY EXPANSIONARY MONETARY POLICY SETS OFF INFLATION**

Increasing the money supply shifts the aggregate demand curve to the right as in panel A. There is upward price pressure. As prices rise, output increases along the short-run aggregate supply curve. As output increases, so does employment. Panel B. The unemployment rate falls below the NAIRU level, and as a result inflation accelerates.

employment. Panel B shows that the unemployment rate falls below the NAIRU level, and as a result inflation sets in. Thus, an increase in the money supply can begin an inflationary episode.

Monetary policy may also play a role in sustaining inflation inertia. If monetary authorities adopt an accommodating policy and let money supply increase in tandem with prices, inflation can persist. However, if monetary authorities act quickly to squelch inflation by restrictive policies, they can clamp it down. Whether monetary policy is being restrictive or accommodative depends to a large extent on the rate of increase in the money supply relative to the increase in the demand for money. In Chapter 14, we saw that normally the demand for money (at any interest rate) increases with *nominal* income. If the economy's real growth is, say, 2 percent, and prices are increasing at 3 percent, then if the money supply is increased at

the rate of 5 percent per year, the increased supply of money will just equal the increased demand at an unchanged interest rate. If the money supply increases less rapidly, then for demand to equal supply, interest rates and the value of the Canadian dollar must rise, and this reduces investment and net exports. The aggregate demand curve shifts to the left and inflationary pressures are reduced.

## EXPECTATIONS AND FOREIGN EXCHANGE RATES

In Chapter 14 we saw that there were two channels through which monetary policy affected the economy: it affected interest rates and thus investment,

INFLATION INERTIA

Inflation once started perpetuates itself.

Increases in prices lead to increases in wages, which in turn lead to further increases in prices.

Expectations of inflation get built into wage formation.

Monetary policy can dampen or accelerate inflation.

The central issue of the macroeconomic policy debate in the 1990s concerned the risk involved in the use of monetary policy to reduce unemployment. The unemployment rate was running high, but was gradually decreasing from over 11 percent in 1992 to 9.5 percent in 1995 as the expansion of the economy continued, owing to buoyant demand. Should the expansion be further fueled by monetary policy? That would help to bring unemployment down to more acceptable levels, but would it set off an inflationary episode that would be costly to reverse? There seemed to be little evidence of a "precipice"—a rapid increase in the rate of inflation—should aggregate demand increase further, for inflation rates had remained in the 1–2 percent range for four years.

Moreover, some thought that the costs of reversing any increases in inflation—reducing demand and generating more unemployment in the future—were essentially equal to the benefits the economy received by operating at a somewhat lower unemployment rate now. In this view the costs of slight increases in the inflation rate appeared at most moderate. Thus, the risk analysis focused on questions of timing. With a tighter monetary policy, if it turned out that inflationary pressures would have been triggered by an increase in demand, the economy would have avoided a temporary bout of inflation. But if the economy could have stood further stimulation without increased inflation, it would have had the continued benefit of very low inflation, but at the expense of forgoing employment opportunities. On the other hand, with a more expansionary policy, if it turned out that the economy could withstand more demand without higher

inflation, the increase in output and employment would be a clear gain. If inflation did increase then, the Bank of Canada could return the economy to the old rate of inflation if it wished to do so, by a corresponding increase in unemployment and decrease in output. But because of discounting—the fact that a dollar today is worth more than a dollar tomorrow—even then the present discounted value of this increase in output is positive. The only question is the "price," a temporary increase in the rate of inflation. Many economists thought the risks were too low, the cost of being proved wrong—this small temporary increase in inflation—too low to justify the conservative strategy.

Others worried that although the risk of causing high rates of inflation through monetary stimulation might not be large, the cost of being wrong could be quite severe. They argued that any increase in inflation, even a moderate one, would become built into expectations of future inflation. If the Bank of Canada had to reverse itself and bring the rate of inflation back down, the process of decreasing expectations might take time. So the cost in terms of decreased output and employment would be greater than any temporary gains in output and employment that would occur before the increase in inflationary expectations became evident. In the eyes of this group, the costs of following the more cautious approach to monetary policy—persistently high though gradually decreasing unemployment rates—were lower than the costs associated with pursuing a more aggressive monetary expansion and risking even moderate increases in inflation and longer spells of high unemployment in the future.

and, in an open economy, it affected exchange rates and thus net exports. In our earlier analysis, we noted that a decrease in the interest rate makes holding assets in the country less attractive, decreasing the demand for its currency and thereby decreasing the exchange rate. The lower exchange rate makes the country's goods more attractive abroad, increasing exports, and makes other countries' goods more expensive, decreasing imports. The result is an increase in net exports, shifting the aggregate demand schedule to the right. The same logic applies to a restrictive monetary policy. Higher interest rates lead to a higher exchange rate and a decrease in net exports, shifting the aggregate demand curve to the left.

This analysis ignores one critical ingredient in the determination of exchange rates, a wild card that makes predicting the effect of monetary policy on exchange rates difficult: expectations. If Canadian investors hold yen and the dollar *appreciates*, they make a capital loss. Consider Jack, who spent $1,000 to buy yen in June 1995, when the exchange rate was 60 yen to the dollar. He received 60,000 yen. Four months later, the exchange rate was 75 yen to the dollar. If he cashed in his yen, he would have received $800, for a 20 percent loss in only four months. If investors expect the dollar to appreciate, they sell yen and buy dollars, so the demand for dollars increases. Hence, the exchange rate rises—confirming their expectations. It is easy to see how a spiral of increasing exchange rates can emerge, as each rise of the dollar reinforces beliefs that the dollar will rise further—at least up to a point.

How investors and speculators form their expectations, and how monetary policy affects those expectations, is a complicated matter that is not completely understood—a fortune awaits anyone finding a crystal ball that reveals their psyche. But inflationary expectations are an important determinant. If the price level in Canada is expected to rise faster than the price level of Japan, investors will believe that *in the long run* the dollar must decline in value relative to the yen.

Expectations reinforce the dampening effect of tighter monetary policy when tighter monetary policy leads to an appreciation of the dollar because of its effects on inflationary expectations: if investors believe that the monetary authorities are taking actions to dampen the economy, and hence reduce inflation,

they will expect the dollar to increase in value relative to the yen, compared to what it otherwise would have been. This expectation of an increased value leads to higher demand for dollars today, and a higher exchange rate. The higher exchange rate makes imports more attractive to Canadians, whereas Japanese consumers find our goods more expensive, and so we will export less.

## CAUSES OF WAGE AND PRICE RIGIDITIES

We have described how wages and prices adjust—for instance, how wages increase faster, the lower the unemployment rate. These empirical regularities make sense; after all, the tighter the labour market, the more likely employers will be scrambling to hire workers and the more wages will rise. But to economic theorists these explanations are not fully satisfactory. Why don't wages and prices adjust even faster than they do? If they did, unemployment might not be able to persist for as long as it does. Economists have identified three key reasons that wages and prices adjust slowly: adjustment costs, risk and imperfect information, and imperfect competition, which gives rise to kinked product-demand and labour-supply curves.[3]

### ADJUSTMENT COSTS

The first explanation for price and wage rigidities emphasizes the costs of changing prices. When firms change their prices, they must print new menus and price lists or otherwise convey the

[3] In some cases, these explanations seem to explain too much—they suggest that under some circumstances, prices and wages will not adjust at all to, say, small changes in demand or costs. But the economy consists of many firms in different circumstances. Some may be in a situation where they do not respond at all, while others may respond fully. The *average* for the economy will reflect a *slow* response.

In the next chapter, we consider a set of explanations that pertain particularly to the labour market.

## USING ECONOMICS: EXPECTATIONS FORMATION

Expectations play a major role in perpetuating inflationary episodes, so having some idea of how people form expectations is important for a full understanding not only of how these inflationary episodes work, but, perhaps more important for policy makers, of how to end them. Over the years economists have developed three ways of viewing how individuals form expectations: static, adaptive, and rational. To see how these methods of expectation formation differ, consider how someone would have predicted the inflation rate for 1992, given the rates of inflation in 1990 and 1991:

| Year | Inflation Rate (%) |
|------|--------------------|
| 1990 | 4.8 |
| 1991 | 5.6 |
| 1992 | 1.5 |

*Static Expectations* Under static expectations people assume that the coming year will be just like the past year. In this case, if the inflation rate in 1991 is 5.6 percent, people would expect the same rate in 1992.

*Adaptive Expectations* With adaptive expectations people would look at the data and see that inflation rose from 4.8 percent in 1990 to 5.6 percent in 1991, an increase of some 17 percent. Thus the expectation for the coming year of 1992 might be a further 17 percent increase, to 6.5 percent.

*Rational Expectations* By taking all available information into account, including the announced "zero inflation" stance of the Bank of Canada (holding inflation to between 0 and 2 percent), the behaviour of the Bank in implementing this policy, and the general depressed state of the economy at the end of 1991, people might rationally have expected the inflation rate that actually occurred in 1992, 1.5 percent.

change in prices to their customers. Changing prices costs money, and these costs are referred to as **menu costs.** Similar costs apply to changing wage rates. In fact, if wage costs are determined by negotiated contracts, the cost of changing wages may be even higher than for prices. Menu costs may be large, but advocates of the menu-cost explanation of price rigidities point out that even small costs can have big effects. If each firm in the economy is slow to adjust its prices because of menu costs, even if these costs are small, the cumulative effects could still be significant. There could be powerful aggregate price rigidities.

Still, when firms face a shift in the demand curves for their products, as shown in Figure 16.12, they must choose whether to adjust quantity or price. While there are costs of adjusting either prices or quantity, the costs of adjusting quantity are almost always much greater. Facing such choices, firms will adjust prices rather than quantities. Accordingly, *in most instances* the direct costs of making adjustments do not provide a convincing explanation of price rigidities.

## RISK AND IMPERFECT INFORMATION

Risk and imperfect information are important causes of price and wage rigidities. There is a great deal of uncertainty about the consequences of wage and price changes. When a firm lowers its price, whether sales increase or not depends on how other firms in the industry respond and how its customers respond. If rivals respond by lowering their prices, the firm may fail to gain market share, and its profits may simply plummet with the decline in prices. If other producers fail to repond, the firm may gain

## Figure 16.12 ADJUSTMENT COSTS

Shifts in the demand curve facing a firm necessitate adjustments in either the price charged or the quantity produced. How the firm adjusts depends in part on the costs of adjusting price and/or quantity and the risks associated. If the costs or risks of adjusting prices are high, and of adjusting quantities are low, then the firm will leave price unchanged, and lower quantity: there will be price rigidity.

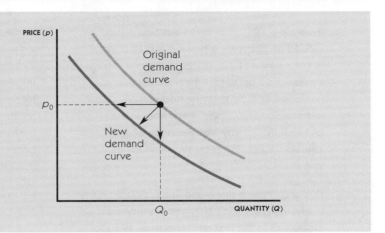

a competitive advantage. On the other hand, customers may think that this is just the first of several price decreases and decide to postpone purchases until prices get still lower; thus, a decrease in price might even result in reduced sales. Similarly, the consequences of a firm's lowering its wages depend on how its workers and rival firms respond. Other firms might leave wages unchanged and use the opportunity to try to recruit the firm's best employees. Alternatively, they might respond by lowering wages in a corresponding manner. In one case profits would rise, in the other, they would fall.

The uncertainty associated with wage and price changes is often much greater than that associated with changing output and employment. When a firm cuts back on its production, provided it does not cut back too drastically, its only risk is that its inventories will be depleted below normal levels, in which case it simply increases production next period to replace the lost inventories. If production costs do not change much over time, there is accordingly little extra risk to cutting back production. Similarly, there is little risk to a firm decreasing its employment simply by not hiring new workers as older workers leave or retire—much less risk than that associated with lowering wages.

Since firms like to avoid risks, they try to avoid making large changes to prices and wages; they would rather accept somewhat larger changes in quantities—in the amount produced or in the hours worked. As a result wages and prices are "sticky."

## KINKED DEMAND CURVES

A third type of explanation attributes price rigidities to the shape of demand curves facing firms under imperfect competition. Recall that with perfect competition, a firm faces a horizontal demand curve. With imperfect competition, a firm faces a downward-sloping demand curve; in particular, the demand

### SOURCES OF WAGE AND PRICE STICKINESS

Adjustment costs

Risks associated with wage and price adjustments

Imperfect competition with kinked product-demand or labour-supply curves

## CLOSE-UP: MENU COSTS AND MAGAZINES

In January 1982, a copy of *Business Week* cost U.S. $2. In February 1991, it still cost U.S. $2. But during that time, prices in general increased by about 50 percent, which means that the real price of the magazine had actually fallen sharply. Surely *Business Week* knows the rate of inflation. So why was the price of the magazine so sticky? Why didn't it move at all for nine years?

*Business Week* is not alone in this pattern. One study analyzed price changes of thirty-eight magazines in the United States from 1950 to 1980 and found that magazines allow inflation to erode their cover prices by nearly one fourth, on average, before raising their price. Over the time of this study, about one third of all magazines were sold in the form of single copies, rather than by subscription.

This pattern of sticky prices is not unique to magazines, and it makes the point that choosing or changing a price can be among the toughest decisions for a business. As Gregory Mankiw of Harvard University has written, "The act of altering a posed price is certainly costly. These costs include such items as printing new catalogs and informing salesmen of the new price. . . . More metaphorically and more realistically, these menu costs include the time taken to inform customers, the customer annoyance caused by price changes, and the effort required even to think about a price change."

No one denies that menu costs exist or that they provide a reason for individual companies to wait for a time before altering prices, rather than raising prices a bit each year. However, economists remain divided over whether menu costs are a powerful enough factor, taken alone, to explain economywide price stickiness.

*Sources:* N. Gregory Mankiw, "Small Menu Costs and Large Business Cycles: A Macroeconomic Model of Monopoly," *Quarterly Journal of Economics* 100 (May 1985): 529–37; Mankiw, "A Quick Refresher Course in Macroeconomics," *Journal of Economic Literature* 28 (December 1990): 1645–60; Stephen G. Cecchetti, "The Frequency of Price Adjustment: A Study of Newsstand Prices of Magazines," *Journal of Econometrics* 31 (April 1986): 255–74.

---

curve may have a kink, as illustrated in Figure 16.13. The kink means that firms lose many more sales when they raise prices above $p_0$ than they gain when they lower prices below $p_0$.

There are two reasons why the demand curve may be kinked—why there are very different responses to price increases and price decreases. First, companies believe that if they raise their prices, their own customers will immediately know it and will start searching for stores selling the good at a lower price. But if they lower their prices without heavy expenditures on advertising, customers at other stores may not find out about their lower prices, so they gain few new customers.

Second, firms worry that if they raise their prices their rivals will not match the increase, and hence they will lose customers as a result of their relatively uncompetitive prices. But if they lower their prices, rivals will view this as a threat and will match the decrease and the firm will gain little from the attempt to beat the market.

Kinked demand curves have one dramatic implication: small changes in marginal costs may have no effect on the price firms charge. Even if a company's costs go down, it will continue to charge the price at the kink, $p_0$ in Figure 16.13, because it will worry that if it cuts its price in response to the lower marginal cost, other firms will simply match it and it will be no better off. Thus, kinked demand curves give rise to price rigidities: small changes, such as those resulting from a fall in wages, have no effect on either the output or pricing decisions of the firm.

A similar analysis applies to labour, in markets where firms have to pay higher wages to obtain

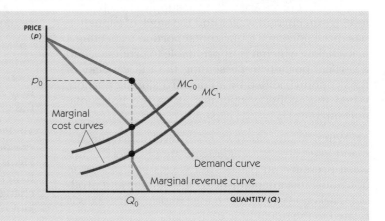

**Figure 16.13 KINKED DE-MAND CURVES AND PRICE INFLEXIBILITY**

If firms lose many more sales from price increases than they gain from price decreases, their demand curve will be kinked. When the demand curve is kinked, the marginal revenue curve has a vertical section, since the extra revenue from price decreases is less than the lost revenue from price increases, and small changes in marginal cost will not lead to any change in price or output.

more workers with required skills. There may be *different* responses to a firm's lowering or increasing its wages. If a firm raises wages, rival firms may match the increase out of fear of losing their best workers; but if a firm lowers wages, the rival firms may not respond, taking advantage of their higher wages to attract the best workers. Thus, the consequences of raising or lowering wages may be costly.

## REVIEW AND PRACTICE

### SUMMARY

**1** Other things being equal, lower levels of inflation are associated with higher levels of unemployment. This relationship is called the Phillips curve.

**2** The level of inflation associated with any particular level of unemployment will increase as expectations of inflation increase. As a result, if the government tries to maintain the unemployment rate at a very low rate, the inflation rate will continually increase, as each increase in inflation is built into individuals' expectations.

**3** The unemployment rate at which the inflation rate is stable is called the natural rate of unemployment, or the non-accelerating-inflation rate of unemployment (the NAIRU). The Phillips curve that reflects the effects of inflationary expectations is called the expectations-augmented Phillips curve.

**4** The NAIRU can change because of changes in the structure of the labour force and in government policies aimed at facilitating worker mobility.

**5** If households and firms have rational expectations, changes in policy can be reflected directly in inflationary expectations; the expectations-augmented Phillips curve can shift up immediately, without waiting for inflation actually to occur. By contrast, if they have adaptive expectations, the expectations-augmented Phillips curve only shifts up in response to recently realized inflationary experiences. With rational expectations, the trade-off between inflation and unemployment may be particularly unfavourable: there may be large increases in inflation with little or no reduction in unemployment in response to government attempts to lower the unemployment rate, for instance, through more expansionary monetary policy.

**6** The short-run aggregate supply curve gives the amount that firms are willing to supply at each price level (given current wages and the stock of capital). It has three portions: a horizontal portion (reflecting a price below which it is unprofitable to produce), and a vertical portion (representing the full capacity of the economy), joined by an upward-sloping portion. When the economy operates along the horizontal portion, there is excess capacity.

**7** When at the current price level aggregate demand is greater than aggregate supply, there is upward pressure on prices. But wages and prices do not adjust instantaneously to clear labour and product markets. The rate of change in prices or wages is related to the magnitude of the gap.

**8** There is considerable inflation inertia. As the price level increases, the aggregate demand for labour shifts up; as the wage level increases, the aggregate

supply curve may shift, so that the "new equilibrium" is at a still higher level. Thus, price and wage increases reinforce each other and give rise to inflation inertia.

**9** Monetary policy may either accommodate the inflation and thus help perpetuate it by allowing the money supply to increase in tandem with prices or it may dampen it by restricting the rate of increase of the money supply.

**10** Prices and wages may be slow to adjust for three reasons. Firms may face large costs of adjustments. Firms may adjust output and employment rather than prices because the uncertainties associated with changing prices may be greater. And firms may face kinked product-demand and labour-supply curves and may not change prices even when marginal costs change, or may not change wages even when the demand for their goods (the price they receive) changes.

## KEY TERMS

cost-of-living adjustments (COLAs)

inflation tax

expectations-augmented Phillips curve

natural rate of unemployment

non-accelerating-inflation rate of unemployment (NAIRU)

rational expectations

long-/short-run aggregate supply curve

demand-pull inflation

cost-push inflation

stagflation

inflation inertia

menu costs

## REVIEW QUESTIONS

**1** Why is there a trade-off between inflation and unemployment in the short run?

**2** What role do changes in expectations play in shifting the Phillips curve? What difference does it make whether expectations are adaptive or rational?

**3** What is the NAIRU? Why, if unemployment is kept below the NAIRU, will the rate of inflation accelerate? Why might the long-run Phillips curve be vertical?

**4** What factors affect the NAIRU?

**5** What is the shape of the typical short-run aggregate supply curve?

**6** What is the relationship between the dynamic analysis of the Phillips curve and the static analysis of aggregate demand and supply curves?

**7** What is inflation inertia? What factors contribute to its existence? How do increases in the price level affect the aggregate demand curve for labour? How do increases in the wage level affect the aggregate supply curve for output?

**8** Why might real wages adjust more slowly than either nominal wages or prices?

**9** What are some explanations for wage and price rigidities?

# PROBLEMS

**1** Why might the inflationary effect of a one-time increase in a tax rate on final goods be different from other events that might start an inflationary spiral?

**2** The sacrifice ratio measures the number of "unemployment-years" required to bring down inflation by 1 percent. If the sacrifice ratio is 2, one can bring down the inflation rate by .5 percent either by increasing the unemployment rate by .5 percent for two years, or by increasing the unemployment rate by 1 percent for one year, or by 2 percent for a half year. If the sacrifice ratio is 1, how long will it take to bring down the inflation rate by 2 percent?

**3** Assume the government maintained the unemployment rate above the NAIRU rate by 1 percent for two years, and the inflation rate increased by 1 percentage point, from 3 to 4 percent. If there are no irreversibilities, what must the government do to decrease the inflation rate to its original level? What is the sacrifice ratio?

**4** If you were the governor of the Bank of Canada in 1994, would you have reduced interest rates with unemployment over 10 percent, other indicators suggesting the economy had excess capacity, and with no strong signs of incipient inflation? Why or why not?

**5** "If expectations adjust quickly to changes in economic circumstances, including changes in economic policy, it is easy to start an inflationary episode. But under the same conditions it is also easy to stop inflation." Discuss. If true, what implications might this finding have for economic policy?

**6** Use aggregate supply and demand curves to explain whether (and when) the following events might trigger inflation:
- (a) an increase in business confidence
- (b) an increase in the interest rate
- (c) the development of important new technologies
- (d) an increase in the price of imports
- (e) an increase in government spending

**7** What would be the effect on the Phillips curve of an announcement that OPEC, the cartel of oil-producing countries, had fallen apart, and thus the price of oil was expected to fall dramatically?

**8** While playing around with old economics data in your spare time, you find that in 1966 unemployment was 3.4 percent and inflation was 1.7 percent; in 1972 unemployment was 6.2 percent and inflation 3.5 percent; in 1979 unemployment was 7.4 percent and inflation 9.1 percent; in 1988 unemployment was 7.8 percent and inflation 4.0 percent. Does this evidence necessarily imply anything about the shape of the short-run or long-run Phillips curve? How might you interpret this data?

# UNEMPLOYMENT: UNDERSTANDING WAGE RIGIDITIES

L arge numbers of people collecting unemployment insurance, huge lines at firms that are hiring workers, plants closing down and laying off workers—all are symptoms of an economy in a recession. Even more than lost output and reduced profits, the human misery that results from unemployment inspires the political commitment to limit both the extent and the costs of unemployment in the economy. But if we are to understand how to reduce unemployment, we must first understand its causes.

If unemployment represents a situation where the supply of labour exceeds the demand, why did the discussion of the macroeconomics of unemployment in Part Three look at the product rather than the labour market? The reason is simple. Variations in output underlie most variations in employment, and variations in aggregate demand underlie most variations in output. Still, one important fact remains, which we emphasized in Chapter 8. No matter what the source of variation in the aggregate demand for labour, if real wages adjusted, full employment could be sustained. Unemployment is fundamentally a labour market phenomenon. It reflects a

## KEY QUESTIONS

**1** What are the reasons that wages may not fall even when there is excess supply of labour?

**2** What policies might reduce either the extent of unemployment or the costs borne by those who are thrown out of work?

**3** What are some of the problems facing the unemployment insurance system?

failure of real wages to adjust to changes in economic circumstances. The last chapter gave several reasons why wages and prices may be sticky. This chapter focuses on special features of the labour market that may contribute to rigidities in wages, particularly in *real wages.*

## THE WAGE-EMPLOYMENT PUZZLE

It turns out to be difficult to reconcile observed changes in employment (or unemployment) and wages with the basic competitive model. If we ap-

plied the basic model to the labour market, we would predict that when the demand for labour goes down, as in a recession, the (real) wage also falls, as illustrated in Figure 17.1. A leftward shift in the demand for labour results in lower wages. If the supply of labour is unresponsive to wage changes (the labour supply curve is inelastic), as depicted by the steepness of the line in the figure, the reduction in the wage is large.

It doesn't seem to happen that way in the real world. In the Great Depression, when the demand for labour fell, real wages actually rose in Canada. While unemployment increased from 2.5 percent in 1929 to almost 20 percent in 1934, real wages *rose* by 8 percent. (In fact, actual wages fell by 14 percent, but the consumer price index fell by 22 percent.) More recently, from 1991 to 1996, real wages fell

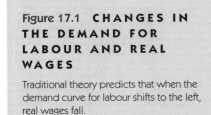

Figure 17.1 **CHANGES IN THE DEMAND FOR LABOUR AND REAL WAGES**

Traditional theory predicts that when the demand curve for labour shifts to the left, real wages fall.

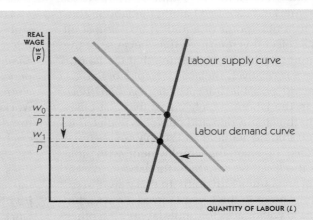

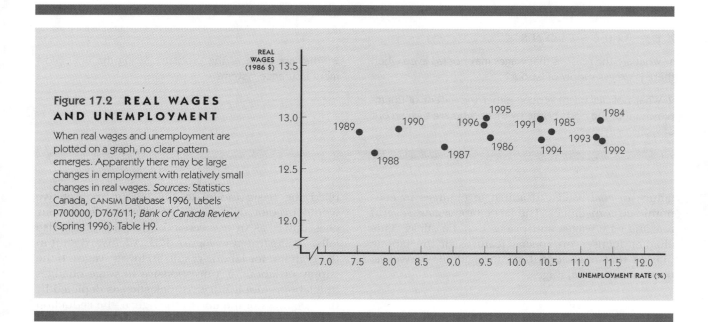

**Figure 17.2 REAL WAGES AND UNEMPLOYMENT**

When real wages and unemployment are plotted on a graph, no clear pattern emerges. Apparently there may be large changes in employment with relatively small changes in real wages. *Sources:* Statistics Canada, CANSIM Database 1996, Labels P700000, D767611; *Bank of Canada Review* (Spring 1996): Table H9.

slightly while unemployment fell from 11.3 percent to 9.5 percent.

Figure 17.2 shows the real wage and unemployment rates during the 1980s and early 1990s. Real wages have not been much affected by changes in unemployment. There are three possible explanations. The first is that the supply curve for labour is horizontal and the demand curve for labour has shifted, as shown in Figure 17.3, panel A. In this case, the labour market has moved along the labour supply curve to a new point of equilibrium. Almost all economists reject this interpretation, because of the huge amount of evidence suggesting that the labour supply curve is relatively inelastic (steep), not flat.

The second possible interpretation is that there are shifts in the labour supply curve that just offset the shifts in the labour demand curve, as depicted in panel B. The shifting demand and supply curves trace out a pattern of changing employment with little change in the (real) wage. Again, the labour market winds up at an equilibrium point. In this view, the reduced employment in the Great Depression was due to a decreased willingness to supply labour—in other words, an increased desire for leisure. Over the past thirty years, there have been marked changes in the supply of labour, as women and baby boomers have joined the labour force. But most economists do not see any persuasive evidence that the supply curve of labour shifts much as the economy goes into or comes out of a recession, let alone to the extent required in Figure 17.3, panel B. And they see no reason why shifts in the demand curve for labour would normally be offset by shifts in the supply curve.

The third interpretation, that there has been a shift in the demand curve for labour, with no matching shift in the supply curve *and no corresponding change in the real wage,* is depicted in Figure 17.3, panel C. The labour market is stuck in disequilibrium. At the wage $w_0/P$, the amount of labour that workers would like to supply remains at $L_0$. But as the demand for labour shifts, the number of workers hired at $w_0/P$ falls from $L_0$ to $L_1$. The difference, $L_0 - L_1$, is the level of unemployment. If the wage does not fall, most economists—and virtually all of the general public—would say the unemployment is **involuntary unemployment.** People are willing to work at the going wage, and the work is not there. The same argument holds even if there is a slight

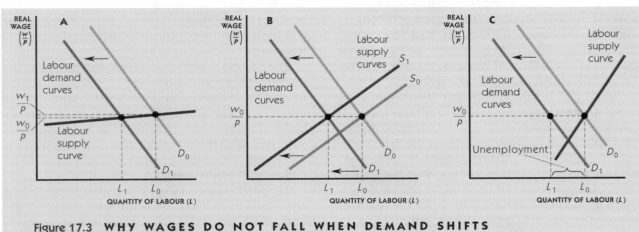

**Figure 17.3  WHY WAGES DO NOT FALL WHEN DEMAND SHIFTS**

Panel A shows a very elastic labour supply curve. A leftward shift in demand for labour from $D_0$ to $D_1$ will decrease employment with little effect on wages. Panel B shows a shift in both supply and demand curves. Although the shift in demand for labour from $D_0$ to $D_1$ would reduce wages by itself, it is offset by a shift in the supply of labour from $S_0$ to $S_1$, leaving the wage level unchanged. In panel C, the demand for labour shifts from $D_0$ to $D_1$, but wages do not fall for some reason. Involuntary unemployment results.

shift in the labour supply curve and a slight change in the wage. The adjustment in the wage is too small to align demand with supply.

The question posed by panel C is fundamental to macroeconomics. How do we explain the apparent fact that wages do not fall in the face of a shift in the demand curve for labour? Reasons abound, as we will see in the following sections.

## EXPLANATIONS OF WAGE RIGIDITIES

Why is it that wages do not fall enough to eliminate unemployment quickly? We looked at several explanations in the previous chapter. Two possibilities are important for the current discussion. First, firms may not be allowed to lower wages, because of union pressure or government legislation. Second,

the efficient wage for the firm (i.e., the wage at which profits are maximized) may be at the current wage level. It may not pay the firm to reduce wage levels, even if the supply curve for labour changes. The reasons for wage rigidity or stickiness may vary from industry to industry and may overlap.

## UNIONS, CONTRACTS, AND GOVERNMENT REGULATIONS

One reason real wages may not decline as employment declines is that contracts and regulations are in place that keep them from doing so. In effect, there are wage floors, like the price floors we encountered in Chapter 5. The most conspicuous example is union contracts.

***Union Contracts***  Labour union power explains wage rigidities in some industries. High wages in parts of the Canadian manufacturing sector have undoubtedly contributed to the high costs of production—and to the decline of Canadian companies in world markets. Studies of the impact of unions on wage rates in Canadian industries have shown that unionized workers earn as much as 25 percent more than nonunionized workers, on average. This is especially true for less skilled workers.[1]

Unions and management share the blame when the high wages called for in their contracts make an industry uncompetitive. In many instances, unions have insisted on high wages even in the face of declining employment. Management has sometimes found it easier to pay the unions what they ask—even if doing so may not be good for the long-term health of the firm—rather than suffer the aggravation of a protracted negotiation or a strike.

It may even be in the interests of those currently employed in unionized industries to demand wages so high that they significantly reduce the demand for workers. If a union demands ever-higher wages, the employer will have an incentive to reduce the work force. But if the decline in the work force is slow enough, it can be accomplished by natural attrition (by workers who choose to retire or quit). In that case, the job security of those still employed is not threatened. Nonunion workers who would be willing to work for less money are shut out by the union contract and have no way of offering to work for a lower wage.

Unions occasionally accept wage cuts in severe recessions. For example, during the recession of the early 1980s, unions in the airline, automobile, and steel industries accepted wage cuts rather than drive their firms into bankruptcy.

Economists may not agree about whether or not unions can obtain higher wages for their members over the long run than would be the case in a competitive labour market. But there is little doubt that unions slow the pace of wage adjustments. The first reason is that union contracts are for a fixed period—three years is typical. If the contract is signed just before an economic downturn, it may be more than two years before any wage adjustment takes

place, even if workers agree to one. And if the economy is back on the road to recovery by the time the contract comes up for renewal, the workers' wages will have been largely insulated from the economic downturn.

The second reason union contracts may slow the adjustment process is through cost-of-living adjustment (COLA) clauses. In periods when some rate of inflation is the norm, union contracts frequently build in clauses to ensure that the wage increases keep pace with the rate of inflation. In consequence, real wages are relatively unaffected by the rate of inflation or unemployment.

The final reason is that, to the extent that unions *are* sensitive in their collective bargaining to the unemployment rate, union wages adjust slowly to changes in unemployment, since different contracts expire in different months and different years.

Union contracts, however, cannot provide the full explanation of rigid wages in Canada. There was high unemployment before unions became important, and there has been high unemployment recently, despite the steady decline of unions over the past thirty years. As the economy went into the Great Depression in 1929, only 7 percent of the labour force was unionized. In the recession of 1982, only 18.8 percent of the work force belonged to unions, and the unemployment rate hit 10 percent.

***Implicit Contract Theory*** Union-contract-style wage rigidities may come about even in the absence of a union or an explicit labour contract. This is because the relations between an employer and her employees are governed by a host of implicit understandings developed over time between the firm and its workers. These implicit understandings are referred to as an **implicit contract.**

Workers are generally risk-averse. Many have fixed financial commitments like the monthly rent or car payments. They do not want their wages to fluctuate with every change in the demand and supply of labour. Firms can bear these market fluctuations more easily. First, the owners of firms tend to be wealthier, with a larger cushion for adjusting to variations in income. Second, in the event of a temporary shortfall of funds, companies can borrow more easily than can most workers.

Given that firms are less vulnerable to economic

---

[1] See Wayne Simpson, "The Impact of Unions on the Structure of Canadian Wages: An Empirical Analysis with Microdata," *Canadian Journal of Economics* 18 (February 1985): 164–81.

## UNION CONTRACTS...

- may reduce unemployment in unionized sectors.
- may slow down real-wage adjustment, thus contributing to cyclical unemployment.

- do not cover enough of the labour force to fully explain unemployment trends.

---

fluctuations than individual workers, it pays companies to provide at least some indirect "insurance" to their workers. Workers will be willing to work for a dependable firm that pays a steady wage, even if that wage is lower on average than the highly varying wages they could get elsewhere. Such a firm provides a form of insurance to its workers through an implicit contract—an understanding that the wages will not vary with the month-to-month, or even year-to-year, variations in the labour market. The firm behaves *as if* it had a contract with its workers guaranteeing the wage. It is called an implicit contract because it is an understanding, not a formal or explicit contract. In these circumstances, the wage workers receive can be thought of as consisting of two parts: the "market" wage (the wage the worker could receive elsewhere) plus an adjustment for the implicit insurance component. When the market wage is relatively low, the wage received by the worker may be higher than the market wage. The worker is receiving a benefit on the implicit insurance policy. When the market wage is high, the wage received by the worker may be lower than the market wage. The difference is the premium the worker pays for wage stability.

For many industries in which long-term employment relations are common, implicit contract theory provides a convincing explanation of why wages do not vary much. But it does not explain layoffs. The risk of most concern to workers is the complete cessation of their income. Thus, implicit contract theory seems to predict that rather than laying people off, firms will engage in **work sharing;** they will reduce the hours each person works. Some firms have in fact experimented with work sharing, but it is not common. Layoffs are.

Proponents of the implicit contract theory try to explain layoffs in two ways, both of which are ultimately unsatisfactory. The first focuses on the fixed costs of employment and the idea that productivity shrinks more than proportionally with changes in the length of the workday. This makes it more costly for the firm to reduce the hours of work per day rather than to lay off workers. If a worker needs the first half-hour to settle into work, the last half-hour to get ready to leave, and a one-hour lunch break, then a six-hour day will lose the same two hours as an eight-hour day. So a firm seeking to cut its labour bill by 25 percent, and to accomplish this by cutting its workday from eight to six hours, would find its productivity reduced by 33 percent. The argument is that this could be avoided by laying off workers instead. This does not, in fact, explain layoffs, however, because the work sharing could simply take the form of fewer days a week rather than fewer hours a day.

The second explanation for layoffs given by implicit contract theorists is that unemployment insurance encourages layoffs. In most places, individuals are not eligible for unemployment compensation in the event of a layoff unless they work full time. (Some European countries now allow unemployment compensation for those who face reductions in their work week.) If a company trims the work week, it and its workers share the cost. If the company lays off workers instead, the government shares the cost. This is an unsatisfactory explanation because it once again only suggests a different form of work sharing—one in which there are short-term layoffs that take the form of job rotations. One group might be laid off for two months, the next group for the next two months, and so on. Job rotations such as these are in fact very rare in the real world.

But the most telling criticism of implicit contract theory is that it does not really explain why wages of job seekers should fail to decline when there is unemployment. Even in the deepest recession, the labour market is like a revolving door, with people quitting jobs and some firms hiring new workers.

Even if implicit contract theory could explain why some workers are laid off, it does not explain why employers do not pay new employees lower wages than they pay to their existing work force. If the wages paid to new employees fell sufficiently, presumably there would be no unemployment.

***Insider-Outsider Theory*** Seeking an explanation for why firms faced with recessionary conditions do not pay lower wages to new employees, economists have devised what is known as **insider-outsider theory.** Insiders in this case are those with jobs at a particular firm. Outsiders are people who want jobs at that firm.

Insider-outsider theory focuses on the importance of training costs. Each firm needs a labour force trained in the special ways that it operates. Most of the training is done by current employees, the insiders. The insiders recognize that by training new employees, outsiders, they are reducing their bargaining position with the firm. The company can promise to continue to pay them higher wages than the newcomers, but the insiders know this promise could be broken. In future bargaining situations, the employer can use the availability of the lower-wage workers to exert downward pressure on the wages of the other employees. Knowing this, the insiders refuse to cooperate with training the outsiders, unless the new employees' interests are made coincidental with their own. The firm can accomplish this only by offering similar pay. This results in wage stickiness and unemployment persists.

Insider-outsider theory holds, further, that even if the current employees were to train new, lower-paid workers, the firm should not take the new workers' willingness to work at a low wage seriously. For once an outsider has been trained, she becomes a trained insider able to extract from the firm higher wages.

Wage systems in which new workers are paid less than established workers doing the same job are called **two-tier wage systems.** Firms do not like two-tier wage systems. Most such experiments—such as the contract between American Motors (Canada) and its workers signed in 1983, which provided that new workers be paid 85 percent of what previously hired workers received—are relatively short-lived. The experiment was abandoned when the contract expired.

***Minimum Wages*** A minimum wage set by the government may result in unemployment. The minimum wage is a government-enacted price floor. To the extent that workers would accept and firms would offer wages below the minimum if they were allowed to, the minimum wage keeps the demand for labour from equalling the supply. Most workers in Canada earn considerably more than the minimum wage, so minimum wage legislation has little effect on unemployment for these workers. However, minimum wage legislation probably does contribute *some* to the unemployment of unskilled workers, including teenagers just entering the labour force. This effect may not be strong, however. Some provincial governments set a special lower minimum wage for teenagers but relatively few firms avail themselves of this opportunity. They pay their teenage employees wages that are in excess of the new minimum wage. Still, it is worth noting that in recessions, unemployment rates among unskilled workers and teenagers often increase much more than among the population as a whole.

## EFFICIENCY-WAGE THEORY

Even in a world without contracts, explicit or implied, wages may not fall enough to eliminate unemployment because firms may find they make more profits by paying a wage higher than the one at which the labour market would clear. If paying higher wages leads to higher productivity, then higher wages may improve a firm's profits.

In Chapter 1, we learned that when Henry Ford opened his automobile plant in 1914, he paid his workers more than double the going wage. He wanted his workers to work hard. He knew that his new technique of production—the assembly line—when combined with motivated workers, would increase his profits. Many modern companies apply the same philosophy.

### WHY DOES PRODUCTIVITY DEPEND ON WAGES?

Economists have identified three main reasons why firms may benefit if they pay high wages: wages affect the quality of the work force, the level of effort, and the rate of labour turnover. Each of these factors has been extensively studied. In each, productivity may depend not just on the wage paid but also on the wage paid relative to that paid by other firms, and on the unemployment rate.

***Quality of the Labour Force***   It is all too common for companies to discover after a wage cut that they have lost the best of their workers. Indeed, this is the reason frequently given by firms for not cutting wages. This is an example of adverse selection: the average quality of those offering to work for a firm is affected adversely by a lowering of the wage. If a firm lowers wages, its best workers are the most likely to find a new job at the old (higher) wage and therefore the most likely to leave.[2]

***Level of Effort***   We can easily see that it would not pay any worker to make any effort on the job if all firms paid the market-clearing wage. A worker could reason as follows. "If I shirk—put out a minimal level of effort—I will either be caught or not. If I don't get caught, I get my pay-cheque and have saved the trouble of making an effort. True, if I am unlucky enough to be caught shirking, I risk being fired. But by the terms of the basic competitive model, I can immediately obtain a new job at the same wage. There is, in effect, no penalty for having been caught shirking."

Firms that raise their wages above the market-clearing level will find that they have introduced a penalty for shirking, for two reasons. First, if their workers are caught shirking and are fired, they will have to take the lower wage being offered by other firms. Second, if many firms offer higher-than-market-clearing wages, unemployment will result, since at the higher wages firms as a whole will hire fewer workers. Now a worker who is fired may have to remain unemployed for a time.

Consider a wage just high enough that workers are induced not to shirk. We know this wage must exceed the wage at which the demand for labour equals the supply. If one of the unemployed workers offers to work for a lower wage at a particular firm, he will not be hired. His promise to work is not credible. The firm knows that at the lower wage, it simply does not pay the worker to exert effort.

The no-shirking view of wages also provides a gloomy forecast for the well-intentioned unemployment benefits policy offered by government. Assume the government, concerned about the welfare of the unemployed, increases unemployment benefits. Now the cost of being unemployed is lower, hence the wage a firm must pay to induce workers to work—that is, not to shirk—is higher. As a result, wages are increased, leading to a lower level of employment. The higher unemployment benefits have increased the unemployment rate.

Higher wages may lead to higher levels of effort for another reason. They may lead to improved worker morale. If workers think the firm is taking advantage of them, they may reciprocate by taking advantage of the firm. If workers think their boss is treating them well—including paying them good wages—they will reciprocate by going the extra mile.

***Rate of Labour Turnover***   Lowering wages increases the rate at which workers quit. Economists refer to this rate as the **labour turnover rate.** It is costly to hire new workers, to find the jobs that best match their talents and interests, and to train them. So firms seek to reduce their labour turnover rate by paying high wages. The lower the wages, the more likely it is that workers will find another job more to their liking, either because it pays a higher wage or for some other reason. Thus, while firms may save a little on their direct labour costs in the short run, if they cut their wages in a recession, these savings will be more than offset by the increased training and hiring costs incurred as demand rises again and they have to replace lost workers. We can think of what workers produce net of the costs of hiring and training them as their *net* productivity. Higher wages, by lowering these turnover costs, lead to higher net productivity.

## DETERMINING THE EFFICIENCY WAGE

If, as we have just seen, net productivity increases when a firm pays higher wages, then it may be profitable for an employer not to cut wages even if there is an excess supply of workers. This is because the productivity of the employer's work force may decline enough in response to a wage cut so that the overall labour costs per unit of production will actually increase.

---

[2] It should be clear that we have now moved away from the assumption that all workers are identical.

## CLOSE-UP: EFFICIENCY WAGES IN TANZANIA

One of the implications of efficiency-wage theory—that employers may be able to get work done more cheaply by *increasing* wages—can lead to some topsy-turvy implications. Or as Alfred Marshall, a famous economist of the late nineteenth and early twentieth centuries put it: "Highly paid labour is generally efficient and therefore not dear labour; a fact which though it is more full of hope for the future of the human race than any other that is known us, will be found to exercise a very complicating influence." The first chapter of this book gave the example of Henry Ford's taking advantage of efficiency-wage theory by paying higher wages in the automobile industry. But the theory can have striking implications in less developed countries too.

Consider the experience of the East African nation of Tanzania, formed by the union of Tanganyika and Zanzibar in 1964. When the area now known as Tanzania achieved independence in 1961, most wage earners worked on large plantations. Most of the workers were migrants, as is commonly the case in Africa, and returned from the plantations to their home villages several times each year. The workers had low productivity and were not paid much. After independence, the government decreed that wage rates for the plantation workers would triple. Plantation owners predicted disaster; such a massive increase in the price they paid for labour, they thought, could only drive them out of business. But the government responded with predictions, based on efficiency-wage theory, that higher wages would lead to a more productive and stable work force.

The government predictions turned out to be correct. Sisal is a plant cultivated because it produces a strong white fibre that can be used for cord or fibre. Overall production of sisal quadrupled under the efficiency-wage policy. This occurred not because of a change in the overall physical capital available but because more motivated and highly skilled workers were better employed by the plantation owners. Over several years following the wage increase, however, employment in Tanzania's sisal industry fell from 129,000 to 42,000, thus illustrating how efficiency wages can increase unemployment.

*Sources:* Mrinal Datta-Chaudhurl, "Market Failure and Government Failure," *Journal of Economic Perspectives* 4 (Summer 1990): 25–39; Richard Sabot, "Labor Standards in a Small Low-Income Country: Tanzania," Overseas Development Council (1988).

The employer wants to pay the wage at which total labour costs are minimized, called the **efficiency wage.** The wage at which the labour market clears—the wage at which the supply of labour equals the demand for labour—is called the market-clearing wage. There is no reason to expect the efficiency wage and the market-clearing wage to be the same. **Efficiency-wage theory** suggests that labour costs may be minimized by the payment of a wage higher than the market-clearing wage.

If the efficiency wage is greater than the market-clearing wage, it will still pay any profit-maximizing firm to pay the efficiency wage. There will be unemployed workers who are willing to work at a lower wage, but it will not pay firms to hire them. At the lower wage, productivity will decline enough to more than offset the lower wage.

If productivity depends on wages because effort increases with the wage—the shirking view of wages—the efficiency wage *must* exceed the market-clearing level. But in some circumstances, the efficiency wage can be less than the market-clearing wage. In that case, competition for workers will bid up the wage to the competitive, market-clearing level. Firms would like to pay the lower, efficiency wage, but at that wage they simply cannot hire workers. In efficiency-wage theory the market-clearing wage thus forms a floor for wages.

In general, the efficiency wage for any firm will depend on two factors: the wage paid by other firms and the unemployment rate. The wage paid by other firms matters because if other companies pay a lower wage, a firm will find that it does not have to pay quite as high a wage to elicit a high level of effort. Workers know that if they are fired, the jobs they are likely to find will pay less. Thus, the cost of being fired is increased, and this spurs employees on to work harder. The wage paid by other firms matters for other reasons as well. If wages paid by other firms are low, the firm will lose fewer workers to other firms if it lowers its wages, and thus the "cost" of lowering wages—increased turnover costs—will be lower. Also, firms will find it easier to hire high-quality workers at any wage if the wages paid by competitors are lower.

The unemployment rate comes into play because as it increases, firms again find that they do not have to pay quite as high a wage to elicit a high level of effort. The workers know that if they are fired, they will have a harder time getting a new job.

Efficiency-wage theory also suggests a slow adjustment process for wages. Each firm is reluctant to lower its wages until others do, for several reasons. The company worries that its best workers will be attracted by other firms. It worries that the morale of its workers, and thus their productivity, will be impaired if they see that their wage is below that of similar firms. No company wants to be the leader in wage reductions. Each therefore contents itself with reducing its wage slowly, and never much below that of other firms. Gradually, as wages in all firms are lowered, employment is increased and unemployment is reduced.

These patterns are in contrast to the basic competitive model, which predicts that with a relatively inelastic supply curve for labour, there will be large and quick changes in wages in response to changes in the demand for labour. It is these wage changes that supposedly prevent unemployment.

## WHY ARE THERE LAYOFFS?

Efficiency-wage theory also helps explain why, if the economy needs a 25 percent reduction in labour employed, workers don't simply work thirty hours rather than forty, and save jobs for the 25 percent of their colleagues who otherwise would be laid off.

According to efficiency-wage theory, the reason workers do not just work thirty hours rather than forty is that by reducing work proportionately among its workers, a firm will in effect be reducing overall pay proportionately. The company will fall back into the traps outlined above. If it lowers overall pay, it may lose a disproportionate fraction of its better workers. These workers can obtain offers of full-time work and full-time pay, and they will find this more attractive than a job with 80 percent of full-time work and 80 percent of the pay. (They may enjoy the extra leisure, but it will not help meet the mortgage payments.) Furthermore, workers now working part time will find that their incentives to exert high levels of effort decline. If they get fired, losing a part-time job is not as serious as losing a full-time job. This ability to explain concentrated layoffs is one feature that sets efficiency-wage theory apart from some of the alternative views of wage rigidity.

## THE IMPACT OF UNEMPLOYMENT ON DIFFERENT GROUPS

As noted in Chapter 6, one striking aspect of unemployment in Canada is that it affects different groups in the population very differently. In competitive markets, wages will adjust to reflect productivity. Groups with higher productivity will have commensurately higher wage rates, while groups with lower productivity will have lower wage rates. But people in both groups will have jobs. There would be no reason for different groups to have different unemployment rates.

The efficiency-wage theory argues that there may be some kinds of labourers, such as part-time workers or those with limited skills, who at any wage have sufficiently low productivity such that it barely pays a firm to hire them. To put it another way, while they may receive a low wage, the wage is only just low enough to offset their low productivity. Paying higher

Immigration to Canada has fluctuated widely over time. The high point was in 1913, when 401,000 immigrants entered the country. By 1930, immigration had fallen to 105,000. From 1932 to 1944, immigration was so low that net immigration was negative (gross immigration was 13,000 in 1933). From the mid-1940s, it rose steadily to reach a peak in 1957 around 275,000. Since then it has been going through phases of rising and falling.

Immigration policy has always been a contentious issue. Historically, immigrants were low-skilled workers and their families. The Diefenbaker government of 1957 shifted the emphasis from a large number of low-skilled immigrants to a small number of high-skilled ones, causing a decline in the number of immigrants to below 100,000. As the economy strengthened, the number of new arrivals began to rise, reaching 200,000 by 1967. A source of discontent with the system was its preference for family members at the expense of independent applicants. In 1967, the Pearson government separated independent from family applicants and adopted a new selection system for the former: the point system. This system, which remains in place today, accepted independent applicants according to a system of points for a variety of educational and occupational skills.

The point system has undergone various refinements over the years. The current assignment of points was adopted in 1985, and is based on the view that immigration should not only be tied to Canada's specific labour-force needs in terms of occupational skills, but also that it should try to smooth out the current age imbalance in the Canadian population and especially should compensate for the fluctuations in domestic fertility rates. Under this system, 60 percent of the points are allotted for economic factors (education, training, experience, occupational demand, and arranged employment). The remainder are divided among several other factors including location, age, knowledge of English or French and personal suitability. The idea is to combine skills and demographic considerations with ease of integration into both the workplace and the society.

A comprehensive study by the Economic Council of Canada published in 1991 listed three types of effects of immigration—economic, political, and social. The study's authors found that the economic and political effects of immigration are relatively small. The impact on both long-term and short-term unemployment and on filling labour market gaps is negligible. If immigration were to increase, per capita incomes of Canadians would rise slightly because of a combination of economies of scale for a larger population and contributions of immigrants to tax revenues. Most other economic benefits would accrue to the immigrants themselves in the form of higher incomes. The political benefit of a larger population, nationally or in some provinces, was judged to be small. The study's authors argued that the real benefits of immigration are social and humanitarian. The country benefits from the increased cultural and ethnic diversity. They judged immigration to be beneficial on humanitarian grounds, since the immigrants gain a great deal and existing Canadians do not lose. On the basis of these conclusions, the council recommended that immigration be raised gradually from the current average of .63 percent of the population over the past 25 years to 1 percent of the population by 2015—from 168,000 in 1991 to 340,000 in 2015. So far in the 1990s, immigration levels have held steady in the 200,000 to 250,000 range.

Source: Economic Council of Canada, *Economic and Social Impacts of Immigration* (Ottawa: Minister of Supply and Services Canada, 1991).

wages would not increase productivity enough to offset the wage increase. And paying lower wages would reduce productivity, making that option unworkable as well.

It is these groups, who lie right at the margin of the hiring decision, who bear the brunt of the fluctuations in the demand for labour. Teenagers and young workers not only have higher average unemployment rates, they bear more than their proportionate share of the burden of variations in employment. Similarly, even if the minimum wage for teenagers is low, most firms continue to pay teenagers more than the minimum wage. Presumably firms are worried that cutting wages by 10 percent would reduce productivity by more than 10 percent, as they lose their best teenagers and as the remaining workers' effort is reduced.

### LIMITS OF EFFICIENCY-WAGE THEORY

Efficiency-wage theory may provide a significant part of the explanation for wage rigidities in a number of different situations: where training and turnover costs are high; where monitoring productivity is difficult; and where differences in individuals' productivity are large and important but it is difficult to ascertain them before hiring and training them. But efficiency-wage considerations are likely to be less important in situations where workers are paid piece rates on the basis of how much they produce, or in situations where training costs are low and monitoring is easy. These situations may indeed exhibit greater wage flexibility, at least if there are no union pressures, implicit contracts, or insider-outsider considerations.

### OKUN'S LAW AND DISGUISED UNEMPLOYMENT

As high as the unemployment rate sometimes climbs, it still may not fully reflect the underutilization of labour. Firms find it costly to hire and train workers. When they have a temporary lull in demand, they may not even lay workers off, for fear that once laid off, the workers will seek employment elsewhere. Thus, firms keep the workers on the job, but may not fully utilize them. This is **labour hoarding,** and can be thought of as a form of disguised unemployment. Employees are not really working, though they are showing up for work. Like open unemployment, it represents a waste of human resources.

The importance of this disguised unemployment

---

### ALTERNATIVE EXPLANATIONS OF WAGE RIGIDITIES

**1** Unions with explicit and implicit contracts prevent wages from falling. Insider-outsider theory explains why firms do not pay newly hired workers a lower wage. Minimum wages explain why wages for very low skilled workers do not fall.

**2** Efficiency-wage theory suggests that it is profitable for firms to pay above-market wages. This is because wages affect the quality of the labour force, labour turnover rates, and the level of effort exerted by workers.

was brought home by the American economist Arthur Okun. He showed that as the economy pulls out of a recession, output increases more than proportionately with employment; and as the economy goes into a recession, output decreases more than proportionately with the reduction in employment. This result is called **Okun's law.** In Okun's original study for the United States, for every 1 percentage point decrease in the unemployment rate, output increased by 3 percent. (In Canada, the current estimate is that output will rise by 2 percent for every 1 percentage point fall in the unemployment rate.) This was a remarkable finding, for it seemed to run contrary to one of the basic principles of economics, the law of diminishing returns, which would have predicted that a 1 percent increase in employment would have less than a proportionate effect on output. The explanation for Okun's law, however, was simple. Many of those who were "working" in a recession were partially idle. As the economy heated up, they worked more fully, and this yielded the unexpected increase in output.

## POLICY ISSUES

This chapter has explored possible reasons why wages do not fall to the level where the demand for labour equals the supply. The truth involves a combination of all the explanations. Minimum wages play a role among very low skilled workers. Unions play a role in some sectors of the economy. And in some jobs, firms do not cut wages because of efficiency-wage considerations.

Wages do sometimes fall, as in the Great Depression, but what is important is wages *relative* to prices. Wages do not fall *fast enough* to equilibrate demand and supply. And all the reasons given in this chapter play a role, not only in explaining why wages do not fall, but also in helping us to understand why, when they fall, they fall slowly.

When the labour market does not clear and involuntary unemployment results, there may be an economic role for government. It is worth reviewing government policies designed to overcome failures

in the labour market. Such policies have included increasing wage flexibility and reducing the costs of unemployment by providing replacement income to the unemployed.

## INCREASING WAGE FLEXIBILITY

Those who see wage rigidities as a major cause of unemployment and believe that they are created by unions or implicit contracts have sought ways of increasing wage flexibility. In Japan, large companies have long-term (lifetime) implicit contracts with their workers, but workers receive a substantial fraction of their pay in the form of annual bonuses. In effect, this means that the wage a worker receives varies from year to year, depending on the fortunes of the firm. Unemployment in Japan is considerably less variable than in North America, and many economists believe that flexible wages are an important part of the reason.

Two features make wage flexibility unattractive to workers. First, workers would have to bear more risk in income fluctuations. Under the current system, workers who have considerable seniority and who often dominate union negotiations face little risk of being laid off during hard times. Their incomes are relatively secure, both from year-to-year variation and from the threat of complete cessation. With the bonus system, however, all employees, including the more senior ones, would face considerable risk. And as the discussion of implicit contracts pointed out, the firm is generally in a better position than the worker to bear the risk of economic fluctuations.

Second, workers worry that the firms most likely to be willing to give large profit shares to their employees in exchange for wage concessions may be those firms that expect the smallest profits. By giving up a share of the profit, they are giving the least away. In effect, when the workers' pay depends on the profits of the firm, workers become much like shareholders—what they receive depends on how well the company does. It does no good to own a large share in the profits of a firm that makes no profits.

This second reason makes it clear why unions do not trust wage flexibility systems. Their concern that firms without profits will be the most willing to offer to share them with their workers proved justified in 1985, when employees of Eastern Airlines in the United States actually accepted a pay reduction in return for a share of the profits. The airline went into bankruptcy soon after.

Still, the fact is that large segments of Japanese industry employ a system with greater wage flexibility, and that system seems to give rise to less variability in employment. Japan appears to have overcome the obstacles to making wages vary with profits. How this happened, whether it is possible for Canada to move to a system with more flexible wages, and what role government should play in encouraging such a move, remain questions of debate among economists.

## REDUCING THE COSTS OF UNEMPLOYMENT

During the past half-century, governments have made it their responsibility not only to reduce the level of unemployment, but also to reduce the costs borne by those unfortunate enough to be unemployed. The difficulty is, how do we do this without giving rise to further economic problems?

### UNEMPLOYMENT INSURANCE

The Unemployment Insurance (UI) programme is the most important one for reducing the cost to the worker of being unemployed. (Beginning in 1996, the name was changed to "Employment Insurance" by the federal government, but the role of the programme as a system of transfers to the unemployed remained the same.) It was started by the federal government in 1941 in the wake of the Great Depression. All employed workers must participate in the scheme. The self-employed are generally not eligible, except for fishermen. UI is financed by premiums paid by both the employer and the employee. In 1996, the rate was 4.2 percent of the wage for employers and 3.0 for the employee, up to a maximum amount. Workers who are laid off receive benefits if they have worked for a qualifying period ranging from 20 weeks in areas where the unemployment rate is 6 percent to 12 weeks where the unemployment rate is 15 percent. Benefit payments are $413 per week for workers earning above a minimum level, and they may be received for up to 45 weeks,

depending on the number of weeks of contribution. They are taxable, and are recovered from high-income recipients. There are special benefits for maternity and parental leave and for sickness.

Critics of the programme worry that it reduces the incentive of unemployed workers to search for jobs. There is some evidence for this. The number of people who get jobs just as their unemployment benefits expire is far greater than can be accounted for by chance. Others worry that when generous unemployment insurance is available, workers have less incentive to exert effort at any given level of wages and unemployment because the threat of being fired is not as fearsome as it would otherwise be. To restore the incentives of efficiency wages, firms must pay higher wages, but when they do, the higher cost of labour induces them to hire fewer workers. By this logic, high unemployment insurance actually contributes to increasing the unemployment rate.

What we have here is another illustration of a familiar basic trade-off. Economic arrangements that diminish risk also diminish incentives. A person who is guaranteed a job will have little incentive to work. If unemployment insurance were sufficiently generous that it fully replaced whatever income he lost if he were fired, a worker would not find any economic incentives for working. And a worker who is laid off would have no incentive to look for a new job. Thus, some critics of the current unemployment insurance system argue that we have gone too far in reducing risk—and also incentives.

Other critics argue that the current Canadian UI system is targeted to the wrong groups—that it does not provide enough support for either the long-term unemployed or new entrants into the labour force, but provides too much for the short-term unemployed. Insurance for unemployment spells of six or eight weeks may be unnecessary in the eyes of many economists. They argue that people should be able to finance these short-term spells out of savings or by borrowing. Though there is a waiting period of two weeks before receiving benefits, they argue that this is far too short. These economists believe that in general, insurance should be designed to cover *large* losses against which individuals cannot self-insure.

One way to overcome some of these incentive problems, particularly those arising from the alleged

# USING ECONOMICS: EXPLOITING UNEMPLOYMENT INSURANCE

Unemployment insurance (UI) payments grew by over 7 percent per year in the late 1980s and early 1990s to become the largest single category of federal expenditure. Much of this growth was due to unusually high rates of unemployment in the period. But some would argue that the system got out of hand financially because the federal government uses the programme not just to provide insurance to laid-off workers but also as a policy for alleviating regional disparities. Eligibility requirements are considerably lower and the length of benefit payments are considerably higher for depressed regions such as the Atlantic provinces and eastern Quebec. Also, the fishing industry, which is a main source of employment in these areas, is given preferential treatment. UI has become a major source of income to these regions, far greater than the value of premiums paid by their residents.

Not surprisingly, such a system with adverse incentives lends itself to potential abuse. A practice allegedly engaged in by some employers, especially those in depressed regions, is to arrange to employ workers for short periods of time, just enough to make them eligible for UI. Indeed, even provincial governments are accused of the practice, and it is easy to see why. Such workers will be temporarily removed from provincial welfare roles and will instead be supported for the lengthy benefit period by the federal UI system. The practice came to be dubbed "Lotto 10-50," a takeoff on the federal government's lottery scheme Lotto 9-49. The 10 refers to the minimum period for which the worker had to be employed to become eligible for UI prior to 1996, and the 50 to the number of weeks for which benefits will be paid.

To appreciate the size of the incentive involved, imagine a worker being hired in a depressed region for the minimum qualifying period of 10 weeks at any wage above $815 per week, the so-called maximum insurable earnings level in 1995. The contribution of the employee and the employer to UI would be 7.2 percent of earnings for 10 weeks, or $586.80 (.072 × $815 × 10). Once laid off, the worker could collect benefits of 60 percent of maximum insurable earnings for 50 weeks, amounting to $24,450 (.60 × $815 × 50). Thus, the net gain from the UI system is $24,450 − $586.80 = $23,863.20! The amount the person would otherwise have been receiving from welfare depends on the province and circumstances. For example, a single employable in Nova Scotia would have received about $7,154 over the same period, while a single person with one child would receive about $12,640. Obviously, it is very attractive for employees to take a short-term job even if it means doing so for a low wage. It is also very attractive for the province to offer such a job, given the savings in welfare payments involved. Unlike Lotto 9-49, Lotto 10-50 was not a game of chance at all; it was a sure thing!

overuse of the system to support temporary layoffs, is to introduce insurance principles into the funding of the programme. This could be done by making premiums "experience-rated," a practice that is followed by some states in the United States. Under experience-rating, the level of the premiums paid by a firm and its employees depends upon the amount of benefits claimed in the past. This reduces the incentive for firms to use layoffs to adjust to temporary declines in the demand for their products. Experience-rating has been frequently advocated in Canada.

There has also been considerable concern with

the fact that eligibility criteria and benefit levels are much more favourable in high unemployment regions than elsewhere. In effect, UI is being used both for addressing regional inequalities and for insuring against layoffs. Critics argue that this discourages workers from moving from depressed regions where permanent jobs are scarce to regions where jobs are available, and that it creates an atmosphere of dependency in depressed regions whereby entire regions come to rely on UI far too much.

## REVIEW AND PRACTICE

### SUMMARY

**1** Involuntary unemployment exists when the supply of labour exceeds the demand for labour at the prevailing market wage. This happens when demand for labour falls but real wages do not decline.

**2** The explanations for why firms may be unable to reduce wages and thus unemployment include union contracts or implicit contracts, insider-outsider theory about why firms do not pay lower wages to new hires, and minimum wage laws.

**3** Reducing wages may actually lead to an increase in labour costs, because (a) it may result in a lower average quality of workers as the best workers leave; (b) it may result in lower effort; and (c) it may result in higher turnover costs.

**4** Firms often do not fully utilize their labour force in economic downturns. This labour hoarding means that as the economy expands, output increases more than proportionately to increases in employment.

**5** Making wages depend more on firm profits might result in less variability in employment. But workers would risk income reductions in hard times, and would worry that the firms most likely to give large profit shares to employees are those with the smallest profits to share.

**6** Unemployment insurance reduces the costs to workers of being laid off, but it also reduces workers' incentives to work hard or to search for a new job. Firms' responses may lead to higher rather than lower unemployment.

### KEY TERMS

involuntary unemployment

implicit contract

work sharing

insider-outsider theory

two-tier wage system

labour turnover rate

efficiency wage

labour hoarding

Okun's law

### REVIEW QUESTIONS

**1** What gives rise to involuntary unemployment?

**2** List reasons why firms may be unable or unwilling to reduce wages.

**3** True or false: "The prevalence of unions and minimum wage laws is the primary reason for wage stickiness, and therefore for unemployment, in the Canadian economy." Discuss your answer.

**4** If an implicit contract is not written down, why would a firm abide by it? Why would a worker?

**5** Why does implicit contract theory predict that work sharing is more likely than layoffs?

**6** Give three reasons why productivity may depend on the level of wages paid.

**7** How does an efficiency wage differ from a market-clearing wage?

**8** How does efficiency-wage theory help explain why different groups may have very different levels of unemployment?

**9** What trade-off does society face when it attempts to expand economic security for workers by means of higher unemployment benefits or greater job security?

## PROBLEMS

**1** How might statistics about (a) the fraction of minimum wage workers who are heads of household, (b) the fraction of minimum wage workers who live in families that are above or below the poverty line, or (c) the fraction of minimum wage workers who are young affect views about the desirability of increasing the minimum wage?

**2** Would you be more or less likely to observe implicit contracts in industries where most workers hold their jobs for only a short time? What about industries where most workers hold jobs a long time? Explain.

**3** A number of businesses have proposed a two-tier wage scale, in which the wage scale for new employees is lower than the wage scale for current employees. Using the insights of insider-outsider theory, would you be more or less likely to observe two-tier wage scales in industries where a lot of on-the-job training is needed? where not much is needed?

**4** Would you be more or less likely to see efficiency wages in the following types of industries?
    (a) Industries where training and turnover costs are relatively low
    (b) Industries where it is difficult to monitor individual productivity
    (c) Industries that have many jobs where individual differences in productivity are relatively large

**5** (This question is based on the chapter appendix.) The following figures represent the relationship between productivity and wages for the Doorware Corporation, which makes hinges.

| Wage per hour | $ 8 | $10 | $12 | $14 | $16 | $18 | $20 |
|---|---|---|---|---|---|---|---|
| Hinges produced per hour | 20 | 24 | 33 | 42 | 52 | 58 | 60 |

Graph the productivity-wage relationship. From the graph, how do you determine the efficiency wage? Calculate output per dollar spent on labour for the Doorware Corporation. What is the efficiency wage?

## APPENDIX: DERIVATION OF THE EFFICIENCY WAGE

Figure 17.4 depicts a curve that represents one possible relationship between productivity and wages. We refer to this curve as the **wage-productivity curve.** Productivity here can be thought of as "the number of pins produced in an hour," or any similar measure of output. There is a minimum wage, $w_m$, below which the firm will find it difficult, if not impossible, to obtain labour. At a very low wage, $w_1$, the company can only hire the dregs of the labour market—those who cannot get jobs elsewhere. Worker morale is low, and effort is low. Workers quit as soon as they can get another job, so labour turnover is high.

As the firm raises its wage, productivity increases. The company earns a reputation as a high-wage firm, attracting the best workers. Morale is high, turnover is low, and employees work hard. But eventually, as in so many areas, diminishing returns set in. Successive increases in wages have incrementally smaller effects on productivity. The firm is concerned with wage costs per unit of output, not wage costs per employee. Thus, it wishes to minimize not the wage but the wage divided by productivity.

This can be put another way. The company wishes to maximize the output per dollar spent on labour (we are assuming that all other costs are fixed). Since productivity is defined as output per unit of time (pins per hour), and the wage is labour cost per unit of time (dollars per hour), dividing productivity by the wage produces the equation

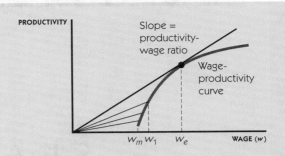

**Figure 17.4 THE RELATIONSHIP BETWEEN PRODUCTIVITY AND WAGES**

As wages rise, productivity increases, at first quickly and then more slowly. The efficiency wage is the wage at which the ratio of productivity to wage is highest. It is found by drawing a line through the origin tangent to the wage-productivity curve.

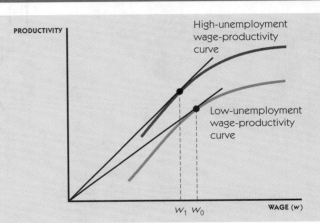

**Figure 17.5 SHIFTING THE PRODUCTIVITY-WAGE RELATIONSHIP**

If unemployment is low, workers have many alternative job possibilities. With the threat of being fired reduced, at each wage workers work less hard, so productivity is lower. In the case shown here, the efficiency wage will be lower when there is high unemployment than when there is low unemployment.

$$\frac{\text{productivity}}{\text{wage}} = \frac{\text{output/unit of time}}{\text{dollars/unit of time}} =$$

$$\frac{\text{output}}{\text{dollars spent on labour}}.$$

Thus, a decision to make the ratio of output to dollars spent on labour as high as possible is mathematically equivalent to a decision to make the ratio of productivity to wages as high as possible. To tell what level of wages will accomplish this goal, Figure 17.4 shows the productivity-wage ratio as a line from the origin to a point on the wage-productivity curve. The slope of this line is the ratio of productivity (the vertical axis) to the wage (the horizontal axis).

As we draw successive lines from the origin to points on the wage-productivity curve with higher wages, the slope first increases and then decreases. The slope is largest for the line through the origin that is just tangent to the wage-productivity curve. The wage at this point of tangency is the wage at which labour costs are minimized: the efficiency wage, $w_e$.

Changes in unemployment rates may shift the wage-productivity curve, as shown in Figure 17.5. At each wage, the productivity of the labour force is higher at the higher unemployment rate. Also, the efficiency wage—the wage at which the ratio of productivity to the wage is maximized—is lowered slightly. It falls from $w_0$ to $w_1$. The change in the efficiency wage may be relatively small, even if the shift in the curve relating productivity to wages is relatively large.

# CHAPTER 18

# INFLATION VERSUS UNEMPLOYMENT: APPROACHES TO POLICY

**M**aking economic policy can be like walking a tightrope. Lean too far one way, and unemployment increases. Lean too far the other, and prices rise. It is even possible to have the worst of all worlds: simultaneous inflation, unemployment, and slow growth.

Many of the basic macroeconomic problems stem from variability in the level of economic activity. When the economy is dragging along, a jump start may be required to reignite it. But when the economy is racing, inflation may loom. Both unemployment and inflation cause economic hardship. Unemployment particularly affects the young, who have no cushion of accumulated savings to fall back upon, as well as single parents and unskilled workers. Inflation takes its toll among retired people, whose incomes do not rise commensurately with inflation.

After briefly reviewing these costs, we focus in this chapter on the major policy issues: Should the government intervene to stabilize the economy? If so, how? With monetary or fiscal policy? We then illustrate some of the basic issues by means of a historical review of the major policy debates over the past three decades.

**1** What are the key issues facing policy makers as they decide whether to attempt to stimulate or dampen the economy?

**2** What are the alternative explanations of the pronounced fluctuations in the level of economic activity in the economy? Why does the economy periodically experience a downturn in which unemployment is high, growth slows down, and output actually falls?

**3** Why do some economists believe that the government should not intervene to stabilize the economy? Why do they believe that such intervention is unnecessary, ineffective, or more likely to do harm than good? And why do other economists believe that intervention can be helpful?

**4** How can government attempt to dampen economic fluctuations and to reduce the NAIRU, below which inflation starts to accelerate?

**5** What have been some of the major policy debates over the past three decades? How do they illustrate general principles?

## THE IMPACT OF INFLATION AND UNEMPLOYMENT

When should policy makers act to stimulate or dampen the economy? Each decision involves a trade-off. Consider the problem facing Canadian policy makers in 1994 and 1995, as the unemployment rate decreased from 11.2 percent, to 10.4 percent, to 9.5 percent. Everyone agreed that at some point, inflationary pressures would set in. The question was, when? If the Bank of Canada acted too early and raised interest rates too much, the recovery could stall, throwing the economy back into recession. If it waited too long, inflation would increase. How much would it cost to bring inflation down? What would be the costs of a higher level of inflation?

### THE BASIC TRADE-OFFS

The discussions in earlier chapters have set the scene for how policy makers approach these decisions: the costs of high unemployment—including the loss in output—are apparent. According to Okun's law, lowering the unemployment rate by 1 percentage point (say from 11 to 10 percent) typically increases output by 2 percent. In an $800 billion economy, this translates into $16 billion per year.

Inflation, too, has its costs, though the discussion in Chapter 16 suggested that at the low levels of inflation that have prevailed in Canada during the past ten years, some of those costs are more perceived than real.

Chapter 16 also clarified the trade-off between inflation and unemployment. Today, the focus is not so much on trading off a little more inflation for a temporary lowering of the unemployment rate as on the risk of setting off a bout of inflation. Governments recognize that if they permanently run the economy at a rate lower than the NAIRU, inflation will accelerate; most governments do not seem willing to take advantage of even the short-run gains from reduced unemployment, which typically occur earlier than the inflation costs, which are felt only later. Today, the debate focuses more on risk: If there is uncertainty about the NAIRU, how aggressive or conservative should the government be? How willing should it be to risk an increase in inflation, at the cost of failing to use the economy's resources as fully as possible?

In assessing these risks, the same factors—the costs of inflation and of unemployment—enter in much the same way they did when economists thought there was more of a long-run trade-off between inflation and unemployment. Not surprisingly, those who previously worried about unemployment argue for more aggressive policies, while those who worry about inflation argue for conservative policies.

Key to understanding these two positions is the recognition that unemployment and inflation affect different groups differently.

Unions, which are concerned with unemployment, typically push for aggressive macroeconomic policies. Spokespersons for business, such as the Canadian Manufacturers Association, also support aggressive policies. This is not surprising, since more aggressive policies typically entail a lower value for the Canadian dollar, which increases the demand for Canadian exports, and lower interest rates, which reduce the cost of borrowing to finance inventories and the purchase of plant and equipment. Bay Street bondholders push for more conservative policies, which tend to cause real rates of return on bonds to be higher. The split in views is often characterized as one between Main Street and Bay Street.

Low-wage workers and other disadvantaged groups are most likely to benefit from low-unemployment (aggressive) policies. Since these groups have little savings, they bear little of the costs of inflation. The costs of *unanticipated* increases in inflation are typically borne by those who hold long-term bonds: they see the value of those bonds decrease as nominal interest rates rise, as typically happens when inflation increases.

## PERSPECTIVES ON FLUCTUATIONS AND MACROECONOMIC POLICY

There is widespread agreement on the desirability of high growth, low unemployment, and low and stable inflation. But economists disagree about the role and means of government in pursuing these objectives. Some economists believe that government attempts at intervention have little effect or, worse, only destabilize the economy. Others argue that government interventions are generally successful.

For simplicity, we can split economists into two broad groups on these issues: interventionists and noninterventionists. Noninterventionists tend to have great faith in markets and little faith in government. Some noninterventionists believe that the economy adjusts quickly and efficiently to disturbances and see little role for government action. Other noninterventionists accept that markets may adjust slowly, but argue that government efforts do more harm than good.

Interventionists argue that because markets adjust slowly, there may be extended periods of unemployment, *and* government policies can restore the economy to full employment faster than the market would do on its own.

## ECONOMIC FLUCTUATIONS

Figure 18.1 shows how the rate of growth of output (real GDP) has fluctuated over the postwar period. Panel A shows the movement in the rate of growth of real GDP relative to the **long-run trend.** The long-run trend is shown as the smooth line drawn through the data, tracing out the growth rates the economy would have followed if growth rates had changed according to a steady trend. The actual growth rate is sometimes above this trend line and sometimes below. Panel B shows how both the growth rate and the unemployment rate have deviated from their long-run trends over the same period. The two curves illustrate the negative correlation between these deviations of the growth rate and the unemployment rate from their trends. When the rate of growth of output is above its long-run trend, the rate of unemployment is below its, and vice versa. The term "recession" is reserved for periods in which output actually declines, but even growth at a substantially lower rate than normal represents an economic slowdown, with significant consequences.

The figure illustrates the central challenge in "managing" the economy: its variability. It is not as if there is an isolated episode in which the aggregate demand curve shifts to the left, resulting in unemployment. The prescription then would be simple: use monetary or fiscal policy to shift the aggregate demand curve back to the right. The problem is that

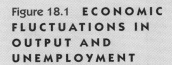

Figure 18.1 **ECONOMIC FLUCTUATIONS IN OUTPUT AND UNEMPLOYMENT**

Panel A shows how the growth rate of real GDP has moved above and below a long-run trend line over the past 50 years. Panel B compares the deviation of the growth rate of real GDP from its trend with the deviation of the unemployment rate from its trend. When the growth rate of real GDP is below its trend, unemployment tends to be above its trend, and vice versa. *Sources:* Statistics Canada, CANSIM Database 1996, Labels D20463, D767611; M. C. Urquhart, ed., *Historical Statistics of Canada,* 2nd ed. (Ottawa: Statistics Canada, 1983).

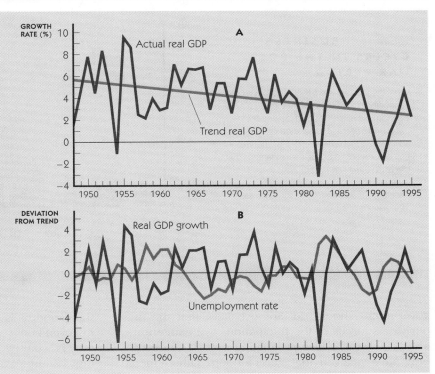

the economy is always changing, always fluctuating. There is a real fear that because of the length of time it takes policies to be put into effect and then for the effects to show up, the government may be stimulating the economy just at the time when it should be dampening it, and conversely. Some economists think that government policies have actually contributed to the economy's fluctuations. Views concerning whether government should or should not intervene depend strongly on views concerning the *origins* and nature of the economy's fluctuations.

At one time, economists thought that there was a certain inevitability to these economic fluctuations—they were so regular that they were called business cycles. But at least since World War II, the length of time between recessions has been extremely variable, as Figure 18.2 shows. The heights of the alternating bars indicate the length of the recessions and

expansions beginning in 1947. Two things stand out. The first is that both recessions and expansions vary considerably in duration, making the business cycle very unpredictable. The second is that economic downturns tend to be much shorter than expansions. The average length of a downturn is only 10 months compared with 54 months for an expansion.

Although the length of downturns and upturns has been highly variable, there are still distinct patterns associated with the economy's fluctuations. In downturns, not only does output growth slow down (and sometimes even become negative), but unemployment increases. Hours worked per worker tend to decline, inflation tends to slow, and in some cases, prices even start to fall.

While economists agree that the economy has been marked by fluctuations exhibiting these distinctive patterns, they disagree about the *causes* and what

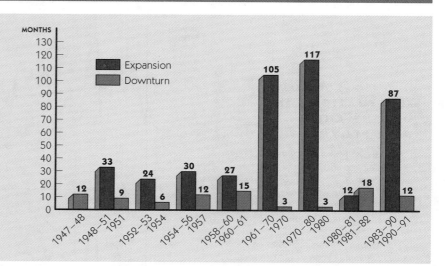

Figure 18.2 **BUSINESS CYCLES IN THE POST-WAR PERIOD**

Over the past 50 years there has been high variability in the length of time that economic expansions and downturns have lasted. The average expansion is 54 months, and the average downturn is 10 months. As this book goes to press, the expansion that began in 1991 has lasted more than 80 months. *Source:* P. Cross, "Alternative Measures of Business Cycles in Canada: 1947–1992," *Canadian Economic Observer* (February 1996): 3.1–3.40.

government should do. Some believe that the underlying sources of the fluctuations are **exogenous shocks,** disturbances originating outside the economy, such as a war that starts a boom. Others focus on **endogenous factors,** properties of the economy itself, such as a tendency of the economy to become overconfident in expansions, leading to overinvestment (including overinvestment in inventories), leading in turn to a downturn as investment slows down once the overinvestment becomes recognized. Today, most economists think economic fluctuations involve a mixture of exogenous and endogenous factors: an external shock such as an increase in the price of oil may hit an economy, but endogenous factors may sometimes amplify the initial effects and make them more persistent.

Some of the variation in economic activity is an inevitable consequence of the inability of anyone to predict the future perfectly. At times firms will overestimate demand and produce too much. When production exceeds sales, inventories build up. As inventories build up, firms are induced to cut back on their production. By the same token, government interventions designed to stabilize the economy may not do so; they may even exacerbate the fluctuations, because government cannot predict perfectly where

the economy is going. Indeed, in many cases it may not even know with much precision where the economy is today. Data indicating the health of the economy become available only with a lag.

Most economic downturns in the postwar period in Canada have been associated with large increases in interest rates by the Bank of Canada, but these increases originally had been motivated by evidence of actual or incipient inflation. In some cases, such as the oil price shock of 1973, exogenous shocks played a role in accelerating inflation. In other cases, the natural buoyancy of the economy has led aggregate demand to outpace aggregate supply. Economists disagree as to whether monetary policy could have more finely tuned the economy: could a timely raising of interest rates have kept aggregate demand moving precisely in lockstep with aggregate supply, so that inflation did not pick up and so that monetary authorities could have avoided "slamming on the brakes"? Or, having failed to stop the inflation, could it have slowed down the economy more gradually, and thus avoided as deep a recession at the same time that it lowered inflation?

Interventionists believe that appropriate policies—for instance, maintenance of the automatic stabilizers discussed in Chapter 15—can both reduce the endogenous forces that either give rise to or help sustain fluctuations and increase the likelihood that interventions actually stabilize the economy.

## THE NONINTERVENTIONIST PERSPECTIVE

Those who share the view that government should not intervene to stabilize the economy differ in their reasons. Some believe that the economy is efficient, so that there is little that government can add; while others believe that governments do have significant effects—but more often make matters worse. We now take a closer look at each of these perspectives.

### REAL BUSINESS CYCLE THEORY: INTERVENTION IS UNNECESSARY

Intervention is clearly unnecessary if the economy always operates efficiently, at full employment. **Real business cycle theorists** attribute the economy's fluctuations to exogenous shocks, such as the 1973 and 1979 oil price increases, but believe that markets adjust quickly—prices and wages are sufficiently flexible for full employment to be restored quickly—and certainly more quickly than it takes government to recognize a problem, take actions, and for those actions to have effect. Since the economy typically operates at full employment, government need only worry about inflation. But recall from our discussion in Part Two that when the economy is at full employment, prices tend to increase with the money supply. Price stability, and full employment, can be attained if the monetary authorities let the money supply expand at the rate of increase in *real GDP*.

### NEW CLASSICAL MACROECONOMICS: INTERVENTION IS INEFFECTIVE

Some noninterventionists claim that the government cannot even have an effect in the short run, as the private sector largely undoes any government action. Thus, if the government increases the money supply, with *rational expectations*, all market participants recognize that this will affect the price level. Price levels adjust instantaneously, so that the *real* money supply is unchanged. The expansionary effects of the increase in money supply are thus completely counteracted, and monetary policy has no *real* effects. Similarly, an increase in the government deficit is perfectly offset by an increase in private savings as households foresee the need for higher taxes in the future.

The view that policies are largely ineffective and what effectiveness they possess is only in the short run and generates no permanent gains is strongly advanced by the **new classical economists.**

### INTERVENTION IS COUNTERPRODUCTIVE

Faith in markets is one thing; faith in the ability of government to improve on markets is another. Some noninterventionists see more shortcomings in markets than do real business cycle theorists and new classical economists, but nonetheless have little confidence in the ability of government to improve macroeconomic performance. Indeed, some hold the view that intervention is counterproductive, for two reasons.

First, they recognize that there are important lags between the time the government recognizes a problem and takes action, and between the time the action occurs and its macroeconomic effects are fully realized. By the time the effects are fully realized, the "medicine" may no longer be appropriate. Lags by themselves would not be a problem if the government could accurately forecast where the economy was going and what the exact effects of policy on the economy would be. But everyone, including the government, foretells the future with a cloudy crystal ball, and as a result, governments risk prescribing the wrong medicine. In recent years, governments have become much more sensitized to the problem of *timing*. One of the reasons for the reluctance of the Bank of Canada to take strong actions to stimulate the economy in 1991, in the midst of an economic downturn, was a worry that given the shallowness of the recession, the economy might quickly recover on its own, making a large increase in the money supply unnecessary and potentially harmful in terms of fuelling future inflation.

Critics of strong interventionist policies argue, further, that there are systematic *political* reasons that interventions are often misguided. Governments want the economy to be strong as they go into an election; they thus tend to overheat the economy: the gains in employment show up before the election, but the costs, in terms of inflation, hopefully show up only after the election.

### RULES VERSUS DISCRETION: THE NONINTERVENTIONIST PERSPECTIVE

Critics of intervention claim that historically, whether because of these political motivations, or simply because of lags in policy making and effect, the government has actually exacerbated the economy's fluctuations. When the government attempts to dampen a boom, its policies reducing demand take effect just as the economy is weakening, reinforcing the downward movement. The opposite occurs when the government attempts to stimulate the economy. Thus, critics of government action conclude that the government should not try to manage the economy. It should simply stick by some simple rules. **Monetarists** believe that the government should expand the money supply at a constant rate. They believe that government should follow set **rules** and not exercise **discretion.** Furthermore, sticking to such rules would, in their judgment, eliminate a major source of uncertainty and instability in the economy: uncertainty about future government policy.

They believe further not only that government should pursue certain rules, but that it should have its hands tied, so that it has no choice. The reason for this is that even if the government today promised to follow certain rules, such as not to try to stimulate the economy should there be a downturn, it will not—or cannot, politically—follow those rules. The problem of whether the government will actually carry out a promised course of action is called the problem of **dynamic consistency.** The government may announce that a particular tax change is permanent—and it might even deceive itself into believing that the tax change is permanent. But when circumstances change, policies will change. And the fact that policies will change, and that individuals and firms expect them to change, has enormous consequences for the behaviour of individuals and firms and the effects of policies. For instance, in 1985

the federal government introduced a generous tax exemption for capital gains earned by Canadians. All capital gains up to a lifetime limit of $500,000 were to be made exempt from taxation. These breaks were intended to be permanent and were intended to encourage savings in equities. In the next couple of years, many persons who already owned shares whose value had increased considerably decided to cash them in. They figured, correctly, as it turned out, that this policy would not last. Better to cash them in now and avoid the tax rather than wait until another government reverses the policy. In fact, only two years later the lifetime exemption was reduced to $100,000, and the rate of tax on capital gains was increased. All the initial exemption did was induce persons to sell their existing shares rather than invest in new ones.

## THE INTERVENTIONIST PERSPECTIVE

The most compelling case for intervention is based on three premises: (a) without intervention, recovery may take an unconscionably long time; (b) certain interventions can improve the *structure* of the economy and enhance overall macroeconomic performance; and (c) discretionary interventions, while not perfect, on balance can reduce the economy's fluctuations.

As a practical matter, governments *must* intervene: political pressures will not allow them to sit idly by if the economy goes into a deep recession, and in any case, monetary authorities have constantly to take decisions about what to do. Even to keep the money supply constant, or to increase it at a fixed rate, requires decisions: forecasts about what would the money supply be in the absence of any action by the Bank, and judgments about the consequences of particular actions.

The underlying assumption of the noninterventionists is that markets adjust quickly and so high unemployment is at most a short-term affair. In some periods this assumption has seemed unpersuasive: in the Great Depression, unemployment persisted for many years. Unemployment rates in some European countries have exceeded 10 percent for more than a decade. Even here in Canada, unemployment has been close to the double-digit level for most of the 1990s. As a practical matter, when unemployment rates are high, governments are under enormous pressures to do something.

Today, the leading school of thought of economists who believe that government can and should intervene to stabilize the economy is called **new Keynesianism.** They share John Maynard Keynes's view that unemployment may be persistent and that though market forces may restore the economy to full employment, those forces work so slowly that further action is required. The new Keynesian theories differ from older Keynesian analyses in their greater emphasis on *microeconomics.* For instance, they share with many real business cycle and new classical economists a view that the economy consists largely of profit-maximizing competitive firms. But they have identified a variety of reasons for markets' failure to adjust quickly to disturbances, such as costs of adjustment and imperfections of information.

Moreover, while they agree that there are forces that enable the economy to dampen and absorb exogenous shocks, there are also forces that sometimes lead it to amplify shocks and make them more persistent. Noninterventionists emphasize the former: when firms cut back production in response to an inventory buildup, prices and wages adjust quickly and fall. At these low prices and wages, firms decide it is a good time to buy new machines; households may decide it is a good time to buy durables and new houses. These decisions help raise aggregate demand, offsetting the dampening effect of the excess inventories.

By contrast, new Keynesian economists emphasize the forces within the economy that amplify fluctuations and help make those fluctuations persist. Thus, the fall in the price of oil in 1985 might have been viewed as a good thing for the economy—the reverse of the increase in the price of oil in 1973 and 1979. But the unanticipated fall in the price of oil led to massive disruptions and bankruptcies in western Canada; these in turn weakened the real estate market and banking system in those provinces, leading to an overall contraction of economic activity. The impacts were felt well beyond the oil industry, and in

the process of being disseminated through the region, seemed actually to be amplified.

## THE MULTIPLIER-ACCELERATOR

The most widely discussed of the systematic endogenous forces that amplify fluctuations is called the **multiplier-accelerator.** We already encountered the multiplier: an upturn in exports is amplified by the multiplier, so that the increase in GDP may be two or more times the increase in exports. But matters do not stop here: the increase in GDP leads firms to want to invest more to meet the increased demand for goods. Typically, it takes around $2 to $3 of capital to produce a dollar of GDP. Thus, if firms expect output to increase by say $10 billion, they will want to increase their capital stock by $20 to $30 billion. This is called the *accelerator.* As firms increase their investment, GDP grows even more. Increased investment of $20 billion results in a further increase in GDP by $40 billion, if the multiplier is 2. But this increase in GDP may give rise to a further increase in the demand for investment. Thus, the multiplier and accelerator help to amplify and propagate what was initially an exogenous shock, an increase in exports.

Not only does the structure of the economy serve to amplify and propagate external shocks, it may also itself convert an expansion into a downturn. To see how this occurs, consider what happens as the economy continues to expand. Eventually it hits constraints; for example, shortages of labour may impose a limit on the expansion of the economy. Once these constraints are hit, the economy stops expanding. Investment slows down, and aggregate demand is reduced by the multiplier effect. A downturn begins that, as in the expansion phase, feeds upon itself through the interaction of the multiplier and the accelerator.

## OTHER SOURCES OF AMPLIFICATION

There are other reasons that the internal structure of the economy may amplify fluctuations. For instance, firms rely heavily on profits as a source of investment. They may face constraints on the amount they can borrow, and they may find it impossible to raise funds by issuing new shares, or feel

## DIFFERING VIEWS OF MACROECONOMIC POLICY

### NONINTERVENTIONISTS

**Real business cycle theorists** believe fluctuations in economic activity are due to exogenous shocks and that markets respond quickly to economic disturbances. Government intervention is unnecessary.

**New classical economists** think that policies can have no long-run effect because the private sector anticipates the effects of policy and undoes them. Policies can only have a real effect in the short run, and then only if prices do not respond quickly.

Others believe that even though markets adjust slowly, discretionary macroeconomic policies make matters worse rather than better because of lags in determining the need for policy and then implementing it.

### INTERVENTIONISTS

**New Keynesians** think markets respond slowly, so periods of unemployment can be extended. Discretionary macroeconomic policy can be effective.

Business cycles are endogenous phenomena and forces exist that amplify fluctuations. Governments should both engage in discretionary macroeconomic policies and design built-in stabilizers that make the economy more stable.

---

that the cost of doing so is so unattractive that they would prefer to rely on internally generated funds. As the economy goes into a downturn, profits fall; decreased profits lead to decreased investment, exacerbating the economic downturn.

New Keynesians agree that adjustments in interest rates and prices may *partially* offset these destabilizing influences—for instance, in a recession lower interest rates provide greater impetus for firms to invest—these adjustments are simply too weak to offset them fully.

## POLICIES TO IMPROVE ECONOMIC PERFORMANCE

Interventionists claim not only that markets by themselves do not ensure full employment but that government interventions can *and have* contributed to the stability of the economy. While acknowledging that to be sure there have been instances in the past where government actions may have exacerbated an economic downturn, they believe that by and large the government's record is a positive one. In the period before World War II, when government did not systematically try to stabilize the economy, the variability of output appears to have been higher and included many more episodes not only when growth slowed down, but also when output actually decreased.

While academic economists often debate *whether* government should intervene, most policy debates center around *when* and *how*. There are three sets of policies designed to improve the economy's economic performance.

First, government intervention should attempt to change the structure of the economy to make it more stable. Automatic stabilizers, which automatically lead to increased government expenditures and reduced taxes when the economy goes into a downturn, are the most important example.

Second, it should use *discretionary* macroeconomic policy to stimulate the economy when output is low and unemployment high, and to dampen the economy when inflation is strong.

Third, it should attempt to lower the NAIRU, so that price stability (stable inflation) can be attained at a lower level of unemployment.

## RULES VERSUS DISCRETION: AN INTERVENTIONIST PERSPECTIVE

Interventionists argue that discretionary macroeconomic policy can and has helped stabilize the economy. They also argue that the historical record shows why it is not possible to follow simple rules. Consider, for instance, the simple rule discussed earlier: the money supply should increase at the rate of increase of *real* GDP. Since the monetary authorities do not directly control the money supply, this still entails some discretion: they must forecast what will be happening to the economy and, on the basis of their forecast, make judgments concerning what policies to undertake so that the money supply will expand at the desired rate. While such policies enjoyed enormous popularity at the end of the 1970s and in the early 1980s, their consequences were largely viewed to be unfavourable. In Canada, the single-minded pursuit of this policy by the Bank of Canada led interest rates to soar to nearly 20 percent and ushered in the worst recession in half a century. Furthermore, as we saw in Chapter 14, the marked changes in the relationship between the monetary aggregates (money supply) and output that have occurred during the past two decades removed the theoretical underpinnings of this approach. Inevitably, central banks must use discretion, if only to judge whether there has been a change in the structure of the economy.

## INFLATION/UNEMPLOYMENT TRADE-OFFS

If government is to intervene actively in the economy using its discretion, the question becomes, what should it do? The analysis of Chapter 16 and the first part of this chapter provides the analytical basis for these decisions. Clearly, we would like to have both low rates of inflation and low rates of unemployment. The question becomes, is there a trade-off: Can we get, say, lower rates of unemployment by allowing the inflation rate to increase?

In the years immediately following the discovery of the Phillips curve, most economists thought that there was a trade-off. Those economists who thought that the costs of inflation were high argued for a high unemployment rate, while those who thought the costs of low inflation paled in comparison with the costs of unemployment argued for somewhat lower unemployment rates. Thus disagreements about policy largely hinged around disagreements about the *costs* of inflation and unemployment. Economists who focused on the hardship that unemployment

imposed on workers advocated low unemployment policies; those who focused on the impact of inflation on investors, including retired individuals who depend on interest payments to live, advocated low inflation policies.

But in the 1970s, as the unemployment rate and inflation rate increased together, and as economists became more aware of the importance of inflationary expectations and inflation inertia, increasingly a consensus developed that the economy could not enjoy a sustained level of unemployment below the NAIRU for long before inflation started increasing.

There still remained two elements of disagreement about the nature of the trade-off. First, while there was agreement that the long-run Phillips curve was at least close to vertical, some economists thought that in the short run—for a period of perhaps several years—the economy could experience lower unemployment while inflation increased only moderately. Others worried that with rational expectations, even short periods of low unemployment, below the NAIRU, could give rise to high levels of inflation. They see the economy as standing on a precipice: leaning toward too low an unemployment level quickly leads to soaring inflation.

The historical experience within Canada over the past fifteen years strongly suggests that those worries were exaggerated. Slight deviations above or below the NAIRU seem to lead to slight increases or decreases in the rate of inflation. The economy does not seem to stand on a steep precipice.

The second disagreement concerned the costs of "disinflation," reducing the inflation rate. Assume policy makers make a mistake; they push the unemployment rate below the NAIRU, and inflation increases slightly. What would it take to reduce inflation? Clearly, the economy would have to operate for a while at a higher level of unemployment, one above the NAIRU. Those who advocate a cautious policy—making sure that the unemployment rate never fell below the NAIRU—would worry that the costs of reducing inflation were very high. In particular, they might recall the experience of the 1970s and 1980s: to wring the inflationary expectations of the 1970s (when inflation hit double-digit levels) out of the economy, the Canadian economy had to go through the deepest recession since the Great Depression.

But the evidence from attempts to achieve more

## CONTROVERSIES IN MACROECONOMIC POLICY

**Values**

How large are the costs of moderate inflation?

How large are the costs of unemployment?

Since the costs of inflation and the costs of unemployment are borne by different individuals, how do we "value" these different costs?

**Trade-offs**

How quickly will attempts to lower unemployment below the NAIRU lead to increases in prices and price expectations? How quickly will runaway inflation set in? Does the economy sit on a precipice?

Are there large costs associated with disinflation? What is the relationship between these costs and the benefits that the economy achieved during the period during which unemployment was lower than the NAIRU?

---

moderate inflation suggests that the costs are low. Indeed, the loss in output and employment from "killing" inflation are matched by the gains in output and employment during the period in which unemployment remains below the NAIRU. This suggests that policies that focus on preventing inflation at all costs are somewhat excessive.

## IMPLEMENTING POLICIES: TARGETS

So far we have focused our discussion on the questions, *what are the trade-offs* and *what should be the objectives of macroeconomic policy?* But even when there is agreement about the objectives of macroeconomic policy, there may be disagreements about how best to achieve those objectives. For instance, the government might believe that the NAIRU is 8 percent, and might wish to keep the unemployment rate at that level, but it does not directly control the unemployment rate. The Bank might want to keep the inflation rate at 2 percent, but it does not directly control the inflation rate. Over the years economists have come up with a variety of "targets"—intermediate variables that are not necessarily of interest for their own sake but that are easier to control than the variables of real interest, and that are (or were thought at the time to be) closely related to the variables of real concern. Thus, in the late 1970s and early 1980s, many monetary authorities focused on the **monetary aggregates,** the statistics describing the money supply (M1, M2, etc.). Controlling these would, it was believed, stabilize the inflation rate. It was believed that there was

a stable relationship between the money supply and nominal income. If the money supply increased by 3 percent, nominal income would increase by only 3 percent. And since most of the advocates of this theory believed that the economy normally operated at full employment, if the economy's full-employment output was growing at 3 percent, that would imply that there would be no inflation. (The rate of increase of nominal income is the rate of increase of real income plus the rate of increase of prices.) But just as the theory came to be widely believed, the empirical relationship fell apart, as we saw in Chapter 14. The ratio of the money supply (say, M2) to nominal income appeared to vary in ways that were hard to predict. Thus, controlling the money supply was not a good target. At other times, monetary authorities have focused on variables such as the real interest rate, the exchange rate, or the rate of inflation. Today, the Bank takes an eclectic approach, incorporating data about all of these variables, including the monetary aggregates, in its analysis.

## STRUCTURAL POLICIES: LOWERING THE NAIRU

Discretionary monetary and fiscal policy, no matter how aggressive and well pursued, will never completely eliminate the economy's fluctuations. Governments therefore try to improve the structure of the economy, to dampen the fluctuations and to reduce the NAIRU, so that the economy can have lower unemployment rates without the threat of increasing inflation. The major set of policies aimed at dampening fluctuations are the automatic stabilizers, discussed in Chapter 15, which automatically lead to reduced taxes and increased expenditures as the economy slows down. Here, we focus on policies aimed at lowering the NAIRU.

The government can try to lower the NAIRU in several ways: increasing labour mobility, increasing the competitiveness of the economy, controlling directly the increase in wages and prices, and moral suasion.

### INCREASING LABOUR MOBILITY

By reducing the time that it takes for people to move from job to job the government can reduce *frictional unemployment* and thus lower the NAIRU. Policies that facilitate labour mobility include government employment centers, which enable individuals to ascertain quickly vacancies for which they might be suited and also provide information about training opportunities. A central part of Sweden's active labour market policies are training programmes that provide those who have lost their jobs the skills required for the new jobs being created. Many economists in Canada have advocated that support for the unemployed be reoriented from "passive" income support policies like unemployment insurance and welfare to "active" policies that stress training and education so that the unemployed are better suited to find the kinds of jobs that are currently available.

Some government policies, particularly in Europe, have probably reduced labour mobility and thus increased the NAIRU. There is concern that legislation intended to increase workers' job security by making it more difficult for employers to fire them has had the side effect of making employers more reluctant to hire new workers, and thus has impeded the process of job transition. Changing these laws may lower the NAIRU.

### MAKING THE ECONOMY MORE COMPETITIVE

A second approach, which received considerable attention in the late 1970s and early 1980s, entails shifting the aggregate supply curve down and out, as illustrated in Figure 18.3. This increases output at any given price level, and thus reduces inflationary pressure. One way of shifting the aggregate supply curve is to reduce regulation. For example, deregulating airline, trucking, and natural gas prices leads to lower prices as competitive forces come into play. These lower prices have a ripple effect as they spread throughout the economy. Industries that use trucks and natural gas as inputs lower their prices, and sectors that use those industries' products are in turn able to lower their prices. Economists applauded these initiatives because they increase the efficiency of the economy. But many economists

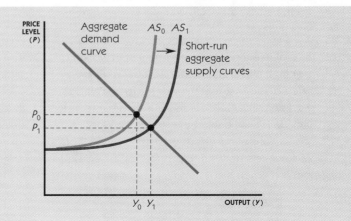

Figure 18.3 **INCREASING OUTPUT BY SHIFTING THE AGGREGATE SUPPLY CURVE**

Policies that make the economy more competitive, such as deregulation, cause the short-run aggregate supply curve to shift down and out. Aggregate output rises from $Y_0$ to $Y_1$, and inflationary pressures are reduced.

POLICY PERSPECTIVE:

GOVERNMENT TRAINING PROGRAMMES: ARE THEY
NEEDED AND DO THEY WORK?

One way unemployment might be reduced without leading to inflationary pressures is to implement policies designed to affect structural change in the labour market—to reduce the NAIRU. Some have argued that a labour-training programme is a key component of both making the Canadian economy more competitive, by increasing our skill levels relative to the rest of the world, and reducing structural and frictional levels of unemployment, by making it easier for the unemployed to find matches with prospective employers. Many economists believe that there is a role for government in worker training due to the existence of an externality (part of the benefit from a firm's spending on worker training accrues to other firms in the economy; see Chapter 7 for a discussion of externalities). Firms are reluctant to spend much on training, since newly trained workers can take the benefits, their increased productivity, to another firm. Considering that all firms have this problem, it is thought that the private markets provide too little worker training relative to the level that would be best for society. Indeed, many of those advocating reform of welfare and unemployment insurance programmes insist that these be linked directly with government training initiatives.

To evaluate the role for government in worker training, several important questions must be answered. Is it true that the externality involved in worker training leads firms to underprovide it? Is Canada lagging behind the rest of the world in the amount of training its workers receive? If private markets do tend to provide too little training, can government training programmes be ef-

fective at filling the gap? Finally, how should the programmes be designed? For example, should training programmes directed at those who are currently unemployed be fundamentally different from those directed at the employed?

A recent study by Constantine Kapsalis looked at the training undergone by current employees in 1991. He found that 30 percent of employees participated in employer-sponsored training programmes and courses and 18 percent undertook some formal training on their own, sometimes in addition to that supported by their employers. In total, about 41 percent of employees received some training, which averaged out to 93 hours per trainee. So it seems that firms and their employees are investing in a significant amount of training, though whether this is at the socially optimal level or not remains an open question. International comparisons show that Canada is among the world's leaders in the incidence of both employer-sponsored training and postsecondary education. Thus, fears that Canada is lagging behind its major competitors around the world in training appear to be unfounded. This would suggest that there is limited need for government intervention with respect to the training of employees. Firms may well be able to avoid the externality problem by providing training whose benefits are specifically designed for its own environment (so-called "firm-specific" training). Or they may be able to induce workers to bear some of the costs of training by keeping their wages low during training periods and rewarding them with higher wages if they stay with the firm after their training has made them more productive.

The above study concerned only those who were employed. But what about those who are unemployed? Surely efforts to reduce the NAIRU must focus on them if structural unemployment is to be reduced. One might also assume that government's role would be greater as regards the unemployed. A recent article in *The Globe and Mail* summarized several studies of government training programmes in various nations. The general conclusion is that large-scale government-run training programmes do not lead to significantly higher probabilities of employment and/or significantly higher wages. It could be argued that this is due to the fact that the unemployed are the least skilled to begin with, and so the benefits would not be expected to be large. Training done through for-profit institutions and small-scale government programmes run in conjunction with specific employers did have greater success, with both the employed and the unemployed.

The lessons seem clear. Beyond providing basic education and training—the kinds of skills most likely to be subject to the externality problem—governments should be wary of becoming involved in large-scale training programmes. If it is deemed that too little training is being provided in an economy, a better option for policy is to concentrate on small-scale programmes linked to specific employers and skills, or to grant education and training vouchers that can be used to help defray the costs of private programmes, which appear to have a better chance of success.

*Sources:* C. Kapsalis, "Training in Canada: Reassessing the Evidence," *Canadian Business Economics* 1 (Summer 1993): 3–11; "The Training Wheels of Government Go Flat," *The Globe and Mail,* April 13, 1996, p. D4.

questioned both the magnitude of the effects and the speed with which they come into play: the time it takes for supply reactions to occur is too long to make supply-side initiatives effective instruments for short-term inflation control.

These and other measures taken to make the economy more competitive may lower the NAIRU: in a more competitive economy, particularly one that is more open to international competition, there will be less pressure to increase prices and wages, even when the unemployment rate is low. For instance, workers worry that if they demand significant wage increases, the products they produce will not be able to compete with foreign imports, demand for what they produce will decrease, and they will face a risk of losing their jobs.

## WAGE AND PRICE CONTROLS AND MORAL SUASION

In the 1950s and 1960s, many believed that competition—market forces—was insufficient to control price and wage increases. Large unions could demand and get large wage increases, regardless of the unemployment rate, and industries that, like the steel industry, were dominated by a few large producers could and would raise their prices, even when there was large excess capacity. In a number of instances, governments tried to reduce the inflationary pressures, at any level of unemployment, by imposing direct controls on wages and prices. Such controls impose high costs on the economy by interfering with how the price system serves to allocate resources and tend to be effective only for short periods of time. When the price controls are removed, prices increase rapidly, largely undoing any benefits from the lower rates of price increases while controls were in place. Today, few economists advocate price and wage controls as a way of lowering the NAIRU, in other words, of improving the economy's inflation/unemployment trade-off.

A less intrusive form of intervention that some governments have tried is "moral suasion," in which they try to *persuade* firms and workers not to raise prices and wages. The government sets wage and price guidelines, with which it hopes workers and firms will voluntarily comply. The government often has considerable leverage beyond its appeal to moral rectitude, because it can threaten not to buy from firms that violate its suggestions. There have been some dramatic episodes where such moral suasion appears to have worked.

In 1983, when double-digit inflation had persisted for three years, the federal government introduced the so-called 6 & 5 restraint programme. Pay increases for federal government employees and price increases in federally regulated agencies were limited to 6 and 5 percent for 1983–84. As an inducement for the private sector to follow suit, government contracts were restricted to firms that abided by the 6 & 5 guidelines. As it turned out, the rate of inflation fell by more than 5 percent in 1983, suggesting to some that the programme was effective. Today, however, most economists are skeptical about the power of moral suasion to have an effect on price setting for long.

## A BRIEF HISTORY OF MACROECONOMIC POLICY

The historical record, illustrated in Figure 18.1, shows clearly that discretionary fiscal and monetary policies have not been able to eliminate the economy's fluctuations. But fluctuations do appear smaller today than they were before World War II, and discretionary policies may have played a role. In the following sections, we review briefly the major policy episodes of the past 30 years.

### FISCAL EXPANSION IN THE 1960s

The heyday of discretionary fiscal policy was the 1960s. Domestic monetary policy was essentially ruled out by the fact that Canada's currency value was tied to the U.S. dollar through a fixed exchange rate from 1962 to 1970.

In 1962, Canada was emerging from a two-year recession. The federal budgets of 1963 and 1964 raised taxes and effectively erased the budget deficit.

Even though real GDP growth remained high in 1965, the government chose to adopt an expansionary fiscal policy. Following the lead of the Kennedy administration in the United States two years earlier, taxes were cut. This made sense in the United States, since in 1963 their unemployment rate was stuck at a relatively high level and their budget was in surplus. But in Canada, when the tax cuts were introduced the economy was already operating near capacity. The expansionary policy resulted in inflation that persisted for the rest of the decade.

Inflationary pressures did emerge in the United States in the late 1960s. The need arose for government expenditures to fight the Vietnam War and to deal with pressing domestic issues by means of new social programmes. President Johnson was unwilling to raise taxes to pay for these expenditures and inflationary pressure ensued. The high demand in the United States spilled over into Canada and increased our levels of output and inflation further.

The 1966 budget responded by reducing government expenditures and raising taxes, with the expected result that output growth slowed moderately. The government quickly reacted in 1967 with further expansionary fiscal policy. This turned out to be an overreaction, since further inflation was induced. Once again restrictive policies had to be undertaken to combat inflation. During the 1960s real GDP growth had averaged 5.2 percent, but the anti-inflation policies of the latter half of the decade had reduced it to 2.5 percent by 1970. Given a decade of high growth and inflation, unemployment was low for most of the 1960s.

### STAGFLATION IN THE 1970s

Canada recovered from the slowdown of 1970, and in 1973 real GDP growth reached a decade high of 7.5 percent. Then a fundamental change in economic conditions worldwide led to a different set of problems in Canada and most other industrialized countries. The main event that precipitated a structural change on the supply side was the oil price shock engineered by OPEC. The dramatic rise in the price of oil induced further inflationary pressures, adding to those that had already been brought on by excess aggregate demand.

The oil price shock, by shifting the short-run aggregate supply curve upwards, caused output and employment to fall at the same time as the price level rose, a combination referred to as **stagflation.** The federal government cut taxes to increase aggregate demand and restore output and employment. If the original decline in output and employment had been caused by a leftward shift in the aggregate demand curve instead of the aggregate supply curve, this type of policy might have been appropriate. In the circumstances, however, the expansionary policy served mainly to induce further inflation.

## THE EMERGENCE OF MONETARISM IN THE LATE 1970s

The adoption of a flexible exchange rate in 1970 opened the door for the use of monetary policy. Initially, the Bank of Canada remained committed to keeping the value of the Canadian dollar at par with the U.S. dollar. By 1975, the price level began to be seen as a more important monetary policy target than the exchange rate. Keynesian prescriptions were losing credibility because fiscal policy, given the inappropriate way it might have been used in the past, had not been effective in stabilizing prices and generating high output and employment. Inflation had reached double digits in 1974 and many called for a new approach to macroeconomic policy, one based on rules rather than discretion.

The doctrine of monetarism became popular. In 1975, the Bank announced target rates for the growth rate of the money supply. This was accompanied by a spell of wage and price controls in 1975, and a reduction in tax rates whose objective was to improve incentives by workers and firms to supply more output. The result was a temporary decline in the inflation rate of almost 3 percent. However, the unemployment rate remained stubbornly high.

The effort to stabilize the Canadian economy was further frustrated in 1979 by turmoil in the U.S. economy. Canadian interest rates were allowed to rise to comply somewhat with those in the United States as the Bank of Canada slowed the growth in the money supply. The value of the Canadian dollar was allowed to depreciate relative to the U.S. dollar. Making imports more expensive caused inflationary pressures to increase.

## SUPPLY-SIDE ECONOMICS

By the time President Reagan took office in the United States in 1981, there was a widespread view that something had to be done to stop inflation. With the unemployment rate approaching double digits, the problem did not seem to be lack of aggregate demand. Economists, who naturally think about markets in terms of demand and supply, thus turned more of their attention to aggregate supply. Indeed, a major cause of the inflationary episode were supply shocks, especially the increase in oil prices in 1973 and 1979. President Reagan wanted to reduce taxes *and* reduce inflation. But reducing taxes without reducing expenditures typically shifts the aggregate demand curve to the right; this would have exacerbated the inflationary pressures. There was an easy solution: if the aggregate supply curve shifted to the right by more than the aggregate demand curve shifted, inflationary pressures would be reduced. A tax decrease that lowered marginal tax rates would increase incentives to work and to save, and thus shift the aggregate supply curve. Deregulation could further increase the efficiency of the economy, again shifting the aggregate supply curve. Most economists were skeptical about the *magnitude* of the effects: in the short run, the shifts in the supply curve would not be large. The evidence appeared to confirm these predictions. Inflation was not halted by the experiments in supply-side economics. The U.S. central bank was forced to adopt a restrictive monetary policy, which caused interest rates to soar.

Though supply-side economics never caught on in Canada to the same extent, its consequences for the Canadian economy were felt because of the strong interrelationship of the two economies. Both unemployment and inflation rates were running above 11 percent by 1982, and once again the Canadian government was forced to focus on inflation as its immediate policy problem. Tight monetary policy resulted in interest rates rising to over 20 percent. This frustrated attempts by the federal government in the latter part of the 1980s to bring the growing budget deficit under control.

## CLOSE-UP: THE SERVICE SECTOR AND THE McJOBS DEBATE

Over the past several years many have expressed concern that most of the new jobs being created in the Canadian economy are in the service sector. This phenomenon is not unique to Canada; it is a worldwide trend among the developed nations. The concern is that these jobs are low-paying—like those at McDonald's, thus the nickname McJobs—unlike the jobs in the goods-producing sector of the economy. This concern is not one that is confined to economists, politicians, and policy makers; it is often remarked upon by the media and the public at large. The debate became intense in April 1996 when it became a major topic at the G-7 "employment summit" in Lille, France. ("G-7" is the name given to the seven largest industrialized countries in the world, the United States, the United Kingdom, Germany, Japan, France, Italy, and Canada.)

It is certainly true that most new job creation takes place in the service sector, but are these jobs low-paying? A recent study by Lee Grenon of Statistics Canada found that the answer to this question is "yes and no." His study found that not all nor even most service-sector jobs are low-paying. In fact, most of them are either high-paying *or* low-paying, with few being in the middle of the weekly earnings distribution. The goods-producing sector has a more even distribution of low-, middle-, and high-paying jobs. This is because the service sector includes not only those who receive relatively low weekly pay— like retail clerks and restaurant staff—but also the relatively well-paid—like stockbrokers, investment bankers, and computer analysts.

Overall average weekly earnings in the service sector are lower than in the goods sector. And the earnings distribution by industry is not only more uneven, but is also uniformly below the earnings distribution in the goods sector. But these differences are somewhat misleading, for two main reasons. First, the study includes only those who are employed by someone else, not the self-employed. In the goods sector, this leaves out farmers and fishermen, whose pay is relatively low. In the service sector, doctors, lawyers, accountants, and consultants are left out, but their office staffs are included. This would tend to understate the averages in the service sector. Second, and perhaps more important, the service sector includes a greater proportion of part-time workers. Thus it is not surprising that average weekly earnings are lower. Nonetheless some disparity likely remains. Whether this is a permanent or temporary state of affairs is an open question.

Therefore, while the move to a more service-oriented economy is certain to bring changes in the labour market and, to a certain extent, in the distribution of income, it is not clear that this will lead to a lower overall wage level. It is also not clear what, if anything, the Canadian government could do about this trend, even if it wanted to do something. The transition to a service-based economy may be just as profound and irreversible as was the earlier shift from agriculture to manufacturing.

*Source:* L. Grenon, "Are Service Jobs Low-Paying?" *Perspectives on Labour and Income* 8 (Spring 1996): 29–34.

## POLICY IN THE 1990s

High interest rates and unemployment rates in the 1980s left an enormous legacy: huge government budget deficits. The national debt was five times as high in 1990 than it had been in 1975. The deficit/GDP ratio reached more than 5 percent.

### MACROECONOMIC POLICY IN A HIGH DEFICIT ENVIRONMENT

In the 1990s a consensus emerged that the deficit had to be reduced and that much of the reduction should be achieved by cutting expenditures rather than raising taxes. This virtually eliminated the scope for discretionary fiscal policy. Governments in the 1990s faced a seeming dilemma. All wanted to reduce unemployment, which continued to run at historically high levels. But they also wanted to reduce the deficit, which in traditional macroeconomic theory would impose a huge drag on the economy, as the aggregate demand curve shifted to the left. Yet after 1993, both the deficit and the unemployment rate began to fall in tandem. How was that possible?

There is a simple answer to this puzzle: reduced deficits lead to reduced interest rates. Lower interest rates, and the lower value of the Canadian dollar that accompanied them, stimulated investment and net exports. Despite reduced employment in the public sector brought on by dramatic cuts in government spending, job creation in the private sector was strong enough to cause unemployment to fall from 11.2 percent in 1992 to 9.5 percent in 1995, the lowest level in five years. It was *as if* monetary and fiscal authorities had coordinated their policies, with monetary expansion more than offsetting fiscal contraction.

Equally important to the effects of macroeconomic policy were other changes in the economic environment that were conducive to business. A buoyant U.S. economy provided a strong stimulus to exports. Furthermore, efforts to make the private sector more competitive by opening up markets at home and abroad to international competition (see Chapter 21) and by deregulating the economy contributed to business confidence. The fact that governments chose to concentrate on cutting expenditures rather than increasing taxes seemed also to appeal to members of the business community. They convinced governments that increased taxes would have impeded incentives and competitiveness, and therefore job creation.

### MONETARY POLICY AND UNCERTAINTY OVER THE NAIRU

The major macroeconomic policy debate focused on how expansionary monetary policy should be. This debate in turn centred on uncertainty over the NAIRU and the risks of aggressive versus conservative monetary policies. In the early 1990s, the prevalent view was that the NAIRU was around 8–9 percent. According to this view, it was not surprising that with double-digit unemployment rates from 1991 to 1994, there was no evidence of inflationary pressures. Many economists argued that interest rates should remain low to encourage the continuation of the expansion. Others worried that there were long lags: the evidence of incipient inflation would only turn up months later. The Bank of Canada, aware that it took six months or more before its policies had full effect, and worried that the economy might become overheated, gradually increased short-term interest rates from 5 percent in early 1994 to 7 percent in early 1995. The economy continued to expand, though at a more moderate pace, and unemployment continued to fall until it reached 9.5 percent—with still no evidence of increasing inflation. The debate over whether there should be monetary easing continued through 1995 and 1996. Monetary conservatives, while revising their estimate of the NAIRU down, were convinced that further decreases in the unemployment rate would ignite inflation; others advocated a gradual exploration of lower unemployment rates, to see whether the economy might operate at 9.0, 8.5, or even 8.0 percent unemployment or lower without inflation beginning. All parties recognized that there was uncertainty about the NAIRU. The critical issue was the possible cost of "conservative" versus expansionary policies. Conservative policies might mean temporarily missing the opportunity for more rapid growth and higher output until evidence as to the level of the NAIRU mounted; expansionary policies might mean risking temporarily higher inflation

## USING ECONOMICS: CALCULATING THE RISK OF AGGRESSIVE MONETARY POLICIES

Throughout the 1990s, a central problem facing the Bank of Canada has been determining the level of the NAIRU. Given its uncertainty about the NAIRU, the Bank must assess the risks—costs and benefits—associated with "overshooting" versus those of setting its sights too low. In 1994, for instance, some economists thought the NAIRU was at 9 percent, while others thought it had dropped to around 8 percent. What would happen if the Bank assumed the NAIRU to be 8 percent when it was actually 9 percent?

Economists have estimated that the unemployment rate has to be maintained at 2 percentage points above the NAIRU for one year in order to lower the inflation rate by 1 percentage point. Conversely, lowering the unemployment rate to 1 percentage point below the NAIRU increases the inflation rate by .5 percentage points. Suppose the unemployment rate was 9 percent, and the Bank, acting on the mistaken assump-

tion that the NAIRU was 8 percent, undertook policies to reduce the unemployment rate to 8 percent. The cost of this error would be an increase in inflation of .5 percentage points.

On the other hand if the Bank assumed that the NAIRU was 9 percent when it had actually fallen to 8 percent, the Bank would not act to cause the unemployment rate to fall, and the economy would suffer a higher level of unemployment than was necessary to maintain stable prices. What would be the lost value of output, assuming the Bank persisted in maintaining the 9 percent unemployment rate for one year? Suppose that reducing unemployment by 1 percentage point increases output by 2 percent. (This is Okun's law, discussed in Chapter 17.) Accordingly, maintaining the unemployment rate at a level that is 1 percentage point too high costs the economy 2 percentage points of GDP. In an $850 billion economy, this translates into $17 billion—a fairly steep price to pay!

should it turn out that the NAIRU was in fact 9 percent or higher.

## DISLOCATED WORKERS

While the overall macroeconomic performance of the economy in the mid-1990s was strong, there were many individuals whose enthusiasm over the economy did not match the economic statistics. Some of these were unskilled workers who saw their wages stagnate or fall, while others were workers who saw their job security threatened and felt anxious about their jobs. This anxiety was enhanced by frequent news stories of major firms "downsizing," or laying off workers. Layoff announcements are common in recessions, but this time they continued well into the recovery.

The statistical evidence painted a mixed picture. Overall there was not strong evidence for significant increases in discharges of employees that had worked at a firm for at least a year (called displacement rates), but among certain groups—especially groups with very low previous rates of displacement, such as white-collar and middle-aged workers—displacement rates were up, though remaining lower than among blue-collar workers.

A discussion developed over the extent to which corporations had a responsibility to provide training to their workers to ensure that they could move onto another job if they were discharged. Since the data suggested strongly that those with higher education could move more quickly to another job, the discussion of displacement placed new emphasis on the importance of education. Finally, concern about dis-

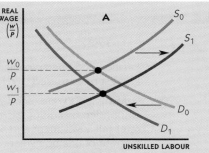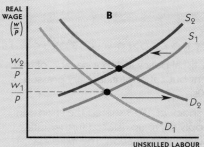

### Figure 18.4 DEMAND AND SUPPLY FOR UNSKILLED LABOUR

In recent years, the supply curve for unskilled workers has shifted to the right, while the demand curve for unskilled workers did not keep pace and may even have shifted to the left as in panel A. The real wage for unskilled workers fell from $w_0/P$ to $w_1/P$. Increased private-sector investment along with training programmes that increase the productivity of unskilled workers would shift the demand curve to the right as in panel B. Training and education would also reduce the number of unskilled workers, causing the supply curve to shift to the left. These effects would cause the real wage to rise from $w_1/P$ to $w_2/P$.

placement focused attention on government policies to facilitate movement between jobs, such as the active labour market policies discussed in Chapter 17, including converting the "unemployment" insurance programme into a "reemployment programme."

### UNSKILLED WORKERS

Our concern here is primarily with macroeconomics, the aggregate performance of the economy as measured by unemployment rates, inflation rates, and growth rates. Yet we have repeatedly emphasized that not all individuals fare the same in different economic environments—inflation may hit investors more, while the burden of unemployment falls disproportionately on the poor. In the mid-1990s, macroeconomic discussions increasingly focused on the fact that while overall performance was good, there were significant groups that did not seem to participate fully in the benefits of economic growth. For a variety of reasons, the wages of skilled workers (especially graduates of postsecondary institutions) rose dramatically compared to those of unskilled workers. Indeed, for the least skilled workers, real wages actually declined. Among economists, there was a widespread recognition that this was simply the working of the law of supply and demand: while the supply curve of such workers may have shifted slightly to the right, the demand curve for

such workers probably had shifted slightly to the left, so the equilibrium real wage was lowered. (See Figure 18.4.)

A debate raged about what, if anything, could be done about this. One school of thought argued that low taxes would lead to high savings and investment, and some of this would eventually get reflected in a shift in the demand curve for labour to the right, increasing real wages. The other school of thought argued that reducing the deficit would lead to high national savings and lower interest rates, and this might eventually lead to a shift in the demand curve; but this process was slow, and possibly uncertain. In addition, government needed to do three other things. First, it had to ensure that more individuals obtain skills by going to postsecondary education institutions; this would indirectly benefit the remaining unskilled workers, by shifting the supply curve to the left. Second, it had to make sure that the relatively unskilled had more skills than they obtained in high school, the kind of training that suited them for the workplace. Interest focused on skills-training schemes used elsewhere, such as the successful apprenticeship programmes that are traditional in Germany, to improve the productivity of less-skilled workers and shift the demand curve for them to the right. And finally, governments had to supplement the income of unskilled workers and maintain other elements of the social safety net (especially health

## CHANGING MACROECONOMIC POLICY ISSUES

1960s  Expansionary fiscal policy led to a decade of low unemployment but caused inflationary pressure into the 1970s.

1970s  The oil price shock of 1973 shifted the short-run aggregate supply curve up, fuelled further inflation, and resulted in stagflation. The fixed exchange rate was abandoned in 1970 and monetary policy assumed prominence. Monetarism, which relied on targets for money growth, was adopted.

1980s  High inflation was handled by means of supply-side policies based on tax cuts. The resulting inflation was met with tight monetary policy.

Inflation and unemployment remained high, and interest rates soared to over 20 percent.

1990s  Governments were faced with high deficits and responded by cutting expenditures. Interest rates fell, investment and net exports rose, and the rate of unemployment fell. Business confidence was helped by the opening up of trade opportunities, strong demand from the United States, and the deregulation of markets. Some new policy concerns arose, including the plight of displaced and unskilled workers and the high level of the NAIRU.

care) so that even if workers' wages were low, their living standards at least approached that of the poverty level. The federal government began to introduce refundable tax credits available selectively to those with low incomes.

## ECONOMIC CHALLENGES OF THE TWENTY-FIRST CENTURY

As we have seen, every period has its own economic problems. Just as it is difficult to predict the performance of the economy a year or five years from now, it is hard to predict the central problems and controversies that will be facing the economy in five or ten years. It is probable that the challenges we have discussed in this chapter—of maintaining full employment with stable prices and of addressing the concerns of dislocated and unskilled workers—will still be there. It is also probable that the two issues to which we turn in the next two chapters, enhancing the rate of growth and reducing the deficit, will also be at the forefront. But whatever the problems, the kinds of analytic tools and ways of thinking that we have taught in this and the preceding two parts of the book will be a central part of the framework policy makers will use as they address those problems.

# REVIEW AND PRACTICE

## SUMMARY

**1** Those who bear the cost of inflation tend to be different from those who bear the cost of unemployment. The latter costs tend to be concentrated especially among unskilled workers.

**2** The economy is subjected to marked fluctuations. These fluctuations may be induced either by exogenous shocks or arise out of the internal structure of the economy. In many cases, the economy may act to amplify and make persistent exogenous shocks.

**3** Those who criticize active intervention argue that markets adjust quickly, so that unemployment is short-lived, and that attempts by government to intervene are not only unnecessary but largely ineffective, since they are offset by actions of the private sector. To the extent that they do have effects, critics say, such policies often exacerbate fluctuations, because of the long lags and limited information of government and because political pressures result in its overheating the economy before elections.

**4** Most governments believe that they should intervene to help stabilize the economy. Without government intervention, there may be long periods of high and persistent unemployment. Generally, government policy can be and has been stabilizing, though policy makers recognize that there are often long lags and that policy is made with imperfect information, so that at times, policy may be ill-timed or be counterproductive.

**5** Critics of discretionary policy believe that government intervention should be restricted by fixed rules. But critics of fixed rules argue that not only does this mean giving up on an important set of instruments, but that fixed rules never work well, because they fail to respond to the ever-changing structure of the economy.

**6** Current policy discussions recognize that the economy cannot be kept at unemployment rates below the NAIRU for long. The debate centres on the following questions: (a) What is the level of the NAIRU? Have changes in the structure of the economy lowered it? (b) What are the risks and rewards of aggressive policies designed to keep unemployment at the NAIRU as opposed to more cautious policies that lower the unemployment rate only after more evidence that the NAIRU is lower has accrued.

**7** Some economists and policy makers argue for aggressive policies to keep unemployment low. They believe that the costs of forgone output and higher unemployment resulting from cautious anti-inflationary policies are significant, while the real costs of low inflation are small, especially when there is indexing. They also believe that it is not too costly to correct mistakes. Those who argue for more cautious policies worry that once started, inflationary episodes are hard to bring under control; to do so typically requires periods of high unemployment. Not only do these people tend to view the costs of inflation as high, but they view the benefits of reduced unemployment as being more than offset by the risks of higher unemployment, should inflation be ignited.

**8** Governments can pursue policies both to stabilize the economy (automatic stabilizers) and to lower the NAIRU (by improving labour mobility, increasing competitiveness of markets, and using moral suasion).

**9** Each period in our economy's history has had its own problems, such as dealing with excess demand in the 1960s during U.S. involvement in the Vietnam War, controlling inflation and avoiding stagflation in the 1970s, responding to the consequences for Canada of supply-side policies in the United States during the 1980s, and facing the huge budget deficits in the 1990s that were the legacy of the previous decade. Also in the 1990s, the Canadian economy and its monetary policy have been affected by uncertainty over the level of the NAIRU, and Canadians have seen growing income inequality between skilled and unskilled workers.

## KEY TERMS

long-run trend

exogenous shocks

endogenous factors

real business cycle theorists

new classical economists

monetarists

dynamic consistency

new Keynesianism

multiplier-accelerator

## REVIEW QUESTIONS

**1** What are the alternative explanations of the sources of the economy's fluctuations? What is the relationship between views about the nature of these fluctuations and views about the role of government?

**2** What is the multiplier-accelerator model?

**3** Describe the rules versus discretion debate.

**4** What is the problem of dynamic consistency? Give an example of it.

**5** What steps can the government take to lower the NAIRU?

**6** Provide some examples of how different policies or instruments affect different groups in society.

**7** Describe the principal macroeconomic problems of the past four decades, how the events of various periods affected the development of economic theories, and how economic theories affected the actions undertaken by policy makers.

## PROBLEMS

**1** Describe the actions of the private sector that might offset the actions of government listed below. In which cases do you think the actions will *fully* offset the government actions?

  (a) The government increases the money supply.
  (b) The government attempts to increase aggregate demand by increasing government expenditures without increasing taxes.
  (c) The government increases transfer payments to the elderly in an attempt to make them better off. (Assume that (1) the elderly currently receive some financial support from their children or that (2) the elderly save for their retirement needs, calculating their level of savings so that they'll be able to maintain a certain standard of living in retirement.)
  (d) The government attempts to reduce inequality by taxing inheritances.

**2** In parliamentary governments such as ours, the prime minister can announce a change in taxation or expenditure and implement that change almost immediately. How might this fact affect the balance between the use of monetary policy versus the use of fiscal policy?

**3** Some critics of indexed bonds have argued that indexing will reduce the government's resolve to fight inflation. Compare the *real* costs to the government of an increase in inflation when it has used long-term indexed bonds to finance its indebtedness with the costs when it has used conventional long-term bonds for this purpose. Compare the real costs to bondholders of an increase in inflation in these two circumstances. Do you think that indexing will increase or decrease the resolve to fight inflation?

Other critics of indexed bonds have argued that indexing imposes a huge risk on the government, because if inflation increases, the government will have to pay more interest. Proponents suggest that indexing reduces the risk faced by the government, because there will be less variability in the *real* payments made by government. Assume the rate of inflation in the future will be either 5 percent or 15 percent (with equal probability). Compare the risks associated with an indexed bond paying 2 percent real interest and a nominal bond paying 12 percent. Which form of bond do you think is less risky from the government's perspective?

**4** If the economy is in a boom, why might a multiplier-accelerator model predict that it will eventually slow down? If the economy is in a recession, why might the multiplier-accelerator model predict that it will eventually speed up?

**5** In the traditional multiplier-accelerator model, an increase in GDP of $10 billion gives rise to an increased demand for additional capital. If the desired ratio of capital to output is 2 to 1, and if the $10 billion increase in output is believed to be permanent, what is the increase in the desired level of capital? Assume firms try to fill this gap in one year. What then is the increase in the desired level of investment? If prices of capital goods rise in booms and fall in economic downturns, why might increases in output give rise to smaller increases in the demand for investment in booms and larger increases in economic downturns. What happens to the demand for investment if firms believe that the economic expansion will not be sustained?

**6** A decision tree outlines the consequences of each decision depending on how some uncertainty is resolved. Below is a decision tree for the Bank of Canada's decision whether to pursue an aggressive or cautious unemployment/inflation policy. The NAIRU is either 7 percent or 8 percent, but the Bank is uncertain about the real value of the NAIRU. Under an aggressive strategy, the Bank will set the unemployment rate at 7 percent; under a cautious strategy, it will set unemployment at 8 percent. Each strategy has different consequences, depending on the real value of the NAIRU. These are outlined in the decision tree below:

Aggressive Strategy: set unemployment at 7 percent
— NAIRU = 8 percent —— Outcome?
— NAIRU = 7 percent —— Outcome?

Cautious Strategy: set unemployment at 8 percent
— NAIRU = 8 percent —— Outcome?
— NAIRU = 7 percent —— Outcome?

Fill in the outcomes for each branch of the decision tree given each of the following assumptions: (a) it takes two years to discover the true NAIRU (if the Bank chooses the aggressive strategy when the NAIRU is actually 8 percent, higher inflation will occur in two years, indicating the real value of the NAIRU); (b) keeping the unemployment rate 1 percentage point below (above) the NAIRU for one year increases (decreases) the inflation rate by 1 percentage point; (c) decreasing (increasing) the unemployment rate by 1 percentage point increases (decreases) output by 2 percent; (d) GDP is initially at $1 trillion; (e) after the real NAIRU is discovered, the Bank changes the unemployment rate so as to return the inflation rate to its original level over two years; and (f) ignore any indirect effect of inflation on output. What happens to output and inflation during the four years for each policy option? Evaluate the trade-offs between aggressive and cautious policies.

# PART FIVE

# Issues in Macro-Economic Policy

**U**nemployment and inflation, the subjects of Parts Three and Four, are not the only economic concerns that make the news. Deficits in Canada, starvation in Ethiopia, and the economic crises in the formerly communist countries of the Soviet Union and Eastern Europe are among other events that have grabbed headlines in the past decade. In this part of the book, we use the principles and insights developed in the preceding chapters to take a look at these and other current public-policy issues.

Chapter 19 discusses a major problem facing Canada: the slowdown in its rate of economic growth. The country is growing neither as fast as it did in earlier decades nor as fast as some of its major economic rivals. We ask, what causes economic growth, and what can be done to stimulate it?

Chapter 20 focuses on two means—fiscal deficits and unfunded public pensions—by which government policy can transfer fiscal burdens from one age group, or generation, to another. The fiscal deficit has been at the centre of public concern for almost a decade and has persisted despite seeming efforts to reduce it. We consider why large deficits are a matter of concern, not only because they entail the transfer of burdens from current to future generations but also because they impose a drag on savings and investment and thus upon economic growth. Unfunded public pensions share with fiscal deficits the feature of being intergenerational transfers from current generations to future generations. The terms of the transfer depend upon demographic trends. With the proportion of retired persons projected to rise dramatically in the near future, the burden imposed on the future young to finance the pensions of the old becomes unreasonably high. Policy options are discussed in Chapter 20.

The Canadian economy is very dependent upon trade, so access to foreign markets for our products is very important. At the same time, our domestic producers are faced with competition from foreign suppliers; naturally, they are concerned with the effect that will have on the fortunes of their firms. Chapter 21 outlines policy issues facing an open economy like that of Canada. The various sorts of barriers to trade are presented as well as arguments for eliminating them. Trade barriers can be reduced unilaterally, bilaterally through negotiation with a single country, or multilaterally through an agreement reached with many countries. Multilateral trade liberalization through the World Trade Organization and bilateral liberalization through the Canada-U.S. and North American Free Trade Agreements are discussed.

Most of the world lives in countries where incomes are but a fraction of those in Canada, the United States, Western Europe, Japan, and the other developed countries. By the standards of these less developed countries, most people who consider themselves poor in the more developed countries are indeed well off. In Chapter 22, we learn some of the major differences between the developed and less developed countries. We also ask, what are some of the major issues facing these poorer countries as they struggle to grow and raise themselves out of the poverty in which they have been mired for centuries? In Chapter 22, we also look at the collapse of the formerly socialist economies of Eastern Europe, why the socialist system failed, and the problems these countries face today in making the transition to capitalism.

# 19

# GROWTH AND
# PRODUCTIVITY

T he changes that have taken place in the standard of living during the past century are hard to comprehend. In 1900, Canadians' level of consumption was little higher than the average citizen's in Mexico or the Philippines today. Life expectancy was low, in part because diseases like smallpox, diphtheria, typhoid fever, and whooping cough were still common. You were fifteen times more likely to catch measles in 1900 than you would be today. The abundance of land meant that relatively few Canadians were starving, but luxuries were scarce. People worked as long as they could, and when they could no longer work, they became the responsibility of their children; there was no easy retirement.

During the nineteenth century, the standard of living in England and a few other European countries was perhaps slightly higher than that of Canada. These countries' standard of living was the highest in the world, but even within Europe, there were famines. In the most famous of these, the Irish potato famine of 1845–48, more than a tenth of the population died, and more than another tenth migrated to North America. For those

## KEY QUESTIONS

**1** What are the principal determinants of growth in the economy?

**2** What factors might account for the slowdown of growth in Canada? What, for instance, might explain the decline in productivity growth?

**3** Are there policies available to the government that might stimulate economic growth?

living in Asia, Africa, and Latin America, as the vast majority of people did then and do now, life was even harder.

Higher standards of living are reflected not only in higher incomes and longer life expectancies, but also in shorter working hours and higher levels of education. Improved education is both a benefit and a cause of higher living standards. Table 19.1 compares Canada in 1926 and 1996, indicating stark contrasts in standards of living. Underlying all these differences is an increase in the output for each hour worked, what Chapter 6 identified as productivity. During the 1980s and '90s, the rate of productivity growth has been markedly lower than in the 1960s. One major goal of this chapter is to understand what causes productivity to increase. A second is to understand the slowdown in growth that has taken place during the last two decades.

### Table 19.1 CANADA IN 1926 AND 1996

|  | 1926 | 1996 |
| --- | --- | --- |
| Population | 9.5 million | 29.8 million |
| Life expectancy | 61 years | 78 years* |
| GDP (in 1996 dollars) | $47 billion | $672 billion |
| GDP per capita (in 1996 dollars) | $4,947 | $27,685 |
| Consumer purchasing power per dollar (in 1996 dollars) | $9.62 | $1.00 |
| Average hours worked each week in manufacturing industry | 50.0 | 38.5 |
| Average hourly pay in manufacturing (in 1996 dollars) | $4.59 | $16.44 |
| Total telephones in country | 1.2 million | 17.5 million |
| Total bachelor's degrees conferred | 4,319 | 123,202* |
| Total doctoral degrees conferred | 28 | 3,356* |
| Percentage of those aged 5–19 enrolled in school | 64.3 | 93* |

\* figures for 1993

*Sources:* Statistics Canada, CANSIM Database 1996, various series; M. C. Urquhart and K. A. H. Buckley, eds. *Historical Statistics of Canada* (Toronto: Macmillan Co. of Canada, 1965); Statistics Canada, *Education in Canada, 1995,* Catalogue No. 81-220, (Ottawa, 1996).

## EXPLAINING PRODUCTIVITY GROWTH

For almost a century, the United States has been at the centre of the technological advances that have changed the world. The telegraph, laser, transistor, airplane, assembly line, jet engine, atomic energy . . . the list of technological achievements goes on and on. Canada's contributions, though much more modest in absolute terms, have nonetheless also been far-reaching, as the example of the telephone shows. More important, we have benefited from our proximity to the United States and from the relatively open border, which has allowed goods and services, capital, and especially knowledge to flow freely back and forth. The country has reaped a huge reward. Levels of productivity increased continually and rapidly. Today, living standards in Canada are among the highest in the world.

The Canadian and American rates of growth of productivity have followed remarkably similar patterns in recent years, as shown in Figure 19.1. Panel

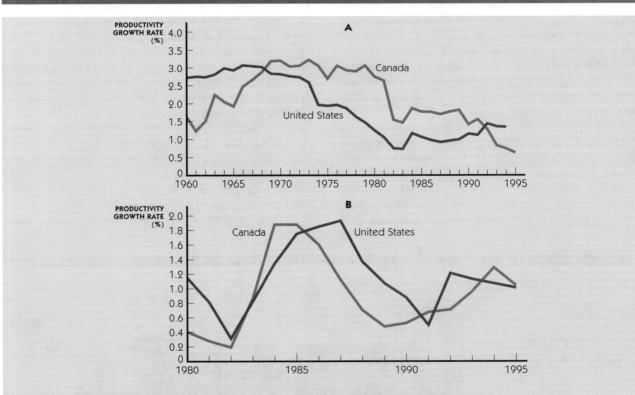

## Figure 19.1 CANADIAN AND U.S. PRODUCTIVITY TRENDS

Panel A shows that the growth rates of GDP per capita in Canada and the United States have dropped sharply in recent years. (The number given for each year represents the rate of growth of per capita output over a decade ending in that year.) Panel B shows that the decline in output per hour worked, a good measure of productivity, has been much less pronounced. (This one is measured as a rate of growth over a five-year period.) *Sources:* Statistics Canada, CANSIM Database 1996, Label D1, D20463, D20884; *Economic Report of the President,* 1994; U.S. Bureau of Labor Statistics Data, 1996, Series ID No. prs84006091.

A shows the growth rates of GDP per capita in Canada and the United States since 1960. In Canada, the rate of growth of output per worker slowed considerably in the eighties and nineties and has fallen below that of the sixties. The decline has been somewhat more precipitous than in the United States, which has also suffered from a long-term decline in productivity growth. Another indicator of productivity is real output per hour of workers, shown in panel B. Here the picture is somewhat less dramatic. While the growth of output per worker has declined since the mid-1980s, it is still about the same as it was in 1980. The difference between these two panels is that output per capita divides GDP by the entire population and not just workers. So if a larger proportion of the population is not in the labour force, say, because they are too young or are retired, this itself would depress GDP per capita. Output per hour worked is a more accurate measure of the true productivity of those who are actually employed, though GDP per capita indicates how well off the average person is.

Productivity tends to vary markedly with business fluctuations. As the economy recovers from a recession, output increases faster than employment, and productivity soars; when the economy goes into an economic downturn, conversely, output decreases faster than employment, and productivity falls. Consequently, economists measure long-run productivity growth from one business cycle peak to the next—points where resources are being fully used—or over sufficiently long periods of time that the cyclical fluctuations become small relative to the long-term trends. Figure 19.1 takes this approach, measuring productivity growth over the previous decade. Cyclical effects are still apparent: the low productivity growth for 1982 is in part attributable to the severe recession of that year.

But do the relatively small differences in rates of increase in productivity shown in Figure 19.1, panel A, make much difference? So what if the average rate of productivity growth fell from about 3 percent to 2 percent—what's so important about a difference of 1 percentage point? In fact, it makes a great deal of difference, because the differences compound over time. Consider this simple calculation. Two countries start out equally wealthy, but one grows at 2 percent a year while the other grows at 3 percent a year. The difference in productivity would be barely perceptible for a few years. But after thirty years, the slower-growing country would be only three quarters as wealthy as the faster-growing one. Lower growth in Canada and the United States compared with the growth of other developed countries in the last two decades explains why many countries have almost caught up to the living standard in North America, as shown in Figure 19.2.

Lower growth in GDP per capita means lower

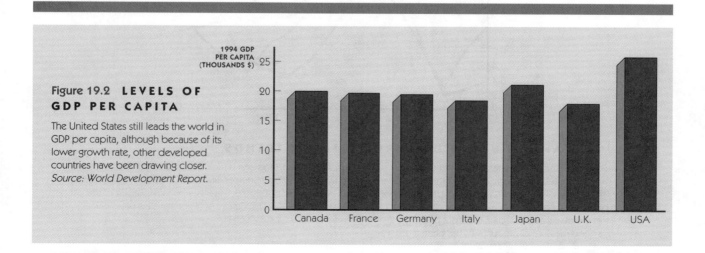

**Figure 19.2 LEVELS OF GDP PER CAPITA**

The United States still leads the world in GDP per capita, although because of its lower growth rate, other developed countries have been drawing closer. *Source: World Development Report.*

growth in standards of living. On average, people will have less of everything—from smaller houses to poorer health care to less travel to fewer government services than otherwise. Many families have been able to sustain increases in their income, but only by having both spouses working—and the reduced leisure itself has put strains on the families and represents a lowering of living standards.

To understand what may have contributed to the productivity slowdown, we need to understand what causes increases in output per hour in the first place. There are four key factors: savings and investment, education and the quality of the labour force, reallocating resources from low- to high-productivity sectors, and research and development. The next four sections discuss these factors in turn.

## INVESTMENT AND SAVINGS

Workers today are more productive than they were twenty or a hundred years ago because they have more and better machines. A Canadian textile worker can produce far more than a textile worker in India, partly because of differences in the equipment they use. Many textile workers in India still use hand-looms, similar to those used in Canada two hundred years ago.

Modern machines are expensive. Someone has to put aside money to buy them—someone has to save. If the savings rate is higher, there will be more in-

vestment; the quality and quantity of machines people have to work with will increase, and so will productivity. One of the distinguishing features of Japan and the other rapidly growing countries of East Asia is their remarkably high savings and investment rates, two or more times that of Canada.

Economists have attempted to estimate the contribution of investment to economic growth—and the extent to which lower rates of growth of GDP have contributed to lower rates of growth of GDP per capita, or productivity. One recent estimate is that about one quarter of the growth in the manufacturing industries in the sixties, seventies, and eighties could be attributed to investment. So a significant part of the slowdown in productivity growth might be attributable to a lower rate of investment.

Higher levels of investment relative to GDP result in more capital per worker. Economists call this **capital deepening.** As the amount of capital per worker increases, output per worker increases. Suppose an economy has an investment rate of 10 percent of GDP, and a low level of capital per worker. Increasing its investment rate to 15 percent will raise the level of capital per worker, and thus productivity and the growth rate. This is illustrated in Figure 19.3. Increasing capital per worker from $k_0$ to $k_1$ raises output per worker from $(Q/L)_0$ to $(Q/L)_1$.

In Chapters 8 and 9 we learned that the level of investment may be related to the level of savings. If the economy is closed to international capital flows, investment must equal savings, as illustrated in Figure

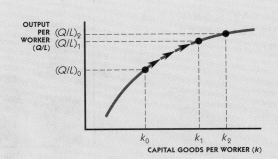

### Figure 19.3 INVESTMENT AND PRODUCTIVITY

An increase in the investment rate (the ratio of investment to GDP) results in capital deepening. As capital per worker increases, output per worker increases.

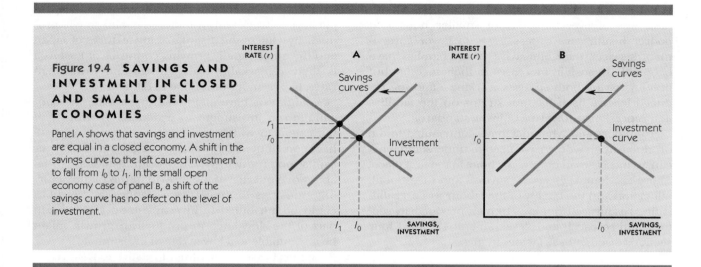

**Figure 19.4 SAVINGS AND INVESTMENT IN CLOSED AND SMALL OPEN ECONOMIES**

Panel A shows that savings and investment are equal in a closed economy. A shift in the savings curve to the left caused investment to fall from $I_0$ to $I_1$. In the small open economy case of panel B, a shift of the savings curve has no effect on the level of investment.

19.4, panel A. At the other extreme, if the economy is a small open one, the country can borrow as much as it wants from world capital markets at the going interest rate, so investment is independent of savings, as shown in Figure 19.4, panel B. Historically, however, we have seen that savings and investment do tend to move together. Even in an open economy like Canada's, a reduction in savings can lead to some reduction of investment.

Figure 19.5 compares aggregate savings as a percentage of GDP for a number of industrialized countries. The Canadian savings rate is less than one half that of Japan and lower than that in many European countries, but is comparable to the American and British rates. By historical standards, the current savings rate in Canada is low. Because of its adverse effect on investment, this low savings rate may underlie part of the slowdown in productivity growth.

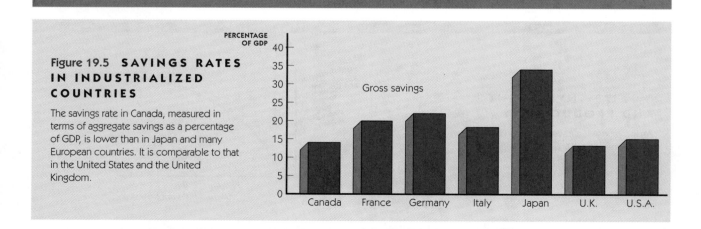

**Figure 19.5 SAVINGS RATES IN INDUSTRIALIZED COUNTRIES**

The savings rate in Canada, measured in terms of aggregate savings as a percentage of GDP, is lower than in Japan and many European countries. It is comparable to that in the United States and the United Kingdom.

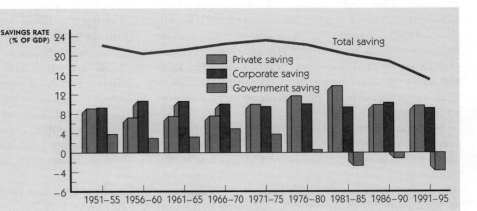

### Figure 19.6 THE DE-CLINE IN CANADIAN SAVINGS

Total national savings has fallen gradually in the past two decades. The most significant decline was in government savings, but household savings has fallen since the early 1980s. Only corporate savings has remained virtually unchanged.
*Source:* Statistics Canada, CANSIM Database 1996, Matrixes 6702, 6705.

## WHY HAVE SAVINGS RATES FALLEN?

To see why Canadian savings rates have fallen, it is useful to separate aggregate savings into three components: personal (or household) savings, corporate savings, and government savings (or dissavings, when the budget is in deficit). Figure 19.6 shows how each of these, as well as aggregate savings, have changed over time. The figure makes clear that much of the decline in aggregate savings is due to the huge government deficits in recent years. Corporate savings rates have been roughly constant over the postwar period. But household savings has fallen off in the past decade. The origins of the government deficits will be discussed in Chapter 20. Here, the focus is on private-sector savings.

We can use the basic framework for consumer choice introduced in Chapter 7 to analyze the determinants of savings. Prices (here, the interest rate) and preferences affect the desire for consumption in the future versus consumption today. People save for future needs—for retirement (called life-cycle savings); to buy a home, pay for their children's university education, or to meet certain other needs (called target savings); for emergencies, for periods in which their incomes may be low, say, because they are laid off from a job, or in which their needs are high, or because they require medical attention (called precautionary savings); and to leave something to their children (called bequest savings).

During the past two decades, virtually all of the

motives and incentives for saving changed in a way so as to discourage saving. Improved public pensions and health programmes reduced the need for private savings for retirement; improved capital markets and insurance—provided by both government and employers—meant that people did not have to save as much for emergencies; improved capital markets also meant that people did not have to save as much for a down payment for a house; and improved government student-loan programmes meant that parents did not have to save as much for their children's education.

But one change should have stimulated savings: an increase in the real after-tax return. In the 1980s, taxes on the return to capital, particularly for upper-income levels, fell, and real before-tax returns soared. Nevertheless, savings fell. Actually, this should not come as too much of a surprise: we also learned in Chapter 7 that the effect of changes in real after-tax interest rates on savings, while positive, is probably small.[1]

But the changes discussed so far by themselves do not seem to account fully for the low levels of savings. Accordingly, economists have looked elsewhere for an explanation.

The **life-cycle theory of savings** emphasizes that

---

[1] There, we saw that while the *substitution* effect leads to increased savings, the *income* effect results in reduced savings. Although on theoretical grounds the *net* effect is ambiguous, the evidence supports a small positive effect.

savings will differ in different parts of an individual's life cycle. The 45–65 age group are typically high savers; no longer facing the burden of caring for children, they recognize the necessity of setting aside money for their retirement. The percentage of the population in this group has been low since the middle 1970s, but has begun to increase in the 1990s. This should provide an impetus for an increased personal savings rate.

Some economists have argued that the huge increase in real estate prices in the 1980s meant that more individuals were saving in the form of home equity; these savings were not recorded in the national income accounts. Though the explanation seemed plausible at the time, it suggested that when real estate prices levelled out, or fell, as they did in the late '80s and early '90s, savings rates would increase. They did not.

Some economists attribute the decline in savings rates to a change in values: the "Now" generation wants its consumption now, and its members put less store in setting aside money for their children. This tendency to spend now rather than saving for the future is reinforced by the much greater variety of consumer durables now available to consumers. These require large outlays of cash up front that might otherwise have been set aside for the future.

Whatever the explanation for low private savings, those who believe that increasing private savings is necessary to stimulate productivity feel stymied: microeconomic instruments to stimulate household savings, such as tax preferences, are likely to have at most small effects.

## INFRASTRUCTURE

Most discussions of the low level of investment in Canada focus on low *private* investment. But government investment is also important. These investments include roads, bridges, airports, and harbours, called **infrastructure.** Without adequate infrastructure, the private sector cannot perform effectively. During the 1980s, not only did the deficit soar, but infrastructure investment declined. In many cases, even maintenance activities were forgone, so that by 1992, the nation's infrastructure was in worse shape than it had been a decade earlier. Where the public capital stock amounted to 63 percent of GDP in 1971, by 1993, it amounted to only about 54 percent. This declining public capital stock has exerted a drag on the economy's productivity, though there are no precise estimates of the magnitude of the drag.

## POLICIES TO STIMULATE SAVINGS AND INVESTMENT

Government has only limited tools to stimulate savings and investment. Reducing the fiscal deficit increases national savings, and in an economy that is not perfectly open, this leads to increased investment. Reducing the deficit by cutting back on infrastructure investment or other forms of investments such as in education may, however, be counterproductive; overall investment (public plus private) may decline, and the forgone public investment may have yielded as high or higher returns than the induced private investment.

When the economy is at full employment, in a closed economy investment subsidies have no effect on aggregate investment. With given government expenditures and consumption, the Bank of Canada simply has to raise interest rates to ensure that aggregate demand equals the full-employment level of output. In an open economy, investment subsidies induce more investment and more borrowing from abroad. If the subsidies lower the before-subsidy marginal return to investment to the point where it is below the cost of capital from abroad, the country (at the margin) is actually worse off as a result of the additional investment. GDP—what is produced in

## EXPLANATIONS OF LOW HOUSEHOLD SAVINGS

Improved public pensions and health care

Improved insurance markets

Improved capital markets

Change in values: Less future-oriented behaviour

Canada—increases, but GNP—subtracting what has to be paid to foreigners (i.e., what Canadians can actually spend)—actually decreases.

GDP can be increased if savings can be increased and consumption reduced, so investment rises. The apparent unresponsiveness of savings to the real interest rate has made most economists skeptical about the potential use of tax policy to encourage savings. There is some evidence that RRSPs (Registered Retirement Savings Plans) have had some effect on increasing savings, largely because banks and other financial institutions have used them as the basis of advertising campaigns to obtain deposits.

## WHY LOWER SAVINGS AND INVESTMENT IS NOT THE WHOLE STORY

As important as the low savings and investment rates are in explaining the low rates of growth of productivity, they are not the whole story. As we have seen, capital accumulation leads to increases in output per worker—in productivity. However, this effect is limited to the short run. After an increase in savings and investment, the economy eventually reaches a new ratio of capital to worker. This is capital deepening. At the new level of capital to worker, the econ-

omy is indeed operating at a higher level of productivity, but the productivity *increase* has run its course. This is illustrated in Figure 19.7, which uses a hypothetical time series for real output to display the economy's growth path. Three segments of the growth path are evident. The first segment (*AB*) represents the economy's growth before the increase in savings and investment. The steep segment that follows (*BC*) represents the period of capital accumulation arising from the increase in savings and investment; as capital per worker increases, so does productivity and the growth rate of the economy. But once the new, higher level of capital per worker is reached, the economy resumes its original growth rate, represented by the third segment (*CD*).

This analysis may suggest that repeated increases in the level of savings and investment, generating continuous capital deepening, will result in a long-run increase in the rate of productivity increase and therefore a long-run increase in the rate of economic growth. This is not the case. The flaw in the reasoning is to overlook the law of diminishing returns, which says that, as the amount of capital goods per worker continues to increase, successive increments of capital increase output per worker by less and less. Eventually, further increases in capital

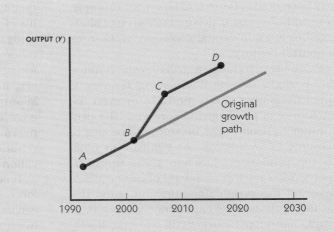

**Figure 19.7 SHORT-RUN AND LONG-RUN EFFECTS OF CAPITAL DEEPENING**

Capital deepening increases output per worker (productivity), and therefore economic growth, but these effects are limited to the short run. The graph shows three segments of a hypothetical growth path. *AB* represents the economy's growth before an increase in savings and investment. *BC*, the steep segment, represents the period of capital accumulation arising from an increase in savings and investment. Once the new, higher level of capital per worker is reached, the economy resumes its original growth rate, represented by the third segment, *CD*.

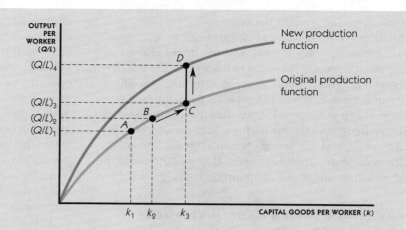

**Figure 19.8 ANALYSIS OF DIMINISHING RETURNS**

With a given production function, the increase in capital goods per worker from $k_2$ to $k_3$ would result in a smaller increase in productivity than the corresponding increase from $k_1$ to $k_2$. But as the economy increases its capital goods per worker, the production function may shift. Rather than moving from $B$ to $C$, the economy would then move from $B$ to $D$. The proportionate increase in output per worker could be as large as or even larger than the movement from $A$ to $B$.

per worker will yield almost no increase in output per worker. Figure 19.8 shows that, as the economy increases capital per worker from $k_2$ to $k_3$, the increase in output per worker is much smaller than when the economy increases capital per worker by a similar amount from $k_1$ to $k_2$.

Productivity growth has not diminished in every period of rapid capital accumulation. Productivity growth increased rapidly in the early postwar period despite high levels of investment. Similar observations have been made elsewhere. Japan, for example, has had steadily increasing productivity growth along with large increases in capital goods per worker for the past quarter century.

The reason that productivity growth can continue over long periods, despite diminishing returns, is that capital deepening is not the only, or even the primary, source of productivity increases. The production function itself might be shifting because of improvements in technology. As Figure 19.8 illustrates, if the production function shifts upwards, output per worker rises at each level of capital goods per worker. If the production function shifts upwards at the same time as capital per worker rises from $k_2$ to $k_3$, output per worker will rise from $(Q/L)_2$ to $(Q/L)_4$ rather than to $(Q/L)_3$. The effect of a shift in the production function will offset the diminishing returns to capital due to capital deepening. If we are

to understand how this is possible, we need to look at these other sources of productivity increase to which we now turn.

## HIGHER QUALITY OF THE LABOUR FORCE

A second major source of enhanced productivity growth, after increased investment, is a higher-quality labour force. Recent discussions of the quality of the labour force have focused on workers' skills and the possibility that Canada is falling behind other countries in training and educating its work force. The general consensus is that running a modern industrial economy requires a well-educated labour force. In addition, an economy on the cutting edge of technological change needs trained engineers and scientists to discover and shape those innovations. This, in turn depends on an effective education system.

It is well documented that a more educated work force has higher productivity. The average income earned by someone with a university degree is over twice that of someone with only grade eight education and about 50 percent higher than someone who only graduated from high school. Furthermore, returns to education have increased markedly in recent

In response to the growing concerns about Canada's prosperity being threatened in the context of a fiercely competitive global economy, the federal government launched the Prosperity Initiative in 1991. It formed an independent Steering Group on Prosperity consisting of 20 Canadians (all volunteers) from a wide range of backgrounds. The Steering Group produced an Action Plan in October of 1992. It reflected the views of thousands of Canadians who had participated in community talks, roundtables, conferences, and forums. The Action Plan set forth 54 specific actions, indicated who should be responsible for them, and even set target dates for undertaking the actions.

The Action Plan consists of three parts. The first part involves creating a growing economy, able to compete in the global economy. The keys to achieving this are an emphasis on innovation and quality along with technological mastery and productivity growth. Among the main recommendations are the formation of a National Quality Institute and the introduction of consumer education courses in schools and adult education centres. To reduce the burden of government, the plan calls for an independent review of federal and provincial taxes and expenditures, a competitiveness impact assessment for existing and proposed laws and regulations, a budget for regulatory oversight to review the economic impact of regulations, and a tough performance review of a number of government departments. The plan recommends a high-speed, broad-band electronic "information highway" to link Canadians to one another and to the world of ideas, and to encourage greater

use of existing technologies and development of new ones. Tax incentives would be given for the use of innovative equipment and technologies, and more dynamic and innovative capital markets would be encouraged, in order to help create new firms and aid small firms in growing larger. A coordinated private-sector strategy would aim to double the number of firms that export. A Centre of Excellence for Sustainable Development would be created to help achieve environmental goals and to enable Canadians to compete in the market for "green" products. A nationwide approach to worker adjustment would be used to prepare the work force to take on new jobs.

The second part of the strategy would improve education and training systems. Though Canada spends over 7 percent of GDP on education, the highest percentage of any developed country, we are not getting value for our investment. To remedy this, the plan calls for a Canadian forum on learning whose purpose is to define goals and to promote innovation and partnerships for excellence in learning. It calls for competence-based systems for all levels of education and training, where success is defined by measurable skills. A concerted effort would be made to build stronger links between schools and the world of work, and to ensure that all young people complete secondary school. Employer-supported training should be increased to be equal to 2 percent of working time. Finally, there should be a 30 percent per year increase in the availability of computers and software in schools.

The third part of the plan aims to make Canada a truly inclusive society in which all persons have the opportunity to achieve their full potential and to share the opportunities that innovation brings. This is important because women, immigrants, and visible minorities will constitute an increasing proportion of Canada's labour force. Key recommendations include an integrated approach to income security that enhances the ability of these groups to find work, while reducing disincentives; a restructuring of the workplace to accommodate family and other social realities; and a new set of training programmes for aboriginal managers at institutions of higher learning.

The Action Plan represents a far-reaching and inclusive set of proposals meant to address the economic and social challenges of the twenty-first century. Its motto is: "Let's get going! Allons-y!"

*Source:* The Steering Group on Prosperity, *Inventing Our Future: An Action Plan for Canada's Prosperity* (Ottawa, 1992).

years—even as the number of educated has increased. The returns to education seem to be significant, even though some of this difference may be attributable to the fact that those who graduate from university are more able (and hence would have had higher incomes even if they had not gone to university) and to factors such as family background and high school performance. Just a year of university raises earnings by 5 to 10 percent or more. One study of identical twins found that each year of additional schooling raised the later earnings of the more educated twin by about 13 percent.

## THE STRENGTHS OF THE CANADIAN EDUCATION SYSTEM

Canada now spends over $50 billion on the formal education of its youth. In recent years there has been a significant increase in the quantity of education in Canada. More students are finishing high school. The high school dropout rate is falling. The percentage of high school graduates enrolling in postsecondary education institutions is increasing. As the new, more highly educated workers have replaced older workers, the share of the labour force with a university degree has increased significantly. And enrollment in graduate schools has increased even more rapidly than undergraduate enrollment.

A particular strength of Canada's education system is its egalitarianism. Other countries such as the United Kingdom, Germany, and China take decisions on whether a particular child is suitable for postsecondary education at a relatively early age (sometimes as young as 11). Early sorting on the basis of test scores gives a distinct advantage to children with more-educated parents or children with parents who are able to afford tutors for them. In Canada such decisions are taken much later, and students typically get repeated chances to demonstrate that they are qualified for postsecondary education.

Another great strength is the Canadian system of community and technical colleges, many of which provide a high-quality education to those who could not afford to go to university, who may not have performed well in high school, or who wish simply to acquire a skill that can be used in the work force. University programmes tend to be of longer duration and more costly than college programmes and are not oriented to the training of technical skills. In many countries, such students would be precluded from further education. Ironically, while in many respects the Canadian educational system is more egalitarian than those of other developed countries, in one respect it is less so. Most European countries charge virtually no tuition to students who are admitted to their universities.

Still another strength is Canada's university system, which ranks among the best in the world. Students from virtually every country come to Canada to study both as undergraduates and graduate students. The discoveries and innovations flowing out of the universities' research laboratories have been an important source of technological innovation.

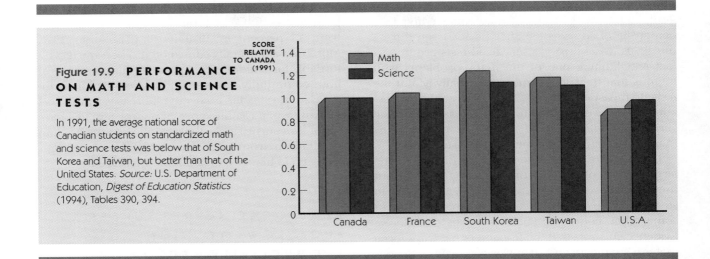

**Figure 19.9 PERFORMANCE ON MATH AND SCIENCE TESTS**

In 1991, the average national score of Canadian students on standardized math and science tests was below that of South Korea and Taiwan, but better than that of the United States. *Source:* U.S. Department of Education, *Digest of Education Statistics* (1994), Tables 390, 394.

## SYMPTOMS OF A HUMAN CAPITAL PROBLEM

Despite the great strength within the Canadian educational system, there are symptoms of some problems—problems that may be contributing to the slowdown of productivity. The concern is that while on quantitative measures Canada looks good, with high levels of expenditure and high levels of enrollment, the quality of education is not as high as it could be. On standardized tests, particularly in science and mathematics, Canadian students perform below students from many other countries, even countries that have until recently been classified as less developed, such as South Korea and Taiwan (see Figure 19.9).

A related cause for concern is that the level of skills learned earlier, in grade school, seems to be declining in recent years. Figure 19.10 shows that

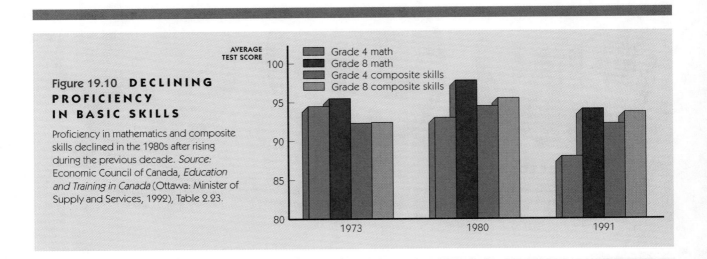

**Figure 19.10 DECLINING PROFICIENCY IN BASIC SKILLS**

Proficiency in mathematics and composite skills declined in the 1980s after rising during the previous decade. *Source:* Economic Council of Canada, *Education and Training in Canada* (Ottawa: Minister of Supply and Services, 1992), Table 2.23.

over the decade of the 1980s both grade four and grade eight pupils' skills in mathematics and in a composite of subjects fell after having risen during the 1970s. Of course, standardized tests are imperfect and limited; one of the many problems with them is that they do not measure creativity. But the tests do measure students' success in achieving certain objectives of education, such as mastery of basic verbal and mathematical skills. The poor performance of Canadian students is thus disturbing.

Canada, like the United States, is unique in the large fraction of its youth that goes to university, but the proportion of Canadian students who choose to study science and engineering is smaller than in some other countries, such as Japan and Korea. Evidence suggests that the fraction of the work force that are engineers and scientists is a major determinant of rapid economic growth.

Finally, a significant fraction of Canada's population is deprived of the opportunity to realize their full potential. The role of family background in determining educational achievement has increasingly been recognized. Children who grow up in poverty are less likely to attain an education commensurate

with their ability, and the number of children in poverty has increased markedly in recent years, from 15 percent in 1980 to 19 percent in 1994. Moreover, a university education has become less affordable for children from poor families. Tuitions at both community colleges and universities have increased at rates far exceeding increases in the cost of living while real incomes of poorer families have fallen. Not surprisingly, the gap between the fraction of children from poor families and rich families going on to higher education has increased.

## REALLOCATING RESOURCES FROM LOW- TO HIGH-PRODUCTIVITY SECTORS

During the past century, Canada has evolved from an agricultural economy to an industrial economy to a service economy. Figure 19.11 shows this dramatic structural change. The service sector, broadly defined, includes not only traditional services such as haircuts and restaurant meals but also the more

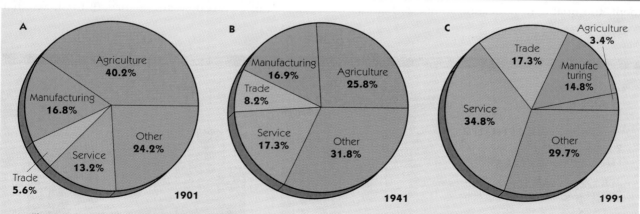

**Figure 19.11** **SECTORAL SHIFTS**

Employment in the Canadian economy shifted out of agriculture to all other industries in the first half of this century, and from agriculture and manufacturing to trade and services in the second half. *Sources:* M. C. Urquhart and K. A. H. Buckley, eds., *Historical Statistics of Canada* (Toronto: Macmillan Co. of Canada, 1965); Statistics Canada, CANSIM Database 1994.

sophisticated services provided by doctors and lawyers, educational institutions, and computer programmers, among others. The medical sector alone has grown to the point where today it accounts for more than 9 percent of GDP.

The movement out of agriculture and into industry explains some of the productivity increase in the early part of the century. While the level of productivity in agriculture was increasing rapidly, it remained lower than in industry. Thus, as workers shifted out of low-productivity jobs in agriculture into high-productivity jobs in manufacturing, average productivity in the economy increased. With almost all labour now out of agriculture, and with agricultural productivity increased to the point where incomes in that sector are comparable to that in the rest of the economy, this kind of shift can no longer be a source of overall productivity growth. But there remain other opportunities. Productivity in the telecommunications and export sectors is substantially higher than in other parts of the economy. Telecommunications deregulation will facilitate the movement of resources into that sector. And recent international trade agreements (see Chapter 21) will open up new opportunities for export growth. Both should contribute to an overall increase in productivity.

## TECHNOLOGICAL CHANGE

This final source of productivity growth may be the most important. Indeed, it has been estimated that as much as 87 percent of all increases in productivity are due to technological progress. One of the major differences between the economy today and in 1900 is the routine nature of change in the modern economy. The prototype of the nineteenth- and early twentieth-century inventors were men like Thomas Edison and Alexander Graham Bell—lone individuals, working by themselves or with a small number of collaborators. Small entrepreneurs and innovators continue to play a role in developing new products, particularly in the computer industry. But the prototype of a modern research effort, like the U.S. programme to put a man on the moon, has thousands of scientists working together to accomplish in a few short years what would have been almost

unimaginable earlier. Technological change in the modern economy is a large-scale, systematic effort. Modern research is centred in huge laboratories, employing thousands of people. Some of these laboratories, such as the National Research Centre, are run by the government and carry out research in basic science, but many are private, like Connaught Laboratories, where insulin was developed. Indeed, most major firms spend about 3 percent of their gross revenues on research and development.

The current level of technological progress has become so expected that it is hard to believe how different the view of reputable economists was in the early 1800s. Real wages of workers were little higher than they had been five hundred years earlier, when the bubonic plague destroyed a large part of the population of Europe and thereby created a great scarcity of labour. After half a millennium of at best slow progress, Thomas Malthus, one of the greatest economists of that time, saw population expanding more rapidly than the capacity of the economy to support it. What was missing from his dismal forecast of unavoidable overpopulation was technological change.

## EXPENDITURES ON R & D

A major determinant of the pace of technological progress is the level of expenditures on R & D. These expenditures are a form of investment: expenditures today yield returns in the future. There are two major sources of research funds, corporations and government. Government has had primary responsibility for *basic* research, the development of new ideas with wide applicability—from developments in mathematics that eventually led to the computer to developments in our understanding of physics that eventually led to nuclear power. Industry has primary responsibility for *applied* research, the kind of research that leads to a new software programme or a newly designed telephone or a better laser. In between, there is a vast gray area, with shared responsibility, and today, research moves from the university to the corporation with remarkable rapidity. Basic advances in understanding genes, often achieved in university labs, quickly spawned firms using genetic engineering to make new drugs.

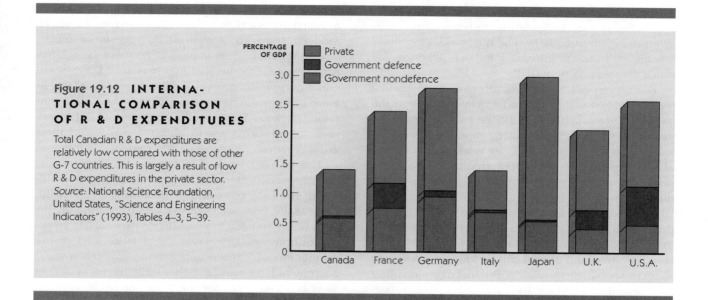

**Figure 19.12 INTERNATIONAL COMPARISON OF R & D EXPENDITURES**

Total Canadian R & D expenditures are relatively low compared with those of other G-7 countries. This is largely a result of low R & D expenditures in the private sector. *Source:* National Science Foundation, United States, "Science and Engineering Indicators" (1993), Tables 4–3, 5–39.

As Figure 19.12 shows, in terms of total R & D as a percentage of GDP, Canada fares badly among the G-7 industrialized countries—only Italy fares worse. On the other hand, much of our standing is due to low private-sector R & D spending rather than low public-sector spending. It is also noteworthy that hardly any of our R & D effort takes place in the defence sector, unlike, say, in the United States, France, and the United Kingdom. Figure 19.13 shows how federal government and total expenditures on R & D have changed since 1970. Federal spending on R & D as a percentage of GDP has actually declined, despite the fact that total R & D expenditures as a percentage of GDP have risen. The fall has been dramatic; federal spending as a percentage of GDP was a third smaller in 1995 than it was in 1971.

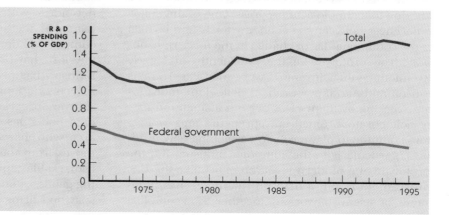

**Figure 19.13 FEDERAL SUPPORT FOR R & D**

The proportion of GDP spent by the federal government for R & D has declined since 1971, while total (public plus private) R & D expenditures as a percentage of GDP have risen. *Sources:* Statistics Canada, CANSIM Database 1996, Label D10011; Statistics Canada, *Service Bulletin: Science Statistics* 19, no. 8 (1995): pp. 3–5.

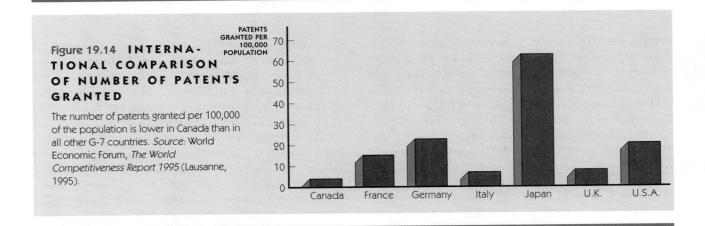

Figure 19.14 **INTERNA-TIONAL COMPARISON OF NUMBER OF PATENTS GRANTED**

The number of patents granted per 100,000 of the population is lower in Canada than in all other G-7 countries. *Source:* World Economic Forum, *The World Competitiveness Report 1995* (Lausanne, 1995).

This underinvestment in R & D is reflected in the Canadian record on patents granted. Figure 19.14 shows that today, relative to the size of the population, Canada is performing more poorly by this indicator than all other large industrialized countries that are in the G-7.

The high rates of return on R & D expenditures support the view that there is underinvestment in research: some estimates put the private returns at over 25 percent, and since many of the returns accrue to firms other than those undertaking the research, social returns are estimated to be even higher. In perfectly functioning capital markets, rates of return on different types of investment would be equalized. If the rate of return is relatively high in one sector, investment funds should flow into that sector until the rate of return is driven down. The fact that rates of return on R & D expenditures are high reflects the fact that for some reason enough investment funds are not flowing into R & D to make rates of return to R & D comparable with other investments. High risk, combined with limitations on the ability to borrow to finance R & D, provide part of the explanation for the seeming underinvestment in R & D.

In one important sense, the shortfall of R & D expenditures in Canada gives a misleading impression as to the extent to which innovations are available to Canadian firms. A high proportion of firms operating in high-tech and innovative sectors in Canada are actually subsidiaries of multinational corporations based elsewhere. These companies tend to do a disproportionate amount of the R & D in the home country, especially the United States. On the one hand, this should be of limited concern since the discoveries that are made become available to Canadian subsidiaries. On the other hand, the fact that R & D takes place elsewhere implies that Canadian scientists may be lured abroad rather than working at home.

Some economists, while agreeing with the evidence concerning underinvestment in R & D, have raised questions about the importance of R & D in explaining the *current* productivity slowdown. It normally takes years for the effects of R & D to show up in productivity statistics. To the extent that the productivity slowdown in the 1970s was due to decreased expenditures on research, assuming such a time lag between expenditures and productivity gains, the relevant decreased expenditures would have been in the 1950s and 1960s. Yet the 1960s in particular was a period of high spending on research.

### OTHER POSSIBLE FACTORS

There may be other factors contributing to the slowdown of the pace of technological progress. Two prominent theories in recent years relate the productivity slowdown to the increased importance of the service sector and the unexpected increase in energy prices in the 1970s.

***The Service Sector*** Some economists contend that the decline in heavy industry—in steel, automobiles, and manufacturing in general—and growth in the service sector help explain the recent slowdown in productivity growth. In fact, in recent years, productivity growth in manufacturing has been quite robust, even higher than in the sixties. But the proportion of GDP attributable to manufacturing is gradually declining, while that of the service sector is rapidly increasing, as we saw in Figure 19.11. If productivity growth in the service sector is low, this will offset high productivity growth in manufacturing, and productivity growth in the economy as a whole will be low.

The issue then becomes whether service sector productivity growth is in fact low. Those worried about the potential for technological change in services cite haircutting as an example: the only major innovation in this field in the past hundred years has been the electric hair clipper. Similar arguments might apply to the services of lawyers and accountants, and to other types of services that are labour-intensive. But other economists are more hopeful. They cite the development by McDonald's of more efficient ways of delivering fast food, improvements by many of the country's major retailers that have reduced the markup of retail prices over wholesale costs, and the computer revolution that continues to open up new technological possibilities in banking, insurance, and design. Finally, as noted in Chapter 6, quality improvements may be inadequately reflected in the price and output measures, leading to the understatement of productivity gains.

The growth in importance of the service sector may, however, affect *measured* productivity. Productivity is calculated by dividing *real* output by hours worked. Calculating real output entails making adjustments for price change; but as we saw in Chapter 6, making those adjustments is not as easy as it seems. How much of the price change reflects improvements in quality? How should we evaluate new products, like automatic tellers? Many economists believe that the way these adjustments are conventionally done understates the importance of quality improvements, and so understates the true increase in productivity. Moreover, these measurement biases are particularly large in the service sector, so that as the service sector has expanded, the extent to which the standard measures understate productivity growth has increased.

*The Energy Crisis* Another factor that may have contributed to the slowdown of technological change is the energy crisis. Some economists have noted the fact that the slowdown seems to have occurred around 1973, when oil prices soared. Much of the existing capital was designed for a world of cheap energy, and much of the investment in the subsequent years went not to capital deepening, but to replacing the old capital with more energy-efficient machines and buildings. According to this view, the standard measuring procedures overestimate net investment since 1973. Moreover, firms diverted more of their research budgets to looking for ways of saving on energy, again at the expense of research that might have increased overall productivity.

Other economists question the importance of the run-up in energy prices, since the real price of oil had declined to earlier levels by the mid-1980s. In any case, energy constitutes but a small percentage of GDP.

### THE POLICY DEBATES OF THE 1990S

Policy discussions have focused on both corporate and public R & D expenditures. There is widespread agreement that government should support R & D through preferential tax treatment (such as the R & D tax credit, under which government in effect pays 25 percent of the cost of R & D expenditures). R & D expenditures are a form of investment, and so the high cost of capital in Canada (as compared to Japan)—a result of the low savings rate in Canada and the United States—puts Canadian firms at a disadvantage in obtaining investment funds. The R & D tax credit may partially overcome this.

More controversial than the R & D tax credit have been direct government expenditures to develop new technologies or to subsidize corporations who do so. Critics label such subsidies **industrial policies:** an attempt by government to intervene in the market's allocation of resources. They claim government is notoriously bad at picking winners, areas with high likelihood of success. In their view, firms driven by the profit motive are more likely to take good decisions than the government, driven by special interests.

Advocates of direct government subsidies for research contend that there are important spillovers from technological research, that there is clear evidence of underinvestment in advanced technology (as one would expect, given such spillovers, and limitations on firms' ability to obtain funds to finance

## Close-up: The Productivity Slowdown and Increased Inequality

The years following 1970 were marked not only by a slowdown in the rate of growth of productivity, but by an increase in earnings inequality as well. The strongest evidence for this has come from studies in the United States. Between 1970 and 1989, real hourly wages for the lowest-paid 10 percent of American prime-aged male workers fell by 30 percent, while those for the top 40 percent increased slightly. One consequence of this wage gap was a significant increase in inequality. The top 20 percent of income earners in the United Sates increased their share of national income from 40 percent in 1970 to about 45 percent in the late 1980s. At the same time, the share of the national income of the poorest 20 percent had decreased from 5.6 percent to 4.6 percent.

The increase in income inequality has not been as pronounced in Canada. Here, the top 20 percent of income earners increased their share of national income from 41 percent in 1965 to 44 percent in 1994. At the same time, the bottom 20 percent changed hardly at all, rising slightly from 4.4 to 4.7 percent. This does not mean that wage inequality did not increase in Canada as well. Indeed, evidence indicates that, of the OECD countries, Canada's earnings inequality is second only to that of the United States. Our relatively generous system of transfers to low-income persons helps prevent a wage gap being translated into an income gap.

Economists have speculated about whether, and in what ways, the decline in productivity growth and the increase in inequality are interrelated. Some look to supply-side explanations, particularly for the decrease in real wages among the lowest decile. They see the decreased quality of education as having decreased the number of well-prepared workers. Others focus on demand-side explanations. They see technological change as having decreased the demand for unskilled workers and increased the demand for those with higher skills. While immigration of unskilled workers, particularly from Latin America, may also have driven down the wages of unskilled workers in the United States, that has not likely been a factor in Canada where immigration has been much more oriented to those with skills needed here. Instead, the increased flow of imports from low-wage countries may have had important effects. To compete with these cheap imports, workers in some industries have had to accept wage cuts or be content with smaller than usual wage increases. Meanwhile, high-wage industries like steel and autos faced a decline in employment as they modernized in the face of competition.

A recent study by Charles Beach of Queen's University and George Slotsve of Vanderbilt University has shown that the idea of the "disappearing middle class" is more myth than reality, much like the notion that the poor in Canada are getting poorer. The study reports, for example, that while the median after-tax family income in Canada did not change much over the last 20 years (primarily due to increases in taxes), the proportion of families with incomes between 50 percent and 150 percent of the median declined only from 61.4 percent in 1972 to 58.9 percent in 1992, and has been rising since 1985.

As the effects of free trade and corporate restructuring continue in Canada, it is certain that the gains in productivity will not be shared equally among all income classes. However, as the numbers point out, Canada has done a better job than the United States of preventing any increases in wage inequality from being translated into further income inequality.

*Sources:* C. John, K. Murphy, and R. Topel, "Why Has the Natural Rate of Unemployment Increased Over Time?", *Brookings Papers on Economic Activity,* (1991); Statistics Canada, *Income Distribution by Size in Canada,* Catalogue No. 13-207, various years; C. Beach and G. Slotsve, *Are We Becoming Two Societies? Income Polarization and the Myth of the Declining Middle Class in Canada* (Toronto: C. D. Howe Institute, 1996).

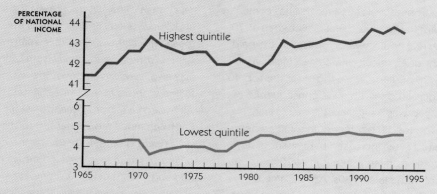

## INCREASING INCOME INEQUALITY

Increasing wage inequality has not contributed greatly to greater income inequality. The share of national income going to the poorest 20 percent has not changed much, and that going to the highest 20 percent has increased by only a small amount. *Source:* Statistics Canada, *Income Distributions by Size in Canada,* Catalogue No. 13-207, various years.

risky research), and that the government has a credible record of picking winners—including, for example, the support of communications satellites, nuclear reactors, and commuter trains. Furthermore, government programmes have provisions to enhance the likelihood of success, including requiring recipients to put up a considerable amount of their own capital and subjecting applicants to a stiff competitive review process in which independent experts judge the likely significance of any spillovers.

Another policy debate has centred around the extent to which basic R & D spending should be cut as part of the government's efforts to address the budget deficit. Advocates argue that deficit reduction is imperative so that more savings are made available for productive investment and interest rates are reduced. There is no particular reason why some expenditure programmes should be spared. Critics say this is shortsighted. Spending on research and devel-

opment acts as much a spur to growth as does the investment induced by deficit reduction. They say that Canada is already spending far too little on R & D, as reflected by the fact that the rate of return on public R & D expenditures is even higher than that of private investment.

## TOTAL FACTOR PRODUCTIVITY

Low and declining rates of savings and investment, low and declining quality of education, and low and declining levels of government investment in R & D may have all contributed to the low and declining rates of productivity increase in Canada. Economists have asked, can we quantify the role of different factors? To do that, they have used a methodology called **total factor productivity analysis,** in which they ask, if there had been no technological change,

## FACTORS CONTRIBUTING TO PRODUCTIVITY GROWTH

Capital accumulation

    Increasing national savings

    Increasing investment

Improved quality of labour force

    Education and training

    Educational reforms

Reallocation of labour from low-productivity sectors to high-productivity sectors

    Movement from agriculture to industry

    Increasing exports

Technological progress

    Increased expenditures on R & D

    Encouragement of private R & D expenditures by means of tax incentives

---

based on what we know about the returns to and increases in the supply of capital (human and physical) and labor, how much would productivity have increased?

Suppose the share of capital in output—the amount of output attributable to capital (the total returns to capital divided by GDP)—is 20 percent, and the growth of capital is 10 percent. The share of capital in output (20 percent) multiplied by capital growth (10 percent) gives us the amount that capital growth contributes to the growth of output (2 percent).[2] The same logic applies to labour. But capital and labour do not account for all of growth. The part of growth which cannot be explained by increases in capital and labour is called the increase in total fac-

---

[2] To see this, consider the change in output, $\Delta Q$, "attributable" to an increase in capital by an amount $\Delta K$; if $r$ is the return to capital,

$$\Delta Q = r\Delta K.$$

The percentage increase in $Q$ is just

$$\frac{\Delta Q}{Q} = \frac{r\Delta K}{Q}.$$

Multiplying the numerator and the denominator of the expression on the right-hand side by $K$, we obtain

$$\frac{\Delta Q}{Q} = \frac{rK\Delta K}{QK}.$$

$rK/Q$ is just the share of capital in GDP ($rK$ is the total return to capital, and $Q$ is output). Hence the percentage increase in output attributable to the increase in $K$ is the percentage increase in capital times the share of capital.

---

tor productivity. The rate of total factor productivity increase is calculated as follows:

$$\text{TFP} = g_Q - (s_K \times g_K) - (s_L \times g_L)$$

where

$s_K$ = share of capital in GDP

$s_L$ = share of labour in GDP

$g_Q$ = rate of growth of output

$g_K$ = rate of growth of capital

$g_L$ = rate of growth of labour.

The increase in total factor productivity reflects the increasing efficiency with which an economy's resources are used. Some of this is the result of R & D, but much of the increase in total factor productivity cannot be easily explained. The part that cannot be explained is referred to as the **residual**—the part of growth that is "left over" after all the systematic sources of growth are taken into account. The spread of new production techniques, such as replaceable parts in the nineteenth century, the assembly line in the early twentieth century, and just-in-time inventory management techniques in recent years, are all examples of technological advances that bear little relationship to R & D expenditures, and thus form part of this "residual."

The fact that productivity growth is in part inexplicable poses major problems for those involved in long-term forecasting. Was the rapid growth of productivity in the 1950s and 1960s an aberration, a result of almost two decades of depression and war

# USING ECONOMICS: CALCULATING TOTAL FACTOR PRODUCTIVITY

Between 1984 and 1994 real GDP rose by 27.4 percent. How much of this was due to increased productivity? To determine this, we must first take account of any increases in the factors of production available to the economy. Over this period, employment rose by 16.6 percent, and it is estimated that the value of capital stock increased by 31.6 percent. Suppose that 70 percent of the value of output produced goes to labour and 30 percent goes to capital. These are the shares of the cost of producing output represented by payment for wages and salaries, and for capital services. Given this, a 1 percent increase in the labour force should cause output to rise by .7 percent, while a 1 percent increase in the capital stock should cause output to rise by .3 percent.

To calculate the increase in total factor productivity, begin with the formula on page 416:

$$TFP = g_Q - (s_K \times g_K) - (s_L \times g_L)$$

The percentage increase in total fractor productivity equals the growth in national output ($g_Q$) minus the growth in output attributable to capital ($s_K \times g_K$) minus the growth in output attributable to labour ($s_L \times g_L$). Substituting the data for the period from 1984 to 1994:

$$TFP = 27.4 - (.3 \times 31.6) - (.7 \times 16.6)$$
$$= 27.4 - 9.48 - 11.62$$
$$= 6.3$$

This framework can be used to identify the sources of economic growth. Between 1984 and 1994, of the 27.4 percent growth in national output, 9.48 percent is attributable to increased capital stock, 11.62 percent is attributable to increased employment, and 6.3 percent is attributable to increased productivity. The table below shows this calculation for ten-year periods all the way back to the time of the Great Depression in the 1930s.

*Sources:* Statistics Canada, CANSIM Database 1996, Label Nos. D14442, D767608; Statistics Canada, *Fixed Capital Stocks and Flows*, Catalogue No. 13-568, various years; M. C. Urquhart, ed., *Historical Statistics of Canada*, 1st ed. (Toronto, 1965), 2nd ed. (Toronto, 1983).

## PROPORTION OF GDP GROWTH FROM:

| Years | Growth in real GDP | Growth in real GDP due to increased capital stock | Growth in real GDP due to increased employment | Growth in real GDP due to increased total factor productivity |
|-------|-------|-------|-------|-------|
| 1984–94 | 27.4% | 9.5% | 11.6% | 6.3% |
| 1974–84 | 36.9% | 12.6% | 17.4% | 6.9% |
| 1964–74 | 67.8% | 17.4% | 26.8% | 23.6% |
| 1954–64 | 65.1% | 22.0% | 18.2% | 24.9% |
| 1944–54 | 34.8% | 18.7% | 11.8% | 4.3% |
| 1934–44 | 115.9% | 3.9% | 14.7% | 97.3% |

during the thirties and forties, with the consequent postponement of the introduction of new innovations into the economy? Or are the 1970s and 1980s an aberration—a period of adjustment as fundamentally new technologies, such as computers, became more widely disseminated, their full benefits to be reaped in future decades?

## THE COSTS OF ECONOMIC GROWTH

Faith in the virtues of economic progress is widespread. Even among people with serious doubts about certain technologies, few will openly embrace the alternatives of economic stagnation and a relatively lower standard of living for Canada. But this does not stop people from complaining (with some merit) that technology takes away jobs.

In the early 1800s, English workmen destroyed labour-saving machinery rather than see it take over their jobs. They were referred to as **Luddites,** after their supposed leader Ned Ludd (who may have been largely mythical). Concerns about workers thrown out of their jobs as a result of some innovation are no less real today.

Technological progress creates jobs as it destroys them. Of course, it can be hard to teach an old dog new tricks, so a middle-aged or older worker who loses her job may have real difficulty in getting another that is even nearly as good. How much sympathy this displaced worker should receive is a matter on which reasonable people can disagree. Does a worker who is used to a certain wage have an inalienable right to this wage? Should we pay more attention to the costs to the worker who loses a job than to the benefits to a worker in the new industry who gets a better job?

It's not surprising that technological progress frequently meets with resistance, and the government often responds positively to the pleas for intervention to help particular groups. Most economists believe that these interventions are harmful when judged from an overall perspective, because they slow down the pace of innovation and, with it, the rate of productivity increase. They believe that the

cost to society exceeds the gains to the protected groups. The objective of the government should be to design programmes that assist in the transition of people displaced by technological change. Such programmes can be thought of as a form of insurance. Most workers face the possibility that their jobs will be made technologically obsolete. Knowing that if they are thrown out of work for this reason they will be at least partially protected adds to a sense of security, something most workers value highly. In the long run, such programmes can actually help increase the rate at which technological changes are adopted by making the prospect of losing a job less fearful.

More generally, we saw in Part Two that in the long run, with flexible wages, the economy will create enough jobs to match the supply. In Part Three we saw that in the short run wage and price rigidity may lead to significant unemployment, but that there were government policies which could help ensure that the economy remained at close to full employment. To the extent that government employs such policies, there will be fewer worries about jobs. There will be less resistance to new technologies that lead to job loss, as workers become more confident that the economy will at the same time generate new job opportunities.

## ARE THERE LIMITS TO ECONOMIC GROWTH?

In the early 1800s, the British economist Thomas Malthus envisioned the future as one in which the ever-increasing labour force would push wages down to the subsistence level, or even lower. Any technological progress that occurred would, in his view, raise wages only temporarily.

Over the past century there has been a decrease in the rate of population growth, a phenomenon perhaps as remarkable as the increase in the rate of technological progress. One might have expected improved medicine and health conditions to cause a population explosion, but the spread of birth control and family planning has had the opposite effect, at least in the more developed countries. Today family

## CLOSE-UP: ACCOUNTING FOR GROWTH

Many economists have used total factor productivity analysis to attempt to quantify the role played by each of the main factors contributing to economic growth: capital accumulation, labour growth, and technological progress. A recent study by Pierre Mohnen of l'Université du Québec à Montréal estimated the contribution of these factors to the growth of Canadian manufacturing industries for the period 1965–83. His findings are summarized in the table below.

At the bottom of the table is a category labelled "residual"—the part of increased productivity that cannot be explained by the other, measurable, factors. Fully half of the growth in output remains unexplained; most of the residual is interpreted as being due to technological change.

The major controversy about these numbers is associated with the role of capital accumulation. Some economists believe that capital accumulation is far more important than these numbers would suggest, partly because without new investment there would not be learning by doing, new techniques would not be introduced into the economy, and the spur to R & D would be reduced.

### THE SOURCES OF ECONOMIC GROWTH

| Fraction of growth of manufacturing output accounted for by | |
| --- | --- |
| Capital accumulation | 26% |
| Labour employed | 11% |
| R & D | 14% |
| Residual | 49% |

*Source:* Table based on Pierre Mohnen, *The Relationship between R & D and Productivity Growth in Canada and Other Major Industrialized Countries* (Ottawa: Ministry of Supply and Services, 1992), p. 30, Table 5.

size has decreased to the point where in many countries population growth (apart from migration) has almost halted. Those who worry about the limits to growth today believe that *exhaustible* natural resources—like oil, natural gas, phosphorus, or potassium—may pose a limit to economic growth as they are used up in the ordinary course of production.

Most economists do not share this fear, believing that markets do provide incentives for wise use of most resources: as any good becomes more scarce and its price rises, the search for substitutes will be stimulated. Thus, the rise in the price of oil led to smaller, more efficient cars, cooler and better-insulated houses, and a search for alternative sources of energy like geothermal and synthetic fuels, all of which resulted in a decline in the consumption of oil.

Still, there is one area in which the price system does not work well—the area of externalities, discussed in Chapter 7. Without government intervention, producers have no incentive to worry about air and water pollution. Furthermore, in our globally connected world, what one country does results in externalities for others. Cutting down the rain forest in Brazil may have worldwide climatic consequences. The less developed countries feel that they can ill afford the costs of pollution control, when they can barely pay the price of any industrialization. They feel it is unfair to ask them to pay the price of maintaining the environment, when the major industrialized economies are the major source of the environmental degradation. Environmentalists argue that we are all in the same boat, and if global warming occurs, it could have disastrous effects on all of us, in both the less and more developed countries. While the scientific community is not in agreement about the significance of these concerns, most economists do not believe that we face an either/or choice. We do not have to abandon growth to preserve our environment. Nevertheless, a sensitivity to the quality of our environment may affect how we go about growing.

This sensitivity is building a new consensus in favour of **sustainable development**: growth that is not based simply on the exploitation of natural resources and the environment in a way that cannot be sustained. In many cases, policies can be devised that improve economic efficiency and thus promote economic growth at the same time that they decrease adverse environmental effects. Such policies include eliminating energy subsidies and certain agricultural subsidies that induce farmers to use excessive amounts of fertilizers and pesticides.

## The Prognosis

Though this century has been marked by large increases in productivity, the rate of productivity growth has not been steady. There have been periods of relative stagnation as well as periods in which the economy has burst forth with energy and growth. Is the decline in productivity growth just a passing phase? Or were the high rates of productivity growth during the 1950s and 1960s the aberration?

The analysis presented in this chapter suggests grounds for both pessimism and optimism. There is no quick or easy reversal of many of the factors hampering productivity growth, such as the low rate of savings. But some of the factors hampering productivity growth are more easily altered. These include the failure of government to improve the economy's infrastructure and the low level of expenditures on research and development, at least expenditures on basic research.

Most economists think it unlikely that North America will ever again be in the position of technological dominance it held for so long. But there is widespread optimism that the Canadian economy can return to a higher level of productivity growth, provided the right government policies are pursued.

## REVIEW AND PRACTICE

### Summary

**1** Canada and the United States experienced a marked slowdown in the rate of productivity growth in the late 1970s and early 1980s. Even seemingly small declines in the rate of increase in productivity will have a powerful adverse effect on the standard of living over a generation or two.

**2** There are four major sources of productivity growth: increases in the accumulation of capital goods (investment); a higher quality of the labour force; greater efficiency in allocating resources; and technological change.

**3** The rate of savings in Canada has declined in recent years. Some of the reasons are improved government retirement programmes, more extensive insurance coverage and greater ease in borrowing, and changes in social attitudes.

**4** The most plausible way to achieve an immediate increase in overall national savings would be to reduce the government deficits.

**5** The Canadian education system has important elements of strength, and there have been significant increases in human capital in the last twenty years; nevertheless, there are serious concerns about the quality of education Canadian students are receiving in preparation for the labour force and about the number of scientists and engineers being trained.

**6** The twentieth century has been marked by shifts in the Canadian economy from an agricultural base to an industrial base and more recently to a service base. Some economists think that the potential for technological progress is less in the service sector than in the industrial sector, and this accounts for part of the productivity slowdown. Others account for the slowdown by focusing on the relatively low level of R & D expenditures.

**7** Government supports R & D through both direct spending and tax incentives, though direct support for R & D as a percentage of GDP has actually declined during the past quarter century.

**8** There has long been concern that certain natural resources (like oil) will someday run out, causing economic growth to halt. However, most economists would argue that the price of resources will increase as they become more scarce, and this will encourage both greater conservation and a search for substitutes.

## KEY TERMS

| | | | |
|---|---|---|---|
| capital deepening | infrastructure | total factor productivity analysis | Luddites |
| life-cycle savings | industrial policy | | sustainable development |

## REVIEW QUESTIONS

**1** True or false: "Since growth-oriented policies might have an effect of only a percent or two per year, they are not worth worrying much about." Explain.

**2** What are the four possible sources of productivity growth?

**3** What are the various explanations of the slowdown of the rate of increase in productivity?

**4** What are the components of overall Canadian savings, and how did they change in the 1990s?

**5** What are some reasons for the decrease in the savings rate in recent years?

**6** Will government policies designed to raise the rate of return on savings, such as exempting interest from taxes, necessarily lead to increased savings? (Hint: You may wish to review the discussion of income and substitution effects in Chapter 7.)

**7** What is the link between changes in savings and changes in investment? What is the link between changes in the level of investment and the rate of growth of productivity in the short run? What is meant by capital deepening? Use the model of Chapter 8 to show how for a closed economy a tax credit may lead to a higher equilibrium level of investment. Show how a government deficit may lead to a lower equilibrium level of investment.

**8** What policies might the government use to increase investment in R & D?

**9** What are some costs of economic growth? Short of seeking to restrain growth, how might government deal with these costs?

**10** What are some of the concerns about limits to economic growth? How have they been overcome in the past?

## PROBLEMS

**1** Will the following changes increase or decrease the rate of household savings?

    (a) The proportion of people in the 45–64 age bracket increases.

    (b) Government programmes provide secure retirement benefits.

    (c) Credit cards become much more prevalent.

    (d) The proportion of people in the 21–45 age bracket increases.

    (e) Government programmes to guarantee student loans are enacted.

**2** Explain how the following factors would increase or decrease the average productivity of labour:

    (a) Successful reforms of the educational system

    (b) The entry of new workers into the economy

    (c) Earlier retirement

    (d) High unemployment rates during a recession.

**3** Suppose a firm is considering spending $1 million on R & D projects, which it believes will translate into patents that it will be able to sell for $2.5 million in ten years. Assume that the firm ignores risk. If the interest rate is 10 percent, is the firm likely to attempt these R & D projects? If the government offers a 20 percent R & D tax credit, how does the firm's calculation change?

**4** Explain why a rapid influx of workers might result in a lower output per worker (a reduction in productivity). Would the effect on productivity depend on the skill level of the new workers?

**5** Explain, using supply and demand diagrams, how a technological change such as computerization could lead to lower wages of unskilled workers and higher wages of skilled workers.

**6** Consider the four sources of economic growth. Discuss the relative importance of the various items. Which are most likely to have a significant effect on growth?

**7** Using the model of Chapter 8, discuss the effect on the level of investment for an open economy of (a) an increased government deficit; (b) an increased government expenditure, financed by taxes on households whose effect is to reduce households' disposable income; (c) an investment tax credit. How will such policies affect future living standards of the country's residents?

# CHAPTER 20

# INTERGENERATIONAL TRANSFERS: DEFICITS AND PUBLIC PENSIONS

W e saw in Chapter 9 that starting in the early 1980s, the federal government began to incur large budget deficits. The increasing deficits led to higher and higher levels of debt and an increasing burden on the government simply to pay interest on the debt. By 1994, when the federal budget deficit levelled off, the amount of debt accumulated had reached almost 75 percent of GDP. Taking the provincial debt into account, that figure was closer to 100 percent. Budget deficits reflect spending for the benefit of current taxpayers that must be paid for by future taxpayers. The public debt represents the value of future tax liabilities left to be paid for by future taxpayers, including the current young and future generations. On grounds of both fairness and economic prosperity, there is widespread agreement that government deficits have to be brought under control rapidly.

Deficits are not the only way that governments redistribute wealth from the young and future generations to older persons. Public pension payments to the old that are financed by taxes on current workers (unfunded pension plans) have the same effect. Just as the public debt represents the

## KEY QUESTIONS

**1** What gave rise to the fiscal deficit? And why is it so difficult to reduce?

**2** What are the central economic issues in the debate about why and how deficits should be reduced?

**3** What have governments in Canada done to address the deficit problem?

**4** What are the problems facing the retirement income system in Canada and how do they compare with the public debt problem?

**5** What are the policy options for reforming public pensions?

future tax liabilities that have been accumulated by past budget deficits, so one can calculate the sum of future unfunded pension liabilities that have been accumulated on behalf of persons currently retired or partway through their working lives and that will have to be paid for by future pension contributors. These unfunded pension liabilities are of the same order of magnitude as the public debt, and are projected to grow very rapidly as the proportion of retired persons in the population rises.

This chapter reviews the origins of the deficit problem as well as the debate about the consequences of deficits and how the deficit problem should be addressed. The final section addresses the related problem of the rapid growth in unfunded public pension liabilities and discusses the options for pension reform.

## THE SOURCES OF THE CURRENT CANADIAN DEFICIT PROBLEM

The current deficit problem began in the 1980s. Federal government spending rose during the 1980s from 21.3 percent of GDP in 1981 to 23.1 percent of GDP in 1991. But taxes failed to rise to match this boost in spending; taxes were 17 percent of GDP in 1981 but by 1991 they had risen only to 17.5 percent of GDP, far less than was required to finance the in-

creased expenditures. As a result the government had to borrow increasingly large sums of money.

What caused government expenditures to rise so rapidly relative to tax revenues? Figure 20.1 depicts the change in each of the main categories of federal government expenditures and of tax revenues as a percentage of GDP since 1950. As the figure indicates, federal government expenditures on goods and services have not been the culprit: they have gradually declined as a percentage of GDP. The main sources of increase have been federal government transfer payments, to persons, businesses, and other levels of government (mainly the provinces). Transfer payments to persons as a proportion of GDP doubled between the 1950s and the late 1970s, and those to other governments tripled over the same period. These more than offset the mild rise in tax revenues over the period.

This figure reflects the four main sources of rapid growth of government expenditures in the past twenty years.

### HIGHER PAYMENTS TO THE ELDERLY

As the number of elderly people in Canada has grown, federal expenditures on programmes like Old Age Security and the Guaranteed Income Supplement have expanded rapidly as well. While the proportion of the federal budget devoted to payments to the elderly has stayed around 12 percent since the late

**Figure 20.1 THE FEDERAL BUDGET**

Federal tax revenues as a proportion of GDP changed relatively little until the 1990s and then rose slightly. On the expenditure side, expenditures on goods and services have gradually declined over the past four decades. Transfers to persons and businesses and transfers to governments both rose significantly from the 1960s and 1970s to the the 1980s and 1990s. Interest on the federal debt began to rise quickly in the 1980s. *Source: The National Finances 1994* (Toronto, Canadian Tax Foundation), Tables 3.6 and 3.8, pp. 3.7–3.09; *Finances of the Nation 1995* ( Toronto, Canadian Tax Foundation), Tables 18.2 and 18.3, pp. 18.3–18.5.

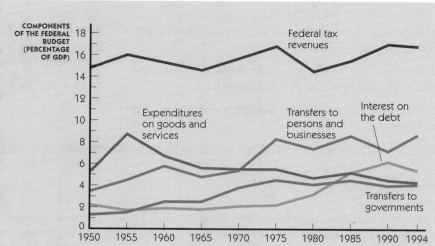

1970s, as a proportion of GDP such payments rose from 2.5 percent in 1981 to over 2.7 percent a decade later. Given the gradual aging of the population, this proportion will increase even further through the rest of the 1990s.

## HIGHER SPENDING ON UNEMPLOYMENT INSURANCE BENEFITS

The Unemployment Insurance (UI) programme was made more generous in 1970. Coverage was expanded to a wide variety of workers, and eligibility requirements for receiving benefits were eased. As long as unemployment rates remained relatively low, as they did in the 1970s, the costs of the programme were contained. But with the dramatic rise in the rate of unemployment into double-digit figures in the 1980s, expenditures on UI benefits escalated rapidly, more than tripling between 1982 and 1992. As a proportion of the federal budget, UI payments almost doubled in that decade. The Mulroney government was finally forced to act in early 1993 and announced that persons who voluntarily left

their jobs would no longer be eligible to receive UI benefits. Furthermore, the amount of benefits paid was reduced for all UI recipients except modest-income individuals with dependents.

## HIGHER TRANSFERS TO THE PROVINCES

Transfers to the provinces have always been an important component of federal expenditures. Traditionally, the federal government has made equalizing transfers to the less well off provinces (essentially all except Alberta, British Columbia, and Ontario). In the 1950s and 1960s, however, the importance of transfers to the provinces in the federal budget increased markedly with the implementation of major shared-cost programmes in the areas of health, welfare, and postsecondary education. In the early 1950s, federal transfers to the provinces amounted to under 1.5 percent of GDP. This rose to 3.2 percent by the end of the 1960s and to over 4 percent by the beginning of the 1980s. Federal transfers remained at those levels for most of the decade, despite the fact that the federal government periodically introduced measures to contain them.

## HIGHER INTEREST PAYMENTS

Like any other borrower, the federal government has to pay interest. During the 1970s, federal government interest payments were about 1.5 percent of GDP (or 12 percent of government expenditures). But from 1983 to 1990 they exceeded 4.5 percent of GDP, and by 1995 they had reached 6.3 percent of GDP and made up 30 percent of federal government expenditures. This reflected not only the increasing size of the public debt, but also the fact that interest rates soared as the Bank of Canada sought to reduce the high inflation rates that had plagued Canada in the 1980s, along with most other industrialized countries. By the 1990s, federal government revenues exceeded its **programme expenditures,** its expenditures not including interest payments on the debt; the deficit problem had become the debt problem. If the debt in 1995 were the same as it was in 1981, the federal government would be running a surplus of $11.5 billion, rather than a deficit of $37.7 billion! Through interest payments, deficits feed on themselves.

## OTHER FACTORS IN DEALING WITH THE DEFICIT

Federal tax receipts as a percentage of GDP have increased only slightly since 1981, rising from 17 percent of GDP in that year to 17.8 percent in 1992. But there is strong political resistance against increasing taxes sharply. Indeed, federal taxes fell to 16.8 percent of GDP by 1994. The Conservative government elected in 1988 took the view that deficit reduction should largely be achieved by expenditure reductions rather than tax increases, a policy that was continued by the Liberal government that succeeded it as well as by most provincial governments. Furthermore, the federal government ruled out reducing transfers to persons (which make up over one third of programme spending) as an instrument as well. This left expenditures on goods and services, transfers to businesses, and transfers to the provinces as the main potential sources of expenditure reduction.

Between 1985 and 1995, expenditures in all three of these categories fell as a percentage of GDP—goods and services, from 5.2 to 4.3 percent; transfers to business, from 2.4 to 1.9 percent; and transfers to the provinces, from 4.5 to 3.3 percent. The result was that federal government programme expenditures actually fell from 19.6 percent of GDP in 1985 to 14.8 percent by 1995.

These efforts to reduce the government deficit succeeded in reducing programme expenditures below tax revenues; the entire deficit could be accounted for by interest on the debt. The deficit control programme suffered a setback with the recession of 1991, which reduced government revenues and increased public expenditures for programmes such as UI. But even without the recession, the slightly higher taxes and decreased programme spending would still not have been enough to bring the federal government budget into balance.

Another source of budget deficit problems is the deficits of the provinces and their municipalities. Like the federal deficit, the deficits of the other levels of government have been increasing since the early 1980s. The combined deficit of all provinces and their municipalities stood at $1.3 billion in 1982. By 1995, it had risen to $20 billion, more than half the size of the federal deficit. Given that provincial expenditure responsibilities in health and education are among the most rapidly growing expenditure areas, the pressures on the expenditure side are likely to continue for some time. In any event, the use of reductions in transfers to the provinces as a way of fighting the federal deficit simply shifts the deficit problem to the provinces since they must now find the money to replace the transfers no longer received from the federal government. The provinces may be no better able to bring their deficits under control than the federal government its own.

## CONSEQUENCES OF GOVERNMENT DEFICITS

Economists have traditionally argued that government borrowing, just like individual borrowing, makes sense or does not make sense according to

## FACTORS CONTRIBUTING TO THE FEDERAL DEFICIT PROBLEM

Higher transfer payments to the elderly

Higher spending on unemployment insurance benefits

Higher transfers to the provinces

Higher interest payments

Resistance to higher taxes

The 1991 recession

the purpose for which the money is used. It makes sense to borrow to buy a house that you will live in for many years or a car that you will drive for several years. In that way, you spread out paying for the item as you use it. It makes economic sense to borrow money for an educational degree that will lead to a higher-paying job in the future. But if you are paying this year for the vacation that you took two years ago, maybe you should chop up your credit cards!

Countries are in a similar situation. Borrowing to finance a road, school, or industrial project that will be used for many years may be quite appropriate. Borrowing to pay for projects that are never completed (or perhaps were never even started) or borrowing to finance this year's government salaries poses real problems. Many governments have taken on more debt than they could comfortably pay off, forcing them to raise taxes sharply and reduce living standards. Others have simply failed to repay, jeopardizing their ability to borrow in the future.

Financing government expenditures by borrowing rather than increasing taxes results in higher levels of consumption, since disposable income is higher. But the consumption must come at the expense of something else. If the economy is at full employment, it cannot come from higher GDP. It must come either from lower investment or from lower net exports, or from a combination of both. In either case, some costs will be borne in the future.

If investment is reduced, less capital will be available to employ workers and produce output in the future, and less capital income will be generated. Economic growth and future living standards will be reduced to pay for higher present consumption. If net exports are reduced, borrowing from abroad must increase to maintain equilibrium in the balance of payments. The increase in foreign indebtedness implies that interest and principle repayments

must be made to foreigners in the future. Again, the higher present consumption made possible by government borrowing entails reduced consumption in the future. That is the opportunity cost of government borrowing.

Reducing the deficit has the opposite effect. It depresses present consumption, but results in increased investment and/or net exports. Future living standards are increased in return for a fall in current consumption.

## HOW FUTURE GENERATIONS ARE AFFECTED BY BUDGET DEFICITS

By borrowing, the government transfers the cost of its spending onto future taxpayers, both the current young and future generations, thereby allowing current taxpayers to maintain a higher level of consumption than in the absence of the borrowing. Thus, when the Canadian government partly financed the enormous costs of World War II by borrowing rather than raising taxes, it spread the burden of the war to future generations.

To see how this works, suppose the bonds the government issues are purchased by 40-year-old workers. Thirty years later, as these 40-year-olds enter retirement, the government decides to pay off the bonds by raising taxes on those who are then in the labour force. In effect, the government is transferring funds from these younger workers to those who were the workers during the war, who are now 70 and retired. Thus, part of the cost of the war is borne by the generation who entered the work force after the war. The lifetime consumption of those who were 40 during the war is little affected. They might otherwise have put their savings into stocks or bonds issued by firms; the war (to the extent that it was financed by debt, or bonds) affects the form of their savings, but not the total amount they have to spend over their lifetime.

## ALTERNATIVE PERSPECTIVES ON THE BURDEN OF PUBLIC DEBT

The notion that public debt reflects consumption benefits enjoyed by current and past generations but whose costs are passed on to future generations represents the current dominant view. But some believe that this view overstates the burden of the debt. Two different reasons are given.

### THE "DEBT DOES NOT MATTER BECAUSE WE OWE IT TO OURSELVES" ARGUMENT

It used to be argued that the fiscal deficit does not matter because we simply owe the money to ourselves. The budget deficit was compared to the effect of one brother borrowing from another on the total welfare of the family. One member of the family may be better off, another worse off, but the indebtedness does not really matter much to the family as a whole. Financing government expenditures by debt, it was argued, could lead to a transfer of resources between generations, but this transfer would still keep all the buying power in the hands of Canadian citizens.

We now recognize that this argument is wrong on three counts. First, even if we owe the money to ourselves, the debt affects investment and thus future wages and productivity, as noted.

Second, today we do not in fact owe the money to ourselves. Canada is borrowing abroad and is becoming more indebted to foreigners. The conse-

quences of the country's spending beyond its means are no different from those of a family's spending beyond its means. Eventually it has to pay the price of the consumption binge. In the case of a national consumption binge, it is future generations that have to pay the price.

Third, simply to pay interest on the debt requires high levels of taxes, and taxes introduce distortions into the economy, discouraging work and savings. (There is some disagreement among economists about the *quantitative* significance of this effect; those who advocate rapid deficit reduction typically argue that these distortionary effects are very large.)

### THE BARRO-RICARDO ARGUMENT

A more recent argument is that in the face of increased deficits, current taxpayers save more rather than increase their consumption. The American economist Robert Barro, developing an argument broached (and rejected) by David Ricardo, the great nineteenth-century British economist, contends that individuals care so much about future generations that they increase their bequests when they see their offspring faced with future indebtedness caused by government deficits. To be able to be more generous in their bequests, they increase their household savings by exactly the amount of the increase in the deficit; national savings do not change. The increased government dissaving is fully offset. This is the so-called **Ricardian equivalence hypothesis:** that households view government borrowing as equivalent to borrowing done on their behalf.

The evidence does not support the Ricardian equivalence hypothesis. Increased government deficits may lead to higher household savings, but far too little to offset those deficit increases. Figure 20.2 shows how personal savings and government deficits have varied since 1950. While there is some correla-

---

## CONSEQUENCES OF GOVERNMENT FISCAL DEFICITS

**1** Some of the burden of current expenditures is shifted to future generations directly.

**2** Issuing government bonds may decrease investment and thus make future generations worse off indirectly.

**3** Foreign indebtedness may increase, reducing future standards of living.

**4** Government dissaving has not been fully offset by private savings.

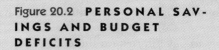

**Figure 20.2 PERSONAL SAVINGS AND BUDGET DEFICITS**

Federal budget deficits and personal savings as a percentage of GDP have varied considerably since 1950. In the 1970s and 1980s they tended to move together, but in other periods they tended to move in opposite directions. *Source:* Statistics Canada, CANSIM Database 1996, Matrixes 6693, 6702, 6705.

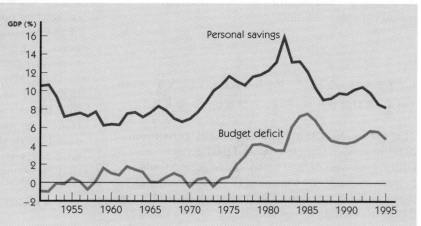

tion between budget deficits and household savings in the 1970s and early 1980s, in other years the two move in opposite directions.

## ADDRESSING THE DEFICIT PROBLEM

At one level of analysis, reducing the deficit is a simple matter: either increase taxes or reduce expenditures. Currently, public taste for tax increases appears to be limited, even for taxes on the wealthy. Consequently, discussions have focused on improving the efficiency of government or cutting back on government programmes.

All through the years that the deficit was rising, politicians were arguing that both of these should be done, and yet remarkably little progress was made until 1995. The question is, why?

### CUTTING BACK ON GOVERNMENT PROGRAMMES

When the Mulroney government ran for reelection in 1988, it was partly on a promise to eliminate the fiscal deficit over a period of time. Despite reducing pro-

gramme expenditures in everything from defence to family allowances and imposing surtaxes on higher-income Canadians, Mulroney's government met with limited success. The federal deficit as a percentage of GDP rose from 4.4 percent in 1989–90 to 6 percent in 1992–93. Understanding how government spends money helps to explain why reducing expenditures proved so difficult during the early 1990s.

Figure 20.3 breaks down federal government expenditures into different categories. Some of these expenditures cannot be cut in the short run: they are nondiscretionary. For example, the government must meet the interest obligations on the bonds it has issued to finance the deficit. In 1995–96, these soared to 30.3 percent of government expenditures. Other expenditures are for entitlement programmes like Old Age Security (OAS) and Unemployment Insurance (UI). These social insurance programmes constitute nearly a third of the budget. Given the rules for OAS, expenditures simply increase as the number of persons aged 65 and over increases. The only way to cut these expenditures is to change the rules, and this has been difficult to do.

UI expenditures could be cut back in a variety of ways, such as reducing the size of the benefit or the length of the period over which payments are made; relating benefits more closely to some measure of need, such as family income; tightening up eligibility requirements, as the Mulroney government did by

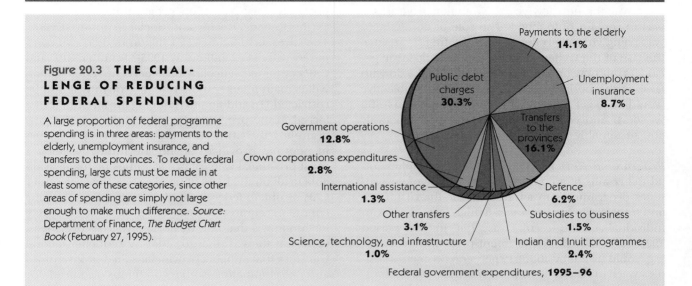

**Figure 20.3 THE CHALLENGE OF REDUCING FEDERAL SPENDING**

A large proportion of federal programme spending is in three areas: payments to the elderly, unemployment insurance, and transfers to the provinces. To reduce federal spending, large cuts must be made in at least some of these categories, since other areas of spending are simply not large enough to make much difference. *Source:* Department of Finance, *The Budget Chart Book* (February 27, 1995).

Payments to the elderly 14.1%
Unemployment insurance 8.7%
Public debt charges 30.3%
Transfers to the provinces 16.1%
Government operations 12.8%
Crown corporations expenditures 2.8%
International assistance 1.3%
Defence 6.2%
Other transfers 3.1%
Subsidies to business 1.5%
Science, technology, and infrastructure 1.0%
Indian and Inuit programmes 2.4%

Federal government expenditures, **1995–96**

making persons ineligible who quit their jobs voluntarily, or increasing the number of working weeks required before a worker becomes eligible; or making the programme more like a true insurance scheme by introducing experience-rating into the premiums (a firm's premium would vary according to its track record with layoffs). But such savings will only make a small dent in the deficit as long as unemployment rates remain high. Furthermore, politically it is very difficult to implement such changes. All of the aforementioned remedies have been advocated at one time or another in the past, yet few have been acted on.

Nor is there much more scope for cutting back on expenditures on goods and services. Government operations have been pared to the bone. The major category of these expenditures is for defence, and these have already been cut drastically at a time when the Canadian Armed Forces are being called upon to engage in an increasing number of international peacekeeping missions.

The largest single component of federal government programme expenditures is for transfer payments to the provinces. This category has already been asked to bear a disproportionate share of the costs of deficit reduction. Moreover, in a sense, such reductions by themselves do nothing to address the public-sector deficit problem; they simply transfer it from the federal government to the provinces. This will only help solve the problem if the provinces are better able to find ways to reduce the growth of expenditures than the federal government. Given that the most rapidly growing categories of expenditures, health and education, are at the provincial level, this may be possible. Most provinces have made a concerted effort to limit the growth in these expenditures, with some success.

## DEFICIT REDUCTION UNDER THE LIBERALS

When the Liberals took office in 1994, the deficit was virtually out of control. The federal debt was over 70 percent of GDP, having increased from 55 percent only four years earlier. Interest payments were eating up almost one third of tax revenues. The Chrétien government had little choice but to take drastic action. The budget of February 1995 signalled a new approach to economic management. The size of the federal government was to be scaled back dramatically over the next few years. No major programme was to remain untouched. The role of government was being virtually redefined for the first time since the rise of the welfare state in the early postwar period. From now on government would make do with less; as the budget documents put it, the objective would be to get government right so that it can fulfill its social and economic mandates more effectively and sustainably.

*Programme Review*   The 1995 budget implemented the results of a comprehensive review of government programmes in all areas other than UI, OAS, and transfers to the provinces (which were dealt with individually). The result was that in the period 1994–95 to 1997–98, department programme spending would be cut by about 19 percent. Business subsidies were to be cut by 60 percent; in nonagricultural business the cut was over 75 percent. Particularly hard hit was spending in the areas of transportation, industry, natural resources, and regional development. Even defence spending was to be reduced by 14 percent. The only department allowed to increase was Indian and Northern Affairs.

*Transfers to the Provinces*   In 1995–96, federal transfers to the provinces consisted of three main components—Equalization, $8.9 billion; Established Programme Financing (EPF), $9.2 billion; and Canada Assistance Plan (CAP), $8.0 billion. These programmes had been instituted in the 1960s and 1970s. Equalization payments went to the seven less well off provinces (all but Alberta, British Columbia, and Ontario) according to the extent to which their capacity to raise tax revenues fell below the national average. EPF was an equal per capita block grant made to all provinces to support their spending on health and postsecondary education, and was conditional on a province's maintaining comprehensive, universally available, accessible, and portable (across provinces) health insurance systems. CAP was a shared-cost programme whereby the federal government matched provincial expenditures on welfare, provided the provincial programmes were available to all in need and were portable across provinces.

Beginning in 1996–97, the EPF and CAP programmes are to be combined into a single block grant in support of provincial health, welfare, and postsecondary education programmes, referred to as the Canada Health and Social Transfer (CHST). The CHST is to fall to $11.1 billion by 1997–98, compared with $17.2 billion in 1995–96 under EPF and CAP combined, a decline of 35 percent. (Equalization will remain intact, but its rate of growth will also be restricted.) In addition to reducing the amount transferred to the provinces to support their social programmes, the CHST will have fewer strings attached in how the provinces spend the funds. No longer must provincial welfare programmes be made available to all on the basis of need as was the case under CAP, or obtain federal sanction for funding; the only condition required to make the programmes eligible for funding is that they be portable across provinces. Critics of the CHST argue that by reducing federal transfers that support provincial social programmes and by eliminating some conditions required for provinces to be eligible to receive full CHST funding, the federal government is no longer ensuring that social programmes adhere to national standards. They fear that provinces, in an effort to attract businesses from other provinces and to discourage low-income persons from residing in the province, and if left to their own devices, will compete away the social programmes that have provided economic security to Canadians regardless of where they reside.

*Unemployment Insurance*   With the 1995 budget the government announced its intent to undertake a major reform of UI to reduce its costs and also to introduce reemployment benefits to help unemployed workers get jobs. The revised system, complete with a symbolic name change to Employment Insurance (EI), was phased in beginning in July 1996. Under EI, eligibility requirements are tightened up: new entrants to the labour force and those reentering after two years' absence will require a minimum 26 weeks of work to qualify, rather than the standard 12 to 20 weeks, depending on the regional unemployment rate. Maximum weekly benefits fall by about 10 percent (from $448 to $413), except for low-income workers with dependents, and benefits will be available for up to 45 weeks instead of 50. Benefits will be reduced by up to 5 percent for frequent claimers.

There are also a number of measures intended to reduce the disincentives associated with EI.

Reemployment benefits such as wage subsidies, assistance for self-employment and partnerships, and loans and grants for improving skills are introduced. Low-income claimants can earn small amounts without decreasing their benefits. The number of hours of work rather than of weeks will count in accumulating benefits, and there can be gaps in employment. These changes will allow EI premiums to fall slightly for both employers and employees. These measures should improve the flexibility of the labour market, and the government will save $.7 billion in 1996–97 and similar amounts thereafter.

***Transfers to the Elderly*** The current system of transfers consists of a universal payment under the OAS to all persons aged 65 and over, plus a Guaranteed Income Supplement (GIS) payment to the low-income elderly (based on family income). The income tax system also includes a number of measures that affect the elderly: tax credits for persons 65 and over, tax credits on pension income, a graduated elimination of OAS benefits for higher-income recipients, and tax assistance for retirement savings through company pensions (RPPs) and individual accounts (RRSPs). All these are to be affected by deficit-induced reforms. The OAS/GIS transfers as well as the age and pension income tax credits and the OAS clawback will all be eliminated and replaced by a new Seniors Benefit to take effect beginning in 2001 and to apply to those who were under 60 years of age in 1995. The Seniors Benefit will be paid to persons aged 65 and over depending upon their family income; singles with income below $52,000 and couples with combined incomes below $78,000 will receive some payment, depending on the size of their income. The benefits will be tax-free and fully indexed to inflation. The idea of the Seniors Benefit is to target transfers to the elderly who are most in need so as to make better use of a more limited amount of funds. It will also serve to relieve the pressure on the system that is bound to occur as the proportion of the population that is elderly increases. The combination of longer life expectancy and lower birthrates means that the proportion of the population over 65 will rise from 12 percent in 1995 to 23 percent in 2030.

In addition to this major structural change in the system of transfers to the elderly, other elements of the retirement income system will also change. As part of the deficit-reduction package of the 1995 budget, the amounts that could be deducted from income for RRSPs and RPPs were restricted. The federal government along with the provincial governments also launched a major review of the other element of pensions, the Canada Pension Plan. We return to that programme later in this chapter.

***Tax Measures*** Almost all of the burden of deficit reduction was put on cutting expenditures rather than increasing taxes. Between 1995 and 1998, expenditures will fall by about seven times as much as taxes will rise. Tax rates applicable to corporations, especially large ones, and financial institutions will rise by a small amount, and excise taxes on tobacco and gasoline will also increase. At the same time, various measures will be introduced to strengthen Revenue Canada's ability to enforce the tax laws and to eliminate various tax shelters.

This package of stringent measures is meant to provide a start in the long-run process of bringing the deficit and debt under control. The deficit/GDP ratio

FEDERAL DEFICIT-REDUCTION MEASURES, 1995–98

Programme review: Cuts in departmental spending and business subsidies

Transfers to the provinces: Merge EPF and CAP into the Canada Health and Social Transfer and reduce the amounts transferred

Employment insurance: Reduce benefits, tighten eligibility, reduce disincentives to seek employment

Transfers to the elderly: Replace OAS/GIS with the Seniors Benefit, targeted to those most in need

Tax changes: Small increases in taxes combined with measures to make the tax system fairer and better enforced

During the 1980s, the annual federal budget deficit hovered in the range of $20 billion to $29 billion. This caused the federal public debt to rise much more rapidly than GDP. Debt as a percentage of GDP rose roughly from 20 percent to 60 percent. Eventually, the debt/GDP ratio would have stabilized at some higher level, had the budget deficit stayed in the same range. However, as the stock of debt rises, maintaining the same size of deficit becomes more difficult, because the cost of servicing the debt rises as well. Interest on the debt rose from $5.6 billion, or 13 percent of government spending, in 1978 to $42 billion, or 26 percent of government spending, in 1995.

Governments can maintain different debt/GDP ratios over the long run. But different debt/GDP ratios impose quite different obligations on government budgets. To see the orders of magnitude involved, consider an economy that grows at an average annual rate of 3 percent, that faces an average interest rate of 8 percent, and that spends 30 percent of its GDP on government programmes. If the debt/GDP ratio is constant, debt will also grow at 3 percent annually. If debt is $B$, this implies that the annual change in debt, which is simply the deficit, is $\Delta B = .03 \times B$. If the debt/GDP ratio ($B/Y$) is .2, the deficit must be .6 percent of GDP ($.03 \times .2 \times 100\%$). Moreover, the interest on the debt must be 8 percent of $B$, or 1.6 percent of GDP ($8 \times .2$). Thus, the interest on the debt is larger than the size of the deficit, implying that the federal government must be running a structural surplus, that is, collecting more taxes than it spends on programmes. The structural surplus is 1 percent of GDP ($1.6 - .6$). Finally, since programme spending is 30 percent of GDP, total government spending on programmes and interest is 31.6 percent of GDP ($30 + 1.6$). Interest payments make up 5 percent of government spending ($1.6/31.6 \times 100\%$). These numbers are summarized in the following table alongside similar calculations for the case in which the debt/GDP ratio is 60 percent.

| | Debt/GDP Ratio 20% | 60% |
|---|---|---|
| Deficit as a percentage of GDP | .6 | 1.8 |
| Interest as a percentage of GDP | 1.6 | 4.8 |
| Structural surplus as a percentage of GDP | 1.0 | 3.0 |
| Interest as a percentage of government spending | 5.0 | 13.8 |

If GDP is $800 billion, a debt/GDP ratio of .2 implies a budget deficit of $4.8 billion with interest payments of $12.8 billion; a debt/GDP ratio of .6 implies a deficit of $14.4 billion and interest payments of $38.4 billion. It is easy to see why budget deficits in the range of $20 billion to $29 billion in the 1980s caused the debt/GDP ratio to rise so rapidly in a short period of time. It is also clear that simply stabilizing the ratio of debt to GDP at the relatively high level of .6 requires significant deficit cutting.

is to decline abruptly to 3 percent by fiscal year 1996–97, the lowest level since the mid-1970s. The debt/GDP ratio, which has risen steadily since 1980, will finally begin to decline after 1996–97. At the same time, the face of government in Canada will have changed considerably. Programme spending will fall to about 13 percent of GDP by 1996–97, its lowest level since 1950–51. The kinds of services that the federal government provides will be much more limited than before, and those that are provided will more often be charged to the user. The government will get out of the business of providing many goods and services that it reckons the private sector can do better, such as in the transportation area. Transfers to persons will be much more selective to those in need, and transfers to business will be cut back drastically. The federal government will play a much smaller role in financing the social programmes delivered by the provinces. The responsibility for designing, delivering, and financing health, welfare, and postsecondary education programmes will lie much more with the provinces. The imperative of deficit reduction will have served to change significantly what Canadians can expect from their government.

## PUBLIC PENSIONS AS INTERGENERATIONAL TRANSFERS

The accumulation of public debt to be repaid by future generations of taxpayers is not the only form of intergenerational transfer resulting from government policy. Even if governments maintained balanced budgets, their spending and taxing policies would benefit some generations relative to others. Many government expenditure policies favour people of particular ages. The education system favours the young; the health care system favours especially the old; measures to clean up the environment favour future generations. Since most tax revenues come from the working-age population, the combined tax and expenditure policies of the government involve a mix of transfers from those of working age to the old, to the young, and to future generations.

In principle, one could calculate which generations gain on balance and which ones lose as a result of government policies. Such a calculation is referred to as **generational accounting,** an example of which is discussed in the Close-up on page 436. Generational accounting is a fairly recent innovation, but one that could prove to be extremely useful to policy makers. By informing them of which generations systematically gain and which lose as a result of tax and expenditure policies, those policies can be modified so that accepted norms of intergenerational fairness are served. Generational accounting can also be used to infer how major demographic trends impose burdens on particular age cohorts. For example, it can

be used to indicate the fiscal consequences of the aging of the large baby boom generation, born in the early postwar period. As this population bulge approaches retirement age, what burden will it impose on the smaller working-age population as a result of the intergenerational transfers from the working to the retired population that are built into government expenditure policies?

We focus on one such programme in this section, the system of income transfers to the elderly, or public pensions. Public pensions constitute one of the largest components of intergenerational transfers from the young to the old in Canada. On the basis of projected trends in life expectancy and fertility, it has been predicted that by 2030 there will be only about three workers for every retired person in the population, compared with five in 1995. As the proportion of the population that is retired rises, policy makers must decide how to deal with the increasing burden that the existing system of transfers to the retired would impose on the succeeding, smaller generation of workers.

### THE CANADIAN SYSTEM OF TRANSFERS TO THE ELDERLY

Transfers to the elderly are part of a more general set of federal government policies designed to ensure that the retired have adequate incomes to support them when they have finished working. The system is based on the so-called **three pillars,** a combination found in many industrialized countries.

One pillar, constituting about 30 percent of pension income in Canada, is a set of transfers to the elderly intended to ensure that they have enough income to satisfy their basic economic needs. In Canada, as we have seen, this has consisted of Old Age Security (OAS), an equal per capita transfer payment made to all persons aged 65 and over, supplemented by the Guaranteed Income Supplement (GIS), paid only to those whose income from other sources, including pensions, is low. Like other components of government redistributive policy, OAS and GIS are financed out of general tax revenues. In 1996, the OAS was $4,760 per year. It is both taxable and subject to clawback through the tax system for persons with higher family incomes. The GIS payment is

## Close-up: Generational Accounting—Measuring Intergenerational Transfers

It is clear that many government programmes and policies, including the accumulation of government debt and the existence of unfunded public pensions, involve transfers among different generations. But what is the magnitude of these transfers? Recently, a procedure called generational accounting has been devised to find an answer to this question.

Generational accounting is based on understanding the government's "intertemporal budget constraint," that is, the requirement that all expenditures must eventually be paid for. The idea is that government expenditures need not be paid for by taxes as they are incurred; they can be postponed and paid for by borrowing. In the case where borrowing is used, the amount borrowed corresponds to the present value of the future taxes that must be raised to cover the amount borrowed plus interest. This implies that the sum of government expenditures undertaken this year must be covered by taxes now or in the future whose present value equals the expenditures. The same applies to expenditures undertaken next year, the year after, and so on. The intertemporal budget constraint involves summing up all current and future expenditures discounted to the present plus the current stock of public debt (which must also be paid by future taxes) and setting that equal to the taxes needed to finance them. The intertemporal budget constraint can be written as

present value of all current and future government purchases of goods and services

+ present value of all current and future transfers paid to all living and future generations

+ value of government debt as of now

= present value of current and future taxes paid by all living and future generations.

The left-hand side represents the present value of everything that must eventually be paid for—expenditures on goods and services, transfer payments, and the amount of debt that has been accumulated in the past. The right-hand side is the present value of all the taxes that must be raised to pay for these obligations.

This expression can be rearranged in a useful way by taking the term involving transfers to the right-hand side and referring to *net taxes* as taxes minus transfers. Then by distinguishing between living and future generations, the intertemporal budget constraint becomes

present value of all current and future government purchases of goods and services

+ value of government debt as of now

= present value of net taxes paid by all living generations

+ present value of net taxes paid by all future generations.

If the present value of expenditures on goods and services remains unchanged, any decrease in net taxes paid by generations currently alive must be made up by increases in net taxes on future generations, and vice versa.

By making assumptions about productivity growth rates, population projections, and the future paths of government taxation, transfer, and spending programmes, one can calculate the stream of future net taxes that will have to be paid by each age cohort in the living generations. So, for example, the present value of all future net taxes of persons currently aged 45 can be calculated. If that is done for persons of all different ages currently alive, the sum across all such age groups yields the first term on the right-hand side of the above expression. One can then infer the net taxes for future generations, the amount sufficient to balance the intertemporal budget constraint.

These calculations have recently been done for Canada by Philip Oreopoulos of the Institute for Research on Public Policy and Lawrence Kotlikoff of Boston University. Using 1994 data, and assuming that expenditures on goods and services grow at the same rate as productivity, they calculate that the present value of future taxes is positive for men aged 0 to 55 and women aged 0 to 50 in 1994. It reaches a maximum of $290,100 for men aged 25 and $135,400 for women aged 25. The present value of future net-tax payments is negative for persons older than these ages in 1994. These results should not be surprising. Those who are older have already paid the bulk of their lifetime taxes and are now set to collect many of the transfers that primarily go to the elderly, especially public pensions and Old Age Security. What is more revealing is to compare those who are just born with those who will be born in the future. For men, newborns in 1994 will pay net taxes over their entire lifetimes with a present value of $131,200. Members of future generations will pay $267,900 over their lifetimes, a difference of 104.2 percent. For women, the comparable numbers are $56,700 and $115,800.

Another way to look at this is to calculate what proportion of lifetime income would have to be paid as taxes by members of different generations. For those born in 1994, Oreopoulos and Kotlikoff find that 32.4 percent of lifetime income would have to be paid in taxes. For those born later than that, the average lifetime tax rate is 64.9 percent, more than twice as high. These figures reflect a significant imbalance of tax obligations in favour of current generations at the expense of future ones. Moreover, an imbalance continues to exist even if the growth rates of government expenditures are much slower than the rate of productivity growth.

Generational accounting brings out into the open what choices are available. To avoid encumbering future generations with significantly higher lifetime tax obligations, some fairly stringent measures would have to be undertaken involving some combination of tax increases, transfer cuts, or reductions in government expenditures. And the longer the delay before acting, the more stringent the changes would have to be. Whether the changes would be politically palatable to current voters remains to be seen.

*Source:* P. Oreopoulos and L. J. Kotlikoff, "Restoring Generational Balance in Canada," *IRPP Choices, Public Finance,* vol. 2, No. 1, February, 1996.

based on family income. The maximum GIS payment an individual can receive on top of OAS is $5,660.

As discussed above, beginning in 2001, the OAS/GIS programme will be replaced by the Seniors Benefit, a transfer to the elderly geared entirely to family income. The maximum benefit for single seniors with no income will be $11,420, about $120 higher than the maximum combined OAS/GIS. But it will fall off as income increases, especially rapidly beyond incomes of $30,000. By restricting payments only to those in need, the cost to the federal treasury can be contained despite the burgeoning growth in the elderly population. This completes the transition from what was originally a universal pension payable in equal amount to all persons 65 and over to one that is completely targeted to those with lower family incomes.

The second pillar, constituting another 30 percent, is the compulsory contributory pension plan that all employed Canadians must participate in. In all provinces but Quebec, this is the Canada Pension Plan (CPP). Quebec workers are subject to the Quebec Pension Plan (QPP), whose structure is similar to that in the rest of Canada. The CPP and QPP ensure that working Canadians have a minimal amount of income to replace their earnings from employment after they retire. The contribution rate in 1996 was 5.6 percent of pensionable earnings (earnings between $3,500 and $35,400 per year), and is paid in equal amounts by employers and their employees. The size of pensionable earnings, which rises each year at the rate of growth of average wages, determines the size of pension payments. For person retiring in 1996, the CPP provides pension benefits of $8,725 per year for those who contributed the maximum; the benefit is then fully indexed to inflation. CPP benefits also include a supplementary benefit to surviving spouses, orphans, and disabled contributors and their dependents, and there is a lump-sum death benefit, paid to survivors of CPP recipients.

The significant feature to note about the CPP and QPP systems is that they are not fully funded. Contributions by current and past workers to CPP and QPP go into a fund, which is drawn on to pay benefits. But the money in the fund is not sufficient to finance the future benefits of those who have contributed. As the proportion of the population that is retired increases, the fund will dwindle to nothing and benefits will have to be paid by those then working. Since there will be a relatively small number of workers supporting a large number of retirees, the contribution rates will have to rise dramatically to maintain the existing level of benefits.

Figure 20.4 shows the extent to which past contributions are insufficient to pay for the benefits that have been promised to those who have retired or will retire in the future. The figure compares the **unfunded liabilities** of the CPP—the current value of future CPP obligations to pay for all the benefits that have been promised by the plan—with the size of the federal debt for three recent years. This unfunded liability is the amount that future taxpayers would have to pay in order to make good all the benefits that have accumulated to date and that cannot be covered by the CPP fund that does exist. It is analogous to the national debt, which also shows the taxes that must be raised in the future to pay for the accumulated federal debt. The size of the unfunded liability in 1995

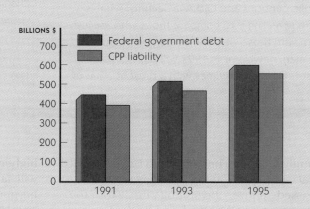

**Figure 20.4 UNFUNDED CPP LIABILITIES AND THE NATIONAL DEBT**

The federal government debt has risen from $445 billion in 1991 to $600 billion in 1995. At the same time the size of CPP unfunded liabilities, the current value of all future pension obligations not covered by the CPP fund, has risen from $390 billion to $556 billion. *Sources:* Statistics Canada, CANSIM Database 1996, Label D469409; *An Information Paper for Consultations on the Canada Pension Plan,* released by the Federal, Provincial and Territorial Governments of Canada (Ottawa: Department of Finance, February 1996).

THE THREE PILLARS OF THE PENSION SYSTEM

OAS/GIS: Basic retirement income support for the elderly financed out of general revenues

CPP/QPP: Contributory public pension scheme for the employed to provide partial replacement income when retired

RPP/RRSPs: Tax-sheltered savings for retirement to supplement income provided by public pensions

was $556 billion, comparable to the national debt of $600 billion—and growing as rapidly. If one were to include the QPP, the unfunded CPP/QPP liability combined would far exceed the size of the national debt. Another way to look at the emerging financial problem with CPP is to project how much the contribution rate would have to rise in order to pay for future CPP benefits under the existing system. The current contribution rate of 5.6 percent of pensionable earnings, which itself has risen gradually from 3.6 percent in 1966, would have to increase to 14.2 percent in 2030. What could or should be done about this is a topic we will return to shortly.

The third pillar is the system of private pension plans that individuals participate in to provide their own income for retirement over and above what is provided by the two public pillars. It accounts for the remaining 40 percent of pension income. Private pension savings take two forms. Some private pensions are provided by firms to their employees as part of the package of benefits of employment. These company pensions are called Registered Pension Plans (RPPs). Alternatively, persons can accumulate savings for retirement individually through Registered Retirement Savings Plans (RRSPs). These are particularly helpful for the self-employed, for those working in small firms that do not offer pension plans, or for part-time workers.

The reason why RPPs and RRSPs are included as one of the pillars of government policy is that they are encouraged by the tax system. Contributions to RPPs and RRSPs up to an allowable limit are fully deducted from income before taxes are applied. Their invested returns are then allowed to accumulate tax-free until retirement, and are only taxed as they are taken out in retirement.[1] The fact that they are allowed to accu-

mulate tax-free means that they are "sheltered" from income tax and are therefore treated preferentially relative to other forms of savings, which are neither deducted from income when saved nor allowed to accumulate tax-free. The limit for yearly RRSP and RPP contributions is $13,500 in 1996, but will rise to $15,500 by 1998. Of course, persons are free to save additional amounts over and above that for their own retirement, but such savings are not eligible for tax-free status. Any interest, dividends, or capital gains earned on such saving is taxed as income.

The arguments for sheltering savings for retirement from taxation are twofold. First, if current income is not consumed now but is saved only for retirement, the saver is not currently benefiting from the income. It is argued by some that it is fairer to tax a person according to the benefits they receive from their income rather than from the income itself. They say that people should be taxed according to what they "take out of the social pot" (what they consume) rather than what they "put into the social pot" (what income they obtain from their productive efforts). Taxing retirement savings only when they are used for consumption achieves this. Second, by encouraging people to save more for their own retirement, the retired will have more funds to support themselves and there will be less need for government support through the first pillar.

## POLICY PROBLEMS AND OPTIONS

The existing three-pillar system of pensions has been in place since the mid-1960s with relatively little change, and there is growing concern that it is no longer suitable for today's circumstances. For one thing, as the population ages, the cost of these

---

[1] In the case of RRSPs, individuals have the option of taking funds out before retirement. But if they do so, the funds taken out are taxable.

programmes rises rapidly. Given the fiscal constraint that governments are facing as a result of the large public debt that has accumulated, it is natural to look to large expenditure items such as transfers to the elderly for savings. For another thing, the first two pillars of the system are not fully funded. This has two adverse consequences. First, it implies that substantial transfers are being made from the young, whose tax payments finance the transfers, to the elderly, who receive the transfers. As the number of old relative to young rises, this imposes an unfair burden on the young. This burden is compounded by the fact that the young face considerable difficulties breaking into a job market in which the large cohort of old persons hold the top, best-paying jobs.

The second adverse consequence of the lack of funding is that it tends to depress the savings rate. Contributions to the CPP or QPP that could otherwise have been saved for retirement and have found their way onto capital markets are instead used to pay for the retirement consumption of the old. The lower amount of savings by Canadians reduces the funds available for investment, at least some of which would have taken place in Canada. Lower investment means less capital available to employ workers, lower growth rates, and probably less opportunity for enhancing productivity growth by the discovery and use of new techniques of production.

For these reasons, pension reform is an item high up on the policy agenda, not only in Canada but in many other industrialized economies as well, including especially the United States. In considering the reform options, it is again worth focusing on the three pillars.

### BASIC INCOME SUPPORT FOR THE ELDERLY IN NEED

Reform of the first pillar, that which provides a basic amount of income support to those 65 and over out of general tax revenues, is well under way. The OAS/GIS system combined a universal transfer programme paying the same amount to all elderly persons (OAS) with a supplemental payment to those of low income that gradually fell in size as income rose above a floor amount. The problem with this system, as with any universal transfer system, is that it made the same basic OAS transfer to all persons whether they were needy or not. The size of the transfer could be reduced, and the payment to those most in need enhanced, by better targeting the payments to those elderly with little or no income of their own.

The proposed Seniors Benefit outlined above does precisely that. It increases the benefits to those with the lowest incomes, and gradually eliminates them as income rises. In the process, the total cost of the programme declines. This new system is not actually scheduled to take effect until 2001. The transition period between the announcement and the implementation is intended to enable future retirees that are still under 60 to adjust to the new system. If the new programme were implemented immediately, those who are now about to retire would not have the opportunity to save to make up for the sudden reduction in their retirement income. They will therefore be protected from any adverse effects of the new system.

### CONTRIBUTORY PUBLIC PENSION TO REPLACE EMPLOYMENT EARNINGS IN RETIREMENT

Most of the concern with reform focuses on the second pillar of the system involving CPP and QPP. As we have seen, the CPP/QPP system is not fully funded. The unfunded liabilities of the CPP system amounted to $556 billion in 1995, roughly equivalent to the national debt. Moreover, the ratio of retired to working population is expected to continue to grow dramatically; so too will the burden imposed on future workers to make good on the pension expectations of the large cohort of retirees. If no policy action is taken, future working generations will be faced with enormous obligations to pay the CPP or QPP pension benefits that the retired will expect to receive on the basis of the current plan.

How can this problem be avoided? A number of options have been proposed, but they are all variants on one of two main alternatives. One is to fix the CPP/QPP system by building up the fund and seeing that it is invested wisely. The other is to phase out the system entirely and rely on some other means for ensuring that workers have enough replacement income available in retirement. Let us consider these in turn.

Building up the CPP (or QPP) fund implies either

increasing contributions, reducing benefits, or some combination of the two. Benefits could be reduced in a number of different ways. The proportion of earnings replaced by pension benefits could be reduced. The age of full eligibility could be increased over 65. Or some of the ancillary programmes, such as disability benefits, the death benefit, or spousal benefits, could be cut either totally or in part. Which of these routes is taken depends on the extent to which policy makers view the CPP as a programme of retirement savings that ought to be based on actuarial principles. Actuarial principles require that the amount each person contributes over her working life is just sufficient to finance what she expects to receive in benefits during retirement, so that each type of contribution stands on its own financial feet. If actuarial principles are followed, there would be a fund of past contributions just sufficient in size to cover future benefits. The existing programme is not only unfunded but also contains some elements whose relative cost is not reflected in the contribution rate. For example, all contributors pay the same rate regardless of whether they have spouses or have a high chance of drawing disability benefits. Thus, the programme is partly one of social insurance rather than being a pure pension system.

Contribution rates could be increased in different ways to build up the fund. The employer or employee contribution rate could rise, or the cutoff level of income could be increased to get more financing from higher income earners. Both of these options—increasing contribution rates or decreasing benefits—will serve to build up the fund and in so doing will relieve the future young of what would otherwise be an enormous financial burden.

Building up the fund is only part of the solution. Full benefits of the fund will only be achieved if the fund is invested wisely in the capital market. The fund that currently exists to finance part of future CPP benefits is not so invested. Instead it is lent to the provinces at interest rates that are lower than could be achieved by sound financial management. In addition to the fact that investment returns are not maximized, it is argued that easy access to loans from the CPP fund makes provinces more inclined to use it to increase their current spending. The larger the rate of return the funds earned on capital markets, the smaller the size contributions would have to be in order to cover

future CPP benefits fully. Some have suggested that this can best be done by having the fund managed by the private sector, since the government has no particular expertise at financial management.

The alternative to reforming the CPP/QPP system by building up the funding is to do the opposite—phase the system out by ceasing to build up future obligations. Those who would advocate abolishing the CPP and QPP argue that no amount of reform will bind future governments to behave so as to maintain a reasonable fund. That would involve behaving with much more foresight and with a longer planning horizon than recent governments have done. These people argue that governments that have to be reelected periodically are unlikely to have longer-term outcomes always in mind. After all, aren't governments responsible for the massive buildup in unfunded liabilities as well as the public debt that are the sources of the current problem? And, isn't it the case that no government in an industrialized country has succeeded in maintaining a funded public pension plan?

As attractive as abolishing CPP and QPP might be from the point of view of avoiding problems caused by lack of long-term planning by the government, such a drastic move would also be faced with some transitional problems. The main one would be what to do with the existing unfunded liabilities, which are promises that have been made to past contributors. It would presumably be necessary for the government to retain whatever obligation it feels is justified towards persons who have contributed in the past.

And if CPP were phased out, how would one ensure that people have enough replacement income available to live on when they leave the labour force? One answer might be that workers should be responsible for saving for their own retirement. The problem is that evidence and past experience suggests that, for whatever reason, most people simply do not set aside enough for their own retirement. Perhaps they are too myopic, or perhaps they know that if they do not save for retirement, government will provide for them. Either way, with too little set aside for retirement, government will have little choice but to come to these people's rescue. For this reason, it is widely accepted that government has some role in ensuring that workers save something

When the Canada Pension Plan was begun in 1966, contribution rates were 3.6 percent of pensionable earnings and were projected to rise to 5.5 percent by the year 2030. That rate was surpassed in 1996 and is now currently projected to rise to 14.2 percent. How could planners be out by a factor of almost three?

One reason is demographics. People are living longer; on average, benefits will be paid out for 4.5 years longer than in 1966. Also, the birthrate has fallen since 1966 following the baby boom in the twenty years before that. There will be far fewer workers to support each retired person when the baby boomers start to retire. This accounts for 2.6 percentage points of the rise in the projected contribution rate.

Another reason is changes in economic conditions. The rate of growth in incomes has slowed considerably as both the labour force and per capita incomes have grown less rapidly than was expected in 1966. Wages and salaries grew at the average annual rate of 5.1 percent in the 1960s, but were stagnant in the early 1990s. At the same time real interest rates have almost doubled, rising from 2.4 percent to 4.6 percent over the same period. This makes the opportunity cost of not having an adequate CPP fund higher. About 2.2 percentage points of the increased contribution rate is due to economic factors.

Yet another reason is the improvement in benefits enacted over the years: CPP benefits were fully indexed in 1975; survivor benefits were extended to widowers instead of just widows; earnings tests for retirees were eliminated; a

child-rearing dropout provision was added; disability benefits were enhanced and eligibility requirements were relaxed. This accounts for the remaining 3.9 percentage points of the rise in the projected contribution rate.

What are the policy options? A recent study undertaken jointly by the federal, provincial, and territorial governments (excluding Quebec, which runs the QPP alongside CPP) outlined ways of keeping future contribution rates from rising to 14.2 percent, as projected under the current system, by building up a fund through combinations of higher contributions and lower benefits and investing it more wisely. Various scenarios were presented in which CPP rates could be increased quickly—over a six-to-eight-year period—to a higher level, which would be a "steady-state" contribution rate that could be maintained indefinitely. This would entail accumulating a fund equal to about six years of future benefits which, when well invested, could support enough of the benefits to enable contribution rates to fall.

The table below illustrates some of the options available. If benefits were left unchanged, but contribution rates were to increase quickly, a fund could be built up that would allow the steady-state contribution rate to be held to 12.2 percent rather than 14.2 percent, as under the current unfunded financing regime. If the overall cost of benefits were reduced by 7 percent, the steady-state contribution rate could fall to 11.3 percent, while if benefits were reduced by 15 percent, the contribution rate could fall to 10.3 percent. Deciding among these options is obviously difficult, especially since any reduction in

| Benefit scenario | Steady-state contribution rate (percent of pensionable earnings) |
| --- | --- |
| Existing benefits | 12.2% |
| 7 percent benefit reduction | 11.3% |
| 10 percent benefit reduction | 10.9% |
| 15 percent benefit reduction | 10.3% |

Source: An Information Paper for Consultations on the Canada Pension Plan, released by the Federal, Provincial and Territorial Governments of Canada (Ottawa: Department of Finance, February 1996).

benefits must entail some provisions becoming less generous. But not deciding could be more costly, since these figures depend upon changes being instituted beginning in 1997.

for their own retirement. If a public pension system like the CPP is not used, the alternative is to make individual saving for retirement mandatory. The most likely way of doing this is to mandate employers to provide pension schemes for their employees. While this is a feasible alternative to a public plan, it does impose a burden on the private sector, especially on small employers and on sectors with high labour force turnover. Moreover, it has the potential for reducing the flexibility of the labour market and reducing the incentive of firms to take on employees.

## TAX SHELTERING OF RETIREMENT SAVINGS

The third pillar of the retirement income system is the system of personal pensions either provided by employers (RPPs) or contributed to individually (RRSPs). In most industrialized countries, RPPs and RRSPs are sheltered from taxation in the sense that they are allowed to accumulate free of tax until they are taken out in retirement. As mentioned, support for this form of tax sheltering is based on two arguments. For one, since private pension savings are meant to provide consumption benefits only in retirement, it is argued that it is fairer to tax them according to what they pay out at that time rather than taxing them before they are used. Second, if persons

are encouraged to save more for their own retirement, they will be less reliant on the government. Moreover, increasing the savings rate is itself a worthy objective, since it makes more funds available to finance investment and so encourages growth, job creation, and productivity improvements. So it is worth providing an incentive for retirement savings.

While many economists are satisfied that the current system meets both these objectives, others argue that the tax treatment of RPPs and RRSPs is unfair. Because it relies on a person's being able to deduct pension contributions from income for tax purposes, it provides more benefits to higher-income persons; not only are they in a position to save more and obtain higher deductions, but also since they are in a higher tax bracket, each dollar deducted from taxable income saves more in taxes. Supporters respond that this emphasis on the redistributive effects of RPP/RRSP contributions is misplaced. If consumption really is a fair base for taxation, then allowing deductions for retirement savings is a suitable way to ensure that it is consumption that is actually taxed. If one is worried about redistribution, the appropriate response is to increase the steepness of the income tax rate structure rather than focus on what enters the tax base. On the other hand, if the intent of the tax assistance is to encourage saving for retirement by those who would otherwise end up relying on government support, providing higher rather than lower incentives to low-income persons might be preferred. Higher-income persons hardly need an incentive to save enough for their own retirement: their retirement savings don't compete with current financial needs. While the debate goes on, the government seems for now to have accepted the principle of allowing RPPs and RRSPs to be deductible from income.

## REVIEW AND PRACTICE

### SUMMARY

**1** The early 1980s were marked by a surge in the size of federal budget deficits. There appear to be five main causes of the increase: higher transfer payments to the elderly, higher spending on unemployment insurance, higher transfers to the provinces, higher interest rates, and resistance to higher taxes.

**2** Government borrowing can be an economic burden for future generations in several ways. First, future generations have to bear the burden of paying off debt left to them. Second, government borrowing can crowd out investment, which will reduce future output and wages. Third, when the money is borrowed from foreign investors, Canadians as a whole must pay some of their national income each year to foreigners, resulting in lower living standards. The current generation may mitigate the effects of the deficit by saving more and passing more wealth on to its heirs.

**3** Reducing the federal budget deficit has proved to be politically difficult. Two thirds of federal spending goes to transfers to individuals, transfers to provinces, and interest payments. Without tax increases or large cuts in these areas, the deficit cannot easily be reduced.

**4** The federal government initiated a major reduction in all categories of government spending beginning in 1995. Expenditures by government departments were reduced by 19 percent over three years; transfers to the provinces for health, welfare, and postsecondary education were consolidated into the Canada Health and Social Transfer and cut in size; Unemployment Insurance was renamed Employment Insurance, benefits were reduced, and the system was made more flexible; and it was announced that transfers to the elderly would be replaced by the Seniors Benefit and eligibility would be determined by full income testing.

**5** Public pensions and other programmes represent intergenerational transfers of comparable magnitude to the federal debt.

**6** The retirement income system consists of three pillars: basic income support for the elderly (OAS and GIS), an occupational pension to replace earnings lost by retirement, and tax assistance for retirement savings (RPPs and RRSPs).

**7** Because of the aging of the population and reduced economic growth, the unfunded liabilities of the CPP have increased rapidly. To prevent contributions from rising to high levels, a fund could be built up by increasing contributions and possibly reducing benefits in the near future.

### KEY TERMS

programme expenditures

generational accounting

three pillars

unfunded liabilities

Ricardian equivalence hypothesis

## REVIEW QUESTIONS

**1** What happened to the size of the budget deficits in the 1980s? Had there ever been such large deficits in peacetime?

**2** Name five factors contributing to the large budget deficits of the 1980s.

**3** What is the relationship between the deficits and the federal government debt?

**4** What are the consequences of an increased deficit in a closed economy? in an open economy? How can borrowing from abroad affect future generations for the better? How can it affect future generations for the worse?

**5** What is the argument that "the debt doesn't matter, since we owe it to ourselves"? What is wrong with this argument?

**6** Since it is politically or legally difficult to cut transfers to the elderly, unemployment insurance, and interest payments, why can't federal spending be cut substantially by focusing on all other government programmes?

**7** In what sense is the unfunded liability of the Canada Pension Plan equivalent to federal government debt?

**8** What is the reason for the predicted rise in CPP contribution rates and how can it be avoided?

## PROBLEMS

**1** Canadian foreign indebtedness is comparable to that of Mexico. But does this necessarily mean that Canada has a similar debt problem as Mexico? Why or why not? Can you think of a situation in which an individual with debts of larger value than another individual may actually have less of a debt problem?

**2** True or false: "Government borrowing can transfer resources from future generations to the present, but it cannot affect the overall wealth of the country." Discuss.

**3** Suppose a certain country has private savings of 6 percent of GDP, foreign borrowing of 1 percent of GDP, and a balanced budget. What is its level of investment? If the budget deficit is 1.5 percent of GDP, how does your answer change?

**4** Imagine that a nation's budget deficit increases while its foreign borrowing remains unchanged. What factors would you expect to change in this situation?

**5** Explain how reducing the budget deficit would contribute to long-term growth, using the savings-investment identity.

**6** If the federal government cuts transfers to the provinces, explain whether this will affect the deficit of the public sector of all levels of government combined.

**7** Put yourself in the place of the minister of finance. How would your deficit-reduction measures differ from those that recent governments have enacted?

# CHAPTER 21

# TRADE POLICY

Go into any trendy clothing store and look at the labels: some items are made in Canada and others come from the United States, but many others come from Hong Kong, Malaysia, China, Taiwan, India . . . Today more than ever, Canadians enjoy products from around the world, and those in other countries eat pasta made from Prairie wheat, travel in Bombardier commuter trains, and listen to Bryan Adams or Céline Dion.

In Chapter 3 we saw that there are gains to be had by all countries when they produce and trade according to their comparative advantage. But in spite of the gains from trade, countries have imposed a variety of barriers to trade. In recent years, Canada has worked with other countries both bilaterally and multilaterally to lower these barriers to trade. This chapter explores both the barriers to trade and the major initiatives to remove them.

**1** Why and how do countries erect barriers to trade?

**2** What is meant by fair trade laws? What is dumping, and why are economists often critical of anti-dumping laws?

**3** Why are government subsidies to industries considered a barrier to trade? To what extent do countervailing duties correct this problem?

**4** Why is protection so popular? Who are the winners and losers from free trade?

**5** What is the GATT? The WTO? What is NAFTA?

## COMMERCIAL POLICY

Countries that have *no* barriers to trade are said to practice **free trade,** but virtually all countries engage in some form of **protection:** in one way or another they restrict the importation of goods. Policies directed at affecting either imports or exports are referred to as **commercial policies.** This section considers the forms trade barriers take, their economic costs, and their economic and political rationales. The next section explores international attempts to reduce these trade barriers.

There are three major categories of trade barriers—tariffs, export subsidies, and nontariff barriers. The latter includes quotas, voluntary export restraints, and penalties that are imposed on foreign firms for allegedly engaging in unfair trading practices but that often actually serve to impede trade rather than promote fair trade.

### TARIFFS

A tariff is simply a tax on imports. Since it is a tax imposed only on foreign goods, it puts the foreign goods at a disadvantage. It discourages imports and protects domestic producers from foreign competition.

Figure 21.1 shows the effect of a tariff. The figure shows a downward-sloping demand curve for the product, and an upward-sloping *domestic* supply curve. For simplicity, we consider the case of a country sufficiently small that the price it pays on the international market does not depend on the quantity purchased. In the absence of a tariff, the domestic price is equal to this international price, $p^*$. The country produces $Q_s$, consumes $Q_d$, and imports the difference, $Q_d - Q_s$. With a tariff, the price consumers have to pay is increased from $p^*$ to $p^* + t$, where $t$ is the tariff. Domestic production is increased to $Q'_s$—domestic producers are better off as a result. But consumers are worse off, as the price they pay is increased. Their consumption is reduced to $Q'_d$. Since production is increased and consumption reduced, imports are reduced: the domestic industry has been protected against foreign imports.

Using the concepts of consumer and producer surplus first introduced in Chapter 3, we can quantify the net loss to society due to the tariff. The consumer surplus measures the difference between the amount consumers are willing to pay and what they have to pay. In the absence of the tariff, it is given by the triangle *ABC*. After the price increase, it is given by the triangle *ADE*. The net loss to consumers is the trapezoid *DBCE*. Part of this represents a gain to producers. In the initial situation, producer surplus is *BKJ*—the difference between what producers receive for producing $Q_s$ and what it costs them to produce that amount. For example, the first unit produced costs them only *0K*, but they are paid *0B*; the supply curve shows the cost of producing the various units of output. When the tariff is imposed, producer surplus becomes *DKH*, a gain of *DBJH*. The government also receives tariff revenues of *HGFE*, which is

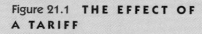

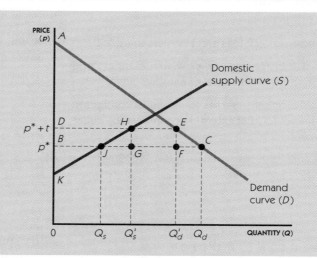

**Figure 21.1 THE EFFECT OF A TARIFF**

The curves labelled $S$ and $D$ are domestic supply and demand curves for an imported product. The international price is $p^*$. Under free trade, imports are $Q_d - Q_s$, the difference between demand and domestic production. When a tariff at the rate $t$ is imposed on each unit of good imported, consumption falls, domestic production rises, and imports fall to $Q'_d - Q'_s$.

a gain to society that can be used to purchase goods and services or to reduce taxes elsewhere. The net loss to society is the differences between the loss to consumers and the gains to producers and the government, $DBCE - DBJH - HGFE$. Thus, the societal loss is represented by two triangles, $EFC$ and $HGJ$. These are deadweight losses, the net loss to society in the value of output produced as a result of interfering with the price system. The triangle $EFC$ is similar to the deadweight loss to consumers arising from a monopolist's raising his price. The triangle $HGJ$ is the waste of resources resulting from the fact that as the economy expands production as a result of the tariff, the cost of the increased production exceeds the cost of purchasing the good abroad.

## QUOTAS

Rather than imposing tariffs, countries may use **non-tariff barriers** (NTBs) to protect domestic producers against imports. One form of NTB is to set **quotas**—limits on the amount of foreign goods that can be imported. In Canada, import quotas have been widely used as part of the supply management system for some agricultural products, including eggs, butter,

and milk. Supply management policies were intended to stabilize the market for these goods by applying quotas to all domestic farmers as well as to imports. In the case of imports of dairy products, the quotas were set so low almost to preclude imports entirely.

Producers often prefer quotas to tariffs. With limitations on the quantity imported, the domestic price increases above the international price. With quotas, domestic producers know precisely the magnitude of the foreign supply: foreigners cannot sell any more even if they become more efficient or exchange rates change in their favour. In that sense, quotas provide domestic producers with greater certainty than do tariffs, insulating them from the worst threats of competition.

Quotas and tariffs both succeed in raising the domestic price above the price at which the good could be obtained abroad. Thus, both protect domestic producers. There is, however, one important difference: with quotas, those who are given permits to import get a profit by buying goods at the international price abroad and selling at the higher domestic price. The government is in effect giving away its tariff revenues. These profits are referred to as **quota rents.** In Figure 21.1, if an import quota of $Q'_d - Q'_s$ were imposed instead of a tariff, the quota rent received by importers of the protected product would be *HGFE*, the same amount that would otherwise have gone to the government as tariff revenue.

## VOLUNTARY EXPORT RESTRAINTS

In recent years, international agreements have succeeded in reducing the level of tariffs and restricting the use of quotas. Accordingly, countries have sought to protect their industries from the onslaught of foreign competition by other NTBs. One that became popular in the 1980s was **voluntary export restraints** (VERs). When imports of automobiles from Japan to North America soared, Canada and the United States, rather than limiting imports by tariffs or quotas, persuaded Japan to limit its exports "voluntarily."

There are two interpretations of why Japan was willing to go along with this VER. One is that they worried that Canada and the United States might take stronger actions, like imposing quotas. From Japan's perspective, VERs are clearly preferable to quotas because the quota rents accrue to them rather than to importers in North America. A second interpretation is that VERs enabled Japanese producers to act collusively. It might have been in their interest to collude to reduce production and raise prices, but such collusion would have been illegal under anti-combines laws in Canada and antitrust laws in the United States. The VER "imposed" restrictions on the Japanese car producers that they might have chosen themselves if they had been permitted to under the law. No wonder, then, that they were willing to go along! The cost of protecting North American producers was high: not only did Japanese cars become more expensive to consumers, but also the quota rents were transferred to Japanese producers.

Quotas and VERs are the most transparent NTBs: they explicitly restrict imports by a stated amount. But there are many others that, though less transparent, are still important. A host of regulations have the same effect of imposing barriers to trade. Product quality, health, or safety standards intended to protect consumers can wittingly or otherwise discriminate against imports. Labelling regulations involving language content of packaging can as well. Federal and provincial government procurement practices can favour domestic suppliers, and so on. The breadth of protective options available makes the liberalization of international trade a daunting task.

## RESPONSES TO UNFAIR TRADING PRACTICES

Most people believe in competition. But most people also believe that competition should be fair. When foreign firms can undersell domestic firms, they suspect foul play. The federal government has legislated anti-combines laws to ensure that there is effective and fair competition domestically. Laws have also been enacted by most industrialized countries to ensure "fair competition" in international trade. But most economists believe that *in practice* these laws are often used as protectionist measures, reducing competition and restricting imports. To ensure *fair* competition, economists argue that the same sorts of laws

## COMPARISON OF TARIFFS, QUOTAS, AND VOLUNTARY EXPORT RESTRAINTS

All can be used to restrict imports by the same amount, with the same effect on consumers and domestic producers.

With tariffs, the difference between domestic price and international price accrues to government as tariff revenues.

With quotas, the difference accrues to importers, who enjoy quota rents.

VERs are equivalent to quotas, except that the quota rents are given to foreign producers.

In February 1996 Canada and the United States reached an agreement on the thorny trade issue of Canadian softwood lumber exports. The dispute arose because timber interests in the United States claimed that Canadian provincial governments were unfairly subsidizing exports by charging forestry companies stumpage fees (the fees paid to cut down trees on Crown lands) that were below the price that would prevail were the land owned privately rather than publicly. Some years earlier the United States had applied countervailing duties on softwood imports from Canada; it was threatening to do so again, despite having lost two cases before binational trade panels under the Free Trade Agreement.

In the originally negotiated agreement, each exporting province would restrict its exports in a manner it most preferred. British Columbia was to limit its exports by imposing an export quota. Quebec, on the other hand, would increase its stumpage fees. Some months later, the agreement was modified because the Canadian government feared that such a system would be too difficult to administer. In the final settlement the Canadian government would levy an export tax on all softwood lumber going to the United States, regardless of its province of origin.

Though these three export restrictions seem different, their effects on the market are actually quite similar. This can be seen by reexamining Figure 21.1. Consider the United States as the domestic country. If it imposes a countervailing duty of $t$ per unit, the price will rise to $p^* + t$, the quantity of imports from Canada will fall from $Q_d - Q_s$ to $Q'_d - Q'_s$, American domestic production will rise from $Q_s$ to $Q'_s$, and the U.S. government will collect revenue equal to the area $HGFE$, or $t$ times the quantity of imports. Suppose instead that to avoid the duty Canada agrees to some form of export restriction. First, if it imposes a quota on its exports of $Q'_d - Q'_s$ units, the outcome in the market is the same. The quantity of Canadian lumber imports falls to $Q'_d - Q'_s$, the quota amount, and the price rises to $p^* + t$. Second, suppose that the Canadian government raises its stumpage fees. A stumpage fee of $t$ per unit of output increases the cost of producing Canadian lumber and the price of lumber going to the United States to $p^* + t$, and lowers imports to $Q'_d - Q'_s$. Finally, an export tax of $t$ per unit also raises the price of Canadian lumber in the U.S. market to $p^* + t$, and the quantity sold there falls to $Q'_d - Q'_s$.

What is different about the three forms of export restraint is what happens to the area $HGFE$, $t$ per unit on sales of $Q'_d - Q'_s$ units, the revenue that would have been obtained by the United States government by a countervailing duty. With an export quota, the increase in price means that the exporting companies in Canada receive this area. If each exporting province raises its stumpage fees, the revenue goes to the provincial governments according to how the exports are divided among them. The federal government takes in this revenue if an export tax is imposed. So, while all three forms of export restraint achieve the same outcome in the American market, the revenue they generate goes to different parties.

that apply domestically should be extended internationally. There should not be two standards of fairness, one applying domestically, one internationally.

Unfortunately, progress towards achieving this goal has been limited, even among countries that have formed free trade areas or economic unions with one another. Perhaps one reason is that the allegedly unfair trading practices can emanate from government policies as well as the anticompetitive behaviour of firms. Two important responses to unfair trading practices have emerged in recent years. One, anti-dumping duties, is directed at firms whose trading practices are said to be unfairly harming the importing country. The second, countervailing duties, is aimed at countries whose government policies are said to be giving their exporting firms unfair advantages.

## ANTI-DUMPING DUTIES

**Dumping** refers to the sale of products in foreign markets at prices lower than those in the home country, where the price difference is not justified by cost differences. Normally, consumers greet discounted sales with enthusiasm. If Italy is willing to sell shoes in Canada at low prices, why should we complain? One legitimate reason might be **predatory pricing.** By selling below cost, the foreign companies hope to drive Canadian firms out of business. Once they have established a monopoly position, they can raise prices. In such a case, Canadian consumers gain only in the short run. But in competitive markets, predation simply cannot occur; in such markets, firms have no power to raise prices. In most of the cases where dumping has occurred, markets are sufficiently competitive that predation is not of concern.

**Anti-dumping duties** are the penalties countries impose on foreign firms found to be dumping. It is tempting for a country to use anti-dumping duties as a means of protecting domestic producers against low-cost imports, especially if tariffs are ruled out because of international agreements or because they cannot be easily applied selectively to particular firms. It is not a simple matter of distinguishing dumping as a predatory practice from selling at low prices because of excess supply or because of cost conditions. The fact that distinguishing between

them is in the hands of the government of the importing country makes it tempting for the government to take the side of the domestic firms against the importers.

Not surprisingly, the application of anti-dumping duties has varied over the years. In Canada, a federal agency called the Canadian International Trade Tribunal (CITT) is responsible for conducting inquiries into whether Canadian producers are injured by imports that are dumped or subsidized. Anti-dumping duties can be imposed on the basis of their findings. A recent report of the CITT found that the number of anti-dumping actions initiated increased rapidly in 1983 after the 1981–82 recession, then fell off rapidly after 1987, only to increase again in the early 1990s. The number of total actions in place was at a peak, 156, in 1985, but a large number of existing actions were revoked in the late 1980s. Footwear, leather, textile, and clothing products accounted for over 60 percent of the value of goods covered by anti-dumping actions in recent years. In previous years, primary metals tended to be the most affected. Anti-dumping actions against American firms represented only about one fifth of the total value of goods subject to such actions during the 1980s, though this proportion increased considerably in 1991 as a result of two particular cases, one involving beer introduced into the British Columbia market, and the other, carpeting. Overall, these findings confirm that anti-dumping duties tend to be used more during recessions and tend to be directed at low-cost countries rather than at the United States, which is by far our largest trading partner.

## SUBSIDIES AND COUNTERVAILING DUTIES

A second trade practice widely viewed as unfair is for governments to subsidize domestic firms' production. For example, the government may give certain domestic industries tax breaks or pay for a portion of a firm's costs. These subsidies give the firms receiving them an unfair advantage over foreign firms. Trade is determined not on the basis of comparative advantage, but of relative subsidy levels.

The usual logic of economics seems to be reversed by viewing subsidies as unfair: If some foreign government wants to subsidize domestic firms, why should the consumers complain? Presumably only if the subsidies are part of a policy of predation—if subsidies are used to drive domestic firms out of business and establish a monopoly position, after which prices will be raised. Most foreign subsidies do not fall into this category.

Opposition to these subsidies arises from the domestic companies who see their businesses hurt. While the gains to consumers outweigh the losses to businesses, the gain to each consumer is small, and the number of consumers affected is large and they are not well organized. The losses are concentrated on a much smaller number of producers, who are far more organized and are able and willing to take their case to the domestic government. In response, the domestic government may impose **countervailing duties,** taxes imposed on the imports that offset any advantage thought to be provided by the subsidies.

Whereas anti-dumping duties are commonly used in Canada, countervailing duties are more commonly used by the United States, a practice that has been the source of some trade friction with Canada. Its use is triggered by a complaint by a producer of unfair competition because of foreign subsidies. Given the extent to which Canadian government policies, including general regional subsidies and investment tax credits, impinge differentially upon various industries, the use of countervailing duties is potentially almost open-ended. For example, the U.S. government found the Canadian softwood lumber industry to have been subsidized by virtue of the fact that the stumpage fees charged by the British Columbia government for the right to cut trees were too low. In other words, low tax rates were deemed to be equivalent to a subsidy.

Governments may preach against other countries' providing subsidies to exporters, but often they engage in the practices themselves, sometimes in indirect ways. The Canadian government has provided large subsidies to transport Prairie grain to ports for export. Favourable loans and guarantees may be provided to Canadian exporters through the Export Development Corporation. The mining industry has benefited from generous tax breaks through the corporate tax system. And regional development subsidies have supported exporting industries in Quebec and the Atlantic provinces.

Are there any circumstances in which subsidies might be justified? In principle, the answer might be yes. Governments may be able to use subsidies to enable its country's firms to establish a dominant position in a market. There are relatively few firms that are involved in supplying urban transit systems, and Canadian firms happen to be among them. With some government assistance, it may be possible for these firms to achieve a dominant position in the market. Or governments might subsidize an industry where production involves a steep learning curve: the more one produces, the lower the marginal cost of production. The Japanese government subsidized makers of computer chips to the point where almost no other country could compete with them. As it turned out, research by American producers enabled them to more than offset the advantages of Japanese subsidies. Of course, as is often the case, the U.S. government also responded by offering its own subsidies. Governments might also subsidize industries that might produce techniques and knowledge of benefit to other industries, or that are of strategic or military significance. Examples include high-tech and aerospace industries.

The trouble is that it is often difficult for governments to know for which industries subsidies are really justified. Picking winners may be little different than a lottery. And, more often than not, several countries end up subsidizing firms in the same industry. In the end their subsidies neutralize each other: no firm is able to gain an advantage over

## UNFAIR TRADE PRACTICES AND GOVERNMENT RESPONSES

Dumping: Firms selling abroad at lower prices than at home for reasons unrelated to cost differences

Response: Imposition of anti-dumping duties on the imports of firms found to be dumping

Subsidies: Governments subsidizing the production of exporting firms either directly or indirectly

Response: Imposition of countervailing duties on imports of firms found to be subsidized others. The issues are much the same as those involved in the question to which we now turn: whether to protect domestic industries from foreign competition.

## PROTECTIONISM IN CANADA—POLITICAL AND ECONOMIC RATIONALES

Canada is no stranger to protectionism. Tariffs were used as long ago as the 1870s explicitly to protect manufacturing industries from foreign competition. Subsequently tariffs were supplemented by a variety of other instruments designed to give Canadian firms a leg up on potential foreign competitors in the Canadian market. These included quotas on imports, subsidies and special tax breaks for manufacturing industries, restrictions on foreign investment, subsidized rail transportation, and cheap energy pricing. Protectionism was directed largely at the United States, our largest trading partner. Great Britain was spared to some extent by a mutual system of preferential treatment that existed among Commonwealth countries.

This long-standing policy of protectionism against foreign imports has come to be questioned in recent years for a number of reasons. Within Canada, primary producers, especially those in the West, complained because the tariff served largely to protect manufacturing industries located primarily in central Canada. Thus, they were forced to purchase their machinery and equipment at protected prices rather than importing them from lower-cost sources. Also, it was argued that although the protective tariff encouraged the growth of a large manufacturing sector, the result was a series of manufacturing industries that consisted of too many small-scale firms designed to serve the relatively small domestic market. Studies showed that a more competitive and open environment that forced the manufacturing industries to operate more efficiently and take advantage of large-scale production could cause GDP to be as much as 10 percent higher.

Finally, and perhaps most influentially, it was argued that Canadian exporters had more to lose than import industries had to gain by a policy of protecting the latter. The reasoning was as follows: Tariffs are largely applied to merchandise imports. However, Canada's merchandise trade balance has been in surplus for several years. Not only that, but the merchandise trade balance with the United States has been largely responsible for that. At the same time, the U.S. trade deficit was increasing at an alarming rate, resulting in a threat of protectionist policies in the United States. This threat was seen by many as more than negating any benefits that might accrue to Canadian producers from domestic protectionism. This recognition led the Royal Commission on the Economic Union and Development Prospects for Canada—better known as the Macdonald Royal Commission, after its chairman, the former finance minister Donald Macdonald—to recommend a system of free trade with the United States in 1985. This recommendation led to negotiation two years later of the Canada-U.S. Free Trade Agreement (FTA), which was later expanded to the North American Free Trade Agreement (NAFTA) with the inclusion of Mexico.

While the FTA removed most trade barriers between Canada and the United States, a trade deficit remained with the rest of the world. Imports from overseas, especially from low-wage countries, were seen as taking away jobs from Canadian workers. Not surprisingly, protectionism retained some popular support as a way of dealing with the problem.

Chapter 3 showed how free trade, by allowing each country to concentrate production where it has a comparative advantage, can make all countries better off. Why, in spite of this, is protection so popular? The basic reason is simple: protection allows domestic producers to sell at higher prices by shielding them from foreign competition. Even though the losses to consumers from higher prices exceed the gains to producers in higher profits, producers are well organized and consumers are not; hence producers' voices are heard more clearly in the political process than are consumers'.

There is an important check on firms' ability to use the political process to advance their special interests: the interests of exporters, who realize that if Canada closes off its markets to imports, other countries will reciprocate. Consequently, exporting firms have been at the forefront of advancing freer and

The Canadian economy has always relied heavily on foreign investment for its growth. Indeed, capital raised abroad, mostly in Britain, was instrumental in the construction of the railways that made Confederation possible. But attitudes to and policy stances regarding foreign investment have changed several times over the years.

During Canada's early development, most foreign investment took the form of borrowing; Canadian bonds were purchased by foreigners. In the postwar era, more and more foreign investment in Canada was direct investment—investment by foreign firms in branch plants or subsidiaries in Canada and the takeover of Canadian firms by multinational corporations. This direct investment came increasingly from the United States, some of it designed to "jump" the tariff barrier that Canada had long thought necessary to ensure the existence of a domestic manufacturing industry. This foreign ownership of Canadian industry led to concerns on the part of economic nationalists that important economic decisions in the "branch-plant economy" would be taken by non-Canadians.

In response to these concerns, in 1974 the Foreign Investment Review Agency (FIRA) was created to screen foreign takeovers of Canadian firms with assets of $250,000 or more. The following year its authority was extended to include new investments in Canada by foreign firms to ensure that they were accompanied by benefits to Canadians and the protection of Canadian jobs.

Over the next ten years attitudes towards both trade and foreign investment changed as globalization of the world economy occurred. Reductions in tariffs and other trade barriers, more efficient global transportation and communications systems, and deregulation of some industries contributed to the rapid growth in world trade and investment—by now deemed responsible for economic growth and rising standards of living. Investment was seen as essential for facing the challenges of an increasingly competitive world economy. Though the review-free limits on firm size had been raised several times, the public perception was that the need to seek FIRA approval discouraged much needed investment from coming into the country.

In response to this, the Mulroney government saw the need to stimulate the private sector with a more open business climate and expanded investment opportunities. It replaced FIRA in 1985 with a new agency called Investment Canada whose purpose was to encourage new investment in Canada from foreign and domestic sources alike and to undertake research and provide policy advice on matters relating to investment. Almost all new investments were allowed without review, the exceptions being takeovers of firms with assets worth over $5 million and investments in "culturally sensitive" areas. Today, Investment Canada continues to promote foreign investment in Canada and by Canadians abroad.

The North American Free Trade Agreement (NAFTA) has had further important impacts on investment in Canada and on the work of Investment Canada. Canadian and Canadian-based foreign firms have freer access to the large markets south of the border; fewer investments between Canada, the United States, and Mexico will be reviewed and stopped (the review threshold for direct investments has risen to $150 million); takeovers of one foreign-controlled firm by another foreign-controlled firm are no longer subject to review; and each country has agreed to treat investors from the other countries on the same basis as domestic firms when it comes to regulating both new businesses and ongoing operations. Overall, NAFTA provides for a much more hospitable investment environment in all three countries by encouraging a freer flow of capital among them.

These changes in policy have had some apparent success in encouraging Canadian investment both at home and abroad. In the ten years prior to the birth of Investment Canada, Canadian direct investment abroad grew by $39.4 billion, and foreign direct investment in Canada grew by $47.3 billion. In the ten years since, Canadian direct investment abroad grew by $75.2 billion, while foreign direct investment in Canada in-

creased by $62.1 billion. These flows are quite large for a country the size of Canada.

The attitude towards foreign investment in Canada has come full circle. Foreign investment, first encouraged, then rigourously reviewed, and perhaps even actively discouraged, is once again viewed favourably by the government. This saga provides an example of how policy is changed over time in response to changes in economic conditions and to changes in how various phenomena are viewed by both economists and the public at large.

Sources: "International Investment in Canada," *Investing in Canada* 6, no. 1 (Summer 1992), published by Investment Canada, Ottawa; Statistics Canada, *Canada's International Investment Position, 1995*; External Affairs Canada, *The Canada-U.S. Free Trade Agreement: Synopsis*, (Ottawa: External Affairs Canada, 1987); External Affairs and International Trade Canada, *NAFTA: What's it all about?* (Ottawa: External Affairs and International Trade Canada, 1993).

fairer trade through international agreements of the kind that will be described in the next section.

But before turning to a review of these international agreements, we need to take a closer look at some of the other economic aspects of protection. Although the country as a whole may be better off with free trade, certain groups may actually be worse off. Those especially affected include displaced firms and workers, low-wage workers, and those in industries in which competition is limited without free trade.

## DISPLACED FIRMS AND WORKERS

China has a comparative advantage in inexpensive textiles while Canada has a comparative advantage in natural resources and manufacturing complex goods and services, like engineering services and urban transit systems. If Canada starts to import more textiles from China, Canadian textile manufac-

turers may be driven out of business, and their workers will have to find work elsewhere. More than offsetting these losses are the gains to the export industries. In principle, the gainers in those industries could more than compensate the losers, but such compensation is seldom made: hence the opposition of the losers to opening trade.

Typically, economists shed few tears for the lost profits of the businesses that are hurt by opening trade. After all, that is just one of the risks that businesses face and for which they are typically well compensated. New innovations destroy old businesses: the introduction of the automobile hurt the carriage trade. But barring the door to new technologies is bad economics—and bad economic policy.

There is, however, often more sympathy towards workers affected by trade—though there is no reason why there should be greater concern for workers displaced by more open trade than by new innovations. When the economy is running at close to full employment, workers who lose their jobs typically do find new employment. But they often go through a transition period of unemployment, and when they eventually do find a new job, there is a good chance that their wages will be lower. While these particular labourers are worse off, workers as a whole are better off, because those who get newly created jobs in the export industries on average get paid more than the average for the economy. Concern about the transitional costs borne by displaced workers has motivated governments to provide special assistance for these workers to help them find new jobs and obtain the requisite training.

Sensitivity to the problems of displaced workers is particularly strong when unemployment is high because those who lose a job cannot easily find alternative employment. Auto workers in Ontario who see their jobs lost as a result of imports of Japanese cars view the Japanese as "stealing" their jobs. Indeed, in such situations, trade is *blamed* for the high unemployment rate. If we restrict imports, it is argued, we will keep jobs in Canada.

## BEGGAR-THY-NEIGHBOUR POLICIES

In Chapter 10 we saw that output may be limited by aggregate demand. Aggregate demand depends on consumption, investment, government expenditures, and net exports. Net exports equal exports minus imports. Increasing imports thus reduces net exports—reducing aggregate demand, national output, and employment. Policies that attempt to increase national output by reducing imports are called **beggar-thy-neighbour** policies, because the jobs gained in one country are at the expense of jobs lost in another. If Canada imports less, foreigners export less. Restricting imports into Canada may *initially* have a positive effect on Canadian output. But the gains are typically a mirage. Other countries will import from us only if they can sell goods to us. Even without retaliatory measures by other countries, if Canada restricts imports, typically exports fall in tandem. Without exports to Canada, other countries' incomes fall, and with the fall in income, they import less, including from Canada. Moreover, when other countries see reduced exports as a result of active policies by other countries to restrict imports, they tend to respond by retaliating, playing tit-for-tat.

The worst instance of these beggar-thy-neighbour policies occurred at the onset of the Great Depression when, in 1930, the United States increased tariffs on many products to prohibitive levels. As U.S. imports declined, so did incomes in Canada, Europe, and elsewhere in the world. As their incomes declined and as they imposed retaliatory tariffs, they bought less from the United States. U.S. exports plummeted, contributing further to the economic downturn in the United States. With incomes in the United States plummeting further, U.S. imports declined even more, contributing still further to the decline abroad, which then fed further into the decline in U.S. exports. The downturn in international trade that was set off by the U.S. tariffs is often pointed to as a major contributing factor in making the Great Depression as deep and severe as it was.

## WAGES IN AFFECTED SECTORS

Beyond these short-run problems of transition and unemployment, there may be longer-run problems facing workers in affected sectors. Canada has a comparative advantage in producing goods that require highly skilled workers. As Canada exports more of these goods, the demand for these skilled workers increases in Canada, driving up their wages. Similarly, Canada has a comparative disadvantage in producing goods that require a high ratio of

### INTERNATIONAL TRADE AND JOBS

Opposition to imports is strongest when the economy is in a recession, but restricting imports as a way of creating jobs tends to be counterproductive.

unskilled labour, such as lower-quality textiles. As imports compete against these industries and their production decreases, the demand for unskilled labour decreases. This drives down the wages of unskilled workers.

These decreased wages for unskilled workers are often blamed on imports from Third World countries like China, where wages are but a fraction of those in Canada. The consensus among economists who have looked closely at the matter is that international trade explains a relatively small part of the decline in wages—perhaps 20 percent. Nonetheless, those who see their livelihood being threatened are among the most ardent advocates of trade restrictions. Again, economists argue that the appropriate response is not to restrict trade, but to increase skills: workers who receive the skills become better off as their wages rise commensurate with the increase in their productivity, and as more workers become skilled, the remaining supply of unskilled workers is reduced. With a smaller supply of unskilled workers, the real wages of unskilled workers increase, offsetting the adverse effects of trade.

## INCREASED COMPETITION

International trade also has other adverse effects in industries where competition is limited. With limited competition, firms enjoy monopoly or oligopoly profits, some of which are often passed on to workers. Particularly when those industries are unionized, workers may receive wages far higher than workers of comparable skills working elsewhere in the economy. International trade introduces more competition; with the increased competition, monopoly and oligopoly profits get competed away. Firms are forced to pay competitive wages—that is, the lowest wage that they can for workers of the given skill.

## OTHER RATIONALES FOR PROTECTION

Job loss and decreased wages and profits from international competition provide much of the *political* motivation behind protection. To an economist these are not compelling reasons for protection since the gains to the protected sectors are more than offset by losses elsewhere in the economy, especially to consumers. Are there any *legitimate* arguments for protection? Are there circumstances where protection may be in the *national* interest, and not just in the interest of those being protected? Three arguments have been put forward.

### INFANT INDUSTRY

The first is the **infant-industry argument.** Costs in new industries are often high and come down as experience is gained. The infant-industry argument is that, particularly in less developed countries, firms will never be able to get the experience required to produce efficiently unless they are protected from foreign competition.

Economists have traditionally responded to this argument skeptically. If it pays to enter the industry, eventually there will be profits. Thus, the firm should be willing to charge today a price below cost to gain the experience, because today's losses will be more than offset by the future profits. Recently, however, the infant-industry argument has found more favour. Firms can only operate at a loss if they can borrow funds. If capital markets do not work well, firms may not be able to borrow even if their eventual prospects are reasonable. This is a particular danger in less developed countries.

This is a legitimate conclusion, but it is an argument not for protection but for assistance, which can take the form of loans or direct subsidies. Economists argue for direct assistance rather than protection because it is transparent: everyone can

## EFFECTS OF TRADE ON WAGES

International trade may lower wages of unskilled labour and those working in industries where competition is limited. International trade raises wages of skilled workers.

see that it is a subsidy to producers. Economists criticize protection because it is a hidden tax on consumers, the proceeds of which are transferred to producers. The lack of transparency encourages what economists call rent seeking: the expenditure of resources by industries to persuade government to impose hidden taxes that benefit themselves.

### STRATEGIC TRADE THEORY

Another argument for protection is that it can give a country a **strategic trade advantage** either by (a) helping reduce domestic costs of protected sectors below those of rivals or (b) forcing foreign firms to reduce their prices in order to overcome the tariff barrier. Domestic costs may be reduced if there are economies of scale: the larger the level of production, the lower the average cost. Protection ensures a large domestic sales base and therefore a low average cost of production. The instances in which strategic considerations based on economies of scale might provide a rationale for protection appear relatively rare. Examples might include capital-intensive manufacturing products such as transportation and communications equipment. Even then, protection would be effective only when foreign governments do not retaliate by taking similar actions.

The use of tariffs to force foreign firms to reduce their prices, the second type of strategic trade policy, relies on the protecting country having some influence on the price at which it purchases its imports. As a major producer of aluminum, Canada may purchase a significant proportion of bauxite, the ore containing aluminum, in world markets. If so, restricting the purchase of bauxite by a tariff may induce bauxite suppliers to lower their prices. This is referred to as the **optimal tariff argument** for protection. It too is rarely likely to be effective. Few countries are likely to be large enough in any one market to have an influence over price. Even if they are, other countries are likely to retaliate with their own "optimal tariffs."

### EXTERNALITY-GENERATING INDUSTRIES

A final argument for protection is that certain types of firms provide external benefits to others. For example, firms that use advanced technologies may produce innovations or new types of products that can be made use of by other firms. Firms producing these so-called knowledge externalities are not fully compensated for the costs they incur, so, as occurs with any externality, the firms produce less than the socially optimal amount. Tariff protection, it is argued, will enable them to produce more, and society will benefit from the new knowledge they generate.

This argument is rather difficult to evaluate and respond to. By their very nature, knowledge externalities are difficult for the policy maker to observe. There is little certainty as to which firms or industries are deserving of support on these grounds. To the extent that the argument is legitimate, it calls for direct assistance rather than tariff protection.

## INTERNATIONAL COOPERATION

The decade of the 1980s produced a dramatic rise in the use of trade barriers. The combination of the growth in world trade and the recognition that restrictive trade policies are shortsighted and ultimately self-defeating has led to a recent emphasis on negotiating freer trade internationally. Two approaches have been pursued in tandem. On the one hand, there are global approaches aimed at achieving **multilateral agreements.** The most prominent of these is known as the **General Agreement on Tariffs and Trade,** or **GATT,** which was set up soon after World War II and has since been replaced by the **World Trade Organization (WTO).** The second approach involves small groups of countries negotiating freer trade agreements among themselves. Such **bilateral** or **regional agreements** include the Canada-U.S. Free Trade Agreement and its successor, the North American Free Trade Agreement (NAFTA), and the European Union.

## GATT AND THE WTO

After World War II, the countries of the world realized that there was much to be gained from establishing an international economic order in which barriers to trade were reduced. They established the General Agreement on Tariffs and Trade, or GATT. In 1995, this was replaced by the World Trade Organization, or WTO.

GATT was founded on three guiding principles. The first was *reciprocity:* if one country lowered its tariffs, it could expect other countries in GATT to lower theirs. The second was *nondiscrimination:* no member of GATT could offer a special trade deal that favoured only one or a few other countries. The third was *transparency:* import quotas and other nontariff barriers to trade should be converted into tariffs, so their effective impact could be ascertained.

GATT has proceeded in a number of stages, called **rounds** (the Kennedy Round, completed in 1967; the Tokyo Round, completed in 1979; and, most recently, the Uruguay Round, completed in 1993). Collectively, the rounds have reduced tariffs on industrial goods markedly. The average tariff on manufactured goods was 40 percent in 1947; by 1993, it was less than 5 percent, and the Uruguay Round reduced it still further.

The Uruguay Round was remarkable for two achievements. First, it began the process of extending the principles of free and fair trade to a number of much more difficult trade areas. There were agreements to reduce agricultural protection, and particularly quotas and export subsidies, and to ensure that intellectual property rights—patents and copyrights—were respected. Trade in services as well as goods was covered. Second, it created the World Trade Organization to help enforce the trade agreements. Previously, a country that believed that it was suffering from an unfair trade practice could bring a case to a GATT panel, which would examine the evidence. But even if the panel was unanimous in finding that an unfair trade practice had occurred, there was little available in the way of effective enforcement. Under the WTO, a country injured by an unfair trade practice will be authorized to engage in retaliatory actions.

The liberalization of world trade is obviously of great importance for a country that relies as much on exports as Canada. It opens up potential markets for our products around the world. At the same time, the rules of the WTO require us to change our own remaining protectionist practices. To comply with the principles applying to agriculture, Canada is gradually abandoning the system of quotas against imported foodstuffs that supported our supply management system, and is replacing them with tariffs with much less protective impact. The provinces have had to give up their policies of allowing only locally produced beer to be sold in provincial outlets. Rules protecting intellectual property have resulted in stronger patent protection being given to the pharmaceutical companies to prevent their drugs from being copied by generic companies.

## REGIONAL TRADING BLOCS

GATT and the WTO have made considerable progress in reducing trade barriers among all countries. But the difficulties of reaching agreements involving so many parties have meant that progress has been slow. In the meantime, many countries have formed **trading blocs** with their more immediate neighbours, not only to eliminate trade barriers but also to facilitate the unimpeded flow of capital, and in some cases even labour. The largest and longest-standing one is the European Union (EU), the successor to the European Common Market, whose origins go back to the Treaty of Rome in 1958. It has evolved to become a single market involving most of Western Europe, in which goods, services, labour, and capital are free to move across borders. In addition, a central authority is responsible for certain EU-wide policies in areas such as agriculture, regional development, transportation, and competition policy. Taxes have been harmonized, and the EU is working towards eliminating border controls and establishing a monetary union with a single currency and monetary policy.

The North American Free Trade Agreement (NAFTA), which replaced the Canada-U.S. Free Trade Agreement in 1994, is evolving towards a free trade zone encompassing Canada, the United States, and Mexico. Within these countries, goods, services, and capital (though not labour) will be free to move across borders without tariffs or other impediments. There are also many smaller free trade zones, such as between New Zealand and Australia, and among

## CLOSE-UP: FTA AND NAFTA

To gain easier access to the U.S. market, Canada entered into the Free Trade Agreement (FTA) with the United States on January 1, 1989. The FTA was innovative in several respects. First, it created the largest free-trading bloc in the world. Second, the FTA covered agricultural trade, a sector that had eluded international trade negotiators, such as those of the GATT, in the past. Third, the FTA was also the first trade agreement to encompass trade in services, business travel, and investment. Finally, the agreement contained rules and mechanisms for settling disputes between the trading partners. Five years later, after over three years of negotiations, the FTA was expanded to include Mexico and became the North American Free Trade Agreement (NAFTA) encompassing a market of 360 million consumers.

According to NAFTA, virtually all tariffs and nontariff barriers (such as quotas and licences) are to be eliminated, some immediately, others to be phased out over periods of up to ten years. There are two sorts of exceptions to this. The first is that NAFTA has adopted the provisions of GATT listing reasons for which import or export control measures can be used to protect national interests. The second sort involves exceptions negotiated specifically for NAFTA. Examples of this include measures to promote and strengthen cultural industries, basic telecommunications services, public-sector health care and social service programmes, and water in its natural state.

Two important provisions exist to ensure that the elimination of import and export controls between the three countries will actually lead to the freeing of trade. First, so-called "rules of origin" apply, limiting the traded goods that are eligible for free trade treatment. The rules of origin state that 60 percent of the manufacturing cost of most items must be incurred in one of the three member countries. Without this provision, other countries could take advantage of the North American free trade zone. Suppose, for example, that Japanese bicycles are duty-free in Canada but not in the United States. The rules of origin prevent Japan from moving bicycles duty-free into Canada and then into the United States to avoid the U.S. tariff.

Second, trade among the three countries is also subject to the principle of "national treatment" under the FTA. This means that each country's domestic policies must apply without discrimination to the producers of the other two countries. That is, Canada cannot apply taxes or regulations that discourage the consumption of Mexican goods, if these do not also apply to domestically produced goods.

Key areas covered by NAFTA include:
*Goods Trade*   Special attention was devoted to three sectors: automobiles, agriculture, and energy. Trade in cars, trucks, and parts is duty-free, provided 62.5 percent of direct production costs are incurred in North America (compared with 50 percent under the Auto Pact between Canada and the United States, whose other provisions remain in effect). Export subsidies on agricultural products are eliminated, and most import licences and quotas are replaced by tariffs that will be gradually phased out. Exceptions to the tariff phase-out include the dairy, egg, and poultry industries. Virtually all bilateral barriers to trade in energy are eliminated, including import quantity restrictions. The control and licensing of exports is maintained. So is the ability to cut back oil exports in times of tight supply,

provided that such restrictions do not reduce the proportion of energy output that is exported to the other party. For constitutional reasons, Mexico retains the right to limit foreign participation in the energy sector.

*Services* The FTA and NAFTA are innovative in freeing trade in several service sectors, such as banking, architecture, engineering, tourism, and computing. National treatment applies to trade in services as well as in goods, though rules of origin do not. Notably, NAFTA commits each country to providing effective protection and enforcement of intellectual property rights. But some services are exempt from free trade, including telecommunications services and government-provided health, education, and social services. Environmental, health, safety, and labour standards also remain under domestic control.

*Investment* National treatment is also extended to business investment. This will lead to greater ease in establishing new firms and acquiring existing firms in the other countries. Canada can still review large foreign takeovers, and foreign ownership can be restricted in culture, social services, basic telecommunications, and some transport sectors. Crown corporations are protected from sale.

*Government Procurement* For reasons of regional development, government goods and services contracts are often made available only to local or national firms. Under the GATT, federal government goods contracts worth over U.S. $171,000 must be tendered internationally. The NAFTA lowers this cost threshold for competition between the United States and Canadian suppliers to U.S. $25,000 for most government departments. A significant proportion of the Mexican procurement market is also opened up.

*Dispute Settlement* NAFTA defines problem-solving procedures in advance so that the implementation and operation of free trade will be smoother and more assured. When necessary, a NAFTA Trade Commission will set up panels to resolve bilateral trade disputes, consisting of two panelists from each country and a jointly chosen fifth member from neither country. NAFTA does not preclude the use of countervailing and anti-dumping duties against firms from member states as ways of penalizing what are regarded as unfair trade practices. These can also be reviewed by binational trade panels, which can make binding determinations as to whether or not they are in accordance with domestic legislation.

Not surprisingly, given such a wide-ranging agreement, there are those who argue that NAFTA will cause harm to Canada. Some focus on the dislocation that the opening of trade will have on domestic manufacturing industries. For example, some firms which produced on a relatively small scale largely for the Canadian market, such as clothing and beer firms, may no longer be able to compete against larger American firms. Others argue that sovereignty over domestic programmes will be threatened, especially over social programmes and programmes to protect cultural industries.

Supporters counter by saying that the benefits from gaining access to the large North American market more than outweigh the costs. They argue that Canadian manufacturing firms are too small and inefficient precisely because they have been induced by the protective policies of the past to concentrate on the small domestic market. They also point out that present and future social programmes will not be threatened as long as they are not designed primarily to protect domestic producers. And they maintain that the cultural sector is being provided with all the protection it needs.

countries in Latin America and Central America. None of these are on as grand a scale as the EU. For example, none involve central authorities with responsibility to take some policy decisions, though they typically do have a formal mechanism for settling disputes and enforcing the provisions of the regional agreement. And none involve free movement of labour.

## TRADE DIVERSION VERSUS TRADE CREATION

The gains from internationally coordinated reductions in trade barriers are clear, but the gains from regional trading blocs are more controversial. Reducing trade barriers within a region encourages trade between members of the trading bloc. Some of this is **trade creation:** newly created trade involving goods and services that were previously domestically produced. But some of it represents **trade diversion:** goods and services previously purchased from countries outside the bloc, which might have a comparative advantage, are diverted to firms in member nations whose production costs are higher. Trade creation results in gains from trade, so it is mutually beneficial. Trade diversion involves substituting purchases from a lower-cost nonmember to a higher-cost partner and is detrimental. The net benefits of the regional trade bloc will be positive only if trade creation exceeds trade diversion. The lower the level of trade with nonmember countries is to begin with, the better the likelihood that trade creation will exceed trade diversion; and the more dissimilar the member countries are, the greater the opportunities for trade creation that exist.

## INVESTMENT

Expanding regional trading blocs to cover investment flows, as in the case of NAFTA, raises particular anxieties. When the Canada-U.S. Free Trade Agreement took effect, there was some concern that firms would relocate in the United States, taking jobs with them. The thinking was that many firms in the manufacturing sector had set up plants in Canada to gain access to the Canadian market. Under free trade, that was no longer necessary since market access was guar-

anteed. Moreover, it was feared, the lower taxes in the United States as well as less restrictive labour laws and fewer and weaker unions would encourage capital to flee Canada. The fears multiplied when NAFTA was formed and Mexico became a member of the bloc. Labour costs were lower in Mexico given the low level of wages; as well, employment and environmental standards were alleged to be lax, and this would attract firms from both Canada and the United States to Mexico. The diversion of investment to Mexico would cost Canadian and American jobs.

Such arguments are based on some important misconceptions. They fail to take account of the distinction between absolute and comparative advantage, discussed in Chapter 3. The process of plant relocation and rationalization is a two-way street. If plants in Canada were inefficient or operating on too small a scale, that implies that the gains from trade were not being fully exploited. The process of shutting down small, inefficient plants and consolidating operations in larger-scale operations need not imply that all such operations be south of the border. They are as likely to consolidate operations in Canada as in the United States. And, any systematic differences that might have existed in costs between Canada and the United States because of differences in wage rates or tax levels would not persist in the presence of free trade. The pressures of competition might serve to eliminate them. If not, the exchange rate will settle down such that the balance of payments is in equilibrium and each country is producing what its comparative advantage dictates. It is simply not sensible to suppose that economic activity will move in one direction only.

These arguments also fail to take account of the fact that capital markets are already global. Capital will flow to good investment opportunities wherever they are. If good opportunities exist in Canada, capital will flow there regardless of how much Canadians invest in Mexico. Investment barriers impede the flow of capital to its most productive uses, thus lowering world efficiency.

The argument that investment in Mexico must come at the expense of Canada and the United States is based on a "zero-sum" view of the world. It is similar to the one that says when a country imports, it loses jobs: the gains to foreigners from their exports

## TYPES OF INTERNATIONAL COOPERATION

**Multilateral agreements—GATT and WTO**

- Based on principles of reciprocity and nondiscrimination.
- Uruguay Round extended trade liberalization to services and agricultural commodities, and helped establish intellectual property rights.
- The WTO replaced GATT.

**Regional trade agreements—NAFTA, EU**

- Risk exists that trade diversion will outweigh trade creation.
- May be better able to address complicated issues, such as those involving investment.

are at the expense of domestic firms, which otherwise would be producing these jobs. In Chapter 3, we saw what was wrong with this argument: the theory of comparative advantage says that when countries specialize in what they produce best, *both* countries are better off. Workers gain in higher wages from moving into those sectors where their productivity is highest; and consumers gain from the lower prices. So too with investment. When investment flows to where its return is highest, world output is increased. Since the return to capital is increased when it is efficiently allocated, savings rates may also increase, so that the overall supply of funds will be higher. Higher savings rates and more efficient use of available savings will combine to give a higher world economic growth rate.

But just as not everyone necessarily gains from trade according to comparative advantage, so too not everyone will necessarily gain from the flow of capital to Mexico. There will be some investment diversion from other countries to Mexico, as Mexico becomes more attractive to investors throughout the world because of its improved access to the huge North American market. Most economists believe that the net effect on investment in Canada will be negligible, and could even be positive. Industries within Canada who see their opportunities expand by selling more to Mexico will invest more, more than offsetting the reduced investment from firms that decline in the face of competition from Mexican imports.

In fact, investment flows augment the gains from trade that would occur in their absence because there are important trade-investment links. Canadian

companies producing abroad tend to use more parts from Canada, just as French companies producing abroad tend to use more French parts. Thus, flows of investment often serve as a precursor to exports.

### TRADE-OFFS BETWEEN REGIONAL AND GLOBAL AGREEMENTS

The potential economic trade-off between trade within a region at the expense of reduced trade outside the region has led some economists to oppose regional trade agreements. There is also a concern about political trade-offs. Recent Canadian governments seem committed to the idea of reducing trade barriers everywhere. Should the government use the limited political resources and goodwill it has to focus on regional or worldwide agreements? A pragmatic approach has been pursued. They actively participated in multilateral negotiations leading to the formation of the WTO. But Canada is only one of many medium-sized players internationally, and the bulk of our trading is concentrated in a few regions. The government's main efforts have been directed at pursuing regional trade agreements involving broad removal of barriers in areas of prime interest. This began within the hemisphere, starting with the United States, moving on to Mexico, and then aiming for Chile and beyond. The next priority is the Asia Pacific area, a region of high growth and large markets. Finally, there has been an attempt to reduce the barriers that exist between the European Union and the members of NAFTA. The hope is that a successful regional strategy will bring pressures to bear that will hasten fully international agreements.

# REVIEW AND PRACTICE

## SUMMARY

**1** Countries protect themselves in a variety of ways besides imposing tariffs. These nontariff barriers (NTBs) include quotas, voluntary export restraints, and regulatory barriers. Though there have been large reductions in tariff barriers in recent years, there has been some increase in NTBs.

**2** Actions nominally taken to counter unfair trading practices—anti-dumping and countervailing duties imposed on foreign firms—are often used as protectionist measures.

**3** Concern about imports is particularly strong when unemployment is high, but beggar-thy-neighbour policies that attempt to protect jobs by limiting imports tend to be counterproductive.

**4** Although all countries benefit from free trade, some groups within a country may be adversely affected. In Canada, unskilled workers and those in industries where trade substantially increases competition may see their wages fall. Some workers may lose their jobs and may require assistance to find new ones.

**5** Global trade agreements provide a framework within which trade barriers can be reduced. The Uruguay Round of GATT negotiations extended trade liberalization to new areas, including services, agriculture, and intellectual property, and established the World Trade Organization to enforce regulations.

**6** Difficulties in arriving at trade agreements involving all the nations of the world have resulted in more effective regional agreements, including NAFTA. These regional agreements cause trade creation among member countries, but they may also induce trade diversion from nonmembers, which represents losses to member-country economies.

**7** Under NAFTA, barriers in markets for goods, services, and capital are removed. Concern has been raised that this will cause capital to move out of Canada and into the United States and Mexico as firms try to rationalize production and produce in the lowest-cost location. But the principles of trade do not support this concern.

## KEY WORDS

| | | | |
|---|---|---|---|
| free trade | voluntary export restraints | infant-industry argument | World Trade Organization (WTO) |
| protectionism | | strategic trade theory | |
| commercial policies | anti-dumping duties | optimal tariff argument | bilateral/regional agreements |
| nontariff barriers | countervailing duties | General Agreement on Tariffs and Trade (GATT) | trade creation |
| quotas | beggar-thy-neighbour policies | | trade diversion |
| quota rents | | | |

## REVIEW QUESTIONS

**1** What are the various ways in which countries seek to protect their industries against foreign imports?

**2** How do tariffs and quotas differ?

**3** Why are consumers worse off as a result of the imposition of a tariff?

**4** What are the actions taken against foreign firms to ensure fair international trade? How have they worked in practice?

**5** What is meant by voluntary export restraints? How does this differ from tariffs? from quotas?

**6** How is it possible that some groups are adversely affected by free trade? Which are the groups in Canada that are most adversely affected?

**7** What are beggar-thy-neighbour policies? What are their consequences?

**8** What do GATT and the WTO do? What are their basic underlying principles? What have been GATT's achievements? What further advances were accomplished under the Uruguay Round?

**9** What is NAFTA? What are the advantages of regional free trade agreements?

**10** What is meant by trade diversion versus trade creation? Why is trade diversion harmful?

## PROBLEMS

**1** Suppose Canada decides to protect its magazine industry by restricting the import of American magazines. Compare the amount of gains and losses that accrue to various parties as a result of implementing the protection by means of
   (a) tariffs
   (b) quotas
   (c) persuading U.S. magazine producers to restrict their exports voluntarily.

**2** In the early 1990s, the U.S. softwood lumber industry persuaded the U.S. government that exports of softwood lumber from British Columbia were being subsidized. The stumpage fees charged by the B.C. government were said to be so low as to constitute an unfair subsidy. The U.S. government threatened to impose countervailing duties on Canadian softwood lumber exports to the United States. To preclude this, the B.C. government agreed to impose an export tax on softwood lumber sold to the United States. Explain whether this was a sensible response.

**3** In 1993, the world price of aluminum fell, partly because of the worldwide recession, partly because new techniques allowed aluminum cans to be produced using 10 percent less aluminum, and partly because Russia, no longer using its aluminum to make airplanes, began exporting it. The possibility existed that anti-dumping duties would be levied against Russia, although Russia was selling the aluminum at world prices. What do you think might have been the consequences if the anti-dumping duties had actually been

filed? (Some background facts: Japan is a major importer of aluminum; and Alcan is a major owner of non-Canadian production facilities.)

**4** If you were a minister of international trade intent on discouraging exports, how might you use regulatory policies to further your objectives?

**5** If Mexican workers receive a quarter of the wages that Canadian workers do, why don't all Canadian firms move to Mexico?

**6** Under NAFTA, the removal of import barriers and barriers to capital mobility removed the incentives that companies had to locate in Canada in order to serve the Canadian market. Is Canada likely to end up being harmed as a result of companies relocating south of the border?

**7** When Canada and the United States signed the Canada-U.S. Free Trade Agreement in 1989, do you think there was more trade creation than trade diversion? What about when NAFTA was created in 1994 by expanding the Free Trade Agreement to include Mexico?

**8** Should NAFTA treat Japanese firms producing cars in North America differently than North American–owned firms?

**9** Should the free trade provisions of NAFTA apply to the cultural industries? To the educational and health sectors? To the purchase and sale of water? Movement of labour?

# CHAPTER 22

# DEVELOPING AND TRANSITIONAL ECONOMIES

Our focus until now has been on the industrialized economies of the world that enjoy high standards of living, consisting of North America, Western Europe, and Japan. Most of the world's population live in much poorer countries. Three quarters of them live in **less developed countries,** or LDCs, countries that simply have not been able to achieve rates of growth high enough to raise the living standards of the average person above poverty levels. Others live in **transitional countries,** the formerly communist countries of much of Eastern Europe, including what used to be the Soviet Union. These are countries that eschewed the market system, opting instead for a socialist system in which private property was replaced by state ownership and in which resources were allocated by centralized planners rather than decentralized markets. Some countries, like China, can be viewed as both an LDC and a transitional economy. China attempted, unsuccessfully, to achieve development through socialist economic principles. Although the sources of their present economic difficulties are different, both LDCs and transitional countries strive to improve the lives of their citizens by economic growth.

KEY QUESTIONS

**1** In what ways, besides their poverty, do less developed countries differ from industrialized ones?

**2** What are the impediments to growth in LDCs?

**3** What policies can LDCs pursue to improve their standard of living?

**4** What were the economic conditions that gave rise to the socialist idea?

**5** How did Soviet-style socialism differ from the market system and why did it fail?

**6** What problems do the former socialist economies face in making the transition to market economies?

The LDCs pose some of the most poignant problems in economics. There are no simple answers, no easy formulas that, if followed, would ensure successful solutions. Still, as this chapter explains, economists have learned a lot during recent decades about the process of economic development. The problems of the transitional economies are somewhat different. They are involved in overhauling their entire economic systems, making them more market-based. Even China, the most populous country in the world, has committed itself to using markets in its economic life. This chapter contrasts socialist-style economies with those of developed countries, highlighting the major differences that might account for their divergent growth paths and standards of living, and pointing out some of the problems that have arisen in the difficult period of transition to market economies.

## LDCs: SOME BACKGROUND

Statistics can provide some indication of what it means to live in an LDC. In Canada, life expectancy at birth is about 78 years. In Peru, it is 66 years; in India, 61 years; in Nigeria, 51 years. In Canada, 6 infants die for every 1,000 live births; in Brazil, 56; in Pakistan, 95; in Ethiopia, 122. The average Canadian completes 12 years of schooling, while the average African gets only 5 years. India, with a population thirty-one times larger than that of Canada, has a GDP roughly one half of that of Canada. This means that per capita income in India is about 1.5 percent of that in Canada.

The United Nations and the World Bank (an institution established by the major industrialized countries after World War II that provides loans to LDCs) group countries into three categories: low-income countries, with a GNP per capita of U.S. $725 or less in 1994; high-income countries, with a GNP per capita above U.S. $8,955; and middle-income countries, with GNP per capita in between. The low-income countries are the LDCs, while the high-income countries are industrialized, or **developed, countries.** Figure 22.1 shows the countries in the various income categories. Table 22.1 compares some of the relevant statistics for Canada (a high-income country), Mexico (middle-income), and India (low-income).

While over the past hundred years the income gap among the high-income countries has narrowed considerably, that between the high-income and low-income countries has not. However, there are signs that change is possible. Some countries have made notable progress in recent years.

First, several countries have moved from the circle of LDCs to the ranks of middle-income countries. These are referred to collectively as **newly industrialized countries,** or **NICs** for short. These success stories include the "gang of four": South Korea, Taiwan, Singapore, and Hong Kong. In the forty years since the devastating Korean War, South Korea has moved from the category of backward country to that of major producer—not just of simple products such as textiles but of automobiles (the Hyundai) and computers (many of the IBM clones

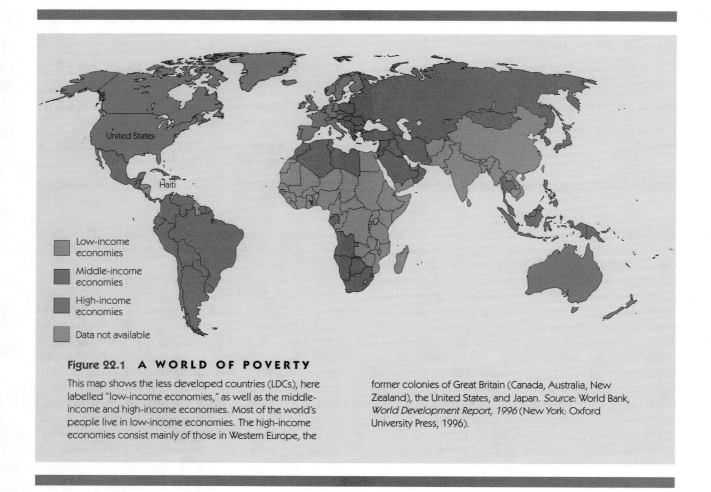

**Figure 22.1  A WORLD OF POVERTY**

This map shows the less developed countries (LDCs), here labelled "low-income economies," as well as the middle-income and high-income economies. Most of the world's people live in low-income economies. The high-income economies consist mainly of those in Western Europe, the former colonies of Great Britain (Canada, Australia, New Zealand), the United States, and Japan. *Source:* World Bank, *World Development Report, 1996* (New York: Oxford University Press, 1996).

are made in South Korea), which require a reasonably high level of technological expertise. Even more impressive, Japan has moved from the ranks of middle-income countries to the position of one of the most prosperous in the world.

Second, there have been pockets of remarkable progress *within* the LDCs. In the early 1960s, agricultural research centres around the world developed new kinds of seeds, which under correct conditions increase the yields per hectare enormously. The introduction and dissemination of these new seeds, accompanied by enormous improvements in agricultural practices—known as the **green revolution**—led to huge increases in output. India, for example, finally managed to produce enough food to feed its burgeoning population, and now sometimes exports wheat to other countries.

Third, even the grim statistics for life expectancy—55 in Bangladesh and 44 in Malawi (compared to 78 in Canada)—represent improvements for many countries. But these improvements have a darker side in some—a population explosion reminiscent of the Malthusian nightmare. Malthus, you will recall from Chapter 19, envisioned a world in which population growth outpaced increases in the food supply. In Kenya during the early 1980s, improved health conditions enabled the population to grow at the remarkable rate of 4.1 percent a year, implying a doubling of the population every eighteen years, while output increased only at the rate of 1.9 percent a year.

### Table 22.1  STANDARD OF LIVING IN CANADA, MEXICO, AND INDIA

| Category | Canada | Mexico | India |
|---|---|---|---|
| GNP per capita (U.S. $) | 19,510 | 4,180 | 320 |
| Life expectancy (years) | 78 | 71 | 62 |
| Agriculture as percentage of GDP | 2 | 8 | 30 |
| Energy consumption per capita (kilograms of oil equivalent) | 7,854 | 1,453 | 243 |
| Food as percentage of total household consumption | 11 | 35 | 52 |
| Medical care as percentage of total household consumption | 5 | 5 | 3 |
| Average annual inflation (GNP deflator) 1980–92* | 4.1 | 62.4 | 8.5 |
| Average annual growth of population (percentage), 1980–92 | 1.3 | 2.0 | 1.8 |
| Infant mortality rate per 1,000 live births | 6 | 35 | 70 |
| Population per physician | 450 | 1,242 | 2,460 |
| Population in cities of 1 million or more as percentage of total population | 35 | 28 | 9 |

*Source:* World Bank, *World Development Report* (New York: Oxford University Press, various years). Data are for the most recent years available, in most cases 1994.

\* Like the GDP deflator discussed in Chapter 6, the GNP deflator is the measure of the price level used to adjust GNP for inflation.

Output increases do nothing to improve per capita income when the population grows even faster.

The 1980s were a particularly hard decade for some of the poorest countries, as Figure 22.2 shows.

Sub-Saharan Africa had basically stagnated over the past quarter century, but during the 1980s per capita income actually fell 2.4 percent per year. Latin America had grown a little more than 2 percent a

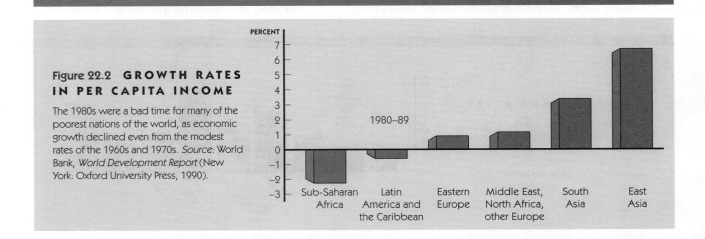

### Figure 22.2  GROWTH RATES IN PER CAPITA INCOME

The 1980s were a bad time for many of the poorest nations of the world, as economic growth declined even from the modest rates of the 1960s and 1970s. *Source:* World Bank, *World Development Report* (New York: Oxford University Press, 1990).

year in per capita income over the previous quarter century. During the 1980s per capita income fell by .7 percent a year.

## EXPLANATIONS OF UNDERDEVELOPMENT

Part of the poverty of LDCs arises from their lack of resources. They have less physical capital per capita and less human capital, with high illiteracy rates and low average years of schooling. The lower levels of physical capital per capita are not the result of low savings rates—in fact savings rates of many are comparable with that of Canada (see Figure 22.3). But their high population growth rates mean that they have to save a lot just to stand still.

High population growth rates have had another effect. They have increased enormously the proportion of the young, who are dependent on others for their income. They have also made the task of improving educational levels even harder. There is a vicious circle here. Typically, more educated women have smaller families. This is partly because they are more likely to be informed about family planning, but it is also partly because the opportunity cost of having children is higher for them: they must forgo more income.

Low education levels and lack of capital means that these economies cannot avail themselves of much

of the most advanced technology. With some exceptions, they specialize in low-skill, labour-intensive industries (products that require much labour relative to the amount of equipment they employ), like textiles. In turn, the reliance on labour-intensive techniques of production means that there is less opportunity for productivity improvements that come with new capital investment, opportunities that account for much of the growth in per capita incomes in industrialized countries.

## THE IMPORTANCE OF CAPITAL

How much of the difference between developed and less developed countries can actually be attributed to lack of capital, as opposed to inefficient use of capital? If a shortage of capital in LDCs were the major difference between the developed and less developed countries, the law of diminishing returns would predict that the return to capital in the industrialized countries would be much lower than the return in LDCs. The more capital a country has relative to its population, the lower is the output per machine and the lower is the marginal return to capital. In other words, the shortage of capital should make the return to capital greater. This difference in returns would naturally result in a movement of capital from the more developed to the less developed countries, as business firms searched out profitable investment opportunities.

The evidence shows some differences in the return to capital. But these differences are too small to

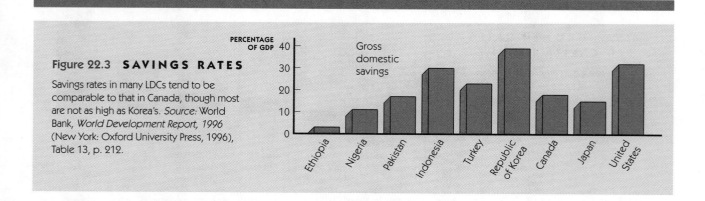

**Figure 22.3 SAVINGS RATES**

Savings rates in many LDCs tend to be comparable to that in Canada, though most are not as high as Korea's. *Source:* World Bank, *World Development Report, 1996* (New York: Oxford University Press, 1996), Table 13, p. 212.

# CLOSE-UP: THE INTERNATIONAL DEBT CRISIS

Borrowing from abroad can make sound economic sense. For instance, much of the development of the Canadian transcontinental railroad in the nineteenth century was financed by bonds issued in Europe. Over the past two decades, many firms and governments of less developed countries borrowed billions of dollars from banks in Canada, the United States, and other developed countries, as the table here shows. But while the nineteenth-century railroad companies were able to repay investments, it became apparent in the 1980s that some of the countries that had borrowed heavily—particularly Brazil, Argentina, and Mexico—could not repay what they owed. The resulting crisis threatened the economic prospects of the LDCs and the financial viability of many Western banks.

The immediate cause of the problem was simple. In the 1970s, real interest rates were low, and

banks were flush with "petro-dollars"—dollars that oil producers, particularly in the Middle East, had earned from selling their oil at the high prices that prevailed beginning in 1973—and wanted to invest or deposit abroad. Both borrowers and lenders were optimistic that the loans would create economic growth, and repayment would be easy.

Then three things happened. First, nominal and real interest rates soared in the late 1970s, and the interest payments rose far beyond any level that the borrowers had imagined. Second, the world entered a recession in the early 1980s, and the worldwide slowdown in growth made it even more difficult for the LDCs to pay back what they owed. Third, oil prices fell in the early 1980s. Some of the largest borrowers had been oil producers, like Mexico and Indonesia, which had intended to repay their loans by selling oil.

| Country | Public or publicly guaranteed external debt in 1989 (U.S. $) |
| --- | --- |
| Brazil | $84 billion |
| Mexico | $76 billion |
| India | $54 billion |
| Argentina | $51 billion |
| Indonesia | $41 billion |
| Egypt | $40 billion |
| China | $37 billion |
| Poland | $35 billion |
| Turkey | $35 billion |
| Nigeria | $32 billion |
| Venezuela | $25 billion |
| Algeria | $24 billion |
| Philippines | $23 billion |
| Morocco | $19 billion |
| Korea | $17 billion |

*Source:* World Bank, *World Development Report, 1991*, Table 21.

But bad luck is not the only culprit. The banks are also to blame for failing to take into account the risks associated with the loans they were making. They should have realized, for instance, that prices for goods like oil are volatile. The banks also placed too much trust in the assurance of foreign governments that the loans would be invested productively. Much of the money was invested in projects that were probably not economically viable from the start. By contrast, some better-managed countries like the Republic of Korea borrowed heavily but invested the money wisely and have been able to repay it.

Massive defaults on loans were avoided only by debt rescheduling. As a payment came due, the banks lent the country more money, in effect postponing the date at which repayment is to occur. As a condition for this rescheduling, the lenders insisted that the borrowers "put their house in order"—cutting back, for instance, on their huge budget deficits. But this strategy of squeezing the LDCs to pay had its own problems: the only way the countries could repay was for them to grow more. But growth required additional capital, which foreign lenders were reluctant to provide. The only way out was to forgive some of the debt and then count on the rest being repaid.

Debt forgiveness, which amounts to a gift to the debtor countries, also has its problems. For example, will forgiveness encourage countries to borrow more in the future than they have the capacity to repay? Is Brazil more deserving of such a multi-billion-dollar gift than many poorer countries in Latin America or Africa, just because it borrowed more?

demonstrate that a capital shortage is the major problem faced by the LDCs. Moreover, if a capital shortage were the major problem, the LDCs would use what capital they have very intensively. But this does not typically happen. For example, factories run extra daily shifts more often in developed countries than in LDCs.

A much more important impediment to growth in many less developed countries is the lack of efficiency in how scarce funds are used. In Venezuela, which tried to invest its oil dollars as fast as they came in during the 1970s, output increased by 10 cents for every dollar invested in capital equipment. In contrast, in the developed countries, each extra dollar of investment results on average in an output increase of between 30 and 50 cents—three to five times higher. In many LDCs, greater investment simply does not lead to much increased output.

There are a number of reasons for this. Some economists have argued that at any moment a country has only a limited absorptive capacity for more capital. It lacks the human capital, the experience, and technological know-how to pursue many projects simultaneously. The absorptive capacity is most limited in the poorest countries. When investments are pushed beyond absorptive capacity, they yield very low returns.

Many economists, however, believe that there are two more fundamental reasons for the low returns to capital: the lack of developed capital markets to allocate capital efficiently, and well-intentioned government interventions that nonetheless support low-return projects. At least in the past, many countries thought that a symbol of development was a steel mill or some other big factory or plant, even if such a factory was unsuitable for the economic conditions of the country.

## INEQUALITY

Many LDCs are also marked by high levels of inequality. Thousands of homeless people sleep in the streets along which the wealthy travel in Mercedes

FACTORS CONTRIBUTING TO UNDERDEVELOPMENT

Lack of capital equipment

Lack of education

Lack of technology

Lack of developed capital markets

Government interventions that impair efficient resource allocation

Great income inequality

cars. Some of this inequality is simply the workings out of the laws of supply and demand. There is an abundance of unskilled labour and a scarcity of capital, so that wages are low and those who have capital do well.

Indeed, earlier theories suggested that inequality contributed to economic growth. Sir Arthur Lewis, who received the Nobel Prize for his work on development economics, argued that what he called the *surplus of labour* kept wages low and profits high. Workers earning subsistence wages could not save, but capitalists could, so that the higher profits contributed to a higher savings rate. In this view, there was a trade-off between growth and equality.

Today, many economists believe that growth and equality are really complementary, as evidenced by the East Asia miracle discussed later in the chapter.

## FAILED GOVERNMENT POLICIES

Most of the countries of Asia and Africa were colonies of the European powers until World War II. As they got their independence in the aftermath of the war, the new governments took upon themselves the responsibility of promoting economic development. Almost all believed that strong government action would be required, and some, such as India, took an avowedly socialist strategy. These ideas were partly in revulsion to what they saw as the exploitive capitalism of their colonial masters, partly a reflection of the seeming success of the Soviet Union's rapid industrialization.

## PLANNING

In many LDCs, the government attempted to direct the overall course of the economy by "planning." A "Ministry of Planning" would draw up a detailed plan, typically for five years, specifying how much each sector of the economy would grow, how much investment would occur in each sector, where the output of each sector would go, and where each sector would receive its inputs. The Ministry of Planning had enormous powers, among them allocating investment funds and the foreign exchange required to import raw materials from abroad.

In the last decade, there has been considerable disillusionment with government planning—a disillusionment that set in even before the failures of the Soviet-style system became evident. The issue is not whether planning is needed—it surely is—but whether the most effective place to do the planning is in a government centralized bureau or at the level of the firm. Today most economists are skeptical about the ability of a centralized bureau to do effective planning.

One of the main arguments for centralized planning was its presumed greater ability to coordinate. But the experience of the past quarter century has shown that centralized planning offices generally do not do a good job at coordination. One reason is that they often lack the requisite information. Another is that firms can more easily deal with the details of investment projects—deciding what kind of plant to construct, how to construct it, making sure that it is constructed in an efficient way, and so on—than can government bureaucrats. And these details, more than anything else, determine the success of the projects.

## TILTING THE ECONOMY

The purpose of planning, of course, was to do more than just substitute for the markets' role in coordinating economic activity. It was at the very least to tilt the economy in ways that would enhance growth.

Some ideas on how this might be done were borrowed from the Soviet Union, such as an emphasis on capital-intensive industries like steel. Many countries pursued a policy known as **import substitution,** stressing the substitution of domestically produced goods for goods previously imported. In this view, the hallmark of a developed country is modern industry. Rather than importing steel, automobiles, TV sets, computers, and other such products, a nation should produce them itself in order to develop the skills necessary for modernization. In other words, it should produce all the goods it had previously imported from the industrialized economies. This is the road to development that most of the larger LDCs, including India, China, and Brazil, undertook in the years after World War II. At times, each of these countries has taken import substitution to extremes, insisting, for example, on domestically produced computers even when they might not be able to perform the functions of imported computers.

But the import substitution approach has disadvantages of its own. Trade barriers set up to protect domestic firms can end up protecting inefficient producers. The absence of foreign competition means that there is an insufficient spur to innovation and efficiency. The profits to which trade barriers frequently give rise provide a source of government corruption. And the trade barriers remain in place years after they were introduced.

The problems are particularly evident when the protected industry is one like steel, whose product is used in other industries. An Indian car manufacturer might be profitable if it could only purchase steel at international prices. But if it is forced to pay inflated prices to buy Indian steel, it cannot compete with foreign producers. The government might try to offset this by subsidizing the car manufacturers. A subsidy or trade protection in one sector thus grows into a complex of subsidies and trade protection in other sectors.

Although trade protection to stimulate import substitution generally leads to massive inefficiencies, it has proved successful for a time in some countries such as Brazil, which enjoyed several decades of rapid growth before the debt crisis of the 1980s tainted that picture. Also, advocates of import substitution note that many of the most rapid bursts of growth of the current developed countries occurred in wartimes, when the economy was inwardly directed, not export-oriented. These same advocates, looking at the experience of Japan, argue that at least for industrial goods, import substitution—the development of a domestic market—must precede exports. Before Japan was able successfully to sell cars abroad, it first had to develop a market for Japanese cars at home.

## WHEN GOVERNMENT BECOMES THE PROBLEM

Sometimes government has actually impeded the development process. It has done this both by allocating inefficiently those resources over which it has direct control and by interfering in the function of markets so that *they* could not efficiently allocate resources.

Mao Tse-tung, perhaps because he saw that wheat was the predominant grain consumed in the more developed countries, directed that vast areas of China be converted from rice to wheat. This land was not suited for wheat, and agricultural productivity suffered. Moreover, the conversion to wheat fields actually depleted the land of its fertility, so that when it was eventually returned to growing rice, productivity was lower.

The government, unlike the private sector, can support an unprofitable firm for many years. Also, the scale of mistakes governments make sets them apart from the mistakes of private firms. If a single farmer mistakenly decides to grow wheat rather than rice, the costs he faces are not comparable to the costs borne by China when Mao made his mistake.

Mao's mistake was an honest mistake of judgment, not a consequence of his pursuit of private interests. But some problems facing the LDCs arise from governmental corruption, and here private interests conflict with public ones. Corruption is often associated with the large role government plays in an LDC, particularly in restricting foreign trade. When the government imposes a high tariff or otherwise protects an industry, the protected firms can raise their prices and increase their profits. If there are only one or two such firms, they will be tempted to share some of the resulting profits with the government official responsible for the protection. And the government official, knowing this, has a strong incentive to ask the private firms to share some of the profits.

Between honest mistakes and corruption lies a third category: rent-seeking activities. If government has the power to confer special benefits, people will seek those benefits for themselves. Firms will try to persuade government that they deserve protection from foreign competition, knowing that such protection will increase their profits. They may give outright bribes, or they may simply spend funds to help elect officials who are sympathetic to their views.

## THE EAST ASIA MIRACLE

As development strategies based on planning, import substitution, and heavy industrialization were failing in India, China, and many countries in Africa and Latin America, the countries of East Asia were pursuing a different set of strategies and achieving growth rates of 7 percent or more year after year.

Several ingredients were essential to their success. Governments in these countries took an active role, but their role was to pursue market-oriented policies that encouraged the development of the private sector. They sought to augment and "govern" the market, not to replace it. A key policy was to ensure the macroeconomic stability of the economy, avoiding for the most part high inflation. As part of this strategy, governments maintained a high level of fiscal responsibility, eschewing the huge budget deficits that characterize many LDCs.

They sought to augment all the ingredients of growth, including fostering high savings rates—often in excess of 25 percent. In Japan, more than a third of these savings was garnered through a system of postal savings banks established by the government

that provided a secure and easy way to save, particularly for those in the rural sector. In Singapore, the government established a "provident fund" to which all workers were required to contribute 40 percent of their income.

These governments also influenced the allocation of capital in a myriad of ways. Banks were discouraged from making real estate loans and loans for durable consumption goods. This helped to increase private savings rates and discouraged real estate speculation, which often serves to destabilize the economy. As a result, more funds were available for investment in growth-oriented activities, like new equipment.

In addition, governments established development banks, to promote long-term investment in activities like shipbuilding, steel mills, and the chemical industry. These interventions have been more controversial and their success has been mixed. The steel firms in Taiwan and Korea are among the most efficient in the world. But soon after the chemical industry was established in Korea, the price of oil, an essential ingredient, soared, and the industry suffered losses for almost two decades. With the decline in oil prices, it is now doing better. Proponents of these initiatives argue that they have technological benefits for other sectors and are necessary as part of a long-run growth strategy.

The Japanese government took a variety of other initiatives to promote certain industries. Among its most noted successes were its entry into the computer chip market. By the early 1980s, Japan looked as if it would completely dominate that market, before Intel and other American producers reasserted American leadership. A noted failure was Japan's attempt to discourage Honda, a manufacturer of motorcycles, from entering the auto market, arguing that there were already too many producers.

### EXPORT-LED GROWTH

One factor that distinguished the countries of East Asia from less successful LDCs was their emphasis on exports. A growth strategy focusing on exports is called **export-led growth,** in contrast to the import substitution policy described earlier. Firms were encouraged to export in a variety of ways, including being given increased access to credit, often at subsidized rates.

In export-led growth, firms produce according to their comparative advantage. This is not current comparative advantage, based on current resources and knowledge, but dynamic comparative advantage, based on acquired skills and technology and recognition of the importance of learning by doing— of the improvement in skills and productivity that comes from production experience. With exports, demand for the goods produced by an LDC is not limited by the low income of its citizens. The world is its market.

Advocates of export-led growth also believe that the competition provided by the export market is an important stimulus to efficiency and modernization. The only way a firm can succeed in the face of keen international competition is to produce what consumers want, at the quality they want, and at the lowest possible costs. This keen competition forces specialization in areas where low-wage, less developed countries have a comparative advantage, such as labour-intensive products.

Export-led growth has also facilitated the transfer of advanced technology. Producers exporting to developed countries not only come into contact with efficient producers within those countries, they also learn to adopt their standards and production techniques. They come to understand better, for instance, why timeliness in production and quality are important.

## FOSTERING EQUALITY

Another distinctive aspect of East Asia's development strategy is its emphasis on equality. We have already noted several aspects of these egalitarian policies: Singapore's home ownership programme; the almost universal provision of elementary and secondary education, including to women; and the land redistribution programmes that were the precursor of growth in several of the countries, including Taiwan and Japan. In many of these countries, government has also tried to curb excessive wage inequality and to discourage conspicuous consumption by the rich.

Their experience has shown that one can have high savings rates without either the oppressiveness of Soviet-style governments or large inequalities.

The equality measures actually promoted economic growth. The land reforms resulted in increased agricultural production; the sharecropping system previously in place in Taiwan had had the effect of a 50 percent tax on output. The high education levels increased productivity directly and facilitated the transfer and adoption of more advanced technology. More education for women is, as we have noted, associated with declining rates of population growth.

But the greatest boon of equality for development may be through its political effects. Inequality frequently gives rise to political instability, and political instability has strong adverse effects on the economic climate. In such an atmosphere, both domestic and foreign firms will be reluctant to invest. The countries of East Asia not only managed to have remarkable political stability, but as their incomes grew, there was a strong trend towards democratization.

## REDEFINING THE ROLE OF GOVERNMENT

The central question many LDCs are asking today is, what can we learn from the success of the East Asia countries and the failures elsewhere? What can governments do or refrain from doing to effectively facilitate growth?

*Actions to Take* Governments should act in a fiscally responsible way, constraining expenditures in line with their tax revenue base. They should maintain macroeconomic stability. More broadly, they should work to create a favourable climate for investment, including foreign investment, which provides not only additional capital but also the transfer of valuable technology.

They should do whatever they can to reduce the rates of population growth and to increase the quantity and quality of education. The evidence suggests that the most reliable way of controlling population is to increase the opportunity cost of having children. Educating women does exactly that. That is why female education has not only a direct benefit in increased productivity, but an indirect benefit, in reduced population growth.

Why is it that the economies of some countries grow faster than others? An important question for industrialized nations like Canada, it is a crucial one both for developing nations and for those nations in transition from planned to market economies. Until recently economists have not been able to account for differing rates of economic growth among nations with any degree of certainty.

Traditional, or "old," growth theory predicts that poor countries should grow faster than rich ones. Since poor countries have less capital per capita than rich countries, capital should flow to the poor countries where its rate of return should be higher, thus leading to higher growth rates and convergence of per capita GDPs. "New" growth theory, focusing on the technological advantages possessed by rich countries, predicts that these should have higher rates of growth. In particular, the use of more advanced and capital-intensive techniques of production leads to more rapid productivity growth through "learning by doing," spillovers of knowledge from one industry to another, and the discovery of new products and innovative techniques of production. According to this view, productivity growth is lower in economies relying on more labour-intensive techniques of production. This could explain why convergence of GDP per capita between low-income and high-income countries is rarely observed. If anything, the income gap between high-income and most low-income countries is rising. Though the predictions of these two schools of thought are different, both are based on the notion that economies operate on their production-possibilities frontiers. That is, both types of

economies are doing the best they can given their productive resources.

Economists have begun to ask whether either the old or the new growth theories can adequately explain observed growth patterns. Over the last quarter century, some, but not all, of the poorest nations have been the fastest-growing economies. Perhaps the best-known of these are the Southeast Asian "tigers." On average, poor countries fail to grow as fast as rich countries, but the fastest-growing subset of poor nations always leads the way for all. The fact that growth rates are not systematically related to national income levels does not fit either of the above theories. The American economist Mancur Olson has suggested that countries with low growth may simply not be operating efficiently. He rejects the notion that growth patterns can be explained by differences in access to private knowledge, the existence of overpopulation in some nations, or differences in capital, and instead concludes that the most important factors may lie in specific institutions and economic policies. In his view institutions that are designed for the enforcement of property rights and that ensure that contracts are honoured, and economic policies that allow individuals access to free markets are essential if nations are to operate on their production-possibilities frontiers and achieve maximum rates of growth.

Evidence has recently come to light that supports this view of economic growth and suggests some additional factors. In their study of economic growth between 1970 and 1989, Jeffrey Sachs and Andrew Warner of Harvard University have shown that developing nations that are considered to be open—having low tariff and nontariff barriers to trade and investment flows—grow faster than those where domestic producers are highly protected. Though concerned with international trade and investment, this notion of "openness" may also serve as a proxy for other market-oriented policies that Olson considers to be so important. Political stability is identified by Sachs and Warner as a significant factor. Again this lends support to Olson's contention that institutions that reassure investors that their money faces only an acceptable level of risk are important. The level of government spending on goods and services tends to affect growth rates adversely. Apparently, the more important the market is relative to the public sector, the more conducive economic policy is to growth, a finding that is consistent with Olson's theory.

Sachs and Warner also uncovered some other factors that suggest that the determinants of growth are multifaceted. Two important ones are the level of investment and the economy's endowment of natural resources. That high investment should lead to high growth rates should not be surprising. Virtually all growth theories would predict that. The effect of natural resource wealth is more surprising. Larger resource endowments tend to pull growth rates down despite the fact that they make a country wealthier. This may be partly because the country is induced to direct large amounts of its investment to developing the resource wealth rather than to sectors like manufacturing, where productivity growth may be higher. It might also be that resource wealth provides a source of funds that governments find irresistible to use in unproductive ways.

The implications of these findings for policy makers in developing and transitional economies are potentially profound. Fostering institutions that ensure well-defined and stable property rights and pursuing economic policies that promote (or at least do not hinder) access to international markets would seem to be prerequisites for good economic growth. Restraining the public sector from attempting to do things that are best left to the private sector seems also to be good for growth. Countries that are able to establish these fundamentals seem likely to be the ones that will grow the fastest.

*Sources:* M. Olson, "Big Bills Left on the Sidewalk: Why Some Nations are Rich, and Others Poor," *Journal of Economic Perspectives* 10, no. 2 (Spring 1996): 3–24; J. D. Sachs and A. Warner, "Economic Reform and the Process of Global Integration," *Brookings Papers on Economic Activity,* no. 1, 1995: 1–107; Ibid., "Natural Resource Abundance and Economic Growth," *National Bureau of Economic Research,* Working Paper No. 5398, December 1995.

Governments also need to provide a basic **infrastructure,** not only physical infrastructure, like roads and ports, but also institutional infrastructure, like an effective legal system through which contracts can be enforced. Even here, however, the direct role of government versus the private sector has been evolving. Many countries have discovered that parts of the infrastructure, like toll roads, can be provided privately, relieving the government of both fiscal and managerial burdens. In some areas, such as telecommunications, what is most needed is a regulatory structure that promotes competition at the same time as it ensures that consumers are not being taken advantage of by what monopoly power remains.

Finally, they should aim to create a competitive export sector appropriate to the resources of the economy, as most of the countries of East Asia did.

***Actions to Avoid*** Governments should avoid policies that inhibit growth. These include trade protection, which insulates firms from competitive forces that enhance efficiency, and unnecessary regulations, which restrict competition, deter entry, and increase costs and prices.

***What Advanced Countries Can Do to Help*** Foreign aid can be of immense help. There is general agreement that technical assistance and education have been extremely valuable. These forms of assistance have become more important as international capital markets have become more developed so that even LDCs can obtain funds for high-return investment projects.

The poorest of the LDCs, including many countries in Africa, cannot borrow on private capital markets. But that is mainly because the risk of default is high. In many of these countries, there are few good investment projects. The World Bank channels multilateral aid to investment projects in poor countries through an arm of its operations referred to as the IDA (International Development Assistance) programme. Unlike with private loans, IDA funding is not expected to earn commercial rates of return. Its intention is to increase the effectiveness of foreign aid.

Some forms of foreign aid are actually counterproductive. Thus, food aid sometimes depresses local prices, harming farmers and discouraging domestic production. Some large projects sponsored by the World Bank have been criticized as being bad for the environment, yielding economic returns that in some cases are barely enough to pay the interest on the loans, and leaving many poor countries with an enormous debt load.

Many economists continue to emphasize the importance of trade for LDCs and developed countries alike. Giving LDCs access to markets in industrialized countries is, in their view, a "win-win" policy. Consumers in the latter win by having a greater variety of goods at lower prices. The LDCs benefit from having a large market for their goods. But such a view is not universally held. Spokespersons for labour complain that admitting goods produced by low-wage countries, especially those with inadequate employment standards, results in lower wages and even job losses to Canadian workers. However, as we argued in Chapter 21, the total gains from trade generally outweigh the losses to certain groups.

## THE TRANSITIONAL ECONOMIES

In industrialized countries today, there is widespread confidence in markets and in the efficiency with which they allocate resources. To be sure, there are market failures, periods of unemployment, and pockets of poverty. But we have seen in this book how markets by and large allocate resources efficiently. We have seen as well how selective govern-

---

### AN AGENDA FOR DEVELOPMENT

How the developed countries can help

    Reduce trade barriers

    Increase foreign aid

    Facilitate foreign investment

Growth-oriented policies for LDCs

    Reduce population growth

    Increase quantity and quality of education

    Provide a basic infrastructure (roads, ports, a legal system)

    Provide a favourable climate for investment, including foreign investment

    Facilitate development of capital markets (financial intermediaries)

    Develop a competitive export sector

    Promote equality

Policies that may inhibit growth

    Trade protection

    Regulations, licensing

ment interventions can remedy the market failures and address the problem of the inequality of income generated by the market.

But this confidence has not always been present; neither is it universal now. When North America went into the Great Depression in 1929, not to recover fully until World War II, hundreds of thousands of Canadians lost their jobs. The capitalist economic system did not seem to be functioning well. Today, to the billions of people still living in abject poverty in India, elsewhere in Asia, and in Africa and South America, markets have failed to meet their rising aspirations. And even within the industrialized countries, there are many who have not partaken of the general prosperity. For them the market system does not seem to have worked well.

It is not surprising, then, that many have sought an alternative economic system, which would generate faster sustained economic growth at the same time as it promotes greater equality. Throughout much of the twentieth century, many saw communism as the answer. They believed that if the govern-ment controlled the economy, recessions would be eliminated, as well as what they saw as the chaos of the marketplace, for instance, the excess expansion of capacity in one industry accompanied by short-ages in another industry.

The countries that came under the domination of the Soviet Union and China after World War II adopted various forms of communism as their economic and political systems. This involved both state ownership of most property—not only the factories, but also the houses and the land—and considerable central control of economic decisions. Because of the important role played by central planning, these economies are referred to as **planned economies,** in contrast to the market economies of North America and Western Europe.

In 1991, the system began to crumble. The Soviet Union was dissolved and one by one the communist countries began to move towards market-based economies. Table 22.2 compares living standards in the Soviet-style economies just before this with those in the rest of the world.

### Table 22.2 COMPARISON OF LIVING STANDARDS BETWEEN PLANNED AND MARKET ECONOMIES

|  | GDP per capita (1988 U.S. $) | Annual GDP growth rate (%) 1965–1988 | Life expectancy at birth | Adult illiteracy (%) |
|---|---|---|---|---|
| Soviet-style economies |  |  |  |  |
| USSR | 2,660 | 4.0 | 70 | < 5 |
| China | 330 | 5.4 | 70 | 31 |
| Hungary | 2,460 | 5.1 | 71 | < 5 |
| Market economies |  |  |  |  |
| Canada | 16,960 | 2.3 | 77 | < 5 |
| USA | 19,840 | 1.6 | 76 | < 5 |
| India | 340 | 1.8 | 58 | 57 |
| Italy | 13,330 | 3.0 | 77 | < 5 |
| Egypt | 660 | 3.6 | 63 | 56 |
| Sweden | 19,300 | 1.8 | 77 | < 5 |

*Source:* World Bank, *World Development Report* (1990).

# HOW SOVIET-STYLE ECONOMIES WORKED

Private property, prices, and the profit incentive play a central role in market economies. If these are abandoned, what replaces them? Three major components are central planning, force, and political controls and rewards.

In Soviet-style economies, decision making, including coordination of economic activity, was done by government ministries through **central planning**. Five-year plans with detailed targets were drawn up: how much was steel production to be increased, food production by how much, and so on. Individual plant managers were told not only what they were to produce but how they were to produce it.

Market incentive schemes were also replaced by force. We saw in earlier chapters that some incentive schemes take the form of the carrot, some of the stick. The Soviet Union under Joseph Stalin preferred the stick. Those who did not meet their targets were rewarded with a sojourn in Siberia.

Political controls and rewards also helped replace the lack of economic incentives. Key positions in the economy went to faithful members of the Communist party. In the early days of the revolution, these included many who really believed in socialism as an alternative, superior form of economic organization. Given their ideological commitment, economic incentives to work hard to meet the goals were relatively unimportant. And to the extent that incentives were important, they were provided by the potential for promotion. But as the years went by, membership in the party came to be seen as the vehicle for getting ahead. The party faithful not only received goods jobs but enjoyed other benefits, including access to special stores at which goods not generally available could be acquired.

A basic aspect of market economies, competition, was shunned. No competition with government enterprises was allowed, and the government enterprises did not compete with one another. Not all competition was eliminated, though—there was still competition to be promoted to top positions and thus receive higher incomes and better access to desirable goods. But success in this competition was not based on how efficiently you produced the goods that consumers wanted, or how innovative you were in devising new products. Rather, success was measured by how well you complied with the bureaucratic targets and requirements and how well you performed in the politics of the bureaucracy and party.

Central planning failed miserably in replacing markets. The central planners simply did not have the requisite information. Workers, for instance, were often mismatched with jobs. They were given job security, but this reduced their economic incentives. Pay, and even promotion, were generally not related to performance, and incentives were undermined. Without economic incentives, workers often exerted the minimal level of effort that they could get away with.

Similarly, firms had no incentive to produce beyond the quotas assigned to them. Indeed, they had an incentive not to do so, because if they showed that they could produce more with fewer inputs, in subsequent years their quotas would be increased. In the absence of a price system, shortages often developed, not only of consumer goods, but also of inputs into production. Hence, firms squirreled away any extra raw materials they could get their hands on.

The absence of prices and profits had further debilitating effects. In market economies, returns to investment are the signals that determine how capital should be allocated. The quest for profits provides the incentive for entrepreneurs; equally important, losses are a signal for firms to close down. In socialist economies, with the state owning all firms and therefore all profits, profits provide little incentive, and losses are seldom used as a basis for shutting down establishments. If a firm makes a loss, the government meets the deficit. This phenomenon is referred to as **soft budget constraints,** to contrast them with the harsh reality of budget constraints facing firms in a market economy. For the firm in a socialist system, there is no penalty for making losses, and no incentive to conserve on resources or to innovate.

In a way, it made sense for the Soviet government not to pay too much attention to profits, since the prices firms received for what they produced and the prices they paid for the inputs they used (including labour and capital) were not market-clearing prices. They did not represent the scarcity value of the resources used nor of the goods produced. Thus, the profits were not a good measure of the benefits or costs of the firm's production. By the same token, since prices were not set at market-clearing levels, they did not reflect true scarcity. Hence returns to investment—measured in rubles—were not a sound guide for allocating investments. Prices and wages provided little guidance for whether firms should try to economize more on labour or capital or other inputs.

In the absence of prices and interest rates to guide investment, those decisions were taken on the basis of beliefs about the "correct" path of development. The Soviet leader, Joseph Stalin had two basic ideas. First, he recognized that resources that were not allocated to consumption could be given to investment. In terms of the production possibilities curve depicted in Figure 22.4, his first objective was to reduce consumption and move the economy from a point such as $E_0$ to $E_1$. One of the aims of the collectivization of agriculture was to do just that, to squeeze the farmers as much as possible. But urban workers' wages were also kept low. By keeping wages low and the supply of consumer goods limited, the Soviet planners in effect "forced" the economy to have high savings.

Stalin's second idea was to focus investment on heavy industry. Stalin considered huge factories, such as steel mills, the central symbol of modern economies, which distinguished them from less de-veloped, agrarian economies. He therefore invested primarily in heavy industry, providing little support for agriculture, consumer goods, or housing. The two ideas were in a sense intertwined. With low wages and low consumption, there was little need to invest in industries to provide consumption goods.

## SOVIET-STYLE SOCIALISM AND INEQUALITY

The Soviet government, through its planning ministry, not only decided what was to be produced and how, it also provided the answer to the "for whom" question. In answering this question, three aspects of Soviet ideology played an important role. First, Soviet-style economies were committed to heavy industrialization and a deemphasis of agriculture. Not surprisingly, then, a large part of the burden of the costs was borne by agriculture. Forced collectivization in agriculture kept agriculture wages low. In effect, there were high taxes on agriculture.

Second, the programme of high savings and low consumption could be interpreted as putting an emphasis on the consumption of future generations at the expense of the consumption of the current generation.

Third, an attempt was made to reduce the inequality in society, at least according to the leaders'

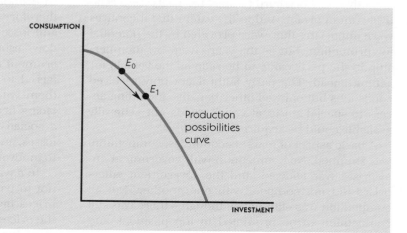

Figure 22.4 **RAPID INDUSTRIALIZATION: MOVEMENTS ALONG THE PRODUCTION POSSIBILITIES CURVE**

Soviet-style socialists believed that rapid growth of heavy industry was desirable, so they increased investment. But as the production possibilities curve shows, this can only be done at the expense of consumption. Central planners tried to move the economy towards a point such as $E_1$, with a high output of investment goods and a low output of consumption goods.

## THE BASIC ECONOMIC QUESTIONS UNDER SOVIET-STYLE SOCIALISM

**1** What is produced?

    Heavy industrial goods

    Other goods as the state sees fit

**2** How are goods produced?

    With technologies and inputs decided upon by the state (often capital-intensive technologies)

**3** For whom are they produced?

    For future generations (high forced savings rates)

    For present generations according to the wages set by government (high "taxes" on agriculture)

    For government officials, who get high rewards

**4** Who takes the decisions?

    Central planning authorities

---

rhetoric. The government determined everyone's wages. It decided how much more a skilled worker got than an unskilled worker. Some goods it allocated directly, such as housing and medical care.

To what extent Soviet-style socialist systems were successful in reducing inequality remains debated. On the one hand, after all land and other property had been confiscated, there were no longer any very rich people. Also, free medicine and highly subsidized food and apartments provided subsistence for the poor. Moreover, one of the major sources of poverty, unemployment, was eliminated. But on the other hand, differences in life-style between the worst-off members of society and high party officials remained enormous. Whole families of ordinary citizens lived crowded together in one room, and though no one starved, they spent long hours in lines to obtain the barest necessities of life. By contrast, high party officials enjoyed vacations along the beaches of the Black Sea, could buy goods unavailable elsewhere at stores reserved for party members, and had chauffeur-driven cars and other powers and perquisites enjoyed by relatively few within the capitalist world.

## THE FAILURE OF SOCIALISM

For several decades, Stalin's programme appeared successful. He was able to force net investment rates up to almost unprecedented levels, more than 23 percent of net national product in 1937, for example. Many factories were built. The official statistics suggested a path of rapid industrialization and growth. There is growing doubt about the reliability of the statistics, but there is little doubt that the gains were accompanied by political repression. The U.S.S.R.'s economic progress was interrupted by World War II, in which 20 million Russians are believed to have died, and the economy was greatly disrupted.

The ensuing decades witnessed several changes in attitudes towards the Soviet-style socialist experiment. At first, the "efficiency" virtues of the system were lauded. The planning mechanism replaced the perceived chaos of the marketplace. Investment could be directed in a rational way. Resources could be quickly mobilized. Moreover, the government could force the high levels of savings required for a successful development programme. Strong central control was thought to be necessary for rapid growth. Moreover, it was thought that Soviet-style socialism could make possible a level of equality the market economy had not been able to attain. Basic human services like health and education could be brought to the masses.

But as economies like Czechoslovakia and Hungary, which had been prosperous before the war, fell behind other European countries, concerns about the efficiency of the system were raised. Such systems could force their citizens to save more because they could repress consumption, but could they allocate resources efficiently? It became increasingly clear that the countries were not growing as fast as one would have thought. The higher savings rates did little more than offset the higher levels of inefficiency.

By the mid-1970s, inklings of an impending economic crisis became more and more apparent. While agricultural productivity in the United States and Western Europe had boomed, in the Soviet-style socialist countries it had stagnated. In 1973, the Soviet Union began buying massive amounts of wheat from Canada, the United States, and other Western countries to feed its people.

By the mid-1980s the magnitude of the problems the country faced became ever clearer. It was evident that many of the statistics on industrial production and well-being had been highly exaggerated. In most economists' judgment, the Soviet-style socialist experiment had been a failure. More than seventy years after the experiment began, income per capita was a tenth of what it was in Canada and the United States.

As the failures of Soviet-style socialism became more evident, various reforms were discussed. Three tacks were possible: try harder to make the socialist system work; combine elements of socialism and capitalism; or give up on socialism completely and move to a market-based system. For three decades, the Soviet Union tried the first strategy. Workers were exhorted to work harder. Money poured into agriculture but left few traces of enhanced productivity. Shortages continued and black markets flourished.

Elsewhere attempts were made to combine what were seen as the strengths of capitalism with those of socialism. Hungary made some attempt to introduce market principles into the socialist system. China implemented the so-called "responsibility system" in agriculture, which essentially allowed farmers to sell most of what they produced in markets and to keep the proceeds. It proved to be a successful experiment—the annual growth rate of grain production in the six years after the responsibility system was adopted was 5 percent, compared with 3.5 percent in the thirteen years before the new system.

Another type of experiment occurred in Yugoslavia. The ownership of firms was turned over to the workers, who were responsible for choosing their own managers. Firms became workers cooperatives, and they assumed responsibility for much of the decision making in the economy. But the system proved to have its problems. The incentive to work seemed to be enhanced only for smaller enterprises. For those with many workers, each worker felt she had a negligible amount at stake. Workers cooperatives seemed reluctant to hire new workers, since this would dilute the share of profits going to existing ones. Unemployment rates soared, and the willingness to change jobs suffered. Investment posed yet another problem. When workers left the firm, they received nothing. Thus, they had little incentive to invest for the long term. Of course, these problems are not inherent in cooperatives. In the industrialized world, when a person joins a cooperative, he has to buy a share; when he leaves, he takes his capital out. This provides an obvious incentive for the cooperative to take good investment decisions.

Despite the partial success of some of these experiments, in the end it was the third tack that was taken. In October of 1990, President Gorbachev announced that the Soviet Union would be converted to capitalism in five hundred days. He soon dropped this programme, whereupon the economists who had been advising him resigned. It appeared as if there would be another attempt to make socialism work. But then, following an attempted coup in August 1991 and the dissolution of the Soviet Union, the country changed direction again: most of the newly created republics seemed committed to adopting some form of market system.

## THE TRANSITION TO MARKET ECONOMIES

Many former socialist countries, including Hungary, the Czech Republic, and Poland, are today committed to becoming market economies. Others, such as Bulgaria, Romania, and Albania, want *some* market reforms, but how many and how fast remains uncertain.

### MACROECONOMIC PROBLEMS

The first transition hurdle Eastern European economies face is a period of disruption in which living standards, at least for some, fall below even the low level that they had been under socialism.

A central problem with socialism was that

resources were inefficiently allocated. If the economy is to move from a point inside its production possibilities curve (such as *A* in Figure 22.5) to a point on the curve, resources will have to be reallocated. Factories will have to be shut down. Workers will have to be let go. These disruptions will be reflected in high transitional unemployment. Transitional unemployment is like frictional unemployment—the unemployment that occurs as workers move between jobs—magnified many times over. Poland, the first country to attempt the transition, experienced unemployment rates estimated at 25–35 percent.

Unemployment is particularly serious in Eastern European countries, because they do not have the same kinds of safety nets that protect people forced out of jobs as industrialized countries. This is not surprising, since under the previous regime unemployment was not a problem. Firms retained workers even when they were no longer needed, for they had no profit motive, no budget constraint. But now, in the transition, firms do face budget constraints. Moreover, since capital markets are not yet working well, new firms are not being created and old firms are not expanding production to absorb the workers who have been laid off.

Inflation receives considerable attention in Eastern Europe these days, because typically wages do not keep pace with prices so that living standards fall. But the fall in living standards is not really caused by the inflation. It is caused by the economic disruption of the transition process, which simultaneously reduces output, leads to inflation, and lowers living standards. Rates of inflation have been extremely high. In Russia, for example, inflation exceeded 20 percent *per month* for much of 1992.

The reason inflation always seems to arise in the transition is easy to see. The Soviet-style economies were run with prices below market-clearing levels. In Russia, indeed, the price of bread was kept so low that farmers found it cheaper to buy bread than grain to feed their pigs. Shortages were endemic. Hence, once prices were freed, price increases were inevitable. A one-time price increase is not the fundamental worry, however. The danger is that it will lead to inflationary expectations, which, once established, perpetuate inflation.

Huge government deficits contribute to inflationary pressures. As the government's control over the economy weakens, its revenue sources often diminish. Under socialism, it could simply seize corporate profits. If it wanted to increase profits and thus its revenues, government could just increase the prices charged or reduce the wages paid. As government abandoned its role in wage and price setting, it lost its ability to raise revenues in this way. But cutting back on expenditures seems no easier in Eastern

Figure 22.5 **INEFFICIENCIES UNDER SOCIALISM**

The Soviet-style socialist economies seemed to use their resources inefficiently, so that they operated substantially below the production possibilities curve, such as at point *A*. Moving the economy from *A* to a point like *B*, on the production possibilities curve, will entail substantial improvements in efficiency.

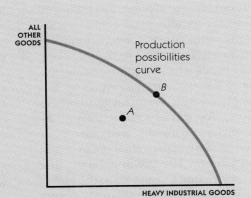

Europe than elsewhere. Food subsidies are a major drain on the budget, but government threats to reduce them have met with stiff opposition.

As profits shrank, and for huge numbers of enterprises turned into losses, the economies in transition faced a dilemma: they could either subsidize enterprises making losses or allow them to shut down. With limited revenues, subsidies required deficit financing. If the enterprises were not shut down, the economy faced inflationary pressures. If they were shut down, unemployment increased.

## PRIVATIZATION AND COMPETITION

Competition is at the centre of the market economy. One important way for Eastern European countries to promote competition is through trade liberalization. Although most economists believe that trade liberalization will enhance economic efficiency in the long run, some are concerned about those who lose out in the competition, including people who lose their jobs. They make a variant of the infant-industry argument, which goes like this: enterprises in the former socialist economies have been insulated from competition for decades. It is unfair to suddenly subject them to competition and make their survival depend on this market test. They need time to learn how to compete.

Another way to promote competition is to sell off different parts of existing state enterprises to private entrepreneurs. There are few problems in selling off small businesses—barbershops, retail stores, restaurants. The real difficulties come in selling large enterprises like automobile or cement factories. Selling them to foreigners raises a host of thorny problems. No country likes to see its factories owned by foreigners. And if a country sells the factories to buyers abroad at too low a price, it is as if the country is giving away its hard-earned savings to foreigners.

Different countries have approached the problem of privatization differently. The Czech Republic first privatized stores, restricting purchases of the stores to citizens and prohibiting their resale to foreigners for two years, and accepted the grim fact that many of the hated Communist bosses would now become capitalist bosses. Economic efficiency, in the minds

of Czech reformers, was more important than revenge. The country distributed vouchers to all citizens, which the citizens used to bid for shares in the larger, privatized firms. Thus, in one stroke, the Czech Republic hoped both to privatize and to establish a viable stock market. With the widely distributed ownership of firms, they hoped to establish a people's capitalism. The next problem the Czechs face is that, with no shareholders having a large stake in a firm, managers will run the firm with little outside check on their actions. There have been proposals to deal with this problem, such as the establishment of holding companies or investment banks, but no consensus has emerged.

Hungary, by contrast, has taken the view that the advantages of foreign ownership—in particular, the advantage of foreigners' expertise—outweigh the disadvantages. Government officials point out that almost 40 percent of Belgian firms are foreign-owned with no adverse effects. They envisage a similar role for foreign ownership within their own economy.

Russia, like the Czech Republic, used vouchers, but a large fraction of the shares were distributed to the workers and managers of each enterprise, raising questions about the extent of outside control to which managers will be subject.

## SPEED OF TRANSITION

The pace of privatization has also varied greatly across countries and sectors. In Russia by 1995 over 55 percent of the large enterprises outside of certain key sectors, such as energy, had been privatized. In the Czech Republic, over 70 percent had been privatized. But in Romania and Bulgaria, privatization is proceeding at a very slow pace.

The former Soviet-style socialist economies face a difficult problem in deciding how fast to make the transition to capitalism. One approach is "cold turkey," or shock therapy: take the plunge, live through a short, nightmarish period, and then enjoy future prosperity. The other approach calls for a more gradual transition and considers political as well as economic issues. For instance, will the pain caused by cold turkey be so great that support for the market will erode?

Poland tried the cold turkey approach, at least with respect to its macroeconomic adjustment.

Inflation was brought under control, but at the expense of a drastic drop in output and employment, and the defeat of the government that undertook the plan. And even after the macroadjustments are made, the microeconomic problems—for instance, making factories more efficient, reallocating labour and capital—remain. Most of the other countries have moved more cautiously.

The problem is that the success of market economies depends on a host of long-established institutions, not just on the abstract concept of markets. And all these institutions have to be functioning reasonably well if the economy is to prosper. There must be credit institutions to sort out potential loan applicants, to monitor the loans, and to see that funds go where they are most productive and are used in the way promised. There must be a legal structure to ensure that contracts will be enforced and to determine what happens when one party cannot fulfill its contract (bankruptcy). There must be a competition policy to ensure that firms compete against one another.

Beyond that, the more advanced countries have developed a set of safety nets to help certain segments of society, such as the unemployed. Since unemployment was not a problem in socialist economies, these societies do not have such safety nets. There may be a huge human toll if the transition, with its attendant unemployment, proceeds before the safety nets are in place. Yet the budgetary problems facing all of these governments make it hard to institute such programmes quickly.

Those who advocate a more gradual transition to market economies believe that the long-run success of these economies will be enhanced by thinking through each of the components, trying to design the best possible institutions, adapting to the particular situations in which they find themselves, and borrowing where appropriate from the developed countries.

Even with rapid reforms, for most of the countries in transition it will take years, perhaps decades, to overcome the problems bequeathed them by their communist systems.

## REVIEW AND PRACTICE

### SUMMARY

**1** Most of the world's population lives in either less developed economies (LDCs) or in countries that are in the process of transition from socialist to market economies. In both cases, the main policy issue is how to increase per capita income.

**2** In LDCs, life expectancies are usually shorter, infant mortality is higher, and people are less educated than in developed countries. Also, a larger fraction of the population lives in the rural sector, and population growth rates are higher.

**3** In recent years, newly industrialized countries (NICs) such as South Korea, Singapore, Hong Kong, and Taiwan have managed to improve their economic status dramatically. Other LDCs, like India, have expanded food production considerably. But the standard of living in some of the poorest LDCs, such as many African nations, has actually been declining, as population growth has outstripped economic growth.

**4** Among the factors contributing to underdevelopment are a rapidly growing population, a lack of educated workers, market failures such as the absence of markets to efficiently allocate capital, and extremes of inequality.

**5** Central planning has not been effective in LDCs. Governments lack the requisite information and often misdirect resources. On the other hand, governments have played an important role in providing an economic and legal infrastructure.

**6** Some economists believe LDCs should tilt the economy by pursuing export-led economic growth.

Others advocate a strategy of import substitution, where the goal is to develop skills and self-sufficiency by replacing imports. Both groups agree that resources should be allocated on the basis of dynamic comparative advantage.

**7** Soviet-style socialism used central planning, under which government bureaucrats took all major decisions about what would be produced, how it would be produced, and for whom it would be produced. Competition was banned. Prices, set by the government, often did not reflect relative scarcities. Private property was restricted.

**8** In Soviet-style economies, the government decided where investment funds went—forcing high savings rates (which meant low consumption) and heavy industrialization.

**9** In socialist economies, firms had little incentive to make profits since profits went to the state, and little incentive to avoid losses since the government would meet any deficits. Socialism protected workers against layoffs. The trade-off was that this greater security created a lesser incentive for efficiency.

**10** Most of the countries with Soviet-style socialist economies have chosen to move their economies to market-based systems. Among the problems faced are high unemployment and inflation. These countries do not have in place a safety net to protect those hurt in the transition process.

**11** Privatizing state-owned firms has proved difficult in practice. For instance, there is reluctance to sell factories to foreigners or former party bosses.

## KEY TERMS

less developed countries (LDCs)

industrialized or developed countries

newly industrialized countries (NICs)

green revolution

import substitution

export-led growth

infrastructure

planned economy

central planning

soft budget constraints

## REVIEW QUESTIONS

**1** List some important ways in which LDCs differ from more developed countries.

**2** Why may a land reform increase agricultural output? What factors would hinder the success of a land reform?

**3** What are the most important factors inhibiting growth in the LDCs?

**4** What can be done to help overcome the problems of capital shortage and the inefficient allocation of capital?

**5** How does rapid population growth make it more difficult to increase a country's standard of living?

**6** What can explain the East Asia miracle?

**7** What are some of the central characteristics of Soviet-style socialism?

**8** How is the rate of national savings determined in a socialist economy, as opposed to a capitalist economy? How is the allocation of capital determined in a socialist economy, as opposed to a capitalist economy? Who determines what goods are produced in a socialist economy?

**9** Why are budget constraints "soft" in socialist countries and "hard" in market economies?

**10** What effect do the job-security policies of Soviet-style socialism have on the incentives of workers to put forward their strongest effort?

**11** What are the central problems facing countries trying to move from Soviet-style socialism to market economies? Why are inflationary pressures common in a socialist country that is moving towards a market economy? Why is rising unemployment common?

**12** What benefits do socialist economies hope to gain from privatization? What are some of the problems facing privatization programmes?

## PROBLEMS

**1** In Canada, the economy grew by 3.3 percent per year (in real terms) during the 1980s. In India, the economy grew by 5.3 percent during the 1980s. However, population growth in Canada was .8 percent annually, while population growth in India was 2.1 percent annually. Which country increased its standard of living faster for the average citizen? By how much?

**2** Nominal GDP in Kenya was 9 billion shillings in 1967 and 135 billion shillings in 1987. The price level in Kenya (using 1980 as a base year) rose from 40 in 1967 to 200 in 1987. And the population of Kenya increased from 10 million to 22 million in those twenty years. What was the total percentage change in real GDP per capita in Kenya from 1967 to 1987?

**3** How might each of the following present obstacles to entrepreneurs in LDCs?
   (a) A lack of functioning capital markets
   (b) Pervasive government control of the economy
   (c) A lack of companies that offer business services
   (d) A tradition of substantial foreign control of large enterprises

**4** What is the economist's case for having the government be responsible for providing infrastructure? (Hint: You may wish to review the concept of externalities discussed in Chapter 7.)

**5** If many LDCs simultaneously attempted to pursue export-led growth, what would be the effect in world markets on the quantities and prices of products mainly sold by LDCs, like minerals, agricultural goods, and textiles? What effect might these quantities and prices have on the success of such export-led growth policies?

**6** Why might a family in an LDC feel economic pressure to have more children than a family in a developed country?

**7** Explain how each of the following differs in a socialist and a market economy:
   (a) The incentive of a manager to take wise decisions
   (b) The incentive of workers to exert their best effort
   (c) The incentive of a bank manager to screen prospective borrowers carefully

**8** Queues form when there is a shortage of goods. Use a supply and demand diagram to explain why socialist price controls tend to lead to queues.

**9** Why did the Soviet-style socialist economies have almost no safety nets of unemployment and welfare benefits?

**10** In the Soviet-style socialist economies, housing was very scarce, and much of it was controlled by firms. What consequences might this have for labour mobility?

**11** Imagine that you are 60 years old and you work for a workers cooperative in Hungary. If you consider only your own self-interest, are you likely to support hiring more workers? Would you support long-term investments in capital?

# GLOSSARY

**absolute advantage:** the advantage one country has over another country in the production of a good if it can produce that good more efficiently (with fewer inputs)

**accelerated depreciation:** a provision of the income tax system that allows for deductions from income for the purpose of calculating tax liability for the depreciation of capital goods

**accelerator:** the effect on GDP of the increase in investment that results from an increase in output. Greater outputs lead firms to believe that demand for a product will rise in the future; this belief results in increased investment, which leads to growth in output and still further increases in investment, accelerating the expansion of the economy

**accommodative monetary policy:** monetary policy that allows fiscal policy to have its full effect on the macroeconomic performance of the economy

**acquired endowments:** the resources a country builds for itself, like a network of roads or an educated population

**adaptive expectations:** expectations based on extrapolation from events in the recent past

**aggregate consumption function:** the relationship between aggregate consumption and aggregate income

**aggregate supply:** the amount of goods and services that firms would be willing to supply, given their plant and equipment, assuming that wages and prices are flexible and adjust to keep the labour force fully employed

**aggregate supply curve:** the curve relating the total supply of the economy's goods and services at each price level, given the level of wages

**aggregate expenditures schedule:** the curve tracing the relationship between expenditures—the sum of consumption, investment, government expenditures, and net exports—and national income, at a fixed price level

**anti-dumping duties:** penalties imposed by importing countries on producers who sell products at lower prices abroad than they do in their home economy

**appreciation:** a change in the exchange rate that enables a unit of currency to buy more units of foreign currencies

**arc elasticity:** an elasticity calculated for large changes in price

**asset:** any item that is long-lived, purchased for the service it renders over its life and for what one will receive when one sells it

**automatic stabilizers:** mechanisms that automatically take money out of the economy when the economy is booming and put money in when its slowing down.

**autonomous consumption:** that part of consumption that does not depend on income

**average costs:** total costs divided by total output

**balance of payments:** the summary of transactions of all types between Canadians and foreigners, comprised of the sum of current and capital accounts

**balance of trade:** the difference between the value of exports and the value of imports in a given year

**balance sheet:** the accounting framework that shows a firm's assets, liabilities, and net worth

**balanced-budget legislation:** legislation that prohibits the government from deficit spending

**balanced-budget multiplier:** the increase in GDP from a dollar increase in government expenditures matched by a dollar increase in taxes

**Bank of Canada:** the public institution that conducts monetary policy in Canada

**bank rate:** the interest rate paid by chartered banks on loans from the Bank of Canada

**bank run:** the attempt by a large number of depositors to withdraw money from a bank in which they have lost confidence

**barter:** trade that occurs without the use of money

**basic competitive model:** the model of the economy that pulls together the assumptions of self-interested consumers, profit-maximizing firms, and perfectly competitive markets

**beggar-thy-neighbor policies:** restrictions on imports designed to increase a country's national output, so called because they increase that country's output at the same time that they hurt the output of other countries

**bilateral agreements:** agreements between two countries to reduce trade barriers, such as the Canada–U.S. Free Trade Agreement

**bilateral trade:** trade between two parties

**black market:** the market for buying and selling illegally

**boom:** a period of time when resources are being fully used and GDP is growing steadily

**branch banking system:** a banking system with national banks that have a large number of branches across the country

**budget constraints:** opportunity sets whose constraints are imposed by money

**budget deficit:** the excess of government spending over taxes in any given year

**business cycle:** fluctuations up and down in economic activity that occur with some regularity

**capacity:** the amount of output available if resources are fully employed

**capital-account surplus:** net borrowing (borrowing minus lending) by Canadians from foreigners

**capital adequacy requirements:** limits placed by the Bank Act on the ratio of assets to equity of chartered banks

**capital cost allowance:** the deduction from taxable income allowed for the cost of a machine each year to reflect the fact that over time the machine is becoming worth less due to wear and tear and obsolescence

**capital deepening:** an increase in capital per worker

**capital gain:** the change in the value of an asset due to a rise in its price between the time it is purchased and the time it is sold

**capital goods:** the machines and buildings firms invest in with funds obtained in the capital market

**capital inflow:** the money coming from abroad to buy assets in Canada

**capital investment:** the purchase of new buildings, machines, and equipment by firms

**capital market:** the market in which savings are made available to those who need additional funds, such as firms that wish to invest, and in which ownership claims on different assets and their associated risks are exchanged

**capital outflow:** money from Canada going to other countries for the purchase of assets

**cartel:** a group of producers with an agreement to collude in setting prices and output

**causation:** the relationship that results when a change in one variable is not only correlated with but actually determines a change in another variable: the change in the second variable is a consequence of the change in the first variable, rather than both changes being a consequence of a change in a third variable

**central bank:** the bank (Bank of Canada) that oversees and monitors the rest of the banking system and serves as the bankers' bank

**central planning:** the system in which central government bureaucrats (as opposed to private entrepreneurs or even local government bureaucrats) determine what will be produced and how it will be produced

**centrally planned economy:** an economy in which most decisions about resource allocation are made by the central government

**circular flow:** the way in which funds move through the capital, labour, and product markets between households, firms, the government, and the foreign sector

**classical economists:** economists prevalent before the Great Depression who believed that the basic competitive model provided a good description of the economy and that, if short periods of unemployment did occur, market forces would quickly restore the economy to full employment

**classical unemployment:** unemployment that occurs as a result of too-high real wages; it occurs in the supply-constrained equilibrium, so that rightward shifts in aggregate supply reduce the level of unemployment

**clearing the market:** the circumstance in which demand equals supply

**closed economy:** an economy that neither exports or imports

**commercial policies:** policies designed to alter either imports or exports

**communism:** an economic system in which the government owns and controls virtually all property except personal property

**comparative advantage:** the advantage one country has over another country if its *relative* efficiency in the production of a particular good is higher than the other country's

**competitive equilibrium price:** the price at which the quantity supplied and the quantity demanded are equal

**complement:** a good the demand for which (at a given price) decreases as the price of another good increases

**compound interest:** interest earned on interest previously earned and saved

**consumer price index (CPI):** a price index in which the basket of goods is defined by what a typical consumer would purchase

**consumer surplus:** the difference between what a person would be willing to pay and what he actually has to pay to buy a certain amount of a good

**consumption:** the purchase of goods and services by individuals

**consumption function:** the relationship between disposable income and consumption

**correlation:** the relationship between variables such that a change in one variable is consistently associated with a change in another variable

**cost-of-living adjustments (COLAs):** provisions in wage contracts for wages to rise automatically with inflation

**cost-push inflation:** inflation whose initial cause is a rise in production costs

**countervailing duties:** duties imposed on imports subsidized by the exporting country

**coupon rationing:** the rationing of items by giving out coupons entitling the bearer to buy a certain number of the items in question

**credit availability:** the amount of funds made available by the banking system for financing borrowing for investment and consumer durables

**credit constraint effect:** the decreased investment that, under credit rationing, results from falling revenues (due to price drops), which decrease the amount a firm is able to reinvest

**credit rationing:** limiting the amount lenders are willing to extend to borrowers, even if the borrower is willing to pay more than other borrowers of comparable risk for more

**crowding out:** the decrease in private investment resulting from an increase in government expenditures

**Crown corporations:** firms that are owned by the federal or provincial governments

**current account:** the sum of the merchandise trade, invisibles, and investment income accounts

**cyclical unemployment:** unemployment that increases with a downturn in the economy and decreases with a boom

**debt:** capital, such as bonds and bank loans, supplied to a firm by lenders; the firm promises to repay the amount borrowed plus interest

**debt/GDP ratio:** public debt as a proportion of GDP

**decentralization:** an organizational structure in which many individuals or subunits can make decisions

**deficit:** the amount by which government expenditures exceed tax revenues in a given year

**deficit spending:** government expenditures that exceed revenues

**deflation:** a persistent decrease in the general level of prices

**demand-constrained equilibrium:** the equilibrium that occurs when prices are stuck at a level above that at which aggregate demand equals aggregate supply; output is equal to aggregate demand

**demand curve:** the relationship between the quantity demanded of a good and the price, whether for an individual or for the market (all individuals) as a whole

**demand deposits:** deposits that can be drawn upon instantly, like those in chequing accounts

**demand-pull inflation:** inflation whose initial cause is aggregate demand exceeding aggregate supply at the current price level

**demand shock:** a rightward shift in the aggregate demand curve, which will initiate inflation in an economy operating at full capacity

**demographic effects:** effects that arise from changes in characteristics of the population such as age, birthrate, and location

**depreciation:** (a) the decrease in the value of an asset; in particular, the amount that capital goods decrease in value as they are used and become old; (b) a change in the exchange rate that enables a unit of one currency to buy fewer units of foreign currencies

**depressions:** severe downturns in the economy

**deregulation:** the lifting of government regulations to allow the market to function more freely

**developed** or **industrialized countries:** the wealthiest nations in the world, including the United States, Canada, Japan, Australia, New Zealand, and those in Western Europe

**diminishing returns:** the principle that as one input increases, with other inputs fixed, increases in output get smaller and smaller

**discouraged workers:** workers who would be willing to work but have given up looking for jobs and thus are not officially counted as unemployed

**discretionary expenditures:** government expenditures that are decided annually

**disposable income:** what households have available to spend out of their incomes after paying income taxes (income minus income taxes)

**division of labour:** the dividing up of jobs among workers so that each can specialize on fewer tasks

**double coincidence of wants:** the situation in which one individual has what another wants and vice versa, thus making trade possible

**downward rigidity of wages:** the situation that exists when wages do not fall quickly in response to a shift in the demand or supply curve for labour, resulting in an excess supply of labour

**drawdown:** the transfer of funds from government accounts in one or more banks to a government account in the Bank of Canada

**dual economy:** the separation in many less-developed countries (LDCs) between an impoverished rural sector and an urban sector that has higher wages and more advanced technology

**dumping:** the sale of a product abroad at a price less than the cost of production

**durable goods:** goods that provide a service over a number of years, such as cars, major appliances, and furniture

**dynamic consistency:** a situation in which the government announces a policy and then has the incentives actually to carry out that policy

**econometrics:** the application of statistics to economics

**economic growth:** the annual rate of change of national income

**economic rents:** payments made to a factor of production that are in excess of what is required to elicit the supply of that factor

**economics:** the study of how individuals, firms, governments, and other organizations determine the way society's resources are used

**economies of scope:** the situation that exists when it is less expensive to produce two products together than it would be to produce each one separately

**efficiency wage:** the wage at which total labour costs are minimized

**efficiency wage theory:** the theory that paying higher wages (up to a point) lowers total production costs, for instance by leading to a more productive labour force

**elasticity of supply:** see **price elasticity of supply**

**endogenous factors:** properties of the economy itself, such as overconfidence in expansions, which tend to generate or exacerbate economic fluctuations; more generally, any variable that is determined within the model itself

**equilibrium price:** see **competitive equilibrium price**

**equilibrium quantity:** the amount demanded and supplied when a market is in equilibrium

**equity concerns:** concerns about equality among individuals

**equity, shares, stock:** terms that indicate part ownership of a firm; the firm sells these in order to raise money, or capital

**excess capacity:** production capacity that is greater than that currently needed

**excess demand:** the situation in which the quantity demanded at a given price exceeds the quantity supplied

**excess supply:** the situation in which the quantity supplied at a given price exceeds the quantity demanded

**exchange rate:** the rate at which one currency (such as dollars) can be exchanged for another (such as marks, yen, or pounds)

**exiting the market:** ceasing to sell or buy in a given market

**exogenous effects:** sources of business cycle fluctuations that originate in events outside the economy, such as an oil price shock

**exogenous shocks:** disturbances that originate in events outside the economy, such as a war that starts a boom

**expectations:** predictions of future events using currently available information

**expectations-augmented Phillips curve:** a Phillips curve that takes into account the impact of inflationary expectations; as inflationary expectations increase, the inflation associated with any level of unemployment increases

**expected return:** the average return—a single number that combines the various possible returns per dollar invested with the chances that each of these returns will actually be paid

**experimental economics:** the analysis of economics in laboratory settings

**export-led growth:** growth resulting from governmental encouragement of exports in which the country has a comparative advantage

**exports:** goods produced domestically but sold abroad

**federal debt:** the cumulative amount that the government owes as a result of past borrowing

**fiat money:** money that the government creates and declares to have value

**final goods approach:** measuring GDP by the total dollar value of goods and services produced, categorized by their ultimate users

**financial intermediaries:** institutions that form the link between savers who have extra funds and borrowers who desire extra funds

**financial investments:** purchases of stocks, bonds, and other financial assets

**financial system:** all institutions involved in moving savings from households and firms whose income exceeds their expenditures and transferring it to other households and firms who would like to spend more than their income allows

**fiscal policies:** policies that affect the level of government expenditures and taxes

**fiscal stimulus:** a government effort to stimulate the economy through fiscal policy

**fixed** or **overhead costs:** the costs resulting from fixed inputs

**flow statistics:** measurements of a certain rate or quantity per period of time, such as GDP, which measures output per year

**four-pillar system:** the four different types of financial institutions devoted to banking, insurance, corporate trusteeship, and stock dealing

**fractional reserve system:** a banking system in which banks hold a fraction of the amount of deposits as reserves

**free trade:** trade among countries which occurs without barriers, such as tariffs or quotas

**frictional unemployment:** unemployment that reflects the movement of workers between jobs

**full-employment deficit:** the budget deficit that would prevail were the economy at full employment, with higher tax revenues and lower unemployment-insurance expenditures

**full-employment** or **potential output:** the level of output that would prevail were labour fully employed (with output exceeding that level were workers to work more than the normal level of overtime)

**gains from trade:** the benefits that each side enjoys from a trade

**GDP deflator:** a weighted average of the prices of different goods and services, where the weights represent the importance of each of the goods and services

**GDP per capita:** the value of all final goods and services produced in the economy divided by the population

**General Agreement on Tariffs and Trade (GATT):** the agreement among the major trading countries that created the framework for lowering barriers to trade and resolving trade disputes; established after World War II, it has now been succeeded by the World Trade Organization (WTO)

**general equilibrium:** the situation in which all markets clear—the demand for each good equals its supply, the demand for each kind of labour equals its supply, and the demand for capital equals its supply

**generational accounting:** calculations showing the extent to which government programmes yield net benefits to different age groups, including future generations

**government regulation:** rules imposed by government that affect the way the economy's resources are used

**government spending:** expenditures undertaken by the government

**green revolution:** the invention and dissemination of new seeds and agricultural practices that led to vast increases in agricultural output in less-developed countries during the 1960s and 1970s

**gross domestic product (GDP):** the total money value of all final goods and services produced by the residents of a nation during a specified period

**gross national product (GNP):** a measure of the incomes of residents of a country, including income they receive from abroad but subtracting similar payments made to those abroad

**home equity loan:** a loan individuals can obtain based on the equity in their houses

**human capital investments:** expenditures to improve the education or skills of workers

**hyperinflation:** extremely high rates of inflation

**imperfect information:** a situation in which market participants lack information (such as information about prices or characteristics of goods and services) important for their decision making

**implicit contract:** an unwritten understanding between two groups involved in an exchange, such as between employer and employees that employees will receive a stable wage despite fluctuating economic conditions

**import function:** the relationship between imports and national income

**import substitution:** the strategy of substituting domestic goods for imported goods

**imports:** goods produced abroad but bought domestically

**imputed rent:** the consumption services obtained by owning one's house rather than having to pay rent

**incentive-equality trade-off:** the fact that the greater the incentives given to individuals to produce, the more inequality there is

**income approach:** the calculation of GDP by measuring the income generated by selling products, rather than the value of the products themselves

**income effect:** the reduced consumption of a good whose price has increased due to the reduction in a person's buying power, or "real" income; when a person's real income falls, she will normally consume less of all goods, including higher-priced goods

**income-expenditure analysis:** the analysis that determines equilibrium output by relating income (output) to aggregate expenditures

**incomes policy:** a government-mandated program of constraints on wage and price increases

**indexing:** the formal linking of any payment to a price index

**industrial policy:** government policies aimed at fostering certain sectors of the economy

**industrial products price index:** an index measuring the average level of prices of goods sold by producers

**industry:** the collection of firms making the same product

**infant industry argument for protection:** the argument that fledgling industries must be protected from foreign competition until they acquire the skills needed to compete

**infinite elasticity of demand:** the situation in which any amount of a good will be demanded at a particular price, but none will be demanded if the price increases even a small amount

**infinite elasticity of supply:** the situation in which any amount of a good will be supplied at a particular price, but none will be supplied if the price declines by even a small amount

**inflation:** the general upward movement of the average of all prices

**inflation inertia:** the tendency of inflation to persist

**inflation rate:** the percentage increase in the general level of prices

**inflation tax:** the decrease in buying power (wealth) that inflation imposes on those who hold currency (and other assets, like bonds, the payments for which are fixed in terms of dollars)

**inflationary spiral:** a self-perpetuating system in which price increases lead to higher wages, which lead to further price increases

**infrastructure:** the roads, ports, bridges, and legal system that provide the basis for a working economy

**inputs:** resources used by firms to produce their products

**insider-outsider theory:** the theory that firms are reluctant to pay new workers (outsiders) a lower wage than current workers (insiders), because current workers will fear being replaced by the new, low-wage workers and will not cooperate with or train them

**interest:** the return a saver receives in addition to the original amount deposited (loaned), and the amount a borrower must pay in addition to the original amount borrowed

**interest elasticity of savings:** the percentage increase in savings resulting from a 1 percent increase in the interest rate

**interest rate effect:** the situation that exists when lower interest rates (resulting from an increase in money supply or a fall in the price level) induce firms to increase investment

**intermediate goods:** goods produced in one firm that are used as inputs by other firms

**inventory:** goods that a firm stores in anticipation of its use later on as a product for sale or an input to production

**inventory correction:** a change in production to restore inventories to their customary volume relative to sales

**inventory cycles:** cyclical variations induced by changes in inventories

**investment:** the purchase of an asset that will provide a return over a long period of time

**investment schedule:** the relationship between the level of investment and the (real) rate of interest

**investment tax credit (ITC):** a provision of the tax law by which government reduces a company's tax bill by an amount equal to a percentage of its spending on investment

**investors:** individuals who supply savings to the capital market

**invisible hand:** the expression coined by Adam Smith (1723–1790) to describe the way prices are determined in competitive markets: self interest leads to social good through the functioning of the market

**involuntary unemployment:** the situation that occurs when the supply of those willing to work at the going market wage exceeds the demand for labour

**Keynesian monetary theorists:** see **traditional monetary theorists**

**Keynesian unemployment:** unemployment that occurs as a result of insufficient aggregate demand; it occurs in the demand-constrained equilibrium (where aggregate demand is less than aggregate supply), so that rightward shifts in aggregate demand reduce the level of unemployment

**labour force participation rate:** the fraction of the working-age population that is employed or seeking employment

**labour hoarding:** the situation in which firms keep workers on the job in a downturn without fully utilizing them

**labour market:** the market in which labour services are bought and sold

**labour turnover rate:** the rate at which workers leave jobs

**lags:** the time difference between when an action, such as a government policy, occurs and when its effects are fully realized

**land reform:** the redistribution of land by the government to those who actually work the land

**law of supply and demand:** the observation that actual prices tend to be equilibrium prices, the prices at which demand equals supply

**leakages:** income generated but not spent within the economy, such as imports, savings, or taxes

**learning by doing:** the increase in productivity that occurs as a firm gains experience from producing and that results in a decrease in the firm's production costs

**learning curve:** the curve describing how costs of production decline as cumulative output increases over time

**legal entitlement:** a right given by law to engage in some activity

**less-developed countries (LDCs):** the poorest nations of the world, including much of Africa, Latin America, and Asia

**liabilities:** what firms owe to others

**life-cycle savings motive:** the impulse to save during one's working life so that one can consume more during retirement

**linear demand curve:** a demand curve that is a straight line

**lines of credit:** agreements by banks to lend customers money automatically up to some limit

**liquidity:** the ease with which an asset can be sold

**long run:** the length of time required for a market to adjust fully to changes in demand or supply conditions

**long-run aggregate supply curve:** the aggregate supply curve that applies when wages and prices have sufficient time to adjust fully to ensure full employment

**long-run trend:** a smooth line drawn through the data, tracing the growth rate the economy would have followed had the growth rate changed steadily

**long-term bonds:** bonds that mature in ten years or more

**Lorenz curve:** a curve that shows the cumulative proportion of income that goes to each cumulative proportion of the population, starting with the lowest income group

**Luddites:** early nineteenth-century workmen who destroyed labour-saving machinery rather than see it take over their jobs

**M1, M2, M3, M2+:** measures of money supply: M1 includes currency and demand deposits; M2 includes M1 plus savings deposits, daily interest chequing accounts, and nonpersonal notice deposits; M3 includes M2 plus nonpersonal fixed-term deposits and foreign currency deposits; M2+ includes M2 plus deposits in near banks

**macroeconomics:** the top-down view of the economy, focusing on aggregate characteristics

**marginal benefits:** benefits associated with an incremental change.

**marginal cost:** the additional cost corresponding to an additional unit of output produced

**marginal costs** and **benefits:** the extra costs and benefits that result from choosing a little bit more of one thing

**marginal propensity to consume:** the amount by which consumption increases when disposable income increases by a dollar

**marginal propensity to import:** the amount by which imports increase when disposable income increases by a dollar

**marginal propensity to save:** the amount by which savings increase when disposable income increases by a dollar

**marginal rate of transformation:** the additional amount of one product that can be produced by reducing production of another

**marginal revenue:** the extra revenue received by a firm for selling one additional unit of a good

**market:** the institution through which trades are made among buyers and sellers

**market clearing:** the situation that exists when supply equals demand, so there is neither excess supply nor excess demand

**market demand curve:** total quantity of a good demanded by all individuals at each price

**market economy:** an economy that allocates resources primarily through the interaction of individuals (households) and private firms

**market for risk:** markets, like those for insurance and capital, in which households or firms can transfer risk to others

**marketplace:** the location where buyers and sellers meet

**market risks:** uncertainties associated with investment decisions

**market supply:** the total amount of a good or service that all firms in the economy supply

**market supply curve:** the total quantity of a good supplied by all firms at each price

**medium of exchange:** any item that can be commonly exchanged for goods and services throughout the economy

**menu costs:** the costs to firms of changing their prices

**microeconomics:** the bottom-up view of the economy, focusing on individual households and firms

**minimum wage:** a law that sets the lowest wage that can be paid to employed labour

**mixed economy:** an economy that allocates resources through a mixture of public (governmental) and private decision making

**model:** a set of assumptions and data used by economists to study an aspect of the economy and make predictions about the future or about the consequences of various policy changes

**monetarists:** economists who emphasize the importance of money in the economy; they tend to believe that an appropriate monetary policy is all the economy needs from government, and market forces will otherwise solve any macroeconomic problems

**monetary aggregates:** the statistics describing the money supply (M1, M2, M3, M2+)

**monetary policies:** policies that affect the supply of money and credit and the terms on which credit is available to borrowers

**money:** any item that serves as a medium of exchange, a store of value, and a unit of account

**money multiplier:** the amount by which a new deposit into the banking system (from the outside) is multiplied as it is loaned out, redeposited, reloaned, etc., by banks

**money supply:** the quantity of money in the economy

**monopolistic competition:** imperfect competition in which the market has so few firms that each faces a downward-sloping demand curve, but enough so that each one can ignore the reactions of rivals to what it does

**monopoly:** a market consisting of only one firm

**moral suasion:** attempts by the Bank of Canada to persuade chartered banks to take certain actions to achieve monetary policy objectives

**multilateral agreements:** agreements among more than two countries to reduce barriers to trade, such as the General Agreement on Tariffs and Trade

**multilateral trade:** trade among more than two parties

**multiplier:** the factor by which a change in a component of aggregate demand, like investment or government spending, is multiplied to lead to a larger change in equilibrium national output

**multiplier-accelerator model:** a model that relates business cycles to the internal working of the economy, showing how changes in investment and output reinforce each other; the central ingredients of the model are the multiplier and the accelerator

**natural endowments:** a country's natural resources, such as good climate, fertile land, or abundant minerals

**natural rate of unemployment:** the rate of unemployment at which the rate of inflation is zero

**near banks:** financial institutions that take deposits and make loans in much the same way as banks

**negatively sloped:** the description of a curve whose value on the vertical axis falls as the value on the horizontal axis rises

**net capital inflows:** capital inflows minus capital outflows

**net domestic product (NDP):** GDP minus the value of the depreciation of the country's capital goods

**net exports:** the difference between exports and imports

**neutrality of money:** a situation in which changing the money supply increases all prices proportionately and has no real effects on the economy

**new classical economists:** economists who, beginning in the 1970s, built on the tradition of classical economics and believed that, by and large, market forces, if left to themselves, would solve the problems of unemployment and recessions

**new growth economists:** economists who, beginning in the 1980s sought to understand better the basic forces that led the economy to grow quickly at one time and slowly at another or that caused some countries to grow more quickly than others

**new Keynesian economists:** economists who, beginning in the 1980s, built on the tradition of Keynesian economics and focused attention on unemployment; they sought explanations for the failure of wages and prices to adjust to make labour markets and possibly other markets clear

**newly industrialized countries (NICs):** nations that have recently moved from being quite poor to being middle-income countries, including South Korea, Taiwan, Singapore, Malaysia, and Hong Kong

**nominal GDP:** gross domestic prices measured in current prices and not adjusted for inflation

**nominal interest rate:** the interest rate actually paid on a loan in dollar terms, uncorrected for inflation

**nonaccelerating inflation rate of unemployment (NAIRU):** the level of unemployment at which actual (realized) inflation equals inflationary expectations; below this rate of unemployment the rate of inflation increases, and vice versa

**nontariff barriers:** barriers to trade that take forms other than tariffs, such as quotas or regulations that put foreign firms at a disadvantage

**normative economics:** economics in which judgments about the desirability of various policies are made; the conclusions rest on value judgments as well as facts and theories

**North American Free Trade Agreement (NAFTA):** the agreement between Canada, Mexico, and the United States that lowered trade and investment barriers between the countries and established a dispute-settlement mechanism

**Okun's law:** the observation that as the economy pulls out of a recession, output increases more than proportionately to increases in employment

**oligopoly:** the form of imperfect competition in which the market has several firms but so few that each must take into account the reactions of rivals to what it does

**open economy:** an economy that is actively engaged in international trade

**open market operations:**   the central bank's purchase or sale of government bonds in the open market

**opportunity cost:**   the cost of a resource, measured by the value of the next-best alternative use of that resource

**opportunity sets:**   a summary of the choices available to individuals, as defined by budget constraints and time constraints

**output per capita:**   the national output of goods and services divided by the population

**outputs:**   products produced by firms

**overnight interest rate:**   the cost of borrowing on the overnight market

**overnight market:**   the market specializing in one-day (overnight) loans

**Pareto-efficient allocations:**   resource allocations such that one person cannot be made better off without making someone else worse off

**peak:**   the top of a boom

**perfect competition:**   a situation in which each firm is a price taker—it cannot influence the market price; at the market price, the firm can sell as much as it wishes, but if it raises its price, it loses all sales

**permanent income hypothesis:**   the theory that individuals base their current consumption levels on their permanent (long-run average) incomes

**Phillips curve:**   the curve describing the trade-off between unemployment and inflation such that a lower level of unemployment is associated with a higher level of inflation

**physical capital:**   a business's investment in plant and equipment

**planned economy:**   an economy in which the government takes responsibility for economic decision making, including developing plans for economic growth

**planned inventories:**   those inventories that firms choose to have on hand because they make business more efficient; **unplanned inventories** result when firms cannot sell what they produce

**plant and equipment:**   buildings and machines that a firm uses to produce its output

**point elasticity:**   an elasticity calculated for small changes in price

**policy ineffectiveness proposition:**   the proposition that government policies are ineffective—policies aimed at stimulating aggregate demand at most change the price level

**portfolio theories of monetary policy:**   theories that argue that monetary policy affects output through its effect on various asset prices, in particular the prices of stocks

**positive economics:**   the branch of economics that describes how the economy behaves and predicts how it might change—for instance, in response to some policy change

**positively sloped:**   the description of a curve whose value on the vertical axis rises as the value on the horizontal axis rises

**potential GDP:**   a measure of what the value of GDP would be if the economy's resources were fully employed

**present discounted value:**   the amount a sum of money to be received in the future is worth right now

**price:**   the amount of money that is given in exchange for an item

**price ceiling:**   a maximum price above which a market's price is not legally allowed to rise

**price elasticity of demand:**   the percentage change in quantity of a good demanded as the result of a 1 percent change in price (the percentage change in quantity demanded divided by the percentage change in price)

**price elasticity of supply:**   the percentage change in quantity of a good supplied as the result of a 1 percent change in price (the percentage change in quantity supplied divided by the percentage change in price)

**price floor:**   a minimum price below which a market's price is not legally allowed to fall

**price index:**   a measure of the level of prices found by comparing the cost of a certain basket of goods in one year with the cost of the same basket of goods in a base year

**price maker:**   an individual or firm that can influence the prices it faces by changing its behavior

**price system:**   the allocation of products and resources from sellers to buyers using prices

**price taker:**   an individual or firm that cannot influence the prices it faces

**principal:**   the original amount a saver lends or a borrower borrows

**principle of substitution:**   the principle that, as the price of one input increases, firms will substitute other inputs for it

**private property:**   property that has an owner with a right to use or sell

**privatization:**   the process whereby functions that were formerly undertaken by government are delegated instead to the private sector

**producer price index:**   an index that measures the average level of producers' prices

**producer surplus:**   the difference between what a firm receives for selling a product and what it would be willing to sell it for

**product differentiation:**   the fact that similar products (like breakfast cereals or soft drinks) are perceived to differ from one another and thus are imperfect substitutes

**product market:** the market in which goods and services are bought and sold

**production-facilitating function:** the holding of inventories of inputs to facilitate production

**production possibilities curve:** a curve that defines the opportunity set for a firm or an entire economy and gives the possible combinations of goods (outputs) that can be produced from a given level of inputs

**production-smoothing function:** the holding of inventories of outputs to even out production between peak and slack selling periods

**productivity,** or **GDP per hour worked:** the amount an average worker produces per hour, calculated by dividing real GDP by hours worked in the economy

**profits:** total revenues minus total costs

**programme expenditures:** expenditures by the government for purposes other than interest payments on the debt

**protectionism:** the policy of protecting domestic industries from the competition of foreign-made goods

**quantity theory of money:** the theory that velocity is constant, so that changes in the money supply lead to proportionate changes in nominal income

**quota rents:** profits that accrue to those firms holding the right to import goods subject to quotas that result from the artificially created scarcity

**quotas:** limits on the quantity of foreign goods that can be imported

**rational choice:** decisions taken by weighing the costs and benefits of all options

**rational expectations:** the expectations of individuals that are formed by using all available information

**real balance effect:** the situation in which, as prices fall, the real value of people's money holdings increases, and consumption increases

**real business-cycle theorists:** economists who attribute the economy's fluctuations to exogenous shocks to which markets adjust quickly.

**real exchange rates:** exchange rates adjusted for changes in the relative price levels in different countries

**real GDP:** the real value of all final goods and services produced in the economy, measured in dollars adjusted for inflation

**real income:** income measured by what it can actually buy, rather than by the amount of money

**real interest rate:** the actual interest rate minus the rate of inflation

**real wage:** the nominal wage divided by the average price of the goods a person buys (as reflected, for instance, in the consumer price index)

**recession:** two consecutive three-month periods (quarters) during which GDP falls

**redeposit:** a transfer of funds from a government account in the Bank of Canada to a government account in one of the chartered banks, causing chartered bank deposits in the Bank of Canada to rise

**Registered Pension Plans:** pension plans operated by firms for their employees in which contributions up to a predescribed limit are deductible from income tax when paid into the plan but taxable when taken out in retirement as a pension

**Registered Retirement Savings Plans:** savings by individuals for their retirement that are deductible up to a prescribed limit from income tax when paid into the plan but taxable when taken out in retirement

**relatively elastic demand:** a situation in which the quantity demanded increases more than in proportion to price reductions

**relatively inelastic demand:** the demand for a quantity that increases less than in proportion to price reductions

**relative price:** the ratio of the prices of two goods, reflecting how much of one must be given up to get more of the other

**reserve ratio:** the proportion of a bank's deposits that are not loaned out

**reserves:** money kept on hand by a bank in the event that some of those who have made deposits wish to withdraw their money

**risk:** uncertainty about what future outcomes will be

**savings account:** a bank account that pays interest, that can be withdrawn at any time, and against which cheques typically cannot be written

**scarcity:** the fact that there are not enough resources to satisfy all wants

**seasonal unemployment:** unemployment that results from seasonal variations

**sectoral free trade:** free trade between countries in the products of a particular industry, such as automobiles

**settlement balances:** accounts that chartered banks must keep at the Bank of Canada

**shortage:** the situation in which people would like to buy something that is not available at the going price

**short-run:** the length of time required for a market to adjust partially but not fully to changes in demand or supply conditions

**short-run aggregate supply curve:** the aggregate supply curve that applies when wages and prices do not have sufficient time to adjust fully and ensure full employment

**short-run production function:** the relationship between employment and output with a given set of machines and buildings

**short-term bonds:** bonds that mature within a few years

**simple interest:** interest that is paid on the principal but not on interest previously earned

**slope:** the amount by which the value along the vertical axis increases as the result of a change in one unit along the horizontal axis; the slope is calculated by dividing the change in the vertical axis (the "rise") by the change in the horizontal axis (the "run")

**small open economy:** an economy that has no influence over the prices it faces on world markets, including both product prices and the interest rate

**social insurance:** programmes to protect citizens against unexpected economic adversity

**socialism:** an economic system in which the means of production are owned and controlled by the state

**social safety net:** the set of government programmes designed to protect citizens against adversity

**social science:** the study of social interactions using scientific methods

**soft budget constraints:** budget constraints facing a firm for which government subsidizes any losses

**stagflation:** a situation in which high inflation exists alongside high unemployment

**static expectations:** the belief of individuals that today's prices and wages are likely to continue into the future

**sticky prices:** prices that take some time to adjust to changes in demand or supply

**sticky wages:** wages that are slow to adjust in response to a change in the labour market

**stock statistics:** measurements of the quantity of a certain item at a certain point in time, such as capital stock, the total value of buildings and machines

**store of value:** something that can be accepted as payment in the present and exchanged for items of value in the future

**strategic trade theory:** the theory that protectionism can give a country a strategic advantage over rivals, for instance, by helping reduce domestic costs through economies of scale

**structural unemployment:** long-term unemployment resulting from structural changes in the economy, such as changes in the composition of industrial output

**substitute:** a good the demand for which increases when the price of another increases

**substitution effect:** the reduced consumption of a good whose price has increased that is due to the changed trade-off—the fact that one has to give up more of other goods to get one more unit of the high-priced good; the substitution effect is associated with a change in the slope of the budget constraint

**sunk cost:** a cost that has been incurred and cannot be recovered

**supply:** the quantity of an item that households or firms offer to sell

**supply curve** the relationship betweeen the quantity of a good supplied and its price, whether for a single firm or for the market (all firms) as a whole

**supply-constrained equilibrium:** the equilibrium that occurs when prices are stuck at a level below that at which aggregate demand equals aggregate supply; in a supply-constrained equilibrium, output is equal to aggregate supply but is lower than aggregate demand

**supply management:** government control of agricultural prices by restricting the amount of a product that can be supplied by farmers

**supply shock:** an upward shift in the aggregate supply curve that can initiate an inflationary episode

**surplus, fiscal:** tax revenues in excess of government expenditures in a given year

**surplus labour:** a great deal of unemployed or underemployed labour, readily available to potential employers

**sustainable development:** development that avoids depleting natural resources and degrading the environment

**tariffs:** charges levied by the federal government on the importation of certain goods and services from abroad

**technological risks:** uncertainties associated with a firm's investment in a new technology

**theory:** a set of assumptions and the conclusions derived from those assumptions put forward as an explanation for some phenomenon

**three pillars of the pension system:** public pensions (OAS), contributory pensions (CPP/QPP), and tax-assisted retirement savings (RRSPs, RPPs)

**time constraints:** opportunity sets whose restrictions are imposed by time

**time value of money:** the value attached to receiving a dollar now rather than at some time in the future

**total factor productivity analysis:** the analysis of the relationship between output and the aggregate of all inputs, calculated as the difference between the rate of growth of outputs and the weighted average rate of growth of inputs, where the weight associated with each input is its share of GDP

**trade creation:** new trade that is generated as a result of lowered tariff barriers among members of a trading agreement

**trade diversion:** trade that is diverted from outside countries as a result of lowering tariffs between the members of a trading bloc

**trade-offs:** the need to give up some of one item to get more of another

**traditional or Keynesian monetary theorists:** economists who hold that the nominal interest rate is the opportunity cost of holding money, that the demand for money decreases as the interest rate rises, and that the interest rate is determined by equilibrium in the demand and supply of money

**transactions demand for money:** the demand for money arising from its use in buying goods and services

**Treasury bills (T-bills):** bills the government sells in return for a promise to pay a certain amount in a short period, usually less than 180 days

**trough:** the bottom of a recession

**two-tier wage system:** a wage system in which new workers are paid less than established workers for doing the same job

**underemployment:** a situation in which employees are not used to their potential

**unemployment rate:** the fraction of the labour force (those unemployed *plus* those seeking jobs) who are seeking jobs but are unable to find them

**unfunded liabilities:** future public pension obligations that are not covered by accumulated funds

**unitary banking system:** a banking system with a large number of banks operating mainly on a regional basis

**unit of account:** something that provides a way of measuring and comparing the relative values of different goods

**unit price elasticity:** a situation in which quantity demanded increases in proportion to reductions in price

**value added:** the difference between the value of a firm's output and the cost of its intermediate inputs

**value of marginal product of labour:** the output price multiplied by the marginal product of labour

**variable:** any item that changes and that can be measured

**variable costs:** the costs resulting from variable inputs

**velocity:** the speed with which money circulates in the economy, defined as the ratio of income to the money supply

**voluntary export restraints (VERs):** restraints on exports not mandated by an exporting country, though often in response to a threat that if such constraints are not imposed, the importing country will impose import quotas

**voluntary unemployment:** a situation in which workers voluntarily drop out of the labour force when the wage level falls

**wage and price controls:** government-imposed restrictions on wage and price increases

**wage-productivity curve:** the graphical relationship between wages and productivity

**wholesale price index:** an index that measures the average level of wholesale prices

**workers:** individuals who sell their labour services

**work sharing:** reducing all employees' hours by equal amounts rather than firing some workers

**World Trade Organization (WTO):** the organization replacing GATT, established in 1995 as a result of the Uruguay round of trade negotiations, and designed to remove trade barriers and settle trade disputes

**zero elasticity of demand:** the situation that exists when the quantity demanded will not change, regardless of changes in price

**zero elasticity of supply:** the situation that exists when the quantity supplied will not change, regardless of changes in price

# INDEX